To Tony

Xmas '93

From Kirk.

Best wishes.

# WELSH NATIONAL OPERA

# WELSH
# NATIONAL
# OPERA

RICHARD FAWKES

Julia MacRae

A DIVISION OF FRANKLIN WATTS

© 1986 Richard Fawkes
Foreword © 1986 Julia MacRae Books
All rights reserved
First published in Great Britain 1986 by
Julia MacRae Books, a division of Franklin Watts
12a Golden Square, London W1R 4BA
*and* Franklin Watts Australia
14 Mars Road, Lane Cove, NSW 2066


Welsh translation of the Foreword
by Eirlys Leader

Fawkes, Richard
Welsh National Opera.
1. Welsh National Opera—History
I. Title
782.1'09429   ML1731.7.W3

ISBN 0–86203–184–2

# CONTENTS

# ILLUSTRATIONS

THE EARLY YEARS: 1946–1969
*(between pages 82 and 83)*


THE MIDDLE YEARS: 1970–1979
*(between pages 178 and 179)*


THE EARLY EIGHTIES: 1980–1985
*(between pages 250 and 251)*

# ACKNOWLEDGEMENTS

I AM INDEBTED to Brian McMaster, Welsh National Opera's General Administrator, for allowing me access to the Company's archives and records in Cardiff, and for his help and encouragement throughout the writing of this book.

Many people have helped me with my research and I am extremely grateful to all those past and present members of WNO who have given so freely of their time and memories. I am also very grateful to those people who have sent me cuttings, programmes and reminiscences. In particular I would like to thank the following:

Rufus Adams, Thomas Allen, Richard Armstrong, Gwilym Beechey, Florence Beese, Francis Brook, Ethel Brown, Stuart Burrows, Edward Byles, Douglas Craig, Zoe Cresswell, Lord Davies, Gerald Davies, Isabel Davies, John Denison, Nigel Douglas, Bryan Drake, Victoria Elliott, Anne Evans, David Fingleton, Victor Fleming, Alfred Francis, Michael Geliot, Stanley Gitsham, Sir Charles Groves, David Gwynne, Ralph Hamer, Raimund Herincx, Tom Hopkins, Anthony Hose, Clive John, Roderick Jones, Ian Keith, John King, Felix Kok, Michael Langdon, Charles Lewis, Judi Lewis, Harry Powell Lloyd, James Lockhart, David Loffler, Sir Charles Mackerras, John McMurray, Peter Massocchi, James Miller-Coburn, Herbert Minett, John and Nell Moody, Janet Morgan, Geoffrey Moses, Robert Musson, Kenneth Pugh, Donald Roberts, Forbes Robinson, Mollie Russell, Christopher Senior, Arthur Servent, Terence Sharpe, Adrian Slack, Vilem Tausky, Robert Thomas, Pauline Tinsley, Dai Trotman, Elizabeth Vaughan, John Wakefield, Eric Wetherell, Sir Huw Wheldon, Gordon Whyte, Cliff Williams, Margaret Williams and Vanda Vale.

I must also express my gratitude to the many critics who have reviewed WNO's productions during the last forty years, especially Kenneth Loveland, who has seen almost every first night and a great many other performances. I would like, also, to thank Gillian Dare of the Arts Council of Great Britain for her help with my research, and Kate Fraser, who transcribed my tapes.

Finally, I must acknowledge the enormous debt I owe to Margaret Moreland, MBE; Muriel Pointon, a founder member of WNO and the

Company's present archivist who has made working in Cardiff such a very great pleasure; Shelagh Nelson, WNO's Press Officer and her assistant, Alison Norman; Paul Hirschman for checking the manuscript, and lastly, Julia MacRae, my editor and publisher, whose enthusiasm for this book has been such an encouragement.

# FOREWORD BY HER ROYAL HIGHNESS
# THE PRINCESS OF WALES

*Patron of Welsh National Opera*

It was over 40 years ago that a small group of opera enthusiasts met together in Cardiff and through their dedication, hard work and drive formed a National Opera Company which gave its first performance in Cardiff in 1946. In the intervening years, the Company has grown in importance and has firmly established itself, not only in Wales, but also on the international Opera stage.

As Patron of Welsh National Opera it gives me great pleasure to introduce Richard Fawkes' book which traces the development and history of a Company whose reputation throughout the world is something of which all concerned can be justifiably proud. I hope that all those who read this history of WNO will find it both informative and enjoyable.

*Diana.*

# RHAGAIR
## GAN EI MAWRHYDI BRENHINOL
## TYWYSOGES CYMRU

Ychydig dros ddeugain mlynedd yn ôl daeth nifer fechan o ffyddloniaid opera at ei gilydd yng Nghaerdydd, a thrwy eu dygnwch, eu llafur caled, a'u brwdfrydedd, ffurfiwyd Cwmni Opera Cenedlaethol. Cafwyd ei berfformiad cyntaf yng Nghaerdydd ym 1946. Dros y blynyddoedd, tyfodd y Cwmni'n flaenllaw, ac yn ddi-os y mae wedi'i sefydlu, nid yn unig yng Nghymru, ond ar lwyfan rhyngwladol yr Opera.

Fel noddwraig Cwmni Opera Cenedlaethol Cymru y mae'n bleser mawr gennyf gyflwyno cyfrol Richard Fawkes. Ynddo y mae'n olrhain hanes a datblygiad Cwmni Opera ag iddo enw da led lled y byd, a gall y rhai a fu'n gysylltiedig ag e deimlo'n gwbl foddhaus. Hyderaf y bydd yr hanes yma am Gwmni Opera Cenedlaethol Cymru o ddiddordeb mawr ac yn fwynhâd i'w ddarllenwyr.

# CHAPTER ONE: 1943–1946

ONE SUNDAY MORNING late in November 1943, John Morgan, a former baritone with the Carl Rosa Opera Company, and his fiancée, Helena Hughes Brown, called at the Llandaff home of Idloes Owen, a well-known Cardiff singing teacher and choral conductor. Their purpose was to discuss the formation of a grand opera company. An hour and a half later, their meeting was over. "It was decided," noted Miss Brown in the minutes, "to form the Company of which Mr Idloes Owen was to be Conductor and General Manager and Miss Helena Hughes Brown Secretary. The name of 'The Lyrian Grand Opera Co.' was decided upon and a list of names was drawn up to be invited to join."

This was not the first time an attempt had been made to form a grand opera company in Wales. In 1890 a company calling itself, rather grandly, the Welsh National Opera had taken Joseph Parry's two operas *Arianwen* and *Blodwen* on a financially disastrous tour and been forced to disband. In the late 1920s and early 1930s the Cardiff Grand Opera Society had flourished before it, too, had folded, and before the Second World War there were a handful of amateur companies throughout South Wales, such as the Barry Grand Opera Company, which staged annual or occasional productions, often using professional principals. Most amateur companies, however, preferred Gilbert and Sullivan or other light opera to grand opera, and although male voice choirs included operatic choruses and individual arias in their programmes, by 1943 Wales was, as it always had been, poorly served for staged grand opera. The music-making tradition in Wales had always been essentially amateur – there was an antipathy amounting to distrust of the professional musical organisation – and without such professional touring companies as the Moody-Manners, the British National Opera Company and the Carl Rosa, there would have been very few opportunities for the inhabitants of the Principality to see any sort of grand opera at all. What made the attempt of Owen, Morgan and Brown to get yet another amateur group off the ground so special was that, although none of them realised it, they were about to give birth to an organisation that within less than forty years would have gained an international reputation and without which British operatic life today would be unthinkable.

Idloes Owen, the driving force behind this new venture, was born in Merthyr Vale in 1895. The son of a colliery worker at the Nixon Navigation Colliery, he had left school at the age of 12 and, as was the custom in those days, followed his father down the pit. A boy soprano, he had always been interested in music and in his spare time taught himself to play the piano and the violin. At the outbreak of the Great War, it was discovered that he had tuberculosis, and he left the mine planning to devote himself to music. His father's death at first made such a possibility seem remote. However, his village staged a benefit concert and raised enough money for him to study for three years at the University of South Wales and Monmouth in Cardiff. In 1925 he became choirmaster of the Cardiff-based male voice choir, the Lyrian Singers, and under him they gained a considerable reputation both inside and outside Wales in concerts and on the radio. It was for the Lyrian Singers that Owen arranged a composition by Mae Jones and Lyn Joshua, and with them gave its first performance. The song was "We'll Keep a Welcome" – Wales's unofficial second national anthem. Owen, in addition to being a composer, arranger and conductor, was also a highly respected singing teacher, possibly the finest in Wales (his best-known pupil was Geraint Evans), and it was from his students that the idea of staging opera first came. So many of them were learning arias and whole sections of operas that they kept suggesting he ought to put on a performance for them. At the same time, people who heard the Lyrian Singers performing operatic choruses were making similar suggestions. While the idea certainly interested him, Owen had, he felt, a greater priority: the formation of an orchestra.

Just before the Second World War, the National Orchestra of Wales, whose principal conductor was Warwick Braithwaite, had been allowed to fold, leaving a gaping hole in the musical life of South Wales which the BBC's Cardiff-based Welsh orchestra, the only other full-time professional orchestra in the whole of Wales, was unable to fill. This had been formed as a studio orchestra and was really too small to be considered a symphony orchestra. It was also unavailable for public concerts or work outside the BBC. If it did perform in public, it was only when a concert was being broadcast. Owen was very much aware of this gap and had decided to try and do something about it. In 1941, the same John Morgan who was later to help him found the opera company introduced him to Victor Fleming, an experienced orchestral conductor from the Midlands whose wartime work with the Treforest firm of Halliwell brought him regularly to Wales. Fleming was already well-known in Wales as a former principal conductor of the Aberystwyth Orchestra and he readily agreed to help Owen find musicians, arrange programmes and obtain music. Unknown to either of them, however, Herbert Ware, a Cardiff violinist, was at the same time in the process of forming his own Cardiff Philharmonic Orchestra. Ware's concerts started well before Owen and Fleming were ready with their scheme and so Owen, realising that wartime Cardiff could not support two orchestras organised upon similar lines, abandoned his plans. During their many conversations about the orchestra, Fleming had mentioned to Owen another idea: the formation of a network of amateur opera choruses throughout Britain which would all learn the same work. Eminent professionals would be engaged to sing the principal roles and would tour the country performing the same production in each centre, with the local chorus. He suggested to Owen that with their reputation for choral singing such a scheme would suit the Welsh admirably. When the orchestral plans fell through, Fleming thought no more about his scheme but clearly Owen, with the constant promptings of his students and from audiences to stage an opera, did, and the idea for an opera company took root.

At 7 o'clock on the evening of 2 December 1943 twenty-eight people, all students or friends and acquaintances of Owen who had sung with him in the past, met at the Cathays Methodist Chapel in Crwys Road to help launch the Lyrian Grand Opera Company. Owen explained what he had in mind: he wanted to form a company of amateur singers to learn six operas in three years; each production to be cast from company members and be produced by a top London producer who might, while in Wales, be prepared to give some private coaching 'in the dramatic art' to those who were interested. The aim was two-fold: firstly to stop the exodus of talent from Wales and secondly to give local singers a chance to appear in grand opera. He proposed that members should pay, as and when convenient, a guinea to join and six pence a week to help cover the cost of hiring rooms for rehearsal. Once the organisation was under way, Owen continued, he did not want to confine it to Cardiff but to play in all the major Welsh cities and towns, picking up local choruses to appear with the company's principals in much the same way that Victor Fleming had suggested to him earlier.

Each proposal was carried unanimously. Owen was confirmed as the company's Musical Director and Helena Hughes Brown as Secretary. Stanley Thomas, manager of the Sun Life Assurance office in Cardiff, was appointed Business Manager, Muriel Pointon was elected Treasurer, and the meeting agreed to form a committee of businessmen to help with the business side of the company. The only major change from the suggestions Owen had agreed earlier with John Morgan and Helena Hughes Brown was over the name. No one now recalls who proposed that the company should not be called the Lyrian Grand Opera. All we know is that by the end of the meeting the new organisation had decided to call itself the Welsh National Opera Company.

The first rehearsal of the new company took place on 6 January 1944.

There were some sixty people present, who had been assembled by word of mouth: members of Owen's Lyrian Singers, members of the BBC Welsh Singers, former members of the Cardiff Grand Opera Society and some of Owen's students. Among them were tenor Frank James, who worked in a Cardiff store and had been singing in the RAF; Herbert Minett, who worked for the Great Western Railway, and his wife, Zoe Cresswell; Muriel Pointon, who worked in the family's butcher's shop; and Tom Hopkins, who ran the Horse and Groom pub in Maesteg. Hopkins was typical of the many excellent Welsh singers of those days who could not afford, through family commitments, to take the chance of travelling to London to become a professional. The one thing that all the founder members of the company possessed in common was a love of singing for singing's sake, and they all had wonderful voices. Although a few could be classed as semi-professional in that they received fees for concert work, most were amateurs and all had full-time jobs. There was never any question that they would expect fees from the company – their reward was to be in taking part. Few, if indeed any of them, realised just what they were starting.

Owen had set himself the task of producing six operas in three years. Before that could happen and to keep the interest alive, he decided to organise a series of concert performances, with orchestra, which, if they were lucky, might also raise funds for the company. His experience of conducting orchestras was extremely limited and he had never before had to book one from scratch, so he wrote immediately to his friend Victor Fleming. "The purpose of my letter is to invite you to Cardiff at the earliest moment you can spare. You will be glad to know that we have formed a Welsh National Opera Company and are making our initial appearance at The Empire Theatre, Cardiff, Sunday 23 April . . . I suggest that perhaps you will conduct the Overtures and Arias . . . I have selected an excellent body of singers from various parts of South Wales and I have no fears in this direction . . . This move I have sponsored entirely alone and it is therefore too late for anyone to cross or kill the company."

Fleming was delighted to help and engaged an orchestra of thirty freelance players for the first concert, which he conducted jointly with Owen at the Empire Theatre, Cardiff, on 23 April 1944, to raise funds for the 11th Glamorgan Battalion of the Royal Engineers. After "God Save the King" and "Land of My Fathers", the orchestra played entr'actes from *Carmen*, Tudor Davies, the popular tenor from the Carl Rosa Company, sang "All Hail, Thou Dwelling" from Gounod's *Faust*, and then for the first time the public had a chance to hear the Welsh National Opera Chorus as they sang a Fantasia on *Die Meistersinger*, with guest baritone Tom Williams and local singers Zoe Cresswell and Tom Hopkins as the soloists. Completing the first half of the programme, Ruth Packer, also from the Carl

Rosa Company, sang "Softly sighs" from Weber's *Der Freischütz*, Tom Williams sang "Eri tu" from *Un Ballo in Maschera* by Verdi, and the orchestra played the overture to Glinka's *Russlan and Ludmilla*. After the interval, Packer and Williams joined Tudor Davies, Doris Russell, Zoe Cresswell and the chorus in a concert performance of *Cavalleria Rusticana*. "The combination of chorus, soloists, and orchestra gave promise of future successful work," wrote the music critic of the *Western Mail*. "The WNOC can be congratulated on the success of their first effort in public. It was a good première, although there were indications at times that better results would have been attained with a few more rehearsals."

After the concert, everybody was filled with enthusiasm to continue. Further charity appearances were arranged, and an approach was made to ENSA (the organisation which had been set up to provide entertainment for the troops) to get on their circuit, starting with a performance for a local RAF Station. In spite of the fact that Margaret Williams, a member of WNO, was in charge of ENSA's musical section in Cardiff, the attempt proved abortive. Walter Legge, the head of ENSA's music section, came down to a concert in the Capitol Cinema on 3 December and although he enjoyed the evening, declared that he was not in favour of concert performances of opera and was certainly not prepared to use ENSA's funds in assisting the formation of a new production company.

Legge's decision was a disappointment rather than a setback. Important though such concerts were in the short term as a way of learning works and getting publicity, the entertainment tax laws meant that any profits from them had to be given to charity rather than be retained by the company. And besides, the whole point of forming the company in the first place had been to *produce* grand opera. Owen was already drawing up plans for staged performances to take place as soon as possible. He had made a tentative enquiry about the availability of the Prince of Wales Theatre for a week in December 1945, and had started to think seriously about which operas should be performed. The chorus already knew *Cavalleria Rusticana*, which became the natural first choice. Victor Fleming suggested *Abu Hassan* by Weber as a possible partner for it; *Carmen*, which he felt could be cast entirely from within the company and would cost no more than £100 a performance; *Tosca*, an opera which, although it would cost £20 a performance more than *Carmen*, had considerable public appeal and had not been seen in Britain since the war began; or Verdi's *Otello*, which Frank Mullings was proposing to put on for the Midland Opera Company with Dennis Noble and Lisa Perli. Fleming felt Mullings could easily be persuaded to restage it in Wales. Owen found these suggestions interesting but too ambitious. They were, he wrote to Fleming, "too much for us. We must travel slowly and tread very carefully."

*Cavalleria Rusticana* had traditionally been played in a double-bill with *I Pagliacci*, and Owen saw no reason to depart from the practice. That solved one problem, but he still needed another work to enable the company to play a varied week. At the Capitol concert on 3 December, at which Legge had been present, the programme was the usual pot-pourri of operatic items, with solos from Joan Cross, Roderick Lloyd, Tom Hopkins and Norman Jones, interspersed with choruses. During rehearsals, Owen had been unhappy with the speed with which the chorus was learning the Finale from Flotow's *Martha*, and, feeling certain that Legge would spot the weaknesses immediately, substituted a chorus from Gounod's *Faust*. This gave him the idea for the remaining piece to be put into production. His next problem was to find a producer. Eric Crozier, the distinguished librettist and Sadler's Wells producer, was approached, but was not interested in either *Cav* and *Pag*, nor in *Faust*. For some time, Owen continued to harbour hopes of persuading a top London man down, but eventually he realised that he simply couldn't afford one. In desperation he asked Norman Jones, a founder member of the company who had been cast as Mephistopheles in *Faust*, if he would take on the job. Jones had been principal baritone with the Royal Welsh Gleemen, with whom he had toured America and Canada twice, and had sung in a *Messiah* at Carnegie Hall. For eleven years he was a member of the Carl Rosa, studying operatic production with Kingsley Lark. Since returning to Cardiff to take up a commercial career just before the war, he had been active not only as a singer but also in helping to train young singers and producing for local operatic and musical societies. He happily accepted Owen's invitation to produce all three operas.

Work on the productions began in earnest, with the chorus rehearsing twice a week in the evenings in rented halls and schoolrooms, and the principals learning their parts with Owen at his home in Station Road. With the exception of Canio in *I Pagliacci* and the title role in *Faust*, which were to be sung by guest star Tudor Davies, brought in as a box-office draw, every solo part was cast from within the company. In April 1945, Owen, whose health had always been fragile, was forced to give up all work for a month. Determined that the operas should not suffer, he asked an acquaintance in Swansea who had considerable experience in operatic conducting, Ivor John, to continue training the chorus. John travelled up to Cardiff to hear a rehearsal and immediately agreed to help.

As with most amateur societies, finding people to work backstage was largely a question of recruiting volunteers from among the members, members' friends and relatives. Cecil Bridge, a member of the chorus who was also a carpenter, was the natural choice to become property master. Mollie Hair, a student of Owen's, had trained as a dancer at stage school and was seized upon to form a ballet group and choreograph the ballet in *Faust*. She managed to find some girls who either knew how to dance or were prepared to try, but no men. At that time, it was not considered manly to want to dance classical ballet, and she had to persuade two of the more gangling females to dress as boys. She also helped out with make-up, showing others how to put it on; and she still sang in the chorus in all three productions.

Sets and costumes (with the exception of one or two principals who used their own clothes, and the ballet, who made theirs) were hired. The sets were ordered from Capes of London, who sent down the nearest thing to Norman Jones's requirements they had available. The costumes proved more difficult to find. Florence Beese, who had been helping out with the wardrobe on various amateur shows in Cardiff, had been approached to become the company's Wardrobe Mistress. She duly measured everyone in the cast and wrote off to the hire firms in London, but received no replies. In desperation, Idloes Owen's wife took her up to London for the day, but because the war had depleted stocks and theatrical costume hire was not uppermost in most people's minds at that time, they were unable to find anything suitable. Eventually, she managed to hire sufficient, though not altogether appropriate, costumes from a firm in Manchester.

One job it was found difficult to fill was that of front-of-house manager. John Morgan and Muriel Pointon approached William Smith, the owner of Morsmith Motors, who had been Secretary of the Cardiff Grand Opera Society in the early thirties and had appeared as a supernumerary, carrying a banner, on one of the Cardiff visits of the British National Opera Company. He thought they were out of their minds even to think of forming another opera company and wanted nothing to do with it.

Vocal and production rehearsals proceeded as planned throughout the autumn and winter of 1945. The December booking for the Prince of Wales Theatre had fallen through, however, and all attempts to rebook it early in 1946 had run up against difficulties. One day, at a Masonic Lodge meeting, Owen mentioned this difficulty to the same William Smith who had already refused to become front-of-house manager. Smith invited Owen to meet him at his office in Frederick Street. After a long discussion about Owen's aims, Smith not only agreed to help but decided to become actively engaged in running the company, consenting to become Business Manager. William Henry Smith, known universally as Bill, was just the sort of dynamic businessman Owen needed. In 1933 he had started Morsmith Motors with the backing of the head of David Morgan Ltd., the Cardiff department store where his father worked in the carpet department, and had turned it into South Wales's leading distributor for Daimler, Lanchester and Rover cars. He was also mad keen on opera. On a tour of Italy after the First World

War, in which he served as a gunner, Smith had visited La Scala, Milan, where he was struck by the similarities in temperament between the Italians and the Welsh. From that moment on, he harboured a dream that one day Wales itself would have an opera house to rival La Scala. It was a dream that had seemed for a time might happen with the Cardiff Grand Opera Society, but when that company folded, he concentrated on his business activities. Once he understood the exact nature of Owen's proposals, he saw a chance to revive his dream, and seized it wholeheartedly. He already knew virtually every person in Cardiff who mattered, and within a few days the hire of the Prince of Wales Theatre had been confirmed for April. He also set about persuading his colleagues in the business world to donate money, supply goods (if not free, at least at a healthy discount) and, by no means least, to buy tickets for the performances. He was determined that the opening season would not be the last, and to give Norman Jones, the producer, time to concentrate on the operas, he took him on as a salesman at his garage, giving him as much time off as he needed.

The first staged performance of the Welsh National Opera Company took place at the Prince of Wales Theatre, Cardiff, on 15 April 1946, with the double-bill of *Cavalleria Rusticana* and *I Pagliacci*. Owen conducted *Cavalleria Rusticana*, and Ivor John, *Pagliacci*. The orchestra for the week, drawn mostly from BBC players, was led by Glen Spiler.

The audience was packed, and not just with friends and relations of the chorus, though they were there in force. Coach parties arrived from the valleys, and people who hadn't booked had to be turned away.

The productions, as might be expected in an almost totally amateur performance, tended to be static. Jones had a sound knowledge of stage-craft but most of the chorus and principals had never appeared on an operatic stage before, and his priority had been to weld them into a cohesive whole. When it came to the singing, however, the audience was given more than its money's worth. Tudor Davies, singing Canio, was a star. He was a founder member of the British National Opera Company and had made his Covent Garden debut as Rodolfo on the opening night of its first London season. He had created the title role of *Hugh the Drover* and leading roles in Holst's *At the Boar's Head* and in Dame Ethel Smyth's *Fête Galante*. For ten years he had been the leading tenor at Sadler's Wells, and for five with the Carl Rosa. There can be little doubt that had Tudor Davies been born into a different age he would have been an international name rather than a national one. Although in 1946 he was nearing the end of his career, he was still a box-office draw and could still turn in a thrilling performance. His co-principals at the Prince of Wales, inspired by his performance, did their best to match him.

"The new Welsh company came through their test with flying colours on their first night," reported the *Western Mail*. "They have started something which promises to become perhaps as important to the art of singing in Wales as the National Eisteddfod itself. Arthur Davies, a baritone with a fine powerful voice and a good actor, scored a double triumph playing leading roles in both operas." In *Cavalleria Rusticana*, the report continued, "the singing of Margaret Williams, who possesses a beautiful soprano voice, made a deep impression. Also outstanding were Phyllis Ash-Child, Helena Hughes Brown (soprano) and Tom Hopkins (tenor). In *I Pagliacci*, conducted by Ivor John, Tudor Davies (tenor), an operatic artiste of first rate power, gave a dynamic performance. No less good were Beatrice Gough (soprano), Frank James (tenor) and John Morgan (baritone). A capable orchestra contributed its share to the marked success achieved during the evening."

And the evening *was* a success, particularly for the chorus, even though the reviews did not mention them. Margaret Williams as Santuzza was so moved by their singing in the Easter Hymn that she was in tears. She remembers Idloes Owen in the pit calling out to her, "For God's sake, leave it to the audience to cry."

On the following night, *Faust*, conducted by Ivor John, was performed with Lilian Evans as Marguerite, Myfanwy Richards as Siebel, and Norman Jones as Mephistopheles. John Morgan sang Valentine, Stanley Gitsham, Wagner, Alice James, Marthe, and the role of Faust was sung by Tudor Davies, who was once again the audience's favourite. The company "confirmed the very good impression they made on their opening night. It was again an excellent performance, lacking nothing in presentation." Like most operatic performances, professional as well as amateur,' it also enjoyed its share of happenings. Norman Jones in his role as producer was so busy talking to the cast backstage that he made an entrance as Mephistopheles on the opposite side of the stage to the puff of smoke, and in the third act, during Marguerite's prayer, Lilian Evans's wig fell off. In spite of her entreaties to the chorus, no one dared pick it up until Mollie Hair finally seized it and, bending over to hide what she was doing, pushed it back on Evans's head.

*Cav* and *Pag* were given again on Wednesday and on Thursday afternoon at a matinée performance for which every member of both casts except Tudor Davies had to get time off work. *Faust* was repeated on Thursday evening with Victor Fleming taking over from Ivor John in the pit. John was not lost to the production, however: he was up on stage singing the title role in place of Tudor Davies, who was unavailable for that one performance. There was no performance on the Friday since it was Good Friday and the theatre was closed; *Faust* was given at the Saturday matinée and *Cav* and *Pag* in the evening.

Because there were still difficulties over the company's tax status and there was no great desire to pay entertainment tax on any profits, it had been decided that all proceeds from the week should go to the Cardiff Royal Infirmary. Unfortunately, the receipts from the box-office were barely enough to cover the costs of the orchestra – £228.9s.6d. plus expenses. But even though the week did not make money, as the curtain fell on the last night, Idloes Owen was already talking of a two-week season the following year, and of adding *Carmen* and *Il Trovatore* to the repertoire. It didn't matter that the productions were perhaps not the most wonderful ever mounted; they were adequate, and the audience had heard glorious singing and been moved by the music and drama as only opera can move people. A heartfelt need in South Wales had clearly been met. The enthusiasm of those on stage is summed up in a memory of Margaret Williams who sang Santuzza. After the performances of *Cav* and *Pag*, which ended at about 11 o'clock, she had to drive home to Brecon and gave a lift to two miners from the chorus. She dropped them off in Abercynon, from where they had to walk fourteen or fifteen miles home. They would have a short rest, get up early for the morning shift and then make their way back to Cardiff in time for the evening performance. They kept this up throughout the week.

In September the company played a week at the Porthcawl Pavilion in an attempt to recover some of the Cardiff losses. Once again the houses were packed for *Cav* and *Pag* (with the same casts as in Cardiff except for Tom Williams singing two performances as Alfio) and for *Faust* (in which Tom Hopkins took over the title role from Tudor Davies for one performance). The reception was again rapturous and people who hadn't booked had to be turned away, but with orchestral costs alone amounting to £268, the week lost even more money. Artistically, if not financially, the company's appearances in both Cardiff and Porthcawl had been an unqualified success and there was absolutely no doubt in anybody's mind that Welsh National Opera would be returning the following year.

# CHAPTER TWO: 1947–1948

T HE SUCCESS of those first appearances in Cardiff and Porthcawl brought a flood of applications to join the chorus from throughout
South Wales, some from as far away as Carmarthen. Miners and colliery
workers, secretaries and housewives, shop assistants and doctors, solicitors
and nurses – anyone with a voice who had ever fancied getting up on stage
and singing in grand opera wanted to be part of the new company. Many of
them could not read stave music and had been brought up on tonic sol-fa;
some could not read either. But as long as they possessed good enough
voices (and many were exceptional) Owen accepted them. Those who knew
only tonic sol-fa could be seen at rehearsals, carefully transcribing their
parts. The lack of formal musical training meant that early rehearsals
consisted of a lot of what is known in choral circles as note-bashing as
Owen and Ivor John, assisted by their patient accompanist, Marjery Pugh
from Barry, strove to drum their parts into the chorus, but it turned out to
be worth it, for the sound they were eventually to produce was to be
something unique in British opera.

Not everyone who joined did so with the approval of family and friends.
The chapel mentality, which thought that appearing on stage in greasepaint
was not just wrong but positively sinful, was still strong outside the main
centres, and many choristers and even soloists took part in spite of incurring
family displeasure.

During the autumn and winter months following the week in Porthcawl,
everyone was hard at work re-rehearsing *Faust*, *Cav* and *Pag*, and learning
the new work for 1947. This was to be Bizet's *Carmen*. It had been decided
that the production would be cast entirely from within the company and
that no guest artists would be engaged for any of the year's performances.
Zoe Cresswell from Rhymney, who had sung in the first concert appearance
three years earlier and had missed taking part in the opening performances
because she was giving birth to a son, was cast in the title role. Frank James,
a student of Idloes Owen, appeared opposite her as Don José. Norman
Jones was again the producer and Mollie Hair was asked to choreograph a
ballet sequence in Act 2 and dance a solo in Act 4.

While Jones concentrated on working with the large and still largely inexperienced chorus, Zoe Cresswell began to worry about her role as Carmen. She was an experienced and popular concert artist, so had no problems with the music, but, never having appeared on an operatic stage, was increasingly concerned about her ability to act the part. One day, while travelling to a concert with Howell Glynne, the distinguished Welsh bass, she confided her fears to him. He suggested she ask for help from an old friend of his, Betty Thompson, who had been an outstanding Carmen with the Carl Rosa Company and was then living in Cardiff. Cresswell did as he suggested and Betty Thompson eventually agreed to coach both her and Frank James in their roles.

*Carmen*, conducted by Victor Fleming, opened Welsh National Opera's second season at the Prince of Wales Theatre on 28 April 1947. During the dress rehearsal on the Sunday, Bill Smith, who was taking over more and more in the running of the company, took a dislike to the singer cast as Escamillo and promptly sacked him. His place was taken by Tom Williams, the only professional guest to appear during the week. The performance was, according to the reviews, "vividly alive" and "spirited". Zoe Cresswell's work with Betty Thompson had paid off. She "was admirably cast as Carmen, portraying skilfully the passionate, fickle gipsy character. Her *Habanera* was remarkably good." Frank James was considered to be an ideal Don José. He did not possess a powerful voice, but he sang lyrically and was a good actor. Their scenes together generated real excitement. Tom Williams, a great favourite in Wales, earned a standing ovation for his powerfully sung Escamillo.

On the following night, *Faust*, conducted by Ivor John, was performed with Tom Hopkins outstanding in the title role and Margaret Williams making a highly praised debut as Marguerite. There was, noted one reviewer, nothing "amateurish" about the production: "By the sheer brilliance of their performance they built up a tremendous atmosphere for the climax . . . It is not only in its principals but also in a well-trained chorus and a capable orchestra that the Welsh company can compare with many of the noted operatic companies." The double-bill of *Cavalleria Rusticana* and *I Pagliacci* completed the week's offerings with Margaret Williams again winning the plaudits, and the applause, for her Santuzza. David Jones as Turiddu and Trefor Phelps as Alfio were the two newcomers to the cast of *Cavalleria Rusticana* which was again conducted by Idloes Owen. The only cast change from the previous year in *Pagliacci* saw Tom Hopkins taking over as Canio.

The week played to full and enthusiastic houses. Looking back on those early productions, it is difficult to judge them by today's professional standards. The reviews they received were of the sort that any reasonably good amateur company might expect from its local papers. "It is a tribute to the care and hard work they have put in that the performances have been of a standard that any of the old-established companies could have been proud to own," one critic wrote. "In addition to the principals there is a first-rate chorus and excellent orchestra, while the shows are well staged." It's probably fair to say that standards were no higher and no lower than for most professional operatic productions at that time. Norman Jones was an experienced producer, but he worked in the old Carl Rosa tradition of allowing principal singers to occupy centre stage and deliver, while the size of the chorus gave him little scope for anything other than getting them on and off at the right time – and every member of that chorus, used to singing in choirs, wanted to stand in the front row and be seen. Jones also had the handicap of working with limited resources, of having to hire sets and costumes, and of working on a small stage at the Prince of Wales which could barely accommodate the numbers he was required to get onto it. Under the circumstances he achieved miracles. And then, of course, there was the chorus, prepared to sing its heart out, producing a volume and tone which staggered many of the professional guest artists. Wales had been starved of grand opera for so long that people were grateful for anything; there was a new audience of ex-servicemen who had seen opera in Italy during the war and discovered it wasn't a long-haired, élitist art form; and there were the relatives of the singers themselves who would travel miles to hear their Blodwen, second from the left in the third row, sing in anything. They, too, found that opera could be fun. Perhaps the most remarkable aspect about those early days of Welsh National Opera was that for the first time in Britain, opera became what it had always been in Italy, a popular art form.

The first of many offers to tour outside Wales was received after the Cardiff season. The Theatre Royal, Brighton, wanted WNO to appear for a week, as did several other English towns and cities, but there simply wasn't the money in the kitty. The week at the Prince of Wales had again failed to recover its costs at the box-office and both Owen and Smith had had to use their own money to pay the bills. Neither of them could afford to subsidise a tour.

In September the company returned to Porthcawl for a sold-out week of *Carmen* and *Faust*, and in October made their first visit to Swansea to give a Sunday concert in the Empire Theatre as part of Swansea's Civic Week. Idloes Owen conducted an assortment of operatic items in the first half and Ivor John took over after the interval for a concert performance of *Cavalleria Rusticana* with David Jones singing Turiddu and Margaret Williams singing Santuzza. Although the house was not full, the evening was greeted with enthusiasm, and both Owen and Smith felt that the time was right to start expanding the company by forming a West Wales section of the chorus based on Swansea. On 23 January 1948, in Christchurch Hall, Owen, Smith and Ivor John addressed a meeting of local singers, many of whom had attended the October concert, and explained that the aim of Welsh National Opera was to produce opera of a professional standard on an amateur basis with an eventual chorus strength of 400 voices drawn from throughout Wales. The best voices would combine to give the major productions while the remainder would provide back-up choruses when the company toured to their region. It was the intention to start with a new Swansea section that would provide the chorus for their own performances, appearing in exactly the same production as the one seen in Cardiff, with the same principals, but with the minor roles cast from Swansea. Rehearsal nights, twice a week, would be on Wednesday and on Friday. The meeting told Owen and Smith what they wanted to hear: that they couldn't wait to get started, and between forty and fifty singers attended the auditions which were held in the last week of February. Those chosen began work immediately on rehearsing *Carmen* for the following year.

It was already obvious that Welsh National Opera, small though it might be, was satisfying a very real need in Wales for both public and performers. The audiences in the second year had been even more enthusiastic than they had been in the first, and interest in some of the principals was already being expressed. Zoe Cresswell had been invited to audition at both Covent Garden and Sadler's Wells (because of family commitments, she decided to remain in Wales) and so had Tom Hopkins, who had already been engaged to sing Faust in Dublin. Owen and Smith were determined that Welsh National Opera would not be allowed to go the way of previous operatic ventures in Wales. Besides, Smith could see the embryo of a company which would fulfil his dream of having a Welsh opera which would be second to none in Britain and known internationally. He could see, as perhaps no one else at that time could, not even Idloes Owen, that they had within their hands the makings of a real Welsh, national, opera. He lost no opportunity to sing the company's praises and to let people know of its existence. During 1946 he had been President of the Motor Agents Association and, for their Jubilee dinner at the Dorchester Hotel in London, had decided to show off his new toy. On the afternoon of Wednesday, 16 October, the entire chorus with soloists had assembled at Cardiff station for the train journey (at theatrical party rates) to London, where they performed operatic choruses and arias as the dinner cabaret. No one was paid, of course, but it did mean that more people outside Wales were hearing about Welsh National Opera.

Smith, the hard-headed businessman, knew, too, that it would take money, more money than could be raised from members' subscriptions and box-office takings, to turn the organisation from eager amateurs putting on a couple of weeks of opera a year into a professional business. He was already spending more time working on the opera than in his garage, and was busy talking to influential local businessmen, looking both for financial help and for contacts. One of the most important of these contacts was the new young director of the Welsh Committee of the Arts Council, Huw Wheldon. "At that time," Wheldon recalled, "I was more concerned about trying to form a Welsh Symphony Orchestra. I remember saying to Bill Smith that an opera company in Wales was madness because it couldn't tour. Bill said it wouldn't tour, it would play for a week in a few chosen towns. Apart from Cardiff and Swansea, I asked, where else? Llandudno, he replied. When I pressed him further, he mentioned Rome and America; male voice choirs go to America, he said, so why shouldn't an opera company?" Wheldon may have been sceptical at first, but Smith's constant badgering, coupled with the enthusiasm he witnessed in the performances, finally convinced him that there might be something in the idea. He not only put Smith in touch with a number of influential people both inside and outside Wales, but also decided that the Arts Council ought to help. He invited the Chairman of the Arts Council in London, Sir Ernest Pooley, to a performance in Cardiff. Pooley duly arrived, but thought the venture very parochial. His attitude (one that was to be met time and time again from London) was one of extreme condescension, and he certainly did not think WNO was worth an Arts Council grant.

But Bill Smith was not a man to let a little setback like that get in his way. In May 1948 he decided to place Welsh National Opera on a permanent footing by forming it into a limited company, on a non-profit sharing basis, "for the promotion and presentation of Grand Opera in Wales and elsewhere, and to contribute to the musical, cultural and educational life of the community", with himself as Chairman, Idloes Owen as Director of Operas, and as many influential people as he could persuade to join (Huw Wheldon and Bernard Morgan of David Morgan among them) on the Board. Smith was at pains to emphasise to everyone connected with WNO that the formation of a limited company did not mean that in future they would be paid for their work. The Morsmith Motors garage in Frederick Street became the company's first real headquarters. A piano was moved in and the first-floor showroom in which he stored cars became the principal rehearsal room. On rehearsal nights, at the end of the working day, the cars would be pushed to one side and the chorus would take over. And as the time of performances approached, one end of the showroom was curtained off to make an area for Florence Beese to store the costumes.

The Arts Council in London may have refused to help with a substantial grant, but fortunately Huw Wheldon in Cardiff was able to distribute small amounts to amateur organisations throughout Wales as he thought fit, simply getting London to rubber-stamp his decisions. Convinced that Welsh

National Opera was just the sort of scheme he ought to be backing, he managed to obtain a grant of £100 to be used, in the official phrase, for professional stiffening. This was a one-off sum which enabled the company to acquire the services of professionals. It was not, like today's grants, intended to cover the cost of a season or even of one particular production.

The formation of the Swansea section and the proposed seasons in Swansea to cater for audiences in West Wales led to the dropping of Porthcawl as a venue in 1948. Since no productions were planned in Swansea, however, until the following year, the 1948 spring season in Cardiff was extended to two weeks and saw the most ambitious planning so far, with performances of six operas. The fortnight opened at the Prince of Wales Theatre on 26 April with a new production of Verdi's *La Traviata*. Sets were again hired, but in order to keep down costs, Norman Jones, the producer, decided to revert to Verdi's original intention and stage the opera in modern dress. He also decided, against the objections of the purists, to introduce a ballet, choreographed by Mollie Hair, between Acts 2 and 3. Since this did not feature in the original score, the music was taken from *The Sicilian Vespers*, the opera Verdi wrote immediately after *La Traviata*. The opening performance got off to a tentative start. Laura Larne, a local concert artist and founder member of the company, making her operatic debut as Violetta, was extremely nervous in the first act and her apprehension seemed to affect the chorus. She was so nervous that in the interval she put on her dress back-to-front and was late for her entrance in the second act. Ivor John, the conductor, repeated the opening music and then placed his baton down while Alice James on stage as Annina the maid kept the action going by opening letters and dusting every piece of furniture and plumping every cushion at least twice. At last Violetta made her entrance and the opera continued. It was a great shame that Larne was unable to conquer her stage nerves, for she had a lovely voice and she could have become a considerable asset to the company. It cannot have helped her confidence that the orchestra too often tended to drown the singers. The interpolated ballet, while not actually getting in the way of the plot, added little to the evening. Tom Hopkins as Alfredo and a Cardiff doctor Arthur Davies, as Germont, stood out with their acting and accomplished singing, but the performance as a whole was not liked, particularly the modern dress. It was not the way most of the audience expected or wanted to see grand opera.

The second new production was of *Madam Butterfly*, the company's first Puccini, which opened at the Thursday matinée on 29 April, starring Victoria Elliott as Cio-Cio-San, produced by Norman Jones, and conducted by Ivor John. A large part of the grant Wheldon had managed to find for the company went on acquiring the services of Elliott, one of the rising stars of the operatic world and the first English artist to appear with WNO. There may have been some initial resentment from a few people who felt that either they or at least a Welsh soprano should have been given the part, but that evaporated the moment everyone heard her sing. Elliott not only possessed a glorious voice, she was one of those artists who threw everything into a performance, and she had very definite ideas about how her role should be played. She coached the Pinkerton (Frank James) in all his moves, even whispering to him what to do during performances. James remembers her saying, quite unknown to the audience, "Now love me a little . . . come on, enjoy yourself," adding, as he clasped her tenderly during the Act 1 duet, "And what are you going to do now?" The chorus were all a little in awe of her when she arrived in Wales, but because she made no concessions to their amateurism, much of her professionalism rubbed off on them.

There was one other English guest principal in the season, Ronald Stear, one of Britain's best-known basses, who took over the role of Mephistopheles in *Faust*, in which Mary Parker from Neath made her debut as Marguerite. The fortnight also included performances of *Carmen*, and of *Cav* and *Pag*. *Cav* saw two cast changes from the previous year amongst the smaller roles. Muriel Pointon sang her first Mamma Lucia and Joan Stephens, Lola. In *Pag*, Rita Davies took over as Nedda and Albert Thomas as Beppe. The operas were, as usual, conducted by Idloes Owen and Ivor John.

The season proved as popular as ever, Victoria Elliott's appearances being a particular attraction. Huw Wheldon had no doubt that his Arts Council money had been well spent, and that Welsh National Opera was worth every penny, and a lot more.

# CHAPTER THREE: 1949–1951

Six PRODUCTIONS in three years was the goal Idloes Owen had set, and in three seasons of performances it had been achieved. The Swansea section had been formed and was preparing to take to the stage in the autumn of 1949. The next target was to start touring, but, without a significant increase in grant from the Arts Council or guarantees from local authorities, that was an impossibility. So, just as in the two years between forming the company and the first staged performances Owen had filled in by organising concert appearances, it was decided that until WNO could afford to take out its productions, concerts would be given in towns and villages throughout Wales. The first such concert, intended to be the start of a tour taking in South, Mid and North Wales, and the first in which the two choruses from Cardiff and Swansea (totalling 120 voices) combined together, was given at the Empire Theatre in Cardiff on 9 January 1949, when *Cavalleria Rusticana* and a selection of operatic excerpts were performed with the BBC Welsh Orchestra under Walter Goehr.

Huw Wheldon was still doing his best to persuade his masters in London to find more money for Welsh National Opera. At the beginning of the year, he had obtained £200 to help hire orchestral players and in May a further £200 to help stage a two-week spring season at the Prince of Wales in Cardiff. This opened with *Carmen* in which Zoe Cresswell, Frank James and Arthur Davies repeated their roles and Eironwen Edwards from Swansea made her debut as Micaela. The orchestra, increased in size from the previous season, was conducted by Peter Gellhorn, a member of the Covent Garden music staff, who had been brought in by Smith to help raise standards. Gellhorn's handling of the orchestra and his forces on stage was highly praised. *Carmen* was given four times during the fortnight (for one performance Blanche Turner travelled from Covent Garden to take over from the indisposed Eironwen Edwards), and although Gellhorn was scheduled to conduct all four, he asked to be released from the last to attend the rehearsals of *Götterdämmerung* at Covent Garden. Victor Fleming, who had already conducted a matinée performance of *The Bartered Bride* that day, took Gellhorn's place without a rehearsal. Gellhorn had adopted quite different speeds from those of Fleming the previous year, and had introduced pauses into the chorus parts. Fleming had a quick word with the principals, assuring them that if they did not stay with him, he would stay with them, and asked the chorus to sing through the pauses. The tension of not knowing whether the evening would be a disaster or not put everyone on their mettle and resulted in the finest, most committed performance of the opera the company had given.

The new production of 1949 was of Smetana's *The Bartered Bride*. The suggestion to stage it had come from Fleming who had already conducted it in the Midlands with considerable success. Neither Owen nor Smith had been happy at first to move away from the standard repertoire and it had taken all Fleming's powers of persuasion to convince them. When they did finally agree, it was a decision they were not to regret. Smetana's portrait of life in a Czech village struck a sympathetic chord in the Welsh and provided an ideal vehicle for the Swansea chorus, which had been given the task of learning the opera.

For the first time, an outside producer was brought in. Norman Jones was spending so much time travelling to Swansea to rehearse the new Swansea section in *Carmen* (and when he wasn't in West Wales he was in Cardiff re-rehearsing the five productions already in the Cardiff section's repertoire) that he clearly could not give a new production the attention it required. Bill Smith, as was increasingly his habit, went straight to his contacts in London to find someone else. The man chosen was John Donaldson, who had produced the opera at Sadler's Wells, where he was resident producer, and Norman Jones became his assistant on the production. Rehearsals took place in Swansea and in Cardiff, which involved everyone concerned in much travelling between the two places. *The Bartered Bride* was not an easy work to cast from within the company, not if it was to make the right impact, and, continuing the policy of engaging guest artists to help raise standards, WNO went outside its own ranks to cast Arthur Servent, a former principal tenor with Sadler's Wells (who had been enjoying great success in the West End production of *Song of Norway*) as Jenik, and Edmund Donlevy as Kecal, the marriage broker.

Donaldson's production, in hired sets and costumes, opened on 4 May. Following immediately after two sold out performances of *Carmen*, it was disappointing to see empty seats in the house but the opera was comparatively unknown and Welsh audiences, as they were to show time and time again, were reluctant to try anything new. Those who were in the audience thoroughly enjoyed themselves. "How the audience rejoiced in Smetana's tuneful music with its exhilarating rhythms and its gay plot," commented the *Western Mail*. The two guest artists did not put a foot wrong. Arthur Servent "made a dashing Jenik, while the other guest star, Mr Edmund Donlevy, was great as the scheming marriage broker."

Donlevy, who compensated for a lack of vocal brilliance by superb acting, showed an excellent sense of timing and delivered his patter songs with impeccable enunciation. Against such artistry, the Welsh singers more than held their own and the evening was a particular triumph for two local artists: Nancy Bateman, a well-known concert singer, who was making her operatic debut as Marenka, and Evan Ellis, her brother, who had been taken from the chorus to play the stuttering Vasek. Bateman was ideally suited to her role, carrying it off with vivacity and charm, while Ellis, although not exceptionally musical (he had to be prompted for many of his cues by his sister), revealed a comic talent which completely won the audience. There was praise, too, for the remainder of the cast, for Donaldson's production and for the competent handling of a difficult score by Victor Fleming, and the performance was frequently interrupted by delighted applause.

The season also included revivals of *Madam Butterfly* and of *La Traviata*, both starring Victoria Elliott and conducted by Peter Gellhorn. Elliott's Butterfly was well known from the previous year; her Violetta proved once more that she possessed a voice of singular strength and beauty. Singing Alfredo opposite her, in place of the indisposed Tom Hopkins, was Tudor Davies who sang forcefully, if at times over-dramatically. Also in the repertoire from previous seasons were *Cav* and *Pag*, both conducted by Victor Fleming.

Apart from disappointing houses for *The Bartered Bride*, every performance had been sold out. Some 15,000 people had seen the productions, and the company's work was being eagerly discussed in Welsh musical circles. There had been a marked improvement in the chorus, which was now more balanced, and in the quality of the orchestra. The guest artists had all contributed much, both as individual performers and in the spur they gave their local colleagues. At the end-of-season press conference, Bill Smith talked eagerly about his plans to engage more vocal coaches and bring in even more notable outsiders to help raise standards still higher.

In August, Walter Goehr returned to conduct two further concerts with a specially assembled orchestra. The first, billed as "the event of the year", took place on 20 August in Central Hall, Newport. The chorus, with principals Zoe Cresswell, Iestyn Harry and Elwyn Adams, were joined in a selection of operatic excerpts by the popular Welsh bass Howell Glynne. The following evening Glynne and Cresswell, together with tenor Edgar Evans from Covent Garden, were the soloists at the second concert at Llanybyther. A small town in mid-Wales with a population of only 800, Llanybyther did not possess a concert hall, and so a marquee was erected in a field. Everyone waited with trepidation to see if anybody would turn up. An hour before the concert was due to start, the roads around the town began to fill up. People came by the coachload, by car, on bicycles, on foot;

some even came on horseback. By half-past seven, 5000 people had filled the marquee to overflowing and hundreds more were left sitting on the grass outside, listening to the chorus and soloists perform selections from *Tannhäuser*, *The Barber of Seville*, *Cavalleria Rusticana*, *I Pagliacci*, *La Traviata*, *The Bartered Bride*, *Carmen* and *Faust*. The evening ended, as it had in Newport, with a rousing *Hallelujah Chorus* from Handel's *Messiah*. Successful though both these performances were, staging such concerts without grants proved to be too expensive, and after Llanybyther the idea was reluctantly dropped.

Three months later, on 21 November 1949, Welsh National Opera made its long-awaited first stage appearance in Swansea, with the West Wales section providing the chorus for a week of opera at the Empire Theatre. Swansea audiences proved to be no more adventurous than those in Cardiff and the house was not full for *The Bartered Bride*, with which the week began. It was the first time, as far as anyone knew, that the opera had ever been performed there. The cast was as it had been in Cardiff and the performance was again conducted by Victor Fleming. Once more, it was Evan Ellis as the stuttering Vasek who managed to steal the show.

People did want to see *Carmen*, however, and all four performances were sold out. This was a company production without guest artists. The title role was taken by Lynne Davies, Iestyn Harry sang Don José, and Elwyn Adams, another chorister, performed Escamillo. The chorus, though smaller than its Cardiff counterpart, was particulary impressive, matching volume with precision, and the audience loved it.

Sadly, Idloes Owen, who had spent so much time training the chorus, was too ill to be present at the Swansea opening. The constant travelling to and from Swansea for rehearsals had proved too great a strain on his already poor health, and he had been ordered by his doctor to take a complete break from opera. There were already signs of a growing rift between Owen and Bill Smith. Owen lived for music; he was not interested in the financial side of WNO (nor of himself, for that matter) and he steadfastly refused to look at the books, concerning himself only with the making of music. He was not, however, keen on conducting orchestras and always used a vocal score, which he understood, rather than a full score. He was also a poor time-keeper: his rehearsals frequently began late and finished early. This was anathema to the ambitious Smith, who insisted that if a rehearsal was scheduled to begin at seven, it should begin at seven, and not end a minute before it was supposed to. Owen's lack of personal ambition was seen by Smith as being detrimental to WNO's welfare and future success. Smith took over more and more, relegating Owen to a secondary, backroom role. In 1949 Owen did not conduct a single opera, and although he was credited with being Music Director, his position had become, in effect, that of training the chorus and principals. And while Smith continued to consult with Owen on artistic matters, he was not prepared to lose the impetus the company was gaining. Increasingly, he was looking for outside help – it was his idea to bring in Peter Gellhorn – and when Owen became ill, he asked Victor Fleming to become more involved on a regular basis. When Fleming said he couldn't because of commitments elsewhere but that he would be happy to conduct any time he was needed, he was never invited back.

Smith was just the sort of ruthless man the company needed. Like any good businessman, he knew that in order to stand still Welsh National Opera had got to expand, and if personalities got in the way, that was too bad. An opera company, if it is to survive, is no place for sentiment.

Opera has always been an expensive art form. No major opera company is able to operate without a subsidy of some kind, and Welsh National Opera, even in those early years, was no exception. Although the chorus were wholly amateur, paying their own expenses to attend rehearsals, and all the backstage helpers gave their services free, rehearsal rooms and music had to be paid for, sets and costumes had to be hired, orchestral musicians, conductors and professional guest artists had to be paid. When WNO became a limited company in 1948, members' subscriptions and contributions towards the cost of rehearsal rooms, a useful source of revenue, ceased. Although the Arts Council had given a further £250 to underwrite the Swansea season, its grants, added to box-office returns, even when playing to full houses, still left a considerable shortfall on each season. Once the Swansea chorus had been established, Smith calculated that it cost £1000 a year to keep WNO alive without it even appearing on stage. These early deficits were cleared by private subscription and by members of the Board. In 1949, for example, Smith himself made a private donation of £100 in addition to providing the facilities of Morsmith Motors and paying, through the garage, the salaries of those people such as producer Norman Jones who worked for WNO full time. During 1949 he had taken another person onto the garage staff to help with the opera's administration, a person whose contribution and dedication to Welsh National Opera cannot be overestimated. Mrs Margaret Moreland had just given up her job in a solicitor's office and was planning to become a housewife, when she was asked to come into Frederick Street for a couple of days to help type out the minutes of a Board meeting. Thirty-five years later, she was still with WNO. If Smith was the general, she was the lieutenant. He may have had the ideas, but it was Peggy Moreland who made them happen. At first she had no title and acted as Smith's secretary, but her organisational skills soon surfaced and before long she was not only Secretary to the Board but was copying out translations, booking singers, sorting out rehearsal schedules, organising tours and doing on her own all those many tasks which are essential for the smooth running of any artistic enterprise. There can be little doubt that without her Welsh National Opera would not have succeeded as it has.

While preparations began for another year, the immediate financial problems were solved by the Arts Council. In 1948 John Denison, a former horn player with the BBC Symphony, London Philharmonic and City of Birmingham orchestras, and Assistant Director of Music for the British Council, had been appointed Music Director of the Arts Council. Huw Wheldon had immediately invited him to a performance of Welsh National Opera in the hope of getting his backing for a more realistic grant. Denison's first impressions were not particularly favourable. While he enjoyed the production he saw, he felt that the company was really too amateur to warrant the kind of grant that would take it out of the music-club category. What made him change his mind was the combined enthusiasm of Wheldon and Smith, who finally convinced him that their plans for Welsh National Opera could happen if only they had the money. And so Denison made his recommendation to the Welsh Committee that WNO should receive an appropriate grant. The Committee responded by increasing the grant for 1950 to £1800.

Smith, determined that WNO would continue to grow, decided to use the increased grant to bring in more outside help, which he felt to be essential to its progress. He was not a musician, indeed he did not know much about music, but he had an almost unfailing instinct for picking talented artists, invariably young people who would welcome the opportunities Welsh National Opera could offer them to extend their repertoires and their experience. He constantly asked advice from singers, musicians and administrators, becoming a frequent visitor to Sadler's Wells and Covent Garden, and always keeping an eye open for people who might fit into his scheme of things. His ability to attract first-rate artists for small fees became legendary. At Sadler's Wells he attended a performance of *The Bartered Bride*, in which two Welshmen, Gerald Davies and Howell Glynne, were singing the roles of Jenik and Kecal. Knowing that WNO's production was to be revived the following season, he went backstage. Both Davies and Glynne were naturally interested in his invitation to repeat their roles in Wales. The conversation soon turned to money. Smith bemoaned the fact that he could not afford to pay large fees, and a figure of 20 guineas a performance was mentioned. Howell Glynne replied that his concert fee was £35, and if other managements found out he had appeared in Wales for less, they, too, would expect to pay him lower fees. "I tell you what," said Smith, "do it for £25 a performance and I won't tell anybody." "I've got a better idea," answered Glynne. "Pay us £35 a performance and tell everybody!" Eventually they settled on a figure of £25.

Shortly after that meeting, Smith was in touch with Gerald Davies again. The 1950 season, he explained, was going to be the longest they had yet had, with two weeks in Cardiff in the spring and two weeks in Swansea in the autumn. Did Davies know of any talented young conductors who would be prepared to go down cheaply? Without hesitation, Davies recommended a young Australian répétiteur who had been on the staff at Sadler's Wells for two years and had created a very favourable impression, Charles Mackerras.

Smith offered Mackerras the job of conducting the two new productions in the forthcoming season, *The Tales of Hoffmann* and *Die Fledermaus*, plus revivals of *Faust* and *The Bartered Bride*. Mackerras, eager to establish a reputation outside the Wells, was delighted to accept. However, he was unable to fulfil all the dates and suggested a colleague from Sadler's Wells to share them with him, South African Leo Quayle.

*The Tales of Hoffmann*, conducted by Mackerras, opened the spring season at the Prince of Wales on 8 May, with Gabriel Todd, a young Welsh tenor who had just left the Royal Academy of Music, as Hoffmann. It was a patchy performance. Mackerras's conducting was praised and won a deserved ovation, and the chorus, which took some time to settle down on the first night, was, by the end of the second week, being compared favourably to that of Covent Garden. Patti Lewis, as Hoffmann's friend Nicklaus, chorister Elizabeth Bowen and Joan Stephens, splitting the roles between them of Hoffmann's lovers (customarily played by the same artist) shared the vocal honours. But against those pluses, Gabriel Todd, while he looked the part, proved a disappointment as Hoffmann. And producer Norman Jones, usually so reliable, also had an off-night. After the high standards set in previous productions, this one seemed decidedly amateur. The general standard of singing was not high, the sets were poor and the costumes dowdy. *The Tales of Hoffmann* failed to delight the public. And, apart from the famous Barcarolle, audiences did not know the opera, which was enough to keep many people away.

The following night *Faust* was revived with William McAlpine in the title role, Margaret Williams as Marguerite and Geoffrey Davies making his debut as Mephistopheles. It was conducted by the BBC's head of music in Wales, Arwel Hughes, and reassured everyone that the company had not lost its touch. *Faust* and *The Tales of Hoffmann* were played for the remainder of the week until the Saturday evening, when *The Bartered Bride*, conducted by Mackerras, was given. Nancy Bateman was once more outstanding as Marenka, while the bargain duet between Gerald Davies and Howell Glynne had to be given an encore.

The second week saw *Die Fledermaus* added to the repertory with Margaret Glyn as Adele, Phyllis Ash-Child as Orlofsky, Frank James as

Eisenstein and Zoe Cresswell as Rosalinda. Edmund Donlevy, the one guest in the cast, sang Colonel Frank, the prison governor. The uncertainties that had marred *The Tales of Hoffmann* had largely vanished. Leo Quayle drew some sparkling playing from the orchestra, and the chorus sang with a lightness, rhythmic precision and spontaneity which surprised many people. The production by Norman Jones (who also played Frosch the gaoler), choreographed by Mollie Hair, who led the ballet troupe, was considered to be the best he had done.

At the end of October, *Faust* opened a fortnight's season in Swansea with Martin Lawrence, the English bass, appearing as Mephistopheles, Iestyn Harry as Faust and Margaret Williams as Marguerite. Iestyn Harry "suffered from faulty make-up and a lack of power in the top register, but his singing of the love duet in Act 2 with Margaret Williams, who had a fine purity of voice, was really effective." Lynne Davies "was miscast histrionically and vocally as Siebel," and "except for rare occasions when the singers selected their own tempo, Leo Quayle, the conductor, maintained a nice control over cast and orchestra . . . Martin Lawrence . . . was a dominating figure throughout, majestically evil, and singing with fine sonority. His diction and demeanour were a lesson to the rest."

The performance of *Die Fledermaus* the following night, with Victoria Elliott taking over as Rosalinda, played to a packed and enthusiastic house, as did *The Bartered Bride* later in the week.

The second week began with *The Tales of Hoffmann*, in which the new Hoffmann, John Myrddin, a principal tenor from the Carl Rosa Company, sang with a strength and quality that had been missing in the Cardiff performances. The remaining production, also new to Swansea, was of *Madam Butterfly*, with Victoria Elliott.

The year had ended on a high note. The Cardiff fortnight in the spring had attracted more than 15,000 people and the two weeks in Swansea had played to mostly full houses (*Faust* and *Ho*,*ffmann* being the exceptions). The chorus strength had increased to 200 (125 in Cardiff, 75 in Swansea), and among the many invitations that had been received for Welsh National Opera to appear outside Wales, Bill Smith announced, somewhat prematurely, that he had accepted one for a European tour the following year. It was his intention, he stated, to take on European opera companies on their own ground. More realistically, he could claim with some justification that the company was moving slowly but steadily towards becoming professional. A start had been made during the year by engaging Betty Thompson, who had coached Zoe Cresswell as Carmen, to become the company's Histrionic Director. The title, possibly unique in opera, was chosen by Smith because he liked its sound. What it meant in practice was that Betty Thompson (with Vera Cook as her accompanist) became the assistant producer, coaching chorus and principals in acting their roles, and eventually becoming responsible for staging revivals. As well as taking on permanent staff, Smith wanted also to start designing and building sets, and making costumes, in house. To hire them was never entirely satisfactory, and to make their own would, in the long run, save money. Some of the costumes used in the year's productions had been made by members of the chorus, and somewhere other than the car showroom was needed to store them. Although a fund to enable WNO's own sets to be built had been launched and nearly £900 had been donated, the plan had to be postponed, for the total cost of the Cardiff and Swansea seasons had come to £7000, a figure well above the annual income, and the fund had to be used to help pay off the debts.

If four weeks of performances during 1950 had seemed ambitious, 1951 was to prove even more eventful. It was the year of the Festival of Britain, a nation-wide celebration designed to demonstrate that Britain had finally emerged from the rigours of the Second World War, and Smith was determined that Welsh National Opera should play its full part in the festivities. The Arts Council's grant was increased to £2000 to enable it to embark on what were termed 'missionary tours' of Wales, with a visit to the National Eisteddfod in Llanrwst and a week in both Aberystwyth and Llandudno, as well as a fortnight in Cardiff and in Swansea. That may not seem much by today's standards, but it was a formidable undertaking for an amateur company. Every member of the chorus and backstage crew had to take time off work to travel the length of Wales to perform. Some took the opportunity of being in Aberystwyth and Llandudno to take their annual holidays and travelled with their families. Others, like Ethel Brown, who worked in Woolworth's in Swansea, had understanding bosses who, in exchange for tickets whenever WNO appeared locally, were quite happy for staff to have time off. Although most people were able to get away, it was very often without pay, and in order to ensure as full a turn-out as possible, a decision was taken to pay compensation for lost wages.

And so at the beginning of 1951 a period of intense preparation began, during which nine operas, including one new work and *Cavalleria Rusticana* in Welsh, were rehearsed. Some people found they were attending a rehearsal five nights a week, but such was the commitment that attendance was almost always 100 percent.

It was clear that Idloes Owen's health would not allow him to keep up such a punishing schedule, and in April, Haydn James from Swansea was appointed Musical Director in all but name to take some of the burden off him. James, who had trained in Italy, was considered by many of the chorus to be the finest choral trainer the company ever had. His great drawback was his temper. If he was not happy with their work, he would fling off his coat and leap up and down in such a rage that everyone fully expected to see him disappear through the floor of the Frederick Street rehearsal room into the showroom below.

The annual appearance in Cardiff began with a two-week season at the Prince of Wales on 30 April. The first night was of the new production of *Il Trovatore*, which had long been one of Bill Smith's favourite operas. Anthony Marlowe, who had appeared at Covent Garden, sang Manrico, while Leonora was the soprano Kyra Vane. Born of Russian parents, Kyra Vane had appeared in *Gay Rosalinda* with Richard Tauber and had sung in Barcelona and elsewhere on the continent as well as in London. Phyllis Ash-Child, who was to become such a WNO stalwart, appeared as Azucena.

On 4 August, a concert performance in Welsh of *Cavalleria Rusticana* was given at the opening of the National Eisteddfod in Llanrwst. Victoria Elliott, singing Santuzza, had not only learnt her role in Welsh but committed it to memory, and gave a passionate rendering of the music which went a long way towards appeasing those members of the audience who were piqued that she and the Turiddu (Heddle Nash, making his only appearance with Welsh National Opera) were both English. The performance received a tremendous ovation.

On 3 September, WNO made its first appearance in Aberystwyth with a week at the King's Hall in which *Faust*, *Cav* and *Pag*, and *Madam Butterfly* were performed. Two weeks later they appeared at the Grand Theatre, Llandudno. The previous occupants had been a circus, as the smell backstage testified, and the first thing the chorus and principals, assisted by Peggy Moreland, had to do was scrub out the dressing rooms. The operas given were *Madam Butterfly*, *Cav* and *Pag*, and *Il Trovatore* in which a young singer who was to go on to international fame made both his debut with the company and his debut as a principal. When Stanley Gitsham, who was singing the part of Ferrando, was unable to appear at the last moment, Bill Smith had great difficulty finding a replacement. Kenneth Loveland, the critic and editor of the *South Wales Argus*, suggested a member of the Covent Garden chorus he had heard in concert with a South Wales male voice choir, and Smith immediately booked him. His name was Michael Langdon.

The Swansea fortnight came at the end of October, with Haydn James in charge of *Il Trovatore*, Warwick Braithwaite conducting *La Traviata* and *Madam Butterfly*, both with Victoria Elliott, and Ivor John taking over for *Cav* and *Pag* and *Die Fledermaus*, and brought to a fitting end WNO's most ambitious and successful year so far. Six weeks of opera had been played to more people than ever before throughout the length and breadth of Wales. The number of people attending the performances in Aberystwyth was equivalent to more than half the total population of the town, while in

Llandudno a fund had been started to bring the company back to the resort the following year. But the success had been bought at a price. In his determination to make Welsh National Opera comparable with any company in Britain or on the continent, Bill Smith had pressed on with his plans even though they could not be afforded. His declared aim was that people should visit Wales to see opera in the same way as they went to Italy. He wanted, he said, "fame for the company". He had estimated the expenditure for the year as being between £21,000 and £22,000, which, even with an increased Arts Council grant and playing to full houses, meant a projected deficit of around £3000. Cardiff Corporation, which had voted to give £1000 to help meet this shortfall, reversed its decision at its next meeting, and the year finished with an overdraft of £12,000. Smith stated the case quite bluntly: either additional funding had to be found, or Welsh National Opera would cease to exist.

SALVATION came in the form of the Arts Council. Whereas London had always thought of Welsh National Opera as just another amateur music club on the same level as the Cardiff Organ Club or the Banbury Co-operative Society's Choir, it now recognised the truth of what first Huw Wheldon and then Myra Owen, Wheldon's successor as Director of the Welsh Committee, had been saying all along – that WNO had the potential to become a major force in Welsh cultural life. 1951 had shown that it was well on the way to achieving that, and so the Arts Council decided to bail out the company by increasing the total grants for 1952 to £6275.

Work began immediately on two new productions of operas by Verdi: *Rigoletto*, which was given to the Swansea section, and *Nabucco*, which both choruses had to learn. *Nabucco* was virtually unknown in Britain. The idea for doing it had come from John Moody, the Arts Council Drama Director and former resident producer at Sadler's Wells, who was one of the many contacts Bill Smith had made during his forays to London. Smith had heard all about Moody's hugely successful production of Verdi's *Simon Boccanegra* at Sadler's Wells, the first time the opera had been staged in Britain, and, hoping to tempt him to stage something for WNO, had invited him to Wales. It was not until November 1949, when one of the drama companies for which Moody was responsible at the Arts Council was in Swansea performing *Ghosts* at the same time as WNO was at the Empire, that Moody was able to see WNO in action. He managed to catch Act 1 of *The Bartered Bride*, Act 2 of *Ghosts* and Act 3 of *The Bartered Bride*, and was immediately struck by the company's enthusiasm, dedication and vitality. However, his commitments at the Arts Council meant he was unable to accept Smith's offer to work with WNO. The following summer he and his wife Nell were on holiday in Switzerland and saw a performance of the rarely staged *Nabucco* in Zürich. Moody knew it was a work that had to be staged in Britain. On his return home, he told Norman Tucker at Sadler's Wells that he must put it on. Tucker replied that he couldn't, firstly because he didn't have a soprano who could sing the taxing role of Abigail, and secondly because the Wells did not have a large enough chorus to do it justice. And there it might have rested but for a chance meeting Moody had soon afterwards with Bill Smith.

*Nabucco*, written when Verdi was 29, was his third opera and his first unqualified success. It tells the story of Nebuchadnezzar's capture of Jerusalem (Nabucco being the shortened form of his name), the intrigues of his adopted daughter, Abigail, against the legitimate Princess Fenena, his blasphemy, madness and recovery after being converted to Judaism, and the freeing of the Jews from Babylonian captivity. It was composed to a libretto by the wonderfully named Temistocle Solera at a time when Verdi was on the point of giving up composition entirely. It was first performed at La Scala, Milan, in March 1842, and four years later was seen at Her Majesty's Theatre in London under the name *Nino* (a sop to the Victorian objection to Biblical subjects being portrayed on the stage). It was given again, this time as *Anato*, at Covent Garden in 1850, the last time it had been seen in Britain.

*Nabucco*, as Moody told Smith, was an ideal work for the Welsh. It is exceptionally rich in choral work, the opening scene being almost exclusively choral punctuated by arias, while the third act, in which the Jews lament by the waters of Babylon in a paraphrase of Psalm 137, contains one of the finest choruses in all opera. The opportunities it would afford the WNO chorus, the Biblical setting and the theme of patriotism made it, Moody was convinced, a perfect choice. Bill Smith needed little persuading.

It had always been the intention, ever since WNO was founded, that it would one day become self-sufficient, and *Nabucco* became the first totally in-house production. Smith managed to obtain the temporary release of John Moody from the Arts Council to direct it. Patrick Robertson, from the Bristol Old Vic, was brought in as designer, and Joan Pyle, who had been working at Glyndebourne, was engaged to supervise the making of the costumes. Moody asked for £1500 to mount the production, agreeing eventually to do it for £1200. It was finally produced for a total cost of £1358.

It was a massive undertaking. There were seven different scenes requiring seven different sets; every member of the eighty-strong chorus had to have two costumes to appear both as Babylonians and as Jews; footwear had to be found, beards made, props constructed. Premises were needed in which the sets could be built. These were found eventually above the coffee business run by stage manager Robert Ernest. Cecil Bridge, from the chorus, took on the job of building the scenery and making the props. Two small cottages which were due for demolition close to Morsmith Motors in Frederick Street, were taken over to house the wardrobe. Patrick Robertson spent hours in the library researching the costumes and hours inventing dyes to find the cheapest way of producing them. He eventually achieved the patterns he wanted by spraying dye through net curtains onto the cheapest material he could find. And when he wasn't working on the costumes, Robertson was painting the sets. Everyone mucked in. Anyone who could wield a needle, including Bill Smith's wife, helped out with making the costumes. Even the guest artists became caught up with the enthusiasm to lend a hand. On the first night, Ruth Packer, who was singing Abigail, was sewing rings onto the temple curtains until ten minutes before she was due on stage.

Work began on the opera long before the principal casting was complete, and chorus rehearsals in both Cardiff and Swansea under Leo Quayle, the new Musical Director, took place over several months. For some time, Smith had been looking for a suitable person to take over the musical side from the ailing Owen, and Quayle had shown himself on previous visits to be a good choral trainer as well as good with orchestras. The chorus liked and respected him. Quayle coached them so thoroughly that by the time of the opening, if the orchestra had struck up with *La Traviata* or any other opera, they would still have sung their parts perfectly. Production rehearsals also started early, but because Moody was unable to take too much time off from the Arts Council, he travelled to Wales only once a fortnight to rehearse with the chorus. In order to use his vast resources to the greatest effect, he had arranged the production as a series of tiers, on which he grouped the chorus simply but strikingly. The opera was being sung in a new translation by Norman Tucker and Tom Hammond, and although Moody had carefully worked out the moves he wanted, his main emphasis throughout the rehearsals was that the chorus should believe the words they were singing, that every movement and gesture they made should come from within.

The small roles were cast from within the company; Joan Stephens as Princess Fenena, Muriel Pointon as Anna (Zaccaria's sister), William Russell as Abdullah (one of Nabucco's officers) and Leslie Wicks as the High Priest of Baal. Tano Ferendinos, a Cardiff-based tenor with a Greek father and a Welsh mother, was cast as the Jewish prince Ishmael. The problems came with the casting of the three leading roles. The taxing role of Abigail, who dominates the opera (first sung by Giuseppina Strepponi, who later became Verdi's wife), requires coloratura singing of a remarkable quality with a span of more than two octaves. Moody decided to cast the English soprano Ruth Packer. Packer had trained in Vienna and before the war had been a *prima donna* in all the usual big soprano roles, but no one had heard her sing a role like Abigail. Moody, who had heard her in *Il Trovatore* in the 30s, thought casting her was a risk worth taking. Appearing opposite her as Zaccaria was the distinguished bass Hervey Alan, with whom Moody had worked at Sadler's Wells. Nabucco proved more difficult to find, and, after a long search, Ronald Jackson, an Australian baritone who had just started singing with the Carl Rosa Company, was given the part. They and the other principals were coached in their roles in London by Edward Downes, then on the music staff at Covent Garden.

While preparations for *Nabucco* were proceeding, events were taking place in an English holiday resort which were to have a profound influence on the musical life of Wales. For some time the Bournemouth Municipal Orchestra had been in financial trouble. Opposition on the local council towards continuing its annual subsidy of £19,000 had been growing steadily, and when the orchestra announced another loss in March, those who wanted to get rid of it went on the war-path. In April the council secretly considered a plan to amalgamate the BMO with the City of Birmingham Symphony Orchestra. The proposal, which came from Birmingham, where the CBSO was also in deep financial trouble, was that an orchestra of seventy-five players should divide its time equally between the two centres under joint musical directors. The plan was rejected, as was another proposal for a smaller orchestra of only thirty-five players. However, that summer the orchestra's opponents finally got their way and the players were told their contracts would not be renewed after September. "I am all for the abolition of a costly toy," stated one alderman. "We are pandering to the tastes of a small minority," declared another. "Some of the people who go to these concerts don't know the difference between Beethoven and Tchaikovsky," opined a third. Such attitudes were ones with which WNO itself was to become all too familiar. Once the news was out, public opinion in Bournemouth was outraged. Money from local residents and businesses poured into a fighting fund and the council finally bowed to the pressure, agreeing to reprieve the orchestra for another year but on a month's notice to quit. During this struggle for survival, John Denison, the Arts Council's Director of Music, had become involved with the orchestra's future and it was Denison, a friend and confidant of Bill Smith, who suggested, as one of the ways it might raise additional revenue, that the BMO might be employed by Welsh National Opera, to become, in effect, its house orchestra. Both Bill Smith and Charles Groves, the BMO's principal conductor, were delighted with the suggestion and the BMO was engaged for the autumn seasons in Cardiff and Swansea.

The first public appearance of the year, on 9 August, was made not with the Bournemouth Municipal Orchestra, however, but with the London Symphony Orchestra in a concert performance of *Carmen* in Welsh which closed the annual National Eisteddfod, held that year in Aberystwyth. Zoe Cresswell sang Carmen, Rowland Jones, Don José, Tom Williams, Escamillo, and the conductor was Leo Quayle. The performance took place in a huge barn of a hall which lacked all atmosphere, and yet, without the aid of costumes or scenery, still managed to provide the capacity audience with a magnificent climax to the Eisteddfod.

The long-awaited Cardiff season finally opened, not at the Prince of Wales, but at a new venue, the Sophia Gardens Pavilion. The Pavilion, a former aircraft hangar, had been acquired by Cardiff Council for the Festival of Britain and they had just spent £400 converting it into a theatre. It seated just under 2000 people and, with only two rows of seats on each level of the raked auditorium, it was promised that everyone, even those at the back, would have an uninterrupted view of the stage. New lighting had been installed to make it comparable to any major theatre in Britain, capable of staging the largest, most spectacular touring shows as well as opera. Not as much attention had been lavished backstage, however. There were only four dressing rooms, and the chorus found they had to change in a room in which the gentlemen were divided from the ladies by a curtain. To add to their problems, in the week of the performances the River Taff overflowed its banks and flooded the room.

Billed as a Festival of Opera, the week began with a full house for *Carmen* on 6 October. Perhaps it was the newness of the surroundings and the size of the hall, or maybe it was the fact that, for the first time, WNO was attracting enormous interest from outside Wales, but the performance did not go well. It was a *Carmen* without passion. Zoe Cresswell, in the title role, had a distinctly off-night, and Rowland Jones delivered a very frigid Don José, clearly saving himself for the climaxes. People who had seen them at the Eisteddfod in August found it hard to believe they were watching the same two artists. The second act was a considerable improvement on the first but even the normally reliable Arnold Davies, a Post Office employee from Aberdare, singing Escamillo seemed daunted by the size of the hall, and much of his part in the lower register of his voice was inaudible. Everything was right except the performance, commented Kenneth Loveland in the *South Wales Argus*. It was, he suggested, frankly not good enough. There was untidiness and indecision in the entries, which may have been due to the singers not being able to see the conductor properly, and there were two minor disasters in both Acts 1 and 2 when the performance had seemed in danger of grinding to a halt. Hard though Leo Quayle tried to bring the performance to life, the whole evening was far too stiff and respectable, saved only by the spirited singing of the chorus in the final act and the excellence of the Bournemouth orchestra in the pit.

Backstage there were problems too. There was no Tannoy in the chorus dressing room to summon the chorus to the stage, and a group of choristers arrived in the wings at the very moment they should have been going on. The stage at the Pavilion was shallower than that at the Prince of Wales and actually getting on quickly in large numbers was difficult. Seeing a gap in the scenery, one of the late choristers hurried through, followed by several colleagues. They had entered through the fireplace.

Although *Carmen* proved to be a disappointing start to the season, it was noticeable that many of the singers in the minor roles had made big advances since their last appearances. Singled out for universal praise was the Micaela of Joan Stephens.

On the following night, 7 October, came the event that everyone had been waiting for: the first night of *Nabucco*. As a matter of historical accuracy it was not, as is often claimed, the first performance of the opera in Britain this century, though that honour still belongs to Wales. Earlier that year, in March, the Clydach and District Operatic Society had staged the work with Serafina de Leo as Abigail and Tom Williams as Nabucco, conducted by Dai Maddocks, a local window cleaner. But it was the Cardiff performance which attracted the interest. The critics descended on Sophia Gardens *en masse* from London and applications for tickets had been received from as far away as Newcastle and Dublin. It was a night to remember for everyone who was in the audience or on the stage. "The result," wrote Cecil Smith in *Opera*, having seen a decidedly poor performance of *Il Trovatore* the previous year and expecting the worst, "should have been something well-meaning but amateurish. Astonishingly enough, the investiture of the opera proved to be wholly professional – and more, for the stage looked handsomer by far than the Covent Garden stage does half the time. And the chorus and principals, skilfully directed by John Moody . . . contributed their share." "One had not come prepared for such handsome and elaborate staging," commented Philip Hope-Wallace in the *Manchester Guardian*.

Ruth Packer as Abigail dominated the stage, displaying a remarkable intensity and thrilling vehemency with singing the like of which had rarely been heard before. "Her voice is admittedly no longer in its first freshness, but it is strange that singing of this calibre has not won wider recognition in the past," wrote Desmond Shawe-Taylor. Very few people in the audience or on the stage were aware that she was singing under the extreme handicap of poor eyesight, amounting to near-blindness. She had spent hours alone on the stage learning her moves so that she would not have to look where she was going. Opposite her, Hervey Alan sang an imposing Zaccaria with all the authority of an Old Testament prophet, and Ronald Jackson, while not perhaps having the ideal voice for Nabucco, made a sympathetic king, especially fine in portraying Nabucco's madness. Tano Ferendinos was a heroic Ishmael, and Joan Stephens, as Fenena, more than held her own amongst the professionals. "It would be impossible to find a single weakness in last night's cast," commented the critic of the *Western Mail*.

The stellar honours for the evening went not to one of the soloists but to the eighty-strong chorus. Verdi's swinging music was sung with a passion and fervour that had not been heard on the British operatic stage before. Their lack of vocal inhibition as they launched into each chorus with an emotion, a "hwyl", usually reserved for rugby internationals at Cardiff Arms Park, reaching a magnificent climax in the "Va, pensiero" chorus of the sorrowing Israelites in Act 3, turned what might have been just an interesting resurrection of a long-lost opera into a triumph.

The decision to revive *Nabucco* turned out to have been a stroke of genius. The company fell on it with a holy joy, proving it to be a masterpiece in its own right. Leo Quayle, in addition to his impeccable training of the chorus, showed a careful mastery of the score, and the Bournemouth Municipal Orchestra played as if it had been accompanying opera all its life.

It would be difficult to underestimate the importance of that night. Welsh National Opera established beyond question its right to be classed among the leading opera companies in Britain. "Remarkable things are going on in Wales," concluded the critic of the *Daily Express*.

The following night was almost bound to be an anti-climax. Charles Groves, the principal conductor of the Bournemouth Municipal Orchestra, made his first appearance conducting *Il Trovatore* in front of a full house. Groves had had considerable experience at the BBC conducting opera in the studio for radio broadcasts, but this was his first time in a theatre and he entered the pit for the evening without having had the luxury of a dress rehearsal, even though several of the cast (Emelie Hook as Leonora and James Johnston as Manrico among them) were new to the production. It may well have been that so much time and energy had been expended on *Nabucco* that *Il Trovatore* had not received as much attention as it deserved, for the performance seemed under-rehearsed and never quite caught fire. Groves occasionally allowed the pace to drag, making it difficult for the singers to sustain their line, and the overall impression was of a good performance in the making rather than a good performance in itself.

On the Thursday afternoon, *Carmen* was performed at a schools matinée with a change of cast, Patti Lewis, the wife of a policeman, taking over as Carmen, and Robert Thomas, the Cardiff-born tenor from Sadler's Wells, as the new Don José. Thomas brought to his arias a fluidity and confidence that had been lacking in Rowland Jones's performance, and he and Patti Lewis made a striking pair in spite of the fact that the house was full of schoolchildren who laughed in all the wrong places. Two further performances of *Carmen* and *Nabucco* and one of *Il Trovatore* completed the week.

In one short season, Welsh National Opera had come of age. It had proved with *Nabucco* that it could stand comparison with any company in Britain. Those critics who had travelled to provincial Cardiff from sophisticated London expecting to scoff had, without exception, stayed to cheer. If there was a single blot on the landscape, it was that while the performances of *Carmen* and of *Il Trovatore* had been sold out, *Nabucco* had not played to a single full house. Cardiff audiences had once more shown a distinct reluctance to try the unknown.

The Bournemouth Municipal Orchestra was again in the pit four weeks later for the two-week season at the Swansea Empire. This opened on 10 November with *Nabucco*, sung by the same principals as in Cardiff, with Leo Quayle conducting. This time, however, the chorus was drawn entirely from the Swansea section. It is quite remarkable to think that not only had Quayle had to coach two choruses in the opera but that Moody had also had to rehearse two productions simultaneously. In spite of the ecstatic reviews *Nabucco* had received in Cardiff, Swansea audiences were also suspicious of a work they didn't know and it did not play to a full house. The performance proved, though, that the Cardiff reaction had not been gratuitously enthusiastic. The chorus, although smaller in size than the Cardiff section, earned praise for their rich tone and committed attack as they, too, allowed themselves to be carried away by the emotion of the story. The "Va, pensiero" chorus was a crowning jewel in an evening that was already an enormous success.

*Nabucco* was followed by a sold-out performance of *Il Trovatore* conducted by Warwick Braithwaite, with Zoe Cresswell, James Johnston, Arnold Davies, Hervey Alan and Phyllis Ash-Child in the leading roles. Braithwaite was cheered repeatedly when he took his place on the rostrum and conducted an impressive and much enjoyed performance. *Carmen* and *La Traviata* were also performed in the first week. *Carmen*, under Leo Quayle, had Patti Lewis as Carmen, Robert Thomas as Don José and Ruth Preece, daughter of the Chorus Mistress, Isabel Davies, and a member of the Carl Rosa Company, making her debut as an excellent Micaela. Braithwaite also conducted *La Traviata* with Victoria Elliott again a superb Violetta opposite Dennis Stephenson's Alfredo.

The second week opened with the other new production, Verdi's *Rigoletto*. It had long been Smith's ambition to stage *Rigoletto* but Quayle had told him there simply was not enough time for the chorus to learn it as well as learning *Nabucco*. Undeterred, Smith asked Isabel Davies to rehearse it instead. The colourful production was put on in only a few weeks by Norman Jones in hired sets and costumes. Quayle, who conducted the first night, must have been both astonished and pleased by the work Isabel Davies had done, for the all-male chorus from the Swansea section sang impressively, securely, and with an obviously increased awareness of the fact that they were an operatic chorus not a choir in costume. Their commitment was total, their enunciation excellent, matching the performances of the principals. Monterone's curse was dramatically delivered by Hervey Alan, chorister Elizabeth Bowen sang sweetly as Gilda, and Dennis Stephenson's Duke of Mantua, though a little insecure at the top, was a great improvement on his Alfredo. Where the production really scored was by having Tom Williams in the title role. Rigoletto was a role which he had made very much his own at Sadler's Wells, and one in which he was considered to be the finest British exponent of his generation. He brought the part vividly to life.

Once *Rigoletto* was safely on stage, Isabel Davies, who had contributed so much to its success, and to the success of WNO since its foundation, decided to resign as Chorus Mistress. Like almost everyone else, she had been combining Welsh National Opera with a full-time job, in her case as a teacher, and increased teaching commitments did not permit her the time to continue.

At the beginning of December, a party was held at the St Mellons Country Club. John Moody was presented with a silver salver in recognition of his work on *Nabucco*, and Cecil Bridge, who had built the sets and made all the props, was presented with a sugar sifter. In his acceptance speech, Moody told his audience how much he admired their qualities of enthusiasm and hard work; his stay with them had been an inspiration. "No other company enjoy themselves so much at work as you do. It is a quality you must never lose," he added. Although there was an air of celebration and congratulation about the proceedings, both Bill Smith and Leo Quayle sounded a warning note. Quayle, while delighted with the achievements, cautioned against complacency; there was, he said, still a lot of work to be done to raise standards. And Smith, ever the realist, pointed out that, eventful though the year had been, the following year was going to be even more important.

Smith was right. It was all very well for visitors to Wales to see an amateur chorus with a sprinkling of professional guests putting on opera and to say how good it was, but he wanted WNO to be judged in the same light as Covent Garden or Sadler's Wells, and that meant taking to the road and going outside the Principality to be seen by audiences whose experience of opera was of those other companies. In April 1953 sets and artists were loaded onto a train bound for Bournemouth. The visit, the first outside Wales, had been arranged the previous year as part of the agreement between the WNO and the Bournemouth Municipal Orchestra, and was not just a first for Welsh National Opera; it was the first made to the provinces by a British opera company not based in London. The short season of one week opened on Monday 13 April at the Bournemouth Pavilion with a performance of *Nabucco*, the first time the opera had been heard in English outside Wales. Leo Quayle's handling of the score was inspired, and both chorus and orchestra responded well to his direction. It was, according to a local critic, one of the best evenings of co-operation between stage and pit ever heard outside a major opera house, and there were nine curtain calls at the finish. The following day, it seemed all Bournemouth was talking about the chorus. WNO, it was agreed, was no longer a deserving provincial enterprise but a British musical institution of stature.

The Pavilion was packed the following night for *Il Trovatore* ("One of the best productions seen in Bournemouth for many years"). Of the two guests taking part (Hervey Alan as Ferrando and well-known tenor Walter Midgley as Manrico) only Midgley received less than ecstatic reviews. The chorus, different from the one that had performed the previous night, sang with precision and firm attack, and the opera was conducted by Charles Groves. The lukewarm reviews Midgley had received led to his indisposition for the second performance, and John Myrddin had to be brought down from London, arriving in Bournemouth only half-an-hour before curtain up. He gave a forthright and heroic performance which was generally preferred to Midgley's.

The week also included performances of *Rigoletto* and *Die Fledermaus*. *Die Fledermaus* played to capacity houses but in spite of good individual performances, failed to capture totally the infectious lilt of Strauss's melodies. The production, felt one critic, "seeks out and penetrates the weaknesses in Welsh National Opera's armour." All the ingredients were there; what was needed was refinement and polish. *Rigoletto*, while being a personal triumph for Tom Williams in the title role, was also not entirely successful, although the production had been tightened considerably since Swansea and the chorus was excellent. The week, however, had played to large and enthusiastic audiences, and after the final performance of *Il Trovatore* on Saturday night, the applause only stopped because the Mayor of Bournemouth went on stage to thank the company. Negotiations began immediately for a repeat season the following year, and invitations arrived for a season in London and a provincial tour, both of which had to be turned down because of the lack of money. Interest in the work of WNO was now national, and its increasing importance was recognised in June by the award of a CBE to Bill Smith.

During the summer, Leo Quayle resigned as Musical Director. His successor was Frederick Berend. Born in Hanover, in Germany, Berend had studied at Munich University and worked as a répétiteur at the Munich Opera under Bruno Walter. He had been musical director of two German opera houses and had worked in Italy for a year and a half before quitting Germany in 1939. Settling in Britain, he had become a British citizen, and as well as conducting several of the famous war-time concerts in the National Gallery, had been a guest conductor with the Carl Rosa Company for three years. His brief for the Welsh was to develop the artistic side without losing the natural quality for which the chorus was becoming famous.

That summer saw the acquisition of the first scenery store. Towards the end of the previous year, the entire stock of scenery and props for eight productions had been purchased from the New London Opera Company, which had appeared at the Stoll and Cambridge Theatres. These included 52 backcloths and a large number of well-made and substantial flats, as well as wooden doors and balustrades, which could readily be adapted to WNO's needs. There was, however, nowhere to store them or the sets of *Nabucco*, and a search for suitable premises had started. These were found eventually in a former bus depot in Penarth.

Since the chorus had taken half their holidays to appear in Bournemouth, it was not possible for Smith to arrange the grand tour he had announced the previous year, and there were no more public performances until the autumn, when a week's season opened at the Swansea Empire on 28 September with performances of *Nabucco*, *Rigoletto*, *Die Fledermaus* and *Madam Butterfly*.

*Nabucco*, which began the week, saw the start of something that was to become commonplace during the next few years. Whether it was because of word of mouth or because the public was at last beginning to believe the reviews, no one really knows, but suddenly everyone decided they wanted to see *Nabucco* and the house was sold out almost as soon as the box-office opened. Queues of people desperate to obtain returned tickets appeared outside the theatre for the first time. *Nabucco* had become a cult.

The following week the company moved to the Palace Theatre, Manchester and 180 people, including 55 orchestral members, the sets and the costumes, made the journey in a train hired for the occasion. The week opened, naturally enough, with *Nabucco*, and it brought the house down. The principals were again outstanding. Their interpretations had by this time become second nature, and many in the audience who had heard the opera before felt that they had rarely sung better. But it was once more the chorus which set everyone talking. The critic of the *Manchester Guardian* did admit to finding their singing "a little disappointing," but even he was forced to admit that *Nabucco* was a production not to be missed. What no one could understand was why it had taken so long for the opera to be performed, and why the Welsh National Opera only performed for six weeks a year.

After the stirring spectacle of *Nabucco*, the more introspective *Madam Butterfly* seemed almost coy in spite of some committed singing by Elizabeth Thielmann, Tano Ferendinos and Tom Williams (who had to appear as Sharpless in a grey suit, his white one having gone astray on the journey). Perhaps it was the lack of choral work the audience found slightly disappointing. They certainly received their fill in *Il Trovatore*, which was constantly interrupted by applause. Conductor Charles Groves had to stop and take a bow halfway through because of the tumultuous reception. The chorus also won the plaudits in *Rigoletto*, the final opera in the season.

Welsh National Opera had been unknown in Manchester before the week started. By the end of it, they had earned a reputation as one of the most exciting operatic companies to have visited the city in recent times. The disappointment of the week was that they had failed to fill the 2500-seat theatre. The opening performance of *Nabucco* had attracted only 60 percent capacity, while *Madam Butterfly* was down to 40 percent. Even *Il Trovatore*, the most popular work in the repertoire, had not attracted a full house.

Three weeks later, on 2 November, a two-week autumn season opened at the Sophia Gardens in Cardiff. The first week was a repeat of old favourites, beginning with *Nabucco*, for which there wasn't a spare seat to be had anywhere, followed by *Rigoletto*, *Madam Butterfly*, in which Zoe Cresswell made her debut as Butterfly, *La Traviata*, with Ruth Packer as Violetta, and *Die Fledermaus*.

The second week began with the only new production of the year, the world première of *Menna*. The first opera to be written by Wales's leading composer, Arwel Hughes, it had a libretto, in English, by Dr Wyn Griffith based on an old Welsh legend in which Gwyn, the day before his wedding to Menna, carves their names on the dead tree, an action which is seen as challenging fate. On the day of the wedding, Alys, an old crone, threatens the village because she has not been invited. Menna, following the ancient custom of hiding until found by the groomsman, disappears. In the third and final act, set many years later, the demented Gwyn is still by the dead tree waiting for Menna. Lightning strikes the tree and reveals Menna's wedding dress. Gwyn throws himself on it and dies.

An international cast was assembled. Richard Lewis, born in England of Welsh parents, played the part of Gwyn, Roderick Jones sang his friend Ivan and Australian soprano Elsie Morison took the role of Menna. The remaining roles were filled by members of WNO, and the performances were conducted by the composer. The producer was Anthony Besch, the designer Rosemary Vercoe.

The opening night was looked forward to as an important event in Welsh musical life, and the first-night audience gave the piece a warm reception. It was Weber who said that the rational thing to do with first operas is to drown them like first puppies. Although that judgement might be too harsh on *Menna*, it contains more than an element of truth. The major problem with *Menna* lay in a plot which was essentially unsuited to operatic treatment. There was a lack of atmospheric variety, what light relief there was being provided by the chorus, which seemed to be dragged into a scene solely for that purpose. Menna, the leading soprano, disappeared in the second act and was not seen again. "An atmosphere of inexperience enveloped it from first to last," wrote Ernest Newman, ". . . its frail strength will not allow it to stand up on its own feet on the stage for a whole evening. The dramatic technique was unsophisticated, the handling of the chorus particularly so; it would stand immobile for long periods of time until we came to regard it as just a piece of stage furniture, then suddenly burst into irrelevantly conventional song and motion. Mr Hughes's music was weakest where it should have been strongest – on the dramatic side. There were some charming lyrical or reflective episodes in each of the three acts which one would gladly hear again; but the composer does not know how to fill up with meaningful music the long stretches between these highlighted moments. In a word, the work is for the most part insufficiently vital for the stage; it leans towards cantata rather than opera." *Menna* was deemed a gallant failure.

# CHAPTER FIVE: 1954–1955

W ITH THE EXCEPTION OF *Menna*, the only new production on offer, 1953 had been a year of consolidation, of trying to improve the standard of the productions in the repertoire. The five weeks had been played to enthusiastic houses, but the Swansea week alone had lost £1900, and the overall deficit was nearly £2500. This amount had been covered by grants from the Arts Council, Cardiff Corporation, Swansea Corporation and by private donations, and over the year as a whole a small operating surplus of £54.14s.7d was made. There remained an overdraft of close on £1500. One of the ways Smith hoped to wipe this off, and at the same time raise money to help form a training school for young singers, was by launching a Friends of the Opera. The target was 20,000 people prepared to subscribe a guinea each, a target which was never remotely approached. For 1954 WNO again had to rely on the Arts Council (with a grant increased to £10,306) and on Cardiff and Swansea Corporations for its main income outside box-office takings.

The 1954 season began in April with a return visit to Bournemouth. This was timed to coincide with Easter in the hope of attracting even larger audiences than in the previous year, and once again everybody took time off work and travelled down by train, many with their families. The season opened with a novel departure. On Good Friday, a performance of the Verdi *Requiem* was given in the Winter Gardens, with Victoria Elliott, Janet Howe, Tano Ferendinos and Tom Williams as the soloists, accompanied by the Bournemouth Municipal Orchestra under Charles Groves. An appropriate choice for Easter, it drew a good house, and the chorus, thoroughly prepared by Berend, gave an assured account of the work.

The season proper began the following Monday with the festive offering of *Die Fledermaus*, the ladies wearing new costumes made by Joan Pyle in the WNO workshops (the men's had still been hired). Although this had never been WNO's most distinguished production, it proved popular with the holiday crowds which packed the Pavilion and was given a better all-round performance than had been seen in Cardiff the previous year, Berend bringing genuine distinction to the conducting. The ballet dancers were provided by the Ballet Rambert. During the Swansea season the previous autumn, Bill Smith had referred to the company's own *corps de ballet* as a "load of cows" and ordered Mollie Hair to find some new dancers immediately. When this had proved impossible, Mollie Hair, who had choreographed all the dance routines up until that time, had ended up doing all the dancing on her own. At the end of the season, she resigned.

The night after *Die Fledermaus*, *Rigoletto* was given with a new cast in a performance which proved to be a long way below the best WNO could give. Obviously there had been too little rehearsal and there were too many mistakes, too many differences of opinion on tempi with conductor Groves and moments of uncertainty throughout the evening. "It was," wrote one critic, "a temporary lapse from grace."

The next night, a new production by Norman Jones of *The Bartered Bride* went a long way towards restoring the balance. The sets had been designed and built using the New London Opera Company stock as a basis, and the work came over as fresh and bright. There was an all-Welsh cast with Nancy Bateman as Marenka, Gerald Davies as Jenik and Howell Glynne as Kecal (confirming that he was one of the finest character actors to be seen on the operatic stage anywhere in the world).

*Nabucco* on the Thursday brought the first changes of cast since the production had opened two years earlier, with Roderick Jones making a distinguished debut in the title role, and Barbara Greenwood, a telephonist at a hospital near Cardiff, coming from the chorus to sing Fenena, her first principal role. Further performances of *Die Fledermaus*, *Rigoletto* and *The Bartered Bride* completed a week which, in spite of the rather sticky start, ended on a decidedly high note. The WNO, claimed Myra Owen of the Welsh Arts Council with visible pride, had enhanced the musical prestige of Wales.

The success was marred by a disturbing event which no one had anticipated. The simmering financial dispute between the Bournemouth Municipal Orchestra and Bournemouth Council, which had brought the orchestra and WNO together in the first place, had finally boiled over. In March the Musicians' Union had put in for a pay rise. This time the council didn't even discuss it; they simply gave the orchestra a month's notice. Its final public concert took place at the Winter Gardens on the Easter Sunday between accompanying the WNO performance of the Verdi *Requiem* and the week of opera at the Pavilion. After the curtain came down on *The Bartered Bride* on 24 April, the Bournemouth Municipal Orchestra simply ceased to exist. Charles Groves, who had been through it all before, was not a man to give in easily and he was determined that professional music-making in Bournemouth should not die. Aided by a groundswell of public opinion, he began yet another fight to save the orchestra. While hopes for some sort of rescue remained high, the Swansea season, for which the orchestra had already been engaged, was less than a month away, and it was impractical for WNO to await the outcome. Bill Smith used his many contacts to obtain a replacement and was fortunate in being able to get the Liverpool Philharmonic.

The Swansea season opened on 17 May at the Empire with the first performance outside Cardiff of *Menna*. Arwel Hughes conducted the same cast that had given the première. Greater familiarity with the score and the smaller Swansea stage increased the dramatic quality of the work, throwing the characterisation into sharper definition, and it was altogether a more powerful, more vivid performance than those in Cardiff, raising expectations that the work might manage to retain a place in the repertoire. But the house was again disappointingly small. Audiences who had not been prepared to try the unknown *Nabucco* certainly weren't going to try an unknown contemporary opera even if it was Welsh. There were even some empty seats for *Rigoletto* the following night. Heaven help Wales, commented one critic, if audiences can't be found for this. The production had been tightened considerably since the previous month, and a full-blooded and exciting performance helped obliterate memories of the ragged Bournemouth appearance. *Nabucco*, played to a capacity house, *The Bartered Bride* and *Die Fledermaus* completed the week.

On 3 July Idloes Owen, the founder of Welsh National Opera, died in the Cardiff Royal Infirmary after a long illness. Although he had remained on the Board of Management, his contribution had been negligible during the previous few years. This was partly because his health had not permitted him to conduct (which he hated anyway) or to train the chorus and principals as he had wished; partly it was because Bill Smith had so effectively taken over that there was no longer a place for Owen. At the time, Smith's actions had produced a deep division within the company. Most of the chorus and many of the principals had been in at the start; they knew and loved Owen, and felt very bitter at the way Smith had treated him. But in their hearts most of them recognised the unpalatable fact that Owen, a man about whom no one ever had a bad or unkind word to say, was not the right man to lead Welsh National Opera. He had striven hard all his life to raise musical standards in Wales; he was a musician to whom music meant everything. But he was not interested in the business side and had a fear and caution of stepping into the unknown which ultimately made him unsuited to running a national company. Smith, on the other hand, had the drive, the ambition and the ruthlessness necessary for success. The basic difference between the two men, apart from their personalities, was in their concept of the direction in which Welsh National Opera should go: whether it should become international or stay parochial. If Owen had remained in charge, there is a strong possibility that Welsh National Opera would have gone the way of all the other Welsh operatic ventures. He probably realised as much himself, but what hurt him, and his many friends, was the manner of his ousting. They felt that Smith might have acknowledged Owen's contribution more, might have given him some post, even if only honorary, that would have kept him involved. When Smith appointed Leo Quayle as Musical Director, Owen had been the last person to find out, and there were those who said that he died of a broken heart. He was to the end, though, a generous man. Personalities don't matter, he told a member of the chorus who had gone to see him in hospital, Welsh National Opera must continue. They were the last words he spoke.

*Menna*, with several cuts and a new overture, was given again at the beginning of August, at the National Eisteddfod at Ystradgynlais. Richard Lewis did not have time to learn it in Welsh and Edgar Evans took over the role of Gwyn. The stage at Ystradgynlais, which had been in constant use for competitions during the afternoon, was converted with scenery and lighting in just over an hour, and although the rain beat a constant tattoo on the roof, 6000 people, the largest audience ever for an opera in Wales, watched the performance, conducted by the composer.

Anthony Besch, who had travelled from Glyndebourne to supervise the performance, returned the following month to start work on Verdi's *The Sicilian Vespers*. The success of *Nabucco* had revealed a very profitable area to explore, and for the next revival another rarely performed Verdi was chosen. *The Sicilian Vespers* was Verdi's twentieth opera, written in 1855, immediately after *La Traviata*, for production in Paris. Apart from a performance in London earlier in the year by the City Opera Club, it had not been performed professionally in Britain for almost 100 years. Verdi did not, apparently, care much for his commission or for the elderly Scribe's libretto (a rehash of one he had written for an unperformed Donizetti work) even though, like *Nabucco*, it dealt with revolution against oppression. The story, which Scribe had originally placed in 16th century Flanders, tells of events leading up to the moment when the Sicilians, on Easter Monday, 1282, turned on their French masters and massacred them. It is short on character and on historical accuracy, but at least it provided Verdi with the basis for a grand opera in the then current Paris style of five acts with ballet. *The Sicilian Vespers* may not be amongst Verdi's greatest works, but it was well worth rediscovering, and offered some magnificent choruses which the Welsh, admirably trained by Frederick Berend, were able to seize upon with fervour.

The production opened in Cardiff on 1 November, not at the Sophia Gardens, which it had finally been conceded was not suitable for opera, but at the New Theatre, which was to become WNO's permanent "home". It was the most expensive production so far and designer John Barker had spent considerable time researching the period. Anthony Besch produced his large forces with great care, grouping them on platforms and rostra which did not meet with every critic's approval but allowed the chorus to sing out, and that's what most of the packed audience wanted to hear. The chorus responded with some magnificent singing, which made visitors from London marvel that they were all amateurs. The difficult role of Elena was played by Ruth Packer, who since her success as Abigail in *Nabucco* had become generally acknowledged to be the finest British interpreter of Verdi. Although she produced some wonderful *sotto voce* singing, her performance on the first night was felt to be too restrained, as though she had not yet learnt how to pace the role. Hervey Alan sang a rich and imposing Procida, the Sicilian patriot, and Roderick Jones as Guido di Monforte, the French governor and villain of the piece, won round after round of applause. The undoubted star of the evening was the young Welsh tenor Brychan Powell from the Glyndebourne chorus, making his debut with the company as Arrigo. He looked impressive and sang in an Italianate style that immediately gripped the audience. His "fresh strong tones and direct confident style predict a famous future," wrote Andrew Porter. "Five years ago he could have been flung, unready, on to the stage at Covent Garden; now he can gain experience in the right way."

Frederick Berend conducted the Bournemouth Symphony Orchestra in a spacious performance of which the only real criticism was the length: some four hours including the ballet.

The Bournemouth Symphony Orchestra was the successor to the Municipal Orchestra. In the months since April, enough money had been raised to keep the players together in the short term, and, with the help of the Arts Council, ways had been sought to establish the new orchestra on a sound financial footing, independent of the local council. One of the solutions was that the orchestra would, like its predecessor, play for WNO. It was an arrangement which benefited both sides, for although the opera company still did not have its own permanent orchestra, it at least had orchestral continuity, a vital factor in helping to increase artistic standards.

*The Sicilian Vespers* was followed by performances of *Rigoletto*, in which the baritone Arnold Davies made a highly acclaimed debut in the title role; *Nabucco*; and then, on the Thursday, by Verdi's *Requiem* with Patricia Bartlett, Pauline Faull, Tano Ferendinos and Howell Glynne as the soloists. The soloists, orchestra and 140 members of the combined Cardiff and Swansea choruses were crowded onto the stage, giving them little room to move. There were almost more people on stage than in the sparse audience. The *Requiem* is intensely dramatic and should have been a natural choice for WNO, but it is one of those works in which it is easy for panic to set in, and panic set in in Cardiff. Many of the chorus could not see conductor

Charles Groves, who had great difficulty keeping the performance together. It was an experiment which was not repeated.

Norman Jones's enjoyable production of *The Bartered Bride* completed the operas on show in the first week, and his production of *Faust*, revived after an absence of three years, opened the second, with the Australian soprano Patricia Bartlett making her debut as Marguerite, Robert Thomas, fresh from his triumph in the title role of Lennox Berkeley's *Nelson* at Sadler's Wells, as Faust, and Hervey Alan as Mephistopheles. *Menna*, with Edith Osler in the title role, was again warmly welcomed by those few people who went to see it, but in spite of the cuts Hughes had made, especially in Act 1, nothing could disguise its basically undramatic form. Audiences had shown they were not prepared to try a new work, and this was to be its last performance in Wales. On Thursday a lively performance of *Die Fledermaus* was presented, the seventh opera of the fortnight. With one totally new production, one revival amounting to a new production and a concert performance of the Verdi *Requiem*, the season was an artistic and administrative achievement of which any opera house could have been proud.

Progress since 1946 had been phenomenal. The announcement of *The Sicilian Vespers* had brought ticket applications from all over Britain, and many leading figures of the musical Establishment in London, as well as critics, had travelled to Wales for the first night. They arrived in Cardiff expecting to see opera of the highest standard. There was no question of allowances having to be made for a semi-professional company. It was now, however, costing £15,000 a year to run Welsh National Opera, a figure which grants from the Arts Council, Cardiff and Swansea, and income from the box-office, were still failing to cover. The attempt to raise money through the Friends' scheme had come to nothing, and 1954 ended, like the previous year, with a loss. There were two answers: the first, which Smith threatened but never seriously contemplated, was to close down; the second, to increase the number of weeks played in order to make each production more viable economically. But this could not be achieved with an amateur chorus which was only available at holiday time or with plenty of notice, and to professionalise the chorus to make it full-time would cost at least £30,000 a year.

WNO could not afford to plunge deeper in debt. *Nabucco*, now recognised as *the* Welsh National opera, had taken time to become popular at the box-office. *The Sicilian Vespers*, which it was hoped would generate the same excitement, was also proving slow to attract audiences, so for the new productions of 1955 it was decided to mount two operas with known box-office appeal, Puccini's *La Bohème* and *Tosca*, and to bring back those old favourites, *Cavalleria Rusticana* and *I Pagliacci*.

A two-week spring season in Swansea opened at the Empire on 25 April with *The Sicilian Vespers*. A certain amount of refurbishing had been done to the set and some pruning had taken place in the earlier acts to tighten the production. The performance was well conducted by Vilem Tausky, making not just his first appearance with WNO but his first as Musical Director. Frederick Berend had resigned at the end of the previous season and Smith had been extremely lucky to have been able to persuade Tausky to take over from him. Born near Brno in Czechoslovakia, Tausky had studied with both Janáček and Suk. During the war, he had joined the Czech army in France and had escaped to England from Dunkirk. His wide experience of opera included conducting not only in his native Czechoslovakia but at Covent Garden, at Sadler's Wells and with the Carl Rosa Company. His quiet, unassuming manner belied his ability. His knowledge of opera was extensive and profound; his beat was clear and decisive, and his acquisition was an immense asset.

*The Sicilian Vespers* was followed by *Rigoletto* and then by *Cav* and *Pag*, which returned to the repertory after an absence of four years. *Cavalleria Rusticana* was given in a new production by Norman Jones with an all-Welsh cast.

The new production of *La Bohème*, with chorus provided by Swansea, opened on 28 April in front of a capacity house. Parry Jones, one of the most famous opera singers ever to emerge from Wales, had been brought in to produce, with Tausky conducting, and a strong cast. Walter Midgley sang Rodolfo; Patricia Bartlett, Mimi; Ronald Lewis, Marcello; Harold Blackburn, Colline; Edmund Donlevy, Schaunard; and Zoe Cresswell, Musetta. Parry Jones's production, using the Alexandre Benois sets which were among those bought from the New London Opera Company, was along traditional lines, concentrating on characterisation, and, with one exception, worked well. The exception was the notoriously difficult second act, which was "poor to frankly bad," and was not helped by poor singing which "failed to come up to the standard maintained throughout the rest of the opera."

The other productions in the first week were of *The Bartered Bride* and of *Faust*. In the second week, *Nabucco*, *Tosca* and *La Traviata* were given. Two hundred people had to be turned away from the single performance of *Nabucco* with which the week opened. The performance was magnificent, and after the famous Jews' lament the audience was so moved it sat in stunned silence and failed to applaud.

*Tosca*, conducted by Charles Groves and produced by Norman Jones, received its first performance on 3 May. Walter Midgley sang Cavaradossi, Kyra Vane, who had sung the role of Leonora in WNO's production of *Il Trovatore* four years earlier, returned to sing the title role and Roderick

Jones was cast as Scarpia. Jones, a stalwart of the Sadler's Wells company, had earned a reputation for being probably the finest British interpreter of the role currently singing. All three principals sang well. The smaller roles, from Edmund Donlevy's Angelotti to William Thomas's comic Sacristan, were equally well taken.

The entire fortnight was a great success and after the final performance of *La Traviata* the audience continued to applaud long after the house lights had come up as if it did not wish the season to end.

In July, Bill Smith realised a long-held ambition: for Welsh National Opera to appear in London. For one week, while the resident Sadler's Wells company was on tour, the theatre in Rosebery Avenue was filled with the lilt of Welsh voices, both backstage and front of house. It had been reasoned, probably correctly, that there were enough expatriate Welshmen in London to fill the Wells for a week but not enough for two, and WNO could not afford to lose money if two weeks did not sell out. Hundreds of nostalgic Welshmen did help pack the theatre, but Englishmen went in equal numbers. Patriotic fervour did not extend to *Menna*, which played to a very poor house. Four operas had been chosen for the visit, which was accompanied by the Bournemouth Symphony Orchestra: *Nabucco* and *The Sicilian Vespers* because they had not been seen in London for many years (and would be likely to arouse much critical and, it was hoped, box-office interest) and because they showed off the chorus to its best advantage; *Menna* because it was Welsh, contemporary, different and a work it was felt should be seen outside Wales; and *Rigoletto* because it was very much a company production and Bill Smith wanted London to see something other than a rarity; he wanted WNO to be judged with the major London companies, not just as a quaint regional purveyor of operatic rarities.

To move everybody and everything up to London was an enormous undertaking for an organisation which, although it nursed professional ambitions and, indeed, was by now semi-professional, was still essentially amateur. The first problem to be overcome was the Equity rule which forbade its members to appear on the London stage with amateurs. Throughout WNO's history, Equity had granted it a special dispensation to employ professional singers with the amateur chorus, allowing it to appear in the English provinces on the strong understanding that the company was moving towards full professionalisation as soon as practicable. This dispensation did not extend to performances in London. A special meeting of Equity's executive committee in March had agreed to a request that the ruling should be waived on this occasion, but in doing so had stressed that it was a one-off decision which set no precedent.

Then there was the problem of getting time off. Out of a pool of 180 voices, a chorus of 75 had been picked, almost every one of them with a daytime job. Some were unable to get time off work but were still determined not to miss out. Muriel Pointon, for example, who had taken over running her father's butcher's shop, would catch the 2.55 pm train from Cardiff to London, sing the performance, then catch the 12.55 am train back, going straight from the station to the market to buy meat, which she then cut up and helped serve until it was time to catch the afternoon train to London again. Throughout the entire week, she did not manage to sleep in a bed once.

There was much curiosity in the press about the visit and advance business at the box-office was brisk, especially for *Nabucco*, which sold out both performances very quickly. *Nabucco*, with its original principals, Packer, Alan and Jackson, opened the season on 11 July. The stage at Sadler's Wells is not ideal for large chorus work, but somehow everyone managed to squeeze on. What no one could have foreseen was that London would be in the middle of a heat wave; conditions backstage were stifling and people had to shower between the acts to keep cool. The packed house (hundreds of people hoping for returned tickets were turned away) witnessed a stirring performance which resulted in five curtain calls at the end of Act 3. "The performance as a whole was a triumph," enthused one critic. Abigail "was sung with astonishing bravura by Ruth Packer . . . here is a singer who is not afraid to let herself go . . . this was an exciting and rewarding evening." The chorus, "inspiring to hear", gave London "a lesson in choral singing." By the time the curtain fell after the ninth and final curtain call, the audience was on its feet, clapping, stamping and cheering.

The following night, *The Sicilian Vespers* was not received with quite the same enthusiasm, partly because the work itself was weaker but also because, as the *Times* critic noted, "it calls for a higher standard of professional singing, and in this respect Tuesday's performance was not free from weakness. Miss Packer again sustained the principal female part of Elena with much skill, but some of the skill had to be devoted to covering up those parts of her voice which are no longer as full in tone as they were." The best singing of the evening, everyone agreed, came from Brychan Powell. Audiences were, however, grateful for the opportunity to see another work which had not been presented in London for many, many years.

By contrast, *Menna* roused little enthusiasm. In spite of being extremely well-sung by the original cast (with the exception of Edgar Evans, who took over the role of Gwyn from Richard Lewis), critics and the sparse public did not warm to the work any more than they had when it was premièred in Wales. The repertoire was completed by *Rigoletto*, giving Arnold Davies his London debut in the title role. He acquitted himself well with his "deeply felt and keenly moving characterisation . . . the voice itself proved strong and flexible enough for the big test of the third act." Gladys Lewis as Gilda, after an uncertain start, improved immeasurably and Walter Midgley as the Duke, who managed to miss an entry on stage because he was busy chatting backstage, enjoyed the unqualified approval of the gallery if not the critics.

Two further sold-out performances of *Nabucco* and *The Sicilian Vespers* brought to a close a highly successful week, which had shown London that Welsh National Opera was a company to be watched. Praise for the chorus was unanimous, and some said it was the best heard within living memory. "Perhaps the most remarkable feature of the various performances was the remarkably pliable singing of the chorus . . . It is to be hoped that, having found its way to London, the Company will pay us further visits in future," concluded the critic of *Musical Opinion*. Ernest Newman, the doyen of music critics, spoke for many when he wrote of *Nabucco*: "I realized that I was confronted by something that demanded to be taken with respectful seriousness. The company seems to have travelled a long artistic way already, and to be likely to go further if it receives the support it deserves in its own country and ours. The performance was an object lesson to a certain other London opera house in unity and integrity of purpose and general competence."

In September the company returned to Bournemouth for a week, opening with *Cav* and *Pag*. On the Monday morning, William Edwards, who was singing Silvio, developed laryngitis. The only replacement who could be found was the Sadler's Wells stalwart Denis Dowling, who caught the train from London to Bournemouth after lunch and spent the journey taking a quick look at a part he had not sung for five years. He arrived in time to meet Patricia Bartlett, the Nedda, and take a glance at the stage before changing into his costume, a mixture of one he had brought from Sadler's Wells and one supplied by the Welsh. No one who did not know would have been aware that he had not been in the the production since it first opened. The week continued with *Faust*, *Tosca* (for which Kyra Vane flew back from Italy), *The Bartered Bride*, *Die Fledermaus* and *Rigoletto*.

A week later, the autumn season in Cardiff opened with performances of *Cav* and *Pag*, *Nabucco*, *Die Fledermaus*, *Faust*, *Tosca*, *La Bohème*, *The Bartered Bride*, *The Sicilian Vespers* and *Rigoletto*. There were no new productions that autumn. It was felt, following the euphoria of the visit to Sadler's Wells, that it would be wise to try and raise the standard of the current repertoire to the same state of excellence as the productions seen there rather than to dissipate energies on a new venture.

# CHAPTER SIX: 1956–1957

Tʜᴇ ʀᴇꜱɪɢɴᴀᴛɪᴏɴ ᴏꜰ Vilem Tausky as Musical Director at the beginning of 1956 came as a surprise. Tausky, who had done so much to raise standards during his short stay, had accepted a position with the BBC's Concert Orchestra, a post which did not allow him the time to continue working in Wales. Smith was again fortunate with his replacement, the highly experienced and extremely popular Warwick Braithwaite. One of the pioneers of professional music in Wales as principal conductor of the National Orchestra of Wales, Braithwaite's operatic experience was extensive, and his understanding of singers and the singer's art was second to none. In the opinion of many knowledgeable people, he was an operatic conductor to be mentioned in the same breath as Giulini and Beecham. A New Zealander who had come to London in 1916 to study at the Royal Academy, he had become a conductor of the O'Hara Opera Company before joining the British National Opera Company at Covent Garden when only twenty-six. He then spent a year in Munich working under Bruno Walter before joining Sadler's Wells, where he had stayed until the outbreak of the Second World War. After the war, he became one of the resident conductors of the newly formed Covent Garden Company, and had made his first appearance with Welsh National Opera, conducting *Madam Butterfly*, in 1951.

Braithwaite was liked and respected by the chorus. When he took the final Sunday rehearsal before the spring Swansea season, scheduled to last from two o'clock until nine, he was astonished when the chorus made no move to leave at the end. Was that all he wanted? they asked, happy to go on for as long as he wished. He made his first appearance as WNO's Musical Director on 16 April at the Empire Theatre in Swansea, conducting the opening performance of the new season. This was a new production of *Il Trovatore* by Harry Powell Lloyd, who also designed the sets. Norman Jones had intended producing the opera himself, but because of illness had been forced to withdraw. Smith turned instead to Harry Lloyd, husband of the celebrated mezzo Edith Coates, and an eminent producer and designer in his own right. The production had to be elementary because Lloyd simply did not have time to attempt anything elaborate. His work with the chorus consisted largely in making sure that they got on and off the stage at the right time, while his production of the principals allowed for little more than the plotting of moves; very little time could be spent on interpretation. In spite of the handicaps, it was an intelligent and well-thought-out production, which gave coherence to a plot which can all too often be baffling if not downright absurd. "The design and the atmosphere," commented Kenneth Loveland, "give gentle but firm emphasis to the theme of superstition and vengeance without delving too deeply into the dangerous strata of melodrama, and there is a life and eagerness about it which makes the opera less of a series of tableaux than it has been known to be. The chorus is used sensibly and the action is compact. The sets are striking and have the added virtues of economy and mobility." It was, everyone agreed, a thundering good production, colourful and imaginative, and Braithwaite conducted the Bournemouth Symphony Orchestra, playing enthusiastically if not always precisely, with a firm grasp of the shape of the piece. Brychan Powell, appearing as Manrico for the first time, continued to make great strides, producing exciting top notes which gave rise to the hope that an important new British tenor had been discovered. The chorus, inspired by Braithwaite, delivered some stirring and robust singing. Disappointingly, the house was not full.

The following night, Braithwaite was in the pit again for *La Bohème*, which had had time to settle down into an efficient and, at times, exciting production, and the week continued with performances of *Nabucco*, *The Sicilian Vespers* and *Madam Butterfly*, in which Victoria Elliott gave her usual committed performance.

The second week included *Tosca*, which was an enormous success due largely to Victoria Elliott in the title role, *Cav* and *Pag*, and *Faust*, and the fortnight ended with everyone well pleased. A slow start at the box-office for everything except *Nabucco* had been followed by full houses throughout the second week and people being turned away.

It was the most successful Swansea season financially, though that did not, of course, mean it was profitable. Although Swansea council had given £1000 towards the season, the cost of hiring the orchestra was double that sum, and that meant the inevitable overall deficit. But what had been particularly encouraging was a noticeable improvement in standards. Whereas, before, all the effort and enthusiasm had tended to be reserved for new productions or for chorus favourites such as *Nabucco*, with revivals left to take care of themselves, the repertory pieces had been sung and performed in a manner which could stand comparison with any outside company's stock productions.

In July, WNO returned to Sadler's Wells for a week. If anybody had thought that their triumphant appearance the previous year had been a fluke brought about by simple curiosity, they were in for a shock. Tickets for all six performances became almost impossible to obtain. Determined to continue the good impression created the previous year, the company opened with a brand-new production of another early Verdi, *I Lombardi*, the first full-scale production of the opera in Britain for over a century. *I Lombardi* (or *The Lombards at the First Crusade*, to give it its full title in English) was Verdi's fourth opera, written immediately after *Nabucco* and premièred at La Scala in February 1843. It tells the story of two brothers, Arvino and Pagano, who both love Viclinda. Pagano kills his father in mistake for his brother and is banished to the Holy Land, where he lives as a hermit. Arvino, accompanied by his daughter, Giselda, arrives in the Holy Land on the first Crusade. Giselda is captured by the tyrant of Antioch and falls in love with his son, Oronte. They elope, Oronte is fatally wounded, baptised a Christian by Pagano, and expires. Pagano then leads the attack on Jerusalem, is himself fatally wounded, reveals his identity to Arvino and dies forgiven in his brother's arms. The idea of staging it had come from George Foa, a BBC television producer responsible for most of the opera seen on television. An Anglo-Italian who had once worked with Toscanini, Foa had televised some operatic excerpts with WNO three years earlier and felt immediately that the company ought to stage the work. Smith, once he knew the subject, agreed and invited Foa to produce. The immediate problem was that the full score could not be found anywhere in Britain. Victor White, a Canadian tenor who had appeared with WNO the previous season and was then studying in Milan, was asked to visit Ricordi, Verdi's publisher. He discovered that the only complete set of vocal and orchestral parts for the opera in existence had been sent to South Africa for a concert performance. While these were being recovered, White managed to buy several second-hand vocal scores for about £2 apiece, and sent them off to Wales. Meanwhile, Ricordi had agreed to release a copy of the full score, which was flown to London to be translated and orchestrated. When Warwick Braithwaite first saw it, he was very excited. "In many respects I consider it to be the finest work Verdi ever wrote," he said. "There are some magnificent choral climaxes – and some of the most beautiful solos, duets and trios he ever wrote." In other words, it was another ideal piece for the Welsh.

*I Lombardi* opened the Sadler's Wells week on 16 July in front of a packed house. It was a daring undertaking to throw themselves in front of the nation's critics without any try-out in the relative safety of Wales. The large chorus (which had been paid eight guineas expenses plus rail fares for the week) began nervously, but soon warmed up. "The performance, which was splendidly conducted by Warwick Braithwaite," according to Philip Hope-Wallace in the *Manchester Guardian*, "was often most moving in its fervour and sincerity – notably the big religious choruses and the trio for bass, tenor, and soprano, with violin obbligato ... But as often in early Verdi, the opera is almost unconsciously comic much of the time. That the crusaders should go off to battle to a perfect set of 'The Lancers' or keep bumping into waltz time, with a flute twiddle to mark the beat, suddenly transports us to the world of Offenbach. And then, what motiveless mishaps, what unexpected stabbings – it is worse than Soho; and each thrust occasions such lengthy singing."

Singing Giselda was the Australian soprano Rosina Raisbeck, with Bryan Drake as Pagano, Paul Asciak as Arvino and Alfred Hallett as Oronte. Apart from the choruses, the musical highlight of the opera was the long Act 3 trio, superbly sung by Raisbeck, Hallett and Drake. In spite of some reservations about the work itself, there was no doubting the critics' enthusiasm for the artists, especially the chorus. "The Welsh singers produced a truly thrilling sound. Opera is indeed alive in Great Britain when the provinces can throw up a performance like this one," wrote Andrew Porter in the *Financial Times*. "It was not merely distinguished by the best choral singing I have heard in any opera-house outside Bayreuth but by an exemplary sense of line," agreed Peter Heyworth in the *Observer*. The opera received a standing ovation at the finish, and the chorus took a separate curtain call.

Foa's stylised production, set on three tiers and looking like an early Italian painting, received a mixed reaction. Hope-Wallace thought it ambitious: "Setting the Lombards climbing all over a miniature zoo of Mappin terraces, gave the crowded house much simple, hearty pleasure," he wrote; but at the other extreme Andrew Porter felt that both production and design (by Louis Kahan) "were below the usual high Welsh standards." Foa and Kahan had "ambitiously essayed a 'stylised' presentation, with a fixed set variously trimmed for the different scenes, but the result was not distinguished enough to come off (it should, however, prove useful when touring). The narrowness of the set had one distinct advantage. It massed the choral tone." Generally speaking, Foa's approach worked well with an opera not noted for its dramatic consistency or shape. There were, however, two distinct failings – the two stabbings, which were so clumsily handled that they provoked laughter (although they certainly did not warrant the boos Foa received from the gallery when he took his curtain call).

*Nabucco* on the second night was also played to a packed house. Charles Groves conducted a spirited performance in which Roderick Jones sang Nabucco in London for the first time. *Il Trovatore*, the only opera in the season which could stand a direct comparison with other productions seen in London, proved disappointing in spite of the excellent teamwork. Too often the orchestra and soloists were at variance, and Braithwaite conducted with such fury that both Zoe Cresswell as Leonora and Phyllis Ash-Child as Azucena found it difficult to make themselves heard. The plaudits were again reserved for the Manrico of Brychan Powell and the Ferrando of Bryan Drake.

The fourth opera, *The Sicilian Vespers*, was also conducted by Charles Groves with enormous gusto but, although the audience cheered long and loud, it failed to reach the expected high standard. Perhaps the exertions earlier in the week had been too much. But, whatever shortcomings the critics found, the packed houses loved every minute of every full-blooded, committed performance. An invitation was immediately forthcoming from the British Travel and Holiday Association for the chorus to tour the United States and Canada, but Bill Smith turned it down. It was, he said, more important to consolidate their success in Britain and to raise the general standard of performance, and that meant continuing the familiar pattern of appearing in Swansea in the spring and Cardiff in the autumn, with visits elsewhere being arranged when and if the company could afford them.

"The heroine was Australian, the conductor and baritone both hailed from New Zealand, the first tenor was English, the second Maltese, the producer was an Anglo-Italian, and the orchestra was the Bournemouth Symphony." So began the review of *I Lombardi* in *Opera*. "The chorus, some eighty strong, it must be admitted was Welsh," the reviewer continued. "I have nothing against this state of affairs at all, especially if it produces good opera, I am merely stating it for the record." The comments may have been flippant, but they were true. Welsh National Opera (to the disgust of those who felt that everything should be Welsh irrespective of quality) had settled into a pattern of employing guest principals (Welsh if available) for most major roles, with smaller roles being taken by members of the company. With a total of five performing weeks a year, professional principals could only be offered contracts for specific productions: for the remainder of the year, those singers had to look outside Wales for their work, so London became the major recruiting ground for guest artists. The expense and logistical problems of bringing singers down to Cardiff or Swansea for rehearsals were also immense, and a system of rehearsing in London was devised, so that they only had to travel to Cardiff for the final few rehearsals or, in the case of a revival, for a dress rehearsal – if one was allotted, which was not always the case. Principals from the company's own ranks would likewise be sent to London to rehearse with the producer (and while there receive vocal coaching from Elizabeth Forini, a former member of the Vienna State Opera). Occasionally, too, they would have to travel to Bournemouth to rehearse with the orchestra. As the first night of a new production approached, it became a nightmare for Peggy Moreland in the office to keep tabs on everyone's whereabouts.

Following its acclaimed visit to Sadler's Wells, WNO was given a triumphant welcome when it appeared at the New in Cardiff that autumn. The season opened in a blaze of glory with *I Lombardi*, the opera's first ever performance in Wales, and continued with *La Bohème*, *Cav* and *Pag*, *Tosca* and *Nabucco*.

As an antidote to its heavier, melodramatic fare, the second week opened with a new production by Harry Powell Lloyd of *The Barber of Seville*, the first Rossini opera to enter the repertoire. It proved a popular choice. Lloyd made no conscious effort to create humour, but relied on the acting skill of a fine cast of principals: William Dickie as a swashbuckling Figaro; Tano Ferendinos as Count Almaviva, singing and acting with an assurance which surprised and delighted everyone; Barbara Wilson, a young Australian, as Rosina; Patti Lewis as Marcellina; Howell Glynne as Dr Bartolo and Michael Langdon, who kept the house in continuous laughter, as a toweringly pompous Don Basilio. With Lloyd's production of *Il Trovatore* being played in Cardiff for the first time, the fortnight ended, as it had begun, with the House Full boards outside the theatre.

Instead of opening with the customary Swansea season, 1957 began with a week in Cardiff in May. This variation to the established pattern was brought about by the closure that winter of the Empire. The only other theatre in the town was the Grand, a repertory theatre which, while it was far from ideal, would at least mean West Wales would not be deprived of grand opera, but it was not available until the autumn. A season at Sadler's Wells had already been booked for June, when it was planned to introduce another rarity into the repertoire. This was to be *Mefistofele* by Boito, and since it was going to be the most lavish, expensive production WNO had yet mounted, Smith wanted to make sure it was in a fit state to be seen in London. So, in place of the lost Swansea date, an additional week was booked in Cardiff. The two other pieces to be played in London were also revived: *I Lombardi* and *Nabucco*, which, it was announced, would be having its last performance in Wales. The production was five years old and showing its age; it was time, Smith felt, to give it a rest. In its place later in the year would be a new production of *La Traviata*.

Boito, the composer of *Mefistofele*, is perhaps best remembered today as the librettist of Verdi's last operas, *Otello* and *Falstaff*, and as the librettist of *La Gioconda*. *Mefistofele*, the first of his two operas, was based, like Gounod's more popular version, on Goethe's *Faust*. It had received its première in Milan in 1868 and caused a riot because Boito was accused, quite unjustly, of being a Wagnerian at a time when things German were far from popular in Italy. Revised and replayed seven years later in Bologna, it immediately became a hit and has remained in the repertoire ever since. It had rarely been performed in Britain, however, its last professional performance being at Covent Garden in 1926, when Chaliapin sang the title role. It was, though, an opera well-known on records and would be likely to arouse considerable interest.

The production was entrusted to George Foa, producer of *I Lombardi*, with designs by the talented young Julia Trevelyan Oman. "I believe we have found a designer of genius," said Bill Smith. The problems she had to surmount were formidable. There were seven scenes, ranging from heaven to hell, which had to be changed quickly, had to be adaptable to stages of differing sizes and had to be easily transportable. There also had to be room to accommodate a chorus of seventy-five, the principals and a corps de ballet of 12 dancers, taken on for the first time since Mollie Hair had resigned in 1953. There were also more than 500 costumes to make, and nearly 100 fibreglass wings for the angels. WNO's own workshops, in addition to preparing two other operas for revival, were unable to cope on their own, and the work was shared between workshops in Cardiff, Manchester and London. It was soon clear to the chorus that this was to be a massive undertaking and everyone was seized with great enthusiasm. Warwick Braithwaite said he had rarely been more moved than by the emotion and sincerity the chorus brought to their work during rehearsals.

Boito had made his protagonist, Mefistofele, a bass, and to sing the role Foa engaged a young, largely unknown Londoner of Belgian parentage, Raimund Herincx. The role of Faust (not nearly so important as in Gounod's version) was given to Alfred Hallett, Marguerite to Solange de la Motte, a French soprano based in London, Martha to Patricia Kern and Helen of Troy to Joyce Barker.

Julia Trevelyan Oman solved the design problems by using a pair of staircases which could be moved around the stage and on which the chorus could be grouped, with other token pieces of scenery being brought on as necessary. Colour was provided by the costumes. It was simple but strikingly effective.

Foa had been careful with his massive chorus. He had gone privately to each member in turn and told them he had singled them out to do something special, but that they should not tell the others in case they were jealous. In this way he involved everyone in acting as well as singing. In one scene he had persuaded a soprano to hang over the top balustrade and sing upside down. She was held by two strong male choristers who in one performance managed to let her go. She was caught by Raimund Herincx below, and forgetting the opera, was so grateful that she flung her arms around Herincx and gave him a kiss. The incident was hailed as a masterpiece of production. By allowing the chorus freedom to develop characters, to joke and to make suggestions, Foa produced real people on stage. He asked for a similar involvement from his principal artists. Herincx, who had been touring on the continent in a series of low-budget productions, was astonished by the demands made upon him. For one aria, Foa wanted him to sing from the top of a large rock placed centre stage. The only way Herincx could get onto it was to run and jump. When on one occasion he missed his footing, a nasty accident was averted only because the quick-thinking Philippe Perrottet (the choreographer and principal dancer) had foreseen what was likely to happen and had positioned himself to catch him and help him onto the rock. Foa thought this "business" looked spectacular and suggested to Herincx that he consider keeping it in.

The opening performance, on 6 May, was rapturously received. "Why has this fine music – so essentially vocal, so essentially singable, and supported by such a spectacular orchestral score – been missing from our opera houses for so long?" wondered Kenneth Loveland. Foa's production was warmly praised as was Raimund Herincx's Mefistofele, which caught both the devilry and the charm of the character and was excellently sung. Alfred Hallett was a smooth, lyrical Faust, and the smaller roles were attractively sung by Joyce Barker, Patricia Kern, Margreta Elkins and Robert Gard. The disappointment was Solange de la Motte, whose voice was too small to be heard.

When the production opened at Sadler's Wells on 24 June, it received an equally enthusiastic reception. Raimund Herincx, making his London debut, was again in commanding form (so good was the impression he made that he was immediately offered a contract by Sadler's Wells). Anne Edwards, replacing Solange de la Motte, although tentative in places, was a distinct improvement as Marguerite, but the other cast change from Cardiff was not so happy. John Carolan as Faust sang patchily – "The tenor playing Faust looked and sounded just like a sheep," wrote one critic. Joyce Barker (a "smooth, ample Helen") and Patricia Kern (a "splendid Martha") again made the most of their appearances.

This was not really an opera for the principals, however, but for the chorus, which was hardly off stage, and rarely had the chorus sung better. After the opening Prologue, the performance was held up for several minutes by prolonged cheering. "There can be no doubt that this chorus has now reached an enviable standard of artistic maturity and Mefistofele is certainly a work to display its abilities."[1] "The hero of the evening . . . was the Welsh chorus, which in all its incarnations – heavenly, infernal, human, legendary – sang superbly."[2] "After ten minutes of this golden-winged all-Welsh celestial choir in full-throated song the audience burst into cheers that must have been heard half a mile away."[3] "They now have an attack

1. *South Wales Echo*                    3. *Daily Mail*
2. Andrew Porter, *Financial Times*

and polish to their singing that many a highly-trained professional chorus would envy."[4] "Eighty lusty Welsh voices gave London its singing thrill of the week."[5]

After such a night, few people would have been surprised if the performances of *Nabucco* and *I Lombardi* which followed had been an anti-climax, but they were far from it. *I Lombardi*, with Joyce Barker as Giselda in the only cast change from the previous year, was as exciting as ever, and *Nabucco*, with Patricia Baird making her debut as Abigail, played to its customary packed house.

From the full, cheering houses of London to a half-empty cinema on the north coast of Wales was quite a comedown. At the end of July, WNO paid its first visit to Llandudno since the not-very-encouraging week in 1951. The Grand Theatre had been closed and the venue this time was the local Odeon cinema. The auditorium was larger than that at Covent Garden and the stage as wide, but it lacked depth and an orchestra pit, and the backstage facilities were almost non-existent. There was no scenery dock and the sets had to be pulled thirty feet into the air to get them into the building. When this was being done on a wet Sunday evening with the rain lashing down and the wind howling, it was not the easiest of jobs; and it did not help the sets much. It was in Llandudno that Florence Beese, the Wardrobe Mistress, was seen chasing choristers along the sea-front trying to recover the *Nabucco* sandals they were wearing. Flo Beese, in her 20 years with WNO, gained a reputation as a bully. But, with 80 choristers taking wigs, beards and bits of costume home, then losing them, she had to be fierce. On one occasion she locked the Swansea female chorus in their dressing-room and refused to let them out until a scarf was found, and she used to stand outside the dressing-rooms collecting wardrobe and preventing people leaving until everything had been returned to her. After *Nabucco* had been running for some time, Bill Smith complained that the beards were dirty. Flo Beese took them home to wash and hung them in the garden to dry. Her neighbours were astonished the following day to see her garden covered with beards.

There were considerable doubts about the wisdom of trying to play grand opera in a seaside resort in the middle of summer, but with the spring and autumn seasons already allocated to Swansea and Cardiff, it had to be the summer, when the chorus could take their holidays, or not at all. And since there had been justified criticism that a company calling itself Welsh National Opera was really only a South Walian organisation, Smith was anxious it should be seen in the north despite the cost of £6000 it took to transport the artists, sets, costumes and orchestra up there. There was an added problem in going in mid-summer; it became very difficult to find

4. *Bournemouth Echo*                        5. Noël Goodwin, *Daily Express*

accommodation for some 200 people, particularly when the allowance was only six guineas a week for full board. Advance bookings were poor, there was a national bus strike on during the week, and when the company's great crowd-puller, *Nabucco*, opened the week, it played to a house less than half full. *Il Trovatore*, another recognised box-office favourite, also failed to attract the public, as did *I Lombardi*. Only *Tosca* played to a house anywhere near respectable. It was a very disappointing visit.

It was a different matter when the autumn season opened in Cardiff with the new production of *La Traviata* by Harry Powell Lloyd, who also designed the sets and costumes. A full house thoroughly enjoyed "a new and adventurous production, set against striking scenery and glowing with colour." Heather Harper as Violetta was making her first appearance with the company. Although she had been seen in the role on television, she was still a comparatively inexperienced stage artist, and this showed in a performance which required stronger projection to make it totally success-ful. She "produced some very sensitive and sweetly tender singing" in a performance "which gave promise of much to come." Opposite her, Tano Ferendinos had an unhappy evening as Alfredo, singing either in front of or behind Braithwaite's beat. Bryan Drake sang Germont with admirable clarity and diction, although his acting on the first night at least was wooden. Raimund Herincx, who had been asked while in Cardiff for Mefistofele to appear as Baron Douphol and sing the optional high notes, made the role much more memorable than in most productions – perhaps a little too memorable. Allowing for first night tensions, it was clear that once the production had settled down, this *Traviata* was going to be extremely good.

The first week continued with *Mefistofele*, *I Lombardi* and *The Barber of Seville*, which brought in Doreen Murray as Rosina and Arnold Matters as a late replacement for Howell Glynne, singing and acting with his usual polish and assurance.

The announcement that *Nabucco* was to be dropped from the repertoire had brought forth hundreds of protests and the opera was brought back for a single performance to open the second week, with Ruth Packer returning to the role of Abigail. The final revival of the season, after a gap of two years, was of *Rigoletto* with John Hargreaves in the title role, Marion Studholme as Gilda, Walter Midgley as the Duke and Michael Langdon, in Cardiff principally for *The Barber*, as Sparafucile.

Enthusiasm for all the productions was as high as ever, and so was the list of people wanting to join the chorus. Ever since the Swansea and Cardiff choruses had become totally integrated, the strength of the full chorus had been maintained at about 120. Of that number, the maximum used in any one performance was 80; the remaining 40 were either back-up voices for

when the regulars were unavailable or were probationers waiting to take
their place in the full chorus. Following the successes of the London, Cardiff
and Swansea seasons in previous years, the number of applicants had risen
to more than 100, of whom only 15 were accepted as probationary
members. It was a matter of considerable pride to be a member of Welsh
National Opera.

The Swansea season which had been cancelled in the spring had finally
been rearranged at the Grand Theatre for November. The Grand posed considerable problems to an opera company. The front rows of the stalls had to be
removed to accommodate even a reduced orchestra, the stage was cramped
and the backstage facilities were atrocious for more than a handful of people.
There was no room for the chorus to change backstage and provision had to
be made for them to use a pub across the road – and the dash to the stage door
was most unpleasant if it was raining. And if artists were required to exit on
one side of the stage and enter on the other, they had to go outside the
building. It was, however, better than nothing, and a grateful Swansea public
flocked to hear *I Lombardi*, *La Traviata*, *Nabucco* and *Mefistofele*.

*Nabucco*, in spite of the efforts to rest it, had again to be brought back
by public demand and was given two performances. At the second, on
the Friday evening, Ruth Packer, who had sung the role of Abigail in all but
one of the performances WNO had given of the opera, announced her
retirement from the stage. She had just sung a superb performance, making
Abigail a creature full of passion and hatred, which caused the disbelieving
audience to wonder if her decision to devote her time to teaching was not
premature. At the end of the evening, Bill Smith went on stage to thank her
for her work with WNO, and paid tribute to the very important part she
had played in helping to develop a public for opera in Wales.

THE GRAND THEATRE in Swansea may not have been ideal but it was the only possible venue for WNO in West Wales. At the beginning of 1958, it was announced that the Grand was about to suffer the fate of the old Empire and be demolished. The fight immediately began to save it, but its future was too uncertain for Welsh National Opera to be able to book a spring season there.

On top of this setback came even more depressing news; a threat to the very existence of Welsh National Opera itself. The previous few years had all ended with a total expenditure which Arts Council grants, local council grants and box-office revenue had never quite managed to match. WNO was caught on a vicious merry-go-round. In order to make each appearance more cost effective, the number of weeks played, both inside and outside Wales, had to be increased, and to do that meant there had to be a chorus which could meet such a commitment. That in turn meant professional choristers, which would require more money. Bill Smith's ideal was for Welsh National Opera to employ professional soloists, have a totally professional chorus and stage staff, and to play a minimum of thirty weeks a year. To do that, he estimated, would require £60,000 a year, a figure which did not include the formation of the company's own orchestra. For the foreseeable future, orchestras would have to continue being hired on a seasonal basis. While Smith realised that such a huge jump in grant was highly improbable, he did have reason to believe that it would be increased gradually; the Arts Council in London had constantly expressed support for the need to professionalise, and Equity had insisted on it as a company goal. The grant for six weeks of performing in 1957 had been in the region of £16,000. To maintain the same number of performances during 1958 would require £17,000. Smith hoped for at least that, and maybe more. Then came news that the Arts Council would not be increasing its grant that year and that its direct grant had, in fact, been reduced by £2000. Welsh National Opera was already taking by far the largest share of the funds allocated to Wales, and the Welsh Arts Council, although staunch supporters of WNO, could not afford to give more. London, facing an operatic crisis of its own, also refused to help. For some time the Carl Rosa

Company, with an annual subsidy of around £60,000, had been losing money at an alarming rate, and it was felt in London that building up WNO at the expense of Carl Rosa would be unwise. Welsh National Opera, it was thought, should not set its sights so high but stay within Wales and remain as a small, worthy provincial venture. Sir William Emrys Williams, the Secretary-General of the Arts Council, and a Welshman who should have known better, even went so far as to suggest that WNO should become a mini-Glyndebourne, presenting an annual festival of opera at a venue such as St Donat's Castle. Bill Smith's reaction was short and pithy: "Stupid," he called it.

One of the suggestions being put forward to save the Carl Rosa was that it should merge for touring purposes with Sadler's Wells. Four years earlier, when the Carl Rosa's financial plight had first become known, Bill Smith, seeing what he felt was a golden opportunity to form the largest touring company in Britain, and with one eye no doubt on their much larger grant, had proposed taking over the Carl Rosa, but the Carl Rosa management had rejected his overtures. Smith now reminded both the Arts Council and the Carl Rosa that his offer was still open. It was again refused. Once more, the survival of Welsh National Opera depended on self-help, and Smith immediately appealed to Welsh local authorities. It took time before their reactions were known, and the overall response was again disappointing. While a few councils gave generously, many refused to give anything, claiming that WNO was too South Wales-based to be of concern to them.

The crisis continued throughout the spring and WNO did not appear in public in 1958 until August, when a performance of *I Lombardi*, translated into Welsh by Sir Thomas Parry-Williams, closed the Eisteddfod at Ebbw Vale. The visit to Llandudno two weeks later, after the disappointing houses the previous year, was viewed with considerable trepidation. Although houses were not full at the beginning of the week, the sense of adversity and concern about the future manifested itself on stage in some impassioned performances. It was as if everyone was determined to prove to anybody who might be watching that WNO must not be allowed to go under. The season opened with one of the best performances of *La Traviata* that WNO had ever given. Elizabeth Fretwell, the young Australian soprano from Sadler's Wells, made a striking company debut as Violetta. Tano Ferendinos had relaxed into the part of Alfredo and sang with genuine Italianate style and feeling, Bryan Drake was a strong Germont and there was excellent support from William Dickie as Baron Douphol and Patricia Kern as Flora. Warwick Braithwaite brought precision and authority to the score, while the City of Birmingham Symphony Orchestra, accompanying a season for the first time, apart from a few blemishes, quickly came to terms with the operatic idiom.

*Traviata* was followed by *Rigoletto* with John Hargreaves in the title role, Marion Studholme as Gilda and Hervey Alan as Sparafucile, and then *Nabucco*. Although the limitations of the stage tended to cramp the production, soloists and chorus sang as if their futures depended upon being liked.

*Die Fledermaus* had been added to the repertoire in the hope that it would attract holiday-makers who might not otherwise go to an opera. It worked. The house was packed for the first time to see Harry Powell Lloyd's new production (which he had also designed) and Warwick Braithwaite set the tone for the evening with a sparkling account of the overture. The entire cast responded with some excellent fooling and fine singing.

The following night, a rain shower sent holiday-makers scuttling for cover and helped boost the audience for *Tosca*. Those who had never seen an opera before (and there were many) were well pleased, for they saw an on-form Marie Collier (who had recently sung Flora to Callas's Violetta at Covent Garden) giving an impassioned and beautifully sung performance in the title role. Ronald Lewis sang Scarpia as a man possessed and Robert Thomas was a vocally thrilling Cavaradossi. Edmund Donlevy and Ronald Stear, as Angelotti and the Sacristan, contributed excellent cameos, and the ever reliable Warwick Braithwaite was in the pit. "Not only did it surpass their excellent performances earlier in the week," wrote Neil Barkla in the *Liverpool Daily Post*, "but finally convinced one that this Welsh National Opera Company are one of the most vital forces in opera today." Opera in Llandudno was still a novelty but there definitely was an audience there, if only it could be persuaded in.

*Die Fledermaus* opened the Cardiff season on 29 September with the House Full boards outside, and they remained there throughout the fortnight. Every single performance, including matinées, was sold out. Not even the triumphant return of Shirley Bassey to her home town a couple of weeks earlier had managed to achieve that. There had been two changes of cast in *Die Fledermaus* since Llandudno: Patricia Bartlett took over as Rosalinda from Zoe Cresswell and Margaret Nisbett as Adele from Marion Studholme. Both delighted the audience, as did the other principals, but it was the chorus the audience really wanted. There was applause for them as soon as the curtain went up on the second act, and it was the choral work that brought the most insistent ovations, and the only encore, of the evening.

Not everyone thought *Die Fledermaus* was an appropriate work to open a season of grand opera. There were no such reservations the following night when the most popular opera singer in Britain made her debut with the company. Tickets for both performances of *Madam Butterfly*, starring Joan Hammond, were sold out weeks in advance. The production had been re-designed by David Tinker and re-produced by Betty Thompson, in Hammond's honour. Opposite her were Robert Thomas as Pinkerton and Bruce Dargavel as Sharpless. The evening "was obviously destined to be an event of outstanding importance, and on this occasion expectations were justified by results." The audience had come to worship Miss Hammond; it did not matter that she was a little too old to be ideally cast as a child-bride or that she towered over Pinkerton; she was received rapturously and she sang beautifully, as did the remainder of the cast. Robert Thomas was "the outstanding musical success of the evening." His Pinkerton was "without serious challenge the best performance of this role heard in Cardiff in recent seasons," and Bruce Dargavel sang superbly as Sharpless. David Tree, a guest from Covent Garden, was a masterly Goro.

Betty Thompson's atmospheric and well-defined production (uncredited in the programme) moved steadily towards its climax and gave the artists a framework within which they could shine. One innovation she made – the introduction of a live, instead of a plastic, baby – did not meet with universal approval. "We had the pleasure of gazing at the pathetic immobility of young Matthew Tinker, who warmed all hearts – not least his stage mother's," wrote one critic; but others found him an unnecessary distraction. The evening, however, was Hammond's. "From the moment Miss Hammond appeared on the stage she dominated it. This is a brilliant voice, certain in its technique, enchanting in its timbre and its ease of production . . . The crowded house was enraptured by her performance and accorded her an immense demonstration at the end of the great love duet and at many other points."

The following night, *La Traviata*, with Victoria Elliott, Tano Ferendinos, and Bryan Drake, also played to a packed and enthusiastic house, and *Il Trovatore* on the Thursday was notable for the fine singing of Paul Asciak as Manrico and Margreta Elkins, the Australian mezzo from Covent Garden, as Azucena. She had previously sung a few bars towards the close of *Mefistofele* with sufficient distinction to cause patrons to wrestle with their programmes in the dark to find her name. As Azucena she emerged as a singer of considerable stature; ". . . the initial nervousness . . . showed in some stiff phrasing, but the richness of the voice and the sense of dramatic urgency about her work had already sent a rustle of pleasure round the theatre . . . it was apparent that here was a young artist of great natural talents."

The first week ended with a performance of *Mefistofele*. The second, containing *I Lombardi* and *Nabucco*, in which Patricia Baird sang Abigail and William Dickie made his debut as Nabucco, closed with *Cav* and *Pag*. It was a fitting finale to a season in which every available seat and standing place had been taken. Although the programming was popular and contained no new works, it must be remembered that even popular operas were new to many people in Wales, especially the young. But even full houses did not cover the fortnight's costs and it ended with a deficit of £4000. Smith felt the decision to go ahead was totally justified. "This current season has proved that if a company provides opera which is good, then the public will flock to see it. And our ambition in Wales is to provide the best opera possible," he said. Although only three weeks had been staged during the year and a prestigious invitation to perform *Nabucco* in Israel, as part of the celebrations for the state of Israel's tenth anniversary, had been turned down, the gloom at the beginning of the year had given way to an optimism that WNO would not be allowed to die. The packed, cheering audiences had shown they wanted WNO to survive and, as the year came to an end, the appeals Smith had made earlier to local councils began to bear fruit. But there was still concern about the future. Each season had added to the accumulated deficit, there was no indication that the Arts Council in London would help the company out of its financial straits, and the appeal for Friends of Welsh National Opera had met with a very disappointing response. Smith decided to attack, to force the Arts Council to recognise the importance of WNO to life in Wales, and so, instead of continuing to cut back on performances, he announced that in 1959 five weeks would be given and would include the production of another rarely heard work.

In the spring, a week was played in Swansea at the Grand which had been saved from closure by the local council. It opened in front of a full house with a good, solid repertory performance of *Die Fledermaus*, and was followed by *Rigoletto*, given by a new cast. John Shaw, the Australian baritone, dominated the performance, singing and acting with an assurance that grew as the evening progressed. Nancy Creighton, the new Gilda, demonstrated a fine voice of much promise, Robert Thomas gave his usual committed performance as the Duke and Harold Blackburn made a convincing Sparafucile. The new ballet sequences, choreographed by Tutte Lemkow, were fresh and attractive, and the male chorus remained consistently excellent. The orchestra, the Bournemouth Symphony, was conducted by Charles Groves.

The following night, Braithwaite took over for *I Lombardi*. The performance was broadcast on BBC radio, the first Welsh production to be broadcast in its entirety, and the largest audience WNO had ever had heard it on top form, with a confident, stirring performance which even took in its stride an exploding light bulb crashing to the stage and showering a violinist in the pit with broken glass in Act 1. The chorus, which was off stage for only short periods, was again the star, but no opera can survive on chorus alone and all the principals (Joyce Barker, Bryan Drake, Paul Asciak and

Tano Ferendinos, repeating their original roles) also sang well. Notable amongst the smaller roles was Glenys Dowdle, a young Swansea soprano, making her company debut as Viclinda.

The hope that *I Lombardi* would become a second *Nabucco* and a work without which no WNO season would be complete, was not materialising and there were far too many empty seats for comfort. The need to attract full houses brought back *Cav* and *Pag* in two full-blooded performances, and *Nabucco*. There was a queue more than one hundred yards long outside the theatre for returned tickets to hear Bryan Drake take over from Hervey Alan as Zaccaria. The disappointment of the evening was Patricia Bartlett's Abigail, which, in spite of her dramatic delivery, failed to master completely the difficult vocal line, and showed just how difficult it was going to be to find a successor to Ruth Packer.

The talking point of *I Pagliacci* was the strongly sung and realistic Tonio of John Shaw, and not just for its musical qualities. Shaw had appeared for the Prologue dressed in a checked shirt and fawn trousers, and had worn the same clothes in the first act. "It is unforgivable," wrote a member of the public to his local paper. The point had been raised by the critic Froom Tyler, who had received a reply from Shaw explaining that the Prologue, being an explanation of what is to follow, does not need to be played in any particular costume; it is often, he pointed out, sung in evening dress at La Scala, "but it is my feeling that as it is preferable to move on with the opera as soon as possible after the Prologue, the less costume changing Tonio has to do the better. As for being rational in opera," Shaw continued, "I very strongly feel that to convince present-day opera audiences one has to endeavour to make situations real and not follow the old-fashioned way of leaving so much to their imagination." Tyler did not agree. Where would it take us, he argued, if we try to make operatic characters "real"? He was, he declared, "against Mr Shaw and progressive producers who are all for rationalisation."

WNO's productions during the fifties and early sixties would hardly be thought of as being progressive today. Certainly they were an advance on the static productions of the early days when everyone was learning their craft, but there was little in them that might be termed radical, even from such guest producers as Harry Powell Lloyd, who sought, when permitted enough time for rehearsal, to people his productions with real, living persons. Norman Jones's productions, too, had, as the chorus's ability had increased, moved more towards making the presentation work logically. Jones, who had produced the bulk of WNO's output during the first ten years, had finally given up his post as Resident Producer. For some time, he had been dogged by ill-health and had been forced to hand over the responsibility for new productions to other producers. Finally he had been unable to cope even with staging revivals, and had instead become the company's first archivist. The task of putting on the Swansea season had been left in the hands of Lloyd, Betty Thompson and Patrick McClellan, the new stage director. McClellan, a tall, bearded Scot, had been brought in by Lloyd. When Bill Smith had first seen him on the station platform heading to Llandudno, he had almost had an apoplectic fit. McClellan was wearing a kilt! "Doesn't he realise this is the *Welsh* National Opera?" Smith had spluttered. Over the next two years, Lloyd, Thompson and McClellan were between them responsible for putting on every WNO performance apart from those by guest producers.

If, as still seemed a distinct possibility, WNO was going to founder, Bill Smith was determined it would not go quietly. The Arts Council grant for 1959 had not been increased to provide the secure base needed; in fact, it had been reduced by £500 to £13,500. However, grants from local authorities, small though some of them were, amounted to £6000 and Smith decided to mount an extra spring season of popular works in Cardiff, hoping again to play to full houses. This opened on 4 May with Gounod's *Faust*, being given its first showing in Cardiff for four years. *La Bohème* the following night was a disappointment, containing long patches of indifferent singing. *Rigoletto* was much more satisfactory, with John Shaw again commanding in the title role, and Joyce Goodwin a striking Gilda. Making his debut as the Duke was Paul Asciak, singing with an intelligence and sincerity which immediately won the packed audience. His rendering of "La donna è mobile" was memorable and not just because he suddenly burst into Italian.

The short season was completed by *Cav* and *Pag* in which *I Pagliacci* stood out due to excellent singing by Joyce Goodwin, Paul Asciak, John Hauxvell and the chorus. Ronald Lewis, taking over as Tonio, was especially good in a performance which was "original and well thought out." "It was," one critic wrote, "an inspired presentation."

The pioneering work in Llandudno was at last beginning to pay off. Banners of welcome hung above the railway station as the specially chartered train arrived for the third successive summer season, and advance bookings were extremely heavy. Audiences were coming not just from throughout North Wales but from much further afield, and many holiday-makers had booked their holidays to coincide with WNO's appearance. Opera was becoming one of the town's tourist attractions and no longer was it necessary to put stickers on the posters proclaiming that the performances were being sung in English so that everyone could understand them. The orchestra for the season was the City of Birmingham Symphony Orchestra. With money so tight, it made sense to have an orchestra in Llandudno which did not have to travel all the way from Bournemouth, and this double partnership of the CBSO playing in North Wales and the BSO in South Wales was to continue for some time. Like the members of the chorus, orchestral players would use the opportunity to take their families on holiday and looked forward to their week by the sea, even when, as on one occasion, they had to play a performance wearing their overcoats because it was so cold.

The Llandudno week opened with *Faust*, in which Michael Langdon (who had just enjoyed the biggest success of his career so far at Covent Garden appearing as the Grand Inquisitor in Visconti's famous production of *Don Carlos*) appeared as Mephistopheles. Langdon's genuine basso voice and commanding stage presence made him ideally suited to the role. Patricia Kern repeated her musical and convincing Siebel, Mary Wells was a touching Marguerite, and Tano Ferendinos an adequate Faust. It was while singing the role of Mephistopheles at a later performance (a schools matinée) that Langdon missed an entrance for the only time in his career. He and Robert Thomas, the Faust, were chatting in the dressing room when they heard some music coming over the Tannoy and realised, simultaneously, that they should have been on stage singing. They arrived in time for Thomas to sing "Be gone!" and for Langdon to reply "I shall wait at the door" before making his exit. As soon as the curtain came down, they apologised to conductor Ivor John. "Don't worry, boys," he told them, "I never realised how beautiful that music was until I heard it without the voices. It was lovely." The week also included *Cav* and *Pag*, *Madam Butterfly* and *Nabucco*, which very nearly didn't get on when the train wagon carrying the scenery was derailed. Fortunately, the sets were not damaged.

At the end of the following month, the autumn fortnight in Cardiff opened with a new production which again excited curiosity throughout Britain: Rimsky-Korsakov's *May Night*. Unlike the other operas WNO had rescued from obscurity, this was a departure in that it was a comic work, not a dramatic piece. Premièred in 1880, *May Night* had received its only professional performance in Britain when it had been sung in Russian at Drury Lane before the First World War, and had last been seen in 1931 in an Oxford Opera Club production. Singing in that Oxford production had been Nell Moody, wife of producer John Moody. Moody, who had retained a close interest in WNO ever since staging *Nabucco* seven years earlier, and was just coming to the end of a five-year tenure at the Bristol Old Vic, felt that it would be another interesting and unusual work and suggested it to Smith. Smith agreed to put it on without consulting Braithwaite, his Musical Director. At the beginning of the year, Braithwaite had arrived in Cardiff clutching copies of Wolf-Ferrari's *The Jewels of the Madonna*, the opera he thought he was about to start rehearsing, only to be told that he was doing *May Night* instead.

In a small way, *May Night* was a minor landmark. It was the company's twentieth production and the first time a Russian opera had been staged. Its announcement aroused considerable interest, for very few people in Britain had ever heard of it, let alone seen it. It did not feature in Kobbé, nor in many musical reference books. Rimsky-Korsakov had based his three-act opera on a short story by Gogol which was, in its turn, based upon an old folk legend in which Pannochka, a water-sprite who was once human but had drowned herself, helps Levko win the hand of Anna and makes sure along the way that Levko teaches his father, the Mayor, a lesson for attempting to seduce Anna. It was the first of Rimsky's fantasy operas and contains much memorably lyrical music, gentle humour, knockabout comedy, ballet sequences, romance, and plenty of work for the chorus. On the face of it, it was another perfect choice. Moody himself was invited to produce and cast Duncan Robertson and Iona Jones as the young lovers, Heather Harper as Pannochka, the water-sprite, Harold Blackburn as the Mayor and Monica Sinclair as his sister-in-law. Stephen Manton, Laurie Payne, Bryan Drake, Barbara Harding, Elizabeth Painter and Valmai Hunter completed the cast. Iona Jones, a 24-year-old from North Wales who had been studying at the Guildhall, was picked for her role from open auditions. Another young unknown, Sally Hulke, was brought in to design the production, which was the most expensive so far staged.

*May Night* opened on 28 September. Moody had deliberately kept his production simple, allowing the folk element full rein. Warwick Braithwaite moved the score along at an appropriately gentle pace and the principals were universally good, with Laurie Payne's drunken Kalenik winning the popular acting award. The packed house gave the cast eight curtain calls. And yet the production was not entirely successful. Partly this was due to the work itself. No matter how many interesting ingredients it contained it was not a work to draw people back time and time again and so could hardly be expected to take a regular place in the repertory. Partly it was the fault of Moody's production and the designs of Sally Hulke. The chorus, many of them without the figures to play convincing water-sprites, looked distinctly uncomfortable in the white leotards they were made to wear, and had to perform dance routines of which they were not completely capable. Their unhappiness showed.

If *May Night* was the season's attraction for the critics, it was the return of Joan Hammond as Madam Butterfly and as Tosca which excited the general public. Her Tosca was everything her adoring fans could have wanted. Opposite her, fellow Australian Ronald Dowd showed why he was fast being regarded as one of the leading tenors in Britain. His Cavaradossi, riding effortlessly over the orchestral climaxes and yet sung with great tenderness when required, was without doubt the best Cardiff had heard for many years. John Shaw provided a powerful, polished Scarpia, and Bryan Drake was an effective Angelotti, though, as one critic pointed out, "he must be careful of points which test the credulity even of opera audiences; it is always well to unlock doors before, not after, passing through them." That apart, this was the sort of full-blooded, committed evening which *Tosca* audiences delight in, and "they capped a very loud evening with a riotous ovation that was even louder than anything that had happened before."

The following night, Lloyd's production of *The Barber of Seville* was given for the first time in two years. For this revival, Lloyd broke with the then current fashion of having a soprano sing Rosina and reverted to the mezzo voice for which Rossini wrote the part, giving the role to the rising young star Margreta Elkins. Other newcomers to their roles were Laurie Payne as Figaro and a young singer making one of her first appearances in opera as the maid, Marcellina: Rita Hunter. She "converted Marcellina's last act aria into a real success."

Also included in the first week were performances of *I Lombardi* in front of a disappointingly small house and *La Traviata* with Heather Harper returning as Violetta and Kenneth Macdonald as Alfredo.

The second week opened on 5 October with a gala performance of *Nabucco*, celebrating its fiftieth performance. The opera was still resisting all attempts to retire it and would have sold out anyway, but the demand for tickets for this very special occasion was enormous. Bill Smith had wanted to celebrate *the* Welsh National opera in as grand a manner as possible and had invited Ann Schneider-Green to sing the role of Abigail. When she pulled out, Ruth Packer agreed to come out of retirement. She and Tano Ferendinos, singing the role of Ishmael, were the only two artists on stage who had sung in the first performance in Sophia Gardens seven years earlier. John Shaw who had been enjoying such success with the company as Rigoletto, sang his first Nabucco, and a young singer from New Zealand, whose career in Britain had been going so badly that he was on the verge of giving up and returning home and was only stopped by the offer from Welsh National, sang Zaccaria. His name was Donald McIntyre. Also new to her role was Glenys Dowdle as Fenena. Shaw was an authoritative Nabucco, but McIntyre had a more limited success: "His voice sounds too youthful for this music, and his artistry is immature, but he is a young singer from whom much can be expected in the future; he sings and acts with intelligence." The chorus sang ardently, and in the pit, controlling the evening superbly, as he had done on so many previous occasions, was Charles Groves. The night, however, belonged to Ruth Packer, recapturing the magic of those early performances as she effortlessly floated Abigail's fiendishly difficult music. At the end of the performance, John Moody went on stage to remind the audience that *Nabucco* had not only made Verdi's reputation but the reputation of Welsh National Opera as well. It was perhaps difficult to recall, in view of its continued popularity, that when *Nabucco* had first been staged in 1952, the opera had not enjoyed such an enormous success and that the Welsh reluctance to try something new had extended to the work they now claimed totally as theirs.

*Nabucco* was followed by performances of *Madam Butterfly*, with Joan Hammond, *Faust*, with Michael Langdon repeating his superb Mephistopheles, *May Night*, *La Traviata*, and a further *Nabucco* to round off a highly successful season.

Despite the fact that WNO was enjoying enormous critical and box-office success, and playing to larger audiences than ever before, its financial state remained parlous. Just before the Cardiff season had opened, news came that the Arts Council in London was again refusing to increase the grant. Bill Smith, who had spent much of the year travelling to London, trying to persuade officials to help WNO, if possible with a direct Treasury grant, had had enough. Minutes before the curtain was due up on the opening performance of *May Night*, he stormed into Braithwaite's dressing room and asked him to announce from the pit that this was definitely going to be the company's final season, that after the Cardiff performances WNO would close down. Braithwaite refused to do any such thing, Smith calmed down, and no more was heard of the threat. But it remained very real. Sir Ifor Evans, the Provost of University College, London, had described WNO as "the most important artistic adventure in Wales today"; its chorus, to quote one leading national critic, had "set an entirely new standard for British opera." And yet London, it seemed, was prepared to allow the organisation to die.

No ANNOUNCEMENT of future plans was made at the end of the Cardiff fortnight, and the short spring season in Swansea, the traditional opening season of the year, was cancelled for 1960. For the first time, the general public realised that Smith was not bluffing, that there was a very real danger Welsh National Opera might follow in the footsteps of every other Welsh operatic venture in the past and disband. Smith had not been idle, however. Aided by Myra Owen and other members of the Welsh Arts Council, he had spent the winter putting pressure on people who were in a position to help, including Members of Parliament. The first results came in March when TWW, the Welsh independent television company, announced that, following discussions between their Managing Director Alfred Francis and Sir William Emrys Williams, the General Secretary of the Arts Council of Great Britain, it was giving WNO a grant of £5000 spread over two years. This was followed in April (after behind-the-scenes interventions by Henry Brooke, the new Minister for Housing, and Lord Brecon, who succeeded Brooke as Minister of State for Wales) by a further announcement that the Arts Council had more than doubled its grant for the year from £14,500 to £32,000. The news, which came too late to save the Swansea season, was greeted with undisguised pleasure. It meant, said a relieved Bill Smith, that the company would no longer have to live hand-to-mouth, but would at last be able to plan properly for the future. "We can now look forward with confidence to the next ten years," he commented. Together with grants from Welsh local authorities the annual income was now in the region of £40,000. The extra money would allow for WNO's steady progress and development, and would be used in the first place to strengthen the top level of the artistic and administrative direction, including the appointment of a full-time Musical Director. Warwick Braithwaite had already told Smith that he had no wish to become involved full-time, and the search to find his successor began immediately. Secondly, it would enable the purchase of premises to house a new headquarters, scenery store, workshop and rehearsal area, and in which there would also be room to run a training centre for young singers. It was the intention to select for full-time training a dozen young singers who would provide the basis of a Welsh Opera for All group and eventually graduate to the main company. "We are not satisfied with being just a provincial opera," Smith declared. "We want to be a national opera in the strict sense."

For twelve years, WNO's headquarters had been Morsmith's garage, with rehearsals taking place there, and in a variety of church halls and rooms above pubs throughout Cardiff. The anticipated growth meant that the garage was no longer suitable, and Smith, who had all but lost interest in it, had decided to sell the business anyway. That meant that Peggy Moreland, Norman Jones and the new administration would have to be found offices and, for the first time, would become full-time employees of Welsh National Opera instead of being, nominally, on the staff of Morsmith Motors.

Since Norman Jones's retirement there had not been a resident Producer, and a second important step came that summer with the appointment of John Moody as Director of Productions. Moody's first production in his new capacity was WNO's first public appearance for ten months. On 1 August 1960, the opening night of the National Eisteddfod, at the Sophia Gardens, Cardiff, Arwel Hughes's new comic opera, *Serch Yw'r Doctor* (*Love's the Doctor*), was given its world stage première under the composer's baton (it had already been broadcast in English). The three-act opera had been commissioned by the Welsh Arts Council for the Eisteddfod. The libretto by Saunders Lewis, in Welsh, was a free updating of Molière's play *L'amour médecin*. The subject – poor boy loves rich girl; father of girl forbids marriage; 'doctor' prescribes marriage to himself as the only answer to the girl's ills and turns out to be, of course, poor boy in disguise – clearly appealed to Hughes, for he produced a flow of melodic music which the company found fun to rehearse and the packed audience thoroughly enjoyed. The problems came when the work was transferred to the stage. Moody and his designer, David Tinker, had set it in a South of France belonging to an earlier age, and yet the libretto contained clear twentieth-century references (to Mercedes-Benz cars, for example) and jokes at the expense of psychiatrists, which made for confusion. In addition, the open stage of the Eisteddfod Pavilion tent, extremely wide but with no depth, did not allow for any great movement of the chorus other than for entrances and exits, and the work, witty though it might have been, was "sadly lacking in movement and action." It contained too many static spells which even Moody's inventiveness was not able to overcome. "No producer on earth could have manipulated the mob which this company gaily turns loose on such a stage just for the sake of maintaining its reputation for chorus singing, which was in fact a notable feature of Monday's performance," commented the *Liverpool Evening Post*. The evening succeeded only because of the delightful vocal writing and some charming singing by the principals: Lucille Graham as Lucinde, the rich girl; Rhydderch Davies as

Sganarelle, her father; Rowland Jones as Clitandre, the poor boy; and Marion Lowe as Lisette, the maid.

Following the Eisteddfod, rehearsals of the current repertoire continued every night in preparation for the week in Llandudno. The interest in the visit, throughout North Wales and from wider afield, was such that train timetables had to be altered to enable people to get to and from the theatre. Free from the worries of an uncertain future, a confidence was displayed which spilled over onto the stage. Harry Powell Lloyd's production of *The Barber of Seville* proved to be an appropriate opening choice, and was followed by *Die Fledermaus*, *La Traviata* with Victoria Elliott as Violetta, *Madam Butterfly* with Marie Collier as Cio-Cio-San and Robert Thomas as Pinkerton, and *Il Trovatore*. The night before *Il Trovatore*, the singer cast as Leonora fell ill. A phone call was made to Zoe Cresswell in Cardiff. Although she had not sung the role for four years, she agreed to help out. She took the score with her on the train, arriving in Llandudno in the afternoon, and was given a brief run-through at the theatre with the Manrico (Paul Asciak) and Count di Luna (Peter Glossop) before being whisked off for a costume fitting. An hour later, she was singing what she felt was the best performance she had ever given. She sang with "an intelligence and conviction that were beyond praise." It was to be her last appearance with WNO.

While the placing of WNO on a sound artistic and financial footing was his priority, Moody had no intention of ceasing to mine the profitable vein he had started with *Nabucco*. For the opening of the two-week autumn season in Cardiff, he came up with another neglected Verdi piece, *La Battaglia di Legnano*. Composed in 1848, the opera tells of the Italian people's fight against the German emperor Frederick Barbarossa in the 12th Century, and was written to rouse Verdi's Italy against her Austrian oppressors. So effectively did Verdi achieve his object that the première in Rome in 1849 created a riot and the opera's performance was banned in Naples. Since that time it had vanished from the repertory in Italy and had been performed only once in the last seventy years (at the Florence Festival in 1959). It had never been staged in Britain. Moody had first come across it seven years earlier while browsing through a second-hand bookshop in London's Charing Cross Road. He found it fascinating, and together with his wife, Nell, set about translating it and updating the action. The opportunity of seeing it on stage had seemed unlikely, but his appointment as Director of Productions suddenly made a production possible. Renaming it *The Battle*, he set the action in German-occupied Italy during the Second World War, making the story the struggle of the Italian partisans against the Nazis, and as technical adviser he brought in an army officer who had helped organise resistance groups. The production opened on 31 October.

Moody's intention in updating *The Battle* was not simply to be gimmicky. He wanted modern audiences to experience something of the fervour which those in Verdi's own day had felt, and with a strong cast of principals – Heather Harper, Ronald Dowd, Ronald Lewis and Hervey Alan among them – he succeeded. "It was a risk, but last night it undoubtedly came off." "The full-throated blaze of choral tone in the big numbers amply justifies this company's choice of the work. It must be suspected that the opera would be perfectly viable in its original setting. Students of Verdi will have no doubt that the musical merits of the score need no special justification, except the good singing that they get here." Moody's production, designed by David Tinker and conducted with great fervour by Charles Groves, was well researched and thought out, and the only real criticism of the updating was that the pace of the original was sometimes a little slow for a modern action drama. At one stage, Hervey Alan, making a brief but striking appearance as the German commandant, had to enter a meeting of partisans without a bodyguard and sing an aria unaware that he was being covered by machine-guns. The shoot-out which followed appeared very contrived. The capacity audience, however, revelled in it and in the spirited choral work, and there were some twenty curtain calls. "Viva Verdi and Bravo Verdi roared the Welsh audience . . . and for a moment we were in Parma, Bologna, or Palermo, or one of those small Italian houses away from the international climate of Milan, where these things really matter." At the close, John Moody went on stage to remind the audience of Verdi's own opinion of the opera: "Among my neglected operas," he once said, ". . . there are two which I should not like to be forgotten: *Stiffelio* and *La Battaglia di Legnano*."

Although the British première of *The Battle* captured the headlines, the Cardiff season was also notable for the company debuts of several young Welsh musicians. Wyn Morris, who had won the Koussevitzky Award and been working with George Szell in Cleveland, appeared in the pit for the first time and drove *Il Trovatore* along at breakneck speed. "In the Anvil Chorus the two gypsies detailed to perform the hammer swinging had to beat away like excited Stakhanovites. One had a momentary vision of a time and motion study having broken out in the Romany camp," observed Kenneth Loveland. Morris's *Bohème*, in the second week, was less successful. A poor performance, indifferently sung and generally lacking in teamwork, was not helped by Morris's brisk approach which lacked eloquent phrasing and too often failed to secure a satisfactory balance between stage and pit; "One lost count of the number of times they parted company."

Another young Welshman making his debut that season was the tenor Edward Byles, cast as Pinkerton opposite Joan Hammond in *Madam*

*Butterfly*. Byles, a former member of the Covent Garden chorus, had spent two years touring with Opera for All, and this was his first major engagement. The pattern of his introduction to the production was typical of the way WNO staged its revivals at that time. He spent two or three mornings and afternoons in London rehearsing with Hammond at Dyneley studios off Marylebone Road, and went to a costumier for wardrobe fittings before travelling down to Cardiff for a rehearsal with local members of the cast under Betty Thompson. After a dress rehearsal in the afternoon, he sang the performance in the evening giving a musically assured performance which "challenged any recent performances we have heard in this role."

The outstanding debutante of the season, however, was a young soprano in *Nabucco*. Since Ruth Packer's retirement, there had been problems in finding a worthy successor as Abigail. For the two performances of the opera that autumn, WNO engaged, on the recommendation of Hervey Alan, a young singer fresh from college who had not appeared on the operatic stage before. Her name was Elizabeth Vaughan. "Her performance, while, not unnaturally showing visible signs of immaturity, suggested potentialities from which a considerable operatic career could be fashioned," commented Loveland.

The season concluded with performances of *Tosca*, *Die Fledermaus* and *May Night*, and was followed by the announcement of Warwick Braithwaite's successor as Musical Director. Once it had been known that Braithwaite did not want to stay on, the company had been inundated with applications, a measure of the prestige WNO was enjoying in the musical world. After much deliberation, the choice fell on Charles Groves, principal conductor of the Bournemouth Symphony Orchestra. Groves had first conducted WNO eight years earlier and had appeared regularly ever since, being associated with some of its greatest successes. He resigned from the BSO and moved his family down to Llandaff to become the first full-time Musical Director. He appeared in his new role in Swansea in March 1961 conducting *The Battle*. During the week he also conducted *La Bohème* for the first time, with Beatrix Edwards as Mimi and Elizabeth Vaughan making her debut as Musetta.

The following month new headquarters were found. The search for premises to replace Morsmith Motors had lasted almost a year. As a temporary measure, the administrative offices had been moved to Union Street while rehearsals continued in a variety of different locations, but then in April, Central Hall in Charles Street, a former Wesleyan Chapel due for demolition, was taken over on a six-month lease prior to its permanent acquisition, made possible by aid from the Arts Council and Cardiff Corporation. It was hardly the grandest building for the preparation of grand opera and needed a lot of work to make it habitable. It had been unoccupied for some time, and even after WNO moved in, its doorways were still used for dumping rubbish. The fabric of the building was in a poor state of repair, the roof leaked and no matter how many coats of distemper were applied to the walls, the damp peeled them off almost immediately. Muriel Pointon was sitting in her office one day when the skylight above her, covered in snow, gave way and ended up on her desk. Heating was by means of gas fires, the flues of which threw flames into the air outside. Twice, Groves was phoned in the middle of the night and told the building was on fire. He had to get out of bed, drive down and explain to the diligent policeman who had spotted the flames that they were simply the exhaust from the fires. It was, however, home.

In May Groves took WNO to Sadler's Wells, its first visit to London since 1957, four years previously. The repertoire consisted of *The Battle*, *May Night*, *Mefistofele* and *Nabucco*.

*The Battle* was generally well received. Andrew Porter found that "... the Welsh production, despite some obvious faults, is very per-suasive ... Moody's production throughout is somewhat rough and ready: but the fire of the piece comes across, and that counts for more than finesses." "There was a great deal in last night's revival that was gripping," wrote the critic of the *Times*, though he was not completely convinced by the updating: "... goodness knows how the problem of pace can ever be solved, for there is no escaping the fact that contemporary drama needs to move at a far quicker speed than that permitted by Verdi's leisurely, spacious music. Welcome as are experiments, perhaps after all the best solution for this work is a courageously inventive production in its own rightful unhurried age ... The performance itself was excellent. Drama-tically, the action was refreshingly simple, direct, and free from all operatic posturing. Musically, there was some superb singing from the chorus, at once vibrant and vigorous, some refined playing from the Bournemouth Symphony Orchestra under Mr Charles Groves (never a tub-thumping Verdian), and last but not least, some powerful solo contributions from Mr Ronald Dowd, a mellow and noble-toned Arrigo, Miss Heather Harper, a clear-ringing, sympathetic Lida, and Mr Ronald Lewis, a suitably storm-tossed, strained-sounding Rolando."

The following night WNO's showpiece, *Nabucco*, was played to a packed house in a performance which had even the critics on their feet cheering. The chorus was as brilliant as everybody expected, Hervey Alan was the excellent Zaccaria and Bryan Drake, who had first sung the role in Cardiff the previous autumn, impressed as Nabucco. But the star of the evening was the unknown Elizabeth Vaughan, making her London debut. "Miss Vaughan seized every opportunity the music gave her with a splendid sense of musical conviction. Her dramatic technique, though fairly rudimentary, is entirely on the right lines, but it was the sheer quality of her singing that thrilled the audience," wrote the *Times* critic. "Miss Vaughan was excellent, and compassed all the role. Her singing was expressive. She dropped cleanly from high C to middle C two octaves lower with exciting effect. The florid arpeggios of the role gave her no trouble, nor did the long legato phrases. She was confident. Her ovation was well deserved," said Andrew Porter in the *Financial Times*. "A Welsh Callas in the making?" asked the *Daily Mail*. "I suggest all operagoers and opera managements note the name," wrote Clive Barnes. They did. Covent Garden immediately invited her to audition and signed her up.

Vaughan was not the only young artist to be snapped up by the London companies that season. The following night, Charles Mackerras, returning for the first time in eleven years, conducted a performance of *May Night* in which tenor John Wakefield made his operatic debut. Duncan Robertson, the original Levko, was unavailable for the revival, and three weeks before the performance a replacement had still not been found. Then Groves remembered Wakefield, a young graduate from the Royal Academy who had sung a performance of *Messiah* with him. Wakefield was contacted and asked if he knew the role of Levko. He had never heard of the opera, let alone Levko, but said he did, and was immediately signed to do it. He went on after a couple of production rehearsals and a dress rehearsal on the morning of the performance. The production received lukewarm reviews: "A somewhat tepid performance," was Donald Mitchell's reaction. "The fantastic element was heavily earthbound and the chorus, grouped stodgily around the stage, sang unfeelingly. They obviously missed the lusty Verdi choruses in which they excel," felt the *Stage*. "A poorly lit set conveyed no sense of time or atmosphere; and, though the male peasant dancing was passable, the dismal cavortings of the water-nymphs were an open invitation to laughter," commented Arthur Jacobs. "You would not want to see it once a month for 10 years; but once in 50 years it is a relaxed, endearing experience, as the performance conducted by Mr Charles Mackerras made quite plain," remarked the *Times*. Wakefield went through the performance in a daze. He was so inexperienced that Stephen Manton, with whom he shared a dressing room, had to help him with his make-up. But his singing was impressive. He "distinguished himself as a Levko charming in voice and deportment." "John Wakefield, a young lyric tenor with an easy stage manner, used his pleasant but as yet undeveloped voice with artistry . . . His love-song in the third act was delightfully sung and sensitively phrased." The following day, he was asked to audition for Sadler's Wells and so began a career which was to make him one of Britain's leading tenors.

The chorus, still visibly embarrassed by what they were required to do in

*May Night*, were on safer, and happier, ground with *Mefistofele*, the fourth production at the Wells that week. "The Welsh National Opera Company very sensibly continues to keep Boito's *Mefistofele* in its repertory," wrote Philip Hope-Wallace; "the fact that it is a shoe-string production of an opera which ought to be a scene shifter's nightmare only emphasises and advertises the sorry lack of money behind this excellently enterprising band. It is here that Zeffirelli and his lavish expenses should be applied, not to Verdi's self-producing *Falstaff* . . . This chorus, backed with Welsh mining valley fervour, raised the roof at the Wells and was cheered to the echo. It makes the ordinary non-critical listener go hot and cold, like the 'Dies Irae' in Verdi's *Requiem*."

WNO had again conquered London. It had, without doubt, become the single most important musical enterprise in Wales, and its contribution to the country's cultural life was recognised in July when Bill Smith was given an honorary Doctorate of Letters by the University of Wales at a ceremony in Cardiff.

After another successful season in Llandudno, breaking its own box-office records with performances of *Nabucco*, *Tosca*, *Il Trovatore*, *La Bohème* and *The Barber of Seville* (which played to the largest house in all the seasons since visits to the town had started), WNO returned to Cardiff for an autumn season with a new rarity: Rossini's *William Tell*. The suggestion to stage it had come from Moody, who felt that Ronald Lewis would make an ideal Tell. The opera, it goes without saying, also contained much for the chorus. *William Tell* was Rossini's final opera and a significant break from the comic operas by which he was, and is, best known. Apart from the overture, which was a regular feature in the concert hall and was being used as the signature tune for a television series, it was hardly known in Britain, having been staged only once (by a touring Italian company at Drury Lane in 1958) during the previous fifty years. One of the reasons for its infrequent appearance was the difficulty in casting the tenor role of Arnold, another was its length: five hours, including the obligatory ballet. Together Groves and Moody cut the running time down to three hours by pruning within scenes rather than by dropping anything complete.

Apart from Lewis as Tell, the 14th Century Swiss patriot fighting against Austrian oppression, the cast included Hervey Alan as Melchtal, Bryan Drake as the villainous Gessler, Glenys Dowdle as Matilda, and Elizabeth Vaughan in the breeches role of Tell's son, Jemmy. Tano Ferendinos was given the fiendishly difficult role of Arnold, and the production was designed by Patrick Robertson. It was intended that both the Swansea and the Cardiff choruses should appear in it, but when it came to the dress rehearsal, Moody discovered that he could not get all his forces onto the stage. Many choristers got left in the wings, and the rehearsal ended in chaos. The following night, an hour or so before the curtain was due up, Moody announced that he was withdrawing the bulk of the Cardiff chorus from the performance, a decision which nearly caused a riot. Thereafter the opera was sung on a rota basis.

It opened to a full house on 2 October. "It has been given an effective, straightforward production by John Moody, and conductor Charles Groves, with the Bournemouth Symphony Orchestra in the pit, directs a spirited performance . . ." "John Moody's production . . . is animated and full of atmosphere." For those who knew only the comic Rossini, the evening was a revelation. Conceived and composed on a grand, epic scale, the work contained some of Rossini's brightest melodic invention. "*Tell* is hardly deserving of the neglect it has met in this country. Though it contains its sterile patches, the opera is remarkably bright, tuneful and dramatic and gave the company's renowned chorus plenty of room to exercise their vocal talents."

Ronald Lewis made a rousing and convincing hero, although he was not robust enough for one member of the audience. At the point at which Tell was seized by the guards, Lewis's mother was overheard to say to her companion, "They wouldn't have been able to grab my Ronnie like that in his younger days." Elizabeth Vaughan's voice soared effortlessly above the ensembles, and Glenys Dowdle, Jean Evans, Hervey Alan and Bryan Drake all seized the opportunities given them. The disappointment was the luckless Ferendinos, who had the greatest of difficulty in coping with a role which involved several high D flats and throwing his voice around the octaves. Tell's famous feat of archery with the apple was skilfully brought off, and although the ballet interludes proved an indifferent intrusion, the revival contained many moments of excitement and enjoyment.

*William Tell* was followed by the much better-known Rossini opera *The Barber of Seville*, with Fernanda Eastwood as Rosina, Kenneth Macdonald as Almaviva, Laurie Payne as Figaro and Derick Davies making his company debut as Dr Bartolo. The fortnight also included performances of *The Battle*, *Nabucco*, *Mefistofele* (with Herincx and Hervey Alan sharing the title role), *Tosca* (which, with probably the strongest cast then available in Britain – Hammond, Dowd and Otakar Kraus as Scarpia – was outstanding) and *La Bohème*, in which Edward Byles sang an impressive first Rodolfo in an otherwise uninspiring evening. The season had been a great success. Demand for tickets, even for the unknown *William Tell*, had been unprecedented, and Groves had good reason to be pleased at the end of his first year as Musical Director.

Idloes Owen, Welsh National Opera's first Musical Director, with William Smith and Norman Jones, drawn by Stanley Gitsham, a chorus member

William Smith, Chairman 1948–68; Norman Jones, the company's first Producer (BBC Hulton Picture Library)

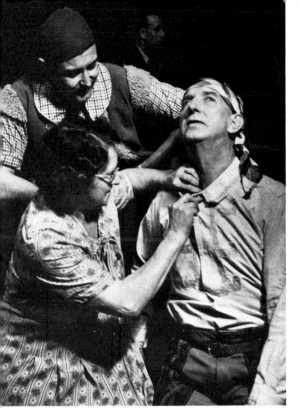

Father and son chorus members, George (right) and Parry Davies. George's wife, Edith, was wardrobe mistress; Norman Jones rehearsing *Cavalleria Rusticana* (BBC Hulton Picture Library)

Ivor John rehearsing the Swansea Chorus

# PRINCE OF WALES THEATRE

## CARDIFF.

Box Office open 10 a.m. to 9 p.m.
Telephone 3528

## Week Commencing APRIL 15, 1946

ONCE NIGHTLY at 6-30. Matinees Thursday & Saturday at 2-30

### WELSH NATIONAL OPERA COMPANY

PRESENTS

# CAVALLERIA RUSTICANA
## I Pagliacci. Faust

| | |
|---|---|
| TUDOR DAVIES | LILIAN EVANS |
| TOM HOPKINS | MARGARET WILLIAMS |
| NORMAN JONES | BEATRICE GOUGH |
| IVOR JOHN | PHYLLIS ASH-CHILD |
| JOHN MORGAN | DORIS RUSSELL |
| ARTHUR DAVIES | HELENA HUGHES-BROWN |
| FRANK JAMES | MYFANWY RICHARDS |
| STANLEY GITSHAM | ALICE JAMES |

Augmented Orchestra

Conductors : Idloes Owen, Ivor John, Victor Fleming

Ballet: Mollie Hair :: Costumes: Smith, Manchester :: Scenery: Capes, London.

Prices of Admission : Pit, 3/-; Upper Circle, 3/6; Centre Stalls, 4/6
Dress Circle, 6/- ; Orchestra Stalls, 6/9

★ PROCEEDS IN AID OF CARDIFF ROYAL INFIRMARY ★

MENNER DE CANTILUPE PRESS CARDIFF & HEREFORD

Poster for the opening night

*Carmen* 1947

*I Pagliacci* 1951 revival: Emrys Jones *Beppo*, Joan Stephens *Nedda* (BBC Hulton Picture Library)

*Il Trovatore* 1951: Betty Thompson rehearses Phyllis Ash-Child and Arnold Davies, Idloes Owen (right) looks on (BBC Hulton Picture Library)

*Nabucco* 1952 Act II

*Menna* 1955 revival: Elsie Morison *Menna*, Edgar Evans *Gwyn*

*Mefistofele* 1957: Raimund Herincx *Mefistofele* (BBC Hulton Picture Library)

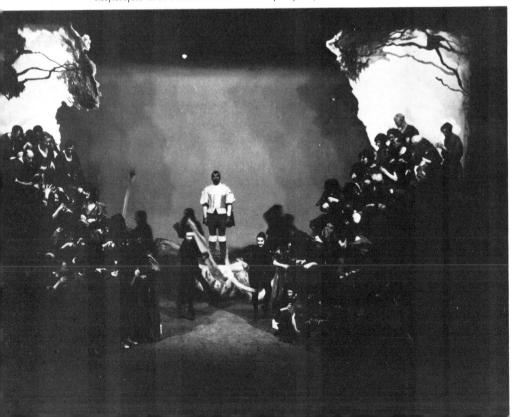

*La Battaglia di Legnano* (*The Battle*) 1960: Heather Harper *Lida*, Ronald Lewis *Rolando* (Alfredo Evan)

*William Tell* 1961: Ronald Lewis *William Tell*, Elizabeth Vaughan *Jemmy* (Reg Wilson)

*The Marriage of Figaro* 1962: Pauline Tinsley *Susanna*, Norma Morgan *Countess Almaviva*, Ronald Lewis *Figaro*, John Shirley-Quirk *Almaviva* (Alfredo Evan)

*Macbeth* 1963: chorus scene (Alfredo Evan)

*Fidelio* 1969 revival: (left) Michael Langdon *Rocco*, Gwyneth Jones *Leonore* (J. A. Jones)

*Don Pasquale* 1966: Geraint Evans as *Pasquale*

*Don Giovanni* 1966: Geraint Evans as a last-minute *Leporello* (see pp. 112–13) (*Western Mail & Echo Ltd*)

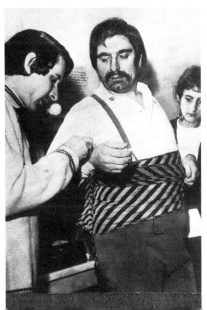

*La Bohème* 1964 The Bohemians: Ronald Lewis, Gerwyn Morgan, Stuart Burrows, Bryan Drake
*La Bohème* 1967: Michael Maurel *Marcello*, David Hughes *Rodolfo*, Elizabeth Vaughan *Mimi* (A. Eva▶

*Carmen* 1967: David Hughes *Don José*, Joyce Blackham *Carmen* (Michael Evans)

*Boris Godunov* 1968: Forbes Robinson *Boris*, Marian Evans *Xenia*

*The Marriage of Figaro* 1969: Delia Wallis *Cherubino* (Michael Evans)

*Falstaff* 1969: Geraint Evans *Falstaff*; Joan Davies, Helen Watts, Margaret Price, Elizabeth Vaughan

*La Traviata* 1969: Josephine Barstow *Violetta*, Thomas Allen *d'Obigny* (Michael Evans)

# CHAPTER NINE: 1962–1963

SINCE 1946 the repertoire had been chosen principally for the chorus. It was on the chorus's strength that WNO's reputation had been founded and it was for the chorus that most people went to the productions. And yet, for some time there had been an undercurrent of dissatisfaction with the sameness of the works on offer, drawn almost exclusively from the Italian repertoire. Not, it is true, from the chorus members themselves, who were happy to sing *Nabucco, I Lombardi* and the other great choral operas night after night, but from critics and sections of the public who kept asking when they were going to hear such operas as *Die Meistersinger*. A company which had never performed a single Mozart opera, or any other German opera, could not be said to have a very balanced repertoire. John Moody had been trying to persuade Bill Smith to stage a Mozart opera, but Smith had always felt that such works were better left to Covent Garden and Sadler's Wells. The closure of the Gaumont Cinema, Cardiff's largest theatre, the previous autumn, bringing a decision by both Covent Garden and Sadler's Wells not to tour Wales again, meant that Welsh National Opera had become the sole purveyor of grand opera in the Principality. Charles Groves also felt that it had a duty to provide a broader repertoire, and of the many gaps to be filled, Mozart was the priority. Between them, Groves and Moody talked Smith into agreeing to stage *The Marriage of Figaro*, in spite of the considerable pessimism of those who said that Mozart would never catch on in Wales and that the style required to stage Mozart effectively was quite alien to the Welsh temperament and character.

*Figaro*, produced by Moody and conducted by Groves, opened at the Grand Theatre, Swansea, on 7 March 1962, with a young cast, several of whom were either making their professional operatic debuts or singing their first major role. Pauline Tinsley, a young artist Groves had worked with on the concert platform, played Susanna, Margaret Price, then a mezzo, made her operatic debut as Cherubino, and John Shirley-Quirk his as Count Almaviva, while the title role was taken by the experienced Ronald Lewis. The spirited production was a revelation to the packed house. "If any came to mock they certainly remained to praise John Moody's fine production," commented one critic. The attractive sets and costumes, designed by

Elizabeth Friendship, who had been engaged originally to make the costumes for *William Tell* and had stayed on as Head of Wardrobe, marked the arrival of a designer of considerable talent, and the evening was guided with exemplary skill by Groves in the pit.

The week's season had opened the night before with *William Tell*, in which Edward Byles took over the difficult role of Arnold, Joy Evans, returning from Germany, sang Jemmy and Olwen Price, Hedda. Byles was a distinct improvement on his predecessor. Also performed were *Tosca*, with Hammond, Dowd and Kraus, *The Barber of Seville* and *Nabucco*, given, with the exception of Bryan Drake in the title role, by an all-Welsh cast. Covent Garden had been unable to release Elizabeth Vaughan, and in her place Anita Marvin, from the Rhondda, sang Abigail. There was also a new Ishmael in Brychan Powell, and at the last moment Gerwyn Morgan took over as Zaccaria from the indisposed Hervey Alan, Morgan's role as the High Priest being taken by chorister Anthony Nowell.

Patrons arriving for the second performance of *William Tell* were in for a surprise. Several of the principals had been laid low with heavy colds, and, with no understudies available, the performance had had to be cancelled, the first cancellation in WNO's history. In its place, *The Barber of Seville* was substituted. The cast were rehearsing that morning in readiness for a performance the following night when they were told they were on a day early. Very few members of the audience asked for their money back. The following night, *The Barber* was again played, as scheduled, and saw the final appearance with the company of Tano Ferendinos, who, after singing in Wales for ten years, had decided to move to Greece permanently. "It was," wrote Kenneth Loveland, "a happy coincidence that it should be this role in which we heard him for the last time, for it has always been one of his best, giving him scope both for attractive singing and comedy."

Two months later, in May, WNO took over Sadler's Wells for a week. Equity had once more granted special dispensation to allow the performances to take place, and in doing so noted that "the hope has been expressed from time to time that the Welsh National Opera will become a fully professional organisation but the realisation of this dream still seems sadly remote." The season opened with *William Tell*. The house was full, as it was for the entire week, and audiences revelled in the full-blooded singing of both chorus and principals as they did for *I Lombardi* and *Nabucco*. For the first time, however, alongside the raves, a note of dissatisfaction crept into several reviews. Allowances were made for veteran tenor Walter Midgley, no longer in fine voice, who got lost in *I Lombardi* and made a hash of his first entry, but some of the other principal singing, with the notable exception of Elizabeth Vaughan in *Tell* and *Nabucco*, was considered to be decidedly ordinary. There was also a certain slackness about some of the choral work, although with 90 voices on stage, the climaxes of *Tell* were as thrilling as ever. More importantly, there was a feeling that the productions themselves were no longer up to the standard expected in London. The sight and sound of the massed forces in *Nabucco* ten years earlier had been a revelation, but the standard and style of operatic production in Britain had changed sufficiently in the intervening years for its staging to look as tired as the old sets in which it still appeared: it was "badly in need of a visual overhaul," according to one critic who spoke for many. And it was not just *Nabucco* that was felt to be sub-standard. "There are signs that choralism is taken too much as an end in itself," summarised John Warrack in the *Sunday Telegraph*. "The productions are now merely desultory and the sets appear to recognise no lines except horizontal ones across the stage; both are in serious need of revision." *William Tell* was deemed unimaginative by Winton Dean of the *Musical Times*. "The earlier part of the performance in fact dragged because it was neither well enough sung nor well enough produced," agreed Arthur Jacobs in the *Financial Times*. ". . . The Welsh National boasts a chorus of 90. Often, but not always, it sang well. But with such numbers, John Moody as producer perhaps felt he could do no more than bring his regiment in, line them up, and bring them out. At any rate the dramatic impact was almost nil."

There were, of course, limitations upon what could be done on the small Sadler's Wells stage, and neither Moody nor George Foa had had a chance to restage their productions. Not that they would necessarily have wished to. Audiences wanted to hear the Welsh singing, and that meant packing the stage with as many people as possible. But such criticisms did raise a question which tied in with Groves's determination to widen the repertoire: where was the company heading? It was a question which had to be faced, and answered, if WNO was to continue to be bold, innovatory, and the leading provincial opera company. For a long time, it had been the only serious contender for the title, but the newly formed Scottish Opera was due to give its first performances in June. No longer would WNO be able to claim priority treatment, and the development of what was seen as an important rival, particularly when it came to Arts Council funding, was viewed with considerable apprehension. "Keeping up with the Macs" was to play an important part in determining future policy.

Following the London season, work began in earnest on the next new production, Wagner's *Lohengrin*. Rehearsals stopped in August for the annual visit to Llandudno, about which there was some doubt until the last minute. A full-time carpenter had been taken onto the staff for the first time in February. One Sunday towards the end of July, while working in the scenery store in a quiet, residential part of Penarth, trying to get the sets ready for Llandudno, he began to use a power saw. Local residents immediately complained to the council about the noise, and a ban was placed on the use of the saw. Permission to convert the premises into a workshop was refused, and a battle began to have them closed down completely. The sets were completed, however, and the season opened on schedule with *The Marriage of Figaro, La Traviata, Nabucco* and *Madam Butterfly*. The week, accompanied by the City of Birmingham Symphony Orchestra, attracted more than 10,000 people and broke box-office records.

There was doubt, too, about the autumn season in Cardiff. During the summer of 1962, Prince Littler, the owner of the New, had closed the theatre and applied for permission to build an office block on the site. Cardiff Corporation, horrified by the thought of losing Cardiff's last remaining live theatre, had refused the application, and while urgent discussions continued about its future (a bingo hall was the next proposal) the New remained shut. It looked as though the autumn season, with no suitable alternative venue, might have to be cancelled, but negotiations with Prince Littler enabled the theatre to be reopened temporarily in time for the curtain to go up on the new production of *Lohengrin* on 1 October.

The driving force behind *Lohengrin* was Charles Groves. Seeking to widen the repertoire with works which were still largely chorus-based, he had first proposed Benjamin Britten's *Peter Grimes*, to which Bill Smith had replied, "Over my dead body." As an alternative, he had suggested *Lohengrin*. It was by no means a unanimous choice for a first essay into Wagner, but Groves had convinced Smith that something by Wagner should be in the repertory and that *Lohengrin* would suit the chorus admirably. Shortly after the decision to stage it had been taken, the Arts Council in London let it be known that they wanted the project cancelled since Sadler's Wells was planning a new production the following year and Covent Garden had announced plans for a revival. Smith, backed by Groves and Moody, decided that since few Welshmen would be likely to travel to London to see either production, they would go ahead. John Moody did not want to produce, and Harry Powell Lloyd was invited to stage it. Robert Thomas was cast as Lohengrin, Russell Cooper as Telramund, Patricia Bartlett as Ortrud, Richard Rees as the Herald and John Holmes as Henry. The casting of Elsa proved more difficult. Whilst throwing around possible names, Groves suddenly remembered the girl who was singing an excellent Susanna for him in *Figaro*, Pauline Tinsley. They auditioned her in London and immediately offered her the role. Production rehearsals began on 5 July, with Lloyd dividing his time between the chorus in Wales and the principals in London. Groves might have been less enthusiastic for the project had he known what was in store for him. It was soon apparent that the chorus were having difficulty with a musical style far removed from the Verdi to which they were accustomed. Groves had opted to prepare the full score in which the chorus divides, often into eight parts, and the choristers, many of whom could not read music, found it impossible to learn. Groves and his accompanist, Alma Myatt, worked all the hours they could with the chorus, but still it would not come right. Attendance at rehearsals became more and more erratic as people felt they would never learn it, and frequently Bill Smith had to read the riot act, threatening to throw out those who failed to turn up. Gloom began to settle over Charles Street, and people no longer referred to *Lohengrin* or the Wagner but to Charlie's Whim or Folly. Harry Powell Lloyd had his first rehearsal with the principals in London on 5 September. On 9 September he rehearsed for the first time with the full company. His diary at that time notes the despair that everyone was feeling: "12th September: I am back from three days of rehearsals in Cardiff. We have covered the whole opera with the usual adventures. One day without Elsa, another without Lohengrin, and two without the Herald. As for the chorus, they come and go and still have scores in their hands." After a long gap comes the next entry: ". . . for the last month I have been travelling between Cardiff and London, mostly by road with Russell Cooper, rehearsing principals in London and chorus in Cardiff. On Sunday we had the dress rehearsal, incomplete as usual as far as scenery, costumes, lights and props . . . As we were lighting the production, I was told, You lit yesterday. I must remember to tell Charlie Bristow at Sadler's Wells where they rightly spend days lighting an opera." After nine months of planning and preparation, opening night appeared to be heading for disaster. Desperately worried about the chorus, Groves placed Ivor John and Alma Myatt in the wings with scores to act as prompters, and as he started the opera, in front of a full and expectant house, many of whom had travelled down from London, he must have wished himself anywhere but in Cardiff. But from the first notes of the prelude it was clear that he had not made the dreadful mistake everyone believed he had. The Bournemouth Symphony Orchestra, enlarged for the occasion, surpassed themselves: "No Welsh National production has ever been better accompanied," wrote Loveland, and while the chorus was naturally hesitant, they provided enough solid singing to please most people. Lloyd's production, backed by the designs of Elizabeth Friendship, went for a straightforward, romantic interpretation which, continued Loveland, ". . . must be ranked as one of the most efficiently mounted things to have been created for the Welsh National." The principals, especially Pauline Tinsley as Elsa and Robert Thomas, singing as well as anyone had ever heard him, as a lyrical and totally committed Lohengrin, helped make the evening a success. "I doubt if there was a better tenor in Germany or one as good for the role," wrote Lloyd in his diary. "The bridal scene was beautifully sung by Tinsley and Thomas and had altogether some magical moments." "It was," concluded Loveland, "a very moving experience."

The biggest cheer of the evening was reserved for Charles Groves. It was already well known that he would be leaving the following year to become Principal Conductor of the Royal Liverpool Philharmonic Orchestra and everyone knew what a great loss his departure would be. Groves was again in the pit the following night for *La Traviata*, which returned in new sets designed by Harry Powell Lloyd, and with Elizabeth Rust and John Wakefield, both new to their roles, as Violetta and Alfredo; and later for *The Marriage of Figaro* in which Derick Davies, singing Figaro for the first time, shared the role with Ronald Lewis. *William Tell, Madam Butterfly, Nabucco* and *I Lombardi* (with Bryan Balkwill, who had first conducted the opera during the Sadler's Wells season in May, making his Cardiff debut) concluded a fortnight for which the House Full boards were out every night.

For many years, WNO had been relying on guest principals, sometimes well known, sometimes talented artists at the beginning of a career and sometimes established performers who simply welcomed an opportunity to try a different role. In the early days, they had been joined in the minor roles by members of the chorus. The opposition of Equity to such a practice and the fact that few of the new, younger singers who had the voices to appear as soloists wished to sing in the chorus meant that some of the casting in these roles had not been as good as would have been wished. Following an Arts Council enquiry into the training of opera singers in Britain (which advocated that trained singers should receive further tuition within a working company) and to help provide a steady supply of potential principals, WNO's Training Scheme came into operation in November. Eight Welsh singers (one had been born in London but had Welsh parents) began a year's course of advanced tuition, working with WNO staff at Charles Street, the first such scheme organised anywhere in Britain. The course was officially opened on 22 November by Lord Brecon, Minister of State for Welsh Affairs, when the students performed the first act of *The Marriage of Figaro*.

*Lohengrin* reached Swansea in March 1963 – without the swan! Although the production had been designed for touring, it was not possible to get the entire set onto the stage of the Grand, and the swan was left behind; Lohengrin had to finish his journey on foot. During the intervening months, it had been announced that Bryan Balkwill was to succeed Charles Groves as Musical Director in September. The night after *Lohengrin*, Balkwill conducted the first performance of *The Seraglio* (given in English as *The Escape from the Harem*). *The Marriage of Figaro*, far from causing audiences to walk out, had played to capacity houses throughout the previous year and had shown that there was indeed a vast audience for

Mozart in Wales. The performance in Llandudno (in which Joyce Blackham had been a late replacement as Cherubino) had played to the largest single audience ever for a Mozart opera anywhere in Wales. That fact, combined with a need to lighten the repertory, led to the choice of *The Seraglio* as the second Mozart production. Moody again produced with a sure touch, taking advantage of the small stages on which the production would be played to turn it into a visually economical piece (superbly designed by Elizabeth Friendship) which emphasised characterisation. Elizabeth Vaughan returned to sing Constanze and Howell Glynne sang, perhaps surprisingly, his first Osmin (he was undecided whether this was his ninety-ninth role in opera or his century). In addition to his superb singing, hitting every low note firmly, his acting revived memories of his marvellous performances as Frosch many years earlier. David Hillman sang Belmonte, Jenifer Eddy, Blonde, and Kenneth Collins, a member of the chorus at Covent Garden, Pedrillo. The production, enthusiastically received, was, according to Loveland, "an encouraging affair, not only for its own sake, but as a pointer to the future," which "should have finally dispersed the remnants who have been fighting a rearguard action in defence of the theory that all Wales really needs is more and more – and if possible louder – Italian opera."

Sadler's Wells that year had extended its season of operetta, and, the theatre not being available in May, a first visit for eight years was made instead to Bournemouth following repeated requests from the town. The week's season opened with *Lohengrin*, conducted by Groves, in which Norman Harper, a Canadian tenor living in Paris, took over the title role and sang powerfully and impressively: his top notes, a member of the chorus remembers, were like shelling peas. Singing Elsa for the first time was Rita Hunter in a performance which was "nothing short of superbly brilliant, imbued with an idealistic, expressive innocence and ringing out unforgettably in the big ensembles." Some of the best singing of the evening came from a third newcomer, Derick Davies, as King Henry. The chorus, too, having at last managed to learn its music, gave a much more assured performance.

The following night *The Seraglio* was presented. Over the weekend, Elizabeth Vaughan had broken a bone in her foot whilst gardening at home. No replacement could be found and, rather than see the performance cancelled, Vaughan agreed to sing from a wheelchair. Elizabeth Friendship hastily prepared an upholstered chair and a costume for John Moody to act as her dumb attendant, pushing her on and off. After a quick rehearsal during the day, the performance began on time. So brilliant was Vaughan's singing that the audience soon forgot her disability and the ever-present Moody, except for once when he left her during a duet with Belmonte and the wheelchair began to roll towards the footlights. There was also an inadvertent laugh when David Hillman as Belmonte also forgot about the wheelchair and hurried to the top of a tower to rescue her just as Moody wheeled her on beneath him!

The week continued with performances of *La Traviata*, in which John Dobson sang his first Alfredo, *William Tell*, and *Nabucco* in which a young Welsh schoolmaster made his professional debut singing the role of Ishmael: Stuart Burrows.

Charles Groves made his final appearances as Musical Director during the Llandudno season in August. He again conducted *Lohengrin* (once more without the swan) and *Tosca* with Joan Hammond, Rowland Jones and Ronald Lewis. His successor, Bryan Balkwill, conducted *Figaro* and *William Tell*.

Groves, throughout his long association with WNO, which had started back in 1952, had been immensely popular both within the company and with audiences. Since he had taken over as Musical Director, his skill as a choral conductor had helped raise standards to heights others had only dreamed of; he had overseen some of WNO's greatest triumphs, and there is little doubt that without his perseverance and hard work *Lohengrin* would have been a disaster. He left with mixed feelings. Most of his career had been spent with symphony orchestras, and he found he was missing the orchestral repertoire. Bill Smith had told him that WNO was well on its way towards acquiring its own orchestra, but, after two years, Groves knew the possibility was remote. Although he had grown to love WNO, the offer from Liverpool proved irresistible.

Bryan Balkwill was a totally different personality. Whereas Groves was always ready to join in, always ready with a joke (he would play a few bars of the national anthem to hurry the choristers back to their seats if they were taking too long after a break), Balkwill was more introverted and difficult to get to know. A Londoner with vast experience – he was on the staff at Glyndebourne, at Covent Garden and at Sadler's Wells and Musical Director of Opera for All – he was known throughout the operatic world as "Mr Opera". His sole concession to taking charge of WNO was to relinquish his post with Opera for All. He was a stickler for accuracy, making few concessions to amateur status and demanding total co-operation from professionals. Shortly after his appointment was announced, Balkwill was quoted as saying that he saw his priorities as being to raise standards and broaden the repertoire. Groves was extremely hurt. Privately, he wondered what on earth Balkwill thought *he* had been trying to do.

Balkwill's first season opened at the New Theatre, Cardiff, on 23 September 1963. After a six-month closure, the theatre had been saved from demolition firstly by the Minister of Housing, Dr Charles Hill, refusing to allow it to become either an office block or a bingo hall, and secondly by Cardiff City Council taking a seven-year lease on the building and forming a trust to run it. £22,000 had been spent on refurbishing it in preparation for the gala opening of the WNO season. Emlyn Williams, the eminent Welsh actor, made a speech from the stage, and then an audience containing local dignitaries, representatives of the Arts Council and the Minister of State for Welsh Affairs, settled back to watch the new production of Verdi's *Macbeth*.

The eighth Verdi opera to enter the repertoire, *Macbeth* was given in a new translation (drawn largely from Shakespeare) by John and Nell Moody, and because of the demands made on the two leading singers and the need to play it frequently, was double-cast. On the opening night, the role of Macbeth was sung by Ronald Lewis and Lady Macbeth by Pauline Tinsley. Lewis "not only sang well; he acted magnificently," reported Loveland, and he was well matched by Tinsley. "Certainly the company is lucky to have in Pauline Tinsley," wrote Philip Hope-Wallace in the *Guardian*, "so unsparing and exciting an interpreter for Lady Macbeth . . . Miss Tinsley brought plenty of conviction to the big scenes and was much applauded." "The finest performance," enthused Clive Barnes in *The Daily Express*, "came from the young Wigan-born soprano . . . Her voice was edged with death, her acting touched with horror."

John Moody's production, with sets by Elizabeth Friendship, was one of his finest. He assembled the chorus (which sang with all its old fervour, raising the roof in the great set pieces) and moved it with consummate skill. Scenes such as the appearance of Banquo's ghost had to be staged without the use of any mechanical contrivances. This was done by having Banquo enter behind the chorus, take his seat and then be revealed. It was simple, but effective. The smaller roles were well taken by Robert Thomas as Macduff, Stuart Burrows as Malcolm and David Gwynne (the first of the trainees from the opera school to be cast in a principal role) as Banquo. Bryan Balkwill drove the orchestra along at a thrilling pace.

The second performance two days later did not receive the publicity of the opening night but is worth more than a passing mention. Delme Bryn-Jones, a young baritone whose only important work before had been at Glyndebourne, made his debut as Macbeth, and Gwyneth Jones, a young Welsh singer whose voice had gone from mezzo to soprano and who had just returned from training in Switzerland, made her debut as Lady Macbeth. Her performance marked her as a singer of outstanding potential.

As well as *Macbeth*, the first week also included performances of *The Marriage of Figaro*, *Lohengrin* (conducted by a warmly-applauded Groves) and *Tosca*, conducted by another former Musical Director, Vilem Tausky.

At the last moment, Otakar Kraus withdrew from *Tosca*, his place as Scarpia being taken by Robert Savoie, who only knew the role in Italian. His scenes with Joan Hammond were sung in that language while she sang with Cavaradossi in English. David Tree as Spoletta opted also for Italian, and the result was a bi-lingual performance which might have been extremely confusing but in fact delighted everyone. Several people were heard afterwards questioning why operas had to be performed in English rather than in the original language. English was restored to the production the following week when Gwyn Griffiths assumed the role.

The Cardiff season was notable not just for its performances but because, for the first time, it ran for three weeks. Smith had been wanting to expand the season for some time and since the 150th anniversary of Verdi's birth fell during that third week, it seemed appropriate, in view of the debt WNO owed to Verdi, to celebrate it with an extended season. The week was devoted entirely to Verdi beginning with *Nabucco* and followed by *I Lombardi*, *La Traviata* and *Macbeth*. On the actual anniversary day, Thursday, 10 October, it was, perhaps not surprisingly, *Nabucco* that was on show. A moving and emotional performance received nine curtain calls. And then a huge portrait of Verdi was brought onto the stage as John Moody talked about the composer's life and the production's early days. Messages were read out from Ronald Jackson, the original Nabucco, then in Australia, and from Leo Quayle, who had conducted and was in South Africa. Hervey Alan, the only survivor of the original 1952 cast who had sung Zaccaria in all but ten of the performances since, stepped forward to announce his retirement from the operatic stage to concentrate on teaching. He had, he said, sung with all the British opera companies and some foreign ones but had never been so happy as with Welsh National. To add to the emotion, Bill Smith brought Ruth Packer, the first Abigail, and Joan Stephens, the first Fenena, on stage to share in the celebrations, and took the opportunity to announce that after 68 performances the production was to be retired gracefully; the performance just witnessed had been its last.

Conducting that memorable evening was Ivor John, another musician with a record of long and distinguished service to WNO. He had started in 1946 and most recently had been working as Groves's chorus master. That night was also to be his farewell. The moment any new Musical Director takes over, he likes to surround himself with people he knows, and that frequently means the departure of those already there. Balkwill was no exception. He brought in Eric Wetherell (a former orchestral player and member of the music staff at Covent Garden, who made his WNO debut that week with *La Traviata*) to be his assistant and there was no longer any place for Ivor John.

One of Wetherell's tasks was to take over running the musical side of the opera school founded the previous year by Groves. A preview of the school's work had been given at the Caerphilly Festival in June with a performance of *La Bohème*, but the tour proper of the first Welsh Opera For All group did not start until 21 October, when the graduates of the first year took *Rigoletto*, *La Bohème* and *La Cenerentola* to over eighty towns and villages throughout Wales and Southern England during a five-month period. The artists, accompanied by a pianist, a company manager and a stage manager, travelled in a minibus; the scenery, costumes and lighting in a lorry. Both vehicles were driven by members of the group. Following this experience, it was planned that the singers would be given minor principal parts in the main productions.

The 1963 autumn season in Cardiff was not only the longest played there or in any theatre, it was also the most successful. The demand for tickets had been phenomenal. More than 500 letters were received before official booking began, and on the day the box-office opened, hundreds of people queued for tickets. Two windows, open from ten in the morning until ten in the evening, dealt with the applications, and staff had to resort to hanging up the telephone, much to the annoyance of the callers. Nine of the twenty-one performances were sold out before opening night, and the average attendance during the season was 92 percent. There was, however, a limit to how far WNO could go. For all the frequently expressed need to widen the repertoire, it was apparent that no great progress could be made while the chorus remained amateur. They had nearly come unstuck with *Lohengrin* and there simply was not the time to spend, nor perhaps the interest, in learning works totally different from those of their beloved Verdi. No real change of direction, or repertoire, could be contemplated until a core of professional choristers, not bound by daytime jobs or family commitments, had been formed. The annual Arts Council report recognised this dilemma. "Wider development of WNO may be difficult to achieve without radical reorganisation," it noted. "The company has reached the limit of development that is possible with an amateur chorus." It was, the report continued, paradoxical that opera should thrive where so few facilities existed for its cultivation, and yet thrive it did. The training scheme ensured a larger supply of soloists but "does nothing to lessen the problems of an amateur chorus." The position of the amateurs was to occupy much thought in the coming years.

# CHAPTER TEN: 1964–1965

Six weeks had been played during 1963 (five in Wales and one in England) and while this was still a long way from a permanent company performing for the greater part of the year, it was a move in the right direction. For 1964 the number of weeks was increased to seven by the addition of an extra week in Swansea. The Swansea fortnight opened with John Moody's new production of *The Barber of Seville*, conducted by Bryan Balkwill. Moody had returned to the original Rossini score to restore the recitatives in place of the spoken dialogue which had often proved an embarrassment in the previous production. He also decided, like Harry Powell Lloyd two years earlier, to revèrt to Rossini's first choice of a mezzo for Rosina, and cast Swansea-born Patricia Kern in the role (one in which she had already scored a great success at Sadler's Wells). Kern, who had once worked in a local bank, was returning to the scene of one of her earliest triumphs: she had tap-danced on the stage of the Grand whilst a schoolgirl. Her performance as Rosina was, wrote Noël Goodwin in the *Daily Express*, "outstanding . . . gifted with a florid technique rare in a voice of her type, she gave a performance of international calibre both in splendour of singing and sense of character." Apart from Derick Davies as Dr Bartolo and Eynon Thomas as the Notary, all the others were new in their parts. Jack Irons sang Count Almaviva, Geoffrey Chard, Figaro, and David Gwynne, Don Basilio. Moody's production (with attractive and ingenious sets by Elizabeth Friendship giving a clever illusion of Spain and space) generally pointed the comedy without too much farce, but there were too many irritating touches of 'business' for it to be considered entirely successful.

The fortnight continued with revivals of *Il Trovatore*, *The Marriage of Figaro*, *Macbeth*, *La Traviata*, *The Seraglio* and *La Bohème*, in which the Musetta of three years earlier, Elizabeth Vaughan, made her debut as Mimi. Singing Rodolfo opposite her, in his first major lead, was the tenor Stuart Burrows. Since his first appearance with the company and the opening of *Macbeth* in which he sang Malcolm, he had successfully auditioned at Covent Garden and had given up his career as a schoolmaster. He sang with refreshing lyricism and ardour, and musically could hardly be faulted: "It was, indeed, in matters of movement and poise that one most often noted deficiencies in his performance," reported a critic who remained blissfully unaware of what was actually happening on stage. During most performances in the tiny Grand, it was customary for the door to the scenery dock, which led directly onto the stage, to be left open to allow fresh air into the building. In the first act, a few moments before Mimi appeared in the attic and as the three other Bohemians made their way off to the Café Momus, a gust of wind blew out the candle with which Rodolfo was supposed to relight Mimi's candle later in the scene. Ronald Lewis, playing Marcello, saw what had happened and returned on stage with a box of matches. Burrows managed to relight the candle, only for it to be extinguished again immediately. When the moment came for him to light Mimi's candle, he was forced to use the matches. It was an awkward moment and no small wonder that Burrows did not appear totally relaxed!

The Cardiff season the autumn before had proved so popular that it was decided to play a week at the New Theatre in May to cash in on the enthusiasm. It opened with *The Barber of Seville*. Elizabeth Friendship's sets fitted well onto the large stage of the New, and Robert Savoie returned to sing Figaro. The French-Canadian baritone had sung the role more than fifty times but always in Italian. For his appearance in Cardiff, he had learnt it in English. He contributed a "lively and bouncing Figaro" which was one of the loudest ever heard in the theatre, and his diction left something to be desired, his performance sounding "oddly out of context in a company where 'opera in English' usually means what it says." *The Marriage of Figaro*, *Macbeth*, *La Bohème* and *Il Trovatore* completed the week.

The same five productions were taken to Bournemouth in May, the performance of *Macbeth* helping to celebrate Shakespeare's 400th anniversary, and then in August to Llandudno, where *Madam Butterfly* replaced *Figaro*. Bill Smith, at the town's official reception, apologised that the programme erred on the side of the unadventurous, but such an apology was hardly necessary; there were, after all, few other places in Britain where one could see *Macbeth*, a new production of *The Barber*, Joan Hammond as Butterfly, *La Bohème* and *Il Trovatore* all within the same week. And it was certainly what the audiences wanted. It was nothing new for bookings for Llandudno to come from outside Wales (Liverpool and Chester had always supplied coach parties, for example), but this year an application was received from two women in New York who had heard about WNO and planned to take their holidays in Llandudno to coincide with the week. So great was the demand for tickets that an extra phone had to be installed in the box-office and every night there were long queues of hopefuls waiting for returns.

To the disappointment of those who had booked for *Madam Butterfly*, Joan Hammond was forced to cancel at the last minute because of an ear infection. She had previously pulled out of a concert at the Swansea Eisteddfod and rumours began to circulate – they were vehemently denied – that, at the age of 52, she was on the point of retiring. Her place was taken by the ever reliable Victoria Elliott. One other artist billed to appear in Llandudno did not make it either. Derick Davies, while on his way to Glyndebourne to take over from the indisposed Benno Kusche as La Roche in Strauss's *Capriccio*, had been involved in a car crash the previous month and had received serious injuries. His place as Schaunard in *Bohème* was taken by Bryan Drake.

Cast changes were frequent at this time, not just for the Llandudno season nor always for such tragic reasons, but throughout the sixties. Not being able to confirm plans until much later than either of the London companies, WNO was often unable to obtain the services of those artists who would have been first choice, particularly once a new production was on the road. "The organisation of WNO is a bit like a jigsaw," Balkwill remarked in an interview. "We have to beg, borrow or steal singers from the other companies." This constant turnover had considerable disadvantages, for it meant that productions rarely had time to settle, and very little in the way of a company style could be imposed on them. It also meant that the standard of singing could be erratic, particularly if a newcomer was not up to the role or was being pushed into a part too early. But there were advantages. Occasionally a top artist would be free for a couple of weeks and Wales would be given the chance to hear the best of the younger Covent Garden singers, performers such as Peter Glossop, who had taken over from Geraint Evans and enjoyed enormous success as Rigoletto and came to Wales to sing Luna in *Il Trovatore*, or Elizabeth Bainbridge; occasionally an up-and-coming singer with little experience had to be engaged – and a new star would appear. At Llandudno, Maureen Morelle replaced Patricia Kern as Rosina in *The Barber* and Michael Maurel took over as Figaro; in Bournemouth, Veronica Dunne had sung Mimi, a role taken in Llandudno by the Covent Garden soprano Jeanette Sinclair with Jenifer Eddy as Musetta; in *Il Trovatore*, Ann Howard, singing her first Azucena, proved to be outstanding.

By the time the autumn season opened in Cardiff further cast changes had had to be made. Veronica Dunne returned as Mimi, while Robert Savoie as Marcello, David Gwynne as Colline and Michael Maurel as Schaunard were all new to their roles. Most interest, however, centred on the professional debut of a 21-year-old tenor just out of college and brought in at the last moment to sing Count Almaviva in *The Barber*: Ryland Davies. He "showed a voice of light texture, which he used with considerable musical feeling, and as the evening wore on one could sense the awakening of a natural response to theatre." *The Barber*, having shed some of its more irksome tricks since opening in Swansea the previous March, had settled down into a polished production.

The major new production was of Beethoven's *Fidelio*. Balkwill had already conducted the work at Glyndebourne and felt it would be ideal for WNO. As John Warrack wrote in the *Sunday Telegraph*: "Every company that wishes to keep in touch with heaven as well as the box office must one day attempt it." The London critics were again in the audience on opening night, 29 September, principally to hear Gwyneth Jones making her debut as Leonore. Neither they nor the rest of the audience were disappointed. "The main reason for a Londoner to undertake the journey to Cardiff," wrote Andrew Porter in the *Financial Times*, ". . . was to hear Gwyneth Jones's first Leonore for she is Covent Garden's most promising young soprano. Soprano, I say, though more accurately she is in that exciting transition period from dramatic mezzo to dramatic soprano . . . Miss Jones, with her wide-spaced, candid eyes, looks beautiful in the part. Her speaking voice is low and attractive. By itself this quality is not enough. Allied to a warm and powerful voice, pure in tone, smooth in emission – and in Leonore of all roles – the result is irresistible." John Warrack in the *Sunday Telegraph* called her "a soprano of rare gifts . . . At present her Leonore has a touching, natural quality that can elude 'larger' artists . . . in the two long calls in the last duet, 'Florestan! Florestan!', a soaring high note softening to a tender cadence, there was a sudden glimpse of greatness." The vocal performance was led but by no means overshadowed by Gwyneth Jones. It had been hoped that, with the exception of Anne Pashley (the former athlete who had won a silver medal at the 1956 Olympic Games) as Marzelline, the production should have an all-Welsh cast. Derick Davies, however, after several weeks in a coma following his car crash, was still too ill to sing Rocco and the role was taken by Dennis Wicks, and on the day of the opening Delme Bryn-Jones, who was due to sing Don Pizarro, lost his voice. His place was taken, without rehearsal, by Raimund Herincx, who rushed down from Sadler's Wells bringing his own costume with him. Robert Thomas sang Florestan, David Gwynne, Don Fernando and Malcolm Williams, Jacquino. All acquitted themselves well. And then there was the chorus. They "set the last scene alight in a way which rarely happens," wrote Loveland in *Opera*. "The great final ensemble shone radiant and serene, the golden crown of the opera, the apotheosis of hope and liberation. Had all that had gone before been routine – and it was a very long way from that – the effect in the opera house would still have been thrilling, and as it was, the cheers went on and on."

John Moody's production (designed again by Elizabeth Friendship) was "straightforward, sensible and satisfying, without tricks or fancy effects, but not without imagination." Both succeeded in conveying faithfully the impression of a police state with its background of fear and suspicion, although, as a minor quibble, the last-act transition from imprisonment to freedom was not projected with the same visual brilliance as the artists on stage gave musically. *Fidelio* had produced one of the most exciting first nights the company had ever known, and the curtain calls lasted for a full five minutes.

*Fidelio* was a sell-out. There were full houses, too, for all the remaining productions with the exception of *Macbeth*, which for some reason had failed to capture the public's imagination. WNO's artistic standing was as high as it had ever been. The major headache remained money. It was costing £75,000 a year to play for seven weeks. The Arts Council grant for 1964 was just short of £55,000 and £12,500 came from Welsh local authorities and district councils. Newport, which for so long had refused to help because, in the words of a local councillor, "Cardiff is not a convenient place for Newport people to visit", now gave £250. Others, however, were still giving as little as two guineas, and the bulk of the money came from two authorities, Cardiff, which gave £5000, and Glamorgan, which gave £3000. Box-office receipts failed to make up the difference between income and expenditure, and 1964 ended with a deficit. The euphoria which had greeted *Fidelio* and the season in general could not disguise the fact that there were still many things wrong which could easily have been put right with an injection of more cash. More rehearsal time was required, especially for revivals, which were still being thrown on without any dress rehearsal. The length of the seasons needed to be extended, something which could not happen without a more permanent (and, therefore, paid) chorus. Nor had the need to acquire a permanent orchestra diminished. The CBSO, although an excellent body of musicians, had demonstrated throughout the autumn season the difficulties symphonic players had in adapting to operatic accompaniment. Felix Kok, for many years leader of the Bournemouth Symphony and later the CBSO, said there was always a danger of symphonic players, new to opera, watching what was going on on stage rather than the conductor. What was required was a nucleus of players schooled in opera. In spite of such problems, the gradual broadening of the repertoire, begun under Groves, had been maintained (although it had been galling in 1963 to see the world première of an opera by a living Welsh composer, *The Knife* by Daniel Jones, being given not in Wales but in London, by the New Opera Company. The reason, once more, had been financial. A modern Welsh opera, no matter how good, would not have played to audiences of a size that would have made it a viable proposition, and without either an additional grant or a more realistic budget, WNO could not have afforded to stage it).

At the beginning of 1965, British Rail announced that the concession of transporting theatrical sets and properties free was to be ended. In future a charge of £15 per truck and 2/6d (12.5p) per mile would be made. This meant, immediately, that the cost of playing the same number of weeks in 1965 as in 1964 would increase appreciably, and without a corresponding increase in grants the deficit would climb even higher. All thoughts of extending the seasons would have to be shelved yet again. Bill Smith, in his annual appeal to local councils, outlined the gravity of the situation and begged for higher donations. His appeal produced its usual response: some councils ignored it, others sent their derisory two or ten guineas.

For some time, it was touch and go whether the Swansea season scheduled to open in March would go ahead. It finally did, but, in order to save money, was cut from two weeks to one. Swansea council immediately retaliated by lopping £500 from the city's £2000 grant in protest. Performances were given of *Fidelio*, *Madam Butterfly*, *Tosca*, with Veronica Dunne, and *Macbeth*, in which Bryan Drake sang the title role for the first time opposite Pauline Tinsley. Making a welcome return to the stage was Derick Davies. Following his car crash, in which he had suffered a broken skull, a fractured arm and leg and chest injuries, Davies had been unconscious for several weeks. It had looked as though his career was over, and doctors said that had he not been a singer, trained to breathe properly, he might not have lived. He sang the roles of Rocco in *Fidelio* and Angelotti in *Tosca*.

The short spring season in Cardiff the previous year had proved to be so successful that it was decided to repeat the experiment, partly to help bring in much-needed revenue from the box-office and partly to try out a new production in preparation for Sadler's Wells two weeks later. This was of Rossini's *Moses*, which had not been seen in Britain for more than 100 years. *Moses in Egypt*, to give it its full title, was written in 1817 and had once been part of the staple diet of most European opera houses. It was first produced in Naples the year following its composition, but without its most famous number, the choral prayer "Dal tuo stellato soglio", which later became so popular that it was sung at Rossini's funeral. This had been added for the work's first revival in 1819 (also in Naples) as a prelude to the crossing of the Red Sea, which had been greeted at the première by gales of laughter. "The general merriment was so frank and so open," recounted Stendhal, "that no one really had the heart to turn surly and whistle. In point of fact, however, scarcely a soul in the whole audience listened to the last part of the opera at all; everybody was too busy discussing the astounding *introduzione*." According to Stendhal, on the eve of the 1819 revival, Andrea Tottola, the librettist, told Rossini that he had saved the act by writing a prayer for the Jews in just over an hour. "If it only took you an hour to write the words," Rossini is supposed to have replied, "I will write the music in fifteen minutes!" This story has now been discounted, but the prayer did get written and it had the desired effect. No one laughed any more, and apparently forty women in the audience were so moved by it that they fainted! The opera was first performed in London in 1823, where, to protect it from the charge of blasphemy, it was renamed *Peter the Hermit*. Rossini revised it extensively for Paris in 1827, and it was this version, last seen in London at Covent Garden in 1850 under the name of *Zora*, which John and Nell Moody had used as the basis for their translation for the Welsh.

*Moses* was a religious choral opera similar in spirit and style to *Nabucco*, which led some people to the natural conclusion that WNO was once more actively searching out works which were a subconscious expression of a suppressed nationalism. Bill Smith denied any such intention hotly. It was, he stated, just another work which provided scope for the celebrated Welsh chorus.

The production was again in the hands of Moody and Friendship, with Balkwill conducting, and a strong cast had been assembled with Michael Langdon as Moses, Pauline Tinsley as Sinaida, Lorna Elias as Anna, Edward Byles as Amenophis, Bryan Drake as Pharaoh and Stuart Burrows as Eleazor.

Moody's approach was firmly conventional – it could hardly have been otherwise with an episodic and static story in which the chorus arrived, sang and departed. The parting of the Red Sea was neatly accomplished by light changes, and nowhere did the production get in the way of the music. There were a few untidy moments on opening night: the clattering of the chorus jewellery as the Egyptians approached at the end made their arrival sound like that of the cavalry. And the evening had begun nervously. Balkwill arrived on the podium having left his baton in the dressing room and the curtain had to be held while it was fetched. Stuart Burrows appeared with his beard on back-to-front, much to the amusement of his fellow artists on stage.

No amount of brilliant singing, and there was much, or updating of the libretto could disguise the fact that the musical quality of the work was inconsistent. As an opera it "is often sublime, and also often boring – or so the Welsh production suggests," noted a review in the *Times*. "One tires of Moses's eternal ranting; Pharaoh is a feeble foil to him; the principal Israelite women are colourless. The Egyptian Queen and her proud, sullen son are the most interesting characters." When the production moved to Sadler's Wells, Harold Rosenthal, writing in *Opera*, was forced to agree with Stendhal and others that the piece "is a bore, and with the exception of the famous prayer and the very moving scene at the beginning of the second act, where the Egyptians are sitting in darkness, I felt the music rarely fitted the dramatic situation."

At the centre of the production was the towering figure of Michael Langdon. "Musically he is magnificent, singing with a profound sense of the dignity and beauty of the music . . . The production gains immensely from having his authority at the heart of it," wrote Kenneth Loveland. He was matched by the brilliance of Pauline Tinsley and the excellence of the other soloists, including Noreen Berry, David Gwynne and Malcolm Williams in the minor roles. And then there was the chorus, reviving memories of an earlier decade with its passionate, committed singing of music it clearly enjoyed. *Moses* might not have been elevated to a permanent place in the repertoire, but it had been given a stirring airing for which audiences were grateful.

Bookings were again heavy for the London week. Although everyone agreed that the chorus was magnificent, *Moses* was received with interest rather than enthusiasm. "As befits the work," wrote Peter Stadlen in the *Telegraph*, "the honours of the evening were shared between Michael Langdon's powerful and authoritative Moses (the first serious main part ever to be entrusted to a bass) and the choir." *Fidelio*, on the other hand, given a single performance the following night, brought the house to its feet and received one of the longest ovations heard at Sadler's Wells for some time. Gwyneth Jones, especially, was outstanding. "The evening was dominated by Gwyneth Jones's generously voiced Leonore . . . She is already a moving Leonore; she has it in her, with more careful gradations of tone and more subtle treatment of the text, to be a great one," commented Alan Blyth in *Opera*. Graham Samuel of the *Daily Express* considered it to be the best *Fidelio*, Sadler's Wells and Covent Garden notwithstanding, to have been seen in London for many years. Michael Reynolds of *Music and Musicians*, however, found it rough and ready, "a fault which seemed to derive largely from Bryan Balkwill's conducting. Indeed, a root cause of dissatisfaction was his failure either to balance stage and pit dynamically or to preserve ensemble between them . . . Given these unfavourable factors, the singers battled as best they could against a heavy accompaniment. Best at bestriding the storm was Gwyneth Jones as Leonore . . . Robert Thomas too, as Florestan, rode the sonic tide quite well."

Gwyneth Jones returned two nights later to sing Lady Macbeth. To demonstrate the strength of the production and avoid having to choose between the two principal casts, *Macbeth* was given on consecutive nights with its double cast of Lewis and Tinsley, and Drake and Jones. The overall verdict was that the first cast was the better. "It is Tinsley's Lady Macbeth that will remain longest in the memory," wrote Frank Granville Barker in *Music and Musicians*.

While enthusiasm for the week, and for the choral singing in particular, remained high, some of the criticisms of WNO's work which had begun to creep into previous London seasons were again in evidence. Writing of *Macbeth*, Eric Mason in the *Daily Mail* noted that "in stage grouping and movement, John Moody's production occasionally suggested amateur theatricals. Production and décor are aspects of the Welsh National which most urgently need improvement if the company aspires, as it does, to full-time status." Andrew Porter of the *Financial Times* felt similarly: "*Macbeth* is not a rarity in London; by bringing it here, the Welsh National invite judgement by metropolitan standards; and by metropolitan standards this must be deemed a provincial affair." In his review of the second performance, Porter continued in a similar vein: "Before becoming too severe, I must ask what standards are applicable? This was vocally a good deal better, and dramatically not all that much worse, than a repertory *Nabucco* which I saw at the Berlin Staatsoper last month. The Cardiff opera plays a few short seasons each year, with a devoted amateur chorus; the Staatsoper is East Germany's metropolitan house, and heavily subsidised. Still, I think that this Welsh *Macbeth* could and should have been better. I also get the impression that a certain complacency has crept into their performances, and what they now need is to invite an outside producer to work with them. This is not to overlook John Moody's many merits; but a company easily becomes ingrown."

The second new production of 1965 opened neither in Cardiff nor in Swansea but in Llandudno, the first time such an event had happened and a sign, Bill Smith said, of the importance WNO attached to the annual season there. More importantly, perhaps, it was of *Die Fledermaus* and was expected to attract holiday-makers, which it duly did. A Commonwealth Arts Festival, with events taking place throughout Britain, had been planned for later in the year, and *Die Fledermaus*, with a cast of Commonwealth singers, was to be WNO's contribution. In practice, this meant almost exclusively artists from Sadler's Wells. Representing Wales were Rowland Jones (Alfred) and Patricia Kern (Prince Orlofsky); James Hawthorne (Eisenstein), though born in Lancashire, was domiciled in Canada, from where Milla Andrew (Rosalinda) also came; Denis Dowling (Colonel Frank) hailed from New Zealand and Jenifer Eddy (Adele) from Australia.

WNO had been trying for many years to convince the Welsh public, without any real success, that *Die Fledermaus* was worth a place in the repertoire. With Harry Powell Lloyd's new production, they were still not entirely successful. Elizabeth Friendship's realistic sets were, according to the *Daily Telegraph*, "sensibly designed to make maximum use of the space available," and Lloyd had "exercised considerable ingenuity in moving and grouping his large cast on a small stage." And yet there was a vital spark missing. "Bryan Balkwill obtained some sparkling playing . . . from the

Birmingham Symphony Orchestra, but neither they nor the singers could capture that elusive Viennese lilt."

A similar reaction greeted the production when it opened in Cardiff at the end of September as part of the Commonwealth Arts Festival (an unfortunate clash of dates meant that the Toronto Symphony Orchestra was appearing in the city that same night). As had happened the last time *Die Fledermaus* had opened a season, there was criticism of the choice, and while audiences enjoyed it, the critics remained condescending. "This has never been one of the Welsh National Opera's gems," wrote David Williams in the *Daily Mail*, "and though it is back again in a new production by Powell Lloyd with attractive sets and a fairly strong cast, it failed to give the company's autumn season the sort of exciting, confident start we have come to expect." Williams's review was headed "Closer to the Taff than the Danube" and this was a view shared by the critic of the *Times*: "Mr Powell Lloyd is no more successful than his predecessors in persuading a Welsh chorus to look Viennese and sophisticated; Mr Bryan Balkwill has only slightly more success than his in encouraging them to sound it. One has always the impression that within the company there is a consciousness that this is not a work they are going to do well, while, on the other hand, audiences continue to demand it. It is impossible not to feel that the time spent on *Die Fledermaus* this year could have been diverted to filling in some of the gaps in the Welsh repertory – Donizetti and contemporary opera for example."

There were, in fact, no further additions to the repertoire during the three-week season. Instead, there was a new production of another old favourite, *The Bartered Bride*, which had not been seen for ten years. Vilem Tausky had much more success in persuading the orchestra and singers to sound Czech, but even so, the production, the first by WNO's ballet master, Philippe Perrottet, was only partially successful. "We might have expected his balletic background to produce something more fluid," commented Loveland in the *Times*. And with the chorus turning in a lacklustre performance, the season had not been given an auspicious start.

The decision to play three weeks again in spite of the economic problems was rewarded by full houses. However, without the stimulus of a new and rare piece, a vital element seemed to be missing. What real excitement there was came from individual performances and especially from the revival of *La Traviata* in which the three main principals were all singing their roles for the first time. Elizabeth Vaughan appeared as Violetta, Delme Bryn-Jones as Germont and David Hughes as Alfredo. Former pop star Hughes, who had been making a name for himself at Glyndebourne since turning to opera, had last appeared on the stage of the New in 1952 when he had topped the bill and been preceded by Peter Sellers. He had been invited to sing Alfredo two years earlier, but, because of other commitments, had been unable to learn the role in time. As soon as his engagement was announced, the theatre was besieged by his fans, desperate to get tickets. "Since Alfredo is the biggest role he has undertaken some evident strain in Act 1 was understandable," wrote Loveland in the *Times*; "but in Act 2 we found him singing easily and lyrically, and to this he added in Act 3 a passionate denunciation of Violetta that was among the best things of the performance. For all three principals it was an encouraging evening." One other singer stood out: Anne Howells, a member of the Glyndebourne chorus, as Flora. The *Times* praised her as "a vocally attractive mezzo with an apparent theatrical temperament . . . for whom it is not rash to predict a useful career."

For the general public, the Cardiff season had been much as before: favourite operas, favourite artists and the discovery of new talent. Behind the scenes, however, important changes were about to be made. The need to professionalise the company, especially the chorus, and to increase the number of weeks played had been talked about for so long that people might have been forgiven for thinking they had heard it all before and that, once again, nothing would happen. Careful management and good box-office receipts, allied with an increased grant from the Arts Council (up £6000 to £60,460) and continued support from local authorities, had removed the immediate threat of closure and allowed a full programme to be staged throughout 1965. It had also created a climate in which it was felt that the first vital steps towards professionalisation could at last be taken. Sir David Webster (from the Royal Opera), a long-time supporter of WNO who had frequently helped Smith with advice and suggestions for artists and conductors, was invited to join the Board to give the benefit of his experience during the transition. "Either things go on developing or they go to bits," he told a meeting of the Cardiff Business Club. "It would be a thousand pities if the Welsh National Opera Company went backwards now. The possibility of the company developing into a fully professional one does not now seem as remote as has been expected." A report was submitted to the Arts Council on the cost of becoming professional, and a feasibility study was begun into alternative venues and which operas the public wished to see. While no promises were made that money would be forthcoming for expansion, the indications were that such a move would be considered favourably, and as a gesture of good faith, the government's first grant allocated by the newly-formed Housing and Arts Committee was given to WNO to help find new headquarters. The chapel in Charles Street had long been inadequate. There was not enough room to make or store scenery, not enough room for proper rehearsals, no room for the training school and nowhere for the wardrobe department; all of these activities had to take place in various halls and rented rooms scattered throughout the city; there was very little room for the administration. In desperate need of repair, the building was in any case due for demolition as part of the redevelopment of the city centre. A search for alternative premises large enough to house the entire company had been going on for some time, and at the end of September negotiations were concluded for the purchase of a derelict warehouse in John Street on the edge of the notorious Tiger Bay district for a cost of £20,000.

# CHAPTER ELEVEN: 1966–1967

S TYLES IN OPERA PRODUCTION must change, or the form will die. It is hard to explain that to the person who asks no more of any production than that the artists be allowed to stand in front of the footlights and sing directly to the audience. The trouble with the 'stand-and-deliver' school is that it involves only one aspect of that marvellous art form called opera, and that without the other elements – acting, scenery, and so on – there is little chance of achieving the magical experience that opera, sung live in a theatre, can provide. For some time, there had been growing concern about WNO's production standards. This does not mean that they were bad, rather that constant repetition was beginning to dull their appeal and there was a limit to what could be achieved in works which required a large chorus to enter and fill the stage. Just as Norman Jones's productions were quite acceptable in their time (and would probably have been quite unacceptable twenty years later), so the earlier productions of John Moody and Harry Powell Lloyd were beginning to look as though they belonged to a previous era. Moody, as much as anyone, realised that what was required was fresh blood, a new initiative, a new approach which would take into account what was happening elsewhere in opera and in drama, where, it was generally agreed, the most exciting theatre in Britain was to be found.

The first of the new producers invited to stage a production was Michael Geliot. 1966 was the twentieth anniversary of the first staged performances, and to celebrate the event, four new productions, the most ever mounted in one year, were announced, with Geliot's production of *Don Giovanni*, the third Mozart opera to enter the repertoire, opening the spring fortnight at Swansea in March. "Given the resources of the company and the size of the stage, it proved a good choice and an interesting experience," wrote the critic of the *Daily Telegraph*. Geliot had brought with him the talented young designer Annena Stubbs, who produced a stylised setting incorporating platforms, grilles, bronze panels and floating banners, much of which could be moved by the chorus. "These enable the many scene changes to be done quickly and smoothly and are especially impressive in the ballroom, tomb and garden scenes," commented Noël Goodwin.

Within this framework, Geliot created a fast-moving and fluent production which emphasised the earthy character of the work, underlining the passions in an almost brutal way, which was far from the pretty-pretty aspect most opera-goers were used to seeing. "The result," wrote David Williams in the *Daily Mail*, "is an original and compact *Don Giovanni*. It is also a serious one." The critic of the *Telegraph* found it "fresh, unconventional, within its own terms of reference consistent, and largely successful." Forbes Robinson, making his debut both with WNO and in the role, was a forthright and compelling Don. "His scenes with the bright voiced Anne Pashley (Zerlina) were musically the most attractive," wrote Goodwin. The rest of the cast were, Loveland felt, singing themselves in and any musical impact the evening might have made was weakened by the indifferent playing of the scratch orchestra, which, "with the best will in the world, could hardly be described as a total, corporate instrument."

The rest of the fortnight saw further performances of *Moses*; *La Traviata*, for which the pop fans again turned up in force to hear a much-improved David Hughes and were rewarded with the best orchestral playing of the fortnight under the baton of Myer Fredman; *The Bartered Bride*, with Dennis Wicks as Kecal; *Fidelio*, which saw the debut in the pit of David Gruffydd Evans, who had joined the company in 1963 (after eight years as a répétiteur in Germany) to work with the Opera for All group; and *Die Fledermaus* which had a new Adele in Angela Jenkins and saw a break with the tradition that the role of Prince Orlofsky should be sung by a mezzo – the part was taken by the tenor Kevin Miller, for no other reason than that it had proved impossible to find a suitable mezzo.

With the exception of *Menna* and *Serch Yw'r Doctor*, both by Arwel Hughes, WNO's repertory had been firmly rooted in works from the past, almost entirely composed in the previous century. Although Puccini's *Tosca* and *Madam Butterfly* had both received their premières this century, they could hardly be considered 20th century operas. There were, of course, still glaring gaps in a repertory which had, until recently, been chosen with the chorus in mind. There was still no Donizetti, still no Britten, still no Richard Strauss – one could go on and on.

The undoubted highlight of the Cardiff season that spring was the world première of a new opera, not just by a living composer but by a living *Welsh* composer. On 5 May, Grace Williams's one-act *The Parlour* opened in a double-bill with Puccini's *Il Tabarro* (played as *The Cloak*). Grace Williams, a pupil of Vaughan Williams, was best known for orchestral works such as the popular *Fantasia on Welsh Nursery Tunes*, and this was her first opera. It had been commissioned by the Arts Council seven years earlier to be part of a proposed double-bill with another Welsh commission, Daniel Jones's two-act *The Knife*, a sort of Welsh *Cav* and *Pag*. But with both operas turning out to be around ninety minutes in length, their pairing had seemed impractical, and *The Knife* had been given its première at Sadler's Wells by the New Opera Company in 1963. *The Parlour*, based on the short story *En Famille* by Guy de Maupassant, had a libretto written by Williams herself because her grant did not run to hiring a librettist. The opera had taken her two years to complete. It tells the story of an impecunious lower-middle-class family hoping to acquire Grandmother's money when she conveniently drops dead, and being hopelessly compromised when she is inconveniently found to be still alive, having overheard every word that has been said about her. In two scenes, with an interlude sung in front of the curtain by the chorus, it was produced by John Moody, conducted by Bryan Balkwill and had an exceptionally strong cast. Edith Coates, as the Grandmother, relished every word and communicated her relish to the audience. Edward Byles was excellent as the weak-willed Papa, while Noreen Berry (Mama), John Gibbs (the Doctor) and Anne Pashley and Janet Hughes as a couple of schoolgirls, all sang with conviction and obvious enjoyment. The chorus, too, although tending to overcrowd the stage, revelled in the tunes they had been given. It was all a harmless piece of nonsense which many of those who took part in feel deserves to be revived today. The first-night audience gave it a sustained ovation, and several critics found it tuneful and attractive. Arthur Jacobs, writing in *Opera*, was less enthusiastic: "There is a gaping hole in the plot – not only is it supposed that a doctor could reasonably mistake a swoon for death, but the woman who comes to lay out the body is presumed to do so too . . . The music is singable, jolly and diatonic; it is graphic in an Arthur Benjaminish rather than Brittenish style . . . As a first opera, this is bound to be hailed as 'a good try'. So it is, but we must recognise what that is a euphemism for."

The second half of the double bill, *Il Tabarro*, saw Marie Collier, who had shot to international fame the previous year when taking over from Callas in *Tosca*, and had already sung the role opposite Tito Gobbi at Covent Garden, appearing as Giorgetta. She contributed an intense, passionate characterisation in a production (also by Moody) which seemed to have had too little time spent on it and lacked lustre. "A dull production, dully set," according to the *Times*.

The Cardiff season, lasting two weeks and containing one modern opera and one each by Puccini, Verdi, Rossini, Smetana, Johann Strauss and Mozart, was one of great contrast, showing the traditional choral work (Rossini's *Moses*) set against Geliot's exciting and fluid production of *Don Giovanni*, which had had many of the hiccups of its Swansea performances ironed out. Every seat was sold for every performance.

In spite of full houses, each performance was having to be subsidised to the tune of £2000, and with income from the Arts Council and local authorities falling behind the required rate, the company was sliding deeper and deeper into debt. The Arts Council in London were concerned. They, like Equity, like Bill Smith himself, wanted to see WNO become a full-time company, but felt that Smith's administration was still too rooted in the amateur past. At their insistence, WNO advertised for a professional administrator who would be able to help balance the books and control future expenditure. The man chosen was Douglas Craig. At 49 Craig had had enormous experience in opera, as administrator, performer and producer. He had sung at Sadler's Wells and at Glyndebourne, had worked as a stage director and producer, and had been in charge of the very first Arts Council Opera for All tour, which had opened its programme with a performance at Blaenau Ffestiniog in 1949. He was also Deputy Director of the London Opera Centre. Although the post of General Administrator had been advertised and more than 100 people had applied, Craig, who was well known to the Arts Council, had been approached informally to apply for the job. It was, perhaps, unfortunate that he was seen by Smith and the incumbents in Cardiff as being an Arts Council man, for it meant that he was never really considered to be part of the 'team' and there was resentment towards his presence almost from the start.

At his first meeting with the Welsh Arts Council, Craig was told what was required of him. He had, in the words of Dr Wynn Jones, "to make more noise," otherwise there was a very real threat that grants would not be renewed. "What he meant," says Craig, "was not that the company should sing louder but that we were to give more performances for the money we were spending. The two seasons in Cardiff, one in the spring and one in the autumn, the week in Swansea and the week in Llandudno were simply not enough in terms of expenditure per performance. The company had got to expand."

It once again became clear that in order to increase the number of performances, the chorus would have to be professional; an opera company playing twenty or more weeks a year, on tour, could no longer rely on choristers turning up only if they could get away. Once that decision had been taken, the days of the amateurs were numbered, and in October it was announced that auditions would be held the following summer for the first professional chorus of 36 voices.

Craig's first task was to reduce the operational deficit. He immediately ran up against the problem of the professional versus the amateur. The old way of doing things had been fairly haphazard. Members of the chorus, many of whom were frankly getting long in the tooth, did not always turn up to rehearsals because they knew the opera, having appeared in it many years before. "It did not occur to them," recalls Craig, "that a new producer might have new ideas, might want them to do something different." Used to a more professional approach, Craig decided to put rehearsals on a more formal basis and brought in Vanda Vale as Controller of Planning, to produce schedules telling everyone where they should be, at what time and what was being rehearsed. Meanwhile, in an effort to "create more noise," a member of staff had been touring theatres and possible venues throughout England and Wales with a view to finding new dates. Her researches showed that there would be a market for WNO, particularly in England, and it was duly announced that by 1968 the company would be appearing for at least twenty-six weeks, the minimum number possible to keep the proposed professional chorus occupied.

The first move towards that expansion came in August when the Llandudno season was increased to a fortnight. The confidence that the town could and would support an extra week of opera was immediately borne out by heavy advance bookings, and by the end of the two-week run almost every performance in the 1700-seat theatre had been sold out for a programme that did not include a single *Bohème* or *Butterfly*. *The Bartered Bride* opened the fortnight, which continued with *Don Giovanni*, the double-bill of *The Parlour* and *Il Tabarro*, *Fidelio*, *Moses*, *La Traviata* and *Die Fledermaus*. Once again there were a number of cast changes. Pauline Tinsley and David Kelly took over as Donna Elvira and the Commendatore in *Giovanni*, Elizabeth Fretwell sang the second performance of *Fidelio* in place of Gwyneth Jones, who had been released to sing Sieglinde at Bayreuth, and Milla Andrew and Jon Andrew sang Giorgetta and Luigi in *Il Tabarro*. In *La Traviata* Otakar Kraus appeared as Germont. There was also a last-minute change in *Moses*. The day before the second performance, Margaret Kingsley, who was singing Anna, went down with laryngitis. An emergency call was made to the London home of Lorna Elias, who had sung the role in previous performances, only to discover that she was on holiday – in Wales. A call to the relatives with whom she was staying elicited the information that she was already on a train back to London. A message was left at her home for her to phone as soon as possible. The following day, she caught a train back to Wales, arriving in Llandudno at three o'clock in the afternoon. Half an hour later, she was on stage rehearsing and that evening gave a superb performance.

The 1966 autumn season in Cardiff was to be the most varied and ambitious so far presented, with nine operas being played in three weeks. It opened with a flourish and a long-awaited event: the first appearance with WNO of Wales's best-known singer, Geraint Evans. For many years, opera-goers had been complaining that Evans had never sung with his own national company. The confirmation of engagements came so late that Evans's international and other commitments (he was often booked up for three years ahead) meant that it had never been possible to arrange a mutually convenient date. This was a situation that Balkwill felt ought to be rectified, no doubt prompted by the news that Evans had agreed to sing Falstaff for Scottish Opera, which was still seen as a great rival. Shortly after he became Musical Director, Balkwill had asked Evans to suggest an opera in which he might like to appear, and to give him some dates. Evans had suggested Donizetti's comic opera *Don Pasquale*, which he was then in the process of learning, and Balkwill had agreed, with the proviso that it had to be sung in English. By the time the Welsh production was staged, Evans had already sung the role in Italian in Buenos Aires, but he went ahead with the part in English, recognising that comic opera needs to be understood by the audience.

Dennis Maunder was brought in to produce, with designs by Friendship; Michael Maurel was cast as Malatesta, Jenifer Eddy as Norina, and Stuart Burrows as Ernesto. Rehearsals with the reduced chorus began some time before the principals ventured to Cardiff, and Maunder did an excellent job, turning each chorister into a character. By the time the soloists arrived the chorus knew exactly what was expected of them, but Evans immediately began to alter Maunder's ideas to fit in with his own conception of the work. The chorus were not at all happy but on Maunder's insistence, tried it the way Evans wanted it. They then reverted to the moves they had rehearsed with Maunder.

Opening night, on 26 September, had a real sense of occasion. The demand for tickets had been phenomenal and every one of the six performances was sold out long before the season opened. Evans, who was singing the part for the first time in Britain, rose to the occasion splendidly. Many people may associate Pasquale more with a bass than a dramatic baritone, but the role suited him admirably. He "fitted his actions to both the rhythm and the temper of the music, and strayed neither into gross fooling nor into too much pathos." Both he and Maurel found the very fast patter duet difficult in English, much of it being unintelligible, but that was the only criticism anyone found to make of his performance. When the curtain came down, the theatre rang with prolonged applause and Evans, the undoubted star of the evening, was given a standing ovation.

*Don Pasquale* got the season off to a flying start. It was followed in the first week by *Moses*, *Tosca*, with Milla Andrew in the title role, and *The Seraglio*, in which Michael Langdon appeared as a formidable Osmin, Jenifer Eddy as Blonde and three young singers appeared in their roles for the first time: Patricia Reakes as Constanze, Malcolm Williams as Belmonte and Myron Burnett as Pedrillo.

The second week saw further performances of *The Seraglio* and *Don Pasquale*, and revivals of *The Bartered Bride*, *Die Fledermaus* and *Don Giovanni*. Former Musical Director Warwick Braithwaite was in the audience for the matinée performance of *Don Pasquale* on 8 October, to hear his son Nicholas make his debut with an authoritative account of the score.

The previous night, the performance of *Don Giovanni* had produced one of those emergencies which cause opera managements to break out into a cold sweat. It was discovered during the afternoon that John Gibbs, the Leporello, had a throat infection which would have made it dangerous for him to sing. All attempts to find a suitable replacement came to nothing, and the management was preparing for Gibbs to mime the role with an understudy singing from the wings, when someone remembered that Geraint Evans was due in Cardiff that evening in preparation for the matinée of *Don Pasquale* the following day. A hurried phone call was put through to his home in Kent to find that he had already left for Paddington Station. A second call was made to the Station Master's office. Evans was sitting on the train, waiting for it to leave, when he heard a Tannoy announcement asking him to go to the Station Master's office. He hurried there, fearing bad news from home. On discovering the true reason for the call, he asked in which language the opera was being sung. When told in English, he replied that he had not sung the role in English for many years and probably could not remember it. WNO management was prepared for this: he could sing in Italian. He agreed and, hurrying back just in time to board his train as it was pulling away from the platform, spent the journey trying to remember a role he had not sung for eight months and for which he did not have a score.

The train was due to reach Cardiff forty-five minutes before curtain up. It was early! A car was waiting to whisk him to the theatre, where he was pushed into a costume, made up and allowed a quick consultation with Forbes Robinson, who was singing Don Giovanni. The curtain went up only a few minutes late, with Evans singing in Italian and everyone else in English, in a production he had never seen and with a cast he did not know (apart from Forbes Robinson). Because of the flying scenery and style of presentation, this was not a production which lent itself readily to newcomers. Roger Prout was the stage manager that evening. "Singers of lesser ability than Geraint Evans and Forbes Robinson might have been content with a workmanlike performance to bridge a difficult evening," he recalled in *A Night At The Opera*,[1] "but both went far beyond that. They excelled themselves. Geraint Evans would enter and a new piece of scenery would drop promptly and take him out of sight . . . The Don and Leporello frequently lost each other completely in a maze of scenic bits and pieces, popping up in front of each other without warning. Geraint would manage

[1] By Barry Hewlett-Davies, a collection of behind-the-scenes stories published by Weidenfeld and Nicolson in aid of ENO's Benevolent Fund.

to translate the odd passage or two ad lib into English only to find that Forbes had now switched to Italian. The lyrics have never been more happily abused. Snippets of Welsh, shouted directions: 'Watch out for your head!' were joined by curious lines like: 'Best of luck to you an' all, Butty' and there were various references to the Triple Crown (Wales had lost a major rugby match and most of the nation was in mourning). I was in the corner that evening, getting terribly harassed by a performance which threatened to get out of hand any moment. Inevitably, I missed giving the lighting man one of his cues . . . which would have brought on a light in a window . . . the object of Giovanni's attention during the canzonetta 'Deh vieni'. Forbes had simply stopped singing and was staring up at the darkened window clicking his fingers at it. I hastily hit the light cue, just as Forbes kicked the set. The light came on as if in response to his boot and the audience dissolved into laughter."

Nothing like that happened in the third week, when *Don Giovanni, Don Pasquale, Die Fledermaus* and *Moses* were repeated, along with two performances of the double-bill *The Parlour* and *Il Tabarro. Il Tabarro* still proved to be only run-of-the-mill, but *The Parlour* was again felt to be a lovely and accomplished work. The patriotism that had drawn full houses for Geraint Evans did not extend as far as trying an opera by a Welsh composer, for the houses, though enthusiastic, were very disappointing, being by far the lowest of the season.

If *Don Pasquale* was the undoubted high point of the Cardiff season, Michael Geliot's production of *Don Giovanni* ran it a close second as the most successful both artistically and at the box-office. It had by this time settled down into a rounded and convincing production. The cast, which had not changed substantially since Swansea, worked as a team and blended together superbly, while the arrival of Pauline Tinsley had added dramatic bite and an extra emotional layer to Donna Elvira. The one discordant note to be found in the reviews was that the recitatives were accompanied by a piano. Efforts to enlarge the orchestra pit at the New had had the effect of making it too small for a harpsichord!

Shortly before the 1967 Swansea season was due to open, Eric Wetherell, the Assistant Musical Director, was involved in a car crash. For a time, he was seriously ill in Cheltenham General hospital with rib, leg and arm injuries, and it was obvious that for the foreseeable future he would not be taking part in any rehearsals or performances. His place on the rostrum when *Don Giovanni* opened the Swansea week was taken by Myer Fredman and, for *Don Pasquale*, by Nicholas Braithwaite.

The season itself had been in some doubt. £8000 had been lost on the fortnight the previous year and it was felt that such a loss (which, given the size of the theatre, was inevitable) could not be permitted again. A week was the most that could be risked. There had also been doubt over the future of the Grand itself, which had been losing money. It was rumoured that the theatre was about to close and that the week in March would almost certainly be WNO's last in Swansea.

One of the ways Craig planned to overcome the deficit was by re-introducing known box-office hits into the repertoire. None of the big chorus operas had ever managed to repeat the success of *Nabucco*; indeed, the current chorus work in the repertoire, *Moses*, was already playing to declining houses. The first of the popular works to be given a new lease of life was *La Bohème*, which had not been played for three years. The sets designed by Alexandre Benois and bought from the New London Opera Company were still quite serviceable, and, to save money, producer John Copley was asked to use them. Copley's realisation was straightforward and traditional, containing no surprises. But there was, as with most productions opening in Swansea (due to the cramped conditions and the scratch orchestra) a feeling of under-rehearsal, as if more time was needed than had been available.

The season had opened with *Don Giovanni* – "well worth a visit," felt Andrew Porter – and it continued with *Moses* and *Don Pasquale*, in which Ian Wallace took over from Geraint Evans.

*Nabucco* had always been regarded as *the* Welsh National opera and ever since it had been dropped from the repertoire there had been clamourings for it to be brought back. Continuing the policy of mounting box-office certainties, Craig and Smith decided to comply with public demand. Michael Geliot, whose *Don Giovanni* had revealed a new style of operatic production, was invited to produce it. It was perhaps ironic that as the time approached when the amateur chorus was about to be disbanded, this should be the work to be revived. So much importance was placed on the production that the spring season in Cardiff opened on Wednesday, 10 May, rather than the Monday, in order to allow Geliot two full days of rehearsal in the theatre.

Elizabeth Friendship had designed a single set of burnished gold walls with a black tessellated pavement on a raked acting area. Different locations were depicted by the introduction of a throne, idols, a huge painted Star of David. The only colour was provided by the costumes, also gold. "A little more variation of colour or texture from one scene to another would have been welcome," wrote William Mann, echoing the thoughts of many who found the settings too severe and had difficulty in placing the exact location of a scene without recourse to the programme. It was inevitable that Geliot's concept would be compared with Moody's fifteen years earlier, and the differences were marked, not only in the setting. Moody, playing to the strengths of the chorus, had turned the opera into the Jews' struggle for nationhood, placing the emphasis on the crowd scenes; Geliot, on the other hand, while including a good deal of violent chorus movement, had placed his emphasis on the three-way struggle between Nabucco, his daughter Abigail and Zaccaria, concentrating on their characterisation. This shift was possibly the reason why the famous "Va pensiero" chorus, although beautifully sung, failed to win any applause on opening night. And such an approach threw the onus of carrying the production firmly onto the shoulders of the three main principals. Pauline Tinsley proved to be a worthy successor to Ruth Packer and Elizabeth Vaughan as Abigail, the role suiting her perfectly. She was, commented Frank Granville Barker, "in her dramatic element . . . attacking her formidable music as though it were the natural thing to do every evening before dinner." Tinsley's great strengths as an artist are her dramatic ability allied to superb musicianship; she gets inside the characters she creates. Raimund Herincx, who sang Nabucco opposite her, recalls just how well she knew her music. Some time later, when the production was on tour, Tinsley had gone shopping during the afternoon. Half-an-hour before curtain-up, she still had not arrived at the theatre. She was not at her hotel and no one knew where she was. She finally appeared, having had an accident in which she had hit her head and become concussed. All she knew was that she was supposed to be at the theatre. They managed to get her changed and onto the stage, where, still dazed and not really aware of what she was doing, she sang a performance that was note perfect. "There are," says Herincx, "very few other singers who could have done that."

On opening night, Herincx, after a shaky start, sang with unfailingly expressive and authoritative tone; his descent into madness and return to sanity was handled with consummate artistry. Clifford Grant's deep bass, contrasting excellently with Herincx's lighter-toned baritone, provided a virile Zaccaria, and there were fine contributions from Rhiannon Davies as Fenena and Malcolm Williams as Ishmael. Balkwill conducted the CBSO with firmness and control. "With such a cast and a pleasing production *Nabucco* re-emerged as glorious as ever," concluded Mann. The first-night audience, packed to the rafters, agreed, but there were those who did not like the production, mostly members of the chorus who remembered how it had been done by Moody and could see little reason for change. They had made their feelings quite clear to Geliot during rehearsals, and some of the tenors had, at one point, staged a walkout. Geliot's style of producing was not to everyone's liking. He had a tendency to use five words when one would have done, and both principals and chorus often felt he was talking down to them. It was perhaps not surprising that on opening night the chorus, perched precariously on the heavily raked stage, looked decidedly uncomfortable and did not sing at their best. However, the validity of Geliot's approach and the sheer power of the music eventually won through and the "Gold *Nabucco*" as it became known was to become the success everyone had hoped. *Nabucco* played predictably to packed houses, as did the rest of the fortnight, consisting of performances of *Don Pasquale*, *Don Giovanni*, *La Bohème*, with Elizabeth Vaughan returning as Mimi, and, with both eyes on the box-office, a revival after a lapse of two years of Harry Powell Lloyd's production of *Madam Butterfly* with Elizabeth Robinson and Edward Byles.

The Llandudno fortnight in August, with the same five productions, sold out as well. Douglas Craig's intention of putting on operas he knew would attract audiences was working well. One other work he felt should be revived was Bizet's *Carmen*, which had not been given for fifteen years because, he was told, it had proved impossible to find a suitable singer to take the lead. The most famous British Carmen of her generation was Joyce Blackham, and Craig knew that if he could get her, every red-blooded male in Wales and beyond would be queuing up for tickets. As luck would have it, she was available, and so *Carmen* went into production for the autumn.

By the time of the first night, every seat had been sold for all performances. What was seen and heard was not quite the *Carmen* everyone knew. Since the previous production, the German musicologist Fritz Oeser had produced a new performing edition of the opera based on Bizet's original score, and it was on this that the WNO production was based. This restored the first part of the duel scene, giving the Toreador considerably more depth of character, lengthened the Act 1 quarrelling chorus, and included several musical passages to colour the spoken dialogue (restored in preference to the recitatives). Oeser's version was not used in its entirety. The closing scene was done in its more usual shortened form and there was no extra music before Escamillo's Act 2 entrance. "Where scholarship ends (and scholars' passions have been deeply aroused in controversy over this text)," commented Stanley Sadie in the *Times*, "taste must take over; successfully here, for the changes seemed to be dramatic gains." WNO's production also used a new translation by John and Nell Moody which was spoken and sung so clearly that its merits took up several inches in the reviews. While there was general agreement that it was an improvement on previous translations, there were minor niggles. "It is often self-consciously 'bright' and in many places too excessively literal," wrote Noël Goodwin in *Opera*. "It is a jarring shock, for instance, to hear José explain that his mother wanted him to be a priest, but that he had to join the army because he was 'too fond of tennis'. The French *jeu de paume* in this context surely relates to the Spanish-Basque ball-game of *pelota* . . . but it is good that the translators have avoided contrived rhymes in seeking to preserve verbal sense and musical stress."

Moody was also in charge of the production. He had chosen as his designer Abd'El Kader Farrah, well known for his work at Sadler's Wells and with the Royal Shakespeare Company. Farrah's costumes were outstandingly good, his rough-textured sets, with their omnipresent giant staircase, less so. They worked well for the tavern and the mountain gorge, "less well for the scenes inside Seville. Spain as a heap of grey-white dust has become as much a convention as the old riot of picture-postcard colour," commented Ronald Crichton of the *Financial Times*. The opening night betrayed traces of first-night nerves. "John Moody's staging . . . is full of thoughtful ideas, let down by a few false moves and (which will surely improve after the first night which I saw) by a stiffness in handling the chorus," wrote John Warrack in the *Sunday Telegraph*. "The children were plainly nervous; but the main chorus itself lacked the usual superb confidence in Act 1, and too many of the individual moves were made with the mechanical caution that reflects uncertainty."

At the heart of the production was Joyce Blackham's Carmen. Because of her other commitments, she had not had time to learn the new translation and reverted to the old one for her arias. "Her flagrant sex-kitten act, claws well out and tail a-swish, is just what is needed," continued Warrack. ". . . when a role is stormed frontally by a singer with neither doubts nor fears, the only thing to do is sit back and applaud." David Hughes, singing his first José, "started uncertainly," according to Stanley Sadie in the *Times*, "but the voice warmed and grew; not much phrasing, nor personality, but perfectly acceptable." Bryan Balkwill drew excellent and vivid playing from the Bournemouth orchestra, and, in spite of initial reservations, it was clear that the production would be a worthy and popular addition to the repertoire. "This is already a *Carmen* of more than average interest and vitality," concluded Ronald Crichton in the *Financial Times*.

*Carmen* was to be the last new production conducted by Bryan Balkwill. Shortly before the season opened, he had announced his resignation as Musical Director. His engagements elsewhere, particularly at Sadler's Wells, were increasing, and with proposals to extend the number of weeks played being so close to fruition, he knew he would not be able to devote enough time to WNO. His decision to leave came as such a surprise to the Board that they had no idea whom to invite to succeed him.

Plans for expansion were proceeding well, though not as fast as had been hoped. At the beginning of 1966, a five-year plan had been forwarded to Jennie Lee, the Minister with special responsibility for the Arts, outlining proposals to increase both output and the number of venues played, and pointing out that to achieve such targets an annual subsidy of at least £250,000 (rising to almost £350,000 by the fifth year) would be required. Although no firm promises were made and the Arts Council did not commit themselves to providing all that was asked for, they let it be known that they would provide a significantly increased percentage of the total needed. At least £85,000 a year would then have to be found from other sources (current grants from local authorities totalled just over £13,000). As a sign of good faith the Arts Council grant for 1966/67 had been increased from £60,000 to £90,000. For the financial year 1967/68, it had been raised again to £150,000. This had led WNO to push ahead not only with new productions and fix up its first real English tour (taking in Bristol, Birmingham, Liverpool and Stratford) for 1968, increasing the total number of weeks played to fourteen, but also to proceed with plans to raise the nucleus of a professional chorus without which no additional performances could be contemplated. Every member of the amateur chorus was invited to audition and more than 200 outside applications had been received following the public announcement the previous October. Auditions were held in both London and Cardiff in July and thirty singers were chosen. The formation of the professional chorus did not mean jettisoning the amateurs; they would still be required for all the big chorus operas for many years to come. It was just that WNO had to have a small chorus which could be relied on to turn up for every rehearsal and all performances, for in addition to the increased touring commitment, Douglas Craig was working on plans to take small-scale productions with an orchestra of no more than 25 players to towns such as Wrexham, Rhyl, Aberystwyth and Haverfordwest, where the main company could not play.

In spite of these moves, some immediate problems remained. The conversion of the premises in John Street was continuing, but the cost of completion had risen to £120,000. Although Cardiff City Council had already given a generous donation of £30,000, no one knew where the remainder of the money was to come from, and the Arts Council were asking to see definite plans that WNO's work would be increased three-fold before they could justify such an enormous expenditure. And then there was the question of an orchestra. For many years, everyone had been talking about the desirability of WNO having its own orchestra. The previous few years had demonstrated time and again the limitations of using more than one orchestra. Not only did conductors have to travel to Bournemouth or Birmingham to rehearse, there was little time available when they got there for more than a run-through of the season's works. Most productions other than new ones went on without a full dress rehearsal; the majority were played without even a complete orchestral run-through, and while the musicians were skilled and could play the notes in the score, there was little a conductor could do other than to try and keep them and the stage together during a performance. This did not help create a high standard of orchestral accompaniment. There was another, more convincing argument as to why

WNO should have its own orchestra, and that was cost. During 1967 £40,000 was spent on hiring three orchestras. The following year, with five additional weeks, that cost would rise appreciably. To form and run an orchestra of fifty players would, it was estimated, cost only an additional £50,000; and when the new orchestra wasn't required for opera, it could, by being augmented, help enrich the cultural life of Wales by giving symphony concerts, as did the Vienna Philharmonic, which it was planned it should resemble. In December, Craig announced that an application had been made to the Arts Council for a grant to form just such an orchestra. "It has been economically and artistically disastrous to employ so many different orchestras," he said. "We've been pedalling away at rehearsals of the same thing like a man on a keep-fit machine – not getting anywhere."

# CHAPTER TWELVE: 1968–1969

O N I JANUARY 1968 the thirty members of the new professional chorus met in an old chapel in Windsor Road, Cardiff, to begin rehearsing *Rigoletto*. Some of them, like John Myrddin, were already experienced singers. Myrddin, a former member of the Carl Rosa who had sung leading roles with the Welsh in the past, had retired to Wales and was anxious to pass on his knowledge to younger singers. Others had come straight from music college. Ten had been members of the amateur chorus. Suddenly they had been given the chance to do something they loved and be paid for it without having to leave Wales. Terry Lake, for instance, had been a postman, Gordon Whyte had been a clerk at a steelworks, Jean Sugrue was a housewife, Gabrielle Capus a teacher, Carol Davies a secretary, Neville Ackerman a factory worker, Kenneth Pugh a miner. The arrival of the professionals did not mean the immediate end of amateur involvement. The Voluntary Chorus (as they became known) would still be essential for several years in mounting the large-scale choral works, and efforts to keep their number to around 100 were intensified. The professionals were also given a new name: the Welsh National Opera Chorale. This was both to differentiate them from the Voluntary Chorus and because it was proposed that they should fill in those months when not working on opera by giving concerts. It was thought that a name such as the Chorale would be a better box-office draw than a title such as the Chorus of Welsh National Opera, from which the public might expect just operatic excerpts. The presence of the Chorale naturally made a difference to the mood within WNO, especially amongst those amateurs who had been its backbone for so long. The younger members were still pleased to have the opportunity to appear with top artists and top conductors and felt that singing alongside professionals would do nothing but raise their own standards. Some of the older members, however, were resentful. WNO, they felt, had been taken over by outsiders and the very people for whom it had been formed and upon whom its reputation was founded were being pushed aside. It was a natural reaction but one which failed to acknowledge that WNO as it had always been could no longer continue. Gordon Whyte, who had been with the amateur chorus for fourteen years before joining the Chorale, summed up the main difference between the amateurs and the professionals in the following way: "We no longer sang on the bus," he recalled.

The arrival of the first professional choristers was not the only major change at the beginning of 1968. After 22 years Bill Smith had decided to step down. The decision was not entirely of his own making. During negotiations with the Arts Council about the increased funding necessary for professionalisation, it had been impressed upon Smith quite forcefully that Welsh National Opera was considered to be a one-man band, and that until that situation changed, the Arts Council (unofficially, of course) would not be happy to see too many changes. Smith was deeply hurt by this attitude, but he was 73 and, after nearly a quarter-of-a-century of crisis after crisis, he'd had enough of the constant battle to raise money. He realised that perhaps a younger man was needed to help pilot WNO through the undoubtedly stormy waters which lay ahead, and he decided to call it a day. It was ironic – and an irony that would have escaped him – that what he had done to Idloes Owen all those years ago was now being done to him.

At the beginning of March, Alfred Francis, the former Managing Director and Vice-Chairman of TWW, the Welsh independent television station which had just lost its franchise, was appointed Executive Chairman. Francis had known Smith for many years, had helped WNO obtain grants, and had become one of Smith's many unpaid advisers. Born in Liverpool (where he had once managed the band in David Webster's Bon Marché store), he had had a long and distinguished career in the theatre as an administrator. For seven years, he had worked at the Old Vic, helping create the conditions from which the National Theatre could emerge, and had served on the boards of the Bristol Old Vic, the D'Oyly Carte and the London Festival Ballet. He had been on Arts Council and Welsh Arts Council committees. A talented composer of light music, he was a noted after-dinner speaker and, what was more important, knew just about everyone who was worth knowing. Following the demise of TWW, he was planning a long rest before beginning to write his memoirs, when Smith asked him to become Executive Chairman. If there was one person, Smith said, who knew the workings of the Arts Council and could stand up to them, it was Francis. Francis, who had a great affection for both Smith and the WNO, agreed but only on a part-time basis, for two days a week, providing Smith was not lost to the company and agreed to remain as its first Life President.

The Swansea week, the first featuring the Chorale, opened in March with a new production of *Rigoletto* by Tom Hawkes, designed by Jane Kingshill. Singing the title role for the first time in his career was local boy Delme Bryn-Jones. One could almost feel the audience willing him to succeed and they gave him a fine reception. "For the first act and a half," wrote Noël Goodwin in *Music and Musicians*, "he sang with a passionate flood of warm and expressive tone, but thereafter he seemed to tire, and his voice lost its lustre and feeling." Despite this, it was a performance of considerable promise. Tom Hawkes's production "had a stiffness in the joints," according to Goodwin. He had grouped his chorus well but failed to imbue the drama with any real tension. The male section of the new Chorale was excellent. "At present," concluded Ronald Crichton of the *Financial Times*, "this *Rigoletto* isn't nearly as interesting or as well performed as last autumn's *Carmen*."

The following night, *Nabucco* was given, followed by *Carmen* with Glenys Louli, a young student from the London Opera Centre who had been born of a Greek mother and an English father in Cairo, making her debut in the title role. She possessed a beautiful voice, which she used intelligently, but her inexperience showed and the performance never caught fire.

Two weeks later, following months of negotiation and planning, WNO paid its first visit to Bristol, accompanied, as in Swansea, by the Ulster Orchestra. Two articulated trucks and a five-ton van had been bought in readiness for the increased touring and these were used for the first time to transport the sets and scenery of *Carmen*, *The Barber of Seville*, *Rigoletto*, *Don Giovanni* and *Nabucco* to Bristol, making several journeys to get everything there. There were two changes in the advertised cast for the opening performance of *Carmen*, although the first-night audience was unable to read about them since the programmes did not arrive at the theatre in time. Joyce Blackham flew back from Germany to take Glenys Louli's place as Carmen, and John Hauxvell was a last minute replacement for John Gibbs as Escamillo. Business in the 2000-seat Hippodrome was poor to start with, but by the second week the houses were beginning to fill and the final performances were played to near-capacity. The graph of attendances, remarked Craig, looked like the ascent of a jet aircraft, and the fortnight was considered sufficiently successful for a second visit to be arranged the following year.

As soon as Balkwill announced his intention to leave, Smith had contacted his friends, especially David Webster at Covent Garden, for their opinions on a successor. He wanted someone who was not just a good enough musician to continue expanding the musical side, but a man who was prepared to fight all and sundry for his beliefs. Time and again the same name came up: James Lockhart. A 37-year-old Scot, Lockhart was on the staff at Covent Garden, where he had established himself as an excellent répétiteur, a fine conductor, and a person who could be difficult if he didn't get his own way. Smith had never met him or heard him conduct, but as Webster, William Walton and Alfred Francis (before he became Chairman) all said that Lockhart was the right man, Smith was prepared to take their word. Lockhart returned from an English Opera Group tour of Canada to be sounded out unofficially by John Moody. He duly met Smith and was appointed Musical Director in March (the last appointment Smith was to make before handing over to Alfred Francis). In their preliminary talks, Smith had made it quite clear that Lockhart would be expected to assist in the professionalisation not just of the chorus but of general attitudes. "I remember Bill Smith telling me, 'Don't look for a fight, but make sure you win all the battles. You will have to break some windows, but don't break three when two will do.' "

Lockhart had several professional engagements to fulfil before he could begin work, so could not take part in the spring season in Cardiff. This opened with a new production of another favourite which had not been seen for two years, *La Traviata*, produced by John Copley (who was concurrently rehearsing Visconti's black-and-white production for Covent Garden) and designed by David Walker. Their intention, in which they succeeded brilliantly, was to set the production as close as possible to its period of composition, and, following the precedent set by Covent Garden, Copley reverted to the names of the Dumas original so that Violetta became Marguerite, Alfredo became Armand, Giorgio Germont became Georges Duval, and so on. Apart from showing that Copley had read the original story, these name changes added little to the production and merely served to confuse the critics, who were uncertain which names to use in their reviews. The actual production was imaginatively conceived and designed. The chorus in particular, attacking its music crisply, was handled with great effect. "Mr Copley's staging is excellent," wrote John Higgins in the *Financial Times*. "It has unity, it has understanding, and like David Walker's equally admirable sets, it looks sturdy enough to stand up to wear, tear and travel. This is not in any way a grand *Traviata* . . . he has produced a domestic tragedy with excursions to the demimonde of Paris. The theme is suggested immediately." Singing the role of Violetta/Marguerite was Ava June. "The most affecting I have heard from her," commented Higgins, "it is very much in key with the production in being neither brilliant nor flashy but in coming from the heart." David Hillman was in excellent voice as Alfredo and Geoffrey Chard was Germont. The playing of the CBSO, under John Matheson, was frequently untidy at the first performance, but, wrote Higgins, "this was one of those evenings when the eyes were on the stage rather than on the pit, and it belonged to John Copley and his designer."

The following night saw a revival of *Tosca* with Milla Andrew in the title role. It was during the opera's second performance, on 31 May, that an incident took place which all those in the theatre that night remember as either the funniest or the most disastrous they have ever seen. Towards the close of the second act, as Tosca was placing the candles around the body of the dead Scarpia and singing the line "This is the man before whom all Rome trembled," the curtain came down. It immediately went up again and Gwyn Griffiths, the Scarpia, was discovered getting to his feet. He sat, totally bemused, wondering what to do next, while the orchestra (conducted by Balkwill) continued playing before the curtain descended to end the act. What had happened was that the Cavaradossi, who was well known for his wandering hands, had, at that moment, approached the stage manager. Startled, she had accidentally pressed the button to bring the curtain down. Realising what she had done, she immediately pressed the button to bring the curtain up, hoping it would cancel out her first action, but it didn't!

Performances of *Nabucco*, *Rigoletto* (with Keith Erwen, the former member of Welsh Opera for All and recent Cinzano Prize winner, taking over at short notice to sing his first Duke) and *Carmen* completed a fortnight, for which, once again, every ticket was sold. The season in Swansea had also played to full houses, and although in Bristol it had taken time to attract an audience, the general feeling was that the fortnight there had been a good start to the increased touring commitment. The enthusiasm with which the year had started quickly evaporated, however, with the news that the Arts Council's grant, which everyone was certain would be doubled from £150,000 to £300,000 to reflect WNO's growing national importance, was to be held at the same level as in the previous year. There was nothing the Welsh Arts Council could do about it. They had confidently expected an increase in their own allocation from central funds, but the economic squeeze that held the entire country in its grip prevented this, and with 36 percent of WAC's budget already going to WNO, there was no room for any increase. Colonel William Crawshay and Aneurin Thomas of the Welsh Arts Council immediately appealed directly to Lord Goodman, the Chairman of the Arts Council in London, to make up the difference, but Lord Goodman refused, suggesting instead that an approach be made to the Welsh Office for a supplementary grant. The Welsh Office did not want to know. WNO's plans for the year had already been made on the assumption that the grant would be doubled. Productions had been cast, theatres had been booked, the Chorale was on the point of having its strength increased to sixty, moves were proceeding to establish an orchestra; and there was still the shortfall on the previous years which needed to be wiped off. Alfred Francis, whose brief when he had taken over as Chairman had been to oversee WNO's professionalisation from top to bottom, suddenly found himself embroiled in a fight for survival.

The immediate effect of the crisis was to postpone all thoughts of forming an orchestra and the hurried engagement of the Bournemouth Symphony, the CBSO and the Royal Liverpool Philharmonic, to accompany the later seasons. It also looked as if the number of weeks played would have to be cut back to eight and certainly all other plans for expansion had to be shelved. Gloom descended yet again on Cardiff.

Urgent talks continued throughout the spring. The Arts Council in London was severely censured for dragging its feet on the report on which all Welsh National's forward planning had been based, and Lord Goodman hotly denied that the sum of £150,000 which had been found to help Sadler's Wells move to the Coliseum had been money originally allocated to WNO. A panic reappraisal of budgets showed that strict economies could cut the predicted deficit on the year's planned operations from £175,000 to £80,000, but that was the minimum extra figure required to allow WNO to meet its current commitments. The Welsh Committee of the Communist Party made a formal complaint to Jennie Lee about the decision to withhold the promised grant, and Renee Short, MP, arrived in Cardiff to chair a public enquiry into WNO. The outcome solved nothing. WNO was informed that only Manchester and Scotland had been designated for opera development outside London and that no additional help could be found.

In spite of these problems, WNO was determined to fulfil its commitments. In August, *Nabucco* was given at the opening of the Eisteddfod in Barry with Tinsley, Herincx, Gwynne, a chorus of 120 and the Sadler's Wells Orchestra conducted by Bryan Balkwill. A week later the Llandudno season opened with *Carmen*, in which Joy Davidson, the American singer and first holder of a foreign passport to appear with WNO, made her British debut as Carmen. There were also cast changes in *Rigoletto*, with Annon Lee Silver appearing as Gilda and Keith Erwen singing the Duke for the first time in his own right. *La Traviata*, *Nabucco* and *Tosca* completed the fortnight.

The new production for the autumn might almost have been chosen to prove to the amateurs that they still featured large in WNO's plans. It was Mussorgsky's *Boris Godunov*, given in a new translation by David Lloyd-Jones and, following the lead set by Scottish Opera a few months earlier, in the original version without Rimsky-Korsakov's "improvements." The first-night saw the debut in the pit of the new Musical Director, James Lockhart, and of Forbes Robinson singing the title role for the first time in his career (a combination which produced a squeak of protest from a Welsh Nationalist politician who publicly attacked WNO for opening its season with a Russian opera conducted by a Scot with an English singer in the title role!).

Having opted for the Mussorgsky original, Lockhart and John Moody, the producer, decided to combine the two versions of 1869 and 1874, omitting the Polish scene but including both the St Basil and a reduced Kromy Forest scene, a decision which drew some criticism for altering the overall shape of the work.

Within this framework, however, Moody produced one of his most creatively imaginative works for WNO. He was helped enormously by Elizabeth Friendship's sumptuous costumes and evocative settings, the only criticism of which was that a large staircase split the small stage and made it difficult for the chorus to move easily. Inhibition was, in fact, the keynote of the first night. There were some first-rate characterisations from the principals, showing Moody's customary care in that department. Anne Pashley's Feodor, Keith Erwen's Grigory and John Dobson's oily, serpentine Shuisky ("a virtuoso piece of actor-singing of a kind quite rare on the opera stage," according to the *Observer's* Stephen Walsh) were outstanding. The chorus took time to warm up, and Forbes Robinson in the title role did not display the depth of characterisation he was to achieve in later performances. "In spite of all his intelligent enunciation, his firm tone and his attention to musical refinements, at present the interpretation lacks the magnetic element to set an audience alight," wrote Alan Blyth in the *Financial Times*. James Lockhart had prepared the musical side meticulously and his conducting, a trifle subdued and slow at the beginning but growing in intensity, provided an auspicious start to his reign as Musical Director. In spite of the first-night reservations, *Boris* (and Robinson in particular) received an enormous ovation, the loudest and most sustained since Gwyneth Jones had made her debut in *Fidelio*, and it was to settle down quickly into one of WNO's most accomplished productions.

After the excitement of the *Boris* first night, *Don Giovanni* came as something of a let down. A far from capacity audience failed to respond to the early scenes which were sluggishly played by the orchestra (under Eric Wetherell) and performed by the singers, and much of Geliot's original taut direction seemed to have lost its cutting edge. The stagehands were slow changing scenes, and the lighting was haphazard, "reaching a climax of incompetence when Geliot's marvellously conceived graveyard scene was ruined by the Statue being seen walking off into the wings." There was only one newcomer to the cast, Marie Landis, who sang Donna Anna neatly and musically but seemed, not unnaturally, to be ill at ease in the production. The teamwork that had marked the earlier performances was missing (which may not be surprising since the cast had not appeared together for six months and then in a different theatre).

The following night, Forbes Robinson repeated the title role in *Boris* which was already showing improvement, and then appeared as an over-the-top Basilio in a lively performance of *The Barber of Seville*. Stuart Burrows appeared as the Duke in *Rigoletto* for the first time in Wales, and the season was completed by *Carmen, Tosca, Nabucco* and *La Traviata*. Making her company debut as Violetta was a young soprano, one of Lockart's first contracted principals, who had been working with Opera for All and had appeared in the Glyndebourne chorus: Josephine Barstow. From the moment the curtain went up, it was apparent that here was a rare talent. She impressed Kenneth Loveland with "a study that was original, impassioned, and beautifully sung." In later performances, she was partnered by Keith Erwen, making his debut as Alfredo. "In a strange way," wrote Loveland, "both gained from fallibility, for the faults were those of impetuosity and this was an ingredient essential to both studies. Miss Barstow was inclined to undisciplined intonation in moments of stress; Mr Erwen was prone to waste energies where they were not needed instead of pacing their deployment with the economy that comes with experience. But these were small prices to pay for the excitement of watching two singers of such strong potential and growing authority."

Both the Llandudno fortnight and the Cardiff season had been tinged with sadness. In July, Bill Smith had returned from holiday and entered hospital for an operation. He had died there on Sunday, 9 July. Not even Smith had realised just how ill he was, and the news came as a terrible shock both to his wife and to the company. On 19 October, one week after the close of the Cardiff season, a memorial service was held at Llandaff Cathedral. Elizabeth Vaughan, Patricia Kern, David Hughes and Forbes Robinson, all artists who had either started their careers with WNO or been given important opportunities by Bill Smith, were the soloists in a performance of Verdi's *Requiem*. In his address, Alfred Francis referred to a man unique in his time. Smith was certainly that. He had created enemies; he had created even more friends. His meanness with money had become legendary, but it was a meanness on behalf of WNO, not himself. He had used his personal funds to balance the books in the early days, had provided the rehearsal room over his garage and kept the company alive when others might have pronounced it dead. His treatment of Idloes Owen had produced deep bitterness and there were those who never forgave him, but without him, as Muriel Pointon has said, there would have been no Welsh National Opera: "Had it not been for the tremendous foresight, business acumen and great drive of this remarkable man, the WNO would have undoubtedly died a natural death in those early years – not from lack of ability or enthusiasm, but from the bane of us all – money."

"The choice of music was perfect," wrote Kenneth Loveland in his review of the memorial service. "The Verdi *Requiem* was a work close to his big heart. The Welsh National Opera chorus first sang it at Bournemouth on Good Friday, 1954, when it was fashionable to say that they were more close to perfection than they really were. 'I thought they might have given us full marks for that,' he said the next day as he read the notices, and then realised that reservations meant that the company was at last being criticised on the higher level . . . Surely these tremendous, defiant choruses were an exact expression of the fighing spirit of a man who faced up to the

Philistines and won, whose tireless courage and advocacy was the inspiration which brought the Welsh National Opera from a small provincial group to its present status as the most important operatic venture outside London? In all the years, I never once heard him talk about 'my company,' though he often coupled himself with them to talk about 'us.' On Saturday night, that ghost might have looked over its glasses at the rows of opera lovers and muttered, 'Singing all right tonight, aren't they, eh?' . . . Bill Smith, whom I once saw weep in the last act of *La Traviata*, would have loved it. In fact he probably did."

It was a great pity that Smith did not live long enough to see the real expansion of the organisation to which he had given so much. He had missed hardly a performance since that April day in 1946 when Welsh National Opera had made its first stage appearance, and it would have filled him with pride to have seen the curtain go up at the Alexandra Theatre in Birmingham at the end of October, at the start of WNO's first major English tour. After Birmingham came the Royal Court in Liverpool, accompanied by the Royal Liverpool Philharmonic Orchestra, and then, on Boxing Day, the Red Dragon flew proudly over the Royal Shakespeare Memorial Theatre at the start of a two-week season in Stratford. The productions taken on tour – *Traviata*, *Carmen*, *The Barber of Seville*, *Rigoletto* and *Boris Godunov* – were all played to large and enthusiastic audiences. Some people still thought that WNO was a totally amateur company and were surprised to find that it was not. Others, brought up on the tours of Sadler's Wells and Covent Garden, had heard good reports of WNO but still went with an attitude of "show us". And that is exactly what WNO did. The Welsh Tourist Board, recognising the impact made in England, gave Welsh National Opera its annual award for the organisation which had done most during the year to enhance the prestige of Wales abroad.

In December, Eric Wetherell had resigned to become Musical Director of Harlech Television, and Lockhart invited Richard Armstrong, a 26-year-old répétiteur at Covent Garden with no experience of professional conducting, to succeed him as Assistant Musical Director.

In February 1969 the first small-scale tour began, under the umbrella title "Opera on Tour", with visits to Haverfordwest, Aberystwyth, Rhyl and Wrexham. This was not designed to supersede the work of Opera for All, but to provide "specially prepared productions of high quality, tailored to fit into theatres unable to accommodate the full Welsh National Opera Company," and give people in Wales who otherwise had no opera a chance to see the company at work. Accompanied by the 25-piece Bournemouth Sinfonietta, the company took with them John Copley's production of *La Traviata*, re-rehearsed by Malcolm Fraser with scenery adapted from David

Walker's originals by Pauline Whitehouse, and *The Marriage of Figaro* in a new production by John Moody especially devised for the tour. It was with *Figaro* that the tour opened in a Haverfordwest school hall. The following night, *La Traviata* was performed with Josephine Barstow as Violetta and Ramon Remedios as Alfredo. Making his professional debut in the production as Baron Douphol was a young singer Lockhart had just signed on contract: Thomas Allen. Allen had been a student at the Royal College when Lockhart had first heard him and persuaded him to become an opera rather than a concert singer. In addition to singing Douphol, he had been asked to understudy Figaro, and when John Gibbs was unavailable for the performance in Wrexham, Allen went on in his place. In front of a half empty hall, he made an enormous impression as a singer to watch.

While the theatres and halls of Rhyl, Wrexham, Aberystwyth and Haverfordwest were providing new outlets, one familiar venue was not being visited that spring. As part of the cost-cutting brought about by the reduced grant, and the fact that it was not known until well into January whether the Grand would be open, it had been decided not to schedule a season in Swansea. There were immediate protests from Swansea Council (which had taken over running the theatre) and a threat to withhold its annual grant of £2000. As a compromise, an alternative week was offered for November.

In March the new John Street headquarters was finally opened by Member of Parliament Renee Short. The building, comprising two large rehearsal rooms (one large enough to use scenery in), two smaller ensemble studios, four coaching studios, a wardrobe department, carpenter's shop, paint shop, scenery store and administrative offices, had been completed at a cost of £120,000. Funding for these alterations had been provided by Cardiff Council, which had bought the premises, paid half the cost of conversion (the other half being met by the Arts Council) and then leased the building back to WNO. Many former members of the company were present at the official opening, at which Muriel Pointon, still after 25 years a member of the Voluntary Chorus, was selected to present a bouquet to Miss Short.

The spring season in Cardiff opened at the New on 21 April with a stirring revival of *Macbeth*. Pauline Tinsley repeated her formidable Lady Macbeth, but Terence Sharpe as Macbeth, Richard Van Allan as Banquo and Ramon Remedios as Macduff were all new to their roles. "In last night's performance," wrote David Evans in the *Western Mail*, "the contributions of cast and chorus made the opening night a total success." In particular, Evans praised the wisdom of retaining a more permanent chorus. Lockhart, conducting the opera for the first time, brought an expressive flow to the score, although "there must have been much gnashing of teeth in the orchestra pit, for the audience, thinking that the music ended when the singers stopped, clapped through every orchestral coda." In a later performance of *Macbeth*, Van Allan was to have the unique experience of singing his and Macbeth's role in the same scene. The Tannoy system backstage had broken down, so no one could hear what was happening on stage. Terence Sharpe was in his dressing room, checking his make-up, when he ought to have been waiting in the wings with Van Allan to make an entrance. When Van Allan realised that Sharpe was not coming, it was too late to find him, and he went on alone, performing both roles. He had just reached the point where a duet was about to begin and was wondering how he could cope, when Sharpe arrived on stage. "He was completely disorientated," recalls Van Allan. " 'Where should I be?' he whispered. 'Downstage left,' I replied. And then the duet began."

The season continued with *Boris Godunov*, *Carmen* (in which Josephine Barstow and Thomas Allen played Frasquita and Morales) and *Nabucco*. Delia Wallis, who had made her debut in *The Marriage of Figaro* as Cherubino on the short spring tour, sang her first Fenena and Richard Van Allan his first Zaccaria. "Previous singers have played him as a father figure, an Abraham-type patriarch among the Jews," wrote Loveland in the *Times*. "Richard Van Allan seems to see him more as a kind of John the Baptist, wild of eye, threatening and primitive, dangerously objective." It was, Loveland concluded, a "study strong on Old Testament fury." At the end of the first act, in a carefully rehearsed move, Van Allan deliberately fell on the heavily raked set with such conviction that many in the audience were surprised to see him reappear after the interval.

It was this performance which produced a story which has become part of operatic legend. It runs as follows: Just as Zaccaria steps forward to sing his first aria, he hears a loud "pssst" in his ear. Turning round, he finds himself face to face with a male stalwart of the Voluntary Chorus, in full Jewish garb and very unhappy. "Do you realise," asks the chorister, clearly agitated, "you're standing in my place? I've been standing in that spot for eleven years." The offending guest artist, without a word, moves over and begins to sing. The artist to whom it actually happened was Richard Van Allan. All his rehearsals had taken place with the Chorale and there was no full dress rehearsal. He was merely warned that the stage would be slightly more crowded during the performance because 70 or 80 amateurs would also be there. "I had never even met them before," he recalls. "On the first night, I made my way on amongst all these hordes and prepared to sing my first line. I was just about to take a breath when this little voice at the side of me said, 'I stand there.' I was a bit thrown by this and looked down at him. He took this as a challenge and said, 'Been standing there for years.' I just had time to say, 'Well, you are not standing here tonight,' before I sang. It wasn't until then that he realised I was one of the soloists. He thought I was a member of the Chorale standing in his place."

A cast all under 30 gave Copley's production of *Traviata* a striking immediacy. Josephine Barstow as Violetta/Marguerite "was sometimes guilty of wild singing, but so was the young Callas and this British soprano discovery has the same kind of exciting dedication. An artist of outstanding promise," reported David Williams in the *Daily Mail*. "So is Keith Erwen, the Cinzano prizewinner just returned from La Fenice in Venice, to sing before his home audience. His Armand matched the passionate femininity of Miss Barstow's Marguerite with an eloquent urgency of its own. Even the conductor was under 30. Nicholas Braithwaite, talented son of a famous father, produced just the kind of glowing playing from the Bournemouth Symphony Orchestra to go with the ardent singing."

Another young conductor was in the pit for *The Marriage of Figaro* which had been repainted and refurbished since the tour. Richard Armstrong, who had made his conducting debut with the opera in Rhyl, had been given the task of conducting in Cardiff without even a dress rehearsal. Although there were no new productions in the fortnight's season, the first presentation in a major theatre of Moody's production attracted the attention of the national critics. According to Alan Blyth, writing in the *Financial Times*, "Armstrong, recently appointed head of Welsh National's music staff, takes a very serious, rather Germanic view of the score. This led him into some heavy sounding speeds and lumpy accompaniments, not helped by loose playing from the Bournemouth Symphony. However, he often handled detail well, in Cherubino's arias, for instance, and the fourth-act finale was evenly paced, eloquently articulated."

While much of the attention centred on Armstrong, there was equal interest in Josephine Barstow's first Countess. She sang, wrote Blyth, "with nicely poised full tone – even when lying uncomfortably on a chaise-lounge during 'Porgi amor' – and a beautifully arched line; only the last refinements are still missing. She acted unobtrusively but pointedly too; I have seldom seen the Countess's affection for Cherubino – a winning, fresh portrayal by Delia Wallis – so subtly expressed."

Touring began the following week in Bristol with performances of *Macbeth*, *Boris Godunov*, *La Traviata* and *Carmen*, and then resumed, after a break of two months, in Llandudno, where advance bookings were again a record and the prospect of a record-breaking fortnight looked very good. 1969 will best be remembered in Wales, and beyond, as the year of the Investiture of the Prince of Wales. Members of the Voluntary Chorus and the Chorale joined with choirs from all over Wales to sing during the ceremony at Carnarvon Castle, and WNO decided to mount two special events to celebrate the occasion. The first of these was a gala performance of

*Fidelio* which opened the Llandudno season on 12 August, and for which every ticket had been sold weeks before. Gwyneth Jones flew back from Bayreuth to sing Leonore, and Michael Langdon, who had learnt the role in English for the performance, sang Rocco. "It is grand to be back with Welsh National Opera," Jones told a reporter. "You have to go abroad to realise what a very good company this is. The chorus, with the large amateur element, are in a class all of their own." Jones herself was in superb voice and was ably supported by Langdon, Robert Thomas (Florestan), Gwyn Griffiths (Pizarro), Anne Pashley (Marzelline), Robert Tear (Jacquino) and a chorus on top form. "The ultimate strength of a sound, if not inspired performance," wrote Neil Barkla in the *Liverpool Post*, "lay in James Lockhart's authoritative musical direction and faithfulness to the score; some excellent vocal ensembles and the consistently reliable playing of the Bournemouth Symphony Orchestra." "Any British version of *Fidelio* including that of the Welsh National Opera must expect to stand comparison with Klemperer's large-scale version at the Royal Opera House," wrote Graham Samuel of the *Western Mail*. "The Welsh company's account could stand this apparently fearsome challenge. It even comes off best in certain aspects. One of these is the conducting of James Lockhart. Of course, this young conductor's concept of this opera has not yet the ripe maturity, the splendid scope of Klemperer's. Nevertheless it presents a great vision of this noble score. It has inspiring grasp, and above all, is free from the little inattentions to detail that now bedevil Klemperer's work."

The second celebratory event was a new production of *Falstaff* starring Geraint Evans. The idea of staging *Falstaff* had come from Douglas Craig and Kenneth Loveland. Naturally, everyone wanted to put on something special starring Welsh singers and, if possible, Geraint Evans. More than a year earlier Craig and Loveland were discussing what it should be. Their first thought was *The Magic Flute* with Evans as Papageno, but then they hit upon the idea of *Falstaff*, one of his most famous roles. Evans said he would be delighted to do it but did not have time to learn the part in English. Craig was ready for that. It would be performed in Italian, the first time WNO had sung in anything other than Welsh or English. And so Evans agreed, provided he was allowed to produce as well. Craig did not feel that he would be able to combine the two effectively, and they settled on John Copley to co-produce with him. Thoughts then turned to other eminent Welsh singers who might take part. A premature announcement of the ideal cast led to newspaper reports that Stuart Burrows would be singing Fenton, but Burrows had already signed a contract to appear as Tamino in San Francisco. It was this type of enthusiasm for naming ideal casts which sometimes led to premature press reports. Once, Geraint Evans, Stuart

Burrows and Margaret Price had been appearing together in *Don Giovanni*, and Evans remarked how nice it would be if they could sing the same roles in Wales. The conversation got out and before anyone knew it, least of all WNO's management, the production had become a fact. When, of course, it never happened because it was impractical, word spread that WNO had turned down an offer which had never actually been made.

Even without Burrows, one of the finest all-Welsh casts ever assembled, and one which would have graced any operatic stage in the world, was engaged for *Falstaff*. In addition to Evans, Elizabeth Vaughan sang Alice Ford; Margaret Price, Nannetta; Helen Watts, Mistress Quickly; Joan Davies, Mistress Page (in place of Patricia Kern who had to drop out); Gwyn Griffiths, Ford; David Gwynne, Pistol; Robert Thomas, Bardolph; Keith Erwen, Fenton; and Edward Byles, Dr Caius.

Sir Geraint Evans (he was knighted in the Investiture honours) had made the role of Falstaff very much his own since he first sang it in Carl Ebert's 1957 Glyndebourne production and it was inevitable that the production should revolve around him. It was, according to Sir Geraint (perhaps not surprisingly), the best-designed and most "workable" *Falstaff* in which he'd ever sung. It borrowed unashamedly from other productions in which he'd appeared, and brought a mixed reaction. "This *Falstaff* is, fundamentally, played as a rapid farce," wrote John Warrack in the *Sunday Telegraph*, "The rowdy element is allowed to dominate rather too much, especially in the Tabard slapstick; but it is all neatly carried out, and has a proper purpose in keeping the texture of the comedy airy." Frank Granville Barker, writing in *Music and Musicians*, was less happy. "The staging was generally direct and telling, with a number of happily inventive touches. At times, however, it indulged in tiresomely excessive stage business – either in an attempt to point jokes that would otherwise be missed by an audience with little or no Italian, or because the producers had not been able to shake off the influence of the over-fussy Zeffirelli staging with which they have long been familiar at Covent Garden."

There was, however, universal praise for the delightful settings of Carl Toms and the subtle lighting of Charles Bristow, and the musical side of the evening provided great pleasure. Evans, in spite of having to take pain-killing drugs for a shoulder complaint, was in excellent form. "It was the quality of the singing – dominated, of course, by Evans' superb interpretation of Falstaff – that made this a performance to remember," commented Granville Barker. "There was the well-nigh ideal Mistress Quickly of Helen Watts, rich in both voice and characterisation. Margaret Price, who could equally well have been cast as Mistress Ford, made a wholly charming and convincing Nannetta, singing her fairy song in the last scene with a radiance and absolute steadiness of tone that I have heard no other soprano bring to it. And Keith Erwen, displaying a liquid lyric tenor of Italianate warmth, made a thoroughly likeable Fenton." The chorus, crowding the stage in the final scene, added their own brand of uninhibited enthusiasm to the proceedings, which were conducted, for the most part, with fine control and understanding by James Lockhart. The decision to sing in Italian was welcomed by some, attacked by others; the audience, whether they understood Italian or not, certainly enjoyed every minute and gave the artists twelve curtain calls at the finish.

All five performances of *Falstaff* had been sold out to mailing-list subscribers. The one on 14 October was attended by the Prince of Wales himself, who flew to Cardiff for the occasion and spent a considerable time after the performance talking to the cast, surprising everybody by his knowledge of and enthusiasm for opera. The remaining productions during the three-week season included *Nabucco*, *Macbeth*, *The Marriage of Figaro* (which was notable for its teamwork and for the much improved conducting of Richard Armstrong), *Boris Godunov* (in which Armstrong also made a considerable impression and Robert Tear, in the one major cast change, made an affecting Simpleton), *La Traviata*, *Carmen* and *The Barber of Seville* (in which Thomas Allen sang his first Figaro opposite Joyce Blackham). "Each season at Cardiff unearths some important new operatic talent," wrote Kenneth Loveland; "Mr Allen could possibly tread the path followed from this stage by such names as Kern, Jones, Vaughan, Burrows, Davies and Howells . . . Only 25, he already possesses exceptional authority as singer and actor."

At the end of his first year in charge, Lockhart began to make changes. He had already brought in Richard Armstrong to succeed Eric Wetherell as his assistant and had engaged Anthony Hose to be Chorus Master of the new Chorale, but he had been biding his time, assessing the strengths and weaknesses of the company, before taking any drastic action. That time had now arrived. He felt that several mistakes had been made with the Chorale and so he got rid of seven choristers, brought in new singers more to his liking, and made several changes to the music staff. Another aspect of WNO about which he was not entirely happy was the style of production. John Moody, recognising that after eight years the time had come for a younger man with fresh ideas, offered his resignation as Director of Productions. A member of the Board straightaway suggested that the post be offered to Franco Zeffirelli, but no one took the suggestion seriously and Moody, on his own recommendation, was succeeded by Michael Geliot. Moody, who had served WNO so well and loyally and had done so much to establish its reputation, was not lost to the company for he agreed to stay on as Artistic Director and as a member of the Council.

The autumn season in Cardiff was followed by visits to Liverpool and

Birmingham, this time under the auspices of DALTA, the Dramatic and Lyric Theatre Association, an organisation set up specifically to tour opera and drama round the regions, and the year ended with a week in Swansea at the refurbished Grand. This was notable for the opportunities it gave to young conductors. Chorus Master Anthony Hose (who had made his debut in Cardiff with a matinée performance of *The Barber of Seville*) conducted *The Marriage of Figaro* for the first time, Lionel Friend, a 24-year-old member of the music staff, was in charge of *La Traviata* and David Gruffydd Evans of *Macbeth*. All three received excellent notices. Word was already getting around that WNO had discovered a new Violetta in Josephine Barstow. Critic Arthur Jacobs travelled to Swansea to hear her and was not disappointed. "Attractively tall and slim, beautifully costumed, she gives a marvellously intense performance. Expressions of love, of loneliness, of the rapture of the moment and the inevitable tragedy ahead, are delivered with supple changes in the colour of the voice, and with affecting acting as well. There are some difficult florid phrases in the music which Miss Barstow has not mastered yet, and her delivery of the brief spoken part in the final scene was oddly chopped-up. But she gives us a real Verdi heroine, make no mistake . . . In itself, this would have been worth the journey from London." Her performance, he concluded, "marked the emergence of a major talent."

# CHAPTER THIRTEEN: 1970–1971

Another short tour to Haverfordwest, Aberystwyth, Rhyl and Wrexham coincided with the most bitter weather of the winter of 1970, making travel for both the company and audiences extremely difficult. However, packed houses were able to forget the snow outside and bask in the sunshine of *The Barber of Seville* in a new production by staff producer Malcolm Fraser, and *Così fan tutte*, in a new production by Michael Geliot, his first since taking over as Director of Productions.

*The Barber of Seville*, designed by Robin Archer, was an enormous success, matching lively teamwork with obvious enthusiasm, and was well sung by Beverley Humphreys (Rosina), Ramon Remedios (Count Almaviva), John Gibbs (Dr Bartolo) and Terence Sharpe (Figaro). The brilliant Don Basilio of David Gwynne demonstrated what a fine asset he had become, and the tumultuous applause grew noticeably louder when he took his curtain calls.

Geliot's straightforward and unfussy production of *Così* showed a good appreciation of the human tenderness as well as the frivolity of the opera. Christine Edzard's sets emphasised the sunny atmosphere, and Geliot, like Fraser, was well served by his young cast: Josephine Barstow as Fiordiligi, Beverley Bergen (making her company debut) as Dorabella and another newcomer, Wendy Eathorne, as the maid, Despina. The roles of Ferrando and Guglielmo were taken by two more rising stars, Keith Erwen and Thomas Allen. Both delighted the audiences with their sense of fun and their fine singing. Only John Kitchiner, who was suffering from laryngitis, proved disappointing as Don Alfonso. By the time the tour reached Wrexham his voice had almost completely gone, but he insisted on appearing even though David Gwynne was in the wings waiting to take over. Brave though it was, many felt he had made the wrong decision.

Back in Cardiff, it was WNO's financial position which was still uppermost in everybody's mind. At a press conference in February, Alfred Francis defiantly announced that although no one knew where the money would be coming from, the year's programme would be the most ambitious ever. Fourteen weeks (eight in Wales, six in England) would be played and would include four new productions: *Aida, Die Fledermaus, Simon*

*Boccanegra* and *The Magic Flute*. Looking even further into the future, an opera had been commissioned from Alun Hoddinott and the first British production of Berg's *Lulu* was in the pipeline. If, Francis went on to say, the Welsh Arts Council's grant stayed at its current level of £162,000, this would mean budgeting for a deficit, since the cost of the proposals would be at least £100,000 more than that. And while he was confident that a way out of the difficulties would eventually be found, he was preparing a self-help scheme. Frank Brown, the former Public Relations director of TWW, was being brought in to mastermind an appeal to industry and commerce, and an Opera Club of Wales was being formed to allow the general public to help support WNO's activities. "If the company cannot develop and make the best possible use of all its assembled talent, it is a waste of the public money spent in the past," he added.

At the same press conference, Michael Geliot outlined WNO's policy as one of Welsh imperialism, not of Welsh nationalism. "We are out to colonise England with Welsh voices," he told the assembled journalists. Sadler's Wells had recently announced its decision to abandon provincial touring; WNO wanted that part of the Sadler's Wells grant which had previously been spent on touring. It was ready, willing and able to take over Sadler's Wells' commitments and was the company in Britain best fitted to tour. "We can provide the most economical use of public money and we will satisfy the undoubted public demand in the provinces," Geliot continued. During the fourteen weeks already announced, visits were planned for Bristol, Liverpool, Birmingham, Southampton and possibly again, Stratford-upon-Avon. WNO was ready, at the drop of a hat, to play a further ten weeks. "We shall take risks with our productions, and possibly even diabolical liberties – but I hope we won't be dull. Our aim will be to make you go to Wales to see the best in modern opera production," he concluded.

For more than two decades, it had been patiently explained to the countless people who kept asking to see it that Verdi's *Aida*, the most spectacular of grand operas, was impossible to stage in the theatres in which WNO played. It was a challenge Geliot decided to meet head on when *Aida* opened the 1970 spring season at Cardiff on 20 April. It was no easy task for him to devise a production which would fit onto stages which were clearly too small for spectacle and still retain the grandeur the audiences would expect. The solution he and his designer (Annena Stubbs) came up with was a set of large, mobile, non-representational polystyrene blocks. They were not universally liked. "It is a claustrophobic *Aida*," wrote Stephen Walsh in the *Observer*, " . . . with little sense of location." Instead of relying on massive spectacle, Geliot opted for characterisation in an interpretation which drew more praise than criticism. "To state, as one broadcast comment did, that the Welsh National Opera bit off more than it could chew," wrote Felix Aprahamian in the *Sunday Times*, "was ineptly patronising. Few features of this generally enjoyable production were unworthy of the work." "Geliot and his designer met the challenge of the opera's more spectacular scenes with skill and common sense," wrote Malcolm Boyd. An *Aida* without the stage or financial resources to include elephants and the Household Cavalry (the production cost only £10,000) must inevitably rely on the quality of the singing, and in this Geliot was fortunate. It had been decided to sing in Italian in order to acquire the services of the best artists available (Lockhart emphasised that the decision did not mark a change in policy), and both Grace de la Cruz and William Johns (two Americans from the Bremen Opera) made auspicious British debuts as Aida and Radames, while Terence Sharpe as Amonasro, Don Garrard as Ramfis and David Gwynne as the King gave strong support. But the star of the evening was Janet Coster, whose Amneris was sung expressively throughout, unifying music and acting to a rare degree. The chorus, too, shone, and the orchestra (the Sinfonia of Wales) were responsive to James Lockhart's driving conducting, apart from the brass section, which should, according to one critic, "have suffered the same fate as Aida, namely to be buried alive, especially the 'processional' trumpets of the triumphal scene." "It was," concluded Andrew Porter's review, "a successful evening, and deservedly so."

The following night, Thomas Allen's first Count in *The Marriage of Figaro* again emphasised what a discovery he was. "He conveyed not only the poise of the aristocrat, but suggested the unscrupulous opportunist beneath the veneer. Opportunity was taken of his high baritone to use the alternative version of the Count's aria that Mozart wrote for the Vienna performances of 1789. Allen negotiated it comfortably," wrote Loveland in *Music and Musicians*.

In the second week, an unscheduled new production took place. A revival of John Copley's *La Bohème* had been announced with a very strong cast, including Josephine Barstow making her debut as Mimi. Copley's production had never really worked, and Ande Anderson had been invited from Covent Garden to re-stage it, but when the Benois sets were removed from storage they were found to be so dilapidated that new ones had to be made. Pauline Whitehouse opted for a traditional approach, retaining many of the elements of the Benois sets that had proved so successful during the more than twenty years they had been in use. Like Copley's hugely successful *Traviata*, Anderson's *Bohème* concentrated on character. The Bohemians were particularly impressive, with an excellently sung Rodolfo from Stuart Burrows, a superb Marcello from Delme Bryn-Jones, and a well-observed Schaunard and Colline from Thomas Allen and David Gwynne. Josephine Barstow's occasional lapses of intonation did not detract from the overall impression she created as Mimi. "In many respects this is a compelling and moving performance," wrote Kenneth Loveland, "touched with that dimension of dedication that makes her work so disturbingly real. It is often beautifully sung ... always absorbing and exciting."

The season had again proved very successful, the first week being played to 86 percent capacity, the second week being sold out with long queues of people waiting for returns. If there was a disappointment, it was in the playing by the Sinfonia of Wales. In an attempt to reduce the wasteful multiplicity of orchestras whilst awaiting the formation of WNO's own orchestra, neither the CBSO nor the Bournemouth Symphony had been engaged for 1970, their place being taken (as it had on the short Welsh tour and in Swansea in March) by the Sinfonia of Wales, a body of freelance musicians, mostly London-based, which had been founded by Anthony Randle. The need for a permanent orchestra, something which had been talked about for almost twenty years, was now becoming acute. Not only was the lack of a permanent ensemble a hindrance to higher standards, but as the commitments increased, the hiring of orchestras was becoming increasingly impractical. The Arts Council recognised this in a report issued at the end of 1969 which emphasised the need for Wales to have both an opera house and an orchestra. The Sinfonia, which had failed to win Arts Council backing and was in financial difficulties, suggested a marriage between itself and WNO, but the Arts Council would not permit it; they had other ideas. The BBC at that time was, like most arts organisations, going through a crisis of its own and was keen to shed some of its regional orchestras, including the BBC Welsh Orchestra. One way of avoiding incurring the wrath of the Musicians' Union was for the Welsh Orchestra to become WNO's house orchestra, and this is what the Arts Council proposed. But Francis and Lockhart could both see that such an arrangement could only be short-term since it would not cease to be a symphony orchestra and would not fit easily into any future plans for expansion. The only real answer lay in WNO acquiring its own orchestra. A careful examination of the figures again showed that a permanent orchestra would not be any more expensive than hiring orchestras, and Francis and Lockhart decided to press ahead. In October 1969, Haydn (Dai) Trotman, a trombonist at the Royal Opera House for 18 years, had been appointed Orchestral Manager, with a brief to form a new orchestra.

Trotman's arrival coincided with the departure of General Administrator Douglas Craig. Craig had never been entirely happy in the job. Apart from the financial worries behind each season, he had had to cope with the antagonism of those who resented his presence, and it was with few misgivings that he left to become the new administrator of the Sadler's Wells

Theatre. No successor was named, partly because those running WNO wished to prove it could be done without him, and partly because the Board wished to re-examine the entire management structure in the light of the rapid expansion.

It was planned that the new orchestra would be engaged initially on a seasonal basis, with the basic personnel providing the core of the permanent orchestra when that was established later (a process which was expected to take at least a year). Trotman's first task was to find a leader. The man he invited was John Stein, the leader of the second orchestra accompanying the Royal Ballet on tour. The ballet orchestra was also seasonal and, having just finished a tour, had no immediate dates. Several of its younger players were asked to join Stein in the new venture, and to balance this younger element Trotman brought in some older, more experienced musicians, ending up with an orchestra of just under 60 strong. It was intended that once the orchestra became permanent, since its operatic work would not, under even the most optimistic forecast, take up more than 40 weeks of the year, the remaining time would be filled in by playing symphony concerts, thus giving Wales something it had lacked for a very long time: its own symphony orchestra. Believing that the name, The Orchestra of Welsh National Opera, would not be a draw in the concert hall if there was no choral or vocal music on the programme, Alfred Francis insisted it be called the Welsh Philharmonia.

With most of its personnel based in or around London, the Welsh Philharmonia's first rehearsal took place in St Pancras Town Hall, London. It was taken by a twenty-seven-year-old American whom Lockhart had engaged to conduct *Aida* and of whom none of the orchestral musicians had ever heard – James Levine. The orchestra made its debut accompanying the Llandudno fortnight in August. Earlier in the year, there had been doubt as to whether the season would take place. The Odeon had been sold and its new owners had agreed to the season, but when the Pavilion Theatre on the pier re-opened as a cinema, they informed WNO that they could not afford to lose business to a rival and the season must be cancelled. The owners of the Pavilion promptly offered their theatre as an alternative venue. The rival managements met and were able to reach a compromise: the Astra (as the Odeon had been renamed) remained the venue, but WNO's future appearances would have to take place in June when there were fewer tourists about who wanted to see films.

Michael Geliot's new production of *Die Fledermaus*, which opened the Llandudno fortnight, was, frankly, a flop, despite an attractive cast. In seeking to brush away the cobwebs of tradition, Geliot had opted for a deliberately sexual approach, showing young people seeking the pleasures of the time. "It will probably shock a lot of old ladies in Shetland shawls," said Alfred Francis before it opened, and there were indeed complaints that it was suggestive. "There is nothing suggestive about it," wrote Loveland in the *Times*. "It is plain statement of fact. Rosalinda is discovered in bed at five in the afternoon and spends Act I in different pairs of male arms and always in her undies. When Mr Geliot's production is not making it clear that she expects to be slept with by Alfred, George Melly's new English text fills in. ('Eisenstein does the rehearsal, I do the performance,' says Alfred with an eye on the bed.) Falke is clearly having an affair with her as well ('Parting is such sweet sorrow,' he says with a glance at her cleavage. 'Back for more tomorrow') and it is marginally possible that he is also having an affair with Eisenstein." Elizabeth Friendship's sets, crowded with nude models sporting black suspenders in Act II, and female bosoms in the Governor's room, backed up Geliot's approach, but somewhere amongst all the smut and innuendo Strauss's music got lost, making the whole evening a leaden affair. "These 'daring' touches were applied with a heavy self-conscious deliberateness – not gaiety – so as to suggest an owlish puritan earnestness of outlook beneath it all," wrote Andrew Porter. The production was, he continued "short on charm, high spirits . . . everything, including Mr Lockhart's conducting, needed to be lighter, more spontaneous, less determined."

The following night, James Levine, whom Lockhart had first heard in the States, where he was Assistant Conductor of the Cleveland Orchestra, made his British debut conducting *Aida*. He controlled a musically satisfying performance. "His insight into Verdi's score and his ability to bring out that indefinable 'something extra' from singers and players mark him as a conductor likely to make a big name in the operatic world," wrote Neil Barkla. The orchestra, wary as always of a conductor they did not know, warmed to Levine almost at once. He was clearly a formidable musician who knew his work, but, more than that, he was prepared to join in with everything. If the company liked him, he, too, liked the company. "To Jim 1," he wrote in the score of *The Magic Flute* which he gave Lockhart as a farewell present, "in remembrance of my first performances with your wonderful company and with deepest thanks for your enthusiastic interest and for the wonderful co-operation and company spirit that made my work here so very pleasant and satisfying. And with hopes that I will have the opportunity to work with you many times to come. Yours, Jim 2."

If Levine was able to demonstrate in Llandudno the talent that would eventually make him Musical Director of the Metropolitan Opera in New York, it was partly due to the presence there of the Welsh Philharmonia. It would not be true to say that the advent of the Welsh Philharmonia made a marked difference to the season (*La Bohème* "exposed the fact that the promising new orchestra . . . have still much to learn about the art of operatic accompaniment which was often far too heavy," wrote Barkla) but they were a definite improvement on the Sinfonia of Wales, and the players Trotman had assembled so enjoyed working with WNO that when he set about re-engaging them for the Cardiff season that autumn, almost every played signed on. The longer they played together, the better at accompanying opera they became.

Although the orchestra had been formed, the other recommendation in the Arts Council report, of an opera house for Wales, was no nearer fulfilment than it had been twenty years earlier. For the foreseeable future, the New remained "home". That summer the orchestra pit was extended and the auditorium given a face-lift, during which dry-rot was discovered in the roof. By the time the theatre re-opened in September, there were 200 fewer (though more comfortable) seats and ticket prices had been raised by up to 60 percent.

The three-week season opened with John Moody's new production of *Simon Boccanegra* at a cost of £9000, less than the amount it took to stage a small-cast play in the West End. As befitted a production by the man who had staged the first British performance of the work (at Sadler's Wells in 1948), Moody's approach was thoughtful and intelligent. It was, however, middle-of-the-road; "neither," according to Andrew Porter, "altogether 'traditional' nor yet experimental, not yet quite a success . . . not specially distinguished or distinctive, but a worthy addition to the repertory." The settings (by Roger Butlin) and costumes (by Richard Davin) were generally disliked. They seemed, wrote Malcolm Boyd, "to test the opera's reputation of being Verdi's gloomiest piece, and probably for this reason they are often at odds with the mood of the music and hardly begin to convey either the period or the location of the drama." Musically the performance was on sure ground with Delme Bryn-Jones and Forbes Robinson singing strongly and expressively as Boccanegra and Fiesco. Josephine Barstow's Amelia was, wrote Porter, "capable, efficient, strongly sung; the voice soared out in the *Requiem*-recalling phrases of the first finale." Keith Erwen contributed a romantic Gabriele Adorno, and Thomas Allen a distinguished Paolo: "Singing and characterization are without exception very sound," commented Malcolm Boyd in the *Musical Times*, "and, in the case of Thomas Allen's vivid portrayal of the ambitious, scheming Paolo, even inspired." It took Lockhart and the orchestra some time to come to terms with the new sunken orchestra pit in an otherwise compelling account of the score. But in spite of the many good parts, the sum failed to produce the response it should have. What the evening really lacked was "some good red-blooded realism."

The remainder of the season, played to invariably full houses, was made up of staple repertory fare and provided much that was rewarding. Keith

Erwen, making his debut in the role, was a creditable Rodolfo in *La Bohème*; Terence Sharpe, singing his first Figaro, impressed in *The Barber*, conducted with great assurance by James Levine; Julian Moyle took over for his first Count Almaviva with less than a day's notice from the indisposed John Kitchiner; Gillian Knight replaced Joyce Blackham with less than forty-eight hours' notice and was a stunning Carmen. And then there was the event everyone had been looking forward to: Pauline Tinsley's first appearance in the title role of *Aida*. Ever since her WNO debut in 1962 she had been a firm favourite with Welsh audiences, who had watched her develop into an international artist singing many roles in which they had heard her first. In the event, it proved to be something of a disappointment, for Tinsley was below par and her performance lacked the expected fire. The compensation, again, was the exceptional singing and acting of Janet Coster as Amneris, while James Levine once more drew some ravishing playing from the Welsh Philharmonia.

Seven productions had been presented during the season (seven different operas in seven days at one stage), an achievement more common on the continent than in Britain. Andrew Porter, writing in *Opera*, summed up WNO's achievements: "The international visitor finds two distinct kinds of opera production: on the one hand a fairly standard sort of presentation of standard works, and on the other something more adventurous: a chance-taking performance which seeks to make a virtue of the special circumstances – small theatre, young singers, a production-budget counted in thousands rather than tens of thousands – and to do something special, reveal some particular aspect of the opera in question." John Moody, he went on, has "in the main been associated with the 'regular' presentations; while Michael Geliot . . . has often been responsible for the other kind . . . Both kinds of presentation are valuable – what the pampered London visitor may deem just another decent *Bohème* or *Barber* or *Fidelio* is after all needed basic repertory, and besides, it may include splendid things such as Gwyneth Jones's first Leonore – but of course the second attracts more attention, and is likely to prove more exciting."

While there was no doubt that the season was extremely successful both artistically and at the box-office, WNO's financial position was worsening at an alarming rate. Even before the curtain went up, it was known that the season would end with a loss. In an effort to save costs a new production of *The Magic Flute* had been cancelled (a raffle designed to raise the £10,000 required for the production had had to be postponed because so few tickets had been sold). The production schedule had already been pruned as hard as was consistent with the maintenance of standards but the constantly increasing travelling and production costs throughout the year had taken WNO heavily into the red; the overdraft had risen to an alarming £100,000 and the banks were demanding that at least £50,000 should be repaid immediately. As Margaret Moreland pointed out, professionalisation meant that everything now had to be paid for; no longer could willing volunteers be relied upon to make costumes, to help with painting scenery, to sing in performances. "The Arts Council has been good enough to make advance grants in this financial year, but even so . . . I am not very optimistic about carrying on until the end of March," she told a reporter in October. Repaying the banks out of advance grants would, if the commitments to visit Manchester, Southampton, Swansea, Birmingham, Leeds and Sunderland were honoured, leave a deficit of up to £70,000. Frank Brown, the Appeals Director, was having as much success at raising money privately as his predecessors had had. Of the 800 businessmen and companies he had written to, many of them national and international, ninety percent had failed to reply, and those who did had either pleaded poverty or sent only a miserly £10 donation. The amount raised by October had not even covered the costs of printing and postage. A massive public appeal was immediately launched for funds to make up the shortfall. Harlech Television produced a documentary on WNO's plight entitled "The Beggars Opera?" Advertisements in the press and letters sent to all the members of the Opera Club (which had been renamed the Friends of the Opera) begged everyone concerned about WNO's fate to invite 20 people into their homes to watch the transmission and collect ten shillings a head for the appeal. Robert Graves, from his home in Majorca, generously sent the manuscript of a poem he had written in Wales to be auctioned, old-age pensioners sent postal orders, school children gave their pocket money, but the overall result was negligible and by December the total raised stood at less than £14,000. Several local councils were also threatening to withhold their grants because, at the Arts Council's suggestion, their issue of complimentary tickets had been withdrawn so that there would be more to sell at the box-office. At a time when WNO was at its height both in stature and in its ability to bring in audiences, it was faced with the stark fact that unless an answer to its problems could be found, there was no alternative but to close down.

One advantage of the adverse publicity was that the Welsh Parliamentary Party, led by Ifor Davies, the MP for Gower, became involved in the cause. On 24 November, Lockhart, Francis, and Bob Bazley, WNO's Treasurer, travelled to Westminster to give Welsh MPs a full appraisal of the situation. The deficit, the MPs were told, had been incurred by success. The expansion plan had been launched and then grants frozen for three years, and yet, ironically, WNO was more in demand than ever. The autumn season in Cardiff had broken box-office records; Birmingham had played to 95 percent capacity after breaking all advance booking records for the

Alexandra; the first appearance in Manchester for seventeen years, where both Glyndebourne and Sadler's Wells had played to small houses, had produced record receipts for opera. The same story was true in Leeds and the reaction in Southampton had been equally encouraging. (It was in Southampton that the only critical note of WNO's work had been sounded: a woman had enquired whether there were elephants to be seen in *Aida* and on being told that there were not, had demanded her money back!) Lockhart went on to outline the difficulties that not having enough money placed on an opera company. It was costing £250,000 a year to keep going and every performance needed, on average, a subsidy of £2000. As an example, he cited the Llandudno season, which had played to three-quarters of capacity and, because of higher seat prices, had taken more money than ever before; the shortfall on the fortnight had been £20,000. Without a realistic grant, it was impossible to plan too far ahead, and that meant Wales would be deprived of seeing artists such as Geraint Evans, Gwyneth Jones and Tito Gobbi because contracts could not be signed until too late. To stay in business, WNO needed £150,000 immediately and its grant for the following year doubled to £320,000. Few of the MPs had realised just how bad things were and they promised to do everything within their power to find a solution.

Within the next few days, three deputations went to the Welsh Office to seek additional Treasury funding, but each time it was pointed out that, in spite of the earnest desire of everyone to see a thriving Welsh National Opera, the government, as a matter of policy, had no say in how the Arts Council allocated its money. Finally, the MPs went to see Lord Goodman, Chairman of the Arts Council. Against all expectations, he promised that help would be forthcoming. There was no question, he stressed, of WNO going out of existence and ways would be found to pay off the deficit. Two days later, on 16 December, Lord Eccles, the Minister for the Arts, announced in the Lords that the government would be giving a further £2.6 million to the Arts Council, part of which would be used to rescue WNO. Everything possible was being done, he said, to save WNO, "one of the greatest opera companies in the world."

The following day, WNO's annual general meeting took place. Alfred Francis had been preparing to announce that the company could no longer continue trading, that the following year's work had been cut to three two-week seasons (in Cardiff, Swansea and Bristol) and that preparations were being put in hand for its winding up. Instead he was able to announce that the deficit had been written off and that the proposed visit to Eastbourne in January 1971 and the small-scale Welsh tour in February would now take place, though only to Haverfordwest and Aberystwyth. Colonel Crawshay, Chairman of the Welsh Arts Council, who had announced the news of the emergency grant, commented that only half the battle had been won. "There is a public demand in England for the Welsh Opera to tour," he said in a public statement, "and money is needed for that. Also we hope that local authorities will give the company more through their church tithe funds (which are separate from the rates) and that really prosperous friends of the Welsh National Opera both inside and outside Wales will give financial help to this very fine company."

Although the Arts Council had cleared off the deficit, it was not prepared to disclose the size of the grant for 1971 nor how favourably the request for a minimum figure of £325,000 would be viewed, and yet the spring season was drawing closer. WNO did, however, know that it would be receiving the same allocation as before from the Welsh Arts Council, and although plans for additional weeks in both Swansea and Cardiff had been abandoned and nothing was confirmed beyond the middle of May, the spring visits to Cardiff, Swansea and Bristol, to include the new production of *The Magic Flute*, went ahead. "These are appallingly difficult times for the company," Francis declared with supreme understatement. At the press conference outlining these plans, Francis drew attention to the reality of the situation. If additional funding was not found, not only would operations for the year have to be curtailed severely, there was, yet again, a very real possibility that WNO would have to close. The alternatives were to limit itself to a season in Cardiff and touring within Wales only; to become a festival company similar to Glyndebourne, or to revert to being entirely amateur. None of these alternatives was considered satisfactory.

From its earliest days, the history of Welsh National Opera had been a story of constant underfunding and the struggle to survive. Somehow the various crises had been overcome, but this time it was different and gradually people outside WNO became aware that it was not just bluff. The Welsh Members of Parliament had been amongst the first to respond, applying what pressure they could in London, and Raymond Gower, the Member for Barry, went further by introducing a private member's bill to allow local authorities and councils to contribute more than the statutory 2.5p maximum to WNO from the rates. In April, shortly before the spring Cardiff season was due to open, the appeal fund suddenly received a flood of money, bringing the total raised to £32,415, the majority contributed over a few days. An opera ball in Cardiff raised £400, £700 came from the Llandudno branch of the Friends, £400 from the Monmouthshire branch, £2000 from the *Western Mail*, £2500 from the Musicians' Union. Tickets for the abortive raffle had suddenly been sold and had raised a further £5000. It was this money that enabled the new production of *The Magic Flute* to be staged.

Produced by Michael Geliot and conducted by James Lockhart, *The*

*Magic Flute* opened in Cardiff on 19 April. Geliot could be relied upon to provide a fresh approach and this he did by setting the production in the South American jungle, the exoticism of which was richly evoked by Roger Butlin's designs. Papageno (beautifully sung by Thomas Allen) was portrayed as a noble, half-dressed savage (there were queues backstage to help Allen with his body make-up). The wise, enlightened civilisation of the 16th century Incas was threatened by the invasion of dark superstition in the form of the Catholic church. Monostatos (a very striking performance from Alexander Oliver) became a rascally monk, the Queen of the Night a painted processional Madonna and the three Ladies predatory nuns in, as Rodney Milnes described them, "early stages of decomposition." It was an interpretation which did not endear itself to everyone. "Mozart's vision of the battle between darkness and light is diminished rather than enhanced by this facile anti-clericalism," concluded Milnes, but even he was forced to admit that within its own context the production was lively and dramatically effective. While most of Geliot's touches were imaginative, not everything worked. The trial scene (with Tamino and Pamina mounting pedestals and standing there) went for little, although a sense of danger was glimpsed when Margaret Price (Pamina) unintentionally fell and bruised her leg as the result of a mis-timed scene shift. On opening night the lighting cues also went wrong. "It was," wrote Andrew Porter in the *Financial Times*, "a patchy performance, which touched greatness at times . . . and was pretty rough in others." Thomas Allen's Papageno took time to establish a relationship with the audience in his comic asides (delivered in Geliot's updated translation with a Geordie accent) but of the quality of his singing there was no doubt: "the best non-German Papageno I have seen for some time," enthused John Higgins in the *Times*. Margaret Price was an unaffected Pamina, pouring forth steady, pure and flawless tone, Keith Erwen a strong, direct Tamino and Glynne Thomas a first-rate Speaker. Clifford Grant contributed a noble Sarastro, there was a genuinely funny Papagena from Lillian Watson and the chorus was outstanding. The only real disappointment was Jessica Cash's undersung Queen of the Night. The orchestra, after an undistinguished overture, responded to Lockhart's capable direction with some stylish playing.

Performances of *Aida*, *Simon Boccanegra*, *The Barber of Seville* and *Boris Godunov* completed the fortnight, which was followed by visits to Bristol and Swansea. The arrival of the Arts Council grant, although much smaller than requested, meant that the remainder of the year could continue as planned, and in June a fortnight was played in Llandudno. Fears that the change of month from the traditional August would result in much smaller houses were not borne out. Advance bookings were as high as ever and the season, consisting of *The Magic Flute*, *Aida*, *Boris Godunov*, *Simon*

*Boccanegra* and *The Barber of Seville*, played to near-capacity. The season also saw the start of what were to become regular features of WNO's visits to North Wales: workshops, with musical illustrations, to explain the productions in the repertoire. One hundred people enrolled for the first all-day event in Rhyl (organised by Workers' Educational Association tutor Rufus Adams, whose brainchild it was) to hear Lockhart talking generally about opera, Geliot on *The Magic Flute*, Moody on *Simon Boccanegra* and an informal concert by WNO soloists including Margaret Price.

The autumn season in Cardiff opened with a revival of *Falstaff* starring Geraint Evans and conducted by Franco Mannino. Mannino, who had arranged and conducted the score for the film *Death in Venice*, was making his British debut. Evans, in splendid voice, "shouted and hammered more outrageously than was good for Verdi or this singer's art, but always to exhilarating effect," wrote William Mann in the *Times*. "Delme Bryn-Jones was the new Ford, Johanna Peters, Mistress Quickly, and Elizabeth Robson, Nannetta. Mannino in the pit was not entirely successful, frequently allowing the orchestra to race away."

Mannino achieved greater success later in the season with a lively *Aida* in which his Italian compatriot Renato Francesconi sang Radames. It proved impossible to judge Francesconi's ability, for it was obvious from his first notes that he was suffering from bronchial trouble and by the end of the performance he was hardly singing at all. His place in the remaining performances was taken by Luigi Ottolini.

The highlight of the Cardiff season was the British première of Alban Berg's *Lulu*. Lockhart had wanted to stage a work which, by moving away from the familiar territory of Verdi, would show the direction in which he believed WNO ought to go whilst at the same time changing the public image of the company, and the opera he chose was Berg's incomplete masterpiece. Many people considered the choice to be suicidal at a time of financial crisis.

*Lulu*, translated by Stuart Hood and Richard Armstrong, received long and intense preparations. Cast in the taxing title role, one of the longest and most difficult in all opera, was Carole Farley, a 24-year-old former Miss Junior America from Moscow, Iowa, who had made her operatic debut in Vienna only two years earlier. The role of Alwa was given to Nigel Douglas, one of the few British tenors capable of sustaining the fiendishly difficult high passages. In the months leading up to the production, Douglas was working in Zürich (as was American John Modenos, the Dr Schön) and Armstrong, who taught their roles to all the principals with the exception of Lulu herself, commuted to Switzerland regularly to coach Douglas and Modenos. Douglas remembers the rehearsal period as being extremely difficult. "It was a way-out work, very challenging, but everyone knew that something special was under way – that if we could get it right, it would explode into life."

Part of the difficulties with *Lulu* stemmed from the large number of principals required and from the fact that Berg's widow would not permit the final act to be completed. Producer Michael Geliot decided to play it as music theatre, taking as his cue the circus prologue and reworking the third act using the composer's completed *Lulu Suite*. It was a gripping concept, supported by Ralph Koltai's imaginative steel-and-mesh sets and Freda Blackwood's striking costumes. On opening night, the cast seemed to be more concerned with getting the notes right than with interpretation, and only Stuart Kale (the Prince), Noreen Berry (Countess Geschwitz) and Eric Garrett (Schigolch) were entirely at ease with the music. Carole Farley looked perfect and "she can sing the part, too, but at present strains her higher tones (much demanded by Berg) into anti-sexual screaming; some men's switch-on, perhaps, not mine," wrote William Mann. Nigel Douglas (who remembers that during their love-making scene Farley, who has perfect pitch, was giving him his notes) sang and characterised Alwa strongly, making every word tell. He made, wrote Ronald Crichton, "a more definite impression than most tenors do" in the role. The real triumph of *Lulu*, however, was the teamwork in which everyone was clearly working towards a goal. It was an exciting evening, conducted with skill and conviction by Lockhart. "This is James Lockhart's grandest adventure as Musical Director of the company," concluded Mann. "If it fell short of optimistic expectation, it was still full of promise and a feat to be congratulated already." "*Lulu* confers on the WNO a visiting card which they can confidently leave with any operatic Intendant abroad," wrote Felix Aprahamian. Far from being an act of suicide, *Lulu* was an act of faith on the part of everyone concerned, especially Lockhart, which represented a major landmark in WNO's history. The entire company had been stretched right up until opening night, and had emerged triumphant. "There was a sense of make-or-break about that first night and I didn't know until the end whether we could bring it off or not," recalls Armstrong, who had spent almost nine months working on the production. "When the performance was over, there was a party. I was still so involved with what had happened on stage that I walked the streets for half-an-hour before I dared go or even speak to anyone." *Lulu* had shown what could be achieved by an ensemble company using techniques which had not been seen in WNO productions before; and yet, in spite of the sustained applause that greeted the first night, not everyone approved of the opera. Several regulars walked out complaining of filth, but their loss was balanced by a new, younger audience and it was this new element that WNO was determined to attract in future.

The future, however, was far from secure. WNO was still having to live from day to day. The Arts Council grant for 1971/72 had been £187,000, including £60,000 from the Arts Council in London for touring in England. Together with revenue from the box-office and other sources, the total income for the year was £281,000, an improvement on the previous year, but still insufficient to meet an expenditure of just over £300,000. As part of the conditions attaching to the writing-off of the £150,000 overdraft, the Arts Council had insisted that there should be no deficit budgeting, and the government had warned that, no matter what happened, they would not under any circumstances bail them out a second time.

It was still in a state of financial uncertainty that WNO, following the Cardiff season, set out on a two-month DALTA-backed tour to seven English cities. Prior commitments meant that several cast changes had to be made, and no tour was ever free from occasions when an artist fell ill and a replacement had to be found. The previous year in Southampton, a sore throat had prevented Joyce Blackham from making her debut as Amneris and Lyne Dourian, a principal mezzo at the Paris Opéra, had been flown in to take her place; in Leeds, when Pauline Tinsley was forced to withdraw from *Aida* at the last moment, the only replacement who could be found was Margaret Tynes, an American living in Italy. Fog in Milan prevented Miss Tynes's plane from leaving on time and she arrived in Leeds only an hour before curtain-up to be met by touring manager Ian Keith in his battered old car. They braved the rush hour to reach the theatre in time for the performance to begin as scheduled. During the 1971 tour it was Elizabeth Tippett who saved the day by appearing for Alison Hargan as Pamina in Birmingham, and Julian Moyle who stood in for Thomas Allen in *The Barber* in Liverpool. There was also a fair share of things going wrong on stage because of working in unfamiliar theatres without adequate time to rehearse. In the performance of *The Barber* in Leeds, Ramon Remedios hit a fountain cherub with his cloak and dislodged it so that it played water not into the pool but onto the stage for the rest of the scene. It was, commented a local critic, the highlight of a performance which was otherwise unmemorable. But the accolade for *the* disaster of the tour has to go to the performance of *Falstaff* in Oxford. During the scene in which Geraint Evans was bundled into the basket and tipped through the window into the Thames, the window refused to open. Everybody thought somebody else had undone the travelling clamps, and no one had. The ladies simply had to put the basket back down on the stage and carry on as if it wasn't there. James Lockhart, who was conducting, was absolutely furious and at the end of the performance seized the hapless John Moody and attempted to throttle him!

The tour finished in Sunderland and ended a year in which WNO, still teetering on the brink of extinction, had played a total of eighteen weeks.

# CHAPTER FOURTEEN: 1972–1973

O<small>N 26 J</small>ANUARY 1972 the Lord Mayor of Cardiff, Alderman Ferguson Jones, called a meeting of fifty officials from the nineteen Welsh local authorities to appeal for £100,000 to help WNO out of its financial difficulties. "Unless the company's financial dilemma can be solved there is little hope of the Opera being able to make the progress rightly expected of them in new productions appearing regularly," Alfred Francis told the meeting. Box-office receipts had already reached near-saturation, and without new productions "a fall in support for the company would then follow as surely as night follows day." WNO, he continued, would prefer a planned winding up rather than stagnation. "Art must move forward as a creative force or stand still and become a folk culture relying upon endless repetition." Having become part of the Welsh way of life, WNO must, he said, replenish its repertoire faster than ever before; its ambition was no fewer than four new productions in each of the next three years. His words, backed by the enthusiastic support of Alderman Jones, produced a sympathetic response, and a target of £80,000 was agreed. Collecting it was a different matter. Several councils refused point blank to donate anything to an organisation which, they claimed, did nothing for them, and many Welshmen would actually have welcomed the opera company's demise. A small glimmer of hope came with the news that the Welsh Arts Council, recognising "a very efficient and economic organisation whose record in tight budgeting is equal to, and probably better, than any other in Britain," was planning to increase its annual grant to £210,000, a rise of 12.5 percent.

While the problems of finance continued to occupy the administration in Cardiff, the short Welsh tour opened in February 1972 at Haverfordwest with John Moody's new production of *Rigoletto*. Terence Sharpe sang the title role, and Elizabeth Lane, a promising member of the Chorale who had won the Geneva Prize the previous year, took her first important role as Gilda. Keith Erwen sang the Duke, David Gwynne, Sparafucile, and another member of the Chorale, Bridget Bartlam, Maddalena. The musical side, under James Lockhart, had been soundly prepared. The audience gave it a tumultuous reception as they did *The Marriage of Figaro* the following evening.

From Haverfordwest, the tour continued to Aberystwyth, Wrexham and Rhyl. It had been a bitterly cold winter and neither travelling nor performing was easy. In Haverfordwest, the St David's Day performance of *Rigoletto* had to be cancelled because of a power cut, and it was so cold in Rhyl that the orchestra wore overcoats throughout the performance.

The second new production of the year was of *Turandot*, which opened the spring season in Cardiff on 24 April. Produced by Michael Geliot, with designs by Alexander McPherson, this was the first new production to be entrusted to Assistant Musical Director Richard Armstrong, largely as a result of his successful work on *Lulu*. Singing the title role for the first time in her career was the ever popular Pauline Tinsley. William Johns, last seen in *Aida*, returned from the Bremen Opera to sing Calaf, and Yvonne Fuller, whose first appearance with WNO had been as Cherubino in *The Marriage of Figaro* on the short tour, sang Liù.

Geliot's production, wrote Elizabeth Forbes in *Opera*, brilliantly solved all the mechanical problems of Puccini's unfinished work, and most of the psychological ones, too, though the central paradox remained: "After the death of Liù, the drama is over and no amount of sumptuous singing in the final duet can disguise the fact. Up to that point, Geliot and his designer, Alexander McPherson, never put a foot wrong." The action took place on a steeply raked set, painted to look like burnished copper, which was dominated in the first act by a huge gong and in the riddle scene by the tiered wedding-cake throne of the Emperor. Around these central symbols, the crowds swarmed effectively, at times masked by gauzes and banners which sealed off the front and centre of the stage. "The lighting, plotted with stunning virtuosity by Robert Bryan, constantly changed with the shifting mood of the music." Not everyone approved of the gauzes, and the tight lighting cues, with the almost inevitable imprecision of a first night, tended to irritate some critics. The overall impression, however, was that Geliot had succeeded admirably in capturing the essence of the work and in translating it to a small stage. "In all, this is one of Geliot's finest Welsh National productions," concluded Malcolm Boyd in the *Musical Times*. It took this production to remind those critics who knew the work only from Covent Garden that the chorus, increased in numbers to 100 for the occasion, is the real protagonist of the piece. They sang magnificently. "The precision and brightness of the women's voices, the warmth and fullness of tone of the men's, provided a most impressive quality and volume of sound that . . . was all but overwhelming," commented Forbes. The sectional rehearsals for both chorus and orchestra, upon which Armstrong had insisted, more than paid off. Armstrong, displaying remarkable assurance, conducted a fluent and idiomatic performance which was rightly hailed as a personal triumph.

The following night, Moody's production of *Rigoletto* was seen in Cardiff for the first time. A cramped feeling that had been noted at Haverfordwest disappeared in the New Theatre, and Moody's intention, to show Rigoletto as a revolutionary against the establishment, was seen more clearly. Delme Bryn-Jones, taking over in the title role, sang powerfully and excitingly until towards the end of the evening when bronchial trouble began to overtake him. Lockhart conducted a strong, sensibly balanced and thoroughly enjoyable performance, though his inclination towards slow tempi occasionally proved difficult for the singers.

Lockhart was in the pit again the following evening for *Aida* with Grace de la Cruz and a new tenor singing his first Radames, Kenneth Collins. Since his first WNO appearance in the 1963 production of *The Seraglio*, Collins had continued singing in the chorus at Covent Garden and working hard to improve his voice. His big chance came in December 1970 when he stood in as a late replacement for Robert Thomas as Arturo opposite Beverly Sills in *Lucia di Lammermoor*. In the audience that night was an executive of WNO, and Collins was quickly offered a two-year contract as a principal. His Radames began nervously but soon improved and demonstrated that the Welsh had again "discovered" a major talent.

Both *Turandot* and *Aida* were sung in Italian, a fact that brought considerable criticism from those who felt that Welsh National Opera should sing in Welsh and from those who felt that all provincial performances of opera ought to be in the language of the majority of the audience – that is, English. While Lockhart had considerable sympathy for the latter view, he felt strongly that if WNO was to become international, it had to attract international artists; and in the economic climate of the time, that meant performing in the language of the original so that singers who did not have the time or inclination to learn a role in English could still be engaged. His point of view was borne out the following night when *Falstaff* was revived, in Italian, with Tito Gobbi. Gobbi's reason for consenting to appear in Wales was, as he put it quite simply, Jimmy Lockhart. He had been singing at Covent Garden on the night Lockhart had made his conducting debut there, and had followed his subsequent career with great interest. Shortly after Lockhart's appointment as Musical Director, Gobbi had expressed a wish to sing in Wales. With his appearances booked far in advance and WNO's constant financial crisis not permitting singers to be engaged far into the future, the prospect had seemed highly unlikely. But then Lockhart had visited Gobbi in Venice and asked him how serious he was. Very, Gobbi replied. Dates, of course, proved a problem, but Gobbi had cleared his diary especially. To acquire him was a major coup for Lockhart; it demonstrated to people beyond the borders of Wales, and outside the British Isles, that Welsh National Opera was a force to be reckoned with, and that a star with an international reputation need not fear for it by being seen in Wales.

It was Gobbi's first operatic appearance in Wales, although he had given a recital at the Empire Theatre in 1953, and he was in fine form. The other cast members were in no way eclipsed by his presence. Elizabeth Vaughan radiated assurance and good humour as Alice, Johanna Peters was an imposing Mistress Quickly and Terence Sharpe sang Ford's monologue with a real feeling of despair. Elizabeth Robson was a sweet Nannetta and Wynford Evans as Fenton sang lyrically. The smaller roles were well characterised by David Gwynne, Robert Thomas, Edward Byles and Noreen Berry, and Lockhart in the pit ensured an integrated performance. "For sheer energy, high spirits and enjoyment, without a trace of vulgarity," wrote Elizabeth Forbes in *Opera*, "this was a *Falstaff*, as well as a Falstaff, that would be very hard to beat." It was interesting for Welsh audiences to be able to compare their own Geraint Evans with Gobbi in a role with which they were both so much associated. Evans was, perhaps, more comic than Gobbi, which appealed to a great many people, but for many others Gobbi, in the autumn of his career and singing a character in the autumn of his life, got deeper beneath Falstaff's skin. In the end, it came down to personal preference. Gobbi so enjoyed his stay with the Welsh and was so impressed by the working atmosphere that he refused to accept his full fee and donated part of it to the Appeal Fund.

There were cast changes, too, for *The Magic Flute*, conducted by Anthony Hose. From the original cast, Thomas Allen was again the quick-witted Papageno around whom the production flowed, Keith Erwen, Tamino, and Glynne Thomas, the Speaker. Of the newcomers, Stafford Dean sang Sarastro, Alison Hargan, winner of both the Kathleen Ferrier and Cinzano prizes, sang Pamina, Margaret Haggart, the young Australian winner of the Sun Aria competition, the Queen of the Night, Terence Walters, Monostatos, and Celia Jeffreys, Papagena. It remained a spontaneous and inventive production and attracted the biggest demand for tickets, notwithstanding the appearances of Tito Gobbi in *Falstaff*. Critics were quick to point out that it was given in English.

Following the Cardiff fortnight, the company set out on tour to Bristol, Swansea and Llandudno. The move of the Llandudno season to June had not been entirely successful. Although box-office takings had stayed constant during the two previous seasons, that was due entirely to an increase in the higher seat prices: the number of people attending performances had actually fallen. In addition to the new productions of *Turandot* and *Rigoletto*, *The Magic Flute* and *Aida* (with Maria Pelligrini in the title role) were also given, plus two performances of *Don Giovanni*, revived after an interval of four years. Forbes Robinson and John Gibbs sang Giovanni and Leporello, Carole Farley sang Donna Anna, Yvonne Fuller, Donna Elvira, and Stuart Kale, Don Ottavio. During the second performance, David Gwynne, the Commendatore, fell six feet from his pedestal and broke a bone in his foot. In spite of being in great pain, he continued singing to such effect that some people in the audience who did not know the opera thought his fall was part of the production.

For some time, Lockhart and Armstrong had been wanting to stage an opera by Benjamin Britten. Their first choice had always been *Peter Grimes*, but this had proved impracticable and they turned their attention instead to *Billy Budd*, Britten's second opera, written for the 1951 Festival of Britain. The success of *Lulu*, generally considered to be "inaccessible" for the general public, convinced them that the time was right to stage an opera by Britain's most distinguished living composer.

A strong cast of guest principals and company artists was assembled for the production by Michael Geliot. Forbes Robinson, who had sung the role more times than any other singer and was generally considered to be its finest exponent, was cast as Claggart, the evil Master-at-Arms, Nigel Douglas as the upright Captain Vere and in the role of Billy was a former Welsh contract artist who had recently left to join Covent Garden (where his first role, incidentally, was Donald in *Billy Budd!*), Thomas Allen. When offered the role by Lockhart, Allen had serious doubts. "I took one look at the part," he recalls, "and went straight back to Jimmy [Lockhart] and said I can't do this, it's too much for me. He replied that they would not have given it to me if they didn't think I could do it. So I did it."

By the time rehearsals began, Allen was working at Glyndebourne. He remembers travelling to Cardiff to start rehearsals. "I walked into the studio and saw the set. As soon as I saw it I thought to myself, 'This piece is going to be a success; we can't fail.' Roger Butlin's set was so wonderful that we would have been idiots not to make it work. When rehearsals started, everyone, from Geliot down, found the work fascinating and stimulating. It was just like preparing for the launch of a ship itself, with everyone working towards getting the boat on the slipway."

Teamwork and meticulous preparation were the keys to the production's success. Geliot had eschewed a revolutionary approach to the work, opting instead for a scrupulously realistic representation of life aboard an English man-o'-war in the 1790s. He not only went deeply into the characterisation of the principals (generally accepted to be a flaw in the piece) and made them work, he also gave every member of the augmented all-male chorus something to do so that they became members of a ship's crew. "Undercurrents of character and emotion were precisely caught, in a glance here, a sudden stiffening or a catch of the breath there," noted Stanley Sadie in the *Times*. Geliot captured perfectly the claustrophobia of life on board ship, and in this he was helped enormously by Roger Butlin's superb set, a cross-section of a warship which gave the audience an immediate feeling they were on board. "Geliot has followed the composer's and librettists' directions faithfully yet imaginatively," wrote Rodney Milnes in *Opera*. "The characterization and mechanics of this very difficult opera are carefully worked out, and handled with skill and sensitivity . . . a masterly realization. Roger Butlin's exceptionally well thought-out sets and costumes indicate many hours well spent in the National Maritime Museum. There is a gauze throughout (which may worry some, but not me) in the manner of an 18th century print, and the backcloth is given the cracked varnish patina of a nautical seascape. Both are beautifully painted."

The production opened the Cardiff season on 25 September. Almost everyone who saw it that night, and subsequently as the performances grew in stature and confidence, says it is the best staging of the opera that has yet been seen, and it was not the most expensive by a long way. Thomas Allen *was* Billy Budd. "His warm and fluent singing matched his unaffected acting," commented Milnes. Nigel Douglas, not thought by some to be ideal casting as Captain Vere, sang with a conviction and authority which were completely in character, while Forbes Robinson sang Claggart with utter sincerity and great beauty, though his acting, more used to the generous expanses of Covent Garden, was felt to be perhaps a trifle overpowering on the smaller Cardiff stage. All the supporting roles were ably taken, with Bryan Drake (Flint), John Gibbs (Donald), Stuart Kale (Red Whiskers) and Eric Roberts (the Novice's friend) outstanding.

In spite of some roughness in places, the Welsh Philharmonia, inspired by a fervent and committed Lockhart, found itself swept up by the atmosphere and played as it had never played before. The evening was a complete vindication of the choice of a Britten opera and of the role of Welsh National Opera in the musical life of Britain. There was still the nagging feeling that Scottish Opera, which had celebrated its tenth anniversary in April, was receiving the better publicity, and if the Welsh wanted to demonstrate its belief in which really was the best company in Britain, it could not have chosen a better way.

To show just how far WNO had progressed, and taken audiences with it, the season included a revival of *Lulu* with the original cast. Fears that this might prove to be under-rehearsed and hasty were quickly dispelled. The individual interpretations had grown in stature, and the two performances of the opera demonstrated that WNO could now pass that major test of artistic resources: a satisfactory revival of an earlier success.

Just in case *Budd* and *Lulu* should not prove popular at the box-office, that old standby *Nabucco* was also revived with Terence Sharpe as

Nabucco, Victor Godfrey as Zaccaria, Milla Andrew as Abigail, Kenneth Collins as Ishmael and Sandra Browne from Trinidad, the 24-year-old winner of the Kathleen Ferrier Award, making an auspicious operatic debut as Fenena. Also in the season were *The Magic Flute*, with Julian Moyle taking over as Papageno, *Don Giovanni* and *Turandot*. Like all revivals at that time, *Turandot*, having opened in Cardiff in the spring and been played on tour in May and June, went on without a dress rehearsal. The conductor was again Richard Armstrong. "The first act is very complicated," he recalls, "and I was, I suppose, a little nervous and apprehensive. I stormed into the orchestra pit determined to have a jolly good go and gave a strong downbeat completely forgetting that the show began with a blackout. The stage management should have reminded me, of course, but they didn't. They probably thought we'd done so many performances I knew it, but that's just the sort of thing you forget in the heat of the moment. I gave my downbeat just as the lights went out in the pit. One or two members of the orchestra didn't play, but most of them did. We had a very solid first note which petered away as everything ground to a halt. The curtain went up, the pit lights came on again, and we started. By then I was a heap of jelly and I conducted the whole of the first act hanging onto the conducting desk." Later in the performance, one of the bars holding a banner descended onto the stage as Ping, Pong and Pang were singing. It missed them all, landing at their feet. The action then required them to come downstage. Two of them managed to step over the bar without mishap, but the third, who was moving a shade slower, was astride it as it began its ascent, much to the amusement of the audience. At the end of the act, there was a further mishap with the gong. "During all this, it was fairly difficult getting the music impeccably correct," remembers Armstrong. "I left the podium at the end of the act and wanted to leave the theatre. Pauline Tinsley, who was singing Turandot, gave me a large brandy to get me back on, the only time I have ever had a drink during a performance." The third act was negotiated without any further traumas and the evening ended in triumph.

The season had been amongst the most varied and rewarding ever staged and the three weeks played to 90 percent capacity. Most remarkable of all, perhaps, was that *Billy Budd* had been sold out and that people had had to be turned away at the box-office. The autumn tour to England – seven cities, a week in each – began immediately afterwards. The Sunderland date had been dropped, and in its place a visit had been arranged to Norwich where *Billy Budd* was honoured by a surprise visit from Benjamin Britten accompanied by Imogen Holst, the Artistic Director of the Aldeburgh Festival. Although the performance he saw was not one of the best, Britten expressed himself well satisfied. "It is marvellous," he told a local reporter, and he was generous in his praise of Thomas Allen. Both *Budd* and *Lulu* attracted large, enthusiastic houses wherever they were played, and the tour in general was well supported. At the annual general meeting in November, Alfred Francis was able to announce a remarkable turnaround in fortunes: the financial deficit for the previous year, after running at around £25,000 for four years and predicted as being as high as £50,000, had been cut to a mere £5000. As Francis pointed out, this was 1 percent of total turnover. The improvement was the result of two main factors: increased subsidies from the Welsh Arts Council and from Welsh local authorities, and an increase in box-office revenue due to the increased number of venues. It meant that the immediate future was, for the first time in more than four years, secure. However, to ensure survival it was absolutely essential that the number of playing weeks, the only way in which further income could be generated, should be increased. In August, James Mowat, whom Francis knew from the Old Vic, had been appointed General Manager. A 47-year-old Scot, Mowat had trained as an accountant and had worked extensively in theatre administration for the Howard and Wyndham touring empire in Scotland, at the Theatre Royal, Newcastle, and at the Old Vic, before becoming General Manager of Pay TV and then administrator of the Crafts Council. Whilst taking over responsibility for all matters of finance and administration, thus filling the gap left by the departure of Douglas Craig three years earlier, Mowat's priority was to expand the number of performing weeks to twenty-five. Together with a minimum of twelve weeks of rehearsal, WNO was. for the first time, approaching a full year's workload.

Francis also announced at the annual general meeting that the first overseas visit, a trip to Switzerland underwritten by the British Council, would take place in June the following year; and that an invitation to appear at the Proms had been accepted (although this was later called off because of the BBC's financial difficulties). "I am reasonably optimistic for this year and the next year for the first time," he said. The stage seemed set for one of the most successful periods in WNO's twenty-five year history.

But the problems were not yet over. Following the production of *Lulu* the previous year, Lockhart had received a semi-official approach to see if he would be interested in becoming Musical Director of the opera house in Kassel, Germany. He had turned the suggestion down, preferring to remain in Wales, but the Germans were insistent and invited him to Kassel to conduct a performance. Once he had seen the possibilities there, Lockhart's resolve began to waver. A few days after his return, he received a firm offer and an invitation to meet the Kassel Intendant in London. At the meeting, Lockhart agreed to accept the post, provided he could combine it with his duties in Wales. He fully expected the suggestion to be rejected, but, to his surprise, the Intendant agreed. Alfred Francis did not like the idea, having serious doubts as to whether Lockhart could combine the two jobs effectively, but both the orchestra and chorus felt that to have as their Musical Director the Musical Director of a German house would do nothing but reflect glory on WNO. And so Francis, somewhat reluctantly, agreed to an arrangement whereby Lockhart would take a cut in salary from WNO and divide his time equally between the two companies, with fifty performances a season in each place. At the age of 41, Lockhart became the first British conductor ever to hold such a position in Germany.

On 8 January 1973, as part of the Fanfare for Europe celebrations to mark Britain's entry into the European Economic Community, a concert was staged at the Capitol Theatre in Cardiff. The programme was planned to include, in the first half, Walton's *Belshazzar's Feast* and in the second Carl Orff's *Carmina Burana* with the choruses of WNO and Lockhart's other company in Germany combining to sing both works. After the programmes had been printed, the Kassel chorus announced that they had been unable to learn the Walton in time, so *Belshazzar's Feast* was replaced in the first half by Walton's overture *Portsmouth Point*, Britten's *Sinfonia da Requiem* and Wotan's Farewell from *Die Walküre*, sung by Forbes Robinson. *Carmina Burana*, with Robinson, Hildegard Uhrmacher, Kenneth Bowen and Julian Moyle as soloists, was performed as planned. Not everyone was happy to celebrate the event, however. During the concert, four people protesting against Britain's entry into the EEC were arrested.

Alfred Francis had been right to be cautious about the effects of Lockhart's appointment in Germany. Musically the development of WNO was at a crucial stage and needed a strong guiding hand. But Lockhart was spending so much time abroad that many people began to feel WNO was no longer his first concern. In December 1972 a deputation from the music staff had gone to Germany to urge him to return full-time. He was placed in a difficult position. He had lavished five years of love and affection on the Welsh, he had helped guide them through perilous waters and had seen them emerging as a fully professional company, the equal of any in Britain. He had no wish to leave WNO, but he had signed a four-year contract with the Kassel Opera. With great sadness, he wrote to the Board, explaining that under the circumstances he felt he could no longer continue as Musical Director.

The Board, with equal reluctance, accepted his resignation, to take effect in September 1973, and were faced with the problem of who should succeed him. Various names were mentioned, including some extremely eminent and unlikely foreign conductors, but Francis was determined not to upset the progress that had been made; an outsider might well have different views on how the company should proceed. To the surprise of the musical world, and of many members of WNO, the choice fell on Lockhart's assistant, Richard Armstrong, who at 30 became one of the youngest-ever musical directors of a British opera company. Few people outside Wales knew of Armstrong, and certainly as far as the general public was concerned he was just another promising young conductor, but both Lockhart, who had recommended the appointment in his letter of resignation, and Francis were convinced that he was the right man to carry on the work they had started.

Performances of opera began in February on the short spring tour with a revival of *Rigoletto* and a new production by Malcolm Fraser of *Madam Butterfly* designed by Shuhei Iwamoto, the first Japanese to design a production of *Butterfly* in Britain. Iwamoto, domiciled in London for the previous ten years, had started his professional career as a photographer before going on to study art. Fraser had by chance seen a poster he had designed for the visit of the Korean State Dancers to Sadler's Wells and decided to engage him to do his first stage production. Iwamoto set his designs in Japan of 1904, the year of the world première of *Madam Butterfly*, and every effort was made to make the stage picture authentic. Japan Airlines flew in the props and many of the costumes, and Iwamoto helped teach the chorus Japanese deportment: how to sit and walk properly, how to hold a fan and how to wear a kimono. His designs gave the work an authentic feel, and Fraser's production allowed the music to speak for itself. He was well served by his cast: Elizabeth Vaughan as Butterfly, Kenneth Collins as Pinkerton, Julian Moyle as Sharpless, Moira Griffiths as Suzuki and Arthur Davies, a young member of the Chorale, as Goro. The production, which opened in Haverfordwest, was conducted by James Lockhart, and he and the cast were applauded for fully ten minutes at the end.

After further performances in Aberystwyth, Wrexham and Rhyl (where Nina Stefanova took over as Cio-Cio-San) both productions were taken to the Theatre Royal in Bath, the first grand opera to be played there for twenty years. In *Butterfly*, Norma Newton, an American who had been heard by Lockhart at an opera workshop he had directed at Texas University and was then a principal soprano at Graz, made her first appearance with WNO in the title role and Henry Newman, a member of the Chorale, sang his first Sharpless. The same production opened the spring season in Cardiff, the last under Lockhart's direction, with Elizabeth Vaughan back in the title role. Also in the repertoire during the two week season were *Rigoletto*, *Turandot*, with Kenneth Collins sharing the role of Calaf with William Johns, *The Magic Flute*, which was distinguished by the brilliant conducting of György Fischer from Cologne, *Billy Budd*, with Terence Sharpe singing Billy and John Shaw as Mr Ratcliffe, and a new production of Verdi's *Don Carlos*.

*Don Carlos* was given in English, in a new translation commissioned from Andrew Porter, and was based on the four-act revision Verdi had made for La Scala in 1884. The opening Fontainebleau scene was omitted (not to everyone's pleasure) and several other minor cuts were made, thereby reducing the length to nearly four hours. Michael Geliot's naturalistic production proved to be well paced. It again had a single basic set designed by Annena Stubbs. This had been designed with the spectacular Act 2 *auto da fé* scene in mind, and the "scaffolding used to accommodate the company's large chorus in that scene became something of an embarrassment elsewhere, especially in the rather drab garden set," noted Malcolm Boyd. "There is surely something amiss when the palace dungeon emerges as the lightest and most spacious set in the whole piece," he concluded. Geliot had again gone for characterisation and for static groupings, lit as in the paintings of El Greco. The principals, warming to such an approach, sang with great vigour. Josephine Barstow, after appearing as Natasha in *War and Peace* and Violetta at the Coliseum, as Lady Macbeth on television and in *The Knot Garden* at Covent Garden, returned as an acknowledged star to sing an impressive and intense Elizabeth de Valois. "Barstow has not the range of colour, the flexibility or the sheer grandeur needed for Elizabeth's exhausting music," wrote Ronald Crichton of the *Financial Times*, "yet her singing is so intense, so musical, her depiction of the Queen's misery so convincing, that she seemed to me . . . to be the most touching exponent of the part since Gré Brouwenstijn." Keith Erwen, having made a sensational debut at the Coliseum in *Carmen* (which led one critic to say the opera should be renamed *Don José*) also returned to sing Carlos, and singing Philip was Forbes Robinson, fulfilling a lifelong ambition to sing the third of what he considered to be the three finest bass roles: Don Giovanni, Boris and now Philip (all, incidentally, performed for the first time with WNO). "His command of the role," wrote Crichton, "is impressively complete." Terence Sharpe as Posa, after a husky start and using a pause to cough significantly, was, at his best, thrilling and David Gwynne made a dignified Inquisitor. Janet Coster sang with immense gusto as Eboli. James Lockhart conducted with real feeling for the music and kept a good balance in the ensemble; "he obtained a committed performance from the Welsh Philharmonia and glorious singing from the chorus." The overall opinion was that the production was a triumph. "It is clear that the Welsh National attain standards as remarkable for their quality as their enterprise," remarked David Fingleton in the *Tatler*.

It had always been Bill Smith's ambition to take WNO on a foreign tour, to show continental Europe just how good the company was. There had been the offers to take the chorus to America, the suggestion that *Nabucco* should be performed in Israel, and half-a-dozen other proposed tours, none of which had come off. But in 1973, Welsh National Opera finally became international. On Friday, 22 June, 166 singers, musicians, backstage crew and administrators, accompanied by a delegation from the Development Corporation of Wales (which used the trip as an opportunity to invite Swiss businessmen to the performances as their guests before talking about business potential in Wales), flew out of Cardiff airport on two Viscounts bound for the Lausanne Festival in Switzerland. Two days earlier, the set for *Billy Budd*, all eight tons of it, had been taken by road.

The planes landed at Geneva in torrential rain, and in the rush to the coaches which were to take them on to Lausanne some members of the orchestra left their luggage behind, though none forgot their instruments. Accommodation in Lausanne, where, in addition to the Festival, the world judo championships were taking place, was scarce and the company were split over five hotels. Terence Sharpe sang the title role for the two Lausanne performances with the same cast as in Wales. The huge audience was overwhelmed by *Billy Budd* and by the superb choral singing, and both performances received sustained applause, with much cheering and shouting.

From Lausanne the company travelled to Zürich by road. The set was erected in the Opernhaus (the first custom-built opera house in which WNO had ever appeared) in a record two hours. Thomas Allen, who was appearing as Papageno at Glyndebourne, flew in on the morning of the performance to sing Billy, returning to England the following day. His model interpretation won the audience's warmest appreciation. The other principals also rose to the occasion, with Forbes Robinson's Claggart sending shivers down the spine and Nigel Douglas singing "a Vere in a million". James Lockhart, making his final appearance as Musical Director, went out in a blaze of glory, conducting an emotion-filled evening. "Last night the Welsh company not only furthered their own reputation, they also performed a service for modern British music . . . this was a triumph for the whole company," wrote Chris Stuart in the *Western Mail*. So successful was the Swiss visit that a suggestion was made that WNO might take part in the next Hong Kong Festival and an invitation was received to make a five-city tour of the United States in 1976.

One of the many highlights of the Swiss performances had been the superb playing of the Welsh Philharmonia which had now developed into a fine operatic orchestra. During that summer the players were offered their first permanent, full-time contracts. Some, who preferred the freelance life, did not accept, but the majority did, keeping much the same nucleus of players who had been in the orchestra since its formation. Since the operatic work the Philharmonia was required to do still left some 20 weeks free a year, the original proposal to fill in with concerts was revived. To get Wales used to the idea of having a fully-fledged symphony orchestra in its midst, three experimental concerts were arranged during the autumn season in Cardiff. On the last three Wednesdays of the month-long season (the longest ever staged in one theatre), instead of an opera the New was given over to an orchestral concert, each one beginning with a short piece by a living Welsh composer. At the debut concert on 26 September, John Metcalf's *Intrada* was given its world première; at the second, William Mathias's *Celtic Dances* and at the third, Hoddinott's 4th Symphony.

The season proper had opened on 18 September with Mozart's *Idomeneo*, produced by Michael Geliot and conducted by Richard Armstrong in his first season as Musical Director. It was a bold choice. Mozart's second opera had long been considered "difficult" to stage (because of its lack of dramatic action) and those difficulties were in evidence in Geliot's production. The opera (in a new translation by Eric Crozier, the librettist of *Billy Budd*) was given in the new edition which had been seen at Salzburg, using additional material discovered by the publishers, Bärenreiter, and keeping some of the changes Mozart himself had made for Vienna. It received mixed reviews. There was almost universal condemnation for the stark, metallic set by Jenny Beavan, "a blank back wall of silver rectangles, like a tray of Swiss bitter chocolate," was how William Mann described it, although he conceded that it did suggest the confined drama of the characters without matching the humanity of the music, except when the panels opened for special effects. The clanking of the set's component parts as they were shunted into position certainly did not help maintain concentration. There was praise, and condemnation, for Geliot's production in almost equal measure. Jeremy Noble of the *Sunday Telegraph* found the set "less destructive than the insensitivity or sheer perversity which has led Michael Geliot to produce several crucial passages, including the finales of all three acts, with a fine disregard for the meaning of words and music." Peter Heyworth of the *Observer* agreed: "At moments his lack of insight reaches grotesque proportions. A single example must suffice. In the final number of the second act the chorus sings 'Away, away,' and to make the point doubly plain, the closing bars end with a diminuendo. At Cardiff the chorus here stands motionless, so that the entire effect so clearly intended in the score is lost. Could lack of dramatic sensibility go further?" William Mann of the *Times*, however, found the production "visually most thoughtful, abundant in grand drama, which enlarges the conflicts of humanity and destiny," and Felix Aprahamian thought the choral tableaux stunning, highlighting the drama of an intrinsically static piece. Once more, in trying to produce a large-scale work in a manner suitable for touring, Geliot had attempted to throw the focus onto the characters, and while not everyone thought him entirely successful, most agreed with Ronald Crichton of the *Financial Times* that *Idomeneo* was "definitely worth seeing . . . this is more than a routine mounting of the piece." There was almost unanimous praise for the cast. Veteran tenor Alexander Young brought experience, artistry and understanding to the role of Idomeneo. Janet Price, in her first major role with the company, sang an accomplished Ilia. Anthony Roden sang well as Idamante, but did not prove to be sufficiently contrasted vocally with Young and his acting, not helped by his make-up or costume, was wooden. Rae Woodland, though lacking the power of former years, was a lyrical and dramatic Electra, while Alexander Oliver, in a brief but telling appearance, made people wish Arbace's second aria was heard more often. There was praise, too, for the excellent chorus, and the most impressive moments in the production were the crowd scenes "not merely due to acutely sensitive ensemble work from both the chorus and orchestra, but because movement was minimised to an occasional mass, stylised gesture." *Idomeneo* was generally thought to have been a disappointing opening to the season.

After revivals of *Madam Butterfly*, with Grace de la Cruz and Ermanno Mauro; *Rigoletto*, conducted for the first time by Julian Smith, a member of the music staff; and *Don Carlos*, with Evelyn Brunner making her British debut as Elizabeth de Valois, the second new production of the season opened on 4 October. This was of Bizet's *The Pearl Fishers*, which had not been seen in Britain since Sadler's Wells had staged it in the 1950s. Opening night coincided with the tenth anniversary of the New Theatre Trust, the body formed to save the theatre from closure. The choice of *The Pearl Fishers*, Bizet's first performed opera (though not the first he had written), was a deliberate attempt to revive those days when WNO had pioneered the early works of Verdi by looking at the less-well-known operas of a popular composer. Although most people knew the famous duet "Au fond du temple saint", a long-time favourite on radio request programmes, very few knew the complete work. It possesses an improbable plot "which leaves Hollywood standing in its crass emotionalism," as Helen Tentelow wrote in her review in the *Guardian*, but contains much music of great originality. The production reverted to the original 1863 score, giving what was believed to be its first performance since the première without the customary melodramatic trio added by Benjamin Godard for the final act. In its place a duet for Leila and Nadir, written by Bizet and scored (in the absence of the original orchestral material) by Arthur Hammond, was restored.

It was a perfect choice for Wales. "Plenty of chorus work, a small cast to budget for, and a finish before the last buses go," a friend commented perspicaciously to Stanley Sadie in the interval. David Atherton, a young member of the Covent Garden staff, was brought in to conduct.

The production by John Moody (who also supplied the translation with

Nell Moody) was well worked out in terms of character and relationships, and the chorus was effectively handled. "Only the dancing – a go-go version of the Turkish Delight advert – jarred," felt Tentelow. Sue Plummer's simple sets used the inescapable steel tubes so beloved by designers of that time, but, commented Stanley Sadie in the *Times*, "do so imaginatively, to make palm trees; otherwise the sets are plain but practical and evocative, and the costumes have style and well used colour. The make-up people did an excellent job in converting these Welsh into Sinhalese." The four principals, perhaps surprisingly, seemed the least assured element of the first night. If *The Pearl Fishers* demands anything, it is four superlative artists in the leading roles. Delme Bryn-Jones as Zurga (celebrating ten years since his debut with WNO) was the most accomplished, and Paul Hudson, another young singer on his way to the top, was a strong Nourabad; but both Kenneth Collins as Nadir and Barbara Shuttleworth, a young Canadian who had been scheduled to sing with WNO in 1970 but had been prevented for family reasons, as Leila, seemed below their best. The capacity audience, though, gave the performance a prolonged ovation, and Rodney Milnes, writing in the *Spectator*, was moved to say that he considered WNO "definitely the best regional buy in my admittedly limited experience. Unlike some, they do not aim too high and therefore have a better chance of avoiding the downward plummet into the muddy waters of prestige flops. *The Pearl Fishers*, their latest Cardiff offering, can be recommended without reservation."

The season ended with a revival of *Die Fledermaus*, which, in Geliot's production and George Melly's coarse translation, still seemed contrived and in poor taste. A welcome feature was the new Adele of Lillian Watson.

The Cardiff season had again proved attractive at the box-office and excellent houses were maintained on the autumn tour to Swansea, Bristol, Oxford, Liverpool, Manchester, Leeds, Birmingham, Norwich and Southampton, during which only *Billy Budd* and *Idomeneo* failed to draw large numbers. The previous year had ended with an overspend of £292, producing a total deficit of £12,391 (brought about by £47 less income from the box-office than had been budgeted for and smaller contributions from local authorities than had been anticipated). It was, however, expected that WNO would break even very soon and there was a buoyant optimisim about the future. The touring schedule was to be maintained and plans for two new productions each spring and autumn were announced.

The increase in touring, particularly within England, had placed a great strain on the members of the Voluntary Chorus. Recruiting new choristers had become almost impossible. Few young amateurs who were good enough were prepared to devote the time required to learning, rehearsing and performing operas with no more reward than expenses paid, compensation for loss of earnings (for those with regular jobs) and the opportunity of appearing with some of the finest singers on the British operatic stage. Since the formation of the professional Chorale in 1968, the strength of the Voluntary Chorus had dropped to sixty, many of them with twenty years or more of service, and some of them were, to be polite, a little long in the tooth. And they were not always available. Coaches were laid on to take them to English theatres for performances of the large-chorus works, but the number turning up would never be known until the last minute. When the coach arrived in Liverpool for a performance of *Nabucco*, there was only one bass on board. Together with the eight basses of the Chorale, that meant a work which was usually performed with at least twenty basses had only nine. In Sunderland, *Aida* was given with only three Voluntary Chorus tenors. When one of them, Cliff Williams, marched on at the head of his army, he was accompanied by one soldier! *Boris Godunov* was another opera frequently performed with half the chorus missing. A performance of *Turandot* in Norwich coincided with a rail strike on Eastern Region. So desperate was WNO for numbers that the curtain was held for a quarter of an hour while a taxi rushed three members of the Voluntary Chorus, who were making their way there independently, to the theatre. This was clearly not the way to run a professional opera company. Equity was still pressing for full professionalisation of the chorus, and the plans for four new operas a year meant that such haphazard arrangements could no longer be tolerated; the time had finally arrived to disband the Volunteers.

During the autumn tour, the news was broken that the services of the Voluntary Chorus would no longer be required and that from the spring of the following year, the chorus, its strength increased to forty-eight, would be entirely professional. Most volunteers were aware that this had to come but that did not reduce the sadness felt by many who had been with WNO since its formation. There was some talk of trying to form a group which would be run along the lines of the original WNO, but it remained only talk. The Volunteers' last appearance was in Southampton on Friday, 14 December 1973 in *Don Carlos*. It was an emotional evening. Peggy Moreland changed into costume and went on for her one and only stage appearance – though she had promised not to sing and only mimed. When the curtain came down, most people repaired to a pub or to their hotel bars and drank to the end of an era.

At a dinner for the Voluntary Chorus given at the Park Hotel the following March, Muriel Pointon, on behalf of the amateurs, made a speech in which she spoke of the pride they felt in "all the years spent building the company, and the great part played in finding the recognition it enjoys today." She paid tribute, too, to those many backstage helpers who had also given freely of their time and their love for no financial reward, and without whom the performances could not have taken place. "It is our heritage, gentlemen," she concluded, "I ask you – please guard it well." Barbara Harding, another Voluntary Chorus member of long standing, wrote an Ode which summed up the feelings of the many amateurs who had appeared with Welsh National Opera. It ended with the words:

> *The young professionals will never know,*
> *Through all the struggling we've had to go.*
> *The laughter, the jokes, the time freely given,*
> *To get to the Wells all the hours we have striven.*
> *So make way for the new, don't heave a sigh,*
> *It would not have been possible*
> *Without you and I.*

THE DEFICIT accumulated during 1973 had sounded a warning bell and in order to avoid further losses, the short small-scale Welsh tour, which had become the traditional opening of the year, was postponed at the beginning of 1974 for three months until the new grants came through. In its place, visits to Leicester and Peterborough, funded by DALTA and the Eastern Arts Association, were arranged. Leicester saw *The Magic Flute* and *La Bohème* (in what was virtually a new production, a restaging of Ande Anderson's original by Malcolm Fraser) with the Italian soprano Ileana Sinnone as Mimi making her British debut and Barbel Edwards singing her first Musetta. Peterborough saw the same two operas and Michael Geliot's new production of Donizetti's *L'Elisir d'Amore* (given in English as *The Elixir of Love*) with Forbes Robinson in excellent voice and high spirits as the itinerant quack Dulcamara, Lillian Watson as a delightful Giannetta, and Terence Sharpe as the bumptious Sergeant Belcore, a role he had previously sung at Glyndebourne. Making their debuts in principal roles were Arthur Davies as Nemorino and Susan Dennis as Adina.

Davies, a former factory draughtsman from Wrexham, had appeared with Opera for All before joining the Chorale and singing the occasional small role. He was already married before deciding to become an opera singer, and the move to Cardiff had meant keeping two homes going, something he could not afford on a chorister's salary. He bought an old van, converted it into a mobile home and parked it in Pontcanna Fields, where he slept in a sleeping-bag and lived on a diet of sausages and bacon. It was there, at a time he was thinking of giving up singing and returning home, that Richard Armstrong came to offer him a principal's contract. "I don't think," said Armstrong, "we can have a principal tenor living in a caravanette," and he offered Davies accommodation until he found somewhere for his family. Although his Nemorino was clearly the creation of an artist at the beginning of his career, it contained indications of the stature he would later attain. His singing of "Did not a tear unwillingly" earned him a well-deserved ovation. Geliot's assured production, complemented by Jenny Beavan's simple yet effective sets, captured the mood of *L'Elisir* perfectly; Anthony Hose conducted with fervour and the chorus clearly enjoyed themselves. The stars of the show for many, however, were the mechanical sheep which propelled themselves about the stage with rare abandon.

Although it was the first time grand opera had been staged in Peterborough for almost twenty years, and notwithstanding the close proximity of Cambridge, the nine-day visit was poorly supported. The opening night of *L'Elisir* played to a disappointingly small house; full houses for the two Saturday evening performances of *Magic Flute* and *La Bohème* failed to increase the overall attendance figures to anything approaching respectable. There had also been problems finding accommodation. The few local hotels were full up and the orchestra had had to be booked in outside the city. Used though WNO was to performing in less than perfect conditions, the theatre in Peterborough (a cinema adapted for the occasion) proved to be quite inadequate. Sets had to be stored in vans since there was no space on stage; the cramped dressing rooms were up two flights of stairs and the stage could only be reached through one tiny door. There was nothing to make WNO wish to return in future years. To cap the visit, the sets of *The Magic Flute* were destroyed when the van returning them to Cardiff caught fire.

Ever since he had been commissioned to write a work for Welsh National Opera, Alun Hoddinott had been toying with the idea of producing a piece based on the story of Rawlins White, the first Welsh martyr of the Inquisition. But eventually he settled on a short story by Robert Louis Stevenson about intrigue amongst traders on a South Sea island, entitled *The Beach*. Dylan Thomas had adapted the same story as a film script, and Hoddinott sent both the original story and Thomas's script to the Cardiff novelist and poet Glyn Jones, asking him to provide a libretto. Jones refused to read the Thomas adaptation and instead made his own. The story opens with the arrival on the island of Falesá of John Wiltshire, a copra trader. Wiltshire, enchanted by the beauty of the place, meets Case, the resident trader, who arranges for him to marry Uma, a beautiful half-caste. After the marriage, Wiltshire finds that nobody will trade with him, the result, he later learns, of Case having told everybody that Uma is taboo. The two men become deadly enemies, an enmity which leads to Case's death. The role of Trader Case was written for Geraint Evans, and a strong cast was assembled to support him. Appearing as Uma was Sandra Browne, Forbes Robinson sang Black Jack; Rowland Jones, Randall; Edward Byles, Father Galuchet; and Delme Bryn-Jones, Wiltshire. The producer was Michael Geliot, the designer Alexander McPherson, and the conductor Richard Armstrong.

*The Beach of Falesá* received its world première on 26 March at the opening of the spring Cardiff season. It was billed as the most important musical event in Wales for many years but that did not make it a success. The cast, aided by the decision of HTV to record the work for television before opening night, knew it well, and Geliot's production brought out the romantic nature of the piece, but, although the critics found much to praise, the general feeling was that it was a worthy but flawed first effort. "Hoddinott," wrote William Mann in the *Times*, "not only an experienced but a sensible composer, decided (I guess) that his first opera must be capable of winning enthusiasm among audiences outside any big cultural metropolis, appealing to those who love Puccini, can enjoy Britten, but do not want to go much further. Yet a new opera in 1974 cannot, honestly, retread the old well-worn ground. *The Beach of Falesá* is a well-made, interesting opera in the tradition of *Peter Grimes*, not experimental nor yet talking down to audiences; the accent of the music is Hoddinott's own, not borrowed. It lacks romantic arias but is not unmelodious . . . I found my attention held throughout." The main problem lay with the characterisation, or, rather, lack of it. Geliot had made the characters interact (rehearsals had not always been entirely happy; Geraint Evans's strong views on how Trader Case should be played did not always coincide with Geliot's), and the production contained some strongly dramatic moments such as the destruction of the jungle temple. Alexander McPherson's sets ably captured the feeling of a South Seas isle. But, apart from Case (thanks largely to Geraint Evans's interpretation), there was no one on stage with whom the audience could sympathise, not even the hero, John Wiltshire, who, commented Edward Greenfield in the *Guardian*, was "altogether too much of a ninny to carry conviction, too solemn in self-analysis." Forbes Robinson could do little with the cardboard character of Black Jack, Case's tame thug, and the tenors were reduced to character roles: the drunk, the priest, the native chief. The role of Uma was little more than a cipher, and Sandra Browne felt that if she had never appeared on stage, she would not have been missed. And in spite of Hoddinott's protestations that it was not avant-garde, and that he had written a lyric work, the general public did not take to his style of writing. Four and a half million people tuned in to the television broadcast; only 400,000 remained to the end. "Most people enjoy a tuneful opera," stated one writer in the correspondence columns of the *Western Mail*, "but it is difficult to understand how anyone can really enjoy this one." "A monologue with music," claimed another.

The novelty of *Falesá* attracted good houses. *Idomeneo*, which followed, received a very poor response, in spite of a strong cast – Kenneth Bowen, Anthony Roden, Janet Price and Rae Woodland – and Geliot's thoughtful production. The season was completed with *La Bohème*, *The Pearl Fishers* and the first Cardiff performances of *L'Elisir*. Geliot's brisk, active production never faltered in pace, and audiences were delighted by Forbes Robinson's outrageous Dulcamara, by Lillian Watson (taking over the role of Adina) negotiating Donizetti's intricate runs and trills in thrilling style, and by the pleasantly sung and well-acted performance of Arthur Davies as Nemorino. The season also contained two orchestral concerts, including a performance of Bach's *St Matthew Passion* on Good Friday with Thomas Allen as Christus and Kenneth Bowen as the Evangelist.

Following Cardiff, *La Bohème* and *L'Elisir* set out on the postponed Welsh tour to Haverfordwest, Aberystwyth, Wrexham and Connah's Quay, a new venue (replacing Rhyl), before arriving in Swansea in May, where they were joined by *The Pearl Fishers* and *Falesá*. *The Pearl Fishers* had replaced *Nabucco* as the one opera guaranteed to sell out wherever it was played and was included as a counter to *Falesá*. which was not expected to attract large numbers in spite of the presence of Geraint Evans. In the event, the single performance was reasonably full, although at the last moment Evans was forced to withdraw and his cover, the admirable Julian Moyle, took over. Moyle succeeded in making Trader Case as formidable a figure as Evans had done, and at the final curtain, the attentive audience applauded warmly. But it was the work's last performance. *Falesá* was not felt to be attractive enough to remain in the repertory.

Touring continued with first visits to Southsea and Wolverhampton, and a week at Bristol, in which *L'Elisir*, *La Bohème* and *The Pearl Fishers* continued to attract capacity audiences. In Bristol, Forbes Robinson took over as Colline, his first time in the role for fifteen years, when Gwynne Howell had to return hurriedly to Covent Garden. The disappointment, once again, proved to be *Idomeneo*.

By May the books for the previous season had been worked out, and they made chilling reading. Far from having turned any financial corner in the previous three years, an accumulated deficit of almost £150,000, the same amount as that the Arts Council had wiped out earlier, was revealed. This had arisen because of two main factors: a sudden, unexpected reduction of income after plans for the year had been made, artists engaged and when it was too late to make any major alterations, coupled with an unprecedented rise in production costs. This time the Arts Council would not, could not, bail the company out and it was made quite clear that it was WNO's own responsibility to reduce the deficit, if necessary, from its current grant. The Arts Council was itself going through a troubled period. A government cutback at the end of 1973 had meant it was some £6 million short of its requirements, and this had been reflected in reduced grants for 1974. WNO's own grant had been reduced by £55,000, and an Arts Council plan to present a short Easter festival of British opera at Sadler's Wells (in which *The Beach of Falesá* was to have been included) had been cancelled because the Arts Council could not raise the necessary £7500. Inflation, currently running at just over 17 percent, was also affecting local authorities and councils. They could not be asked to help out yet again; indeed, there was a very real danger that when seeking to make their own economies, some might choose to cut or even cancel the grants they had in principle already agreed.

James Mowat, WNO's General Manager, denied that there was any threat to the company's future but swift action had to be taken. The autumn production of *Peter Grimes*, the least advanced of the new works, was immediately cancelled, some planned orchestral concerts were called off and the autumn season in Cardiff was cut from four weeks to three, postponing by a week the opening of the new production of *The Flying Dutchman*, which was to have been a gala evening in aid of the Royal National Lifeboat Institution. In spite of these measures, £160,000 had to be found in a hurry just to keep going. For the first time that still fashionable word *sponsorship* was talked about. A brochure outlining WNO's financial position and asking for sponsorship was sent to all major Welsh industries. For the sum of between £15,000 and £20,000, a sponsor could mount a completely new production. At the other end of the scale, for £150 a string quartet could be hired. In his accompanying statement, Chairman Alfred Francis acknow-ledged the gravity of the situation. "For how much longer," he wrote, "must these achievements be taken for granted?" The need to raise sponsorship amounted "to a struggle for survival. *It is a battle which must be won.*" It was a battle few wanted to join. No one was prepared to sponsor a production. One well-known razor blade manufacturer replied to the appeal that they were unable to donate money but offered instead some garden tools. There was a better response to the idea of hiring musicians. ICI Fibres booked two concerts for its factory in Pontypool; a Cardiff businessman sponsored a performance of Handel's *Messiah* in the Capitol; and the brass consort proved extremely attractive, especially in the Working Men's Clubs. Friends of the Opera, particularly in North Wales, once more rallied round, arranging fund-raising activities.

In an attempt to raise the awareness of just what goes into the staging of an opera, a rehearsal of *The Flying Dutchman* was opened to the general public.

The delayed autumn season in Cardiff finally opened with *The Flying Dutchman* on 10 September. The production, his first for the opera company, was by Ian Watt-Smith, with designs by William Dudley. Both had been faced with an enormous challenge, for Richard Armstrong wanted to perform the opera as a single act as Wagner had intended. Although this had been the custom at Bayreuth since 1901, it had never been done in Britain, but Armstrong was convinced that it made greater musical sense than splitting the work into three separate acts. The problem was that Wagner had written only ninety seconds of linking music between acts, during which massive scene changes are required. A single set had to be used, and William Dudley provided a curved, sloping wooden surface covering much of the stage, part of which could be raised when appropriate and augmented in the first scene by rigging and a helm, in the second by a doorway and portrait of the Dutchman, and in the third by an upturned rowing boat. "It was persuasive enough," wrote William Mann, "as the Norwegian craft, particularly with some of the imaginative lighting effects which made its surface flicker and glisten; less so as the shore, where the rake and the shape are awkward, the sense of location unconvincing." During the scene changes (carried out by the stage crew dressed as sailors) and during the overture, a curtain was lowered on which rolling waves were projected. The production itself was simple and straightforward, and worked effectively. David Ward was engaged to sing his internationally acclaimed Dutchman. It was a wise choice, for he was, Mann felt, "better than ever: occasionally inclined to a ferocious bark, but generally in full and rich voice, dark-coloured and haunted on his first appearance, much warmer in the affirmative major-key music of the love duet, and always strong in outlining the shape of a phrase." Singing Senta opposite him, and making her debut with WNO, was Anne Evans, London-born of Welsh parentage. She gave a radiantly powerful and dramatic performance. Kenneth Collins, improving with every appearance, sang Erik, David Gwynne, Daland, and Arthur Davies, the Steersman. Richard Armstrong, after an extravagantly stormy account of the overture, paced the opera well, bringing colour and vigour to the storm music and the sailors' revels. The chorus, the men in particular, sang marvellously.

The decision to perform the opera as a continuous act was totally vindicated. "I never want to hear it in three again," wrote Rodney Milnes in *Opera*. The decision to sing the piece in German (a language unknown to the majority of the first-night audience and to future audiences on tour) was not so happily received and brought forth some harsh criticism.

The following evening, a revival of *Don Carlos*, given in English, was played before only a small band of devotees. They saw the familiar Philip of Forbes Robinson, Eboli of Janet Coster, Posa of Terence Sharpe and Carlos of Keith Erwen, but new to the production were the Inquisitor of Richard Van Allan and the Elizabeth of Anne Edwards, whose last appearance had been in *Mefistofele* seventeen years earlier. An integrated performance was conducted by another newcomer, the gifted young American John Mauceri, a protégé of Leonard Bernstein who had conducted the New York revival of *Candide*. It was an impressive debut.

The remaining revivals also brought cast changes. Greek soprano Vassilia Papantoniou and Romanian tenor Emil Gherman took over the leading roles in *La Bohème*, though neither made an outstanding impression. At the second performance, Sharman Shepherd, a member of the Chorale and understudy for Musetta, having finished singing at the end of the second act and preparing to go home, suddenly had to replace Margaret Haggart for the final two acts. She received a standing ovation. *Simon Boccanegra*, which had re-entered the repertory at Llandudno in June after a gap of three years, was performed with Eugene Holmes, a black Texan who had sung with the Metropolitan's touring company and was currently with the Deutsche Oper am Rhein, singing the title role and Barbel Edwards as Amelia. In *L'Elisir*, Thomas Allen sang his first Sergeant Belcore.

Cast changes were inevitable, too, on the autumn tour. In Swansea, Robert Bickerstaff, already a well-established Verdian baritone, appeared in his first major Wagnerian role as the Dutchman. In Birmingham, Malcolm Fraser's production of *The Barber of Seville*, which had been seen previously only on the small Welsh tour, was introduced to the repertory with John Mauceri using a rarely performed score based on Rossini's original manuscript, and saw the British debut of Japanese soprano Hiroko Kashiwagi as Rosina, Arthur Davies singing his first Almaviva and Michael Rippon, Dr Bartolo. In Birmingham, the lights in the orchestra pit fused midway through the performance of *The Dutchman*, causing a five-minute delay, the first time the opera had not been given continuously.

Earlier in the year, an invitation had been received to take part in the Barcelona Festival in January 1975 with *Billy Budd* and *Peter Grimes*, neither of which had ever been seen in Spain. The cancellation of *Grimes* had, for a time, put the tour in jeopardy, but the Spaniards were finally persuaded that Hoddinott's *Beach of Falesá* would be an appropriate substitute. Three performances of each work were planned. But the inflation that was raging in Britain was also to be found throughout Europe and the Barcelona authorities, who were funding the entire venture, found that they could no longer afford to pay for the Welsh orchestra as well, a prerequisite to the performance of *Falesá*. Since the Festival orchestra could not possibly learn the score in time and attempts to arrange a concert for the Welsh Philharmonia, which would have helped defray costs, had fallen through, the plan to take *Falesá* was dropped, much to the annoyance of Hoddinott, who felt that it should not have been announced until everything was settled. Even then, the visit looked doubtful until a Liverpool shipping firm offered to transport the props and sets free of charge. As compensation for missing out, the Welsh Philharmonia was sent on a sixteen-day tour giving twenty-one concerts for schools.

*Billy Budd* was given three performances in Barcelona in the beautiful Gran Teatro del Liceo. Although the Festival orchestra had been studying the score for two months, they had found it extremely difficult to play and there were rumours that they might strike. In the event, the resulting sound left much to be desired. In spite of the poor orchestral playing, and the fact that several cast members were stricken by upset stomachs, the first night was a triumph. The cast and the conductor, Richard Armstrong, received a fifteen-minute ovation, and the Barcelona critics unanimously gave the Festival Director's Award to Michael Geliot, stressing that it was a tribute to the entire company "which left such a superb impression with its première performance in Spain of Britten's *Billy Budd*."

The year at home began with a visit to Fishguard where *The Grand Duchess of Gerolstein* was given its first performance in the secondary school hall. The venue led to considerable problems backstage, where the principals had to change in classrooms. "Afterwards there was only one small washbasin to have a washdown," remembered Forbes Robinson, who was more used to the facilities of Covent Garden or La Scala, Milan. "I was left standing on the stairs in my jockstrap because there was nowhere else to go." The success of Bizet's *The Pearl Fishers* had convinced Welsh National Opera that the policy of selecting lesser-known works by well-known composers was a sensible one. Offenbach's operetta, although popular with amateur societies, had not been given professionally in Britain since before the war. Producer Malcolm Fraser decided to play it as an Edwardian musical comedy, and for his designers he went outside the conventional theatre to engage Robert St John Roper for the costumes and Tod Kingman for the sets. Both men were well-known for their work at London's Talk of the Town, and St John Roper had designed for the Folies Bergère. Fraser's lighthearted pantomime approach did not please everyone. It was most successful in the military and political satire (the chorus had been coached in their drill by a Regimental Sergeant Major), less so in the bedroom scenes. Forbes Robinson was a formidable General Boum and Ann Howard, returning to WNO after ten years, was perfect as the nymphomaniac Grand Duchess, combining superb vocal and visual style with a kittenish sexuality. There was also lively support from Lillian Watson as Wanda, Terence Walters as Fritz and Eric Roberts as Prince Paul, but no amount of tinkering or licence could detract from the fact that the score was simply not one of Offenbach's best.

The following night Julian Hope's new production of *Manon Lescaut* opened, sung in Italian. The reason for this decision was that the work was still in copyright and no one liked the authorised translation. Hope's production was solid, sensible and straightforward, like the designs of Bruno Santini, but, it was felt, without any real distinction. Richard Armstrong conducted with the warmth and ardour the score demands, obtaining full-blooded and responsive playing from the Welsh Philharmonia, but the real honours of the evening went to Kenneth Collins as des Grieux, revealing at last the stature he had promised for so long: "a first rate performance," wrote Stephen Walsh of the *Observer*, "accurate and sensitive in manner, touching in matter." Elizabeth Vaughan as Manon was, according to David Gillard in the *Daily Mail*, "musically secure but dramatically a little undernourished."

Both productions moved on to Aberystwyth and then to Leicester before joining the repertory in Cardiff in April. Here the third new production of the year, *Così fan tutte*, opened the three-week spring season. American soprano Kay Griffel made her British debut as Fiordiligi; Sandra Browne sang Dorabella; Arthur Davies, Ferrando; Julian Moyle, Alfonso; Terence Sharpe (replacing the American baritone Dale Duesing who had pulled out of the production), Guglielmo; and Lillian Watson, Despina. Geliot's production opened with the three friends leaving a brothel rather than the more usual coffee house. "He will keep popping at least one naughtiness into each of his productions to make us sit up," commented Rodney Milnes in the *Spectator*. ". . . The intention is half-sound; he sought to point the double standard of morality, to the fact that the officers have little moral justification for testing their girl friends' constancy and that the opera should really be called *Così fan tutti*." Liz King's sets and Freda Blackwood's costumes were more suggestive of Regency England than Naples, being "firmly English in style and prettily so in a Gainsborough sort of way. As a point of reference, this seems sensible," wrote Milnes. "Geliot's interpretation of this much-interpreted opera is sincere, and straightforward, avoiding burlesque, caricature, fancy psychology and harsh philosophy," wrote Gillian Widdicombe in the *Financial Times*. ". . . But there is one place where Geliot puts a foot terribly wrong. The set cannot be converted without dropping the front curtain between scenes; and we wait each time, while potted hydrangeas, white stocks, pink climbing roses, the English lawn and the large green watering can are carted off, or on . . . it means a disastrous interruption of the sparkling continuity of *Così fan tutte*, which like *Don Giovanni* is deliberately constructed with linking solo scenes." This reservation apart, the opera was a triumph of teamwork, the singers, not all ideal for Mozart, blending together well. "Sandra Browne's vivacious Dorabella was a perfect foil to Kay Griffel's more dreamy Fiordiligi, and Lillian Watson's Despina must rank with the most engaging of the decade," wrote Denby Richards. "Julian Moyle's Alfonso and Terence Sharpe's Guglielmo were always satisfactory, and occasionally thrilling." Arthur Davies, admirably expressive as an actor and singing attractively for much of the evening, found the role of Ferrando rather too taxing, his voice tiring towards the end. The greatest single asset of the performance, Milnes felt, was the supremely stylish conducting of György Fischer, which was rewarded by playing of like quality from the Welsh Philharmonia.

Also new to Cardiff that season was Malcolm Fraser's production of *The*

*Barber of Seville.* A crowded house was there largely to see Thomas Allen's Figaro. Since his debut in the role five years earlier, Allen had developed into an international star, and the audience was rewarded by a superlative performance. "Always human, dramatically compelling, vocally secure and expressive, he dominated the action without once losing character," noted Denby Richards in *Musical Opinion.* "Rossini unashamedly wrote music to please his audience," commented Christopher Powell of *Music and Musicians*; "his audience unashamedly enjoyed it." The other revival was a re-cast *Flying Dutchman*, with Norman Bailey as the Dutchman, Siv Wennberg as Senta and Michael Langdon as Daland, conducted with a sense of spaciousness which sacrificed nothing in the way of excitement, by Edward Downes.

The first new production for the autumn was of Verdi's *Otello*, which brought James Lockhart back to Cardiff for the first time since his resignation as Musical Director. It was the thirteenth Verdi opera WNO had staged, and, sadly, fate dealt its traditional blow. All the cast were singing in the opera for the first time, and it was soon apparent that the time required to coach them into their roles had been wildly underestimated. Alberto Remedios, in the title role, had to be prompted constantly. "In each act, even the first, where he was screwed-up with nerves, there were glimpses of what his Otello should become, when his unique tone, at once heroic and lyrical, rang out through the theatre. There was also a good deal of ugly, ill-formed singing, with uncomfortable straining for high notes and with Verdi's long phrases gasped out in short Wagnerian snatches. The last act was the best so if Mr Remedios did not pull it off on Tuesday it was not for lack of staying power," wrote Ronald Crichton of the *Financial Times.* Delme Bryn-Jones as Iago, in spite of his strong singing, seemed unsure whether to be cruel and sinister or charming and devious. "The producer appeared to see Iago as an honest trooper who had taken a wrong turning," commented David Fingleton in the *Tatler*, "but in Bryn-Jones' realization this became a cheerful oaf who grinned his way through the great *Credo* – most unconvincing." Judgement on Evelyn Brunner, the Swiss soprano who sang Desdemona, was not, according to John Higgins in the *Times*, easy. "She constantly promised well, shaping a phrase delicately, and then disappointed by singing as though through layers of muslin. The confrontation with Otello in the third act struck real Verdian fire, as did the finale a little later with the WNO chorus in tremendous form."

Geliot's simple and direct production also suffered from this seeming lack of preparation, and from a tendency to underline points too heavily – Iago waved Desdemona's handkerchief like a lone warrior all too anxious to surrender to the enemy – but, as John Higgins reminded his readers, "sophisticates . . . would do well to remember that the three principals were singing their roles for the first time. Experienced managers fielding inexperienced teams cut out the fancy passes." "He blocks out the action clearly enough, but the detail – the business with the handkerchief is an example – is crude. Some of the blame should perhaps go to the designs of Annena Stubbs," wrote Crichton. "Her two interiors are passable, but the ramparts of Cyprus, apparently made out of shining blue-green stone, are gloomily unevocative (with the principals' faces in almost total darkness) and the second act terrace, Otello's golden robe clashing abominably with bronze lions, is hideous. Occasional flights into strong colour, such as the Moor's shocking pink in act three, are regrettable. For the rest the costumes interpret 16th century Venice and Cyprus as far as possible in terms of today's high street, which means they are not only messy but genteel. Even stringent economy is no reason for drabness." The Welsh Philharmonia did not enjoy one of its best nights under Lockhart. The playing was acceptable but lacked tension, "and there was scarcely a dynamic below *mezzoforte* to be heard (the singers, alas, followed suit)," wrote Rodney Milnes in *Opera*. "In short, this production needs a little more running in before final judgement can be passed," concluded John Tyrrell in the *Musical Times*.

The fourth performance of *Otello*, on 24 September, was notable for two things: it was the 200th performance James Lockhart had conducted for WNO and it saw the debut of Barbel Edwards as Desdemona. She had been learning the role in order to take over on the autumn tour, but the sudden return of Evelyn Brunner to Switzerland following her mother's death brought Edwards in with 36 hours' notice and without a proper stage rehearsal. "Hiding any nervousness she might justifiably have felt, Miss Edwards sang with praiseworthy composure and complete security," recorded Elizabeth Forbes in *Opera*. "For a first try at a difficult part it was a very considerable achievement."

The Cardiff season had been divided into two fortnights, with a week separating them. The second fortnight had opened on 23 September with the fifth and final new production of the year – in many ways, the most important production WNO had seen in recent years. Armstrong had long wanted to stage the work of the Czech composer Janáček, but the financial strictures under which WNO was working had made that impossible. In an effort to reduce costs while continuing to mount new and innovative work, WNO entered into an agreement with Scottish Opera to share costs on a new production of *Jenůfa*, the first such arrangement the company had ever made. David Pountney, Scottish Opera's Director of Productions, was to produce (bringing with him Maria Björnson as designer), with Richard Armstrong as conductor, and after being seen in Cardiff and on tour, the same production, with the same cast, was to be presented in Scotland.

*Jenůfa* was the opera with which Janáček, after years of struggle, first

*Simon Boccanegra* 1970: Delme Bryn-Jones *Boccanegra*, Josephine Barstow *Amelia*, Keith Erwen *Adorno* (Alfredo Evan)

*Lulu* 1971: Carole Farley *Lulu*, Ramon Remedios *The Painter* (Michael Evans)

*Billy Budd* 1972: Forbes Robinson *Claggart*, Nigel Douglas *Captain Vere*; chorus and set

*Turandot* 1972: Pauline Tinsley *Turandot* (Alfredo Evan)

*Nabucco* 1972 revival: Sandra Browne *Fenena*, Milla Andrew *Abigail*, Terence Sharpe *Nabucco*

*Idomeneo* 1973 (facing): Rae Woodland *Electra*, Alexander Young *Idomeneo* (Julian Sheppard)

*Madam Butterfly* 1973: Elizabeth Vaughan *Cio-Cio-San*, Julian Moyle *Sharpless*

*The Flying Dutchman* 1974: Anne Evans *Senta*, David Ward *The Dutchman*

*L'Elisir d'Amore* 1974: Arthur Davies *Nemorino*, Lillian Watson *Adina* (Julian Sheppard)

*The Magic Flute* 1974 revival: Paul Hudson *Speaker*, Ryland Davies *Tamino*

*Jenůfa* 1975: Pauline Tinsley *Kostelnicka*

*The Midsummer Marriage* 1976: Felicity Lott *Jenifer*, John Treleaven *Mark*

*Albert Herring* 1976: Henry Newman *Sid*, Arthur Davies *Albert*

*The Barber of Seville* 1977 revival: Della Jones *Rosina* (Julian Sheppard)

*The Marriage of Figaro* 1977: Meryl Drower *Susanna*, Felicity Lott *Countess Almaviva*

*The Makropoulos Case* 1978: A rehearsal, with Elisabeth Söderström *Emilia Marty* (Julian Sheppard)

*Elektra* 1978: Debria Brown *Klytemnestra* (Julian Sheppard)

*A Midsummer Night's Dream* 1978: Geraint Evans *Bottom*, with David Gwynne, John Harris and Julian Moyle (Julian Sheppard)

*Madam Butterfly* 1978: Magdalena Falewicz *Cio-Cio-San*, John Treleaven *Pinkerton* (Julian Sheppard)

*Tristan und Isolde* 1979: John Mitchinson *Tristan*, Linda Esther Gray *Isolde* (Julian Sheppard)

*Turandot* 1979 revival: Kenneth Collins *Calaf*, Rita Hunter *Turandot* (Julian Sheppard)

achieved fame outside his native Moravia. Set in a lonely water mill in the mountains among a small peasant community, it is a powerful tale of love and pain, blinding hatred and sublime forgiveness. A handsome cad refuses to marry his girlfriend when she becomes pregnant; the illegimitate child is drowned by her stepmother; the rejected suitor (the cad's half-brother) ends up with the girl he never stopped wanting. The score is full of glorious, dramatic music. For Rodney Milnes, writing in *Opera*, the arresting opening set the style of Pountney's naturalistic production. "A bare, diagonally wooden-planked stage, a huge millwheel turning; sitting at a long table, a group of women, Jenůfa among them, absolutely still; Laca, his back to the audience, stares at the wheel that should by rights be his. At the first orchestral *forte* Jenůfa jumps to her feet and runs to look in the direction of the recruiting station; at the same moment the group unfreezes and starts to scrub, not peel, potatoes (brilliant – the faster action is more fitting to the nervous music)." "To describe the production as straightforward," wrote Christopher Powell in *Music and Musicians*, "is in no way to decry or underestimate his thoughtful and thoroughly professional approach. Especially welcome was the absence of novelty for novelty's sake, and the care with which the chorus had been rehearsed. Always so excellent vocally, it was a pleasure to see them dramatically effective too, instead of wondering how to stand and where to look, as in Geliot's production of *Otello*."

Pauline Tinsley was superb as Kostelnicka, the stepmother. "She sang the role better than anyone I have heard either on records or in the theatre," wrote Milnes; "her exquisitely sensuous phrasing in the second-act scene with Steva made the situation almost unbearably poignant, especially as it leads directly to the drastic action she is about to take. She pared down her naturally flamboyant dramatic technique, and all her best moments were those of complete stillness, whether steeling herself to kill the baby or sustaining the long Act 2 postlude by sitting in her chair frozen in wide-eyed terror." Josephine Barstow as Jenůfa matched Tinsley with a bravura performance of great intensity, though her voice was not to everyone's liking. Milnes found "her idiosyncratic vocal delivery and externalised acting slightly alienating."

There was an affecting Laca from Allen Cathcart, the American former baritone turned heldentenor, in his British debut, which contrasted nicely with the amiably feckless Steva of Gregory Dempsey (the only member of the cast to have sung in the opera before), and the many smaller roles were well taken by company members. Armstrong, in the pit, drew powerful and vehement playing from the orchestra. "From time to time he errs, perhaps, on the side of stridency. But much of the credit for the coherence and impact of the performance must go to him," reported Stephen Walsh. "There were those who thought that he and the Welsh Philharmonia (on absolutely top form) made the music sound too beautiful – an attitude I cannot begin to understand," wrote Milnes. "The impact of the orchestral sound was overwhelming in this theatre, yet only very occasionally in the first act did it cover the singers. Mr Armstrong risked two long pauses – one between the arrival of the lynching party and the Kostelnicka's confession, the second just before the arresting key change that launches the final duet. In both cases the audience held its collective breath in transfixed silence, so the risk was well taken." There were a few minor quibbles with Pountney's production (as there always seem to be), but there could be no denying the impact *Jenůfa* made on the first-night audience and on subsequent ones. The cheers went on and on. "I doubt if, at the end," concluded David Cairns in *Sunday Times*, "many of the audience still thought of Janáček as a remote, obscure and unappealing composer."

The sharing of production costs with Scottish Opera on *Jenůfa* brought great benefits to both companies, but especially to WNO, where the financial problems were still acute. The cancellation of *Peter Grimes* and other actions taken the previous autumn had staved off the immediate crisis, but there had been additional casualties during 1975. The North Wales Arts Association had had its grant cut and could no longer help finance the spring visits to Wrexham and Connah's Quay, which had had to be cancelled. The autumn visit to Liverpool was also cancelled. The previous November there had played to a total capacity of only 56 percent, with two performances during the week being as low as 40 percent, and, under the circumstances, another such week could not be risked. Box-office returns generally were falling. Inflation and the imposition of VAT meant higher seat prices, which resulted only in less demand for tickets (the first nights of both *Otello* and *Jenůfa* had not played to full houses). WNO was a touring company, even when playing at the New in Cardiff, and there was little that could be done to cut down on overheads. The chorus was only 42 strong, a dangerously low number, and for the bigger works was still having to be supplemented by members of the old Voluntary Chorus who had been given special Equity tickets. The year's commitments had been fulfilled but against a constant background of worry. In May it was thought that the visit to Wolverhampton might be WNO's last appearance, and the Birmingham season had also had a question mark hanging over it until the last moment. The Arts Council's insistence that previous deficits should be met from current funding had simply meant that another deficit had been run up during 1975.

On the surface, there was little to show that WNO was beset by financial concern. Its work on stage was of a company that had not a care in the world. But behind the scenes, much was going on. The Arts Council finally decided that it would help – but at a price. In August, Chairman Alfred Francis had confirmed the rumour (circulating for some time) that he was to retire. He was 66, his wife was ill and he had spent the best part of the previous seven years working and fighting for the company he loved. His brief had been to oversee WNO's professionalisation from top to bottom. He had asked for ten years in which to achieve it and had succeeded in seven. But the Arts Council had decided that he must go. This was a decision not against him personally but against his position. What concerned the Arts Council was that an executive chairman who lived in London and was not with the company full-time could not maintain sufficient financial and artistic control. And with a triumvirate of general manager, artistic director and musical director also helping make decisions, WNO was, it was felt, top-heavy in senior management. As part of its condition for rescuing WNO, the Arts Council insisted on three things: that all future chairmen should be non-executive, that a general administrator or chief executive should be brought in to run WNO, and that a complete overhaul of senior management should be undertaken.

Francis was deeply hurt by the manner of his enforced departure, but agreed to stay on until a successor could be found. At the annual general meeting in October, his deputy on the Council of Management, Lord Davies of Llandinam, was elected Welsh National Opera's first lay Chairman. It was Lord Davies's 35th birthday. An Old Etonian and civil engineer, he had been on the Council of Management for two years, and it was his family trust that had provided the money for a press officer. He took over formally as Chairman on 10 December. His first task, in addition to ensuring that WNO continued to exist, was to find a new chief executive. A selection committee had already been set up and an advertisement placed in the national press, and it had been hoped that the two appointments could have been named simultaneously. But, of the thirty-five applicants, not one was deemed suitable and in December the post was re-advertised.

# CHAPTER SIXTEEN: 1976–1977

Two weeks before the 1976 spring season in Cardiff was due to open, there was still no news of the size of the annual grant. The rumour was that it would be in the region of £1,250,000 and plans had been made on that assumption, for 1976 was to be a year of celebration. It was thirty years since Welsh National Opera had staged its first production, and the occasion was to be marked by twenty-seven weeks of opera (the most ever given) in fifteen venues throughout Wales and England, and by five new productions: *Albert Herring*, *The Seraglio*, *Il Trovatore*, *Orpheus in the Underworld* and the first performances of Tippett's *The Midsummer Marriage* to be staged outside London. A special booklet was printed commemorating the previous thirty years, and messages of goodwill arrived from around the world.

The celebrations had begun on 23 January with *Albert Herring* at the Sherman Theatre in Cardiff. Britten's comic chamber opera, with its cast of thirteen and reduced orchestra, had been chosen not only because it was worth doing but also because it could happily tour to those new small theatres which had recently been opened throughout Wales but could not take large-scale productions. It was not staged, however, without distinct qualms as to whether, being a "modern" work, Welsh audiences would take to it. There was little need to worry, as packed houses in Cardiff gave it an enthusiastic reception. Ian Watt-Smith's delightful production, aided by Alexander McPherson's designs, created a perfect picture of life in a small town, and struck just the right balance between comedy and character. The cast, with the exception of two guest artists (Rae Woodland and Johanna Peters), was drawn entirely from the company, with many from the Chorale making their debuts in principal roles. Rae Woodland, though lacking weight of voice, looked perfect as Lady Billows, less bossy and Amazonian than some interpreters of the role but radiating a sense of authority and superiority that was equally effective. Johanna Peters (who had sung the role on Britten's own recording of the work) was exactly right as Florence Pike, the housekeeper, unsure of her station in life and perpetually on her dignity. Arthur Davies as Albert "fitted the part ideally; a nice, polite boy with no problems but his mother and his shyness." There were skilful contributions from Julian Moyle as the Vicar, Henry Newman and Margaret Morgan as Sid and Nancy, Menai Davies as Mrs Herring, Rita Cullis as Miss Wordsworth, John Harris as the Mayor and David Gwynne as Superintendent Budd. The Welsh Philharmonia, reduced in size to thirteen, responded well to Anthony Hose's forthright conducting. The production was, above all, a triumph of teamwork, clearly enjoyed by the cast and an audience noticeably younger than those drawn to the New Theatre.

After two nights in Cardiff, *Albert Herring* moved north to Bangor, Aberystwyth and Mold, where the performance was almost cancelled due to the weather. The two trucks taking the scenery to Mold got stuck on a mountain road near Dolgellau and only got free because the drivers used parts of the set to clear away the snow. A journey that should have taken them two hours took six.

The main anniversary celebrations began with Michael Geliot's new production of *The Seraglio* which opened the spring season in Cardiff on 1 April. It was perhaps ironic, in view of the occasion, that the production did not contain a single Welsh principal. In WNO's defence, however, it must be stated that the production had been plagued by withdrawals, having had three Belmontes and one Constanze drop out before the first night. Janet Price, as Constanze, was replaced with four days' notice by Lois McDonall, and Keith Erwen, the third Belmonte, by Alexander Young.

Under such constraints, it was perhaps inevitable that Geliot's production, adapted from one he had done in Geneva and using the Geneva sets designed by Serge Marzolff, should have been less than assured on opening night. Neither Lois McDonall nor Alexander Young was entirely at ease, "though Mr Young's sure sense of style and authoritative delivery were as impressive as ever, and even in rather husky voice Miss McDonall makes a formidable heroine," commented Rodney Milnes in *Opera*. "Otherwise," he continued, "the first act passed with those singers who were not falling over either the set or their own costumes pacing nervously round the stage in a classic display of first-night jitters. Even taking that into account, I could not see what Geliot was seeking to do with this difficult piece." The production produced the mixed response that Geliot's work always seemed to inspire. David Murray of the *Sunday Telegraph* found it easy and graceful; others felt it lacked Geliot's usual ingenuity and missed the sparkle of his previous *Così*. "The slightly disappointing result may have been the result of illness and late substitution of two principals, but stemmed more, I feel," wrote David Fingleton in the *Tatler*, "from the difficulties of adapting an original production for a purpose-built opera house to the technical and temporal exigencies of Cardiff's New Theatre ... For, pleasant though it was, *Seraglio* lacked the incisiveness and insight one normally obtains from Geliot in Mozart." Tom Sutcliffe went further in the *Guardian*: "It certainly deserves more care, sensitivity, and precision than Michael Geliot has brought to it ... he shoved the characters around as if he felt a certain activity within the confines of the sets was likely to keep the audience from getting bored." Much interest attached to the British operatic debut of the Jamaican bass Willard White as Osmin. His performance was, according to Ronald Crichton, "both a delight and a nonsense. A delight, because the voice is splendid and is used with instinctive musical grace (it is still light at the bottom for this music, but Mr White's marking of the low notes is more pleasant than many basses' growling of them), and because he is a 'natural', incapable of an ungainly or ill-timed movement. A nonsense, because instead of a pot-bellied, vicious old bully, he presents a young, agile, friendly tiger of a man whom no Pasha in his senses would allow within ten miles of his harem." There were other excellent performances from Lillian Watson as Blonde and Alexander Oliver as Pedrillo, and the orchestra responded marvellously to the direction of György Fischer.

Backstage on opening night, a second drama was taking place. Rather than leave her rings, including a diamond solitaire (a family heirloom), in her dressing room, Lillian Watson had tucked them into the top of her tights for safe-keeping, and accidentally flushed them down the toilet. She realised they had gone only seconds before she was due on stage. Three council workmen were summoned and, while she was singing, began a search of the sewers outside the theatre. By an incredible chance, the diamond solitaire was recovered.

The run of bad luck with the Belmontes continued when the production went on tour. For Swansea and Southsea, Anthony Roden took over from Alexander Young. In Oxford, Roden sang the first performance, but on the afternoon of the second he developed a sore throat and was unable to appear. No replacement could be found until Kenneth Bowen, who had not sung the role for three years, was contacted in a London recording studio. He rushed down to Oxford and prepared to sing from the wings while Roden mimed on stage. Meanwhile, Willard White's car had broken down and he was nowhere to be found. Richard Armstrong was just explaining to the audience how it could get its money back when White arrived half an hour late and the performance could begin. Thomas Leherberger took over as Belmonte for the third performance.

The second new production of the anniversary season was of *Il Trovatore*, sung in Italian. It was appropriate that thirty years should be celebrated with an opera by Verdi, and since *Il Trovatore* had not been seen for twelve years and had not been given a new production for twenty-five, it was deemed the best choice. It also allowed a cast of international and national singers, all of whom owed WNO some debt in their careers, to be assembled. Elizabeth Vaughan was cast as Leonora, Kenneth Collins as

Manrico, Janet Coster as Azucena, Terence Sharpe as Luna, and David Gwynne as Ferrando.

Julian Hope's production was straightforward, a fact applauded by some critics, disliked by others. "Hope got his crowds to make their exits and their entrances and that was about that," commented Tom Sutcliffe in the *Guardian*. Max Loppert of the *Financial Times*, in common with most critics, disliked David Fielding's permanent set. Its twin watchtowers and tilted V-shaped platform, "supplied the evening with a certain visual consistency," he wrote, "by being equally suitable in none of their adaptations to any of the scenes. To which must be added a zoo-cage of an iron frame clanked down for first and last episodes, and some incomprehensible underfloor lighting, all natty cut-out squares – and the result both failed Verdi's dramatic design and was unpleasing in itself." Opinion was less divided about the singing, especially the Azucena of Janet Coster: "one of the most vivid portrayals I've seen in years, singing with an easy flow of golden tone and a wealth of character," reported Frank Granville Barker. Of the other soloists, Kenneth Collins contributed an outstanding Manrico and David Gwynne's Ferrando reminded people that if there is any truth in Caruso's assertion that all *Trovatore* requires is the four greatest singers in the world, he ought to have amended it to five. The musical side had been meticulously prepared by Richard Armstrong, who reinstated some bars usually cut, and with the Chorale in fine form, it was a full-blooded and exciting performance. The audience cheered long and loud. "Performances such as this," one critic enthused, "are rare."

Two days before the Cardiff season opened, it had been announced that Brian McMaster, the controller of opera planning at English National Opera, had been appointed WNO's new General Administrator. The announcement "caused a communal tizzy in a company where not all prima donnas are on stage." McMaster, a 33-year-old Englishman, had read law at Bristol University, qualified as a solicitor and spent five years in EMI's classical record division before joining ENO in 1973. His selection was not universally welcomed, especially by those who used it as further evidence of WNO losing touch with its roots. Why, they wanted to know, had an Englishman been appointed to the top Welsh administrative post?

McMaster arrived at the beginning of July. It had been made clear to him that one of his first tasks must be to make the thorough examination of the management structure required by the Arts Council to bring it into line with that of other major companies throughout Britain. He had not been given a specific brief as regards artistic direction or policy, but was quite clear in his own mind as to the direction in which he saw WNO going. As it was a touring company and played to many audiences who did not know opera, he felt a keen responsibility to cater for these newcomers. They had been brought up on television and a thriving dramatic tradition in the straight theatre, and he felt that unless such excitement could be brought to operatic production, it would remain a dying, museum art form. To achieve this, he was determined to engage leading directors from the theatre. "I have this rather unpopular idea at the moment that this is the age of the opera producer," he told an interviewer; "it's not the age of the great singer." The policy of developing new talent would be continued. "We've very little money," he explained, "and we've got to make that money go a long way. But we do have a really good musical staff, and we will catch the singers young."

The autumn season, planned before McMaster's arrival, was to include new productions of *Orpheus in the Underworld* and *The Midsummer Marriage* plus revivals of *La Bohème*, *Il Trovatore*, *Boris Godunov* and *The Seraglio*. On 29 July, less than twenty-four hours after the plans had been announced, a fire swept through the main scenery store at the old Roath coal depot on the Newport Road. During the previous eight weeks, there had been nine reported break-ins at the depot and sets had been damaged, but they were nothing compared to the events of that afternoon. More than forty firemen and eight appliances helped fight the blaze, which was soon brought under control, but when officials from WNO entered the building to take stock, they were horrified. Twenty-five sets had been totally destroyed, including those for *Jenůfa* (the joint venture with Scottish Opera), *Don Carlos* (due to be loaned to Netherlands Opera), *Billy Budd* and all the revivals required for the autumn season. The few pieces that had been saved had been so battered by the heat and water that they were unusable without extensive renovation. The only prop to survive unscathed was Albert Herring's bicycle. Within less than an hour, the work of thirty years had disappeared. The damage was estimated as being in the region of £400,000, and although everything had been insured, increased costs meant that only half the true value could be recovered.

Within minutes of the news becoming public, McMaster's phone began to ring. Covent Garden offered props for *Boris*, Glyndebourne offered its touring sets of *La Bohème*, the Music Club of Birmingham offered money, Cardiff's Little Theatre offered spears and swords. Every major company in Britain declared itself prepared to help out. McMaster, accepting only the offer of the *Bohème* sets from Glyndebourne, announced that the autumn season, only a month away, would still go ahead. The sets of the two new productions had not been in the store and so were untouched, and emergency plans were immediately put in hand to rebuild the other productions needed for Cardiff and the subsequent tour: *Il Trovatore* (which had only opened in April) at a cost of £12,000, *Boris Godunov* at a cost of £5,000 to remake the sets and properties, *The Seraglio* and *Albert*

*Herring* (new in January and ruined beyond repair) at a cost of £10,000. From that moment on, every revival became, in effect, a new production. The cost of a new production varied between £20,000 and £40,000, and sympathetic though the Welsh Arts Council was to WNO's plight, it did not have any surplus funds. Once again an appeal was launched to raise the £200,000 needed to bridge the gap between the insurance money and the cost of rebuilding, and once again it produced a derisory response.

The immediate problem was to acquire sets in which to rehearse. Five additional craftsmen were taken on in the workshops and working flat out, under Technical Director John Harrison, they managed to get everything ready for the season to open on time, on 31 August, with *Orpheus in the Underworld*. It might have been better had *Orpheus* been one of the works to be consumed by the fire. Although the opera had already been cast by the time of McMaster's appointment, no producer had been named, and McMaster saw this as an opportunity to begin introducing talent from the straight theatre. Wanting to stage *Orpheus* in the grand style of which the French are sometimes capable, he approached the leading French theatrical director, Jean-Louis Barrault. Barrault expressed interest and for a time it looked a distinct possibility that he might accept the invitation. But then, with the opening night only a month away, he said no. In desperation, McMaster turned to a veteran French producer he did not know, but who had already produced *Orpheus* several times in France, Louis Ducreux, formerly of the Marseilles Opera. He brought with him Denis Martin, for thirty years designer at the Belgian National Theatre, Jean-Denis Malclès, who had designed the costumes for Barrault's highly acclaimed Odéon production of *La Vie Parisienne* ten years earlier, and Gigi Caciuleanu, the Romanian Director of Dance at the Grand Theatre, Nancy, to choreograph the restored ballet. But it required more than their combined talents to achieve the style McMaster sought. In spite of their Gallic approach, the opera was given in a "new and resolutely unfunny translation by Wynford Vaughan Thomas and George Barker, whose stretches of ponderous dialogue – despite 'witty' references to the current Welsh water shortage – made the evening seem very lengthy." This lengthiness was not helped by Ducreux's decision to move the overture from the beginning to cover the scene change between Acts 1 and 2, giving the audience more than an hour and a half before the interval. Certain aspects of Ducreux's production undoubtedly worked well, but most critics complained that the production lacked bite, that he seemed to have had problems conveying his intentions to the cast and had been unable to evoke a sufficiently energetic response. There's no doubt that he had had problems. The other new production of the season, Tippett's *The Midsummer Marriage*, was receiving the greater attention, and in many people's minds *Orpheus* had been relegated to a secondary position. Several times Ducreux threatened to leave rehearsals and return to France. The threat was always received by a chorus of offers to drive him to the airport. The end result, not surprisingly, was not a success. "French poise and precision are out. The style is broad, fat and weighty as a German sausage, without delicacy of touch, without nuance, without elegance." The inclusion of the complete ballet score was generally welcomed, but the dancers, with one exception, proved to be inadequate, and although the audience clapped in time, of the famous can-can "the less said the better." Musically the production was on firmer ground, despite some savage cutting of the score which left Johanna Peters, as Public Opinion, with very little to do. Norma Burrowes as Eurydice and Arthur Davies as Orpheus sang stylishly and well, and Emile Belcourt played an amiably cynical Pluto. Perhaps the most encouraging feature of the entire production was that all the inhabitants of Mount Olympus, with the exception of Jupiter (WNO stalwart Julian Moyle), were portrayed by members of the Chorale. Most of them showed remarkable assurance, none more so than Rita Cullis, whose Diana was an object lesson in stagecraft and projection. How many other choruses could so satisfactorily fill no less than nineteen solo roles?

The following night, *Il Trovatore* was given. There had been no time to rebuild the sets, so it was performed against flats and black drapes with a minimum of props to identify locations. It was, many felt, a distinct improvement on the original designs and brought out the best in Hope's production by throwing the emphasis totally upon the singers. Carl Suppa, the Artistic Director of the Opera Company of Philadelphia, made his British debut in the pit. In spite of his pedigree, his conducting, lacking cohesion between pit and stage, was undistinguished.

The sets for *Boris Godunov* had taken just three weeks to rebuild, although there had not been time to finish the St Basil scene, which was dropped for the revival. *The Seraglio* was also performed in makeshift sets, using backcloths and lighting for effects, designed by Alexander McPherson, who had done the costumes for the original. Geliot took the opportunity of revising his production for a largely new cast which brought in Michael Langdon as Osmin, Vinson Cole as Belmonte and Suzanne Murphy, a young Irish soprano who had been singing with a folk group, making her operatic debut as Constanze. There were important debuts, too, in the revival of *La Bohème* using the Henry Bardon sets borrowed from Glyndebourne and rehearsed by Malcolm Fraser. Guido Ajmone-Marsan, the young American winner of the 1973 Rupert Foundation competition and of the Solti contest in Chicago, made a very favourable impression, nursing the score with considerable love and drawing some highly polished playing from the orchestra. Celestina Casapietra, who had been winning accolades in Germany, made her British debut as Mimi. In spite of some pleasurable phrasing, she generally sang too loud for the house, a fault shared by Romano Emili as Rodolfo, "proving at the end to be a better actor than we had imagined at the start. It is an exciting voice, but one wished," wrote Kenneth Loveland, "he could have shared the conductor's views about taking time over the expansion of the music; too often he seemed determined to push ahead on his own." When it came to the top notes of "Che gelida manina", he quite forgot poor Mimi and sang to the gallery, which adored him. Cristina Carlin as Musetta sang in spectacular but crude fashion, which led David Fingleton, writing in *Opera*, to question the need to have imported all three. "It is casting of this kind that brings into question the policy of our regional opera companies. For one cannot but feel that neither Casapietra, Carlin, nor Emili were assets to this revival, nor improvements upon home-grown singers … all three were deplorably casual over intonation, and far too inclined to opt for volume at the expense of tone."

While the rush was on to rebuild as much as possible and to re-rehearse the productions required for the season, work had been progressing on the second new production of the autumn, Michael Tippett's *The Midsummer Marriage*. For some time Richard Armstrong had been wanting to stage an opera by Tippett and his initial choice had been *King Priam*. When that had proved impracticable, *The Midsummer Marriage*, on which Armstrong had worked as a répétiteur with Colin Davis on the 1968 Covent Garden production, was chosen instead. The opera had not been successful either at its 1955 première at Covent Garden, when it was widely dismissed as being both hopelessly problematic and obscure, or in 1968, but Armstrong had come to believe in it. After two years of preparation, it opened at Cardiff on 22 September. With its wealth of exultant choral music and its poetic imagery mined often from Celtic ritual and romance, it was an excellent, if brave choice. When the curtain came down on the first night, Tippett went on stage and received sustained applause from a wildly enthusiastic audience. "The applause was deserved, by the WNO company as well as by the composer," wrote William Mann in the *Times*. "The famous Welsh chorus covered itself with glory, singing Tippett's celebratory choral music, and the various dramatic exchanges with principal characters, not only as lustily as we expect, but with fine rhythmic pointing and intonation and nuance, and with the natural affection it brings to middle-period Verdi." The soloists, too, came in for their share of praise. Raimund Herincx astonished Bayan Northcott of the *Sunday Telegraph* by achieving the remarkable feat of characterising Tippett's hubristic tycoon, King Fisher, from an entirely new angle to that of his Covent Garden performances. He was, agreed Mann, "easier in manner, bearded and almost bohemian-

looking, though as unscrupulous as ever." Jill Gomez as Jenifer seemed to
be suffering from first-night nerves, but still managed some delectable, soft
high notes. John Treleaven, making his debut with a professional company,
"negotiated Mark's soaring cantilenas with warmth and conviction," while
Mary Davies (a member of the Chorale in her first major role) and Arthur
Davies found a most touching naïvety in their Act 2 duets as Bella and Jack.
The invisible Sosostris was superbly sung by Helen Watts, and Paul Hudson
and Maureen Guy as the Ancients looked and sounded formidable.

The orchestra, under Armstrong, played with an assurance which left no
one in any doubt that it had become an operatic orchestra of a very high
standard. Ian Watt-Smith's production did not meet with total approval;
there were those who deplored his decision not to show Mark and Jenifer in
the guise of Shiva and Parvati in the final scene, as suggested in the libretto,
but to replace them by abstract projections. But within the abstract multi-
purpose set with a sunken grassy amphitheatre at its centre, surrounded by
an assortment of revolving perspex discs and doors, designed by Ralph
Koltai and imaginatively lit by Robert Ornbo, Watt-Smith went a long way
towards making Tippett's rather shallow characters into human beings, and
making the opera clear to an audience that did not already know it. The
evening was a triumph, demonstrating that a major work of the 20th
Century could be done in repertory. Tippett himself was delighted with the
production; it was, he felt, the first time the opera had really worked on
stage. "One left the theatre," wrote David Fingleton in *Music and
Musicians*, "feeling that, for all his occasional lapses in libretto and plotting,
Tippett at any rate knows what music-theatre is about, and that in this
production the Welsh National Opera had fully realised his vision." "It was
a magnificent achievement in practically every department," agreed Hugh
Canning, "... this was a red-letter WNO night: the company is to be
congratulated for choosing such a difficult masterpiece and then for
performing it so well."

Immediately after the Cardiff season, WNO embarked on its autumn tour
with *Orpheus*, *Trovatore*, *The Seraglio*, *La Bohème*, *Boris Godunov* and
*The Midsummer Marriage*. Among the cast changes was one worth noting:
in Bristol, Helen Field, the 24-year-old winner of the Young Welsh Singers
Competition, made her operatic debut as Eurydice in *Orpheus*. She was
"charming and very visual". Also in Bristol, in a move designed to attract
audiences, *The Seraglio* was offered at £1 for all seats. It resulted in a full
house to hear Jerome Pruett as the new Belmonte and Frank Olegario
replacing Forbes Robinson as Osmin. The same ploy was tried for *The
Midsummer Marriage* in Birmingham, Liverpool, Leeds and Manchester,
and again produced full houses. In Leeds, where the entire week was sold
out in advance, there were queues for returns and people had to be turned

away. In Manchester, which did not do so well with the other operas, the Tippett, at £1.50 a seat, also proved to be the most popular work of the fortnight and would probably have sold out a second performance had there been one. If *Orpheus* was the disappointment of the autumn, *The Midsummer Marriage* was the undoubted hit, playing to hugely enthusiastic audiences wherever it went.

After thirty years, Welsh National Opera was still the only major company in Britain not to have a permanent home. The need for an opera house had always been a topic for discussion; Geraint Evans had even threatened never to sing again in his native land until a proper opera house was built. "It's second best all the time," he had raged; "I am fed up with seeing second best in Wales." And he was right. Wales, with its musical tradition so firmly rooted in the amateur, did not really want an opera house and certainly was not prepared to pay for one. While an opera house of its own would have been highly desirable for WNO (the lack of a suitable theatre meant that Wales had always been denied the opportunity of seeing major works by Wagner and Richard Strauss, for example), acquiring one had had to take second place to the actual staging of opera. One by one, suitable possibilities had come and gone. The Prince of Wales Theatre, where WNO had begun its existence, had become a cinema showing sex films, the Empire had been demolished. Now the Capitol Cinema, the Cardiff venue for rock concerts, was threatened. Its owners, the Rank Organisation, had applied to convert it into a multi-cinema and bingo-hall complex, and there were rumours that it was to be sold or possibly even demolished. The Capitol had been considered as a potential opera house in the past, but nothing had come of it because of the lack of money. Now, with the building's future in doubt, a feasibility study was carried out to see whether it could become WNO'S new home. The idea caught the public imagination; local papers were full of letters from individuals and organisations (including the Welsh TUC) supporting the proposal, and a petition signed by 12,000 people was sent to the Welsh Office demanding support for the scheme.

The feasibility study showed that the building could be converted into a 1700-seat theatre suitable not just for opera but to take the big touring shows for which there was no venue in Cardiff, at a cost of £3.2 million. Since the Arts Council's Housing the Arts Fund had only recently given £70,000 to the New Theatre to enlarge the orchestra pit and stage, and knew it would be required to come up with the funding necessary to run a new building, the proposal received little official support. And then in the autumn came news that the fight was over. Cardiff City Council had given Rank the go-ahead to convert the Capitol into a two-cinema complex and bingo-hall.

The failure to acquire the Capitol was, perhaps, a blessing in disguise. The annual cost of running a building would have been a vast drain on resources and might well have affected WNO's artistic output. By remaining as a touring company without a home base, it spent its annual income almost entirely where it matters most: on productions.

The programme for 1977, the first on which McMaster was able to stamp a personal imprint, opened at Mold on 25 January with a production of *The Barber of Seville* by William Gaskill. Gaskill, a distinguished stage-director making his debut in opera was an inspired choice. He avoided the hackneyed business which had become an ingrained way of performing *The Barber* and returned to basics. This resulted in a delightful concentration on character, from which the humour flowed naturally. William Dudley provided the excellent sets. Simple and economical, they permitted the singers to use the stage whilst at the same time being attractive and highly atmospheric. "For once," wrote David Fingleton in *Music and Musicians*, "one was left with the feeling that here was a production team who had really thought out an opera in terms of what it would convey to an audience." The singing was worthy of the production. Returning to sing Almaviva, the role in which he had made his debut thirteen years earlier, was Ryland Davies. Thomas Allen as Figaro was, quite simply, superb, confirming that he was the finest British Figaro then appearing on stage. Beverley Humphreys as Rosina, Thomas Hemsley as Bartolo and Geoffrey Moses (a chorister making a notable debut as a principal) as Don Basilio completed an excellent ensemble, conducted by the Assistant Chorus Master, Wyn Davies.

The first new offering of the spring season, continuing the long line of pioneering productions of lesser-known Verdi, was of *I Masnadieri* which, apart from some performances at the Camden Festival in 1962, had not been performed professionally in Britain since its London première in 1847. Written for London, it was first performed, with the composer conducting and Queen Victoria in the audience, at Her Majesty's Theatre. In Cardiff it was played as *The Robbers* in an especially commissioned translation from composer Stephen Oliver, who returned to the German names of the original Schiller play on which Verdi's libretto was based. The work contains a ludicrous plot and for once it might have been better to have sung it in Italian. Two brothers, one good, the other bad, are in love with the same girl. The good brother runs away to become the leader of some brigands, the bad attempts to marry the girl and incarcerates his gullible father, who spends most of the opera entombed. At the close, the good brother, reunited with the girl, unexpectedly kills her rather than let her share the shame of knowing he is a brigand. Producer Julian Hope attempted to make sense of this nonsense on a spare, murky, raked set designed by Hayden Griffin. That he could not always succeed was demonstrated by his decision to line up the bandit chorus, bathe them in light and have them sing directly to the audience as if in a concert performance. But, as with most early Verdi, the plot and characterisation are secondary to the opportunities it offers for grand singing, and although the music of *I Masnadieri* is not Verdi's finest, most of it is direct and accessible and Hope permitted his cast to put it across unencumbered by needless stage business. The chorus sang lustily and there was zestful singing from the principals: Kenneth Collins, in magnificent voice, as good brother Karl, Richard Van Allan as an authoritative Count Maximilian, particularly striking as he emerged from his subterranean prison, and Terence Sharpe as the villainous Franz. Suzanne Murphy took time to settle as Amalia (a part written for Jenny Lind) but went on to reveal a voice of exceptional strength, richness and agility, marred only by a tendency to scoop and by poor diction. There was strong support from Geoffrey Moses, John Treleaven and Mark Hamilton in the smaller roles. Richard Armstrong, conducting a score prepared by Julian Smith from original manuscripts, kept the performance sweeping along. It may have been nonsense, but it was stirring nonsense. Audience reaction, however, was disappointing. After a full auditorium for the opening, the production played to houses only a third full.

The remainder of the Cardiff season saw revivals of *The Barber of Seville*, with John Brecknock taking over as Count Almaviva, *Albert Herring*, with reconstructed sets and Ava June as the new Lady Billows, *Orpheus*, *The Midsummer Marriage* and *Il Trovatore*. For the second performance of *Trovatore*, Kenneth Collins was unable to sing Manrico and Tom Swift, who was appearing with ENO in Leeds, raced the 200 miles to Cardiff to take over. He did not know the role in Italian, and so, while the rest of the cast sang in the original language, he sang in English.

As if the disastrous fire in 1976 had not caused enough problems, another crisis now began to loom large. A series of incidents, some seemingly unconnected, had drawn together at the start of 1977 to plunge the company into an internal feud which was to bring with it much heartache. They centred on the position of Michael Geliot.

The first hint that something might be wrong had come at the press conference announcing McMaster's appointment. "One did not have to be a professional psychologist to plug into the mild undercurrents of anxiety about the exact pecking order in the new hierarchy, particularly as they affect Mr Geliot," wrote Chris Stuart of the *Western Mail*. "The General Administrator will bear ultimate responsibility for all company policy, including artistic policy, we were told by the chairman, Lord Davies. 'What my name is on, I answer for,' countered Mr Geliot politely, but seeming to imply a contradiction. 'When I can't answer for it, then I have to go. It's as simple as that.' Does that mean you're thinking of going? 'No, it doesn't. I'm very happy at the appointment. It has to be a team effort and I'm sure we'll work together very well as a team.' " An awkward moment appeared to have passed, and when McMaster took up his post in July, one of the first things he did was to offer Geliot a new contract guaranteeing him a minimum of three new productions a year, a first refusal on any planned production, selection of designers and at least one major revival.

Behind the public calm, however, a private dispute was raging. At the time Lord Davies had become Chairman, Geliot had offered to resign, as he put it, to give Lord Davies a free hand to assemble the production team he wanted. Davies, on the advice of some senior WNO members, had refused to accept the resignation telling Geliot to wait until the new General Administrator had been appointed. Geliot agreed, but left his resignation on the table, and as far as Davies was concerned, this still stood. He told McMaster as much, and McMaster accepted his job with the understanding that Geliot would be leaving. By the time McMaster's appointment was announced, Geliot had decided not to resign and McMaster, not wishing to change a winning team, agreed to work with him, hence the new contract.

Meanwhile, another situation involving Geliot was coming to a head. In 1971 he had become the Artistic Director of the Welsh Theatre Company based at the Casson Theatre in Cardiff. Two years later, the Welsh Arts Council asked it to give up the Casson and become a touring company. Because of Geliot's position within Welsh National Opera as Director of Productions it had seemed a logical and cost-effective move to combine the two organisations so that the Welsh Drama Company (as it had become known) could make use of WNO's production facilities at John Street. And so the Welsh National Opera and Drama Company, the largest body of its type within the British Isles, had been formed.

For some time, the position of the Drama Company within the organisation had been causing consternation. Its work had come in for much criticism (some justified, some unjustified) with regard to repertoire and standards. Theatre managers throughout Wales who had to take its product were not happy, and several preferred to mount their own productions rather than give room to an organisation they felt had nothing particularly Welsh about it, other than its title. This unhappiness was also felt by the Drama Committee of the Welsh Arts Council, most of their antagonism towards the company being directed at Geliot, whose out-spoken criticism of the Council's funding policies had raised many hackles.

At the beginning of 1977, at a private dinner with Lady Anglesey, McMaster was informed that the Welsh Arts Council had decided not to increase the funding of the Drama Company for the new financial year; the most it could expect, he was told, would be £100,000: enough to cover overheads without allowing it to do any actual work. If this were true, and McMaster had no reason to suppose it not to be, it meant the end of the road for the Welsh Drama Company. (When the grant came through, it was in fact for £80,000, half the previous year's allocation. This was in response to a request for £242,000.) Although the Arts Council had never formally asked for the removal of Geliot (privately it had been suggested that it would be a good thing), both McMaster and Davies believed that Geliot's departure would be to everyone's advantage. On Sunday, 24 January, McMaster and Lord Davies met Geliot to discuss the situation and understood him to say that he would be willing to resign if it was in the best interests of the company for him to do so. The following day, Lord Davies wrote to Geliot accepting his offer. Three days later, Geliot wrote back pointing out that he had not offered to resign but would be willing to accept the termination of his contract with the Drama Company if the company felt that because of outside hostility, whether aroused by his own actions or by the unjustifiable malice of others, the company would be likely to suffer harm by retaining his services. Both Davies and McMaster sensed from the tone of the reply that Geliot was preparing a public attack upon the Arts Council, which neither of them could condone, and at a further meeting they made this view clear to Geliot, Lord Davies insisting that they did not want to get rid of him simply at the behest of the Welsh Arts Council. It was agreed that a suitable way for Geliot to go without any blemish on his professional reputation would be found. Two days later Geliot contacted Lord Davies again, withdrawing all offers to resign. By this time, McMaster had come to the conclusion that he could not work with Geliot, either in the Drama Company or in the Opera Company, and that his and Geliot's ideas on production and repertoire were irreconcilable. With Geliot refusing to go of his own free will, Davies and McMaster wrote to the Board recommending that Geliot be asked to resign or else have his contract terminated. The Board, taking at face value Arts Council assurances that they were not out to kill off the Drama Company, rejected the recommendation at its next meeting in March. McMaster in turn offered to resign. This, too, was refused, Geliot himself being one of the people who helped persuade McMaster to stay, and McMaster was told to find ways of making the partnership work.

In April the Welsh Drama Company, having run out of money, closed after a short season in Aberystwyth. On 14 April, McMaster produced the report asked for by the Arts Council, outlining the new management structure he proposed in relation to the budget for 1977–1978 season. He could, he concluded, no longer find any justification for the post of Artistic Director. "Since the present structure came into being on 1 July 1976, I have attempted to make a potentially difficult situation work, but in effect the artistic policy has been formulated over the past eight months by Richard Armstrong and myself and fundamental areas of disagreement between our thinking and Michael's have become apparent and considerable tension has developed between him on the one hand and Richard and me on the other," he wrote. He recommended that the posts of Artistic Director (which, he claimed, was not a recognised one within opera) and of General Manager should be abolished. He did stress, however, that "it should be our intention to maintain a continuing association" with Geliot. The General Adminis-trator would have overall control of WNO with the Musical Director; the post of General Manager would be superseded by that of Financial Controller and the responsibility for the production activities of the opera company should, he suggested, be vested in a Director of Productions wholly responsible to the Opera Company and on a level of responsibility comparable to that of the Head of Music Staff. The abolition of the post of Artistic Director, would, he estimated, save £13,516 a year.

McMaster's proposals were accepted by the Council of Management in May, and the top administration of the Opera Company was restructured accordingly with McMaster as General Administrator, making decisions jointly with Richard Armstrong, the Musical Director, and a new appointment of Financial Controller to run the administrative side. There was clearly no room in such a set-up for either a General Manager or an Artistic Director. Privately, James Mowat, the General Manager, admitted that his career with WNO was over. Geliot, however, was determined not to go without a fight, and in this he was backed by the chorus. As soon as the proposed changes became known, the chorus met Lord Davies to complain about Geliot's removal and a memorandum was sent to the Board which stated: "Having thoroughly examined the restructuring report, we can find no possible ground for the redundancy of the post of Artistic Director." This was reported in the press as a "we'll-strike-if-Geliot-goes" ultimatum. Equity, too, joined in the argument, opposing both Geliot's dismissal and the abolition of his post. Geliot, angry with both WNO and the Welsh Arts Council, threatened to sue the Arts Council for defamation of character. They hurriedly denied that they had asked for Geliot to be sacked. At a meeting on 11 July, WNO's Board decided to refer the matter to arbitration before issuing redundancy notices.

While this wrangling was going on, performances were still taking place throughout Wales and England. For the Llandudno fortnight in June, a revival of John Moody's production of *Rigoletto* was scheduled, with two American singers making their company debuts. Catherine Malfitano was to sing her first Gilda in Europe and Neil Shicoff to make his British debut as the Duke before going on to sing Don Carlos in Vienna. Three weeks before the production was due to open, the Department of Employment, on the advice of Equity, refused to give either of them a work permit because "neither was of sufficient international status" and, according to Equity, British artists would be just as good. Despite strong representations from WNO, Equity refused to alter its position, and at the last moment two Italian artists, neither of whom needed a work permit since they came from a member country of the European Economic Community, were engaged. There were to be no great revelations or discoveries. Milena Dal Piva as Gilda sang brightly but acted abominably and Antonio Bevacqua was a lightweight Duke. The greatest pleasure of the evening came from the return of Walter Susskind to British opera after too long an absence. He conducted a leisurely reading, injecting the score with just the right amount of tension and consideration for his singers.

In order to give more variety to the seasons in Cardiff and to relieve the pressure of long weeks spent on tour, it had been decided to divide the Cardiff seasons into four appearances of a fortnight each. The first of these fortnights began in September with a new production of Tchaikovsky's *The Queen of Spades*. McMaster and Geliot had been unable to agree on a producer, and at the eleventh hour David William, at the suggestion of the conductor, David Lloyd-Jones (who also provided the translation), was brought in. With so little time to get everything together, William naturally wanted a designer who knew the work already, and the East German Wilfried Werz, who was in Cardiff to discuss the following year's production of *Elektra*, was engaged. He asked his compatriot Erika Simmank-Heinze to provide the costumes. In spite of all the money spent on it (£23,000), the result was, to say the least, disappointing. "Having ridden a crest for some time now they brought one back to earth with a bump with this production, which would have done little credit to an ad hoc company working on a shoe-string, let alone one of our national ones," raged David Fingleton in *Music and Musicians*. The designs were, according to Fingleton, "pretentious and frankly hideous . . . Despite heavy sets requiring two long intervals and four lengthy scene changes which utterly dispelled any dramatic atmosphere that might otherwise have been achieved, the pictures created never actually felt anywhere near Russia, remaining solidly planted in ugly, artificial theatre-land." And while some of the staging was effective, William seemed at sea with the chorus, which remained extraneous to the action throughout the evening. The forty-five-second appearance of retired ballerina Svetlana Beriosova as the Empress Catherine was "yet another sorry miscalculation". Allen Cathcart as Hermann sang powerfully and dramatically, though with little beauty, and Evelyn Brunner as Lisa sang well only fitfully. The best characterisation came from Maureen Guy as the aged Countess, even though her false nose fell off during the performance! The reminiscence of her youth was touchingly sung and her death particularly well acted. Maureen Guy apart, the outstanding contributions were to be found amongst the smaller roles, especially Russell Smythe's beautifully sung, dignified and distraught Prince Yeletsky, Patricia Price as Polina, Arthur Davies as Tchekalinsky and Henry Newman as Tomsky. The Chorale were sometimes over-enthusiastic but sang with gusto, and the performance was adequately conducted by Lloyd-Jones. It was one of WNO's less memorable opening nights.

Equity, finally realising that Neil Shicoff could not be dismissed as an unimportant singer, had withdrawn its opposition and he made his belated British debut as the Duke in the revival of *Rigoletto*. "His voice is full-blooded and heroic," commented Chris Stuart in *Classical Music*, "with plenty in reserve for the climactic moments, and his relaxed, assured dramatic awareness made this a most convincing, as well as a most musicianly, characterisation." Singing Gilda was the promising young soprano Suzanne Murphy. Her performance grew in confidence and she displayed considerable technical skill and artistry in her first attempt at the role.

Ever since the fire, it had become important to restage as many as possible of the lost productions. During the fortnight, *The Pearl Fishers* and *Jenůfa* had reappeared in new sets while on the autumn tour in Leeds (where WNO was making its last appearance prior to the formation of English National Opera North) *Billy Budd* was remounted with complete fidelity to Roger Butlin's original designs and with its original cast. It was this performance which remains in the memories of all those who took part or who saw it, as the best any of them had ever experienced. Quite why it should have happened at that time and on that stage, is one of those operatic mysteries. By this time, five years after the production had first opened, the cast knew their roles perfectly and could concentrate on performing; there was also the excitement of coming together after a break of almost three years to recreate a work in which everyone believed so fervently. But those two factors alone are not sufficient to explain an evening when, even though the house was half empty, near-perfection was achieved. Nigel Douglas feels he has the answer. His schedule saw him in Leeds for a dress rehearsal on the Tuesday, in Düsseldorf for a performance of a new Swiss opera, *An Angel Comes to Babylon*, on the Wednesday and back in Leeds for *Budd* on Thursday. Because of a flight controllers' dispute, there was considerable doubt as to whether he would make it back in time, and since there was no understudy, the performance would have had to be cancelled if he was not there. The fact that he made it with very little time to spare produced such a feeling of relief that everyone relaxed into the performance. "Never did a Phoenix rise more splendidly from the flames than last night's revival," wrote John McMurray.

Douglas did, however, fail to make the performance when the production opened the second, winter season in Cardiff, because of illness, and Stuart Kale, who had understudied the role earlier and was currently working at the Coliseum, was asked to deputise. He did so with twenty-four hours' notice and score in hand. He gave, according to Hugh Canning, "a searing, beautifully sung reading." "It was a plucky effort," commented Kenneth Loveland, "and whenever he could permit himself the freedom to expand, enough was heard to suggest that he should now be given a scheduled appearance."

*Billy Budd* was followed by Geliot's new production of *The Marriage of Figaro*. If he was worried about his position within the company (which was still under negotiation), Geliot did not allow it to affect his work. After his disappointing *Seraglio* the previous year, he was back on form. *The Marriage of Figaro*, using Geliot's own up-to-date and colloquial translation, deliberately pointed up the social differences between the servants and the aristocrats. It was an approach which Meirion Bowen of the *Guardian* felt was laid on too thick, though others found it refreshing, especially since the production was almost totally free of gratuitous comic business. The predominantly young cast, almost all making their debuts either in their roles or with WNO, responded well to Geliot's direction, acting and singing for the most part with considerable style and conviction. John Rawnsley, a former student of the Royal Northern College who had sung with the Glyndebourne Touring Company, appeared as Figaro, Stuart Harling as Count Almaviva, Meryl Drower as Susanna, Patricia Parker as Cherubino, John Treleaven as Basilio and Felicity Lott as the Countess. Lott's rapturous singing was, musically, the high point of the performance.

Geliot's interpretation was superbly supported by Alexander McPherson's set, an elegant baroque framework based on revolves which allowed for swift scene changes, although Max Loppert found by the last act that the constant revolving began to jar, "and the rumble of machinery disturbs the nocturnal atmosphere." György Fischer conducted with just the right amount of care and attention to detail without ever losing the freshness or pace to match what was happening on stage. The evening was, in the words of Max Loppert, exhilarating, restorative and moving.

The second new production that winter was of *La Bohème*. The destruction of the old sets meant that a new production had become imperative, and William Gaskill, whose *Barber of Seville* had been such a revelation, was invited to work his magic again, with Hayden Griffin and Michael Stennett as his set and costume designers. With the production of *Figaro* and the restaging of revivals taking place simultaneously, it was always touch-and-go whether *Bohème* could be got ready in time; it turned out not to be possible. On the Sunday when the production ought to have been receiving its dress rehearsal in the New Theatre, a television show was being recorded there. Because of this the final technical rehearsal had to be held on the Monday and it did not proceed smoothly. A further complication was that most of the production rehearsals had been held on the stage of the nearby Sherman Theatre, and in transit some of the scenery had been damaged. Rehearsals continued into Tuesday and went on so long that the evening performance of *Jenůfa* was held up for twenty-five minutes and had to be given without a complete set for Act 1. It was evident that *Bohème* would not be ready, and the unprecedented step was taken of declaring that Thursday night's opening (which had been sold out for weeks) would instead be a public preview. Patrons were offered the choice of their money back or seeing the preview and being given priority for the production in the next booking period. The second performance on Saturday, 26 November, the last night of the season, became the official first night. It was not perhaps surprising that the production should have had an unfinished feel about it. Gaskill had attempted, as he had with *The Barber*, to take the work back to basics, and therein lay much of the problem. Griffin's sets were sombre, grey and very cardboard-looking, falling uneasily between stylisation and realism. An ever-present Parisian backcloth made a nonsense of Act 3 by placing it outside the gates: why should the guards be searching the women's baskets outside the gates? Gaskill's updating of the action to the 1890s also created problems since there would not have been searches at that time. By returning to the Henri Murger story on which Puccini's opera was based, Gaskill emphasised the squalor of Bohemian life but ignored the warmth of the score. "One was ultimately left regretting the coolness and lack of emotional involvement throughout," wrote David Fingleton. Such a dispassionate approach might not have mattered so much had it been accompanied by superb singing, but unfortunately it was not. The Mimi of Vivien Townley and Rodolfo of Mark Hamilton remained curiously indifferent to each other, partly because of the production, partly because Hamilton, a former member of the Chorale recently upgraded to principal, was more intent on watching the beat than his Mimi. She, too, was stiff and inhibited. The Marcello and Musetta of Terence Sharpe and Catherine Wilson were altogether better, Henry Newman was an excellent Schaunard and there were lively cameos from two Chorale members: Peter Massocchi as Alcindoro and Derek Barnes as Benoit. But in the end, although it contained moments of real drama, the production did not live up to expectations.

Few opera critics are used to having to forsake their interval drink for an ice-cream, but that's what those who attended the afternoon performance of Benjamin Britten's *Let's Make an Opera* had to do when it opened at the Sherman Theatre, Cardiff, on 12 January 1978. Britten's work, written for the 1949 Aldeburgh Festival, was considered to be an ideal introduction to opera for young people of all ages. For its first professional production in more than a decade, Eric Crozier had updated his own libretto, the main change being that in the first scene the children were discovered watching television. The only other concession to contemporary taste was that the name Guy was substituted for Gay.

Sally Day's production, her first for WNO, like the work itself, took time to get going, and conductor Julian Smith had to work hard to involve the audience. He eventually succeeded and in the final act everyone, adults included, overcame their self-consciousness to join in. Of the adult professionals, Helen Field made a superb Rowan, and Peter Massocchi, Mark Hamilton, Caroline Baker and Margaret Baiton all contributed neat cameos.

The work of the main company began with a new production of another opera by Britten, *A Midsummer Night's Dream*, which opened in Mold on 24 January. This had been written for performance in Aldeburgh's Jubilee Hall and benefited greatly by being staged on a similarly small stage. Alexander McPherson had designed a simple, evocative set based upon a series of circles in various shades of green, contained within a tree-top arch on which the signs of the zodiac were painted, the air of magic being greatly enhanced by the subtle and effective lighting of Robert Ornbo. Within this framework, Ian Watt-Smith had produced the opera as a ritual, "suggesting that midsummer is the period when human relationships are in the melting pot, that it is a timeless, spaceless limbo, where mysterious influences are whimsically, even hurtfully active." It was "an ambitious and for the most part brilliantly inventive production" which, Max Loppert felt, enhanced Britten's music although it perhaps lost the peculiar Englishness of the work. "The strengths of the production compensate for this," he continued; "its imagination, its visual fascination, and, happily married to these, its quick, unexaggerated treatment of all the various confusions, altercations, and emotional upsets." Many people went to *A Midsummer Night's Dream* just to see Geraint Evans as Bottom, one of the great comedy roles of the 20th Century. Evans, a seasoned performer in the role, did not put a foot or note wrong. His performance was outstanding and it was natural that he should steal the show. But although he was the lynch-pin of those scenes in which he appeared, he by no means dominated them, and one of the strengths of the production was the assurance displayed by the remainder of the cast, drawn, with the exception of James Bowman as Oberon and Sylveste McCoy as Puck, from the company. Bowman, who had been suffering vocal difficulties, was still not in his best voice on opening night, but managed to convey the imperiousness of Oberon. Rita Cullis sang beautifully as Titania and there was an eloquent quartet of lovers: Margaret Morgan (Hermia), Suzanne Murphy (Helena), Arthur Davies (Lysander) and Henry Newman (Demetrius). The mechanicals, led by David Gwynne's fatherly Quince, included two outstanding performances, from John Treleaven as Flute and Julian Moyle as Starveling. Sylveste McCoy, the actor who once held the world record for the number of ferrets stuffed down his trousers, played Puck as a bearded, older-than-usual, acrobatic satyr, which removed all traces of coyness from the part and Anthony Hose, the conductor, drew some richly textured ensemble and solo playing from the orchestra, which sounded especially well in the Theatr Clwyd. "It sounded so organic and seamless," wrote Michael Kennedy in the *Daily Telegraph*, "that one resented the intervals as violent intrusions."

*A Midsummer Night's Dream*, with the same cast (Paul Hudson, who sang one performance in Mold, was to take over the role of Bottom later in the season and Rosalind Plowright that of Helena) opened the first Cardiff season of the year on 14 March. The following night Richard Strauss's *Elektra* was given its first performance outside London for more than sixty years (apart from some foreign performances at the Edinburgh Festival) and its first ever in Wales. The production was possible only because of the alterations that had been made to the orchestra pit and stage of the New. As part of a deal in which WNO lent the Netherlands Opera its sets for *Don Carlos*, McMaster had persuaded Harry Kupfer, Director of the Dresden Opera and a disciple of Felsenstein, to recreate in Cardiff (using a new translation by Anthony Hose, WNO's Head of Music Staff) the staging he and designer Wilfried Werz had done in Amsterdam the previous year. Cardiff audiences were hardly prepared for their first real taste of continental opera. In Amsterdam the sacrifice of a naked slave girl had caused outrage, not because of the violence but because the critics thought it was the Fifth Maid. Kupfer pointed out that since both girls were black, the critics hadn't looked hard enough to see that they were different people. He avoided such confusion in Cardiff by casting a white girl (Rita Cullis) as the Maid. Kupfer opened the opera in an abattoir, a sign of his emphasis upon the violence and cruelty of the characters. The five maids, who in the libretto are drawing water, here moved aside rotting carcasses before scrubbing away the blood. This emphasis was maintained throughout, including the sacrifice of the naked slave girl and the on-stage murder of Aegisthus, just two of the many liberties Kupfer took with the libretto.

Werz's set was unrecognisable from his work in *The Queen of Spades*. He used the entire stage area, swathing it in crumpled polythene sheeting and covering the floor in bumpy polystyrene. Dominating everything was a huge, crumbling statue of Agamemnon. The only serious miscalculation was the siting of this statue, which obscured crucial entries from too many members of the audience. It was a very physical production, the members of the cast suffering repeatedly from bumps and bruises during rehearsals. Pauline Tinsley as Elektra, who was on stage for almost the entire performance, spent much of that time clinging to ropes dangling from the statue, resulting in blistered and swollen hands, an injured ankle, burns on the neck from rubbing ropes and a dislocated shoulder. The physiotherapist who treated her and other cast members also treated the Welsh rugby team; opera, he concluded, was infinitely more dangerous.

The reaction of the critics when the production opened was, predictably, divided between those who were invigorated by it and those who hated it. Hugh Canning found it a shattering theatrical experience "infinitely preferable to the charade regularly dragged out at Covent Garden since 1952 to show off a handful of stentorian singers." "Crude sensationalism dominates," agreed Nicholas Kenyon in the *Sunday Times*, ". . . but the crude sensations it reflects are precisely those of the music."

At the other extreme, Rodney Milnes and Noël Goodwin loathed everything Kupfer and Werz did. Werz's set, wrote Goodwin in *Music and Musicians*, "looked like the interior of a municipal swimming-bath, and ought, in my opinion, to forfeit any further invitation to work in opera after putting the entire cast at risk by designing a false stage floor of deliberately irregular surface, which had already cost one principal singer a leg injury before the first night and looked a nasty trap for the unwary." Of Kupfer – his programme note in which he described Elektra as "the first terrorist, a psychological terrorist" was dismissed as "a manifesto of intellectual megalomania" – the best Goodwin could find to say was that the production was "an arrogantly imposed view of *Elektra* as another document of social relevance for our time, but which only serves to demean its classical stature in the interests of cheap sensationalism . . . What is sad is that such a production is likely to repel potential audiences from realising the calibre of an outstanding work of musical theatre." Milnes also dismissed the programme note as "the purest, most highly refined horse manure," and the production as "fatuous . . . Indeed it would be possible to laugh the whole contemptible thing off if the musical side were not so brilliant."

There was, however, almost unanimous praise for the cast, not one of whom had sung his or her role before. Tinsley's Elektra was a thrilling and unqualified success. American mezzo Debria Brown as Klytemnestra (replacing Anny Schlemm, the original choice) was dramatically and vocally excellent, and a female trio of unsurpassed quality was completed by Anne Evans singing superlatively as Chrysothemis. Willard White was a noble Orestes and John Mitchinson, too heavily built to play Aegisthus as the usual fop, sang with refreshing vigour. The supporting roles, taken mostly by company members, were all strongly sung. Richard Armstrong, conducting an orchestra augmented to eighty-five (less than that specified by Strauss, but still the largest yet used by WNO), produced a reading of the score which, commented Milnes, was little short of miraculous.

There were a few boos at the end (not, remembering *I Lombardi*, the first time this had happened to a WNO production but a new experience for most of the company) but, for the majority *Elektra* proved to be an unforgettable experience and a major landmark in WNO's development. "With this production," wrote Tom Sutcliffe in the *Guardian*, "the new management at WNO come into their own: Kupfer's work ranks with the very best operatic productions there have been in Britain in the seventies." McMaster's policy of bringing in overseas producers to create a true music theatre had been totally vindicated.

For those who liked their opera less sensational and more traditional, the fortnight included revivals of *La Bohème*, for which the sets still seemed realistic to the point of monotony but saw the debuts of Helen Field as Musetta, Henry Newman as Marcello and Christopher Booth-Jones as Schaunard, and of *The Marriage of Figaro* with Russell Smythe and Jennifer Smith as the new Count and Countess, Mary Davies as Cherubino and Paul Gyton as Don Basilio. Although everyone knew it was Geliot's production, and it was reviewed as such, his name did not appear on the programme, the reason being that his position still had not been resolved. The arbitration requested by Equity and agreed upon by the Board the previous July had broken down since neither side could agree upon an arbitrator. At the beginning of January, the Board had decided to go ahead with the implementation of McMaster's restructuring proposals and to give Geliot notice that as from 17 January he would be redundant. He was asked to cease work immediately on rehearsals of *Figaro* which he was preparing for Mold on 25 January. WNO's Equity deputy, chorister Charles Lewis, went to see McMaster and Armstrong to ask that Geliot be allowed to continue work on the production, and a telegram from the cast – all, without exception, on Geliot's side – brought Lord Davies hurrying to Cardiff. The Chorale and principal singers issued a press statement calling upon the Chairman and Council of Management to "withdraw his notice; to maintain the post of Artistic Director, and Mr Geliot in that post." After hurried consultations, Davies announced that Geliot would be allowed to resume work, but on what basis or for how long he refused to say.

The division within WNO over the "Geliot affair" was almost total. Those who supported him (and the orchestra had decided to back him as well) did so not because of any great affection for him – he had a manner which was not designed to win friends – but because they felt he had been responsible for some of WNO's greatest artistic successes and did not wish to lose him; his continuing presence was seen as essential to the future. Others, recognising that it had come down to an either/or situation between Geliot and McMaster, considered that the loss of McMaster would be a more tragic blow even if they felt he had bitten off more than he could chew. Friends took opposite views and sides, no longer speaking to one another. An emergency Board meeting was called to discuss rescinding the dismissal notice, but the motion was not accepted.

The matter had reached an impasse. Neither side was prepared to give way and the only answer lay with an Industrial Tribunal. The Tribunal met in Cardiff in July. Last-minute negotiations between Geliot's counsel and WNO lawyers over a three-day period caused ten adjournments before, on 20 July, Geliot withdrew his claim for unfair dismissal, to the obvious irritation of the Chairman, who remarked that while he was pleased that agreement had been reached it was a pity it hadn't happened earlier. Under the out-of-court settlement, Geliot stayed with WNO to become Artistic Consultant and Principal Producer for a period of five years, during which time it was agreed he would produce not less than eight operas. On the face of it, it was a total victory for Geliot. His artistic reputation was intact and he had achieved an honourable settlement. But, in fact, neither side could have been said to have won; and McMaster had succeeded in ousting him from the post of Artistic Director.

It had been intended that Geliot should produce the new production of *Peter Grimes*, which was finally scheduled for May. His sacking in January had produced a last-minute search for a replacement and the person chosen was John Copley, who had played the boy apprentice in Tyrone Guthrie's Covent Garden production of 1947. Geliot's original designer, John Gunter, who had already started work on the project, was paid off and Henry Bardon (sets) and Michael Stennett (costumes) were brought in to replace him. With only two months in which to plan and rehearse the production, it was perhaps inevitable that Copley should play safe. Bardon provided him with serviceably realistic, though possibly too intricate and flimsy, sets in which to portray life in the Borough. Copley's handling of the chorus was clearly achieved and the individual characters were carefully delineated. And yet, in spite of many striking moments and fine detail, the overall result was disappointing. To Alun Davies writing in *Musical Opinion*, it was "dour rather than stimulating." "This is not a version of *Peter Grimes* that springs any revelations, but it is a solid honest workmanlike account," concluded Tom Sutcliffe in the *Guardian*.

Singing the title role for the first time in his career was John Mitchinson. Although he sang strongly and with great clarity, his characterisation was too bluff and slow-witted to reveal any of the visionary aspects of Grimes's nature, and much of the dramatic force of his being an outsider was lost. Josephine Barstow, also singing her role for the first time, was an unusually young and sympathetic Ellen Orford, her concern for Grimes being more than neighbourly compassion. Terence Sharpe made a sterling Balstrode, and there was strong support from John Treleaven as Bob Boles, David Gwynne as Justice Swallow, Menai Davies as Auntie and Rita Cullis and Mary Davies as her nieces. Maureen Guy (in real life Mrs Mitchinson; they were appearing on stage together for the first time) provided a finely sung and well characterised Mrs Sedley. The performance was predictably exciting in the choral outbursts and Armstrong, especially evocative in the orchestral interludes and the lyrical passages, conducted with an obvious affection for, and understanding of, the drama.

One of McMaster's principal concerns upon his arrival in Wales had been to rationalise the touring programme. It was, he felt, ridiculous to play in such distant places as Sunderland (which was closer to Scottish Opera and also to the newly formed English National Opera North in Leeds) and Norwich (which received visits from Glyndebourne Touring). His decision to axe Norwich from his schedules the previous year had produced howls of outrage, but financially it made sense. What he envisaged was that each of the major companies should have a sphere of influence, a touring circuit for which it alone would be responsible. The Arts Council looked favourably upon the scheme, especially since both Scottish Opera and Glyndebourne had turned up in Wolverhampton with productions of *La Bohème* at the same time as WNO was playing the same piece in Birmingham. The previous year, aided by a grant of £10,000 from the West Midlands, WNO had rescheduled its visits to Birmingham and had announced that Birmingham would become WNO's English headquarters. What this meant in practice was that an organiser had a desk and a phone within the Hippodrome from which to arrange and co-ordinate ancillary activities. The rumour that WNO would be moving its entire operation to the Midlands because of the failure of Wales to provide a permanent home was not true, but it did demonstrate the strength of the disappointment felt at losing the Capitol. At the same time as these moves were announced, many of the larger, most suitable theatres were themselves in difficulties and there was talk of the Southampton Gaumont and even the Birmingham Hippodrome being closed down. The June season in Llandudno was also in doubt because of WNO's complaints about poor facilities, but a modernisation programme was undertaken which permitted the fortnight to go ahead.

Following the enormous success of the co-production of *Jenůfa* with Scottish Opera in 1975, both companies decided to continue the collaboration by mounting a cycle of Janáček's major works using the same production team: Richard Armstrong from WNO, David Pountney, Scottish Opera's Director of Productions, and designer Maria Björnson. The second work chosen was Janáček's penultimate opera, *The Makropoulos Case*, based on a play by Karel Čapek (best known in Britain for his play *R.U.R.* which gave the word *robot* to the English language) which had been written to show another side of longevity to that of Bernard Shaw's optimistic approach in *Back to Methuselah*. This opened at the New Theatre on 6 September. Cast as Emilia Marty, the 339-year-old opera singer who needs to find the formula for the potion which will give her an even longer life, was one of the great exponents of the role, Swedish soprano Elisabeth Söderström. Her performance, beautifully sung and superbly acted, once again demonstrated that as a singer-actress she was in a class of her own. Among the other guests artists were Thomas Hemsley as the authoritative lawyer Dr Kolenaty, and Nigel Douglas as the elderly, demented Count Hauk-Sendorf. Both gave excellent performances. The two rivals for Marty's love were sung by Neil Howlett and Mark Hamilton, and there were rewarding cameos from Edward Byles as the overworked and worried clerk Vitek, Helen Field as his daughter, Kristina, and Arthur Davies as Janek.

Pountney viewed the work as a psychological thriller and his production employed many aspects of thriller technique. His cast were not allowed to make any concessions to sentimentality, although two of the minor roles, a cleaner and a stage hand (sung by Menai Davies and Russell Smythe), were, it was felt, unnecessarily caricatured. His approach was heightened by the brooding sets of Maria Björnson (the rising tiers of the lawyer's office being particularly effective) and the imaginative lighting of Nick Chelton.

Richard Armstrong conducted a fiery performance, and after the second performance on 9 September, the Czech ambassador presented him with the Janáček Medal for his services to Czech music.

The reintroduction of productions lost in the fire continued with a revival of *Don Carlos* in Bristol, "restudied" by staff producer Jonathan Clift. The decision to rebuild Annena Stubbs's set, one element of the original production that had evoked almost universal dislike, was not welcomed. "My heart goes out to Clift for having to make do with the dreadful building site structure and Marley-tiled bathroom floor which form the permanent setting for this grandest of operas," wrote Hugh Canning in *Music and Musicians*. "I can hardly believe that, when Fate, in the form of the 1976 fire, had been so compliant as to rid the company of such a visual disaster, the management should have decided to rebuild it, and send it off to Amsterdam in exchange for the Netherlands Opera's *Elektra* set." The production had been recast, with Stafford Dean singing Philip, Suzanne Murphy as Elizabeth de Valois and Thomas Allen singing his first Rodrigo, an event which brought the national critics to Bristol. Allen's was, wrote Canning, "the kind of performance one expects at Covent Garden, but which one so rarely encounters there. He sings Verdi like a great French singer of the past with a scrupulously clean line, completely free of Italianate bulges and sobs, and his beautiful effortless tone-quality fits this elegant role like a glove. A performance such as would grace any opera house in the world."

The performance of *Bohème* in Bristol was notable for an impromptu speech after the interval about the theatre's bar facilities, made by a disgruntled member of the audience who had been unable to purchase a drink. He was quickly hustled out and the performance was allowed to continue.

The highlight of the winter season in Cardiff was the new production of *Madam Butterfly*, produced by Joachim Herz and sung in a new English translation by Peter Hutchinson. Ever since his appointment, Brian McMaster had been keen to get Herz, successor to the legendary Felsenstein as Intendant of Berlin's Komische Oper, to work for WNO. The problems had revolved around Herz's wish to stage *Butterfly*, a work already in the repertory in a perfectly acceptable production and his insistence upon a rehearsal period far in excess of anything WNO could afford. The destruction of the original sets in the fire removed the first obstacle and the agreement of the National Westminster Bank to sponsor the production to the tune of £15,000 permitted Herz to have the eight weeks of rehearsal he demanded. This, the first major sponsorship WNO had acquired, had taken fifteen months of negotiation to achieve.

As preparation for the production, an entertainment entitled *An Evening with Puccini*, devised by Financial Controller Nicholas Payne and produced by John Moody, was taken on a short tour to small auditoria unable to stage traditional opera, including such places as Builth Wells and Machynlleth. The idea was both to introduce opera to areas not normally reached by the main company and, at the same time, to whet the appetite for seeing a major work. This was not a concert performance but an entertainment in its own right, using Puccini's letters and the reminiscences of friends in between excerpts from eight of his operas, to tell the story of the composer's life. As a sign of the importance attached to the project, an extremely strong quartet of singers – Helen Field, Suzanne Murphy, Kenneth Collins and Terence Sharpe – was sent out with Assistant Chorus Master Wyn Davies at the piano and actor Eric Flynn as Narrator.

Herz's was to be no ordinary *Butterfly*. It is thought that of all his operas *Butterfly* was Puccini's favourite, and after the disastrous first night at La Scala in 1904 he had worked hard rewriting the opera to make it more palatable. Herz, in his 1977 production at the Komische Oper, had sought to strip the work of the sentimentality which had surrounded this amended version, and had gone back to the first score in order to emphasise the tragedy of Puccini's original conception. In this, Cio-Cio-San knows from the start that she is nothing more than a casual affair for the philandering Pinkerton. Her great mistake has been to fall in love, and the only person permitted to show sympathy to her is Suzuki. Pinkerton is a complete – to use the old-fashioned word – cad, and Sharpless, being cynical and business-like, sides with him. Much of the music Puccini dropped after the first night was restored, most of it in the first act; and the one piece he added to make the role more attractive to leading tenors, Pinkerton's final aria (the only time in the revised version he shows any remorse), was dropped. It was this original version which Herz planned to stage in Cardiff, designed by his Berlin designers Reinhart Zimmermann and Eleonore Kleiber. By co-incidence, Chorus Master Julian Smith had been commissioned by Puccini's publisher, Ricordi, to prepare a new critical edition of the score, and he was able to use Puccini's autograph score to prepare the orchestral parts for the restored music. Zimmermann's single set of Butterfly's house (with its transparent sliding doors, framed by blossoming trees and overlooking a model of Nagasaki) on which light brought the only changes, was deeply evocative, as were Kleiber's attractive but functional costumes.

Herz's approach to the drama was far from revolutionary, though his view of Pinkerton as little more than an animal with no redeeming features at all struck Stephen Walsh of the *Observer* as loaded and distasteful. "But I've nothing but praise for the way it's mounted," he continued. "Reinhart Zimmermann's sets and Eleonore Kleiber's costumes are by miles the most stylish I've ever seen for *Madam Butterfly*; and Herz's stagecraft is immaculate, with all the attention to timing, musical movement and consistent character-drawing which, one has always heard, typified his teacher Felsenstein's work." The ultimate question of Herz's production, wrote Chris Stuart in the *Western Mail*, "concerns whether or not the opera has sufficient impact as serious drama to justify these musical rearrangements and to survive them . . . I confess myself wholly in accord with this production's philosophy of music-theatre and almost convinced, in practice, by its application to this particular opera. My reservations concern the rather pedestrian dramatic pace of this earlier version." While some critics disliked the "new" version, others, such as Max Loppert, found it stimulating. "The Welsh National production is worthy of the event," he wrote in the *Financial Times*. "Indeed it is one that nobody with access to the theatres on the company's touring circuit (in Oxford, Liverpool and Birmingham) should miss; for it is fresh, dramatically needle-sharp, and musically of unusual distinction. The close focus of Herz's directing methods wins pointed characterisation and tightly meshed ensemble playing at all levels." The eight weeks of rehearsal had paid off.

Herz had brought with him Magdalena Falewicz, a young Polish soprano who had sung Cio-Cio-San in his Berlin production. A fine singer-actress, she gave a most moving performance, despite a tendency for her voice to thin out at the top of her register (due, possibly, to singing in English for the first time). Also making her WNO debut was the Scottish mezzo (later to become a soprano) Phyllis Cannan, who sang a rich-voiced and intelligent Suzuki – a striking impersonation, according to William Mann. John Treleaven was the easy-going and philandering Pinkerton, and there were other solo contributions which contributed much to the success of the evening, including Henry Newman's Sharpless, Rita Cullis's Kate and John Harris's Goro. Geoffrey Moses made a terrifying Bonze. The production was superbly conducted by Guido Ajmone-Marsan, who "invoked a warm and stylish response from the Welsh Philharmonia and the Chorale, whose Humming Chorus at the end of Act II, scene 1, was a model of flawless delicacy." Like it or loathe it, Herz's *Butterfly* was the most important Puccini staging in Britain for many years; "a beautiful, provocative production," Malcolm Boyd called it, "and one which will surely prove to be influential."

1979 began with an unparalleled burst of activity: four new productions opening at three different theatres in eight days. On 12 January, Britten's *The Turn of the Screw* opened at the Sherman Theatre in Cardiff. The following week, a double-bill of two rarely performed Offenbach operettas, *The Song of Fortunio* and *Monsieur Choufleuri's At Home*, opened in Aberystwyth. Two days later, *The Magic Flute* was premièred in Mold.

*The Turn of the Screw*, conducted by Anthony Hose, was produced by Adrian Slack, newly appointed as Director of Productions, with designs by David Fielding, and was based on their earlier successful staging of the opera in Wexford. It received a muted welcome which belied the thought and care that had gone into the production. Slack had opted to differentiate between the visions of the Governess and the appearance of the ghosts by projecting images onto a gauze for the visions and having them appear in the flesh to the children. This was deemed a mistake, as it was to have split the tenor roles of Prologue and Peter Quint. Where the production scored (and it was one that improved with every performance) was in its evocation of atmosphere, its underlining of the ambiguities in the work, and in having a cast in which every singer was just right for his or her role. Philip Langridge set the level with a splendidly sung Prologue. Felicity Lott sang quite beautifully as a gentle and vulnerable Governess, counterpointing the forthright and wholesome housekeeper of Menai Davies, while Arthur Davies and Rita Cullis were excellent as Peter Quint and Miss Jessel. Cheryl Edwards provided a touching study of the young Flora and twelve-year-old David Hubbard was a totally convincing Miles.

In a completely different vein was the Offenbach double-bill, mounted especially for touring by Michael Geliot on his return to the company following the Industrial Tribunal. *The Song of Fortunio* and *Monsieur Choufleuri's At Home* had both been written by Offenbach in 1861 for the Bouffes-Parisiens. Geliot provided his own translation and Julian Smith, who conducted, had reduced Offenbach's orchestration to make it suitable for a chamber ensemble. *The Song of Fortunio* was a slight piece revolving around the attempts of a young clerk to find the romantic song with aphrodisiac powers which his master, a crusty lawyer, had used successfully in his youth. He finds it and uses it to seduce the lawyer's wife. With some of the supporting cast switching sexes (most of the male roles were played by women, the cook by a man), Geliot produced it as an over-the-top pantomime; enjoyable but of no great substance. It provided a marked contrast to the second piece, *Monsieur Choufleuri's At Home*. In this, a social-climbing glue manufacturer decides to stage an At Home, inviting Parisian High Society to hear the three greatest opera singers of the decade. Neither High Society nor singers turn up. Instead, Monsieur Choufleuri's evening (in front of his bourgeois neighbours and the denizens of the local brothel) is saved by the performance of an opera written by his daughter's lover and played by himself, his daughter and the composer. This hilarious parody of early 19th century Italian opera (given as *Norma di Neath*) was the high spot of the evening. In it, Meryl Drower wore traditional Welsh costume, Julian Moyle was dressed as a Druid, waving the Red Dragon and hating the English, while Mark Hamilton sported the cross of St George. Geliot and the cast really let their hair down to send up every operatic convention, and Geliot used the opportunity to fire clusters of arrows at his favourite targets. There were references to his recent troubles with WNO and the Welsh Arts Council, critics (the critic of *L'Opéra* was delighted to review the evening in return for the usual nominal fee of 200 francs plus cab fare), insurance fires, the employment of foreign artists, even the advocates of a Welsh-language opera company. "Some might find the humour too broad," wrote Milnes in the *Spectator*, ". . . I laughed fit to bust . . . The Italian opera parody is so funny that it is easy to overlook how difficult it is to sing: all praise, then, to Meryl Drower and Mark Hamilton for managing it so beautifully as well as reducing the audience to helplessness. Julian Moyle blustered tirelessly as Choufleuri." With eye-catching sets by Steven Gregory (a monument to Monsieur Choufleuri's bad taste), the Offenbach double-bill produced a happy evening's entertainment.

*The Magic Flute*, which opened two days later in Mold, was produced by the Swedish director Göran Järvefelt, making his British operatic debut. A former actor, 30-year-old Järvefelt had had a meteoric career. He had worked as Ingmar Bergman's assistant and directed several stage plays before producing his first opera. His work was so highly regarded that he was soon appointed Principal Producer at Gelsenkirchen where his production of *The Magic Flute* had been seen by McMaster. He was invited to recreate it in Wales using the same designer, Carl Friedrich Oberle. Because of the constraints of touring, there could be no spectacular magical effects, and, indeed, a major criticism of the production was that it was short on magic although the animals, especially the crocodile, were superb. Oberle's set was severely functional, being based on a raked semi-circular platform flanked by colonnaded staircases, with a single symbolic tree and a rock-strewn foreground. Against this background, Järvefelt had gone for character, eschewing the "business" so often associated with *The Magic Flute*. "Its cool, sober production style treats everybody – Ladies, Boys, Queen of the Night, Monostatos – as flesh and blood with motives both comprehensible and in context worth following," wrote Tom Sutcliffe in the *Guardian*. Far removed from the Egypt of so many productions (Järvefelt's community was inhabited by everyday people ruled over by a Sarastro dressed in 18th century breeches and pony tail, a kind of modern American guru), "this *Flute* is played at a sort of Rural District Council level, which does bring the issues closer to home," wrote Rodney Milnes in the *Spectator*. The morals with which the text is studded were sung straight to the audience with the house lights up. Hugh Canning wrote in *Music and Musicians*, that he found the approach refreshing "because it illuminates the characters without offending against the spirit of the work."

Papageno was sung with great charm by Russell Smythe. Suzanne Murphy was a strong, dramatic Queen of the Night, "utterly imperious if not in full command of her thrilling voice," wrote Sutcliffe, "and a healthy change from the usual buzz-saw coloratura." There was a powerful Tamino from John Treleaven, an excellent Speaker from Henry Newman and fine singing from Eilene Hannan as Pamina. More important than the individual contributions, Milnes felt, "was a marvellous company feel to the performance that matched the cohesiveness of the production," and if magic was in short supply on stage, it certainly was not in the pit, where György Fischer "coaxed the best from his cast and much pointed and affectionate playing from the orchestra." "Work of this quality is changing the face of British opera performance," wrote Sutcliffe.

Recognition of WNO's stature as a national, and international, company was given a further boost in February with an invitation to help celebrate the fortieth anniversary of the British Institute in Portugal by performing *Billy Budd* and *The Midsummer Marriage* at the São Carlo Opera House in Lisbon. It took nine months of planning to prepare the documents necessary to transport more than 200 people, including the orchestra, sets, costumes and lights for the two productions (10,000 separate pieces had to be itemised, valued and weighed, right down to the disposable cups for the conductor's interval drink) and then a strike by British lorry drivers almost ruined the transport arrangements. When the trucks towing the sets arrived in Lisbon, they brought traffic to a standstill for two hours as they attempted to reach the theatre through the narrow surrounding streets. Only the manhandling of parked cars onto the pavements by the huge crowd that gathered to watch the fun permitted them to get through. A group of gypsies had been employed to help move the equipment into the building. They were so strong, lifting items bodily rather than sliding them, that the job was completed with six hours to spare.

The house was packed for the opening performance of *Billy Budd* (the first in Portugal of Britten's opera), and the artists were given a ten minute ovation which continued even after the house lights had gone up. *The Midsummer Marriage* was also performed to full houses (with Suzanne Murphy and Felicity Lott alternating as Jenifer), but, although well received, it did not generate the same enthusiasm as *Budd*. There was, however, complete agreement that WNO, "the most inventive and adventurous of British companies," was well worth seeing. "The Lisbon visit," a local critic wrote, "confirmed their excellence."

There were no new productions in the first Cardiff season of the year, which saw performances of *The Midsummer Marriage*, *Il Trovatore*, *The Turn of the Screw*, *Madam Butterfly* and *The Magic Flute* (in which Anthony Rolfe Johnson took over as Tamino for the final performance). There was, however, a major restaging by Sally Day of Geliot's 1972 production of *Turandot* (another victim of the fire) in which Rita Hunter made her debut in the title role. Her appearance attracted full houses, "and she obliged with some thrillingly vibrant singing. But ice-cold detachment," reported Malcolm Boyd in the *Musical Times*, "is not an attribute she can easily cultivate, and perhaps her best achievement in the role was to inspire Kenneth Collins to a truly heroic and impassioned performance as Calaf." "The extraordinary thing about Miss Hunter's Turandot," wrote Rodney

Milnes in *Opera*, "was that she made a role that tests the most accomplished superstars (and sometimes audiences) beyond their limits sound so easy. Her tone never hardened but remained pliant and well rounded throughout, and to her phrasing she brought the beguiling musicianship we admire in her Wagner and Verdi ... Here is an interpretation set to conquer the world."

For the next completely new production of the year, audiences had to wait until the second Cardiff season a month later, when *La Traviata* re-entered the repertory. William Gaskill had been engaged to produce but, following his appointment as an associate director at the National Theatre, he asked to be released from his contract and the job was offered instead to Stewart Trotter. Trotter, principally a theatre director, had worked as Peter Hall's assistant on the Glyndebourne *Don Giovanni* and been responsible for restaging the opera on tour, but this was his first production in his own right. He decided to set *La Traviata* in the 1840s, the time of Dumas' original story on which the opera was based, in sumptuous and very effective sets by Tim Goodchild. It was a straightforward and sensible production without gimmicks. "At a time of bird-brained 'new approaches' bolstered by shameless ignorance, Stewart Trotter's production ... seems almost revolutionary in the general faithfulness to what Verdi and librettist Piave were after," commented Ronald Crichton of the *Financial Times*. "Mr Trotter disclaims expert musical knowledge, but everything he does in this *Traviata* shows intelligent, sensitive musical response." Not everything worked. The first scene was considered by many to go too far in its attempt to portray the world of the demi-monde, and the ebb and flow of the chorus was felt to be sometimes too stagey. Also, the cast, drawn entirely from the company, and conductor (Guido Ajmone-Marsan) were performing *Traviata* for the first time, and the inexperience showed. John Treleaven's Alfredo was disappointing, as was Henry Newman's Germont (Newman was suffering from a throat infection although no announcement was made). But for Suzanne Murphy's Violetta there was little but praise. Her potential had been evident for some time. "The potential has been realised," Tom Sutcliffe wrote in the *Guardian*. "Murphy exceeded the expectations whetted by her virile, passionate Queen of the Night and emerged as an operatic star who will make her mark on the international market. It may be rash to base such a prediction on one beautifully realised Traviata ... But Murphy is not just a pretty voice. She possesses an instrument of great tonal character. She commands the vocal heights with strength, excitement and a ravishing quality of sound ... The individuality of the voice lies in a quality she shares with the late Callas – a kind of wedge-shaped hollowness in the tone of each note that, with a slight upping of the pressure, fills generously and thrillingly with colour, vitality and piercing resonance. Great singers reveal their personalities through their unmistakable voice-prints. Murphy is memorable."

During the fortnight, *Elektra* was revived with two major cast changes – Kerstin Meyer taking over as Klytemnestra and Phillip Joll as Orestes – before being played in Birmingham and Glasgow (when WNO appeared at the Theatre Royal as guests of Scottish Opera) and then being taken to Germany in May for the Wiesbaden Festival. There was considerable apprehension amongst the cast before the opening night in Wiesbaden as to how German audiences, well schooled in opera, would react to a Welsh company performing a German work in English. Kupfer went backstage and spoke to them. "You may have an experience you have never had before," he warned. "You may be booed heavily at the end. Remember, they can't help admiring your singing and playing, so it will be me they are booing." At the end of the performance, there was complete silence. Everyone stood, waiting for the booing to erupt, but instead the house rose and cheered. There were fifteen minutes of curtain calls, and the following day the critics were unanimous in their praise of production and cast. Pauline Tinsley's passionate performance as Elektra won her the Festival award for the best individual artist, and the production itself was voted runner-up to the Zürich Opera's Monteverdi cycle as best production.

Further guest appearances during the year saw WNO at the Cheltenham Festival for the first time in July with performances of the Offenbach double-bill and *The Turn of the Screw*, and taking part in the Proms at the Royal Albert Hall in August with a concert performance of *Billy Budd*.

Apart from *Lohengrin* in 1962 and *The Flying Dutchman* in 1974, the operas of Wagner had never featured in WNO's repertoire. It was a gap that many people regretted and was one that both McMaster and Armstrong (now that the New's orchestra pit had been enlarged) were determined to fill. Their ultimate ambition was to mount a complete *Ring*, and at the spring press conference called to publicise the year's plans, McMaster took the opportunity to announce that the cycle, produced by Göran Järvefelt, would begin in 1982, with the operas being introduced at six-monthly intervals, and be completed in 1984. As a lead up to the *Ring*, two other major Wagnerian epics were to be staged. The first of these, *Tristan und Isolde*, opened the autumn season in Cardiff on 8 September. The staging of *Tristan* anywhere is an event likely to attract attention. When it is conducted by that legendary Wagnerian, Reginald Goodall, it becomes an event of national, if not international, importance.

Despite his reputation, 78-year-old Goodall had never conducted *Tristan* before, apart from a single performance (which he described as "terrible") at Covent Garden in 1949, and it was a considerable coup for

McMaster to get him. As always, he insisted on lengthy preparation, beginning work with his singers nine months before production rehearsals started and with the orchestra three months before. When he arrived in Cardiff to begin orchestral rehearsals, he picked up his baton and stood on the rostrum while McMaster made a speech of welcome and formally introduced him to the players. The orchestra waited, expecting him to say a few words. After a seemingly endless pause, he finally spoke. "Gentlemen," he said, "I have begun." Goodall's beat has often been criticised for not being clear. What this fails to take into account is his ability to inspire both singers and players: the Welsh orchestra played for him as it had never played before. Many people were surprised to see him on opening night conducting without a baton. This came about because he lost his baton during a rehearsal and discovered he rather enjoyed not using one.

Six months before opening night, Margaret Curphey, the Isolde, was forced by illness to withdraw and her place was taken, at Goodall's suggestion, by the young Scottish soprano Linda Esther Gray. Gray, who had been asked to sing Isolde at the Coliseum in 1981, had never sung the role but had already begun studying it with Goodall. Singing Tristan was John Mitchinson, the first British tenor to sing the role since Walter Widdop. Not of ideal build for a romantic lover, Mitchinson nevertheless sang powerfully and with much subtlety when required, making every word tell. There was excellent support from Anne Wilkens as Brangäne, Gwynne Howell as King Mark, Bent Norup as Kurwenal and the artists in the minor roles, but on stage the evening belonged to Linda Esther Gray, "a notable new Isolde." "The production marks the emergence of a new Wagnerian singer of enormous talent and potential," commented one critic. "By the end of Saturday evening," wrote Max Loppert in the *Financial Times*, "there seemed no reason why her Isolde, given further periods of playing-in and study, should not grace the stages of the wider operatic world . . . the security, the stamina, the combination of fullness, warmth, and brilliance in the tone, the thrusting attack and freedom of the high notes, came as the happiest of discoveries."

The producer of *Tristan* was the Austrian Peter Brenner, principal producer of the Bremen Opera and son of the legendary Walter Felsenstein. His designer was the German, Klaus Teepe. The importation of yet another foreign team saw the start of a reaction against overseas producers and designers whose work was not thought to be outstanding enough to warrant the exclusion of the British. Teepe's designs had little to offer. His permanent set of a raked platform in the shape of a shallow bowl with raised sides suggesting the ship, the cup or the castle battlements, tended to be visually boring. His designs were, according to one critic, "ugly, clumsy and inept. Imaginative touches progressed no further than crude shadow-play for the advance of Tristan in Act 1, and his sense of colour and costume was deplorable. The third act had a very hefty Tristan wearing a powder blue romper suit on a violently yellow ground-sheet: hardly the setting for incipient tragedy." And the best that could be said for Brenner's production (based on ones he had already staged in Freiburg, Kiel and Bremen) was that it lacked eccentricity and did not impede the unfolding of a glorious score. While he allowed the singers to develop their own characters, he provided little insight into their motives. On this evidence, remarked Loppert, the production team's merits were mainly negative. Against this must be set a musically unforgettable performance by Goodall and the cast. Goodall's control of the orchestra (now renamed the Orchestra of Welsh National Opera) was, wrote William Mann in *Opera*, "a joy to hear, marvellously stylish in phrasing and balance, scrupulously structured and quite dynamic (by no means slow, witness the music after the potion-drinking, and much of the second act up to the love duet . . .), most attentive to the singers." *Tristan und Isolde* was "the greatest triumph in the Company's short though already glory-crowded history."

In between the emotional first night of *Tristan* and the next major production, scheduled for the winter season two months later, another small-scale venture was launched. The success of *An Evening with Puccini* as a foretaste to *Madam Butterfly* led to similar treatment being given to Tchaikovsky in preparation for the following year's production of *Eugene Onegin*. *Tchaikovsky at the Opera*, devised by Nicholas Payne, produced and designed by Sally Day, did not, however, feature only Tchaikovsky's music. Entertaining four friends at home (including Mussorgsky), Tchaikovsky and his guests discuss the operas they have seen or written, allowing for excerpts from *Boris*, *Carmen* and *Götterdämmerung* to be sung, as well as some of Tchaikovsky's own songs and a generous helping of *Onegin*. Once again, a strong cast was assembled, with Julian Moyle, looking uncannily like the composer, as Tchaikovsky, Rita Cullis, Phyllis Cannan, Arthur Davies and David Gwynne as the singers, and Derek Clark as the accompanist, to produce an enjoyable evening's entertainment.

The orchestra's change of name from the Welsh Philharmonia to the Orchestra of Welsh National Opera was made because the idea of it combining its operatic duties with symphonic work had not been working out; there was too little time for it to appear regularly in the concert hall, and thus little justification in a name which appeared to keep it separate from its main function. In November the Chorale also changed its name. It, too, had not been able to fulfil many engagements outside opera, and with WNO's first recording contract in the offing (of the complete *Tristan*), McMaster wanted it to be known as the Chorus of Welsh National Opera. He put the new name to a vote of the Chorale members, who unanimously decided to stay as the Chorale. The following day a notice went up announcing the change.

The winter season in Cardiff opened with the final new production of the year, Verdi's *Ernani*, staged by Elijah Moshinsky, the young Australian whose work at Covent Garden had been winning much praise. Verdi's fifth opera, *Ernani* had not been seen in Britain since a production at Sadler's Wells in 1967. Its fault, like that of the other early pieces, was generally agreed to be that, in spite of its wonderful music, it was undramatic, being of the "on-sing-off" variety of opera. Its locations range from the mountains of Aragon to the palace in Saragossa via various apartments in Silva's castle and Aix-la-Chapelle in France. Moshinsky and his designer, Maria Björnson, transferred the action from the time of Charles V to that of Velásquez in order to achieve more colour in the costumes, and came up with a permanent three-sided balconied set of no particular date, surrounding a shiny black marble floor, upon which the cast moved ceaselessly. The various locations were suggested by the minimum of props. The costumes of the heroine, Elvira, and the chorus ladies looked stunning against this dark set. (The wide skirts did create some problems, particularly when the production reached Llandudno, for they would not go through all the doors on the way from the dressing rooms to the stage; instead they were delivered to the stage and the ladies had to walk down in their petticoats to change in the wings!) Moshinsky and Björnson solved the problem of changing and linking scenes by using a series of black, reflective panels moved, Kabuki-style, by hooded figures to create new stage areas. It was a device which worked well most of the time but had a tendency to become distracting as did Moshinsky's trick of freezing the stage picture for asides. It was, however, an atmospheric production in which the pace never slackened.

A very strong cast responded with some superb singing. Suzanne Murphy sang "an Elvira of melting loveliness and vocal brilliance. Her voice did everything she required of it," wrote Hugh Canning, "and if she can maintain this superb form she will have few rivals." Kenneth Collins, singing and acting with great assurance in the title role, sent his music sailing confidently over the orchestra and Richard Van Allan in the difficult role of de Silva, Elvira's uncle, guardian and suitor, sang throughout with consummate beauty of tone and persuasiveness. Cornelius Opthof, the Dutch-Canadian baritone, made a strong impression as the King, and there was good support from Mark Hamilton as Don Riccardo, Geoffrey Moses as Jago and Catherine Savory as Giovanna. The Chorale were in fine voice ("other companies have brilliant choruses, but the WNO sound has an immediacy and vitality and precision of its own," commented William Mann) and Richard Armstrong conducted the uninhibited orchestra brilliantly. "He caressed his singers with an attention to their vocal and dramatic needs that Verdi, who left scoring until he knew his singers' capacities, would have approved," noted Tom Sutcliffe in the *Guardian*. "He also showed a feeling for Verdian rubato uncommon in British conductors. But his prime concern was to maintain a sense of urgency and discovery, a freshness in the playing and a sense of steady drive in the pacing that would have relieved Verdi of his eternal dread that the audience might lose interest." The audience, far from losing interest, revelled in the full-blooded approach.

Just as in the early days Bill Smith had wanted to show off WNO in London, so McMaster, for some time, had wanted to do the same. In spite of the acclaim WNO was receiving in Wales, throughout England and on the continent, he knew that its reputation would only be finally established – or broken – by appearing in London; and a successful season there would be of inestimable help in acquiring recording and television contracts, both of which would help raise important funding. The Arts Council would not permit its grant to be used for such a season, and if it was to happen, private sponsorship would have to be found. In 1978 negotiations with a potential sponsor had led McMaster to believe that he had raised the money, so he booked the London Palladium for a week in December. When the sponsor eventually pulled out, McMaster was left with two months in which to find the necessary £20,000. He could not find any alternative backers; a public appeal raised a grand total of £4; and the Palladium booking had to be cancelled. But in 1979 negotiations with the oil company Amoco were to produce the most significant sponsorship deal in WNO's history. Amoco, over a period of five years, guaranteed WNO a minimum of £250,000 to finance work which could not otherwise be afforded, starting with an appearance in London. The only available venue large enough to stage opera at the time WNO could be in London was the Dominion, a former theatre since given over to films. It was here that the first Amoco Festival of Opera was given in December. Festival was an appropriate word, for in five days Londoners were given a chance to see five highly acclaimed and varied productions: *Tristan*, *Madam Butterfly*, *The Makropoulos Case*, *The Magic Flute* and *Ernani*. The demand for tickets to see WNO in its first appearance in London for fourteen years, and its first as a fully professional company, was enormous; the touts had a field day. The Dominion was not ideal for opera. A huge barn of a place, it contained no orchestra pit, little in the way of backstage facilities and little storage space. It did not have a stage crew and the stagehands were recruited (as they still are) from those who worked for WNO on its tours elsewhere. WNO was used to performing in poor conditions; it took, however, some time for everyone to get used to the acoustics. Several critics reviewing *The Makropoulos Case* noted that even an artist as experienced as Elisabeth Söderström was having difficulty in riding the orchestra and that, in trying to project her words into the auditorium, her voice gave out before the final scene. The climax to a memorable week was a long-sold-out performance of *Tristan*, "the most remarkable piece of music making I have heard in a theatre this year," wrote Patrick Carnegy in the *Times Educational Supplement*. Audiences had been generous with their enthusiasm and applause for the preceding productions, but nothing equalled the roar which greeted Goodall's curtain call.

The Dominion season crowned a remarkable year. The most noticeable difference from former London visits was that, with a few exceptions, the visual side of WNO's work, thanks to McMaster's choice of producers and designers, now matched the musical standard. "The plain fact is that Welsh National Opera was here showing the rest of Britain how to produce opera," wrote Robert Maycock in *Classical Music*. "I think the WNO is the most exciting opera company in Britain today," agreed Rodney Milnes. "Their selection of producers, conductors and guest singers is adventurous and constructive. Their chorus and orchestra are amazing." It was with considerable pride, and justification, that WNO could quote on publicity material the comment of Tom Sutcliffe in the magazine *Vogue*. "The pace," he had written, "is now being set by the Welsh National Opera, currently top of the British opera league."

For MANY YEARS, WNO's repertoire had rarely strayed out of the 19th Century. Then, during the Lockhart regime, important strides had been made into the 20th Century with performances of *Lulu* and *Billy Budd* amongst others. McMaster and Armstrong had continued to explore the 20th Century repertory with Britten and Janáček, but one area that had never been touched, and one that had been gaining in popularity, was that of the Baroque era. This balance was partially redressed by the opening at Mold on 19 January 1980 of Monteverdi's *The Coronation of Poppea* in Michael Geliot's new production. Elizabeth Gale had originally been cast in the role of Poppea, and when she withdrew her place was taken by Eiddwen Harrhy, who, since first singing with WNO as a member of the chorus nine years earlier, had gone on to appear as a principal at Covent Garden and the Coliseum. During the dress rehearsal, in the scene in which Poppea seduces Nero while singing the line: "And what of these breasts that I offer so gladly like ripe apples," Harrhy decided to abandon the discreet towel provided by Geliot and appear topless. It was a decision which was to receive much publicity, inspire newspaper cartoons and help ensure full houses. The controversy kept interest in the production alive later on tour when Helen Field took over the role in Oxford and Birmingham. Would she also bare all? (The answer was no; she appeared wearing a body-stocking.)

The score used for *The Coronation of Poppea*, written in 1642, the year before Monteverdi's death, was essentially the realisation of Raymond Leppard adapted by the conductor, Wyn Davies. No attempt was made to go for an authentic period sound: a harpsichord, organ, double bass and cello accompanied the singers, with the full orchestra reserved for the interludes. Annena Stubbs's simple yet evocative designs, set against a background of draped curtains, brilliantly evoked the eroticism of the work and skilfully blended Monteverdi's 17th century Venice with Nero's Rome, frequently using Robert Ornbo's subtle lighting to great effect. A permanent front gauze, embossed with a medallion of Nero and Poppea, proved, however, to be a distracting barrier for some. Geliot, like Wyn Davies with his arrangement of the score, made no attempt to achieve period authenticity, but tried to make the opera work for a modern audience by concentrating on the text and characterisation; conversations and confrontations arose naturally from the dramatic action, which was why no one could object to the nude scenes. His decision to use three dancers (naked except for G-strings) to link scenes was one of the least convincing aspects of an otherwise bold and direct production. An anonymous reviewer from Bristol University was reminded more than once of Robert Helpmann's objection to nude ballet: "The trouble is that not everything stops when the music does." Vocally the evening was of a high standard and there were fine individual performances, from Eiddwen Harrhy, Stafford Dean as a noble and moving Seneca, Catherine Savory, a member of the chorus in her first major role as Ottavia, and Arthur Davies as Nero. The many minor roles were all admirably taken by members of the chorus. It was, wrote Michael Kennedy in the *Daily Telegraph*, a production not to be missed, "and not only because of the three naked dancers and a nude Poppea . . . Monteverdi purists will not be wholly satisfied – are they ever? But for a 1980 audience this is a beautiful and compelling realisation of one of the first great music dramas."

Most productions tend to be slack on opening night and tighten considerably the more they are played. *Poppea* suffered the reverse, for when it opened the Cardiff season in February, everything that could go wrong did: the Goddess Amor floated down in the wrong scene and had to be whisked back up, curtains descended on the heads of unsuspecting baritones, spotlights missed their targets, scenery crashed and banged. It was not surprising that the cast, especially Nicholas Folwell deputising for Russell Smythe as Ottone, should not give of their best, and it became apparent that Wyn Davies's realisation, which had sounded so apt in Mold, provided insufficient support for tired voices as well as seeming too long.

No greater contrast to *Poppea* could have been provided than the production of *Eugene Onegin* which opened the following night. McMaster had seen the work of the young Romanian director Andrei Serban in New York, where Serban had been winning great acclaim for his staging of such works as *The Umbrellas of Cherbourg* and Chekhov's *The Cherry Orchard*, and had invited him to Cardiff, together with his American designer, Michael Yeargan, to stage Tchaikovsky's romantic masterpiece. Neither Serban nor Yeargan had worked in opera before, and the singers found Serban's method of working disconcerting. Thomas Allen, singing his first Onegin, remembers that at early rehearsals all Serban did was to give the principals their entrances and exits, leaving them to work out the intervening action themselves. Serban seemed to them to be quite uninterested. In spite of constant reassurances that this was the way he worked and that everything would be all right eventually, matters reached a point at which the singers were prepared to walk out on the production. It was then that Serban, who had been observing them to see which aspects of their characters he could best utilise, decided to start real work. "It was," says Allen, "a very fruitful experience. I have since sung Onegin in Ottawa and there I drew on so many of the things I learnt from Serban. He gave me a background to the character which will, I think, remain the foundation of any Onegin I ever do."

There were other problems to be overcome before opening night. McMaster, convinced that the best way to obtain an authentic Russian feel to the music was to hire a Russian conductor, approached Gosconcert (the official Russian concert agency through which all Soviet artists have to be booked) and was allocated Mark Ermler, a principal conductor at Moscow's Bolshoi Theatre. Because of the Russian invasion of Afghanistan, there were fears that Ermler might not be allowed to leave Moscow, and then, after his arrival in Cardiff, that he might be ordered to return home as a result of Britain's subsequent ban on cultural exchanges with Russia. And then Serban wanted to open the opera in a cornfield. Because of the time of year, no corn was available in Britain. Designer Michael Yeargan, remembering the cornfield behind his home in Connecticut, sent an urgent message to Yale, where he lectured, for a group of students to cut the field, treat the corn with preservative and send it to Wales. Upon its arrival, it was impounded for a week by Customs while being searched for drugs.

When the production finally opened, the care and attention that had gone into it were more than repaid. Serban's production, in Yeargan's simple but attractive sets, owed much to the romanticism of television commercials, but was none the less effective for that. "He has responded with a staging that does Wales proud," commented Alan Blyth. "The strength of Serban's concept, so telling in a small theatre, lies in making us believe and participate in the feeling of Tatyana and Onegin, taking them far away from being operatic stereotypes. Aided by the arrestingly pointful decor of the young American Michael Yeargan, he also succeeds in placing the heartbreak of the principals against a background appropriate to their dilemmas." "The WNO *Onegin* is not merely acceptable, but an outstanding blend of sensitive music-making, well balanced and interesting characters on stage, and a procession of stage-pictures far beyond the everyday purview of opera production, some of them as unforgettable in visionary imagination as the most beautiful cinematic shots you can remember," commented William Mann. It was, according to Kenneth Loveland, one of the most physically exciting and emotionally vivid productions WNO had ever staged.

Serban's skill as a producer would hardly have worked its magic had it not been for the superb singing and intelligent acting of the principals. Josephine Barstow as Tatyana sang as well as anyone had ever heard her, spinning out pianissimo phrases that held the audience spellbound. She achieved "the improbable feat of a great Tatyana without any special gift for lyrical singing," wrote Stephen Walsh of the *Observer*. "As usual she produces more than her fair share of ugly noises and sprawling lines, though when it really matters (in the letter scene or the final duet) she sings with astonishing intensity and musical grasp, and she seems incapable of an unclear or imprecise stage gesture. In poise and movement she is in my experience unequalled in the part." Thomas Allen's Onegin was no less impressive. "I found it hard to think of another baritone I would sooner hear in the role," continued Walsh. "It's one of those voices one takes for granted – a natural channel for music. But, in fact, he uses it with a lot of subtlety, catching equally the appalling emptiness of Onegin's account of his uncle's death and the desperation of his final appeal to Tatyana, articulated at incredible speed, but without the slightest loss of breath control or verbal clarity." The supporting cast were all good, and some better than that, from Anthony Rolfe Johnson's bookish, bespectacled Lensky to Neville Ackerman's M. Triquet.

Mark Ermler proved to be an inspired conductor. With twenty-five years' experience and more than 100 performances of *Onegin* behind him, he brought a new dimension to the score. He shaped the music "with loving attention to instrumental detail," wrote Canning in *Music and Musicians*, "poetic, flexible phrasing and dramatic fire. The WNO Orchestra were like putty (not really the appropriate word for such lustrous playing) in his hands and gave more, in terms of interpretation as opposed to virtuosity, than do his own players at the Bolshoi on his recent recording of the opera." "It would be hard to imagine a more beautiful or affecting evening at the opera," concluded Walsh.

On stage WNO was hardly putting a foot wrong. There had been criticism of some productions, but, generally speaking, the decisions McMaster and Armstrong were taking were the correct ones, and even when a piece did not meet with total approval (one thinks of the turgid designs and production of *Tristan*, for example) there were compensations such as, in the case of *Tristan*, Goodall's conducting and Linda Esther Gray's Isolde. There was an excitement about opera which had not been felt, except occasionally, for some years, and this had been reflected in growing audiences. Since McMaster had taken over, the number of performances had risen from 130 in 1976 to 156 in 1978, and attendance had increased correspondingly, from 72 percent to 84 percent, more than doubling the box-office revenue to just under £500,000. This had been achieved partly by the increased output, partly by the quality of the productions and partly by a rationalisation of the touring pattern, with additional seasons being played in those English cities to which WNO toured under the "spheres of influence" policy initiated by McMaster, allowing a regular following to be built up. In 1979 at Southampton, for example, following a disastrous visit three years earlier, a special effort was made to win back audiences. Advertising was increased, a subscription scheme (common to all the major touring venues) was started with special offers to subscribers, and a hydrofoil was hired to bring people from the Isle of Wight. The hard work paid off; every opera except for *The Magic Flute* and *The Turn of the Screw* sold out in advance, and with on-the-door sales going well, the week ended by playing to 90 percent capacity, breaking the record previously held for the Gaumont by the Spanish dancer Antonio. It also broke three other house records: it took more money than any other opera company, more people attended than for any other series of performances by a single company, and it used the largest orchestra seen in the theatre (95 for *Turandot*, 75 of whom were in the pit, the remaining twenty under the set).

But this progress had been won at a price. The horrific and recurring deficits which had bedevilled WNO up until the end of 1975 had been overcome by careful housekeeping, an adventurous and stimulating repertoire (in which not all productions were "safe" at the box-office, by any means) and increased receipts. But in 1978, in order to keep the new productions coming and fulfil all touring obligations, a deficit had been incurred of £30,000 and in 1979 of £70,000, both with the full knowledge and approval of the Arts Council, which expected to be able to write them off in future grants. In 1979 McMaster and Financial Controller Nicholas Payne had argued cogently for a productivity increase, pointing to the rise in the number of performances and larger audiences. While the Arts Council did not reject the application out of hand, its subsequent grant did not even match the increase in inflation, and by the spring of 1980 it was clear that if a full programme was to be maintained, the shortfall would rise to £175,000. The only answer, if WNO was not to slide further into debt and have to reduce its activities to a level inconsistent with high standards, was to take some form of remedial action. This was achieved by cancelling the projected new production of *Don Giovanni* (scheduled for the autumn), cancelling two proposed revivals (including *Aida*) and dropping two weeks from the touring schedule (one each in Wales and in England, though no venue missed out completely seeing WNO). Even with these measures, expenditure in 1980 was expected to be some £75,000 more than income.

One method of reducing costs on a new production was to share them. This had been successfully done with *Elektra* (it had cost only £5,000 to transport the sets from Holland and adapt them in Cardiff) and in the extremely successful Janáček venture with Scottish Opera. It had also been done with *Ernani*, which was a joint venture with the Royal Northern College of Music, whereby the costs of costumes, sets, translations and general preparation were split between the two. The second combined RNCM production was of Dvořák's rarely performed *The Jacobin*, produced by Adrian Slack, first at the college with students and then restaged for WNO in Cardiff. Interest in the work of Janáček, Smetana and other Czech composers had led naturally to consideration of the operas of Dvořák. Not known principally in Britain as an operatic composer, Dvořák had, in fact, written ten (*The Jacobin* was his seventh), many of them still in the repertoire in Czechoslavakia. All Dvořák's operas were considered, but McMaster did not feel that his best-known (though rarely performed), *Rusalka*, with its water-sprites and nymphs, would appeal to British audiences, and the choice fell on *The Jacobin* which had never been given a professional performance in Britain. In spite of its title, the opera was not political but a romantic comedy set in a Bohemian village ruled by the Hapsburgs at the time of the French Revolution. To make the production as authentic as possible, Jaroslav Krombholc, the leading Czech conductor, was engaged to edit the score and conduct, and John Cervenka, with whom Slack had worked in Australia, to design.

On the eve of rehearsals, Krombholc suffered a heart attack at his Cardiff hotel and Anthony Hose took over until Krombholc's replacement, Czech conductor Albert Rosen, could get to Wales from Dublin, where he was in charge of the RTE Symphony Orchestra.

It is generally agreed that while *The Jacobin* contains beautiful music, it lacks dramatic timing and character. The hinge of the plot is the Count's disinheritance of his son, Bohus, as a result of prejudice against his wife, Julie, and a false report that he is a political radical (a Jacobin; the modern equivalent might be a Red or a Commie). There are stereotyped villains, a pair of conventional young lovers and a good-natured music master, Benda (based on Dvořák's own early teacher), who is the only really successful piece of characterisation in the opera. "Benda, the young lovers and a string of exquisite melodies supported by luscious orchestration are quite enough to justify occasional revival, and the Welsh National Opera are the right company to undertake it," wrote Winton Dean in *Opera*. "The big choral scenes and frequent ensembles play up to the qualities in which they are pre-eminent." Adrian Slack's production emphasised the enchantment of the score and was full of lively detail, especially with the chorus – Benda's rehearsal of the serenade to be performed before the Count (staged as a local choral society at work) was the comic highlight of the evening. Edward Byles made much of the role of Benda, and there were no weaknesses in the remainder of the cast. Suzanne Murphy sang strongly as Julie, Helen Field and Arthur Davies were excellently matched as the young lovers, Terinka and Jiri, and there was strong support from Julian Moyle, Henry Newman, David Gwynne and Phillip Joll. Albert Rosen conducted with a nice blend of full-bloodedness and sensitivity. If there was one aspect of the production which was not successful, it was the designs of John Cervenka. His tubular metal outlines gave little feeling of a Bohemian village and tended to look like an economy measure. For Hugo Cole of the *Guardian*, they quarrelled with the opulence of the music and emotions. *The Jacobin* proved to be a thoroughly delightful entertainment but one in which the charms quickly palled, and it was never likely to retain a permanent place in the repertoire.

As important as sharing productions in helping to reduce costs was sponsorship. Usually this took the form of direct financial aid, but an equally welcome contribution (worth £95,000) came when Renault presented WNO with a new fleet of tractor units for transporting costumes and scenery. There was a whimper of protest that Welsh National Opera should be using French vehicles, but, in spite of repeated requests, no British firm was prepared to make a similar donation. The Renault trucks were used for the first time in June when WNO became the first British opera company to perform in East Germany, appearing in Berlin, at the Dresden Festival and in Leipzig with performances of *Ernani*, *Elektra* and *The Turn of the Screw*. While WNO was away, a unique exchange brought the Leipzig Oper and Gewandhaus Orchestra to Cardiff and Birmingham with Joachim Herz's productions of Handel's *Xerxes* and Mozart's *Titus* (better known in Britain as *La Clemenza di Tito*). The planes that brought the Leipzig musicians to Wales returned to East Germany with WNO's artists on board. The reciprocal visits were sponsored by the British Council, the East German government, the West Midlands local authority and the Visiting Arts Unit of Great Britain, and had taken two and a half years to arrange. Even so, there were last-minute hitches in what McMaster accurately described as a marathon operation. Most of the props had already been wrapped in newspaper for the journey when word came through that no newspapers should be taken. Each item had to be unpacked and rewrapped in tissue paper.

A previous foreign company appearing in Berlin (and not singing in German) had done so badly that tickets had had to be given away to the local barracks. When McMaster had asked Joachim Herz, the Komische Oper's Intendant, what he thought was likely to happen to WNO performing in Italian and English, Herz had invited him to pick his regiment. There was no need to worry. The two Berlin performances sold out the day the tickets went on sale. *Elektra*, with which the visit opened, received a twenty-minute ovation, a record for the house (though there were a few boos when Kupfer and Werz took their curtain calls), and *Ernani* the following night ended with fifteen minutes of applause. The audiences screamed with delight; it was, recalled one WNO member, more like a pop concert than a performance of opera.

Herz went out of his way to make sure the visit was a success, even issuing instructions to the canteen staff to take lessons in tea-making, and when it was discovered that part of the steps for *Elektra* had been left behind, the Komische technical staff insisted on providing new ones free. Arriving for a rehearsal of *Ernani*, the chorus was greeted by members of the Komische chorus with champagne. But perhaps the most poignant moment came when the Komische canteen staff, who had been unable to see any performances through pressure of work, turned up in Dresden to see WNO in action. The enthusiasm found in Berlin was maintained in Dresden, where *The Turn of the Screw*, in its first performance in East Germany, was played with *Ernani*, and later in Leipzig. It was not only an historic but also an outstandingly successful visit.

After an absence of twelve years, *Tosca* was brought back into the repertory to open the Cardiff autumn season in September. This was, perhaps surprisingly, the first time John Copley had produced the opera (though he had worked on other people's productions at Covent Garden). His skill at handling chorus and principals was evident in a polished production which captured perfectly the essence of Puccini's music. The sets by John Pascoe were old-fashioned and practical, the costumes by Michael Stennett authentically period, and the singing of the three principals was uniformly excellent. If her acting was slightly too reserved, Swedish soprano Helena Döse nevertheless "made the role sound almost too easy," according to Rodney Milnes, "making light of the hair-raising technical difficulties. Her creamy, even voice and musical delivery gave constant pleasure." Kenneth Collins gave his familiar committed performance as Cavaradossi, and Anthony Baldwin made a deep impression as Scarpia. Born in Merthyr, Baldwin was largely unknown in Wales, having built his career in Germany, where he was a member of the Düsseldorf company, because he could not find work in Britain. Previous attempts by WNO to lure him back to Wales had failed because of his prior commitments. His performance was much admired by all the critics. "For once the role was really sung, not barked," commented Milnes. "Mr Baldwin judged the size of the house perfectly and treated us to some beguilingly phrased, poisonously lyrical soft singing. That it should have come from so huge and imposing a man made the character twice as frightening."

Copley's production of *Tosca* was traditional in the best sense of the word, allowing the music to speak for itself. It was followed by a revival of another traditional production, John Moody's *Rigoletto*. This was the version he had staged for touring to small theatres in 1972, and was revived with sets restyled by Roger Butlin from his own originals, since financial exigencies did not permit a full-scale new production. It was none the worse for that. Only Terence Sharpe in the title role had survived from the original cast. Among the newcomers were Norma Burrowes as Gilda and Dennis O'Neill (who had made his WNO debut the previous year on tour as Alfredo) as the Duke, confirming that he was well on the way to becoming an international tenor.

The following week saw the world première of *The Servants*, by William Mathias, based on a play by Iris Murdoch. WNO had been asking Mathias to write an opera since 1970, but he had never found a suitable subject. Then, in 1974, he had heard a radio broadcast of *The Servants and the Snow* and was immediately struck by its operatic possibilities. A month later the idea had not gone away so he wrote to Murdoch asking if she would be interested in having it adapted. Murdoch replied almost by return of post, and began work on the libretto herself. For two years, various drafts shuttled back and forth between composer and librettist, until after some half-a-dozen rewrites it had reached a workable state. Mathias then began to write the music, completing the first pencil sketch in a year. He now contacted WNO to say that he had at last found something suitable, and the new work was promised a production.

*The Servants* is set in an aristocratic mansion, to which the new young master returns, determined to end his father's despotic regime. The servants, however, will not let him; he is offered one of his father's mistresses with whom to exercise the droit de seigneur; and the story ends with a double murder and the arrival of a brutal dictator. When the opera opened on 15 September, it received an almost universally hostile press. The problem lay with Mathias's treatment of the libretto. "As a musical construct," wrote Paul Griffiths in the *Times*, "the work is utterly straightforward and secure. As a piece of theatre, however, it leaves a great deal to be desired. *The Servants* is Mathias's first opera, and no one could doubt after seeing it that his expertise lies above all in the fields of choral and orchestral music. There are splendid almost oratorio-like tableaux for the chorus of domestics that show a surer touch than any of the music for the principals. There is also a vigour to the orchestral writing that draws one's attention straight to the pit and, battering away at the mind, keeps it there." While much of the music showed a sure touch, too often the orchestration drowned the singers, and frequently the music seemed to have little relationship with what was happening on stage.

Adrian Slack, aided by Patrick Robertson's revolving set, directed a fluent production in which any lack of drama must, continued Griffiths, "be attributed to the work itself and not to him." "No one could come up with a riveting spectacle from this cluttered, one-paced score," agreed Andrew Clements in the *Observer*. The cast worked hard to realise the composer's intentions and there were some notable performances from Nigel Douglas as the idealist son, Basil (even though he had to struggle for most of the evening to make himself heard over the dense orchestration), Eiddwen Harrhy as his wife, Oriane, Claire Powell, Henry Newman, Phillip Joll and David Gwynne. Not all first performances of operas are successful, even of many now favourites in the repertoire. Perhaps the critics were wrong about *The Servants*, but, as Rodney Milnes ended his review in *Opera*, "I hate to sound grudging when so many man-years have gone into the making of a new opera, but fear this is a case of 'better luck next time'."

The winter season in Cardiff opened with revivals of *Tristan und Isolde* conducted by Goodall, and *Tosca*. Neither drew full houses. The situation was very different for the performances of *The Cunning Little Vixen*, the third of the Janáček cycle produced jointly with Scottish Opera to be seen in Wales. Tickets were at a premium to see David Pountney's highly original and delightful production (which had first been seen at the Edinburgh Festival in August). Maria Björnson's lush setting of a grassy bank, with its undulating mounds and hiding places for the animals, splitting open to reveal the chicken run and the inn, was strikingly imaginative and gave Pountney the ideal stage upon which to develop the action. His solution to having humans portraying animals was solved not by masks, but by the use of costumes and movement; and in a superbly integrated performance the choreography of Stuart Hopps was an important element. There were excellent performances from the large cast: especially Phillip Joll as the Forester, David Gwynne as the Parson, Geoffrey Moses as the Poacher, Nigel Douglas as the Schoolmaster and Arthur Davies as the Fox. Helen Field was simply magical as the Vixen. "Her performance was of astonishing agility, not the least because it was so fox-like and because the slightly hard edge to her tone well suited the high line, which she encompassed with a consistent coquetry and animation. It was a celebration of the joys of living, in a production that celebrated the joys of nature itself," wrote Mark Morris in *Classical Music*. The success of the evening owed much to the teamwork on stage and to Richard Armstrong's inspired conducting. Armstrong had made some changes to the score, returning to the original manuscript to correct some of the variations found in the published material. He had removed the doublings in the wind parts, put in to thicken the texture, removed a repeat passage in the second act which, he felt, had only been put in to cover a scene change, and the off-stage choruses in the inn scene added by Max Brod for a German production. His main alteration, however, was to the tempi, particularly at the end of the second act. His suspicion that the printed metronome markings were spurious had been confirmed by the original manuscript, and as a result he took some passages at half the conventional speed. "The life-enhancing qualities of the performance were immeasurably enhanced by Richard Armstrong's con-ducting," Milnes had written after the first Edinburgh performance. ". . . I know some colleagues found the production too whimsical, but for me the mysterious parade of life, death and rebirth unfolded in almost child-like terms was unbearably moving." After the first night in Cardiff, few would have disagreed with him.

The revival of *Tosca* had brought an unexpected cast change. At Swansea a fortnight earlier, Anthony Baldwin had gone down with a heavy cold. He managed to get through the first performance but was unable to sing the second, and his place as Scarpia was taken by the Italian baritone Mario D'Anna who flew over from Dublin, where he was appearing with the Grand Opera. Baldwin had still not recovered in time for Cardiff, where the role was taken by Pablo Elvira, the distinguished Puerto Rican singer, making his British debut. Elvira was only available because the Metropolitan Opera in New York had been closed by a strike. He stayed on for the visit to Coventry the following week. The Birmingham Hippodrome had been closed that summer for a major refit and, rather than miss out on a Midlands tour, WNO had booked the Coventry Theatre instead, but not without misgivings. There was no loyal WNO following in the city, no tradition of opera-going, and no one knew how many people would be prepared to travel there from Birmingham. Amoco agreed to underwrite the week, and a special bus service was provided for patrons from Birmingham. In the event, Amoco's first regional Festival of Opera (as it was billed) did remarkably well, playing to 83 percent capacity. At the close of the second performance of *Tosca* it was announced that Amoco had won the ABSA/ *Daily Telegraph* award for the best corporate arts-sponsorship programme in 1980.

Amoco's sponsorship was now a vital ingredient in WNO's planning. The financial year ending in April 1981 revealed, in spite of the cancellation of *Don Giovanni* and other economy measures, a deficit of £75,000 brought about entirely by inflation. This represented less that 1 percent of turnover, but was still alarming enough to throw a shadow over the forthcoming year. Although the Arts Council grant was increased by 11 percent to £2.75 million, this was less than the rate of inflation, and on an estimated turnover of more than £3.5 million, allowing for income from all other sources, WNO expected to end 1981 some £130,000 in the red. The number of proposed performances was again reduced (to 133) and it was now the turn of *Parsifal* to be axed. Hopes of starting the *Ring* in 1982 also receded. There was little more that WNO could do if it was to continue providing opera regularly.

What had made the difference between a heavy and a catastrophic loss the previous year was sponsorship, and in particular that from Amoco. The original agreement between the oil company and WNO had allowed for £500,000 over a five-year period. Halfway through the agreement, Amoco had already handed over £400,000 and had promised to keep its donations at the same level, meaning that by the end of the period some £700,000 would have been contributed to WNO's coffers. It was Amoco money which allowed for the London season, for the making of records, for the award of bursaries to young singers, for the publication at a very reasonable price of the extensive programme booklet which accompanied each production, for the special season in Coventry and for an annual free concert in Sophia Gardens.

It was also Amoco's sponsorship that had made the production of *The Cunning Little Vixen* possible, and made possible WNO's first venture into Handel. *Rodelinda* opened at Mold on 13 January 1981, at the start of a short Welsh tour (all six performances were sold out before the first night), before joining the main repertory in Cardiff the following month. The production had been entrusted to the team that had worked on the successful *Onegin*, in the hope that they would be able to work their magic on what is essentially a non-dramatic work. Michael Yeargan designed some attractive Baroque-based costumes and an elegant, two-levelled composite set, with a classical balustraded gallery reached by a spiral staircase and movable as a whole or in sections, which could serve as an indoor hall or, decorated with trees, as a park or garden, or, with a series of grilles, as a prison. "So far, so good," wrote Stanley Sadie in *Opera*, "but the producer Andrei Serban sadly misused it. Clearly he lacks faith in the music. For this turned into one of those tiresome evenings where the producer would never leave well alone. The two-level set especially proved a dangerous snare. Every Handel aria, almost, has a central orchestral ritornello which offers an appropriate moment for stage movement; in many of them Mr Serban had the singer nip deftly upstairs to deliver part of the aria from aloft. This rapidly became farcical, a sort of musical *Upstairs, Downstairs*. And while the opportunities for using the two levels for characters overhearing or overseeing one another did well enough, it became absurd and anti-dramatic to have characters strolling about on one level while the action continued on the other." Not only did Serban keep his singers on the move, he kept the set going as well, regrouping it during arias, and in the second act finale duet between Rodelinda and Bertarido, both perched high on separate towers, bringing them together to hold hands, parting them, and so on; "lovely for *The Umbrellas of Cherbourg*, I'm sure," wrote Rodney Milnes in the *Spectator*, "but too kitschy an accompaniment to music of this stature. Hindsight suggests that with a liberal application of super-glue to all adjoining sections of the set and a powerful electric current passed through the staircase there might be the basis of a sound staging of *Rodelinda* here. The combination of a peripatetic set and a somewhat inexperienced cast brought further perils. I do not think it fair that young singers performing major roles for the first time – and of extremely difficult music – should be required to have to do so ten feet up in the air and on the move. Near-panic was evident more than once."

Singing the title role was Suzanne Murphy, who looked delightful and sang brightly, her performance marred only by some poor articulation. Eiddwen Harrhy was miscast in the mezzo role of Eduige, which did not allow her to show off her true potential as a Handelian singer. For the high castrato roles of the original, counter-tenor Robin Martin-Oliver was cast as Bertarido and Catherine Savory as Unulfo, both singing beautifully, though Martin-Oliver's lack of stage presence made his character seem rather weak. Richard Morton was a convincing Grimoaldo and Russell Smythe a suitably villainous Garibaldo. The performance was conducted by Julian Smith, who was also responsible for the few judicious cuts made in the score. Whatever reservations there might have been about the production (and Serban was to tone down the movement considerably for later performances) or about the artists, an unqualified welcome was given to the addition of a Handel opera to the repertoire.

The night before *Rodelinda* opened, another production designed for even smaller theatres and halls had received its première in Builth Wells. This was *All for Love*, a compilation of love scenes drawn from a wide operatic repertoire, devised and presented by Nigel Douglas. Fully staged scenes from operas as diverse as *Don Giovanni*, *Simon Boccanegra*, *Don Carlos*, *Lucia di Lammermoor*, *La Bohème*, *Arabella*, Heuberger's *Der Opernball*, *Peter Grimes* and *Die Fledermaus* were sung by Douglas, Helen Field, David Gwynne, John Harris, Robert Dean and Rita Cullis, accompanied by Guy Hamilton at the piano. It played to packed and appreciative audiences, many of whom may have been stimulated to try a full performance later. It was with a similar intention that a short concert tour was sent around Wales of three song cycles by composers whose operas were featured in the main season: Wagner, Janáček and Richard Strauss.

The success of *Elektra* three years earlier had made WNO determined to mount Strauss's *Die Frau ohne Schatten*, possibly the most difficult of all his operas both to stage and to understand. It had never been performed outside London, and the decision was taken to sing it, for the first time ever, in English, using a new translation by Eric Crozier. Cuts were made to reduce the running time to just over five hours. Director of Productions Adrian Slack had been intending to produce, but illness forced him to withdraw and McMaster brought in the young Belgian producer Gilbert Deflo to make his British debut, together with the Italian designer Carlo Tommasi. The constraints of touring and the small stages on which it would have to play (one of the reasons it had never been attempted previously) meant that much of the spectacular magic called for in the libretto had to go. The production was not without its stunning visual moments, however. The episode in which five fish fly on stage and land in frying pans was cleverly handled by black-costumed attendants bringing in the fish on rods; and the emergence of the Emperor from the waterfall in the final act was superbly achieved. Carlo Tommasi had designed a plain stone courtyard, with a monumental rock as a background which split open to reveal Barak's hut. Simple and austere, it allowed Deflo to concentrate on the actors, and, with clever lighting by John Waterhouse, was not without colour. There was only one real drawback: with no furniture, the Empress's nightmare was not nearly so effective when experienced crouching on a bare floor as it would have been had she been in bed. The greatest strength of Deflo's direction lay, felt Rodney Milnes, in the depth and clarity of the characterisation that he and a well-chosen cast managed to bring to the opera. Pauline Tinsley was superb as the Dyer's Wife: "the performance of a lifetime," Milnes dubbed it. "Her voice, a gleaming sword at the top, lusciously coloured at the bottom, has never sounded more expressive. A German critic has recently hailed her as one of the leading Strauss sopranos of the day. We know, we know, but it is good to have it confirmed from her home territory. Just as impressive was the way Miss Tinsley delved beneath the prickly surface of the character, finding the inarticulate discontent, the hidden misery and frustration. This is a profoundly moving interpretation." Anne Evans as the Empress, after a slow start, matched Tinsley in a generous outpouring of warm tone; Matti Kastu, the Finnish tenor, while not wholly at ease singing in English, was a heroic Emperor, and Norman Bailey a masterly Barak. His performance contained, wrote Stephen Walsh in the *Observer*, "a reading of instinctive but not cloying warmth, enriched by some beautiful lyrical singing and a firm authority of character and style." Richard Armstrong, conducting an orchestra increased to 97 in strength, brought out the full splendour of the score. "Not since Böhm and Kempe . . . have I heard the subtle colouring and the overwhelming power of this score realised with such sympathy, understanding and patent relish," concluded Milnes. Criticism of some aspects of the production (not everyone was entirely happy with the staging or the costumes) could not detract from the fact that *Die Frau ohne Schatten* was a towering achievement. "The Welsh National Opera proved again," enthused Alan Blyth in the *Daily Telegraph*, ". . . that it is the most ambitious, most successful of our regional companies and, in matters of a secure ensemble working as a co-ordinated team, it can even surpass anything found in London."

The week after the Cardiff season, WNO found itself back in London a year earlier than expected. When the idea of a regular London season had first been mooted by Amoco, McMaster had countered with a proposal that it should be an annual "Festival of Opera" with WNO appearing in the first, third and fifth years and important foreign companies in the intervening years. McMaster hoped that while such foreign companies were in Britain, WNO might be able to make a reciprocal visit to those companies' theatres (as they had the previous year when WNO paid its vastly successful visit to East Germany while the Leipzig Opera had performed in Cardiff and Birmingham). For the first overseas company to play in the Amoco London Festival, McMaster had been negotiating with the Berlin Komische Oper, and contracts had been exchanged for them to appear in early 1981. The drawbacks of the Dominion as an opera house had led McMaster to look for an alternative venue. The Theatre Royal Drury Lane was a possibility, but it preferred to take the musical *The Best Little Whorehouse in Texas* rather than opera, so the Dominion was again booked. At the last moment, however, the East German government, for internal political reasons, refused the Berlin company permission to travel and WNO (with the blessing of the Arts Council) hastily rearranged its spring touring schedule to appear instead for a week in March, taking *Die Frau ohne Schatten*, *The Cunning Little Vixen* and *Rodelinda*.

Following the London season, touring continued to Oxford, Coventry, Bristol and Southampton. It was in Southampton that Pauline Tinsley, having appeared as the Dyer's Wife on the Tuesday, saved the Saturday performance of *Tosca* by stepping in at the last moment to replace Canadian soprano Heather Thomson. Tinsley had not sung the part for twenty years, and when she forgot the words, turned her back to the audience and "la-la"d. There was a last-minute cast change, too, for *Rigoletto* when Miriam Bowen replaced Helen Field as Gilda.

The spring Cardiff season opened with a revival of *The Barber of Seville*, for which Thomas Allen returned to sing Figaro. The following week Allen made his debut as Germont in Stewart Trotter's production of *La Traviata*. Although he looked too young to be Alfredo's father, his portrayal of a grim-faced, moralistic prig was done with chilling effect, and, as always, he sang impeccably.

The new production that spring was of Bohuslav Martinů's *The Greek Passion*. For his last opera, the Czech composer had turned to the novel *Christ Recrucified* by Nikos Kazantzakis, best known as the author of *Zorba the Greek* (which Martinů had also considered using). He adapted the libretto himself, starting in French and then switching to English when a production for Kubelik at Covent Garden seemed possible. When that fell through, he rewrote it in German for Karajan, who did not want to stage it either, and Martinů died in 1959 without seeing it performed. John Moody, on the lookout for new works, had attempted to acquire it for WNO (although the Board did not permit him to try too hard, thinking it would be too great a risk), and *The Greek Passion*, as Martinů had retitled the opera,

was given its world première in Zurich in 1961. Twenty years later, WNO
became the first British company to stage the opera when *The Greek
Passion* opened in Cardiff on 29 April. The story, beginning with the casting
of a Passion play in a remote Greek mountain village, tells of the effect a
group of refugees fleeing Turkish oppression has on the community and of
how the villagers gradually assume the Biblical roles assigned to them.
Designer John Gunter set the production in a detailed village surrounded by
a parched, stony, inhospitable landscape in which one could almost smell
the Greek air. The costumes were equally authentic (designer Sally Gardner,
while researching for them, had been caught in the Athens earthquake
which killed 13 people) and Michael Geliot's production, complete with a
mechanical donkey and two live goats which did as expected and ate the
scenery, captured the tensions and passions of the mountain people
perfectly. (If there was one criticism to be made of the production it was that
the authentic settings produced enormous longueurs while the scenes were
changed.) "The Welsh staging of the Martinů is quite simply one of the
finest opera productions I have ever seen," wrote Rodney Milnes. Geliot
succeeded in drawing first-rate performances from his large cast. John
Mitchinson was in wonderful voice as Manolios, the man cast as Christ,
commanding the stage with the simple dignity and compassion of his
portrayal. Helen Field was a touching and fervent Katerina (the Mary
Magdalene figure) and there were equally impressive contributions from
Richard Van Allan and Geoffrey Moses as the rival priests and Arthur
Davies as Yannakos, the pedlar cast as Peter. Charles Mackerras, a long-
time champion of Martinů's music, conducted with a burning ferocity and
majesty born of a deep belief in the value of the work. The audience was
held by it and by the excellent performance, and yet, ultimately, *The Greek
Passion* was not the overwhelming experience it had promised to be. The
reason was not the production – Geliot and WNO had given Martinů the
finest advocacy possible – but the work itself. Often moving and
imaginative, it is an uneven opera, swinging erratically from good to less
good and back again. "In the final resort," wrote Peter Heyworth in the
*Observer*, "it fails to fulfil its lofty aspirations . . . one listens with interest
and appreciation. But one is not seized."

   William Mathias's *The Servants* had been the first of three contemporary
operas to be staged under the general banner "A Festival of Welsh Opera".
The second was Alun Hoddinott's *The Trumpet Major*, with a libretto by
Myfanwy Piper based on the Thomas Hardy novel, which had been
commissioned and staged by the Royal Northern College of Music first in
Manchester, then in Cardiff under the auspices of WNO in April. On 12
June, the third new opera by a living Welshman was given its world
première at the Sherman Theatre. This was *The Journey* by 35-year-old

John Metcalf, the best of the younger generation of Welsh composers. Metcalf had previously written a children's multi-media show which used operatic techniques, but this was his first major operatic commission. His brief had been to write a chamber work for small forces. He was determined not to produce a literary adaptation, but to create an original piece which would reflect the excitement and innovation then to be found in fringe theatre. John Hope Mason, his librettist, came up with a story based on the Chinese Book of Changes which required eight singers and a mime artist. Four characters (two men, two women) are on a Journey, accompanied by a storyteller. In the course of their travels from an unnamed city to who knows where, they meet a Father and Daughter with a sack, a Running Man with no clothes on and an Old Man. Their journey, wrote Hilary Finch in the *Times*, lasts "about two hours including interval, and, if at the end neither they nor we appear to have travelled anywhere, no matter. As we know, the Journey is more important than the Destination."

Metcalf's score, played by an orchestra 23-strong under Anthony Hose, was successful in conveying atmosphere and demonstrated an ability to support voices rather than overpower them. It was performed with great enthusiasm by Lesley Garrett, Menai Davies, Timothy German and Henry Newman (as the four travellers), Julian Moyle as the storyteller, David Gwynne, Yolande Jones and Phillip Guy-Bromley, but because it was broken into seven scenes, the work never seemed to get anywhere, and there was little opportunity for the principals to develop character. With its echoes of T. S. Eliot, Beckett, Pinter and Osborne, the libretto might have been the basis for an original and stimulating opera. In the final analysis, it wasn't. "The sad fact that, when the storyteller announces that the four 'have travelled far and may have far to travel', we believe not a word," continued Finch, "continue to disbelieve, and, in the end, could not care less, is due to a libretto of appalling banality and vacuity, an equally derivative and characterless score, and an almost entirely misconstrued sense of musical and dramatic structure."

While most critics tried hard to find something encouraging to say about *The Journey*, Rodney Milnes in the *Spectator* was vitriolic in his condemnation of both the libretto and the decision to stage the opera. "It doesn't matter a damn whether all this is the most appalling clap-trap known to man, or whether it has a deeply meaningful substance way above my muscular Christian head, but it does matter that it is wholly undramatic and should have been rejected out of hand by both composer and WNO management ... What we have here, alas, is the outpouring of the Subsidised Muse. New operas are a Good Thing. Subsidised companies must perform them. Composers must be paid to write them. Since they are paid for by the Arts Council, it doesn't matter whether they are any good or not; they go on for three performances before sinking without trace, playing to audiences, like this one, who fidget with barely disguised boredom throughout but applaud wildly at the end. Only nice, middle-class audiences brought up on fair play behave like this, and only a subsidised company would dare to be so cynical as to put this onanistic rubbish before them."

After the furore that had greeted Harry Kupfer's production of *Elektra* three years earlier, it was inevitable that his staging of *Fidelio*, which opened in Cardiff on 5 September, should also arouse deep antagonism. Kupfer's pronouncement the day before the opening that British critics only wanted to see on stage what they were already familiar with brought forth predictable savagery from the critics. "Lamentable staging," "nonsense," "a whirlwind of stupidity," they raged. The production was shared with Netherlands Opera and several critics had travelled to Amsterdam earlier in the year to see what they were in for. They had not liked what they had seen. Kupfer and his designer Wilfried Werz, had set *Fidelio* in a modern prison camp, hemmed in by curtains, with searchlights mounted on watchtowers at each corner. Within this acting area, the gaolers became symbols of a repressive regime, with Don Pizarro (Richard Van Allan) as an SS-type commandant, Jacquino (Richard Morton) as a sadistic young thug and the guards as Nazi storm-troopers. And if that did not upset the critics – it did – the finale almost caused apoplexy. The back curtain parted to reveal a tableau of freedom fighters drawn from history – from Christ to PLO guerillas. "The realisation is crude and garish," wrote Peter Heyworth in the *Observer*, "and surprise grows into incredulity as the roving eye alights first on a full-frontal nude personifying Winged Victory and then stumbles on, among other grotesque details, turbanned freedom fighters armed with machine-guns." When this tableau receded, it was replaced by two coffins, the symbolism of which caused much speculation. The general consensus was that they were there to show that Leonore and Florestan, too, were mortal and that death comes to us all; Paul Griffiths, in the *Times*, thought it was more likely to be Beethoven and Treitschke (his librettist) rolling and writhing therein. "As an example of People's *Kitsch*," roared Rodney Milnes in the *Financial Times*, "this takes the ruddy biscuit." There were undoubted inconsistencies in Kupfer's production: it was made plain that the prisoners were let out of their cells regularly, thus destroying some of the impact of their marvellous chorus welcoming the light, and those lines in the original libretto (translated by Nicholas Payne) which did not fit with the producer's conception were excised. But there could be no denying that it was marvellous music-theatre.

The cast on opening night were slightly inhibited, possibly due to the intensive rehearsals. Anne Evans, dressed in ankle-length greatcoat, brought dramatic intensity to the role of Leonore but was strained in her upper

register. The American tenor Dennis Bailey produced fine, ringing notes as
Florestan but without any sense of legato. Helen Field as Marzelline,
produced by Kupfer as a girl in the grip of intense emotion, was suitably
edgy though she seemed uncomfortable, and while Richard Van Allan and
Stafford Dean sang strongly as Pizarro and Rocco, only Richard Armstrong
and the orchestra escaped a critical battering of some kind. The public's
reaction was mixed. There were those who loathed it; but there were those
who thought it marvellous, and no other WNO production, not even
Kupfer's own *Elektra*, caused such discussion amongst audiences as to what
the opera actually meant.

A similar radical approach was expected from another East German
when Joachim Herz returned to Cardiff to produce Verdi's *La Forza del
Destino*, the sixteenth Verdi opera produced by WNO, in November. In the
event, the production turned out to be run-of-the-mill. Herz, naturally
enough, had a point of view – that war is evil – and to make his view clear,
he changed the running order in Act 3 and reverted to Verdi's original 1862
ending rather than use the revision Verdi had made for La Scala in 1869
(though he dropped Don Alvaro's suicide leap). These alterations were the
most controversial aspect of a production which surprised everyone by its
general lack of controversy. The anti-Christian sentiment was, after all, to
be expected. Reinhart Zimmermann's sets were considered unusually drab,
though, as Milnes pointed out, *Forza* is a dour piece. Herz, always a master
of stagecraft, managed some dramatic and showy effects – the battlefield
camp scene, with its obligatory naked dancers, for instance – but his
approach was essentially straightforward and might have worked better had
it been a framework for great singing. Unfortunately, it was not. Elizabeth
Vaughan, brought in to replace Elizabeth Ander as Leonora, was not in her
best voice. Moises Parker, the Cuban tenor, looked magnificent as Alvaro,
but had almost no control over a beautiful voice. Acting was the main
shortcoming of the American baritone Norman Phillips who, in the words
of Max Loppert, was "a strong-voiced stick" as Carlo. Only Don Garrard
as the Father Superior, Nicholas Folwell as Friar Melitone and Claire Powell
as Preziosilla achieved notable success in their respective roles. The chorus
sang with its customary fervour and enjoyment, but Richard Armstrong's
conducting seemed ill-at-ease and tended to pressure the music too urgently.
*La Forza* had been eagerly awaited; the production's lack of inspiration
raised once more the question of why WNO needed to import foreign
producers, particularly from Eastern Europe.

# CHAPTER NINETEEN: 1982–1983

The FIRST PRODUCER McMaster brought in for 1982 came not from Eastern Europe but from the Gorbals. Philip Prowse, a co-director of the Glasgow Citizens Theatre, was in charge of designing and producing Handel's *Tamerlano*, which opened at Mold on 15 January in a new translation by Robert David MacDonald, as *Tamburlaine*. Atrocious winter weather played havoc with the rehearsal schedule and delayed the cast's arrival in Mold, so it was not perhaps surprising that the production was not at its best. Prowse, making his operatic debut, had designed a composite set of a grey-and-white brick palace, dominated by statues of two horses. As the curtain went up, strobe lighting and falling bricks symbolised the destructive forces of war against which the opera's events unfolded. "The visual conception," wrote the critic of the *Western Mail*, ". . . is nothing less than stunning . . . Against this beautiful yet disturbing backdrop, Prowse plays out the tragedy of the defeated emperor, Bajazet, with unfailing conviction and dramatic cogency. Unlike many recent producers of Handel's stage works, he has taken the composer's judgement and his theatrical conventions at face value, so that in spite of the ornate trains borne by posturing retainers the five principal characters come to life as believable people. Only once, during a particularly long but rapturous aria, does he poke fun at the conventions by allowing Andronicus's trainbearer to drop his load and join in a game of cards with Leone." He also drew strong acting from his cast – Eiddwen Harrhy was outstanding as Asteria – but Handel is an acquired taste, and the fact that the two male leads were sung by counter-tenors (well though Robin Martin-Oliver as Tamburlaine and Brian Gordon as Andronicus sang) did not make the work readily accessible to those brought up on Verdi. When the production was seen at the Edinburgh Festival in September, prior to joining the repertory in Cardiff, it produced a divided reaction from those who felt that Prowse was right to attempt to make the drama credible and those who disliked his approach.

As Nicholas Kenyon pointed out in the *Listener*, it comes as a surprise to realise that from Handel's death in 1759 until 1920 not one of his operas had been seen on a British stage. Whether the purists liked the WNO staging of *Tamburlaine* or not, it at least gave the public a chance to hear a work very few had even heard of before.

When the production of *Parsifal* planned for early 1982 had had to be postponed, Rudolf Noelte, the eminent West German stage director who had been engaged to produce, suggested replacing it with Smetana's *The Bartered Bride*, a much cheaper opera to put on and one that had not been seen in Wales since 1966. Those people who went along to see the new production in Cardiff that February expecting to see a jolly, folksy romp were disappointed. There was a beautiful set designed by Dutchman Jan Schlubach showing a high barn interior, with open doors at the back through which fields of golden corn could be seen, and attractive costumes designed by Elisabeth Urbancic, but Noelte had opted to show the cruelties that lay beneath the comic surface. "If the production shed some of its customary *joie de vivre*," wrote Malcolm Boyd in the *Musical Times*, "it gained much more in dramatic truth." "Rudolf Noelte's remarkable new production . . . does not deny their proper place to such deceptively familiar elements as jolly, dancing peasants, the comic, stuttering tenor, or the colourful circus diversion of the last act," commented Tom Sutcliffe in the *Guardian*. "But these easy-to-patronise ingredients are only the start of *The Bartered Bride*. Noelte rigorously refuses to allow 'operatic' behaviour. Every minute detail is scrupulously observed, and all relationships and stage movements are treated as 'real' – within the convention of Noelte's stage language, where every gesture has to convince on its own terms. The result: the comedy, every bit as serious as *The Marriage of Figaro* (Smetana's model), comes over with extraordinary theatrical vitality." Noelte, responsible also for the excellent lighting, managed to achieve some brilliant visual groupings and the circus scene was thrilling (with Lesley Garrett as Esmeralda doing her own tight-rope walking). His one mistake was his fascination with the open door, which too often caused him to place too many people (and the chorus) deep in the set and made them difficult to hear.

Helen Field as Marenka added to her growing gallery of excellent portraits. "This is a performance of infinitely touching eloquence," wrote Rodney Milnes in the *Spectator*. Harry Nicoll made the stuttering Vasek a figure of complete sympathy, and there was strong support from April Cantelo, Julian Moyle, Menai Davies and Jeffrey Lawton, a member of the chorus, as an imposing Ringmaster. The disappointments included the first Kecal of Derek Hammond-Stroud, who, although acting well the seedy con-man of Noelte's interpretation rather than the more usual buffoon, was miscast vocally, and the Jenik of Warren Ellsworth (who was scheduled originally to be singing the lead in *Parsifal*). Suffering from a throat infection, he was not in his best voice and was replaced at the second performance by Arthur Davies.

The choral singing was, as expected, full-throated and enthusiastic, and Mark Ermler, returning to Wales for the first time following his triumphant debut with *Eugene Onegin*, clearly enjoyed conducting a work that was not part of the repertoire in Russia. He took the overture at a furious pace and the orchestra responded with superb playing. While not everyone was attracted to the more sober treatment, most found Noelte's *Bartered Bride* a moving experience. "I doubt whether Smetana has ever been better served in Britain, as regards conducting and staging," concluded Sutcliffe.

It is often said that Bellini's *I Puritani* is only revived when an opera company believes it has the exceptional singers to do the work justice. The development of Suzanne Murphy had led to the wish to mount a work by Bellini. The more popular choices of *Norma* and *La Sonnambula* were passed over for *I Puritani*, Bellini's last opera, which had not been seen in Britain for almost twenty years and in Wales for even longer. This opened in Cardiff on 10 March, in a production by Andrei Serban, conducted by Julian Smith. It was a surprising choice, for the opera had long been regarded as either a poor *Norma* or a stand-and-sing opera which would pose insurmountable difficulties for an ensemble company. Serban's production was to prove that it was neither. Julian Smith, following extensive research in Italy, had prepared a new performing edition of the score and had made some cuts to keep down the running time. Both he and Serban were convinced that the opera was more dramatic than received opinion had led people to believe.

Serban's working methods again caused upsets during rehearsals – one of the principals threw a shoe at him – and he had difficulty staging the ending. He tried several ways before discovering a painting contemporary with the opera he wanted to recreate. The fact that this meant altering the end of the opera did not deter him, and McMaster had to step in to ensure he stayed with Bellini's conception. Even after the dress rehearsal, he changed his mind about the ending again, and the first-night audience saw yet another solution. Serban was determined to make *I Puritani* real and not just to provide a platform for singing. He wanted to bring out the background of the Civil War against which the events are set. Members of the Sealed Knot Society were brought in to drill the chorus in the correct use of their muskets. "While I am sure that every hand on hip was deeply authentic," wrote Milnes in the *Spectator*, "when executed to a merry *polacca* the poor chorus was made to look like some nightmare team of gay formation dancers." Serban did, possibly, go overboard with his drilling and counter-drilling of the chorus, but his overall concept undoubtedly succeeded. He was aided by the wonderfully realistic sets of Michael Yeargan, those for the first two acts being based on the Barbican at Plymouth; the final act was transposed to a battlefield, and as the curtain rose on a stagecoach stranded in a snowstorm, it drew a round of applause. "Most producers hope that fine singing and Bellini's ravishing score will obscure the weaknesses of a libretto which has more holes than a rusty colander," commented John Higgins in the *Times*. "Serban prefers to try and plug them himself. His solutions are exciting, provoking and about 80 percent successful." The problem of a heroine who goes mad and then spends most of the opera wandering about mentally disturbed was solved by making Elvira a neurotic from the start. Suzanne Murphy curled herself into all sorts of shapes and still managed to give a performance which was little short of magnificent: "An impersonation that will long remain in the mind's eye and ear," wrote William Davies in *Classical Music*. The singing and acting of all the principals was of an exceptionally high standard. Dennis O'Neill's Arturo, sung against the advice of two doctors, matched Murphy in intensity and skill. "Many a tenor in robust health has given less satisfaction," wrote Desmond Shawe-Taylor. "Not only did he scale the famous heights of the role unscathed as far as C sharp and even D, but his phrasing was throughout shapely, his style musical, and his enunciation clear." Two former WNO choristers, Henry Newman as Arturo's rival, Riccardo, and Geoffrey Moses as Elvira's uncle, Giorgio, both revealed new stature and vocal authority. "This was a production – and that word must include Julian Smith's musical version – which showed that Bellini's last opera is a powerful theatrical piece," wrote Harold Rosenthal in *Opera*. ". . . past stagings of *Puritani* have at their worst been little more than concerts in costume and at their best unviable dramatically. This Welsh National Opera production has changed all that; and as a result of the close collaboration between conductor, producer and designer, and a dedicated cast, became a most exciting evening in the theatre."

While WNO was still achieving great success on stage, the news on the financial front was no less encouraging. At the annual press conference, McMaster was able to announce that the projected deficit of around £130,000 for the current financial year had not been reached due to strict budgetary controls, a 28 percent increase in ticket prices and increased attendance figures, much greater sponsorship than had been budgeted for, and a supplementary grant of £50,000 from the Arts Council. These had brought the overspend down to £20,000, and if similar progress was maintained, there was a strong possibility that the books might be balanced during the forthcoming year. There remained, of course, the accumulated deficit, but the Arts Council, impressed by the steps already taken to avoid further losses, had agreed to make another substantial grant towards reducing it. In a further attempt to save money, there were to be still more casualties. The week scheduled for Swansea in April was cancelled at the request of the Welsh Arts Council, and the June appearance in Llandudno was reduced to five performances, a cut-back which caused the local council to cancel its civic reception in a fit of pique.

In May the fourth opera in the Janáček cycle, *Katya Kabanova*, opened the Cardiff spring season, three years after it had first been seen in Scotland. David Pountney's production, with designs by Maria Björnson and Richard Armstrong conducting, had an almost entirely new cast. Elisabeth Söderström returned to sing Katya, the wife who is unable to bear the shame of an affair and commits suicide by throwing herself in the river. Her Katya, well known on record, achieved a rare subtlety in the theatre, but, though beautifully sung and movingly interpreted, there were times when she failed to involve the audience completely in her emotions, due perhaps to having to sing the role in English. American tenor Dennis Bailey, who had last appeared with WNO in *Fidelio*, cut a striking figure as her lover, Boris, and there were delightful performances from Arthur Davies and Cynthia Buchan (the sole survivor of the 1979 Scottish cast) as the young lovers. Rita Gorr, the veteran Belgian mezzo, made her WNO debut and her first appearance in a work by Janáček as Kabanicha, the harridan mother-in-law, in an inspired piece of casting; her authoritative presence, vocal power and precision of gesture produced a terrifying portrait. There was strong support from Jeffrey Lawton as Tikhon, Katya's husband, David Gwynne as Dikoy and the other singers, proving, as Rodney Milnes wrote, that there are no small roles in *Katya*; Richard Armstrong again conducted with complete assurance. And yet, although Rodney Milnes found it a memorable evening and Pountney's production wholly satisfying, *Katya Kabanova* just missed being sublime. "It was an account of the work of notable distinction, given on a high level of musical and dramatic accomplishment, that left me more distant from, less emotionally over-whelmed by, the opera than several less expertly finished performances have done," wrote Max Loppert in the *Financial Times*, echoing the feeling of several critics. This was partly due to the slight detachment of Söderström in the title role, but owed more to David Pountney's production, which, it was felt, sometimes fell uneasily between realism and symbolism. Björnson's sets, heavily influenced by Munch, made little attempt to specify location, and it required a reading of Pountney's essay on the opera to understand completely the significance of the expressionistic river hanging over every scene. Perhaps the high standard of the previous Janáček productions had led to expectations of perfection. "As it is," commented David Cairns, "to hear this marvellous score performed with such conviction was an experience to be grateful for." *Katya Kabanova* was a worthy addition to the Janáček cycle.

It was followed by a revival of John Copley's production of *Tosca*, with further cast changes. Since it had opened less than two years before, there had been three Toscas (Helena Döse, Heather Thomson and Pauline Tinsley) and four Scarpias (Anthony Baldwin, Pablo Elvira, Henry Newman and Norman Bailey). The only constant principal had been Kenneth Collins as Cavaradossi. He was now joined by the American soprano Marilyn Zschau and Italian baritone Ettore Nova, with Mark Ermler conducting. There was a last minute cast change to the revival of *I Puritani* when Dennis O'Neill was indisposed and Arthur Davies had to sing the role of Arturo. A week later O'Neill still had not recovered fully, but insisted on singing the second performance. He managed to get through the first act but was in no condition to sing the third. A hasty phone call was made to Davies at his Newport home (where he was watching his favourite football team on television), and he drove to the theatre in time to save the performance from cancellation.

In June the season in Llandudno and an additional week in Mold were made possible by Amoco's sponsorship. It was in Mold that the postponed production of *Don Giovanni* finally made it onto the stage. Michael Geliot, who had made his WNO reputation with the same opera sixteen years earlier, now directed *Giovanni* as a boisterous romp. While this produced some novel ideas – Giovanni escaped at the end of Act 1 because Don Ottavio, literally, slipped on a banana skin – the overall approach lacked Geliot's usual inventiveness (though Kenneth Loveland particularly enjoyed the introduction of a coffin, à la Kupfer in *Fidelio*, at the end). Giovanni's descent into hell was made through the top of the dining table while it billowed out smoke furiously, "like an out-of-control food warmer". It was a device which ensured that the production could work on any stage, but one which looked faintly ridiculous, particularly when Leporello had to unplug the table to wheel it off. Paul Griffiths wrote in the *Times*: "There are a great many things wrong ... but they all spring from one basic deficiency: that of style. So, if you can imagine a *Don Giovanni* without glamour, without risk, without excitement, without glorious singing, without suave orchestral playing, this is it." The details of Geliot's production might not have upset some critics quite so much (and audiences certainly laughed in the places Geliot wanted them to) had the musical side been stronger. The cast, all company members (five of them ex-choristers), generally proved inadequate for their roles and only Nicholas Folwell as Leporello added to his reputation. In the title role, Henry Newman, whose Riccardo in *I Puritani* had won such praise, radiated "little sexual energy, or indeed energy of any kind," according to Griffiths. "It is quite a surprise when he manages a bound on to his table in the last scene." David Seaman, an Amoco bursary winner, conducting at a leisurely pace – several times the singers had to stop and wait for the orchestra to catch up – did not help the evening achieve musical tension. It was, wrote John McMurray in *Classical Music*, "one of the unhappiest episodes in the company's recent history ... performed in that atmosphere of rising panic which always suggests cast and producer know they have a shambles on their hands . . . It should be noted that the capacity audience seemed to enjoy it all immensely."

If *Don Giovanni* proved to be a disappointment, the three new productions which followed were to provide WNO with three striking successes. Verdi's *Un Ballo in Maschera* opened the autumn season in Cardiff on 4 September, sung in Italian. Producer Göran Järvefelt returned the setting to Verdi's original choice of Sweden (the censors, objecting to the assassination of a European King being shown on stage, had made him change the locale to America). During the prelude, he had Gustav appear before the curtain to toy with a model theatre. Some critics felt this was superfluous, but Rodney Milnes felt that the stage metaphor was well sustained throughout (Gustav was, after all, fascinated by the stage and by opera). The attractive designs by Carl Friedrich Oberle reinforced Järvefelt's theatrical approach, being based on a false stage decorated with 18th century flats and using a series of beautiful backcloths depicting contemporary prints of Stockholm. "This approach lent an aptly Pirandellian feeling to the proceedings," wrote Milnes in *Opera*. "and together with Järvefelt's sober, understated yet purposeful direction of the singers . . . added up to the most convincing and consistently thought through staging of the opera that I have seen." "The concentrated impact of the action on stage is ideally mirrored in Richard Armstrong's conducting," wrote Peter Heyworth in the *Observer*. "Without overdriving the score, he delivers it with a thrilling intensity that captures its sparkle as well as its blackness. Mr Armstrong must surely be counted among the most authoritative Verdian conductors this side of the Alps." Dennis O'Neill sang with brilliance and precision as Gustav, shaping his phrases superbly, and delivering his high notes with ease; Suzanne Murphy was in thrilling but, as Sutcliffe expressed it, idiosyncratic form as Amelia (her diction was too often indistinct). Donald Maxwell was a powerful Anckarström and Rosamund Illing, a graduate from the National Opera Studio, made the page Oscar into a fascinating monster, "at once odious and touching". "Verdi performances in which there is so little sense of mere routine are rare indeed," commented Sutcliffe in the *Guardian*. Few critics or members of the audience disagreed with Paul Griffiths of the *Times* when he wrote that WNO "have opened another hugely ambitious season with a winner."

*Un Ballo in Maschera* was followed on 27 October by Giordano's *Andrea Chénier*, a *verismo* work not seen on British stages for more than twenty years and made possible by NatWest's sponsorship. Michael Geliot, eschewing a revolutionary interpretation, produced an admirably straightforward account of the work, concentrating on character and atmosphere. His handling of the chorus was especially effective. John Gunter provided realistic period sets and Sheelagh Killeen attractive costumes. "It is *verismo* presented in the only way that really works," commented Kenneth Loveland in *Country Life*; "with frank acceptance of its style for its own sake, complete commitment and no punches pulled." Like *I Puritani*, *Chénier* requires strong principals, and received them with Kenneth Collins as the poet/revolutionary Chénier, Elizabeth Vaughan as Maddalena and Ettore Nova (sharing the role with Terence Sharpe) as Gérard. Collins sang with his customary ardour and he and Elizabeth Vaughan gave a thrilling account of their ecstatic final duet. Vaughan was singing as well as anyone had heard her for some time. She was, wrote William Mann in the *Times*, "singing with a strong, steady, exhilarating warmth and brightness . . . which mark a new, glorious phase in her operatic career." The decision to sing in Italian meant that Ettore Nova could be cast as Gérard, and he delivered a stirring performance. There were pointed contributions from the minor characters, and Julian Smith conducted with obvious admiration for the score and stylish vigour. "Try as I may," wrote Milnes in the *Spectator*, "I can find no evidence to suggest that Giordano's opera is anything other than unutterable rubbish – the characterisation pasteboard thin, the action meretricious at a Baroness Orczy level. But my goodness it was well done, directed by Michael Geliot as if it were a masterpiece by Puccini." "By modern standards this is a straight production," concluded Mann. ". . . It will probably not win prizes for originality, but it may alert British opera-goers to the sturdy, heartening merits of a greatly enjoyable Italian opera that has too long been knocking unanswered at the doors of our repertory." The audience cheers at the end went on and on as curtain call followed curtain call.

Two days later, on 29 October, the scheduled performance of *Don Giovanni* was cancelled and in its place was substituted a Royal Gala in aid of WNO's Benevolent Fund, held in the presence of the Princess of Wales. The Princess, who had become WNO's Patron in February and was on her first official engagement since the birth of Prince William, saw Richard Burton introducing excerpts from *Nabucco* (the "Va, pensiero" chorus), *The Bartered Bride*, *Eugene Onegin*, *Un Ballo in Maschera*, *The Magic Flute*, *The Pearl Fishers* (with Stuart Burrows, a late replacement for Dennis O'Neill, and Donald Maxwell singing the famous duet), *Andrea Chénier*, and Elisabeth Söderström singing one of Strauss's *Four Last Songs* and Grieg's *I Love Thee* (a setting of a Hans Andersen poem, in Danish).

And then, on 10 November, the Janáček cycle was completed with a quite exceptional production of *From the House of the Dead*. Maria Björnson's designs for *Katya Kabanova* had not met with universal approval. Those for *House of the Dead* were among the finest she, or any other designer, had ever done. Richard Armstrong had decided to play the three acts continuously, and Björnson designed an atmospheric permanent set of a cross-section of the prison, seemingly carved from stone and honeycombed with cells. At its heart was the blacksmith's forge. Within this framework, David Pountney turned each one of the large cast into an instantly recognisable character, and achieved the most hard-hitting, intense production. During the opening music to the second act, the prisoners were sent on a stylised march round the set, producing one of the most striking images of a striking production (it was repeated at the close to show that the prisoners' boring, repetitive life would continue). The solo performances were all outstanding, Graham Clark's crazy Skuratov, Donald Maxwell's Shishkov, John Mitchinson's Morozov, Robert Carpenter Turner's Goryanchikov and Nigel Douglas's Shapkin among them; but this was essentially an ensemble work and every member of the cast gave the performance of a lifetime. During rehearsals, Pountney had made the cast wear their stinking costumes and leg-irons to get them used to the idea of being in captivity. The corridors of John Street had echoed to the sound of clinking chains as people had gone to the toilet or the canteen, and shins had the skin rubbed off them by the constant chafing. Such attention to detail helped produce real prisoners on stage, and such detailed concentration, wrote Milnes in *Opera*, "demanded (and received) equal concentration from the audience . . . The cumulative effect was both theatrically gripping and spiritually shattering." The production was, wrote Felix Aprahamian in the *Sunday Times*, a moving masterpiece. Holding the evening together, and more than vindicating the decision to play it without an interval, was Richard Armstrong, who secured playing of rare distinction from the orchestra. His "big, lyrical reading," noted Milnes, "emphasised the score's symphonic content, and the orchestra played as if their lives depended on it. Although the brass spilled over into the stage boxes and the sound was wonderfully 'fat', more of the text came across in Mr Pountney's own translation than in any previous performance I have heard. This, quite apart from all else, suggested the care that had gone into this magnificent company achievement."

It is difficult to explain to someone who did not see WNO's *From the House of the Dead* just how powerful and emotional the work is. On the surface, there is little to relieve the gloom. And yet Janáček's music is inspirational, and at the close, few people remained unmoved by the performance they had just witnessed. Although not all Janáček's operas had been staged in the cycle (there remained *Osud* and *The Adventures of Mr Brouček*), *From the House of the Dead* brought the joint venture with Scottish Opera to a close on the highest dramatic, musical and spiritual level. The series had been a critical triumph and over the seven years since it had started with *Jenůfa*, had built an audience for what was once a specialist interest. On the subsequent tour, *House of the Dead* (a title notoriously difficult to sell at the box-office) played to large and tremendously enthusiastic audiences.

The first major production of 1983 was to be another powerful and emotional work. Thanks to £75,000 sponsorship from Amoco, the postponed production of *Parsifal*, the first time (apart from two performances in Manchester in 1920) the opera had been staged outside London, was to open the early spring season, produced by Rudolf Noelte and conducted by Reginald Goodall. The earlier postponement had not meant that preparations had ceased, and Goodall (who had not previously conducted *Parsifal*) had, as usual, been coaching the principals over the previous eighteen months. Just before Christmas 1982 and only a few weeks before the production rehearsals were due to start, Rudolf Noelte withdrew from the project because of a disagreement over casting, and his designer left with him. It was too late for McMaster to find a replacement of comparable stature, and in desperation he gave the production to Mike Ashman, the staff producer who had been assigned to work as Noelte's assistant. Ashman, a former music journalist who had been on the WNO staff for four years, had produced student performances and been responsible in Cardiff for reviving other people's productions, but he had never produced a major opera on his own. Fortunately, one of his specialisations was Wagner and he had very clear ideas of how he wanted to stage *Parsifal*. The withdrawal of Noelte's designer left Ashman free to choose his own, and he invited Peter Mumford, with whom he had worked on *Noye's Fludde* at the Malvern Festival (and who had designed WNO's *The Journey*) to join him. Together they worked over the Christmas period to get the designs for Act 1 ready for rehearsals to start on 4 January.

The cast were all new to their roles, but with Goodall as the presiding genius, everything seemed to be going well. Then, one week before opening night, Goodall himself was forced to withdraw. He had earlier undergone an operation and, although he had returned to the rehearsals, had been forced to admit that he was not well enough to conduct a performance. His place on the rostrum was taken by Anthony Negus, a member of the music staff and his assistant on the production. Negus had worked at Bayreuth for two years, had assisted Goodall on *Tristan und Isolde* and conducted performances of *Fidelio* and *Rodelinda*, but he had never conducted anything as massive as *Parsifal* before.

What might have become a disaster turned out to be one of the most telling *Parsifals* of recent years. Ashman, aware that many members of the audience would not know the opera (or German – it was being sung in the original language), concentrated on the drama of human suffering, and succeeded in telling the story with great clarity. He played down the Christian aspects: Parsifal did not make the sign of the cross with the magic spear at the end of the second act, merely holding it aloft as Klingsor's kingdom crumbled; and Amfortas's wound was restored to the groin, as it had been in the medieval sources and Wagner's own preliminary sketches before he decided to make the Christian parallel more clear. Parsifal himself, with a thrilling first entrance running through the sacred waters, was characterised as a child of nature set against the order of civilisation (with its attendant corruption and awareness). As with any worthwhile production of an opera by Wagner, there was enough in the production to keep the critics arguing for a long time. Some loved the Burne-Jones costumes of the Flower Maidens; others hated them. Some thought that having Klingsor dressed like Nietzsche was a brilliant stroke; others that it was ludicrous. "The deceased swan," wrote Rodney Milnes in the *Spectator*, "I prefer not to describe in a family magazine." But if the production lacked visual magic, it more than made up for it with its clarity, intelligence and conviction. Ashman's greatest contribution was that he made sense of what was happening on stage. In this he was helped enormously by Mumford's designs. Those who wanted the huge effects made possible by massive stage machinery found them spartan and drab, but, like the production itself, they helped focus attention on the action and, with skilful lighting, enabled scene changes to be made easily and effectively; the transformation to the Hall of the Grail, achieved by lowering a lighting gantry over the pool which dominated the centre of the stage, was brilliantly simple. Ashman's production was, wrote Milnes, "by a very long chalk the most probing and challenging I have yet encountered."

Musically the production was equally distinguished. Donald McIntyre, singing his first Gurnemanz, dominated the cast with his authority, clear projection and the glorious firmness of his singing. Linda Esther Gray brought expressive acting and noble singing to the role of Kundry and Warren Ellsworth as Parsifal was particularly effective as the wild boy of the first two acts. He alternated vocally between insecure half-voice and exciting brilliance, but gave a performance of much promise. Phillip Joll's Amfortas was without doubt the best performance he had yet given for WNO, and Nicholas Folwell contributed an incisive and commanding Klingsor. Naturally enough, most attention was centred on Anthony Negus in the pit. Having learnt the work from Goodall, he made no attempt to alter Goodall's ideas, but neither was he a mere cipher. He clearly understood the structure of the work. "His shaping of the long first act seemed surer than Levine's at Bayreuth last summer," wrote John McMurray in *Classical Music*, "and the flower maidens' music was ravishingly done. The later part of that act was less successful – as so often happens – but the Third Act Prelude, music of Parsifal's suffering but touched with hope, took its proper place as one of the score's great

*The Coronation of Poppea* 1980: Eiddwen Harrhy *Poppea*, Arthur Davies *Nero*

*Eugene Onegin* 1980: Thomas Allen *Onegin*, Josephine Barstow *Tatiana* (Julian Sheppard) with the impounded cornfield (see p. 223)

*The Cunning Little Vixen* 1980: set design by Maria Björnson (Julian Sheppard); Helen Field *Vixen* (Eric Thorburn)

*The Greek Passion* 1981: John Mitchinson *Manolios* (Julian Sheppard)

*Die Frau ohne Schatten* 1981: Norman Bailey *Barak*, with Russell Smythe, Julian Moyle and Arthur Davies (Rhiannon Williams)

*Fidelio* 1981: Richard Van Allan *Pizarro*, Anne Evans *Leonore* and Dennis Bailey *Florestan* (Julian Sheppard); set design by Wilfried Werz for the Finale

*The Bartered Bride* 1981: Helen Field *Marenka*, Warren Ellsworth *Jenik* (Julian Sheppard)

*I Puritani* 1982: Dennis O'Neill *Lord Arthur Talbot*, Suzanne Murphy *Elvira* (Zoë Dominic)

*Parsifal* 1983: Warren Ellsworth *Parsifal*, Linda Esther Gray *Kundry*; Donald McIntyre *Gurnemanz* (Clive Barda)

*Carmen* 1983: Henry Newman *Escamillo*, Jennifer Jones *Carmen*; Helen Field as *Micaela*
(Clive Barda)

*The Rhinegold* 1983: (left) Anne Collins *Erda*, Phillip Joll *Wotan*, Patricia Payne *Fricka* (Zoë Dominic); closing scene (Catherine Ashmore)

*The Valkyrie* 1984: Warren Ellsworth *Siegmund*, Kathryn Harries *Sieglinde*; Anne Evans *Brünnhilde*, Phillip Joll *Wotan* (Clive Barda)

*The Merry Widow* 1984: Suzanne Murphy *Hanna Glawari*, Thomas Allen *Count Danilo* (Clive Barda)

*La Bohème* 1984: Suzanne Murphy *Musetta*; Helen Field *Mimi*, John Fowler *Rodolfo* (Clive Barda)

*Don Giovanni* 1984: William Shimell *Giovanni*, Nicholas Folwell *Leporello*; Anne Evans *Anna*, Laurence Dale *Ottavio*, Elaine Woods *Elvira* (Zoë Dominic); set design by Marie-Luise Strandt (Catherine Ashmore)

*Rigoletto* 1985; Dennis O'Neill *Duke of Mantua*; Donald Maxwell *Rigoletto* (Zoë Dominic)

*Norma* 1985: Suzanne Murphy *Norma* (Zoë Dominic)

*Siegfried* 1985: Anne Evans *Brünnhilde* (Clive Barda)

*Siegfried* 1985: Jeffrey Lawton *Siegfried* (Clive Barda)

*Götterdämmerung* 1986

Richard Armstrong; Sir Charles Mackerras (Zoë Dominic); Brian McMaster

wonders." "Negus clearly has the feel of *Parsifal*," wrote Robert Hartford in *Music and Musicians*. "Much as one had to regret Goodall's absence, one was grateful that it had provided the opportunity for him to display it. To him, as much as anyone, was due the fact that the WNO *Parsifal*, in the face of all handicaps, was a moving statement of Wagner's vision." *Parsifal* was a triumph, though the bad luck that had dogged the production continued until the first night: Mike Ashman turned up for it in a wheelchair, having damaged his back two days earlier.

Negus's control of an outstanding orchestra developed throughout the following tour to Birmingham, Liverpool, Bristol and Oxford (the only theatres on WNO's touring circuit capable of taking the production). In Oxford, Donald Stephenson, a trainee at the National Opera Studio, stepped in to sing Parsifal when Warren Ellsworth was taken ill. While it was not the accomplished performance one would expect had an experienced artist taken over, it was a more than creditable professional debut. *Parsifal* sold out everywhere and WNO laid on a special train (the Parsifal special) to take Londoners to the performance in Liverpool. It was there that Wolfgang Wagner, the composer's grandson, saw the production, having travelled over from Germany because he had heard it was something special. At the end, he announced himself well satisfied. "A very interesting and remarkable production," he said, and his praise for Anthony Negus's conducting was glowing.

*Parsifal* was made possible by the generous sponsorship of Amoco. The next new production was financed by the Friends of WNO through money raised by jumble sales, concerts, social evenings, excursions and sponsored events of all kinds. The Friends had been in existence for eleven years and during that time had provided invaluable support for the company, including manning stalls at most of the theatres on tour. When they decided to raise the money for a new production, their unanimous choice had been *Carmen*, which had not been in the repertoire for thirteen years. Whether they approved of what they were given is not on record. The eminent Romanian theatre director Lucian Pintilie, whose home was in Paris, was brought in to produce, together with his designers, Radu and Miruna Boruzescu. All three were making their British debuts. Pintilie had seen a production of *Carmen* in Bucharest when he was twelve which had put him off opera for a long time, and was determined to give the work new life. *Carmen*, he told the cast at their first rehearsal, is the most popular opera in the world; everyone knows it even if they have never seen it, and a mythology has grown up around the work that needs to be removed. The way he proposed de-mythologising it was to stage it as a post-revolutionary, improvised, unofficial performance (it is, he claimed, always the first opera to be staged after a revolution) during a carnival. Radu Boruzescu came up

with a superb set, containing a sand-bagged auditorium in which the chorus
(dressed as guerillas) stage the opera, and dominated by a revolving
maypole and the underside of a balloon basket. Famous arias – such as the
Toreador's Song – were greeted with pop-style roars of approval, and there
was an endless succession of gags at the expense of traditional presentations.
There was so much going on on stage, with a dwarf, tightrope walkers,
jugglers, transvestites, and a miniature railway running across the front,
that when Jacque Trussel (Don José) fell into the orchestra pit in
Llandudno, none of the audience knew whether it was intended or not. It
was the ultimate in producer's opera, a lively, exhilarating theatrical
experience, and the critics, predictably, were divided in their reactions to it.
Felix Aprahamian called it a "desecration . . . overcooked" and found his
initial indignation soon turning to anger; Alan Blyth thought it "crude" and
"vulgar." Max Loppert also disliked it: "It is not *Carmen* that the WNO
has staged, but rather a single producer's problems in contacting the opera
freshly . . . This is not, however, something to get too heated about, despite
the accompanying intellectual pretensions; for what we witnessed . . . was,
in effect, a jolly undergraduate romp, 'naughty' at moments, with a coarse-
grained vein of farce more to some tastes than others."

Other critics accepted it in the spirit in which it was intended. "I
suppose," wrote Milnes, "[it] is as silly as everyone has said it is, but I found
myself rather enjoying it and certainly admired the spirit with which the
company executed the production." John Higgins of the *Times* thought it
"probably the most exotic and complex staging in the company's history to
date, an evening that is simultaneously exhausting and exhilarating," and
John McMurray, writing in *Classical Music*, found that it was "bursting
with theatrical life" and "rescued the drama from stale tradition, shed fresh
light on the nature of the work and retained the essential truth of characters
and music . . . Pintilie's great achievement was to stage a production which
was immediately striking and wonderfully entertaining, but which had the
intellectual strength to raise important and provoking questions."

Musically *Carmen* did not approach the same intense level. The omnipresent chorus acted superbly and sang lustily, and there were strong
cameos from the supporting principals. But, although the main roles were
well acted, they were vocally lightweight. Jennifer Jones, from Delaware, as
Carmen, looked stunning but lacked the vocal armoury to be memorable;
Jacque Trussel, singing cleanly as Don José, was also vocally thin, and while
Henry Newman clearly enjoyed playing Escamillo as a rhinestoned cowboy,
busy signing autographs and basking in the crowd's adulation, he, too, was
vocally underpowered. Helen Field, forced to sing her first aria on ballet
points, also seemed ill-at-ease as Micaela. Kees Bakels in the pit matched the
stage action with some impetuous tempi, but revealed little of the gentle

lyricism of the score. "But this did little to detract from one of the most stimulating and enjoyable evenings in the theatre I have had," concluded McMurray. "*Carmen* became exciting again in a way it had not done since the first time I saw it." "This *Carmen*, even without solid singing, is a knock-out," enthused Tom Sutcliffe.

Before the opera began, as the audience was contemplating the set, a girl was heard to ask her friend, somewhat concerned, "We are at the right opera, aren't we?" But was it *Carmen*? It certainly was not *Carmen* as Bizet wrote it, but it was an operatic experience which played to packed houses and converted many people to the idea that opera can and should be enjoyable.

A few years earlier large-scale productions such as *Parsifal, Elektra* and *Die Frau ohne Schatten* would have been unthinkable, not just because the idea of a Welsh company staging them in Wales would have been laughed at, but because the facilities and theatres to do such works justice were not available. The only theatre in Wales with the facilities to stage *Parsifal*, for instance, was the New in Cardiff. And yet there remained the rest of Wales for which productions needed to be found. After a Monteverdi and two Handel operas, it had been decided, for those small theatres unable to take full productions, to revert to a more popular, general entertainment, and at the beginning of the year, *Dear Ivor*, a compilation based on the life and work of Wales's best-known and best-loved composer, Ivor Novello, had opened at St David's Hall in Cardiff before being taken on a tour of fourteen Welsh towns, and ending with a brief foray into England to the Nottingham Playhouse (with which it was a co-production). In July, *The Drama of Aida* opened in Mold. The enormous interest aroused by Peter Brook's Paris production of *La Tragédie de Carmen*, his cut-down and intimate version of Bizet's opera, had led directly to WNO's decision to do the same for Verdi's *Aida*. Such a product, without chorus and relying solely on five principals, would, it was argued, be ideal for the smaller Welsh theatres. Daryl Runswick, a double-bass player of both classical music and jazz, had been commissioned to re-orchestrate Verdi's score for a wind, brass, double-bass and percussion group of twenty-four players, and Andrei Serban was brought in to produce, with designs by Michael Yeargan. Serban, together with Richard Armstrong, was responsible for stripping the opera to its essentials.

*The Drama of Aida* was not, it was emphasised, simply a cut-down version of the original but a radical re-thinking, concentrating on the conflicts between Aida, Amneris, Radames, Amonasro and Ramphis. It ran for ninety minutes without interval. "Has the patient survived?" asked Peter Heyworth in the *Observer*. "It is not, I suspect, mere chance that the most drastic elements in the experiment are the most successful. Mr Runswick is

surely right to have rejected a merely reduced version of the original score
. . . The result is of course unlike anything that Verdi wrote. But therein lies
its strength. Instead of producing a pallid copy, Mr Runswick has used the
techniques of a twentieth-century chamber orchestra so as to produce an
instrumentation that stands on its own feet in a way that the remainder of
the experiment does not." Heyworth found Serban's production frequently
lame and even, at moments, clumsy; with singing of only a moderate level,
he thought the experiment was ultimately unsatisfying, largely because there
was no urgent need to fillet *Aida* and the end result, unlike Brook's
reworking of *Carmen*, did not reveal any great, hidden truths. Rodney
Milnes, writing in the *Spectator*, was of the same opinion: "With great good
will, I don't think it works. *Aida* is about private passions in a public
context. Remove the latter and the former are pointless . . . I came away
feeling that those who know the opera will find it all very diverting, and
those who don't will be totally mystified." Mystified or not, the audience at
Mold was outraged at having to pay full prices for a reduced product. "The
production is a travesty," raged Leslie Roberts of the Wrexham *Evening
Leader* under a headline "*Aida première insults theatre*". For the first time,
WNO failed to fill the Theatr Clwyd.

Later in the year, a third small-scale production was sent out on tour.
This was *José's Carmen*, devised and produced by Mike Ashman. It was
naturally assumed to be an attempt to out-do Peter Brook, but had in fact
arisen from the workshops held when Pintilie's *Carmen* had entered the
repertory. Ashman, by returning to the Prosper Mérimée novel on which
Bizet based his opera, had stripped the work of its ensembles, and the story
was told in flashback by Don José in prison, awaiting trial for the murder of
Carmen. The singing, by a cast of four (accompanied by a pianist), was
generally accomplished, the production, in a single set, simple and direct.
"Ironically," wrote Tom Sutcliffe in the *Guardian*, "this *Carmen* . . . is a
more conventional account of the work than the highly controversial and
spectacular Pintilie version." There were inevitable losses in not having an
orchestra, and the melodrama of the original was heavily emphasised,
though Ashman's attempt to point a parallel between Escamillo killing the
bull (normally offstage but here shown in a spotlight) and José killing
Carmen was considered far-fetched. Of course, not all the critics approved:
Kenneth Loveland, writing in *Opera*, found it "tatty, even allowing for the
limitations imposed by touring, and it all seemed to have been thrown
together hastily."

During the summer, Cardiff's New Theatre had been closed to allow the
orchestra pit to be deepened and extended (losing three rows of stalls in the
process), and the theatre to be cleaned and repainted, in preparation for the
start of the *Ring* cycle in October. The first time the public had a chance to

hear the orchestra in the new pit came with *Peter Grimes* which opened the autumn season at the beginning of September. This was a restudied version of the production John Copley had first staged in 1978. Copley had been invited to mount that production at short notice (following the sacking of Michael Geliot); it had never really worked, due mainly to the sets which had cramped the action, and had been withdrawn after only five performances. With starker, less naturalistic new sets by Robin Don, and Michael Stennett's original costumes, Copley was able to give the opera the sweep it had missed in its first form. "This is a *Grimes* traditional in the best sense, true to the text but, more important, truthfully, freshly, and feelingly given," wrote Max Loppert in the *Financial Times*. With the same three main principals – John Mitchinson as Grimes, Josephine Barstow as Ellen Orford and Terence Sharpe as Balstrode – in excellent voice, and with strong characterisation in the supporting roles, *Grimes* was a thrilling, profoundly moving revival. The chorus were again in superb form, and though Richard Armstrong took some time to get the measure of the new pit, he conducted with deep feeling and understanding of the score. The Sea Interludes were especially evocative, matching the rainstorm outside the theatre which flooded backstage and even showered some members of the audience during the performance. "This *Peter Grimes* is worth a pilgrimage anywhere," wrote Felix Aprahamian.

The week after *Peter Grimes* opened, WNO took part in the Frankfurt Festival with a concert performance of *Tristan und Isolde* and a concert of British music which included the first performance of a commissioned song cycle by John Metcalf. The company then returned to Cardiff for the opening night of *The Rhinegold*, the first part of the *Ring* cycle, on 21 October, a year later than originally planned. It received a lukewarm reaction, largely because of the setting. Producer Göran Järvefelt had deliberately not seen the Chéreau *Ring* at Bayreuth, but came up with a similar answer to the problems of staging the work: that the root of evil was ownership and that this was best depicted in an industrial setting. Consequently, Carl Friedrich Oberle's designs depicted a cross between a Victorian railway station and Leadenhall market. This gave the critics ample opportunity for sarcasm. "When Wotan and Loge descend to Niebelheim," wrote Denby Richards, "it is to find a home from home underground, while by the time they get up again, they come out on a different platform where there is a convenient cast-iron type bridge to take them on to the Valhalla train. The Rhinemaidens are living in a drought, since there is no sign of water on their platform, or could it have been the ticket hall?" In an attempt to portray the various social levels of the characters in the context of 19th century industrialism, and at the same time emphasise their symbolic natures, Järvefelt had the gods clothed in white, the Rhinemaidens in green and the humans in black, while Loge had his face half-white, half-black. The giants were presented as a pair of navvies. Few people found much to praise in the production. "By and large it seemed to me so limp and dreary – a ragbag of secondhand, ineffective, or just plain silly Wagnerian notions," wrote Max Loppert, "that to dwell on them would be to rub salt in every wound." Järvefelt's intention was to throw the emphasis squarely onto the singers, and in this he succeeded without question. Phillip Joll made a competent first attempt at Wotan, Donald Maxwell was a secure Donner, Nigel Douglas a dominating Loge, and Nicholas Folwell projected his music as Alberich with great force and poignancy, but nervousness on the first night did not allow the cast to give of its best.

Richard Armstrong was in the pit. Rodney Milnes thought it "stunningly well conducted . . . The pacing was Goodall-like in pulse and flow – not a seam showed throughout the evening, the playing was excellent." Some other critics were less happy, noting that the evening lasted almost three hours, for which they blamed a "ponderous" performance by Armstrong. "The marvellous score sounded – to an extent I would not have credited – uninteresting, so sluggishly unvaried was the pulse, so unresponsive to the changing musical events," wrote David Cairns in the *Sunday Times*.

*The Rhinegold* had received a decidedly mixed reaction with the balance of opinion being against the production. But if Andrew Clements of the *New Statesman* felt that his visit to Cardiff had been "quite without a saving grace", most people were prepared to wait until *The Valkyrie* before passing final judgement and would not have agreed with Tom Sutcliffe, who concluded his review in the *Guardian*: "If WNO must do their own Ring, perhaps the best answer would be to scrap this *Rhinegold* and begin again with a new team."

# CHAPTER TWENTY: 1984–1985

O N 18 FEBRUARY, 1984, *The Valkyrie* opened in Cardiff; reaction was warmer than it had been for *The Rhinegold* but was still lacking real enthusiasm. Most of the critics felt that Järvefelt had no clear idea of where he was going, and were uncertain whether he was trying to achieve a naturalistic or an abstract approach. This dichotomy was reflected in Carl Friedrich Oberle's sets. Act 1 took place in a genuine Scandinavian hut, complete with the door asked for in the libretto (his solution for the eruption of spring was brilliantly effective: the door at the back of the hut opened to reveal a vivid blue sky); Act 2 took place against a background of craggy mountain peaks and rivers of ice; and Act 3, while retaining some aspects of the *Rhinegold* set, consisted largely of scattered blocks. "These sets lack stylistic unity and formal cohesion. Visually the Welsh *Ring* is not shaping well," wrote Peter Heyworth in the *Observer*. "The best one can say," wrote Max Loppert in the *Financial Times*, "is that . . . the producer did not actually get in the way of the music." Rodney Milnes of the *Spectator*, however, disagreed: "Järvefelt is very much directing an English text rather than a German opera in translation: his penetrating and sober production is based firmly on what the characters are saying and nothing else. As in his *Rhinegold*, there is no escaping issues in this exceptionally clear exposition, and the combination of dramatic clarity with such musical richness is something approaching an ideal Wagnerian world." Malcolm Boyd of the *Musical Times* was another who praised the clarity of Järvefelt's direction. "It aims to be faithful to Wagner's intentions without intruding any personal ideology, and it is distinguished by sharp, sympathetic characterization and a clear presentation of plot and motive. One always knows what is going on, and why – something that cannot be said for every *Ring* production." The provincial critics, when *The Valkyrie* went on tour, were almost unanimous in their praise for a production which made the action so clear.

In spite of the reservations expressed about the production and designs, there was total agreement that musically it was one of the most distinguished performances of *The Valkyrie* in recent times. The reason was the presence of Reginald Goodall in the pit. Goodall had once told Brian

McMaster that the opera he particularly wanted to conduct again was *The Valkyrie*, because he had "got it wrong the first time." Following his operation the previous year, few people had thought to see him conducting ever again. But when Richard Armstrong, who was scheduled to conduct *The Valkyrie*, was offered a new production of *Andrea Chénier* at Covent Garden and the dates clashed, Goodall readily agreed to take over. He delivered a compelling account of the score, noticeably faster than the one he had committed to record several years earlier. "The essential changes in Goodall's interpretation lie deeper," wrote Peter Heyworth. "They stem from a new dramatic intensity and the new musical urgency that mirrors it. The great symphonic spans that have always been a feature of his Wagner are as strongly felt as ever, so that climaxes seem to emerge out of the very bowels of the music ... From the very opening bars of the prelude, measured yet urgent, it was clear that it was to be an exceptional evening ... the score unfolded with the inevitability of a huge wheel turning, as phrase mounted on phrase and inner voices flowered." "The most extraordinary thing about Reginald Goodall's new look at *The Valkyrie* ..." Milnes wrote, "is its sheer energy ... those who aspire to conduct Wagner should be corralled from all over Europe and herded into Cardiff's New Theatre to learn how it should be done."

If the singing did not quite rise to comparable heights, Goodall nevertheless managed to draw some remarkable performances from his cast. Anne Evans, singing her first Brünnhilde, was radiantly musical, and Warren Ellsworth, his voice in better control than as Parsifal, was an extraordinarily expressive Siegmund. His first-act scene with Sieglinde (Kathryn Harries) generated real excitement. "This Siegmund and Sieglinde both sang, literally, as though possessed," commented Heyworth. Opinion over Phillip Joll's Wotan remained divided, some still feeling he was too young to have been given the part, others recognising that, although inexperienced, he was potentially a fine interpreter of the role. "It's a tribute to his [Goodall's] miraculous powers as a trainer, and to his great musical wisdom, that the new Welsh *Ring* has so clearly found its form," wrote Sutcliffe.

Ten days later, *The Merry Widow*, Lehár's most popular operetta, opened on 28 February, sponsored by the County of South Glamorgan. In previous years, the county had always given WNO a direct grant, but had decided that sponsoring a production would make better economic sense. Wherever *The Merry Widow* played, a stall was set up to extol the advantages of businesses moving to South Glamorgan, and interested companies were invited to see the performance. By the end of the spring tour, the gamble had paid off with at least one firm committed to opening new premises in South Wales.

Producer Andrei Serban had decided to update *The Merry Widow* to the 1930s. Michael Yeargan provided lavish Art Deco settings, and the dazzling costumes (by Jacques Schmidt and Emmanuel Peduzzi) were authentically period (some had, in fact, been bought in Paris's Flea Market). Serban then staged it as a fast-moving entertainment in which no one was allowed to stand still for more than a minute. The singers had had the unusual experience of having to do dancers' warming-up exercises before every rehearsal. "Everything is in constant motion," wrote Max Loppert. "The choreographer, Kate Flatt, also deserves note in the listing, for the interweaving of popular dance into every nook and cranny of the stage and the action is done with a sense of style that for most of the time keeps complaint of excessive restlessness at bay . . . in general . . . the whole show boasts a finish, of colour, line, and detail, rare in British operetta stagings." In all the frenetic movement, Lehár frequently got lost, but Serban rarely gave the audience time to bother with Lehár. The summer-house duet was backed by a writhing silhouetted dancer; elsewhere, amidst the confetti and the balloons, there were girls on roller-skates, topless violinists, dancing waiters, walking valentines, projected newspaper headlines, people wearing butterflies round their necks or animal masks over their heads; all, as Tom Sutcliffe wrote, "to divert attention from every single number."

"The mirror-flanked space of Act 2 reveals a production spending just a little too much time looking at and admiring itself rather than Lehár," wrote Hilary Finch in the *Times*. "Every set piece now has a little screen-projection of its own . . . 'Vilja' is framed by a screened poster design and animated by a rather tacky *pas de deux* (and you need not think you have seen the last of them: they appear later to help us understand Danilo's narrative)." "Andrei Serban's extraordinary production has produced an operetta for people who hate operetta," commented David Harrison of the Bristol *Evening Post*.

Towering over the rest of the cast was Thomas Allen's Count Danilo, quite making one forget that the role is usually sung by a tenor. Looking like Clark Gable, he enunciated his words clearly, delivered his asides with impeccable timing and sang his music as if it were by Mozart. Brian McMaster had tried to persuade Elisabeth Söderström to play the Widow. Suzanne Murphy, who took the role, looked stunning as a cross between Jean Harlow and Carole Lombard, but did not seem at ease. "The rest of the cast," wrote Hugh Canning, "with the exception of Thomas Hemsley as a Baron Zeta from another production, stood by looking both bewildered and sheepish. Robin Leggate should have been ideally cast as Camille de Rossillon, but under Serban's baleful influence, he wandered aimlessly round the stage like a refugee from *The Damned* . . . All was not lost; György Fischer's marvellously lilting, fizzing way with a score he clearly adores enticed gorgeous, silken sounds from the WNO strings and persistently lifted the musical numbers out of the dialogue doldrums."

Once again a WNO production aroused controversy. "It should be shown to all amateur operatic societies under the heading 'how to destroy a masterpiece of operetta,' " fumed one critic. Alan Blyth, however, welcomed a new look at a faded classic. "Little . . . at least as far as the staging was concerned, seemed to me to run counter to the spirit of the original," he wrote in *Opera*.

Opening night of *The Merry Widow* was followed by further performances of *The Valkyrie* and revivals of *The Magic Flute* and *Jenůfa*, the opera with which the Janáček cycle had started almost nine years earlier. This was much more than a standard revival. During his research into the orchestration of *The Cunning Little Vixen*, Richard Armstrong had come across Janáček's original scoring for *Jenůfa* and had wanted to stage a revival using it, rather than the published score with amendments made by Karel Kavařovic, the conductor of the first performance in Prague. Sir Charles Mackerras had used this original score for his recording of *Jenůfa* and it was on his edition that WNO's revival was based, giving the opera its first staging with the original orchestration in Britain and possibly the first anywhere since the 1904 première in Brno. The major difference from the previously heard score, apart from changes in orchestration that removed the romanticism added by Kavařovic, was the inclusion of an aria in Act 1 in which the Kostelnicka explains why, because of her own unhappy marriage, she has refused to allow Jenůfa to marry Steva.

David Pountney took the opportunity to tighten his production, and it emerged with renewed strength. The newcomers to the cast were in every way as worthy as their predecessors. Whereas Pauline Tinsley had played the Kostelnicka as a moral bigot and religious fanatic, Phyllis Cannan (singing her first role since switching from mezzo to dramatic soprano), with the addition of the new material, was able to underline the strong maternal instinct and create a more sympathetic character. "This is an admirable, rock-secure performance," wrote Paul Griffiths in the *Times*, "to set against the distraught, febrile Jenůfa of Helen Field." Field was also singing her role for the first time. She was, wrote Michael Kennedy in the *Daily Telegraph*, "an ideal Jenůfa in voice and looks, strongly projecting the spirited girl of Act 1, so that the tragic figure of the rest of the opera becomes even more intense. Her voice has flowered into a beautiful dramatic lyricism, her singing of the Act 2 prayer being comparable with the finest exponents of the role." Jeffrey Lawton was ideally cast as Laca, Arthur Davies sang a vocally burnished Steva, and there was excellent support from the remaining principals. Richard Armstrong's urgent and passionate account of the score confirmed him as one of the finest of all conductors of Janáček. "It is," wrote Griffiths, speaking for many, "altogether a stunning achievement."

On 27 March, the Princess of Wales arrived in Cardiff to open the new rehearsal rooms named after her. This £350,000 project, financed by a grant from the Welsh Office and a bank loan, included a full-sized studio, a sound studio, electrical workshop, some office accommodation and a canteen, built opposite the John Street headquarters. For the first time, the full orchestra was able to rehearse under its own roof instead of in a variety of church halls. After unveiling a plaque, the Princess listened to Richard Armstrong conducting an orchestral rehearsal and watched a rehearsal of *The Merry Widow*. She also took part in a surprise presentation to Margaret Moreland of a cheque and card to mark her retirement from WNO after 37 years. Margaret Moreland was WNO's longest-serving official, known to generations of guest singers as the person who booked and paid them and sorted out all their problems. To those who knew the workings of WNO more intimately, she was the person who, over the years, had ensured that WNO kept on the road, single-handedly running the office. After many years as Bill Smith's assistant, she became Secretary to the Board and a member of the Council. Following her retirement, she was created a life member of the Board and a trustee of the company. In his tribute to her, Alfred Francis, the former Executive Chairman, wrote of a person who "was almost unique in the world of the performing arts – utterly selfless and totally committed to the well-being of a company claiming virtually the whole of her working life . . . Such public recognition as Mrs Moreland received during my term of office seemed trivial when set against her record of achievement – most of it anonymous." The Voluntary Chorus later held their own special presentation to pay tribute to a woman who had not just been one of the administration but had become a friend. As Muriel Pointon, WNO's archivist, remarked in her speech, she was "the main cog who, through all trials and tribulations, and there were many, kept the wheels well oiled and running smoothly – it was all this that gave the Welsh National Opera the opportunity to progress, and go from strength to strength to become one of the three great opera companies in this country, and to achieve the international status it enjoys today . . . her duties were always carried out without fear or favour which won the love and respect of us all."

One aspect of WNO life Margaret Moreland had had to live with throughout her long and devoted career was the constant lack of money. This had again become an issue, despite the fact that 1982 had been the most successful year financially WNO had ever had, and it seemed that, at last, the financial base was secure. Grants for 1983 had not been increased sufficiently to meet requirements and WNO had been forced to operate some four weeks below its most cost-effective level. The visit to Oxford in April 1984 had been placed in some doubt and only last-minute local sponsorship saved it. Other venues were also placed in jeopardy, but the publication of a government report suggesting that more money should be provided for opera in the regions led to an emergency grant of £130,000 to be divided amongst the four major regional companies, and it appeared that WNO could safely proceed with its plans for 1984. Then came another report, *The Glory of the Garden*, outlining Arts Council strategy for the next decade, and this specifically excluded the possibility of funding companies outside London to the level needed to maintain existing standards. In addition, a Welsh Arts Council submission to London on its future requirements and policies, while it agreed that WNO was under-funded and that it was looking to WNO "to develop small-scale operatic work aimed at smaller communities," made it quite clear that this had to be achieved without extra money being available. Everyone agreed, said the submission, that "Welsh National Opera is a glorious achievement, of which Wales should be rightly proud." When grants for 1984–85 were finally announced, despite the Arts Council's insistence that touring should be increased by 15 percent, WNO was offered an increase of only 2.6 percent. At the same time, Amoco's generous sponsorship (totalling £855,000) had come to an end, and McMaster was left with no option but to raise seat prices and cut the number of new productions from seven to four, including postponing completion of the *Ring*. An urgent appeal went out to all towns and cities in which WNO appeared asking for a minimum grant of £10,000 to ensure future visits. Few were prepared to help. Bristol responded by cutting its grant on the grounds that other local councils paid nothing, and Mold, still smarting from *The Drama of Aida*, refused to give guarantees to cover the inevitable losses on the proposed visit in June. The visit was cancelled, restored on the intervention of the Welsh Arts Council and then cancelled again, a decision which was to leave a legacy of bitterness in North Wales.

Lucian Pintilie, together with designers Radu and Miruna Boruzescu – the team that had produced the controversial *Carmen* – had been engaged to stage the new production of *La Bohème*, replacing the one by William Gaskill which had never been completely successful. Michael Tilson Thomas, the young American conductor, had been invited to make his operatic debut in Britain. Those who hated Pintilie's *Carmen* (and floods of letters attacking the production had arrived in John Street) trembled to think what he might do to another favourite piece. The sighs of relief when it was announced in February that Pintilie was no longer working on *Bohème* could be heard on the other side of the Severn Bridge. The reason for Pintilie's departure was that Radu Boruzescu had designed sets which relied heavily on hydraulic machinery and would have been quite impractical for touring – they simply could not have been erected or dismantled quickly enough. WNO refused to accept the designs, and then Boruzescu, bringing revised ones to Cardiff for discussions with the technical department, left them on the bus from Heathrow. They were never found. With opening night some ten weeks away, and no sign of any agreement being reached on the way the production should go, McMaster felt he had no option but to find an alternative production team.

The cancellation of *Siegfried* had left Göran Järvefelt free to produce and Michael Yeargan, who was in Cardiff for *The Merry Widow*, was asked to provide the designs. Although they had only a short time to come up with their conception before rehearsals started, the end result, which opened in Cardiff on 8 May, was by no means a compromise. Järvefelt went for a naturalistic approach, playing on the fact that he had a cast of young singers who actually looked as if they might be Bohemians, and Yeargan produced sets to match: a cold, uninviting attic for the first act, an unpretentious café for the second and a realistic gatehouse, with uncollected dustbins, for the third. In the final act, Mimi's death took place on a rough mattress, all the Bohemians could afford. "It is a far cry from the cosy romantic world of portly middle-aged well-fed tenors and even portlier sopranos," commented Jon Halliday in the *Stage*. Some critics thought the settings drab and this was certainly a Paris in which it was no fun to be poor, but it possessed a realism that enabled Järvefelt to develop character and relationships. The Bohemians grew their hair and beards, and cut them off again in subsequent scenes, just as real students might. The key to the staging was, wrote Hugh Canning in *Classical Music*, "the effects of abject poverty on the six young people. The men survived as best they could, fobbing off their fat and foolish landlord . . . and readily taking advantage of Musetta's ruse to make her protector, Alcindoro, pay her bill at the Café. Yet, underneath the surface jocularity, Järvefelt sowed the seeds of uncertainty. Rodolfo was no clean-cut, well-fed Mediterranean hero, but a shambolic drop-out, desperately taking refuge from the pervading misery in sex and alcohol. His treatment of the women, however, marked Järvefelt's staging as a cut above your average *Bohème*. Initially, Mimi and Musetta were presented as antipoles, the former a fresh-faced *ingénue* – though by no means averse to taking the sexual initiative by deliberately extinguishing her candle *and* losing her key – the latter a dazzling *femme du monde* with expensive tastes in clothes and underclothes. By the final act, Mimi had succumbed to the lure of the demi-monde and entered, dying, a painted, richly-attired ruin. The effect was shocking, issuing a profoundly feminist commentary on the response of women to poverty." Helen Field was an intense, moving and utterly believable Mimi. John Fowler, a young American tenor, was less remarkable as Rodolfo, for, although he sang stylishly, his voice lacked weight. Donald Maxwell's effervescent Marcello was well matched by the flamboyant Musetta of Suzanne Murphy, and there were notable contributions from Nicholas Folwell as Schaunard, Matthew Best as Colline, James Miller-Coburn as the capitalist Benoit and Peter Massocchi as Alcindoro. In the pit, Kees Bakels (replacing Michael Tilson Thomas who had asked to be released from his contract) gave the orchestra its head which produced a direct and emotional performance, although occasionally drowning the singers. "This was a model of what a performance of a repertory piece by one of our regional companies should be," wrote Alan Blyth in *Opera*.

*La Bohème* was one of two operas (the other was *Peter Grimes*) taken to the Wiesbaden Festival later that month. It was a rule of the Festival not to invite a foreign company back within ten years, but WNO's appearance with *Elektra* in 1979 had been so successful that the rule was broken. Five members of the orchestra decided to cycle out, the remainder of the company travelling more conventionally by car and plane. There was apprehension that they might not be able to repeat their 1979 triumph; and it was disconcerting to hear that the local production of *Madam Butterfly* had been booed both during and after the performance. All three performances were sold out, however, and were a popular and critical success; the house lights had to be turned on to end the applause.

In July, as part of the Ely Festival (Ely being a suburb of Cardiff, not the East Anglian cathedral city), WNO's education department collaborated in the production of a home-grown operatic venture staged in a disused bus repair depot. Two hundred performers drawn from schools, youth centres, adult education groups, rock groups and choirs in the area got together with an orchestra and two professional artists, Eric Roberts (a former WNO principal) and dancer Peter Wooldridge, to stage two performances of *Poor Twm Jones*, a work based on the story of a local simpleton tormented by his fellows, hounded down and killed in the forest, written by Phil Thomas. John Eaton, formerly on the WNO staff, produced, Richard Maxwell Aylwin from the property department, designed and Geraldine Hurl choreographed.

WNO was also scheduled to take part in another Festival that summer, this time in Edinburgh, replacing an overseas company which had pulled out. It looked at first as though the invitation would have to be refused because of a lack of money, but the Mid-Wales Development Corporation came up with the £15,000 needed to present a concert performance of *Parsifal* and a staged performance of Martinů's *The Greek Passion*. At the last moment, the visit was cancelled by the Festival organisers. Reginald Goodall, who was to have conducted *Parsifal*, had had an emergency operation for appendicitis and the Festival refused to accept a replacement.

Since it was uneconomic to travel to Scotland for a single performance of
*The Greek Passion* (for which, it was rumoured, tickets were not selling
well), the entire visit was called off, leaving WNO to try and obtain some
recompense for wasted time.

The decision taken earlier in the year to cancel new productions and
postpone the *Ring* meant that the autumn season was the first for many years
without a new production. Instead of opening with *Siegfried*, it began with
the *Merry Widow* and then, to commemorate the twenty-fifth anniversary of
Martinů's death, a revival of Michael Geliot's 1981 production of *The Greek
Passion*. Something in the work had struck a chord in Wales and since its first
production this was the opera that most people had asked to see again. It was
surprising, therefore, to find empty seats on opening night. The predominantly new cast was a strong one, with Jeffrey Lawton as Manolios,
Phyllis Cannan as Katerina, John Tranter as Grigoris and William Mackie as
Fotis. The chorus were in thrilling voice, the orchestra, under Anthony
Negus, played well. "This was everything that a revival should be, if anything
more overwhelming in its impact than the original . . . an inspired and
inspiring performance," wrote Rodney Milnes in *Opera*.

Also revived with a new cast was Elijah Moshinsky's production of
*Ernani*. Lando Bartolini sang Ernani, Mario Rinaudo, Silva, Aprile Millo,
Elvira and Donald Maxwell, Carlo. The three foreign artists, all making
their British debuts, gave performances which were dependable and at times
thrilling. Rodney Milnes found it a "rip-roaring, provincial performance,
yet highly enjoyable. Early Verdi can do with some good honest vulgarity,
and this Lando Bartolini and Mario Rinaudo supplied in generous
quantity." What they were not used to was the ensemble tradition of
WNO, and with them the production reverted to a stand-and-deliver
performance. "There were times when one could be forgiven for thinking
that yesterday evening was the first time they had met," wrote Kenneth
Loveland in the *South Wales Argus*.

*Ernani* was, wrote Tom Sutcliffe, "one of the least satisfactory WNO
presentations for some time." Such a comment becomes almost a
compliment when placed alongside the reviews for *Don Giovanni*, which
opened the winter season in Cardiff on 27 October. "Monumentally silly,"
"a ragbag of gimmicks and ridiculous staging," "a tedious and repetitive
misrepresentation," "perverse," "a mess," "a catastrophe," "a mass of self-
indulgence," were just a few of the epithets hurled at the production. The
object of the critics' hatred was Ruth Berghaus, the distinguished German
stage director and former head of the Berliner Ensemble, who was making
her directing debut in Britain. She it was who had staged a notorious *Barber
of Seville* in Munich six years earlier, in which Almaviva sang his serenade
perched on the pudenda of a giant, naked female torso while Rosina popped

her head out of a window in the left nipple. What would she do with *Don Giovanni*?

The permanent set, designed by Marie-Luise Strandt, comprised a sloping surface of irregular shapes which gave the critics a great deal of fun trying to describe. Some thought it represented an inhospitable Spanish landscape, others the human brain. "As I see it," wrote Paul Griffiths in the *Times*, "the cast have taken themselves off to Barry Island where they have struck unlucky with the tide. Indeed, the sea has retracted so far and for so long that they find themselves on a wide crazy-pavement of baked mud." From the gaps between the blocks of the set, the cast constantly produced a bewildering variety of objects, ranging from socks and shoes to a teapot. In the first act, swords protruded from the cracks, looking like crosses but also phallic symbols, as Zerlina showed when she set them swinging during "Lá ci darem." Don Ottavio was dressed in a silver suit and sang his first aria transfixed with arrows in a Saint Sebastian pose, his second in a snowstorm. The chorus were dressed like spacemen, with flashing lights making them look like Christmas trees.

Throughout the performance, the audience sat in stunned silence, and as it finished the booing began. "There's no point in pulling punches," fumed Kenneth Loveland, ". . . *Don Giovanni* is visually an incomprehensible and pretentious mess . . . quite simply . . a thoroughly bad production." "Berghaus . . . made her British debut by removing all traces of romance and glamour, reason and credibility from the opera," wrote Jon Halliday in the *Stage*. "Such a shambolic, pretentious production could not even be defended as controversial – it was silly, tedious, just plain daft."

There were those who attempted to find out what Berghaus was up to, realising that she was employing Brechtian theories of alienation – none of the characters ever related to each other – and while no one could be sure of what she meant all the time, there was recognition that it was, in the words of David Cairns of the *Sunday Times*, "all, of course, compulsively and maddeningly watchable." "I must confess to being flummoxed," wrote Rodney Milnes in the *Spectator*. "While it was going on I loathed it; the moment the curtain came down I started, well, not exactly to like it, but to be fascinated by it. It has haunted me ever since. There is without doubt something there, even if I haven't the remotest idea what it may be." "It would be foolish to pretend that Berghaus's tightly-wrought stage action, much of it hugely entertaining, all of it done with immense conviction (no end of praise to the singers), and providing truly striking images, reveals every one of its secrets at first sight. No, she provides pictures to take away and ponder over. There are few enough producers doing that. No wonder she gets so much stick," commented Robert Hartford in *Punch*.

While the arguments about the production raged – and they continued wherever it played – there was total unanimity that this was one of the finest casts assembled for a *Don Giovanni* in recent years. William Shimell was a powerful, virile and energetic Don, Nicholas Folwell a richly sung Leporello, Laurence Dale a vivid, lyrical Don Ottavio and John Tranter a powerful Commendatore. Anne Evans as Donna Anna, Elaine Woods as Donna Elvira and Beverley Mills as Zerlina were the sharply differentiated ladies. Charles Mackerras, conducting a score he had edited himself to try and obtain a more authentic Mozartian sound (using a fortepiano for the recitatives, 18th Century bowing techniques, calfskin timpani with wooden sticks, and faster-than-usual tempi, for example), began as though he wanted to break all records for getting through the opera and brought considerable energy to the accompaniment. It was, wrote Gillian Widdicombe in the *Field*, "one of those evenings when you hate much of what you see but would not have missed seeing it." "As experimental productions go," concluded Patrick Carnegy of the *Times Educational Supplement*, "this one must be counted a major event, with the very great merit of making a work that has become too familiar seem rich, strange and uncomfortable all over again."

The reverberations over *Don Giovanni* continued long after the curtain came down. In an indignant article in the *Western Mail* John Morgan was scathing about the need to hire in foreign producers, even dismissing Göran Järvefelt, a Swede, as an East German, and his fairly straightforward production of *La Bohème* as left-wing propaganda. And yet, no matter how bitterly *Don Giovanni* was attacked, it succeeded in the way that McMaster had hoped: it found new audiences and played to full houses.

The polarised reactions continued when it was brought to London in December. At the first performance, it was booed; at the second, cheered. This was WNO's fifth visit to London. The ending of Amoco's sponsorship had put the season in doubt. Although Amoco recognised that its association with WNO had been worthwhile and would have liked it to continue, fluctuating oil prices meant they were unable to commit themselves further. However, after some months of negotiation, Amoco (UK) Exploration, an affiliated company, took over sponsoring the London season.

Sponsorship was now vital to allow WNO to schedule a full annual programme. Every production during the year had received sponsorship of some kind. The seasons in Bristol, costing £40,000 more than was recouped at the box-office, were only able to go ahead through a donation from Imperial Tobacco, which brought the anti-smoking lobby out to picket the theatre when WNO appeared there in November. The production of *The Threepenny Opera* for the small tour at the beginning of 1985 only took place because of sponsorship from the Mid-Wales Development Corporation.

The most recent productions designed to tour smaller theatres, *The Drama of Aida* and *José's Carmen*, had not been particularly well received, and it was decided to mount a production of a complete work. Kurt Weill's *The Threepenny Opera* was chosen, and with the exception of two guest artists, Roger Bryson as Peachum and Robert Dean as Macheath, was cast from members of the chorus. On paper it looked a good choice. In practice, it failed to achieve any real distinction. "The main failure is not of talent but of direction," wrote Paul Griffiths in the *Times*. ". . . it is all terribly slow. Lines of dialogue simply do not connect, just as all the kicks and stabs so plainly do not connect. One is left with a great litter of meaningless words and a great litter of meaningless violence, and also a great litter of meaningless eroticism: seldom can so many suspenders have been seen to so sadly little purpose."

After the equivocal reception accorded to *The Rhinegold* and *The Valkyrie*, the postponed production of *Siegfried*, which finally opened in Cardiff on 23 February 1985, was a triumph. Wagner himself described the third opera in the cycle as the *scherzo* of the *Ring* and this was the approach Järvefelt adopted. "It is the light-filled work between two tragedies," he said. "I want it to be transparent in mood with lots of humour and clear in meaning." Carl Friedrich Oberle's designs had now become simple rocky sets with a single realistic tree (deciduous) to denote the forest and another (coniferous) beside Brünnhilde's boulder. The ironwork which had so upset people in *The Rhinegold* had been reduced to a few empty packing cases, used chiefly for characters to clamber onto and strike poses. "In general," Bayan Northcott of the *Sunday Telegraph* felt, "this proves an approach that has got into its stride at last."

The clarity with which Järvefelt had been portraying the action in the previous episodes was at last seen to be the production's great strength. The emphasis on comedy grew naturally from the text. The bear and dragon were almost pantomime in effect, with animal bodies and human legs (though the loss of the dragon's tail was bemoaned by some). This had the result of making Fafner less of a monster and more sympathetic. There was also a mechanical, radio-controlled Woodbird (sung by the invisible Kate Flowers), sitting on a tree branch, nodding in response to Siegfried's questions, which quite captivated the audience. "Järvefelt has managed . . . to make the opera a sensible comedy. So played, it blossoms," commented David Murray in the *Financial Times*. It was, Geoffrey Norris of the *Times* thought, "a production which raises no hackles, overstates nothing and, in the stage direction as much as in the sets, offers a consistently uncluttered, objective view of the opera's development." Denby Richards, writing in *Music and Musicians*, went further: "WNO's new *Siegfried* . . . was a triumph for all concerned . . . The atmosphere in Cardiff's New Theatre during the dinner interval on 23rd February was one of carnival. Indeed, I cannot remember such a thrilled and happy audience for any Wagner opera in the last forty years."

The fact that Järvefelt did not push forward an "interpretation" threw the focus onto the music once more, and, again, cast and orchestra responded magnificently. Anne Evans's Brünnhilde continued to impress by the force of her acting and the vitality and eloquence of her singing. Phillip Joll's Wanderer grew in stature. "It was with justified sadness that he left the stage with the breaking of his spear. His dialogue with the impetuous Siegfried was very well done and exceptionally well sung," wrote Denby Richards. Nicholas Folwell was again an impressively evil Alberich, and John Harris made "a superb Mime, finely projected, not too much of a whiner, with diction clearest of all." The revelation of the evening came in the Siegfried of Jeffrey Lawton. This former businessman, who had come to opera late, had barely given notice in his previous appearances with WNO that he had the vocal resources to make such an impressive debut in the role. Järvefelt had portrayed Siegfried as a child-like innocent. "From Cardiff," enthused Kay Woodhams, ". . . comes heartening news for Wagnerites: there *is* a British Siegfried. Jeffrey Lawton tackles the dubious hero with good humour and relish, and achieves the monumental task of making him likeable . . . blessed with the vocal equipment for the most expressive soft singing as well as the taxing brilliance of the love music, he could come to outstrip many a current *Heldentenor*, Germans included." With the orchestra on top form and Richard Armstrong pulling out all the stops, *Siegfried* gave WNO's *Ring* its first complete success. It was, Denby Richards ended his review, "one of the finest Wagnerian productions to be seen anywhere. The thought of *Twilight* is mouthwatering."

Following the enthusiasm which had greeted *I Puritani* three years earlier, the same production team (Andrei Serban, Michael Yeargan and conductor Julian Smith) turned their attention next to the opera generally considered to be Bellini's masterpiece, *Norma*, in a co-production with Houston Grand Opera and Opera North, sponsored by the Friends, which opened in Cardiff in March. This story of the love of the Druid High Priestess, Norma, for the Roman pro-consul Pollione, and his desertion of her for the novice Adalgisa, is extremely difficult to stage, since little happens: the characters sing about what they have done or what they are about to do, until the end, when they go up in flames. It also requires remarkable singing.

Michael Yeargan came up with four or five different designs before settling on a classical background based on the ruins of Pompeii, with moveable pillars to alter locations. Serban, seeking an alternative to the statuesque poses and attitudes usually seen in the opera, used masks to symbolise the difference between private and public utterances, a device which became tedious and did nothing to help the projection of the music. He also gave the two illegitimate children of Norma and Pollione a distracting amount to do. But the main change he made was to base his production on the relationship between Norma and Adalgisa, altering the end to have Adalgisa rather than Pollione following Norma onto the funeral pyre. His approach did not win total approval. "Nothing has been taken for granted, and such a treatment of the work is, at the very least, refreshing," wrote Max Loppert in the *Financial Times*. "But it has gone too far. More than once one is left wondering whether at some point the producer lost confidence in the expressive force of the music . . . The production has been altogether over-embellished. Norma and Adalgisa must give her children a wash-down while threading their way through the final duet-cabaletta (in the proper high key of F), a hair-raisingly difficult piece; it's as if the audience is being told, 'You see, none of that old prima donna stuff here!' "

It is, however, for the singing and the music that people go to see *Norma* and here the production was on safer ground. "What whipped up the enthusiasm so much," wrote Tom Sutcliffe, "was the energy and commitment of the lead singers and the stylish, superbly paced conducting of Julian Smith, a master in the Italian operatic field." "Orchestrally it is a knock-out," agreed Rodney Milnes in the *Spectator*, "sweeping away all preconceptions about Bellini as a purveyor of delicate, Chopin-esque melancholy. Julian Smith goes for Romantic Agony, finding so much violence in the music as to make your average *Trovatore* sound as if it were by Gounod; time and again his investigation of extraordinarily subtle instrumental colour had one drop-jawed in amazement at hitherto unsuspected orchestral riches. There is nothing mimsy about the singing either." Suzanne Murphy, singing a role associated with Callas and Sutherland, was a worthy successor. She had "one or two cloudy moments vocally, but for most of the evening it was thrillingly full-throated, lacking neither stamina nor the control for the start of 'Casta Diva'," wrote John Higgins in the *Times*. Kathryn Harries's Adalgisa, sung with warmth and acted with accomplishment, complemented Murphy perfectly. The two "spurred each other to greater and greater efforts," continued Higgins, "their voices blended with creamy ease. And that is the starting point for casting any *Norma*." Canadian tenor Frederick Donaldson delivered a forthright and heroic Pollione, and there was an impressive British debut from the American bass Harry Dworchak as the Archdruid, Oroveso. "With productions around as imaginative and as musically invigorating as WNO's *Norma* . . . British opera is looking in good fettle this spring," commented Higgins.

The following night, Lucian Pintilie's controversial but hugely popular production of *Carmen* was revived with a new cast that included Cynthia

Buchan as Carmen, Arthur Davies as Don José and American baritone Tom Fox as Escamillo. Pintilie, together with his designers, Radu and Miruna Boruzescu, had also been invited to stage the new production of *Rigoletto* which opened in May. As expected, or feared, his approach was far from traditional. Set in the Victorian age, the opera opened with Rigoletto, a much travelled actor, arriving in his dressing room to don hump and make-up as the jester before joining in the party at the Duke's, peopled by Fellini-esque drag queens. Monterone, dressed in Victorian frock-coat and looking like Gladstone (or was it Verdi himself?), was debagged and mercilessly kicked by the Duke's retainers; Giovanna was stabbed to death during the abduction scene. In the second act, set in a gymnasium, the Duke sang his first aria while being pummelled by a masseur and his second on an exercise bicycle. The final act took place in a cellar into which the chorus, following Gilda's deflowering, poured coal.

Both critical and public opinion were sharply divided. "Besides his own *Carmen* or Berghaus's *Giovanni* it does not look remotely eccentric . . . ," wrote Tom Sutcliffe. "Pintilie rightly observes that the moral crux of the opera is the character of the Duke, a devil with all the best tunes. If the Duke is simpatico, Rigoletto's misfortune is merely a private tragedy. Pintilie offsets the Duke's musical charms by making his 'court' grotesque, stocked with drag queens and Draculas, and himself a pill-popping, oyster-swilling, self-indulgent, Presleyesque absurdity." "He has provided a *Rigoletto* which . . . does nothing to disguise what is tawdry in the work while yet dealing honestly with what is touching," wrote Paul Griffiths. Taking a diametrically opposed view was Kenneth Loveland: "They've done it again . . . ," he fumed. "The latest victim is *Rigoletto*. The good news first. Musically, it is an outstanding performance. The bad news next. You have to sit through Lucian Pintilie's production to experience it." "It is all too easy to say that at least the production poses questions," wrote David Wyn Jones in *Welsh Music*. "If the questions themselves are irresponsible no amount of inventiveness can make them valid." The energetic cast fitted well into Pintilie's concept. Dennis O'Neill clearly enjoyed the sending-up of the Duke that the producer required from him, singing and acting superbly even when in his long-johns. Anne Dawson, the young winner of the s'Hertogen-bosch competition and Ferrier prize, making her WNO debut, was a radiant and appealing Gilda, bringing out the adolescence of the part. "A nubile Alice in Wonderland with a candid sensuality" who, Stephen Walsh felt, "makes perfect logic of a character that is sometimes elusive, and perfect logic of the music, which is nothing if not sensual. She sings it wonderfully." Donald Maxwell as Rigoletto sometimes sounded strained on the first night but acted with his customary conviction, and there was strong support from Wendy Verco as Maddalena, Sean Rea as Sparafucile and Donald Adams as

Monterone. "Under Richard Armstrong," continued Walsh, "the whole production has a compelling force of musicality." As the curtain came down on the first night, the audience cheered a production which "sometimes illuminates, often infuriates and nearly always fascinates," and one which Malcolm Boyd of the *Musical Times* "would go a long way to see again, and even further to hear."

For those who preferred a more conventional approach to opera, the following night John Copley's production of *Tosca* was revived with Josephine Barstow singing Tosca, Kristian Johannsson, a young Icelandic tenor, Cavaradossi, and Anthony Baldwin, Scarpia. Grzegorz Nowak, the Polish conductor, making his British debut, did not have a completely happy time, losing ensemble on more than one occasion and finding it difficult to adjust to the New's acoustics. "The result may not have been the loudest *Tosca* on record, but it would be a keen competitor for the title," commented Kenneth Loveland. There were cast changes, too, for *Norma*. Reuben Dominguez, who had been engaged to succeed Frederick Donaldson as Pollione on tour, had had to return hurriedly to South America. The role had been taken over at short notice in Bristol by Neville Ackerman and at subsequent performances by Arthur Davies, who sang in Cardiff. Rachel Gettler, born in Paris but brought up in Australia, made her British debut singing Adalgisa.

Two years after it had started, and a year later than originally planned, the *Ring* cycle reached its conclusion when *Götterdämmerung* opened on 14 September. Several London critics, held up by traffic on the Severn Bridge, missed the beginning, and some orchestral players were also late. It was not until after the opera had started that Richard Armstrong knew he had a full complement of musicians. Once again, the production left the critics in two minds. For some, Järvefelt's concentration on the homely, almost domestic side of the text lacked the magic they expected. For others, it was a worthy conclusion to a fresh and sensitive interpretation which had grown in stature as the cycle progressed. "Most of the points WNO has scored for getting the *Ring* operas into its repertoire should be forfeited," wrote Tom Sutcliffe, "on account of . . the dull, unadventurous production and design." "The staging is an irredeemable disappointment," agreed David Cairns. Against such opinions must be placed those of critics like William Mann, writing in *Opera*. "Just in case my colleagues on daily papers, and magazines with earlier deadlines than *Opera*, have got it wrong, I must report that WNO's first *Ring* ends impressively, a distinct improvement in terms of staging on the three preceding instalments, as each of them was in turn earlier."

Oberle's sets continued the austere rock motif he had established in *Siegfried*, adding panels and pillars for the Hall of the Gibichungs, altars for the gods, and a mud-banked Rhine. The collapse of Valhalla was effectively done but the final Immolation was weak with Brünnhilde apparently walking off into a rosy sunset. Apart from Järvefelt's decision to leave Gutrune alone on stage at the end, there was, wrote David Murray in the *Financial Times*, "nothing more eccentric in the staging than Hagen's uncomfortable habit of sitting on the floor."

The late arrival of some of the musicians may well have been the reason for a slightly edgy start from Richard Armstrong and the orchestra. Thereafter, they achieved some impressive playing, though at times it threatened to drown the singers. "Besides the shapely solidity of the whole reading," wrote Murray, "there were four or five passages brought to vital expressive life as I have not heard them before." Anne Evans continued as a distinguished Brünnhilde, Jeffrey Lawton again sang a powerful Siegfried, and there was a strong, attractively sung Gunther from Jacek Strauch (making his WNO debut and London-born, in spite of his name). "The musical achievements of this Welsh *Ring* are not to be underrated . . ." wrote David Cairns. "In general, soloists and chorus comprise a cast many companies would covet."

If reaction to the final instalment of the *Ring*, whilst applauding WNO's enterprise in staging the cycle at all, was muted, it must be remembered that the vast majority of people paying to see it had never seen the *Ring* on stage and that the great virtue of Järvefelt's low-key approach was to make it both accessible and comprehensible. Only when the cycle is performed in its entirety in the autumn of 1986, with both Järvefelt and Oberle having had a chance to return to the earlier parts to make them consistent with their later views, will it be fair to pronounce final judgement on a courageous undertaking.

Both Andrei Serban and Lucian Pintilie had, in frequent press interviews and private conversations, acknowledged the debt they owed to Liviu Ciulei, the doyen of Romanian directors. McMaster had been trying for some time to tempt Ciulei to Cardiff, but his appointment as Artistic Director of the Guthrie Theatre in Minneapolis had prevented it. Finally, Ciulei was prepared to come if he could stage *Così fan tutte* in Italian. Since the opera had not been in the repertory for ten years, McMaster was happy to agree.

*Così* opened at the New on 9 November. The critics feared the worst. They were astonished to find, not a radical production set on a rubbish tip or in a circus, but a straightforward approach which was faithful to the original. The only liberty Ciulei had taken was to place the social station of the principals several rungs lower than was customary. Not that this meant that everyone approved of what they saw. Geoffrey Norris of the *Telegraph* found "the freshness of conception . . . Ciulei brought to his staging proved consistently engaging and stimulating," and Tom Sutcliffe assured his readers, "This is Mozart as you like it . . . a charming *Così fan tutte* . . . But a production that is certainly not just baroque reproduction." Rodney Milnes was less impressed. "The worst that can be said about Ciulei's *Così* is that it is really rather boring, the ideas both diffuse and failing to add up to much." What Milnes and those critics who did not enjoy the production disliked was Ciulei's handling of the arias. "*Così* is a conversation piece, one in which those on stage learn as much by listening as the audience does. But here the conversations are broken up either by taking the light down on those who should be listening . . . or introducing that odious convention, the dropcloth aria. 'Un' aura amorosa' is thus performed as a concert piece in total isolation from its context." The lighting of Radu Boruzescu's attractive set, with its rippling sea in the background, also came in for criticism. Ciulei wanted to create an evening atmosphere with the feeling of a nocturne, but to many the lighting just seemed consistently dim. "This is not only depressing in a general way," remarked David Cairns, "it is manifestly absurd in an opera in which the characters are constantly watching one another, and the eyes play an all-important part."

It is a sign of the change that has taken place in operatic presentations in Britain that reviews of most productions, not just WNO's, now start with an assessment of the producer's contribution rather than of the singers'. If Ciulei's production "outrages only by its ordinariness," to quote *Punch*, the choice of cast was excellent. Mark Holland, who had been making enormous strides since becoming a WNO principal the previous year, displayed considerable style and confidence as Guglielmo; Laurence Dale was an excellent Ferrando; and Delia Wallis and Elaine Woods a well-matched Dorabella and Fiordiligi. Andrea Bolton was a "lively, streetwise Despina, far removed from the usual simpering lady's maid," and Thomas Hemsley, though no longer in fine voice, was a masterly Don Alfonso. "Mr Hemsley is like one of those seasoned tennis players who can no longer move as fast as they once could, but are always in the right place at the right time," wrote Peter Heyworth. "His presence brings the element of experience that such a young cast needs." The most disappointing and, in many ways, the most surprising element of the evening was the conducting of György Fischer, who gave a heavy, unsensual account of the score.

The month before *Così* opened, a new production for the small-scale tour had been given its première at the Taliesin Theatre in Swansea. This marked a considerable departure from previous such ventures. Aware that earlier shows devised for the circuit had not been well received, and of the need to explain the workings of WNO to as wide an audience as possible, Brian McMaster had approached Welsh-based playwright Julian Mitchell (author of the award-winning *Another Country*) to prepare a play showing the development of a production from first rehearsal to first night, to give the public some idea of what goes into the staging of opera. The more Mitchell sat in John Street watching rehearsals and listening to what went on, the more he realised the enormity, if not the impossibility, of the task. Then Richard Armstrong gave him a book of anecdotes about Verdi. He read further books about the composer and was attracted to the story of how, after a long silence following the writing of *Aida*, Verdi came back to write *Otello* and *Falstaff*. The idea for *Verdi's Messiah*, an account of the relationship between Verdi and his librettist, Boito, using excerpts from Verdi's operas, was born.

Directed by Royal Shakespeare Company Associate Director, Howard Davies, with a strong cast of former RSC actors (Richard Griffiths as Verdi, Ian Charleson as Boito among them), four singers and an accompanist, *Verdi's Messiah* was a resounding success. "I am not sure that Mr Mitchell hasn't put in a little too much music in the second part – though in a sense that is the point, and the excerpts, from *Otello*, *Boccanegra* and *Macbeth*, are effectively done by a quartet of singers to the admirably 'orchestral' piano accompaniment of Martin André," wrote David Cairns. "But the main business of the drama – the plot to entice the old man from retirement – is quite riveting." Renamed *After Aida*, the play was later staged at London's Old Vic Theatre.

While *Verdi's Messiah* was touring the Welsh hinterland, the main WNO company was appearing for the first time in Plymouth. The Arts Council, being short of money, had insisted that WNO, along with Scottish Opera, Kent Opera, Opera North and Glyndebourne Touring, should cancel seven weeks of touring between them. For WNO this meant dropping visits to Birmingham, Liverpool and Bristol, and taking over Glyndebourne's week in Plymouth. This was not the only cancellation during the year. 1984 had again covered its costs due to the postponement of *Siegfried* and cuts in touring, but the failure to mount any new productions for the autumn season had led to a drop in attendance. Subscription schemes are a vital source of regular revenue and no one wanted to book for a season that contained only revivals. As a result, £30,000 less than anticipated had been raised on ticket sales. The subsequent controversy over *Don Giovanni* had helped produce an enormous spurt at the box-office: the 1985 spring season of 32 performances had been seen by a record-breaking 48,844 people. But in early 1985 the failure of the Arts Council grant to keep pace with inflation had again thrown the remainder of the year into doubt. In WNO's own attempt to balance the books, two proposed revivals were scrapped and touring was pared back. The Theatr Clwyd in Mold, which had last been visited in July 1983, was again dropped from the schedules amidst howls of protest. It cost £40,000 to stage a week of opera in Mold, a figure that could never be covered by box-office revenue, and without guarantees it did not make economic sense to appear there. North Wales was given further cause for alarm with the announcement made towards the end of 1985 that the Astra in Llandudno, the only theatre in North Wales capable of staging large productions, had been closed down pending the issue of a new fire certificate. With cuts also being made in some local authority grants, and no immediate possibility of an increased Arts Council grant, the future of WNO, both inside and outside Wales, was, and remains, worrying. To maintain its quality and quantity of work, WNO has had to rely more and more on sponsorship – during 1985, the amount raised was increased to more than £350,000 – and on co-productions. McMaster's appointment as Artistic Director of the Vancouver Opera has helped with this, both by selling WNO productions to Vancouver and enabling a series of co-productions to be set up.

A background of financial struggle is nothing new to WNO, and as it enters its fortieth year, it is still making ambitious plans. New productions of *Otello*, *The Barber of Seville* and *Wozzeck* enter the repertory in early 1986; there will be a revival of *Così fan tutte*, sung in English, to tour within Wales; future plans include productions of *Lucia de Lammermoor* and Berlioz's *The Trojans*, a joint production with Opera North and Scottish Opera. In September 1986, WNO becomes the first regional company ever to play at Covent Garden when the complete *Ring* cycle, with its original casts and Armstrong conducting, is performed there. How Idloes Owen, Bill Smith and all those other early pioneers would have relished that! And who, honestly, could have foreseen such an event when the curtain rose forty years earlier on the very first appearance of Welsh National Opera?

WNO was founded to bring opera to Wales and provide an opportunity for Welsh singers. Many of its "discoveries" have gone on to grace the operatic stages of the world, and WNO itself has become one of Europe's leading companies. Much has changed, but the ideals with which WNO was born have not. The enthusiasm for singing and for partaking, engendered by the amateurs, has remained an integral part of WNO; guest artists from around the world are both surprised and delighted by the friendliness and welcome they receive in Cardiff – which is why so many return again and again. The chorus, upon which WNO's reputation was founded, is still one of the finest. The commitment to pioneering forgotten or rarely performed works, started in 1952 with *Nabucco*, continues; who, ten years ago, would have thought that the operas of Janáček, for example, would play to full houses? WNO was the first British opera company in modern times to grow out of popular demand, and the basic belief that opera is not an élitist art form but one for anybody and everybody who enjoys a good night out at the theatre is still fundamental to its philosophy. Of course, it still has no opera house (though an Arts Council report in 1984 stated there should be one by 1990 – which will have to be seen to be believed), but against that must be set the benefits of not owning a theatre, of playing regularly to different audiences and of being able to keep productions in the repertory longer.

One of the major changes WNO's fortieth year will bring is that Richard Armstrong, after eighteen years, fourteen as Musical Director, will be leaving (though not lost to the company, since he remains Principal Guest Conductor) to be succeeded by Sir Charles Mackerras. Whatever new outlook Mackerras might bring, he will want to retain the enthusiasm and spirit that have turned WNO from an adventurous amateur organisation into a great company, the point of which, as Tom Sutcliffe wrote in *Vogue*, "is its vitality and irreverence. The work is serious but not solemn; the aim, to interest a wider public." If, sometimes, WNO does not reach its own high standard, it is because it is, as it has always been, a company that makes one expect miracles.

# APPENDIX A: PRODUCTIONS: 1946–1985

The FOLLOWING is a list of all new productions between the years 1946 and 1985 with first-performance casts.

## 1946

### CAVALLERIA RUSTICANA (Mascagni)
15 April, Prince of Wales, Cardiff

| | |
|---|---|
| Turiddu | Tom Hopkins |
| Santuzza | Margaret Williams |
| Mamma Lucia | Phyllis Ash-Child |
| Alfio | Arthur Davies |
| Lola | Helena Hughes Brown |

conductor: Idloes Owen
producer: Norman Jones
sets: hired

in a double-bill with

### I PAGLIACCI (Leoncavallo)
15 April, Prince of Wales, Cardiff

| | |
|---|---|
| Canio | Tudor Davies |
| Tonio | Arthur Davies |
| Nedda | Beatrice Gough |
| Beppe | Frank James |
| Silvio | John Morgan |

conductor: Ivor John
producer: Norman Jones
sets: hired

### FAUST (Gounod)
16 April, Prince of Wales, Cardiff

| | |
|---|---|
| Faust | Tudor Davies |
| Mephistopheles | Norman Jones |
| Valentine | John Morgan |
| Wagner | Stanley Gitsham |
| Marguerite | Lilian Evans |
| Siebel | Myfanwy Richards |
| Marthe | Alice James |

conductor: Ivor John
producer: Norman Jones
sets: hired

## 1947

### CARMEN (Bizet)
28 April, Prince of Wales, Cardiff

| | |
|---|---|
| Morales | Ewart Rossiter |
| Micaela | Morfydd Lloyd-Davies |
| Zuniga | Stanley Gitsham |
| Don José | Frank James |
| Carmen | Zoe Cresswell |
| Frasquita | Rita Davies |
| Mercedes | Nellie Evans |
| Escamillo | Tom Williams |
| Dancairo | Geoff Davies |
| Remendado | William Russell |

conductor: Victor Fleming
producer: Norman Jones
choreographer: Mollie Hair
sets: hired

## 1948

### LA TRAVIATA (Verdi)
26 April, Prince of Wales, Cardiff

| | |
|---|---|
| Violetta | Laura Larne |
| Flora | Beatrice Gough |
| Marquis d'Obigny | Cecil Bridge |
| Baron Douphol | Stanley Gitsham |
| Dr Grenvil | George Jones |

Gaston            Sidney Jones
Alfredo           Tom Hopkins
Annina            Alice James
Giorgio Germont   Arthur Davies
Giuseppe          Evan Ellis

*conductor:* Ivor John
*producer:* Norman Jones
*choreographer:* Mollie Hair
*sets:* hired

MADAM BUTTERFLY (Puccini)
29 April, Prince of Wales, Cardiff

Cio-Cio-San         Victoria Elliott
Suzuki              Phyllis Ash-Child
Pinkerton           Frank James
Kate Pinkerton      Marjorie Griffiths
Goro                John Sidford
Sharpless           Bruce Wilson
Yamadori            Geoff Davies
The Bonze           Arthur Davies
High Commissioner   George Davies

*conductor:* Ivor John
*producer:* Norman Jones
*sets:* hired

## 1949

THE BARTERED BRIDE (Smetana)
4 May, Prince of Wales, Cardiff

Krusina        Bruce Wilson
Ludmila        Phyllis Ash-Child
Marenka        Nancy Bateman
Tobias Micha   Tom Bateman
Hata           Nellie Evans
Vasek          Evan Ellis
Jenik          Arthur Servent
Kecal          Edmund Donlevy
Ringmaster     Frank Evans
Esmeralda      Margaret Glyn
Indian         Tom Morgan
Strongman      Cecil Bridge

*conductor:* Victor Fleming
*producer:* John Donaldson
*sets and costumes:* hired

## 1950

THE TALES OF HOFFMANN
(Offenbach) 8 May, Prince of Wales, Cardiff

Hoffmann       Gabriel Todd
Nicklaus       Patti Lewis
Nathaniel      Herbert Minett
Hermann        Fred Jones
Luther         George Davies
Olympia        Elizabeth Bowen
Spalanzani     Bruce Wilson
Coppelius      Tom Bateman
Cochenille     John Sidford
Giulietta      Joan Stephens
Dapertutto     Bruce Wilson
Schlemil       Stewart Trevarthen
Pitichinaccio  Frank Evans
Antonia        Elizabeth Bowen
Mother's Voice Anita Sargent
Dr Miracle     Geoffrey Davies
Crespel        Richard Williams
Franz          William Russell

*conductor:* Charles Mackerras
*producer:* Norman Jones
*costumes and sets:* hired

DIE FLEDERMAUS (Johann Strauss, Jr.)
15 May, Prince of Wales, Cardiff

Eisenstein      Frank James
Rosalinda       Zoe Cresswell
Colonel Frank   Edmund Donlevy
Prince Orlofsky Phyllis Ash-Child
Alfred          Evan Ellis
Dr Falke        Arnold Davies
Dr Blind        Herbert Minett
Adele           Margaret Glyn
Frosch          Norman Jones
Molly           Morwen Rees
Ivan            Tom Court

*conductor:* Leo Quayle
*producer:* Norman Jones
*sets:* hired

## 1951

IL TROVATORE (Verdi)
30 April, Prince of Wales, Cardiff

Ferrando       Stanley Gitsham
Leonora        Kyra Vane
Inez           Patti Lewis
Count di Luna  Arnold Davies

| | | | |
|---|---|---|---|
| Manrico | Anthony Marlowe | Gaynor | Patti Lewis |
| Azucena | Phyllis Ash-Child | Menna | Elsie Morison |
| Old Gypsy | Stewart Trevarthen | Alys | Phyllis Ash-Child |
| Ruiz | Herbert Minett | Groomsman | Clifford Bunford |

*conductor:* Haydn James
*producer:* Norman Jones
*sets:* hired

*conductor:* Arwel Hughes
*producer:* Anthony Besch
*designer:* Rosemary Vercoe

## 1952

NABUCCO (Verdi)
7 October, Sophia Gardens, Cardiff

| | |
|---|---|
| Zaccaria | Hervey Alan |
| Fenena | Joan Stephens |
| Ishmael | Tano Ferendinos |
| Abigail | Ruth Packer |
| Anna | Muriel Pointon |
| Nabucco | Ronald Jackson |
| Abdullah | William Russell |
| High Priest | Leslie Wicks |

*conductor:* Leo Quayle
*producer:* John Moody
*designer:* Patrick Robertson

RIGOLETTO (Verdi)
17 November, Empire Theatre, Swansea

| | |
|---|---|
| Duke of Mantua | Dennis Stephenson |
| Rigoletto | Tom Williams |
| Sparafucile | Geoffrey Davies |
| Monterone | Hervey Alan |
| Marullo | Vivian Davies |
| Borsa | Graham Davies |
| Ceprano | Cecil Bridge |
| Gilda | Elizabeth Bowen |
| Giovanna | Edith Davies |
| Maddalena | Phyllis Ash-Child |
| Countess Ceprano | Jean Stevens |
| Page | June Bailey |

*conductor:* Leo Quayle
*producer:* Norman Jones
*choreographer:* Joyce Marriott
*sets:* hired

## 1953

MENNA (Arwel Hughes) World Première
9 November, Sophia Gardens, Cardiff

| | |
|---|---|
| Gwyn | Richard Lewis |
| Ivan | Roderick Jones |

## 1954

THE BARTERED BRIDE (Smetana)
21 April, Bournemouth Pavilion

| | |
|---|---|
| Krusina | Arnold Davies |
| Ludmila | Phyllis Ash-Child |
| Marenka | Nancy Bateman |
| Tobias Micha | Gwilym Yeoman |
| Hata | Patti Lewis |
| Vasek | Evan Ellis |
| Jenik | Gerald Davies |
| Kecal | Howell Glynne |
| Ringmaster | Frank Evans |
| Esmeralda | Jean Stevens |
| Indian | Tom Morgan |
| Strongman | Parry Davies |

*conductor:* Frederick Berend
*producer and designer:* Norman Jones

THE SICILIAN VESPERS (Verdi)
1 November, New Theatre, Cardiff

| | |
|---|---|
| Elena | Ruth Packer |
| Arrigo | Brychan Powell |
| Monforte | Roderick Jones |
| Procida | Hervey Alan |
| Bethune | Thomas Morgan |
| Vaudemont | William Thomas |
| Ninetta | Phyllis Ash-Child |
| Danieli | Tegwyn Short |
| Tebaldo | Eric Morgan |
| Roberto | Frank Brown |
| Manfredo | Mervyn Meyrick |

*conductor:* Frederick Berend
*producer:* Anthony Besch
*designer:* John Barker
*choreographer:* Joyce Marriott

# 1955

## CAVALLERIA RUSTICANA (Mascagni)
27 April, Empire Theatre, Swansea

| | |
|---|---|
| Turiddu | Tano Ferendinos |
| Santuzza | Lilian Prosser Evans |
| Mamma Lucia | Muriel Pointon |
| Alfio | Elwyn Adams |
| Lola | Patti Lewis |

conductor: Vilem Tausky
producer: Norman Jones
designer: Harry Powell Lloyd

## LA BOHÈME (Puccini)
28 April, Empire Theatre, Swansea

| | |
|---|---|
| Marcello | Ronald Lewis |
| Rodolfo | Walter Midgley |
| Colline | Harold Blackburn |
| Schaunard | Edmund Donlevy |
| Benoit | Evan Ellis |
| Mimi | Patricia Bartlett |
| Parpignol | Emlyn Smith |
| Musetta | Zoe Cresswell |
| Alcindoro | Vivian Davies |
| Customs Sergeant | Ben Williams |

conductor: Vilem Tausky
producer: Parry Jones
sets: Alexandre Benois

## TOSCA (Puccini)
3 May, Empire Theatre, Swansea

| | |
|---|---|
| Angelotti | Edmund Donlevy |
| Sacristan | William Thomas |
| Cavaradossi | Walter Midgley |
| Tosca | Kyra Vane |
| Scarpia | Roderick Jones |
| Spoletta | Mervyn Meyrick |
| Sciarrone | Thomas Morgan |
| Gaoler | Vivian Davies |

conductor: Charles Groves
producer: Norman Jones
designer: Giovanni Grandi
costumes: hired

# 1956

## IL TROVATORE (Verdi)
16 April, Empire Theatre, Swansea

| | |
|---|---|
| Ferrando | Hervey Alan |
| Leonora | Zoe Cresswell |
| Inez | Patti Lewis |
| Count di Luna | William Edwards |
| Manrico | Brychan Powell |
| Azucena | Phyllis Ash-Child |
| Old Gypsy | Cecil Bridge |
| Ruiz | Tegwyn Short |

conductor: Warwick Braithwaite
producer and designer: Harry Powell Lloyd

## I LOMBARDI (Verdi)
16 July, Sadler's Wells, London

| | |
|---|---|
| Arvino | Paul Asciak |
| Pagano | Bryan Drake |
| Viclinda | Lilian Prosser Evans |
| Giselda | Rosina Raisbeck |
| Pirro | Leonard John |
| Prior | Tegwyn Short |
| Acciano | Elwyn Adams |
| Sofia | Patti Lewis |
| Oronte | Alfred Hallett |

conductor: Warwick Braithwaite
producer: George R. Foa
designer: Louis Kahan

## THE BARBER OF SEVILLE (Rossini)
8 October, New Theatre, Cardiff

| | |
|---|---|
| Fiorello | Vivian Davies |
| Count Almaviva | Tano Ferendinos |
| Figaro | William Dickie |
| Rosina | Barbara Wilson |
| Dr Bartolo | Howell Glynne |
| Marcellina | Patti Lewis |
| Don Basilio | Michael Langdon |
| Officer | Thomas Morgan |

conductor: Warwick Braithwaite
producer and designer: Harry Powell Lloyd

# 1957

## MEFISTOFELE (Boito)
6 May, New Theatre, Cardiff

| | |
|---|---|
| Mefistofele | Raimund Herincx |
| Faust | Alfred Hallett |

| Wagner | Robert Gard |
|---|---|
| Marguerite | Solange de la Motte |
| Martha | Patricia Kern |
| Helen of Troy | Joyce Barker |
| Pantalis | Margreta Elkins |
| Nereus | Robert Gard |

*conductor:* Warwick Braithwaite
*producer:* George R. Foa
*designer:* Julia Trevelyan Oman
*choreographer:* Philippe Perrottet


LA TRAVIATA (Verdi)
30 September, New Theatre, Cardiff

| Violetta | Heather Harper |
|---|---|
| Flora | Elizabeth Tovey |
| Marquis d'Obigny | Vivian Davies |
| Baron Douphol | Raimund Herincx |
| Dr Grenvil | Leonard John |
| Gaston | David Parker |
| Alfredo | Tano Ferendinos |
| Annina | Phyllis Ash-Child |
| Giorgio Germont | Bryan Drake |
| Giuseppe | Evan Ellis |
| Peasant | Shirley Davies |

*conductor:* Warwick Braithwaite
*producer and designer:* Harry Powell Lloyd


## 1958

DIE FLEDERMAUS (Johann Strauss, Jr.)
28 August, Odeon, Llandudno

| Eisenstein | Kevin Miller |
|---|---|
| Rosalinda | Zoe Cresswell |
| Colonel Frank | Edmund Donlevy |
| Prince Orlofsky | Phyllis Ash-Child |
| Alfred | Tano Ferendinos |
| Dr Falke | William Dickie |
| Dr Blind | Tegwyn Short |
| Adele | Marion Studholme |
| Frosch | Ronald Stear |
| Molly | Valmai Hunter |
| Ivan | David Lewis |

*conductor:* Warwick Braithwaite
*producer and designer:* Harry Powell Lloyd
*choreographer:* Philippe Perrottet


MADAM BUTTERFLY (Puccini)
30 September, New Theatre, Cardiff

| Cio-Cio-San | Joan Hammond |
|---|---|
| Suzuki | Phyllis Ash-Child |

| Pinkerton | Robert Thomas |
|---|---|
| Goro | David Tree |
| Sharpless | Bruce Dargavel |
| Prince Yamadori | Bryan Drake |
| The Bonze | Ronald Stear |
| Priest | Ivor Phillips |
| High Commissioner | John Hauxvell |
| Kate Pinkerton | Valerie Griffiths |

*conductor:* Warwick Braithwaite
*producer:* Betty Thompson
*designer:* David Tinker (sets); costumes hired


## 1959

LA BOHÈME (Puccini)
5 May, New Theatre, Cardiff

| Marcello | Ronald Lewis |
|---|---|
| Rodolfo | Walter Midgley |
| Colline | Donald Campbell |
| Schaunard | Bryan Drake |
| Benoit | Tegwyn Short |
| Mimi | Joyce Gartside |
| Parpignol | Emlyn Smith |
| Musetta | Elizabeth Rust |
| Alcindoro | Vivian Davies |
| Customs Sergeant | Kenneth Rees |

*conductor:* Warwick Braithwaite
*producer:* Harry Powell Lloyd
*designer:* Alexander Benois (1955 sets)


MAY NIGHT (Rimsky-Korsakov)
28 September, New Theatre, Cardiff

| Levko | Duncan Robertson |
|---|---|
| Anna | Iona Jones |
| The Mayor | Harold Blackburn |
| Kalenik | Laurie Payne |
| The Distiller | Stephen Manton |
| Mayor's Sister-in-Law | Monica Sinclair |
| The Town Clark | Bryan Drake |
| Pannochka | Heather Harper |
| Mother Hen | Barbara Harding |
| Raven | Elizabeth Painter |
| Stepmother | Valmai Hunter |

*conductor:* Warwick Braithwaite
*producer:* John Moody
*designer:* Sally Hulke
*choreographer:* Norman Dixon

TOSCA (Puccini)
29 September, New Theatre, Cardiff

| | |
|---|---|
| Angelotti | Bryan Drake |
| Sacristan | Donald Campbell |
| Cavaradossi | Ronald Dowd |
| Tosca | Joan Hammond |
| Scarpia | John Shaw |
| Spoletta | Tegwyn Short |
| Sciarrone | Thomas Morgan |
| Shepherd Boy | Norma Jones |
| Gaoler | Vivian Davies |

conductor: Warwick Braithwaite
producer: Harry Powell Lloyd
designer: Giovanni Grandi (1955 sets)

## 1960

SERCH YW'R DOCTOR (Arwel Hughes)
1 August, Sophia Gardens Eisteddfod
Pavilion, Cardiff

| | |
|---|---|
| Lucinde | Lucille Graham |
| Clitandre | Rowland Jones |
| Sganarelle | Rhydderch Davies |
| Lisette | Marion Lowe |
| Ragotin | Evan Thomas |

conductor: Arwel Hughes
producer: John Moody
designer: David Tinker

LA BATTAGLIA DI LEGNANO (Verdi)
Given as The Battle 31 October, New
Theatre, Cardiff

| | |
|---|---|
| Von Friedrich | Hervey Alan |
| 1st Consul | Cecil Bridge |
| 2nd Consul | Leonard John |
| Mayor | Glanville Davies |
| Rolando | Ronald Lewis |
| Lida | Heather Harper |
| Arrigo | Ronald Dowd |
| Mark | Evan Thomas |
| Imelda | Jean Evans |
| An Officer | David Harding |

conductor: Charles Groves
producer: John Moody
designer: David Tinker

## 1961

WILLIAM TELL (Rossini)
2 October, New Theatre, Cardiff

| | |
|---|---|
| Fisherman | Edward Evanko |
| William Tell | Ronald Lewis |
| Jemmy | Elizabeth Vaughan |
| Hedda | Jean Evans |
| Melchtal | Hervey Alan |
| Arnold | Tano Ferendinos |
| Leutold | Richard Rees |
| Rudolf | David Tree |
| Huntsman | Anthony Nowell |
| Matilda | Glenys Dowdle |
| Walter Furst | Gerwyn Morgan |
| Gessler | Bryan Drake |

conductor: Charles Groves
producer: John Moody
designers: Patrick Robertson (sets) and
Elizabeth Friendship (costumes)
choreographer: Ray Powell

## 1962

THE MARRIAGE OF FIGARO (Mozart)
7 March, Grand Theatre, Swansea

| | |
|---|---|
| Figaro | Ronald Lewis |
| Susanna | Pauline Tinsley |
| Dr Bartolo | Derick Davies |
| Marcellina | Olwen Price |
| Cherubino | Margaret Price |
| Almaviva | John Shirley-Quirk |
| Don Basilio | Stephen Manton |
| Countess Almaviva | Norma Morgan |
| Antonio | Elwyn Adams |
| Don Curzio | David Tree |
| Barbarina | Branwen Williams |
| 1st Girl | Norma Morris |
| 2nd Girl | Marjorie Thomas |

conductor: Charles Groves
producer: John Moody
designer: Elizabeth Friendship

LOHENGRIN (Wagner)
1 October, New Theatre, Cardiff

| | |
|---|---|
| Henry | John Holmes |
| Lohengrin | Robert Thomas |
| Elsa | Pauline Tinsley |
| Godfrey | Simon Davies |
| Frederick | Russell Cooper |

Ortrud              Patricia Bartlett
Herald              Richard Rees

*conductor:* Charles Groves
*producer:* Harry Powell Lloyd
*designer:* Elizabeth Friendship

## 1963

### THE SERAGLIO (Mozart)
5 March, Grand Theatre, Swansea

Belmonte            David Hillman
Osmin               Howell Glynne
Pedrillo            Kenneth Collins
Pasha Selim         Gerwyn Morgan
Constanze           Elizabeth Vaughan
Blonde              Jenifer Eddy

*conductor:* Bryan Balkwill
*producer:* John Moody
*designer:* Elizabeth Friendship

### MACBETH (Verdi)
23–25 September, New Theatre, Cardiff

Macbeth             Ronald Lewis
                    Delme Bryn-Jones
Banquo              David Gwynne
Lady Macbeth        Pauline Tinsley
                    Gwyneth Jones
Macbeth's Servant   Donald Williams
Duncan              Glanville Davies
Macduff             Robert Thomas
Malcolm             Stuart Burrows
Lady-in-Waiting     Noreen Berry
Fleance             Stanley Williams
Murderer            Morgan Jones
                    Cecil Bridge
Doctor              Anthony Nowell

*conductor:* Bryan Balkwill
*producer:* John Moody
*designer:* Elizabeth Friendship

## 1964

### THE BARBER OF SEVILLE (Rossini)
2 March, Grand Theatre, Swansea

Fiorello            Christopher Davies
Count Almaviva      Jack Irons
Figaro              Geoffrey Chard
Rosina              Patricia Kern
Dr Bartolo          Derick Davies

Marcellina          Esther Latter
Ambrogio            Christopher Davies
Don Basilio         David Gwynne
Officer             Duncan Reece
Notary              Eynon Thomas

*conductor:* Bryan Balkwill
*producer:* John Moody
*designer:* Elizabeth Friendship

### FIDELIO (Beethoven)
29 September, New Theatre, Cardiff

Jacquino            Malcolm Williams
Marzellina          Anne Pashley
Rocco               Dennis Wicks
Leonore             Gwyneth Jones
Don Pizarro         Raimund Herincx
1st Prisoner        Myron Burnett
2nd Prisoner        Anthony Nowell
Florestan           Robert Thomas
Don Fernando        David Gwynne

*conductor:* Bryan Balkwill
*producer:* John Moody
*designer:* Elizabeth Friendship

## 1965

### MOSES (Rossini)
3 May, New Theatre, Cardiff

Moses               Michael Langdon
Anna                Lorna Elias
Miriam              Noreen Berry
Eleazor             Stuart Burrows
Amenophis           Edward Byles
Pharoah             Bryan Drake
Sinaida             Pauline Tinsley
Osiridis            David Gwynne
Ophidis             Malcolm Williams

*conductor:* Bryan Balkwill
*producer:* John Moody
*designer:* Elizabeth Friendship

### DIE FLEDERMAUS (Johann Strauss, Jr.)
19 August, Odeon, Llandudno

Eisenstein          James Hawthorne
Rosalinda           Milla Andrew
Colonel Frank       Denis Dowling
Prince Orlofsky     Patricia Kern
Alfred              Rowland Jones
Dr Falke            Michael Maurel

| | | | |
|---|---|---|---|
| Dr Blind | Tegwyn Short | Louisa | Anne Pashley |
| Adele | Jenifer Eddy | Augusta | Janet Hughes |
| Frosch | Emyr Green | Aunt Genevieve | Jean Allister |
| Ivan | Donald Williams | Uncle Steve | David Lennox |
| Ida | Anne Bunford | Dr Charlton | John Gibbs |
| | | Rosalie | Marian Evans |

*conductor:* Bryan Balkwill
*producer:* Harry Powell Lloyd
*designer:* Elizabeth Friendship
*choreographer:* Terry Gilbert

Mr Elderberry — Ralph Davies
Mrs Lillywhite — Beatrice Gough

*conductor:* Bryan Balkwill
*producer:* John Moody
*designer:* Elizabeth Friendship

THE BARTERED BRIDE (Smetana)
1 October, New Theatre, Cardiff

in double-bill with

IL TABARRO (Puccini) given as *The Cloak*

| | |
|---|---|
| Krusina | Evan Thomas |
| Ludmila | Phyllis Ash-Child |
| Marenka | Veronica Dunne |
| Tobias Micha | Emyr Green |
| Hata | Anne Bunford |
| Vasek | Malcolm Williams |
| Jenik | Robert Thomas |
| Kecal | John Holmes |
| Ringmaster | Tegwyn Short |
| Esmeralda | Anne Pashley |
| Indian | Gordon Whyte |

| | |
|---|---|
| Michele | Ronald Lewis |
| Luigi | John Dobson |
| Il Tinca | Edward Byles |
| Talpa | David Gwynne |
| Giorgetta | Marie Collier |
| Frugola | Jean Allister |
| Ballad Seller | Malcolm Williams |

*conductor:* Bryan Balkwill
*producer:* John Moody
*designer:* Elizabeth Friendship

*conductor:* Vilem Tausky
*producer:* Philippe Perrottet
*designer:* Elizabeth Friendship

DON PASQUALE (Donizetti)
26 September, New Theatre, Cardiff

## 1966

| | |
|---|---|
| Don Pasquale | Geraint Evans |
| Dr Malatesta | Michael Maurel |
| Ernesto | Stuart Burrows |
| Nornia | Jenifer Eddy |
| Notary | David Rhys-Edwards |

DON GIOVANNI (Mozart)
14 March, Grand Theatre, Swansea

| | |
|---|---|
| Leporello | John Gibbs |
| Don Giovanni | Forbes Robinson |
| Donna Anna | Patricia Reakes |
| The Commendatore | David Gwynne |
| Don Ottavio | David Hughes |
| Donna Elvira | Veronica Dunne |
| Zerlina | Anne Pashley |
| Masetto | Derick Davies |

*conductor:* Bryan Balkwill
*producer:* Dennis Maunder
*designer:* Elizabeth Friendship

## 1967

LA BOHÈME (Puccini)
14 March, Grand Theatre, Swansea

*conductor:* Bryan Balkwill
*producer:* Michael Geliot
*designer:* Annena Stubbs
*choreographer:* Terry Gilbert

| | |
|---|---|
| Marcello | Michael Maurel |
| Rodolfo | David Hughes |
| Colline | David Gwynne |
| Schaunard | Geoffrey Chard |
| Benoit | Tegwyn Short |
| Mimi | Catherine Wilson |
| Parpignol | John Myrddin |

THE PARLOUR (Grace Williams)
World Première 5 May, New Theatre, Cardiff

| | |
|---|---|
| Grandmamma | Edith Coates |
| Papa | Edward Byles |
| Mamma | Noreen Berry |

Musetta              Alice Robiczek
Alcindoro            David Rhys-Edwards

*conductor:* Frank Doolan
*producer:* John Copley
*designer:* Alexandre Benois (1955 sets)


NABUCCO (Verdi)
10 May, New Theatre, Cardiff

Zaccaria             Clifford Grant
Fenena               Rhiannon Davies
Ishmael              Keith Erwen
Abigail              Pauline Tinsley
Anna                 Marian Evans
Nabucco              Raimund Herincx
Abdullah             Malcolm Williams
High Priest          David Rhys-Edwards

*conductor:* Bryan Balkwill
*producer:* Michael Geliot
*designer:* Elizabeth Friendship


CARMEN (Bizet)
25 September, New Theatre, Cardiff

Morales              Christopher Davies
Micaela              Janette Gail
Zuniga               David Gwynne
Don José             David Hughes
Carmen               Joyce Blackham
Frasquita            Angela Jenkins
Mercedes             Alma Myatt
Lillas Pastia        Tegwyn Short
Andres               Keith Erwen
Escamillo            John Gibbs
Dancairo             Dennis Brandt
Remendado            John Winfield
Guide                David Rhys-Edwards

*conductor:* Bryan Balkwill
*producer:* John Moody
*designer:* Abd'ElKader Farrah
*choreographer:* Terry Gilbert


1968

RIGOLETTO (Verdi)
11 March, Grand Theatre, Swansea

Duke of Mantua       Donald Pilley
Rigoletto            Delme Bryn-Jones
Sparafucile          David Gwynne
Monterone            Patrick McGuigan
Marullo              John Hauxvell

Borsa                Malcolm Williams
Ceprano              David Rhys-Edwards
Gilda                Cynthia Johnston
Giovanna             Phyllis Ash-Child
Maddalena            Janet Coster
Countess Ceprano     Marian Evans
Page                 Alma Myatt
Usher                Brian Elliot

*conductor:* Eric Wetherell
*producer:* Tom Hawkes
*designer:* Jane Kingshill
*choreographer:* Harry Haythorne


LA TRAVIATA (Verdi)
23 May, New Theatre, Cardiff

Violetta             Ava June
Flora                Rhiannon Davies
Marquis d'Obigny     John Hauxvell
Baron Douphol        Patrick McGuigan
Dr Grenvil           David Rhys-Edwards
Gaston               Keith Erwen
Alfredo              David Hillman
Annina               Molly Pope
Giorgio Germont      Geoffrey Chard
Giuseppe             Ieuan Davies
Peasant              Peter Massocchi

*conductor:* John Matheson
*producer:* John Copley
*designer:* David Walker


BORIS GODUNOV (Mussorgsky)
23 September, New Theatre, Cardiff

Nikitich             Patrick McGuigan
Mitiukha             David Rhys-Edwards
2nd Peasant          Jean Sugrue
3rd Peasant          John Myrddin
Schchelkalov         John Hauxvell
Boris Godunov        Forbes Robinson
Feodor               Anne Pashley
Xenia                Marian Evans
Pimen                David Gwynne
Grigory              Keith Erwen
Hostess              Edith Coates
Varlaam              David Kelly
Missail              Robert Bowman
Nurse                Rhiannon Davies
A Boyar              William Joseph
Shuisky              John Dobson
Krushchov            Alan Holdich
Lavitsky             John Hauxvell

Chernikovsky          Patrick McGuigan
The Simpleton         Malcolm Williams

*conductor:* James Lockhart
*producer:* John Moody
*designer:* Elizabeth Friendship

## 1969

### THE MARRIAGE OF FIGARO (Mozart)
3 February, Haverfordwest

Figaro                John Gibbs
Susanna               Anne Pashley
Dr Bartolo            David Gwynne
Marcellina            Molly Pope
Cherubino             Delia Wallis
Count Almaviva        John Kitchiner
Don Basilio           Ieuan Davies
Countess Almaviva     Susan Morris
Antonio               David Rhys-Edwards
Don Curzio            William Joseph
Barbarina             Jennifer Evans

*conductor:* James Lockhart
*producer:* John Moody
*designer:* Elizabeth Friendship

### LA TRAVIATA (Verdi)
4 February, Haverfordwest

Violetta              Josephine Barstow
Flora                 Delia Wallis
Marquis d'Obigny      Thomas Allen
Baron Douphol         David Gwynne
Dr Grenvil            David Rhys-Edwards
Gaston                William Joseph
Alfredo               Ramon Remedios
Annina                Molly Pope
Giorgio Germont       Geoffrey Chard
Giuseppe              Ieuan Davies
Peasant               Peter Massocchi
Flora's Servant       John Davis

*conductor:* James Lockhart
*producer:* Malcolm Fraser
*designer:* Pauline Whitehouse

### FALSTAFF (Verdi)
29 September, New Theatre, Cardiff

Falstaff              Geraint Evans
Pistol                David Gwynne
Bardolph              Robert Thomas
Dr Caius              Edward Byles
Mistress Page         Joan Davies

Alice Ford            Elizabeth Vaughan
Nannetta              Margaret Price
Mistress Quickly      Helen Watts
Ford                  Gwyn Griffiths
Fenton                Keith Erwen
Innkeeper             Anthony Feltham

*conductor:* James Lockhart
*producers:* Geraint Evans and John Copley
*designer:* Carl Toms

## 1970

### THE BARBER OF SEVILLE (Rossini)
23 February, Haverfordwest

Fiorello              John Carr
Count Almaviva        Ramon Remedios
Figaro                Terence Sharpe
Rosina                Beverley Humphreys
Dr Bartolo            John Gibbs
Marcellina            Elaine Hooker
Don Basilio           David Gwynne
Ambrogio              Anthony Feltham
Officer               Rhys Devlin
Notary                John Sheppard

*conductor:* Richard Armstrong
*producer:* Malcolm Fraser
*designer:* Robin Archer

### COSÌ FAN TUTTE (Mozart)
24 February, Haverfordwest

Fiordiligi            Josephine Barstow
Dorabella             Beverley Bergen
Ferrando              Keith Erwen
Guglielmo             Thomas Allen
Don Alfonso           John Kitchiner
Despina               Wendy Eathorne

*conductor:* James Lockhart
*producer:* Michael Geliot
*designer:* Christine Edzard

### AIDA (Verdi)
20 April, New Theatre, Cardiff

Radames               William Johns
Ramfis                Don Garrard
Amneris               Janet Coster
Aida                  Grace de la Cruz
King of Egypt         David Gwynne
Messenger             Neville Ackerman

| | |
|---|---|
| Amonasro | Terence Sharpe |
| Priestess | Tessa Coates |

*conductor:* James Lockhart
*producer:* Michael Geliot
*designer:* Annena Stubbs
*choreographer:* Terry Gilbert

### LA BOHÈME (Puccini)
29 April, New Theatre, Cardiff

| | |
|---|---|
| Marcello | Delme Bryn-Jones |
| Rodolfo | Stuart Burrows |
| Colline | David Gwynne |
| Schaunard | Thomas Allen |
| Benoit | Terence Walters |
| Mimi | Josephine Barstow |
| Parpignol | Eric Maddison |
| Musetta | Anne Linstrum |
| Alcindoro | Peter Massochi |
| Customs Officer | Kenneth Pugh |
| Customs Sergeant | Gordon Whyte |

*conductor:* James Lockhart
*producer:* Ande Anderson
*designer:* Pauline Whitehouse

### DIE FLEDERMAUS (Johann Strauss, Jr.)
11 August, Astra, Llandudno

| | |
|---|---|
| Eisenstein | John Wakefield |
| Rosalinda | Beverley Bergen |
| Colonel Frank | Julian Moyle |
| Prince Orlofsky | Carolyn Maia |
| Alfred | Alexander Oliver |
| Dr Falke | Thomas Allen |
| Dr Blind | Terence Walters |
| Adele | Celia Jeffreys |
| Frosch | Declan Mulholland |

*conductor:* James Lockhart
*producer:* Michael Geliot
*designer:* Elizabeth Friendship

### SIMON BOCCANEGRA (Verdi)
21 September, New Theatre, Cardiff

| | |
|---|---|
| Paolo | Thomas Allen |
| Pietro | David Gwynne |
| Simon Boccanegra | Delme Bryn-Jones |
| Fiesco | Forbes Robinson |
| Amelia | Josephine Barstow |
| Adorno | Keith Erwen |

| | |
|---|---|
| Maid | Molly Pope |
| Captain | Terence Walters |

*conductor:* James Lockhart
*producer:* John Moody
*designers:* Roger Butlin (sets) and Richard Davin (costumes)

## 1971

### THE MAGIC FLUTE (Mozart)
19 April, New Theatre, Cardiff

| | |
|---|---|
| Tamino | Keith Erwen |
| 1st Lady | Beverley Bergen |
| 2nd Lady | Molly Pope |
| 3rd Lady | Patricia Llewellyn |
| Papageno | Thomas Allen |
| Queen of the Night | Jessica Cash |
| Monostatos | Alexander Oliver |
| Pamina | Margaret Price |
| 1st Boy | Celia Jeffreys |
| 2nd Boy | Margaret Baiton |
| 3rd Boy | Bridget Bartlam |
| Speaker | Glynne Thomas |
| Sarastro | Clifford Grant |
| 1st Priest | Leonard Williams |
| 2nd Priest | Glynne Thomas |
| Papagena | Lillian Watson |
| 1st Armoured Man | Neville Ackerman |
| 2nd Armoured Man | Joseph Varney |

*conductor:* James Lockhart
*producer:* Michael Geliot
*designers:* Roger Butlin (sets) and Jane Bond (costumes)

### LULU (Berg)
14 September, New Theatre, Cardiff

| | |
|---|---|
| Animal Tamer | Eric Garrett |
| Dr Schön | John Modenos |
| Alwa | Nigel Douglas |
| Lulu | Carole Farley |
| The Painter | Ramon Remedios |
| Dr Goll | Rhys Devlin |
| Schigolch | Eric Garrett |
| The Prince | Stuart Kale |
| A Theatre Dresser | Janet Hughes |
| Theatre Director | Peter Massochi |
| Countess Geschwitz | Noreen Berry |
| Rodrigo | Paul Hudson |
| Schoolboy | Janet Hughes |

| Manservant | Leonard Williams |
|---|---|
| Clown | Gordon Whyte |

*conductor:* James Lockhart
*producer:* Michael Geliot
*designers:* Ralph Koltai (sets) and Freda Blackwood (costumes)

## 1972

RIGOLETTO (Verdi)
28 February, Haverfordwest

| Duke of Mantua | Keith Erwen |
|---|---|
| Rigoletto | Terence Sharpe |
| Sparafucile | David Gwynne |
| Monterone | Glynne Thomas |
| Marullo | Eric Roberts |
| Borsa | Leonard Williams |
| Ceprano | Ralph Hamer |
| Gilda | Elizabeth Lane |
| Giovanna | Patricia Llewellyn |
| Maddalena | Bridget Bartlam |
| Countess Ceprano | Barbel Edwards |
| Page | Robina Silvolli |

*conductor:* James Lockhart
*producer:* John Moody
*designers:* Roger Butlin (sets) and Sue Plummer (costumes)

TURANDOT (Puccini)
24 April, New Theatre, Cardiff

| Turandot | Pauline Tinsley |
|---|---|
| Liù | Yvonne Fuller |
| Calaf | William Johns |
| Timur | David Gwynne |
| Ping | Julian Moyle |
| Pong | Alexander Oliver |
| Pang | Edward Byles |
| Mandarin | Glynne Thomas |
| Emperor | Ieuan Davies |

*conductor:* Richard Armstrong
*producer:* Michael Geliot
*designer:* Alexander McPherson

BILLY BUDD (Britten)
25 September, New Theatre, Cardiff

| Captain Vere | Nigel Douglas |
|---|---|
| Billy Budd | Thomas Allen |
| Claggart | Forbes Robinson |
| Mr Redburn | Julian Moyle |

| Mr Flint | Bryan Drake |
|---|---|
| Mr Ratcliffe | David Gwynne |
| Red Whiskers | Stuart Kale |
| Donald | John Gibbs |
| Dansker | Frank Olegario |
| Novice | Ramon Remedios |
| Squeak | Arthur Davies |
| Bosun | Glynne Thomas |
| 1st Mate | Ralph Hamer |
| 2nd Mate | Peter Massocchi |
| Maintop | Neville Ackerman |
| Novice's Friend | Eric Roberts |
| Arthur Jones | Gordon Whyte |

*conductor:* James Lockhart
*producer:* Michael Geliot
*designer:* Roger Butlin

## 1973

MADAM BUTTERFLY (Puccini)
26 February, Haverfordwest

| Cio-Cio-San | Elizabeth Vaughan |
|---|---|
| Suzuki | Moira Griffiths |
| Pinkerton | Kenneth Collins |
| Goro | Arthur Davies |
| Sharpless | Julian Moyle |
| Prince Yamadori | Henry Newman |
| The Bonze | Ralph Hamer |
| Priest | David Tagg |
| High Commissioner | Peter Massocchi |
| Kate Pinkerton | Patricia Llewellyn |

*conductor:* James Lockhart
*producer:* Malcolm Fraser
*designer:* Shuhei Iwamoto

DON CARLOS (Verdi)
9 May, New Theatre, Cardiff

| A Monk | Paul Hudson |
|---|---|
| Don Carlos | Keith Erwen |
| Rodrigo | Terence Sharpe |
| Thibault | Lillian Watson |
| Princess Eboli | Janet Coster |
| Elizabeth | Josephine Barstow |
| Philip II | Forbes Robinson |
| Herald | Neville Ackerman |
| Voice | Robina Silvolli |
| Count Lerme | Terence Walters |
| Grand Inquisitor | David Gwynne |

*conductor:* James Lockhart
*producer:* Michael Geliot
*designer:* Annena Stubbs

IDOMENEO (Mozart)
18 September, New Theatre, Cardiff

| | |
|---|---|
| Ilia | Janet Price |
| Idamante | Anthony Roden |
| Arbace | Alexander Oliver |
| Electra | Rae Woodland |
| Idomeneo | Alexander Young |
| High Priest | Neville Ackerman |
| Neptune | David Gwynne |

conductor: Richard Armstrong
producer: Michael Geliot
designer: Jenny Beavan

THE PEARL FISHERS (Bizet)
4 October, New Theatre, Cardiff

| | |
|---|---|
| Zurga | Delme Bryn-Jones |
| Nadir | Kenneth Collins |
| Leila | Barbara Shuttleworth |
| Nourabad | Paul Hudson |

conductor: David Atherton
producer: John Moody
designer: Sue Plummer

## 1974

L'ELISIR D'AMORE (Donizetti)
1 February, Embassy Theatre, Peterborough

| | |
|---|---|
| Nemorino | Arthur Davies |
| Adina | Susan Dennis |
| Belcore | Terence Sharpe |
| Dulcamara | Forbes Robinson |
| Giannetta | Lillian Watson |

conductor: Anthony Hose
producer: Michael Geliot
designer: Jenny Beavan

THE BEACH OF FALESÁ (Alun
Hoddinott) World Première 26 March, New
Theatre, Cardiff

| | |
|---|---|
| Schooner Captain | Terence Walters |
| Wiltshire | Delme Bryn-Jones |
| Trader Case | Geraint Evans |
| Black Jack | Forbes Robinson |
| Randall | Rowland Jones |
| Uma | Sandra Browne |
| Fa 'avao | Peggy Troman |
| Father Galuchet | Edward Byles |

| | |
|---|---|
| Maea | Mark Hamilton |
| Apia | Ieuan Davies |

conductor: Richard Armstrong
producer: Michael Geliot
designer: Alexander McPherson

THE FLYING DUTCHMAN (Wagner)
10 September, New Theatre, Cardiff

| | |
|---|---|
| Daland | David Gwynne |
| Senta | Anne Evans |
| Erik | Kenneth Collins |
| Mary | Peggy Troman |
| Steersman | Arthur Davies |
| The Dutchman | David Ward |

conductor: Richard Armstrong
producer: Ian Watt-Smith
designer: William Dudley

## 1975

THE GRAND DUCHESS OF
GEROLSTEIN (Offenbach)
4 March, Fishguard

| | |
|---|---|
| The Grand Duchess | Ann Howard |
| Wanda | Lillian Watson |
| Fritz | Terence Walters |
| Prince Paul | Eric Roberts |
| Baron Puck | Rowland Jones |
| Nepomuc | Ieuan Davies |
| General Boum | Forbes Robinson |
| Baron Grog | Robert Bickerstaff |
| Iza | Sharman Shepherd |
| Olga | Suzanne Streten |
| Amelia | Menai Davies |
| Charlotte | Clare Stanley |

conductor: John Pryce-Jones
producer: Malcolm Fraser
designers: Tod Kingman (sets) and Robert St
John Roper (costumes)
choreographer: Sally Gilpin

MANON LESCAUT (Puccini)
5 March, Fishguard

| | |
|---|---|
| Manon Lescaut | Elizabeth Vaughan |
| des Grieux | Kenneth Collins |
| Geronte di Ravoir | Eric Garrett |
| Lescaut | Terence Sharpe |
| Edmondo | Arthur Davies |
| Innkeeper | Mark Nelson |

| | |
|---|---|
| Dancing Master | Ieuan Davies |
| Musician | Rita Cullis |
| Lamplighter | John Harris |
| Naval Captain | Ralph Hamer |
| Sergeant | Kenneth Pugh |
| Wigmaster | William Thomas |

conductor: Richard Armstrong
producer: Julian Hope
designer: Bruno Santini

COSÌ FAN TUTTE (Mozart)
15 April, New Theatre, Cardiff

| | |
|---|---|
| Fiordiligi | Kay Griffel |
| Dorabella | Sandra Browne |
| Ferrando | Arthur Davies |
| Guglielmo | Terence Sharpe |
| Don Alfonso | Julian Moyle |
| Despina | Lillian Watson |

conductor: György Fisher
producer: Michael Geliot
designers: Liz King (sets) and Freda
Blackwood (costumes)

OTELLO (Verdi)
2 September, New Theatre, Cardiff

| | |
|---|---|
| Otello | Alberto Remedios |
| Desdemona | Evelyn Brunner |
| Iago | Delme Bryn-Jones |
| Cassio | Gregory Dempsey |
| Lodovico | David Gwynne |
| Roderigo | John Harris |
| Montano | Kenneth Pugh |
| Emilia | Noreen Berry |
| Herald | Henry Newman |

conductor: James Lockhart
producer: Michael Geliot
designer: Annena Stubbs

JENŮFA (Janáček)
23 September, New Theatre, Cardiff

| | |
|---|---|
| Jenůfa | Josephine Barstow |
| Kostelnicka | Pauline Tinsley |
| Laca Klemen | Allen Cathcart |
| Steva Buryja | Gregory Dempsey |
| Foreman | Julian Moyle |
| Grandmother | Menai Davies |
| Mayor | Kenneth Pugh |
| Mayor's Wife | Clare Stanley |
| Karolka | Elaine Hewitt |

| | |
|---|---|
| Maid | Margaret Morgan |
| Barena | Rita Cullis |
| Jano | Margaret Baiton |
| Aunt | Jean Loosemore |

conductor: Richard Armstrong
producer: David Pountney
designer: Maria Björnson
choreographer: Terry Gilbert

## 1976

ALBERT HERRING (Britten)
23 January, Sherman Theatre, Cardiff

| | |
|---|---|
| Sid | Henry Newman |
| Albert Herring | Arthur Davies |
| Nancy | Margaret Morgan |
| Mrs Herring | Menai Davies |
| Lady Billows | Rae Woodland |
| Miss Wordsworth | Rita Cullis |
| Mr Gedge | Julian Moyle |
| Supt Budd | David Gwynne |
| Florence | Johanna Peters |
| Mr Upfold | John Harris |
| Cis | Margaret Baiton |
| Emmie | Mary Davies |
| Harry | Simon Bunce |

conductor: Anthony Hose
producer: Ian Watt-Smith
designer: Alexander McPherson

THE SERAGLIO (Mozart)
1 April, New Theatre, Cardiff

| | |
|---|---|
| Belmonte | Alexander Young |
| Osmin | Willard White |
| Pedrillo | Alexander Oliver |
| Pasha Selim | David Capewell |
| Constanze | Lois McDonall |
| Blonde | Lillian Watson |

conductor: György Fischer
producer: Michael Geliot
designer: Serge Marzolff (sets borrowed from
Geneva)

IL TROVATORE (Verdi)
10 April, New Theatre, Cardiff

| | |
|---|---|
| Ferrando | David Gwynne |
| Leonora | Elizabeth Vaughan |

| | |
|---|---|
| Inez | Barbel Edwards |
| Count di Luna | Terence Sharpe |
| Manrico | Kenneth Collins |
| Azucena | Janet Coster |
| Old Gypsy | Peter Massocchi |
| Messenger | Ieuan Davies |
| Ruiz | Mark Hamilton |

*conductor:* Richard Armstrong
*producer:* Julian Hope
*designers:* David Fielding (sets) and Maria
Björnson (costumes)

### ORPHEUS IN THE UNDERWORLD
(Offenbach) 31 August, New Theatre,
Cardiff

| | |
|---|---|
| Pluto | Emile Belcourt |
| Jupiter | Julian Moyle |
| Orpheus | Arthur Davies |
| John Styx | Stuart Kale |
| Mercury | Terence Walters |
| Bacchus | Ieuan Davies |
| Mars | James Miller-Coburn |
| Morpheus | Neville Ackerman |
| Eurydice | Norma Burrowes |
| Diana | Rita Cullis |
| Public Opinion | Johanna Peters |
| Venus | Carol Barlow-Davies |
| Cupid | Margaret Baiton |
| Juno | Peggy Troman |
| Minerva | Margaret Morgan |
| Vulcan | Ralph Hamer |
| Hebe | Sharman Shepherd |
| Apollo | Mark Hamilton |
| Ceres | Ann Beynon |
| Pomone | Robina Silvolli |
| Neptune | Kenneth Pugh |
| Fortuna | Meryn Nance |
| Iris | Dorothy Hood |
| Flora | Margaret Liddell |
| Pan | Peter Massocchi |

*conductor:* Julian Smith
*producer:* Louis Ducreux
*designers:* Denis Martin (sets) and
Jean-Denis Malclès (costumes)
*choreographer:* Gigi Caciuleanu

### THE MIDSUMMER MARRIAGE
(Tippett) 22 September, New Theatre,
Cardiff

| | |
|---|---|
| Jenifer | Jill Gomez |
| Bella | Mary Davies |

| | |
|---|---|
| Sosostris | Helen Watts |
| Mark | John Treleaven |
| Jack | Arthur Davies |
| King Fisher | Raimund Herincx |
| He Ancient | Paul Hudson |
| She Ancient | Maureen Guy |

*conductor:* Richard Armstrong
*producer:* Ian Watt-Smith
*designers:* Ralph Koltai (sets) and Annena
Stubbs (costumes)
*choreographer:* Terry Gilbert

## 1977

### THE BARBER OF SEVILLE (Rossini)
25 January, Theatr Clwyd, Mold

| | |
|---|---|
| Fiorello | James Miller-Coburn |
| Count Almaviva | Ryland Davies |
| Figaro | Thomas Allen |
| Rosina | Beverley Humphreys |
| Dr Bartolo | Thomas Hemsley |
| Berta | Menai Davies |
| Ambrogio | Ieuan Davies |
| Don Basilio | Geoffrey Moses |
| Officer | Gordon Whyte |
| Notary | David Tagg |

*conductor:* Wyn Davies
*producer:* William Gaskill
*designer:* William Dudley

### I MASNADIERI (Verdi)
29 March, New Theatre, Cardiff

| | |
|---|---|
| Massimiliano | Richard Van Allan |
| Carlo | Kenneth Collins |
| Francesco | Terence Sharpe |
| Amalia | Suzanne Murphy |
| Arminio | John Treleaven |
| Moser | Geoffrey Moses |
| Rolla | Mark Hamilton |

*conductor:* Richard Armstrong
*producer:* Julian Hope
*designers:* Hayden Griffin (sets) and Carol
Lawrence (costumes)

### THE QUEEN OF SPADES (Tchaikovsky)
7 September, New Theatre, Cardiff

| | |
|---|---|
| Hermann | Allen Cathcart |
| Count Tomsky | Henry Newman |

| | |
|---|---|
| Tchekalinksy | Arthur Davies |
| Surin | David Gwynne |
| Tchaplitsky | Neville Ackerman |
| Narumov | Peter Massocchi |
| Prince Yeletsky | Russell Smythe |
| The Countess | Maureen Guy |
| Lisa | Evelyn Brunner |
| Pauline | Patricia Price |
| Governess | Menai Davies |
| Mascha | Mary Davies |
| Major Domo | Ieuan Davies |
| Empress | Svetlana Beriosova |

*conductor:* David Lloyd-Jones
*producer:* David William
*designers:* Wilfried Werz and Erika
Simmank-Heinze
*choreographer:* Angela Hardcastle

THE MARRIAGE OF FIGARO (Mozart)
15 November, New Theatre, Cardiff

| | |
|---|---|
| Figaro | John Rawnsley |
| Susanna | Meryl Drower |
| Dr Bartolo | David Gwynne |
| Marcellina | Menai Davies |
| Cherubino | Patricia Parker |
| Count Almaviva | Stuart Harling |
| Don Basilio | John Treleaven |
| Countess Almaviva | Felicity Lott |
| Antonio | Gordon Whyte |
| Don Curzio | Ralph Mason |
| Barbarina | Gloria Crane |
| 1st Girl | Gillian Clench |
| 2nd Girl | Anne Mason |

*conductor:* György Fischer
*producer:* Michael Geliot
*designer:* Alexander McPherson

LA BOHÈME (Puccini)
24 November, New Theatre, Cardiff

| | |
|---|---|
| Marcello | Terence Sharpe |
| Rodolfo | Mark Hamilton |
| Colline | Paul Hudson |
| Schaunard | Henry Newman |
| Benoit | Derek Barnes |
| Mimi | Vivien Townley |
| Parpignol | John Harris |
| Musetta | Catherine Wilson |
| Alcindoro | Peter Massocchi |

| | |
|---|---|
| Customs Official | Gordon Whyte |
| Customs Sergeant | Kenneth Pugh |

*conductor:* Richard Armstrong
*producer:* William Gaskill
*designers:* Hayden Griffin (sets) and Michael
Stennett (costumes)

## 1978

LET'S MAKE AN OPERA (Britten)
12 January, Sherman Theatre, Cardiff

| | |
|---|---|
| Black Bob | Peter Massocchi |
| Clem | Mark Hamilton |
| Miss Baggott | Caroline Baker |
| Rowan | Helen Field |
| Juliet | Margaret Baiton |

*conductor:* Julian Smith
*producer:* Sally Day
*designer:* Anthony McDonald

A MIDSUMMER NIGHT'S DREAM
(Britten) 24 January, Theatr Clwyd, Mold

| | |
|---|---|
| Oberon | James Bowman |
| Titania | Rita Cullis |
| Puck | Sylveste McCoy |
| Theseus | Roderick Kennedy |
| Hippolyta | Patricia Price |
| Lysander | Arthur Davies |
| Demetrius | Henry Newman |
| Hermia | Margaret Morgan |
| Helena | Suzanne Murphy |
| Bottom | Geraint Evans |
| Quince | David Gwynne |
| Flute | John Treleaven |
| Snug | Ralph Hamer |
| Snout | John Harris |
| Starveling | Julian Moyle |

*conductor:* Anthony Hose
*producer:* Ian Watt-Smith
*designer:* Alexander McPherson

ELEKTRA (Richard Strauss)
15 March, New Theatre, Cardiff

| | |
|---|---|
| Klytemnestra | Debria Brown |
| Elektra | Pauline Tinsley |
| Chrysothemis | Anne Evans |
| Aegistus | John Mitchinson |
| Orestes | Willard White |
| Orestes' Tutor | Peter Massocchi |

| | |
|---|---|
| Confidante | Menai Davies |
| Trainbearer | Anne Mason |
| Servant | Mark Hamilton |
| Old Retainer | Gordon Whyte |
| Overseer | Suzanne Murphy |
| Maidservants | Caroline Baker |
| | Anne Mason |
| | Menai Davies |
| | Vivien Townley |
| | Rita Cullis |

conductor: Richard Armstrong
producer: Harry Kupfer
designer: Wilfried Werz

PETER GRIMES (Britten)
16 May, New Theatre, Cardiff

| | |
|---|---|
| Hobson | Paul Hudson |
| Swallow | David Gwynne |
| Peter Grimes | John Mitchinson |
| Ned Keene | Russell Smythe |
| The Rector | Neville Ackerman |
| Bob Boles | John Treleaven |
| Auntie | Menai Davies |
| Two Nieces | Rita Cullis |
| | Mary Davies |
| Mrs Sedley | Maureen Guy |
| Ellen Orford | Josephine Barstow |
| Capt Balstrode | Terence Sharpe |
| Dr Crabbe | David Tagg |
| John | David Horton |

conductor: Richard Armstrong
producer: John Copley
designers: Henry Bardon (sets) and Michael
Stennett (costumes)

THE MAKROPOULOS CASE (Janáček)
6 September, New Theatre, Cardiff

| | |
|---|---|
| Emilia Marty | Elisabeth Söderström |
| Albert Gregor | Mark Hamilton |
| Vitek | Edward Byles |
| Kristina | Helen Field |
| Jaroslav Prus | Neil Howlett |
| Janek | Arthur Davies |
| Dr Kolenaty | Thomas Hemsley |
| Charwoman | Menai Davies |
| Hauk-Sendorf | Nigel Douglas |
| Chambermaid | Caroline Baker |

conductor: Richard Armstrong
producer: David Pountney
designer: Maria Björnson

AN EVENING WITH PUCCINI
6 October, Builth Wells

| | |
|---|---|
| Cast | Kenneth Collins |
| | Helen Field |
| | Suzanne Murphy |
| | Terence Sharpe |
| | Eric Flynn |

muscial director: Wyn Davies
producer: John Moody

MADAM BUTTERFLY (Puccini)
1 November, New Theatre, Cardiff

| | |
|---|---|
| Cio-Cio-San | Magdaléna Falewicz |
| Suzuki | Phyllis Cannan |
| Kate Pinkerton | Rite Cullis |
| Pinkerton | John Treleaven |
| Goro | John Harris |
| Sharpless | Henry Newman |
| Prince Yamadori | Julian Moyle |
| The Bonze | Geoffrey Moses |
| Priest | Gordon Whyte |
| High Commissioner | Peter Massocchi |

conductor: Guido Ajmone-Marsan
producer: Joachim Herz
designers: Reinhart Zimmermann (sets);
Eleonore Kleiber (costumes)

# 1979

THE TURN OF THE SCREW (Britten)
12 January, Sherman Theatre, Cardiff

| | |
|---|---|
| Prologue | Philip Langridge |
| Governess | Felicity Lott |
| Mrs Grose | Menai Davies |
| Miss Jessel | Rita Cullis |
| Flora | Cheryl Edwards |
| Miles | David Hubbard |
| Peter Quint | Arthur Davies |

conductor: Anthony Hose
producer: Adrian Slack
designer: David Fielding

MONSIEUR CHOUFLEURI'S AT
HOME
(Offenbach) 18 January, Theatr y Werin,
Aberystwyth

| | |
|---|---|
| Ernestine | Meryl Drower |
| Chrysodule Babylas | Mark Hamilton |
| Monsieur Choufleuri | Julian Moyle |
| Petermann | Paul Gyton |

Balandard          Ralph Mason
Mme Balandard      Timothy German

*conductor:* Julian Smith
*producer:* Michael Geliot
*designer:* Steven Gregory

in double-bill with

THE SONG OF FORTUNIO (Offenbach)

Fortunio           Julian Moyle
Laurette           Meryl Drower
Landry             Gloria Crane
Guillaume          Lorna Washington
Saturnin           Gillian Clench
Sylvain            Pamela Geddes
Valentine          Mark Hamilton
Babette            Ralph Mason
Friquet            Timothy German

*conductor:* Julian Smith
*producer:* Michael Geliot
*designer:* Steven Gregory


THE MAGIC FLUTE (Mozart)
20 January, Theatr Clwyd, Mold

Tamino             John Treleaven
1st Lady           Helen Field
2nd Lady           Anne Mason
3rd Lady           Caroline Baker
Papageno           Russell Smythe
Queen of the Night Suzanne Murphy
Monostatos         Derek Barnes
Pamina             Eilene Hannan
Speaker            Henry Newman
Sarastro           David Gwynne
1st Priest         Ieuan Davies
2nd Priest         Henry Newman
Papagena           Mary Davies
1st Armoured Man   Neville Ackerman
2nd Armoured Man   Peter Massocchi

*conductor:* György Fischer
*producer:* Göran Järvefelt
*designer:* Carl Friedrich Oberle


LA TRAVIATA (Verdi)
24 April, New Theatre, Cardiff

Violetta           Suzanne Murphy
Flora              Jennifer Rhys-Davies
Marquis d'Obigny   Russell Smythe
Baron Douphol      Julian Moyle
Dr Grenvil         David Gwynne

Gaston             Neville Ackerman
Alfredo            John Treleaven
Annina             Caroline Baker
Giorgio Germont    Henry Newman
Giuseppe           Timothy German
Peasant            Gordon Whyte
Flora's Servant    John King

*conductor:* Guido Ajmone-Marsan
*producer:* Stewart Trotter
*designer:* Tim Goodchild


TRISTAN UND ISOLDE (Wagner)
8 September, New Theatre, Cardiff

Isolde             Linda Esther Gray
Brangäne           Anne Wilkens
Tristan            John Mitchinson
Kurwenal           Bent Norup
King Marke         Gwynne Howell
Melot              Nicholas Folwell
Shepherd           Arthur Davies
Helmsman           Geoffrey Moses
Sailor             Mark Hamilton

*conductor:* Reginald Goodall
*producer:* Peter Brenner
*designer:* Klaus Teepe


TCHAIKOVSKY AT THE OPERA
19 October, Treorchy

*Cast*              Rita Cullis
                    Phyllis Cannan
                    Arthur Davies
                    Julian Moyle
                    David Gwynne

*musical director:* Derek Clark
*producer:* Sally Day


ERNANI (Verdi)
30 October, New Theatre, Cardiff

Ernani             Kenneth Collins
Elvira             Suzanne Murphy
Giovanna           Catherine Savory
Don Carlo          Cornelius Opthof
de Silva           Richard Van Allan
Jago               Geoffrey Moses
Don Riccardo       Mark Hamilton

*conductor:* Richard Armstrong
*producer:* Elijah Moshinsky
*designer:* Maria Björnson

## 1980

### THE CORONATION OF POPPEA
(Monteverdi) 19 January, Theatr Clwyd,
Mold

| | |
|---|---|
| Fortune | Jennifer Rhys-Davies |
| Virtue | Rita Cullis |
| Amor | Margaret Baiton |
| Ottone | Russell Smythe |
| 1st Soldier | John Harris |
| 2nd Soldier | Derek Barnes |
| Nero | Arthur Davies |
| Poppea | Eiddwen Harrhy |
| Arnalta | Menai Davies |
| Ottavia | Catherine Savory |
| Nutrice | Heather Fryer |
| Valletto | Harry Nicoll |
| Seneca | Stafford Dean |
| Pallas Athene | Cheryl Edwards |
| Drusilla | Mary Davies |
| Damigella | Gloria Crane |
| Liberto | Henry Newman |
| Lucano | Neville Ackerman |
| Lictor | Arwel Huw Morgan |

*conductor:* Wyn Davies
*producer:* Michael Geliot
*designer:* Annena Stubbs
*choreographer:* Selena Gilbert


### EUGENE ONEGIN (Tchaikovsky)
27 February, New Theatre, Cardiff

| | |
|---|---|
| Madam Larina | Helen Watts |
| Tatyana | Josephine Barstow |
| Olga | Cynthia Buchan |
| Filipyevna | Menai Davies |
| Eugene Onegin | Thomas Allen |
| Lensky | Anthony Rolfe Johnson |
| Prince Gremin | David Gwynne |
| Captain | John King |
| Zaretsky | Julian Moyle |
| M. Triquet | Neville Ackerman |
| Guillot | Charles Lewis |

*conductor:* Mark Ermler
*producer:* Andrei Serban
*designer:* Michael Yeargan


### THE JACOBIN (Dvořák)
14.May, New Theatre, Cardiff

| | |
|---|---|
| Julie | Suzanne Murphy |
| Terinka | Helen Field |
| Jiri | Arthur Davies |

| | |
|---|---|
| Benda | Edward Byles |
| Bohus | Henry Newman |
| Filip | Julian Moyle |
| Adolf | Phillip Joll |
| Vilem | David Gwynne |
| Lotinka | Heather Fryer |

*conductor:* Albert Rosen
*producer:* Adrian Slack
*designer:* John Cervenka


### TOSCA (Puccini)
2 September, New Theatre, Cardiff

| | |
|---|---|
| Angelotti | Geoffrey Moses |
| Sacristan | Julian Moyle |
| Cavaradossi | Kenneth Collins |
| Tosca | Helena Döse |
| Scarpia | Anthony Baldwin |
| Spoletta | John Harris |
| Sciarrone | Mark Nelson |
| Shepherd Boy | Margaret Baiton |
| Gaoler | Gordon Whyte |

*conductor:* Guido Ajmone-Marsan
*producer:* John Copley
*designers:* John Pascoe (sets) and Michael
Stennett (costumes)


### THE SERVANTS (William Mathias)
World Première 15 September, New Theatre,
Cardiff

| | |
|---|---|
| Basil | Nigel Douglas |
| Oriane | Eiddwen Harrhy |
| Marina | Claire Powell |
| Patrice | Phillip Joll |
| Peter Jack | Henry Newman |
| Maxim | Timothy German |
| Father Ambrose | David Gwynne |
| Hans Joseph | Julian Moyle |
| Mikey | Neil Rowsell |
| General Klein | Phillip Joll |

*conductor:* Anthony Hose
*producer:* Adrian Slack
*designers:* Patrick Robertson and Rosemary
Vercoe


### THE CUNNING LITTLE VIXEN
(Janáček)
5 November, New Theatre, Cardiff

| | |
|---|---|
| Dragonfly | David Turner |
| Badger | Julian Moyle |

| | |
|---|---|
| Forester | Phillip Joll |
| Mosquito | Paul Gyton |
| Dog | Nicholas Folwell |
| Forester's Wife | Jennifer Rhys-Davies |
| Vixen | Helen Field |
| Forester's Son | Margaret Baiton |
| His Friend | Doreen O'Neill |
| Spirit of Vixen | Elaine Bryce |
| Cock | Richard Morton |
| Chief Hen | Diane Fuge |
| Hens | Caroline Baker |
| | Mary Davies |
| | Menai Davies |
| | Pamela Geddes |
| Parson | David Gwynne |
| Schoolmaster | Nigel Douglas |
| Innkeeper | Phillip Guy-Bromley |
| Fox | Arthur Davies |
| Owl | Gillian Clench |
| Jay | Allison Deakin |
| Woodpecker | Timothy German |
| Poacher | Geoffrey Moses |
| Innkeeper's Wife | Menai Davies |

*conductor:* Richard Armstrong
*producer:* David Pountney
*designer:* Maria Björnson
*choreographer:* Stuart Hopps

## 1981

ALL FOR LOVE (devised by Nigel Douglas)
12 January, Builth Wells

| Cast | Rita Cullis |
|---|---|
| | Helen Field |
| | Nigel Douglas |
| | John Harris |
| | Robert Dean |
| | David Gwynne |

*musical director:* Guy Hamilton
*producer:* Timothy Tyrrel
*designer:* Dermot Hayes

RODELINDA (Handel)
13 January, Theatr Clwyd, Mold

| | |
|---|---|
| Rodelinda | Suzanne Murphy |
| Bertarido | Robin Martin-Oliver |
| Grimoaldo | Richard Morton |
| Garibaldo | Russell Smythe |
| Eduige | Eiddwen Harrhy |

| | |
|---|---|
| Unulfo | Catherine Savory |
| Flavio | Stephen Banbury |

*conductor:* Julian Smith
*producer:* Andrei Serban
*designer:* Michael Yeargan

DIE FRAU OHNE SCHATTEN (Richard Strauss)
21 February, New Theatre, Cardiff

| | |
|---|---|
| Emperor | Matti Kastu |
| Empress | Anne Evans |
| Nurse | Patricia Payne |
| Spirit Messenger | Geoffrey Moses |
| Guardian | Helen Field |
| Apparition | Timothy German |
| Falcon's Voice | Rita Cullis |
| Barak | Norman Bailey |
| Dyer's Wife | Pauline Tinsley |
| One-eyed brother | Russell Smythe |
| Hunchbacked brother | Arthur Davies |
| One-armed brother | Julian Moyle |
| Voice from Above | Catherine Savory |

*conductor:* Richard Armstrong
*producer:* Gilbert Deflo
*designer:* Carlo Tommasi

THE GREEK PASSION (Martinů)
29 April, New Theatre, Cardiff

| | |
|---|---|
| Grigoris | Richard Van Allan |
| Patriarcheas | Julian Moyle |
| Ladas | Arwel Huw Morgan |
| Michelis | John Harris |
| Kostandis | Phillip Joll |
| Yannakos | Arthur Davies |
| Manolios | John Mitchinson |
| Nikolios | Catherine Savory |
| Andonis | Neville Ackerman |
| Katerina | Helen Field |
| Lenio | Rita Cullis |
| Old Woman | Anne Morgan |
| Priester Fotis | Geoffrey Moses |
| Despinio | Lorna Washington |
| Old Man | David Gwynne |
| Panait | Richard Morton |

*conductor:* Charles Mackerras
*producer:* Michael Geliot
*designer :* John Gunter (sets) and Sally Gardner (costumes)

THE JOURNEY (John Metcalf)
World Première 12 June, Sherman Theatre, Cardiff

| | |
|---|---|
| The Story Teller | Julian Moyle |
| Nicola | Lesley Garrett |
| Gwen | Menai Davies |
| Scott | Timothy German |
| Craig | Henry Newman |
| Father | David Gwynne |
| Daughter | Yolande Jones |
| Old Man | Phillip Guy-Bromley |
| Running Man | Francis Roselaar-Green |
| Off-stage voice | Phillip Guy-Bromley |

*conductor:* Anthony Hose
*producer:* John Eaton
*designer:* Peter Mumford

FIDELIO (Beethoven)
5 September, New Theatre, Cardiff

| | |
|---|---|
| Jacquino | Richard Morton |
| Marzellina | Helen Field |
| Rocco | Stafford Dean |
| Leonore | Anne Evans |
| Don Pizarro | Richard Van Allan |
| 1st Prisoner | Ralph Mason |
| 2nd Prisoner | Peter Massocchi |
| Florestan | Dennis Bailey |
| Don Fernando | Phillip Joll |

*conductor:* Richard Armstrong
*producer:* Harry Kupfer
*designer:* Wilfried Werz

LA FORZA DEL DESTINO (Verdi)
3 November, New Theatre, Cardiff

| | |
|---|---|
| Marchese di Calatrava | David Gwynne |
| Leonora | Elizabeth Vaughan |
| Curra | Menai Davies |
| Alvaro | Moises Parker |
| Mayor | Peter Massocchi |
| Don Carlo | Norman Phillips |
| Trabuco | Neville Ackerman |
| Preziosilla | Claire Powell |
| Fra Melitone | Nicholas Folwell |
| Father Guardian | Don Garrard |
| Surgeon | Kenneth Pugh |

*conductor:* Richard Armstrong
*producer:* Joachim Herz
*designers:* Reinhart Zimmermann (sets) and Eleonore Kleiber (costumes)

1982

TAMBURLAINE (Handel)
15 January, Theatr Clwyd, Mold

| | |
|---|---|
| Andronicus | Brian Gordon |
| Bajazet | Richard Morton |
| Tamburlaine | Robin Martin-Oliver |
| Asteria | Eiddwen Harrhy |
| Irene | Caroline Baker |
| Leone | Nicholas Folwell |

*conductor:* Anthony Hose
*producer and designer:* Philip Prowse

THE BARTERED BRIDE (Smetana)
23 February, New Theatre, Cardiff

| | |
|---|---|
| Krusina | Julian Moyle |
| Ludmila | April Cantelo |
| Marenka | Helen Field |
| Tobias Micha | Donald Francke |
| Hata | Menai Davies |
| Vasek | Harry Nicoll |
| Jenik | Warren Ellsworth |
| Kecal | Derek Hammond-Stroud |
| Ringmaster | Jeffrey Lawton |
| Esmeralda | Lesley Garrett |
| Indian | Gareth Rhys-Davies |

*conductor:* Mark Ermler
*producer:* Rudolf Noelte
*designers:* Jan Schlubach (sets); Elisabeth Urbancic (costumes)

I PURITANI (Bellini)
10 March, New Theatre, Cardiff

| | |
|---|---|
| Lord Walton | David Gwynne |
| Sir George Walton | Geoffrey Moses |
| Lord Arthur Talbot | Dennis O'Neill |
| Sir Richard Forth | Henry Newman |
| Sir Bruno Robertson | John Harris |
| Queen Henrietta | Catherine Savory |
| Elvira | Suzanne Murphy |

*conductor:* Julian Smith
*producer:* Andrei Serban
*designer:* Michael Yeargan

KATYA KABANOVA (Janáček)
18 May, New Theatre, Cardiff

| | |
|---|---|
| Kudryash | Arthur Davies |
| Glasha | Elizabeth-Anne Price |
| Dikoy | David Gwynne |

| Boris | Dennis Bailey |
|---|---|
| Feklusha | Anne Morgan |
| Kabanicha | Rita Gorr |
| Tikhon Kabanova | Jeffrey Lawton |
| Katya Kabanova | Elisabeth Söderström |
| Varvara | Cynthia Buchan |
| Kuligin | Julian Moyle |

conductor: Richard Armstrong
producer: David Pountney
designer: Maria Björnson

DON GIOVANNI (Mozart)
24 June, Theatr Clwyd, Mold

| Leporello | Nicholas Folwell |
|---|---|
| Don Giovanni | Henry Newman |
| Donna Anna | Rita Cullis |
| The Commendatore | William Mackie |
| Don Ottavio | Richard Morton |
| Donna Elvira | Jennifer Rhys-Davies |
| Zerlina | Doreen O'Neill |
| Masetto | Phillip Guy-Bromley |

conductor: David Seaman
producer: Michael Geliot
designer: Ralph Koltai

UN BALLO IN MASCHERA (Verdi)
4 September, New Theatre, Cardiff

| Count Ribbing | Arwel Huw Morgan |
|---|---|
| Count Horn | William Mackie |
| Oscar | Rosamund Illing |
| Gustav III | Dennis O'Neill |
| Anckarström | Donald Maxwell |
| Judge | Jeffrey Lawton |
| Mme. Arvidson | Anne Collins |
| Cristian | Phillip Guy-Bromley |
| Amelia | Suzanne Murphy |
| Servant | Ieuan Davies |

conductor: Richard Armstrong
producer: Göran Järvefelt
designer: Carl Friedrich Oberle

ANDREA CHÉNIER (Giordano)
27 October, New Theatre, Cardiff

| Majordomo | John King |
|---|---|
| Charles Gérard | Ettore Nova |
| Maddalena | Elizabeth Vaughan |
| Countess | Menai Davies |
| Bersi | Beverley Mills |
| Fléville | Gareth Rhys-Davies |
| Abbé | Paul Gyton |
| Andrea Chénier | Kenneth Collins |
| Mathieu | Phillip Guy-Bromley |
| L'Incroyable | John Harris |
| Roucher | Henry Newman |
| Old Madelon | Anne Morgan |
| Dumas | Ralph Hamer |
| Fouquier-Tinville | Peter Massocchi |
| Schmidt | Mark Nelson |

conductor: Julian Smith
producer: Michael Geliot
designers: John Gunter (sets) and Sheelagh
Killeen (costumes)

FROM THE HOUSE OF THE DEAD
(Janáček) 10 November, New Theatre,
Cardiff

| Goryanchikov | Robert Carpenter Turner |
|---|---|
| Aleya | Yolande Jones |
| Filka Morozov | John Mitchinson |
| Large Prisoner | Jeffrey Lawton |
| Prison Governor | David Gwynne |
| Small Prisoner | Nicholas Folwell |
| Old Prisoner | Osvaldo Valente |
| Skuratov | Graham Clark |
| Chekunov | Julian Moyle |
| Drunken Prisoner | Derek Barnes |
| Cook Prisoner | James Miller-Coburn |
| Blacksmith Prisoner | Ralph Hamer |
| Priest | Julian Moyle |
| Young Prisoner | Timothy German |
| Prostitute | Heather Fryer |
| Don Juan | William Mackie |
| Kedril | Neville Ackerman |
| Shapkin | Nigel Douglas |
| Shishkov | Donald Maxwell |
| Cherevin | Ralph Mason |
| Guard | Mark Hamilton |

conductor: Richard Armstrong
producer: David Pountney
designer: Maria Björnson

## 1983

DEAR IVOR 8 January, St David's Hall,
Cardiff

| Cast | Simon Butteriss |
|---|---|
| | Rosemary Ashe |
| | Peter Savidge |

Anne Collins
Beverley Mills

*musical director:* Guy Hamilton
*producer:* Richard Digby Day
*designer:* Hugh Durrant


PARSIFAL (Wagner)
1 March, New Theatre, Cardiff

| | |
|---|---|
| Gurnemanz | Donald McIntyre |
| Squires | Mary Davies |
| | Margaret Morgan |
| | John Harris |
| | Neville Ackerman |
| 1st Knight | Timothy German |
| 2nd Knight | William Mackie |
| Kundry | Linda Esther Gray |
| Amfortas | Phillip Joll |
| Parsifal | Warren Ellsworth |
| Titurel | David Gwynne |
| Voice | Caroline Baker |
| Klingsor | Nicholas Folwell |
| Flowermaidens | Elizabeth Ritchie |
| | Christine Teare |
| | Kathryn Harries |
| | Rita Cullis |
| | Elizabeth Collier |
| | Catriona Bell |

*conductor:* Anthony Negus
*producer:* Mike Ashman
*designer:* Peter Mumford
*choreographer:* Caroline Lamb


CARMEN (Bizet)
17 May, New Theatre, Cardiff

| | |
|---|---|
| Morales | Phillip Guy-Bromley |
| Micaela | Helen Field |
| Zuniga | David Gwynne |
| Don José | Jacque Trussel |
| Carmen | Jennifer Jones |
| Frasquita | Mary Davies |
| Mercedes | Beverley Mills |
| Lillas Pastia | Junior Walker |
| Andres | Peter Mandell |
| Escamillo | Henry Newman |
| Dancairo | Nicholas Folwell |
| Remendado | Ralph Mason |

*conductor:* Kees Bakels
*producer:* Lucian Pintilie
*designers:* Radu and Miruna Boruzescu
*choreographer:* Stuart Hopps


THE DRAMA OF AIDA 5 July, Theatr
Clwyd, Mold

| | |
|---|---|
| Aida | Anne Williams-King |
| Amneris | Beverley Mills |
| Radames | Donald Stephenson |
| Amonasro | Hugh Macleod |
| Ramphis | David Gwynne |

*conductor:* Richard Armstrong
*producer:* Andrei Serban
*designer:* Jacques Schmidt


THE RHINEGOLD (Wagner)
21 October, New Theatre, Cardiff

| | |
|---|---|
| Woglinde | Marie-Claire O'Reirdan |
| Wellgunde | Caroline Saxon |
| Flosshilde | Marion McCullough |
| Alberich | Nicholas Folwell |
| Fricka | Patricia Payne |
| Wotan | Phillip Joll |
| Freia | Anne Williams-King |
| Fasolt | John Tranter |
| Fafner | Roderick Earle |
| Froh | Richard Morton |
| Donner | Donald Maxwell |
| Loge | Nigel Douglas |
| Mime | John Harris |
| Erda | Anne Collins |

*conductor:* Richard Armstrong
*producer:* Göran Järvefelt
*designer:* Carl Friedrich Oberle


JOSÉ'S CARMEN 14 November, Maestag

| | |
|---|---|
| Cast | Beverley Mills |
| | Bronwen Mills |
| | Paul Strathearn |
| | Henry Newman |

*pianist:* Jane Robinson
*producer:* Mike Ashman


## 1984

THE VALKYRIE (Wagner)
18 February, New Theatre, Cardiff

| | |
|---|---|
| Siegmund | Warren Ellsworth |
| Sieglinde | Kathryn Harries |
| Hunding | Roderick Earle |
| Wotan | Phillip Joll |
| Brünnhilde | Anne Evans |
| Fricka | Patricia Payne |

| | |
|---|---|
| Gerhilde | Elizabeth Byrne |
| Helmwige | Christine Teare |
| Ortlinde | Evelyn Nicholson |
| Waltraute | Mary Hamilton |
| Rossweisse | Wendy Verco |
| Siegrune | Helen Willis |
| Grimgerde | Caroline Saxon |
| Schwertleite | Anne Morgan |

conductor: Reginald Goodall
producer: Göran Järvefelt
designer: Carl Friedrich Oberle

## THE MERRY WIDOW (Lehár)
28 February, New Theatre, Cardiff

| | |
|---|---|
| Baron Mirko Zeta | Thomas Hemsley |
| Valencienne | Kate Flowers |
| Count Danilo | Thomas Allen |
| Bogdanowitsch | James Miller-Coburn |
| Sylviane | Gillian Clench |
| Kromow | Gordon Whyte |
| Olga | Eirian Davies |
| Pritschitsch | John King |
| Praskowia | Margaret Morgan |
| Njegus | Julian Moyle |
| Hanna Glawari | Suzanne Murphy |
| Camille | Robin Leggate |
| Vicomte Cascade | Peter Savidge |
| Raoul de St Briocha | Timothy German |
| Lolo | Mary Davies |
| Dodo | Cheryl Edwards |
| Joujou | Margaret Baiton |
| Froufrou | Marie-Claire O'Reirdan |
| Cloclo | Lorna Washington |
| Margot | Marion McCullough |

conductor: György Fischer
producer: Andrei Serban
designers: Michael Yeargan, Jacques Schmidt and Emmanuel Peduzzi
choreographer: Kate Flatt

## LA BOHÈME (Puccini)
8 May, New Theatre, Cardiff

| | |
|---|---|
| Marcello | Donald Maxwell |
| Rodolfo | John Fowler |
| Colline | Matthew Best |
| Schaunard | Nicholas Folwell |
| Benoit | James Miller-Coburn |
| Mimi | Helen Field |
| Parpignol | John Harris |
| Musetta | Suzanne Murphy |
| Alcindoro | Peter Massocchi |

| | |
|---|---|
| Customs Official | Ralph Hamer |
| Sergeant | Phillip Guy-Bromley |

conductor: Kees Bakels
producer: Göran Järvefelt
designer: Michael Yeargan

## DON GIOVANNI (Mozart)
27 October, New Theatre, Cardiff

| | |
|---|---|
| Leporello | Nicholas Folwell |
| Don Giovanni | William Shimell |
| Donna Anna | Anne Evans |
| The Commendatore | John Tranter |
| Don Ottavio | Laurence Dale |
| Donna Elvira | Elaine Woods |
| Zerlina | Beverley Mills |
| Masetto | Jonathan Best |

conductor: Charles Mackerras
producer: Ruth Berghaus
designer: Marie-Luise Strandt

## THE THREEPENNY OPERA (Weill)
21 December, Dolman Theatre, Newport

| | |
|---|---|
| Peachum | Roger Bryson |
| Mrs Peachum | Menai Davies |
| Polly Peachum | Yolande Jones |
| Macheath | Robert Dean |
| Brown | James Miller-Coburn |
| Lucy | Margaret Baiton |
| Filch/Matthew | Mark Nelson |
| Jenny | Gillian Clench |
| Smith | Gareth Rhys-Davies |
| Whores | Anne Morgan |
| | Patricia Anne Hughes |
| Pimps | Peter Massocchi |
| | Gordon Whyte |

conductor: Andrew Greenwood
producer: Ceri Sherlock
designer: Simon Banham

## 1985

## SIEGFRIED (Wagner)
23 February, New Theatre, Cardiff

| | |
|---|---|
| Mime | John Harris |
| Siegfried | Jeffrey Lawton |
| The Wanderer | Phillip Joll |
| Alberich | Nicholas Folwell |
| Fafner | John Tranter |
| Woodbird | Kate Flowers |

Erda                Anne Collins
Brünnhilde          Anne Evans

*conductor:* Richard Armstrong
*producer:* Göran Järvefelt
*designer:* Carl Friedrich Oberle


NORMA (Bellini)
8 March, New Theatre, Cardiff

Oroveso             Harry Dworchak
Pollione            Frederick Donaldson
Flavio              Timothy German
Norma               Suzanne Murphy
Adalgisa            Kathryn Harries
Clotilde            Elizabeth-Ann Price

*conductor:* Julian Smith
*producer:* Andrei Serban
*designer:* Michael Yeargan


RIGOLETTO (Verdi)
14 May, New Theatre, Cardiff

Duke of Mantua      Dennis O'Neill
Borsa               Timothy German
Countess Ceprano    Cheryl Baker
Rigoletto           Donald Maxwell
Marullo             Mark Holland
Count Ceprano       Ralph Hamer
Count Monterone     Donald Adams
Sparafucile         Sean Rea
Gilda               Anne Dawson
Giovanna            Patricia Ann Hughes
Maddalena           Wendy Verco

*conductor:* Richard Armstrong
*producer:* Lucian Pintilie
*designers:* Radu Boruzescu (sets) and Miruna
Boruzescu (costumes)
*choreographer:* Niloufar F. Sheybany


GÖTTERDÄMMERUNG (Wagner)
14 September, New Theatre, Cardiff

First Norn          Anne Collins
Second Norn         Caroline Baker
Third Norn          Elizabeth Byrne
Brünnhilde          Anne Evans
Siegfried           Jeffrey Lawton
Gunther             Jacek Strauch
Hagen               John Tranter
Gutrune             Kathryn Harries
Waltraute           Patricia Payne
Alberich            Nicholas Folwell

Woglinde            Eirian Davies
Wellgunde           Deborah Stuart-Roberts
Fosshilde           Patricia Bardon

*conductor:* Richard Armstrong
*producer:* Göran Järvefelt
*designer:* Carl Friedrich Oberle


COSÌ FAN TUTTE (Mozart)
9 November, New Theatre, Cardiff

Ferrando            Laurence Dale
Guglielmo           Mark Holland
Don Alfonso         Thomas Hemsley
Fiordiligi          Elaine Woods
Dorabella           Delia Wallis
Despina             Andrea Bolton

*conductor:* György Fischer
*producer:* Liviu Ciulei
*designers:* Radu Boruzescu (sets) and Miruna
Boruzescu (costumes)


VERDI'S MESSIAH (Julian Mitchell)
24 October, Taliesin Theatre, Swansea

*Singers*           Christine Teare
                    Wendy Verco
                    Michael Burch
                    Jonathan Best
*Actors*            Richard Griffiths
                    (Verdi)
                    Zoe Wanamaker
                    (Strepponi)
                    Malcolm Storry
                    (Ricordi)
                    David Lyon (Faccio)
                    Ian Charleson (Boito)

*musical director:* Martin André
*producer:* Howard Davies
*designer:* Bob Crowley

# APPENDIX B: CONDUCTORS
# 1946–1985

THIS LIST includes only those conductors who have conducted stage performances, not concerts, and gives the year in which they first conducted an opera.

GUIDO AJMONE-MARSAN

La Bohème 1976
Madam Butterfly 1978
La Traviata 1979
Tosca 1980

MARTIN ANDRÉ

The Drama of Aida 1984
Jenůfa 1984
Ernani 1984
Rigoletto 1985
Madam Butterfly 1985

RICHARD ARMSTRONG
(Musical Director 1973–1986)

The Marriage of Figaro 1969
Boris Godunov 1969
Carmen 1969
The Barber of Seville 1970
Aida 1970
La Bohème 1970
Simon Boccanegra 1970
Falstaff 1971
Lulu 1971
Turandot 1972
Nabucco 1972
Billy Budd 1972
Rigoletto 1973
Don Carlos 1973
Idomeneo 1973
Madam Butterfly 1973
The Magic Flute 1974
The Beach of Falesá 1974
The Flying Dutchman 1974

L'Elisir d'Amore 1974
Manon Lescaut 1975
Jenůfa 1975
The Pearl Fishers 1976
Il Trovatore 1976
Otello 1976
The Midsummer Marriage 1976
I Masnadieri 1977
Elektra 1978
Peter Grimes 1978
The Makropoulos Case 1978
Ernani 1979
Tristan und Isolde 1980
The Cunning Little Vixen 1980
Die Frau ohne Schatten 1981
La Traviata 1981
Fidelio 1981
La Forza del Destino 1981
Katya Kabanova 1982
Un Ballo in Maschera 1982
From the House of the Dead 1982
The Drama of Aida 1983
The Rhinegold 1983
The Valkyrie 1984
The Greek Passion 1984
Siegfried 1985
Götterdämmerung 1985

DAVID ATHERTON

The Pearl Fishers 1973
La Bohème 1974

KEES BAKELS

The Magic Flute 1981
Carmen 1983
La Bohème 1984


BRYAN BALKWILL
(Musical Director 1963–1966)

I Lombardi 1962
The Seraglio 1963
The Marriage of Figaro 1963
William Tell 1963
Macbeth 1963
The Barber of Seville 1964
La Bohème 1964
Madam Butterfly 1964
Fidelio 1964
Tosca 1964
Moses 1965
Die Fledermaus 1965
La Traviata 1965
Don Giovanni 1966
The Parlour 1966
Il Tabarro 1966
Don Pasquale 1966
The Bartered Bride 1966
Nabucco 1967
Carmen 1967


CLARK BEDFORD

Rigoletto 1973


STEUART BEDFORD

Idomeneo 1974


FREDERICK BEREND
(Musical Director 1953–1955)

Nabucco 1953
Die Fledermaus 1953
Madam Butterfly 1953
The Bartered Bride 1954
The Sicilian Vespers 1954


NICHOLAS BRAITHWAITE

Don Pasquale 1966
Nabucco 1967
Tosca 1968
La Traviata 1969


WARWICK BRAITHWAITE
(Musical Director 1956–1961)

Madam Butterfly 1951
La Traviata 1951
Il Trovatore 1952
La Bohème 1956
The Barber of Seville 1956
Mefistofele 1957
Rigoletto 1958
Die Fledermaus 1958
Tosca 1958
I Pagliacci 1958
Faust 1959
I Lombardi 1959
May Night 1959


DEREK CLARK

Tchaikovsky at the Opera 1979
Tamburlaine 1982
Così fan tutte 1985


NICHOLAS CLEOBURY

The Marriage of Figaro 1981
La Traviata 1981


WYN DAVIES

L'Elisir d'Amore 1974
Così fan tutte 1975
The Grand Duchess of Gerolstein 1975
The Seraglio 1976
La Bohème 1976
The Barber of Seville 1977
The Marriage of Figaro 1977
Don Carlos 1978
The Magic Flute 1979
The Coronation of Poppea 1980
Eugene Onegin 1980


JACQUES DELACÔTE

Eugene Onegin 1982


FRANK DOOLAN

Die Fledermaus 1966
The Seraglio 1966
La Bohème 1967
Don Giovanni 1967


EDWARD DOWNES

The Flying Dutchman 1975

MARK ERMLER

Eugene Onegin 1980
The Bartered Bride 1982
Tosca 1982
Carmen 1983


DAVID GRUFFYDD EVANS

Macbeth 1969


GYÖRGY FISCHER

The Magic Flute 1973
Così fan tutte 1975
The Seraglio 1976
The Marriage of Figaro 1977
The Merry Widow 1984


VICTOR FLEMING

Faust 1946
Carmen 1947
The Bartered Bride 1949
Cavalleria Rusticana 1949
I Pagliacci 1949


MYER FREDMAN

La Traviata 1966
Don Giovanni 1967


LOUIS FRÉMAUX

The Pearl Fishers 1979


LIONEL FRIEND

La Traviata 1969
The Barber of Seville 1970
La Bohème 1970
The Magic Flute 1971


PETER GELLHORN

Carmen 1949
Madam Butterfly 1949
La Traviata 1949


REGINALD GOODALL

Tristan und Isolde 1979
The Valkyrie 1984


ANDREW GREENWOOD

Don Giovanni 1984
The Threepenny Opera 1984
Carmen 1985
Tosca 1985
Rigoletto 1985


CHARLES GROVES
(Musical Director 1961–1963)

Il Trovatore 1952
Rigoletto 1953
La Traviata 1953
Madam Butterfly 1953
Nabucco 1954
Tosca 1955
The Sicilian Vespers 1956
Cavalleria Rusticana 1956
I Pagliacci 1956
I Lombardi 1957
The Battle 1960
La Bohème 1961
The Barber of Seville 1961
William Tell 1961
The Marriage of Figaro 1962
Lohengrin 1962


GUY HAMILTON

All for Love 1981
Un Ballo in Maschera 1983
Norma 1985


ANTHONY HOSE

The Barber of Seville 1969
The Marriage of Figaro 1969
Nabucco 1970
Die Fledermaus 1970
La Traviata 1971
Aida 1971
The Magic Flute 1971
Simon Boccanegra 1971
Don Giovanni 1972
Rigoletto 1972
Madam Butterfly 1973
The Pearl Fishers 1973
L'Elisir d'Amore 1974
The Flying Dutchman 1974
La Bohème 1974
The Grand Duchess of Gerolstein 1975
Albert Herring 1976
Il Trovatore 1976
Boris Godunov 1976

The Midsummer Marriage 1976
The Queen of Spades 1977
A Midsummer Night's Dream 1978
The Turn of the Screw 1979
Turandot 1979
Ernani 1979
The Jacobin 1980
The Servants 1980
The Journey 1981
The Greek Passion 1981
Tamburlaine 1982
Eugene Onegin 1982

## ARWEL HUGHES

Faust 1950
Menna 1953
Serch Yw'r Doctor 1960

## OWAIN ARWEL HUGHES

Così fan tutte 1970

## HAYDN JAMES

Il Trovatore 1951
Cavalleria Rusticana 1951
I Pagliacci 1951

## IVOR JOHN

I Pagliacci 1946
Faust 1946
Carmen 1947
La Traviata 1948
Madam Butterfly 1948
Die Fledermaus 1951
The Bartered Bride 1954
The Sicilian Vespers 1956
Nabucco 1957

## SIMON JOLY

The Barber of Seville 1977

## JAMES LEVINE

Aida 1970
The Barber of Seville 1970

## DAVID LLOYD-JONES

Carmen 1967
The Queen of Spades 1977

## JAMES LOCKHART
(Musical Director 1968–1973)

Boris Godunov 1968
The Barber of Seville 1968
Carmen 1968
La Traviata 1969
Macbeth 1969
Nabucco 1969
Fidelio 1969
Falstaff 1969
Così fan tutte 1970
Aida 1970
La Bohème 1970
Die Fledermaus 1970
Simon Boccanegra 1970
The Magic Flute 1971
Lulu 1971
Rigoletto 1972
Don Giovanni 1972
Billy Budd 1972
Madam Butterfly 1973
Don Carlos 1973
Otello 1975

## CHARLES MACKERRAS

The Tales of Hoffmann 1950
The Bartered Bride 1950
Die Fledermaus 1950
May Night 1961
The Greek Passion 1981
Don Giovanni 1984

## FRANCO MANNINO

Falstaff 1971
Aida 1971

## JOHN MATHESON

Madam Butterfly 1967
Carmen 1968
La Traviata 1968

## JOHN MAUCERI

Don Carlos 1974
The Barber of Seville 1974

## KENNETH MONTGOMERY

Simon Boccanegra 1974

## WYN MORRIS

Il Trovatore 1960
La Bohème 1960

## ANTHONY NEGUS

Fidelio 1981
Parsifal 1983
The Rhinegold 1983
The Magic Flute 1984
The Greek Passion 1984
Siegfried 1985
Götterdämmerung 1985

## GRZEGORZ NOWAK

Tosca 1985

## IDLOES OWEN
(Musical Director 1944–1952)

Cavalleria Rusticana 1946

## JOHN PRYCE-JONES

The Marriage of Figaro 1970
The Barber of Seville 1971
Aida 1971
L'Elisir d'Amore 1974
The Grand Duchess of Gerolstein 1975

## LEO QUAYLE
(Musical Director 1952–1953)

Die Fledermaus 1950
Faust 1950
The Bartered Bride 1950
Madam Butterfly 1950
Nabucco 1952
Carmen 1952
Rigoletto 1952

## EDWARD RENTON

Madam Butterfly 1951
La Traviata 1951

## JAMES ROBERTSON

Il Trovatore 1964
Don Giovanni 1967

## ALBERT ROSEN

The Jacobin 1980

## DAVID SEAMAN

La Forza del Destino 1981
The Bartered Bride 1982
Don Giovanni 1982

## DAVID SHAW

Rigoletto 1972

## JULIAN SMITH

Rigoletto 1973
Idomeneo 1973
The Magic Flute 1974
Simon Boccanegra 1974
Manon Lescaut 1975
Otello 1975
Orpheus in the Underworld 1976
L'Elisir d'Amore 1977
I Masnadieri 1977
Let's Make an Opera 1978
La Bohème 1978
Il Trovatore 1978
Madam Butterfly 1978
Monsieur Choufleuri's At Home 1979
The Song of Fortunio 1979
La Traviata 1979
Tosca 1980
Rodelinda 1981
I Puritani 1982
Tamburlaine 1982
Andrea Chénier 1982
Peter Grimes 198
The Merry Widow 1984
Norma 1985

## PETER STARK

The Coronation of Poppea 1980
Rigoletto 1981

## CARL SUPPA

Il Trovatore 1976

## WALTER SUSSKIND

Rigoletto 1977

## ALAN SUTTIE

Simon Boccanegra 1971
Aida 1971
Rigoletto 1972
Madam Butterfly 1973

Die Fledermaus 1973
La Bohème 1974
The Pearl Fishers 1974
L'Elisir d'Amore 1976

DAVID SUTTON

La Traviata 1969

VILEM TAUSKY
(Musical Director 1955)

The Sicilian Vespers 1955
Cavalleria Rusticana 1955
I Pagliacci 1955
La Bohème 1955
Rigoletto 1955
Die Fledermaus 1955
The Bartered Bride 1955
Tosca 1963
Il Trovatore 1964

ERIC WETHERELL

La Traviata 1963
The Marriage of Figaro 1964
Macbeth 1964
The Barber of Seville 1964
Il Trovatore 1964
La Bohème 1964
Madam Butterfly 1965
Die Fledermaus 1965
The Bartered Bride 1965
Moses 1965
Il Tabarro 1966
Don Giovanni 1966
Rigoletto 1968
Carmen 1968

EMANUEL YOUNG

Madam Butterfly 1953

# APPENDIX C: SINGERS: 1946–1985

THE FOLLOWING is a list of singers who have appeared with Welsh National Opera in principal roles, and the year in which they first sang the role. It does not include actors or dancers.

(Abbreviations: s = soprano; m = mezzo-soprano or contralto; c-t = counter-tenor; t = tenor; bar = baritone; bs = bass)

NEVILLE ACKERMAN (t)

Guide (Carmen) 1969
Abdullah (Nabucco) 1970
Messenger (Aida) 1970
Curzio (Marriage of Figaro) 1970
1st Armoured Man (Magic Flute) 1971
Boyar (Boris Godunov) 1971
Pang (Turandot) 1972
Maintop (Billy Budd) 1972
Herald (Don Carlos) 1973
High Priest (Idomeneo) 1973
Morpheus (Orpheus in the Underworld) 1976
Tchaplitsky (Queen of Spades) 1977
Rector (Peter Grimes) 1978
Gaston (Traviata) 1979
Aegistus (Elektra) 1979
Lucano (Coronation of Poppea) 1980
Triquet (Eugene Onegin) 1980
Pinkerton (Madam Butterfly) 1980
Andonis (Greek Passion) 1981
Trabuco (Forza del Destino) 1981
Kedril (House of the Dead) 1982
Squire (Parsifal) 1983
Pollione (Norma) 1985
Spoletta (Tosca) 1985

DONALD ADAMS (bs)

Zeta (Merry Widow) 1984
Monterone (Rigoletto) 1985

ELWYN ADAMS (bar)

Escamillo (Carmen) 1949
Valentine (Faust) 1950
Alfio (Cavalleria Rusticana) 1951
Bethune (Sicilian Vespers) 1955
Acciano (Lombardi) 1956
Gaoler (Tosca) 1958
2nd Consul (Battle) 1961
Antonio (Marriage of Figaro) 1962
Guard (Seraglio) 1963

WILLIAM AITKEN (t)

Manrico (Trovatore) 1961

HERVEY ALAN (bs)

Zaccaria (Nabucco) 1952
Ferrando (Trovatore) 1952
Monterone (Rigoletto) 1952
Bonze (Madam Butterfly) 1953
Sparafucile (Rigoletto) 1953
Procida (Sicilian Vespers) 1954
Mephistopheles (Faust) 1954
Mefistofele (Mefistofele) 1957
Von Friedrich (Battle) 1960
Melchtal (William Tell) 1961

THOMAS ALLEN (bar)

d'Obigny (Traviata) 1969
Figaro (Marriage of Figaro) 1969
Morales (Carmen) 1969
Figaro (Barber of Seville) 1969

Guglielmo (Così fan tutte) 1970
Almaviva (Marriage of Figaro) 1970
Schaunard (Bohème) 1970
Falke (Fledermaus) 1970
Paolo (Simon Boccanegra) 1970
Papageno (Magic Flute) 1971
Billy (Billy Budd) 1972
Belcore (Elisir d'Amore) 1974
Rodrigo (Don Carlos) 1978
Onegin (Eugene Onegin) 1980
Germont (Traviata) 1981
Danilo (Merry Widow) 1984

JEAN ALLISTER (m)

Genevieve (Parlour) 1966
Frugola (Tabarro) 1966
Hata (Bartered Bride) 1966
Miriam (Moses) 1966

GRAHAM ALLUM (t)

Curzio (Marriage of Figaro) 1969

JUNE ANDERSON (s)

Violetta (Traviata) 1984

JON ANDREW (t)

Luigi (Tabarro) 1966
Pinkerton (Madam Butterfly) 1967
Otello (Otello) 1976

MILLA ANDREW (s)

Rosalinda (Fledermaus) 1965
Giorgetta (Tabarro) 1966
Tosca (Tosca) 1966
Aida (Aida) 1971
Abigail (Nabucco) 1972

RICHARD ANGAS (bs)

Boum (Grand Duchess of Gerolstein) 1975

GWENYTH ANNEAR (s)

Gilda (Rigoletto) 1972
Anna (Don Giovanni) 1972

PAUL ASCIAK (t)

Arvino (Lombardi) 1956
Canio (Pagliacci) 1956

Manrico (Trovatore) 1958
Duke (Rigoletto) 1959

PHYLLIS ASH-CHILD (m)

Lucia (Cavalleria Rusticana) 1946
Suzuki (Madam Butterfly) 1948
Ludmila (Bartered Bride) 1949
Orlofsky (Fledermaus) 1950
Azucena (Trovatore) 1951
Maddalena (Rigoletto) 1952
Alys (Menna) 1953
Ninetta (Sicilian Vespers) 1954
Annina (Traviata) 1957
Martha (Mefistofele) 1957
Marthe (Faust) 1959
Sister-in-Law (May Night) 1961

ROSEMARY ASHE (s)

Dear Ivor 1983

JANE ATHERTON-McMURRAY (s)

Lola (Cavalleria Rusticana) 1951

HELEN ATTFIELD (m)

Maddalena (Rigoletto) 1973

DENNIS BAILEY (t)

Florestan (Fidelio) 1981
Boris (Katya Kabanova) 1982

JUNE BAILEY (s)

Page (Rigoletto) 1952

NORMAN BAILEY (bar)

Dutchman (Flying Dutchman) 1974
Barak (Frau ohne Schatten) 1981
Scarpia (Tosca) 1981

ELIZABETH BAINBRIDGE (m)

Azucena (Trovatore) 1964

MARY BAINES (s)

Fenena (Nabucco) 1963

PATRICIA BAIRD (s)

Abigail (Nabucco) 1957
Nedda (Pagliacci) 1958

MARGARET BAITON (s)

Fleance (Macbeth) 1969
Ida (Fledermaus) 1970
2nd Boy (Magic Flute) 1971
Olga (Grand Duchess of Gerolstein) 1975
Jano (Jenůfa) 1975
Cis (Albert Herring) 1976
Cupid (Orpheus in the Underworld) 1976
Page (Rigoletto) 1977
Juliet (Let's Make an Opera) 1978
Amor (Coronation of Poppea) 1980
Shepherd Boy (Tosca) 1980
Forester's Son (Cunning Little Vixen) 1980
Son's Friend (Cunning Little Vixen) 1983
Joujou (Merry Widow) 1984
Lucy (Threepenny Opera) 1984

CAROLINE BAKER (m)
(some roles sung under the name CAROLINE
　SAXON)

Miss Baggott (Let's Make an Opera) 1978
Maidservant (Elektra) 1978
Inez (Trovatore) 1978
Chambermaid (Makropoulos Case) 1978
3rd Lady (Magic Flute) 1979
Annina (Traviata) 1979
Olga (Eugene Onegin) 1980
Irene (Tamburlaine) 1982
Voice (Parsifal) 1983
Wellgunde (Rhinegold) 1983
Grimgerde (Valkyrie) 1984
2nd Norn (Siegfried) 1985

ANTHONY BALDWIN (bar)

Scarpia (Tosca) 1980
Germont (Traviata) 1984

PATRICA BARDON (m)

Flosshilde (Götterdämmerung) 1985

CHERYL BARKER (s)

Countess (Rigoletto) 1985

EIRA BARKER (s)

Anna (Nabucco) 1962
Peasant (Traviata) 1963

JOYCE BARKER (s)

Helen (Mefistofele) 1957
Giselda (Lombardi) 1957
Leonora (Trovatore) 1958

CAROL BARLOW-DAVIES (s)

Venus (Orpheus in the Underworld) 1976

DEREK BARNES (t)

Benoit (Bohème) 1977
Prologue (Turn of the Screw) 1979
Monostatos (Magic Flute) 1979
2nd Soldier (Coronation of Poppea) 1980
Cock (Cunning Little Vixen) 1981
Jacquino (Fidelio) 1982
Drunken Prisoner (House of the Dead) 1982

GIULIA BARRERA (s)

Elizabeth (Don Carlos) 1973

MARGOT BARRY (s)

Constanze (Seraglio) 1964

JOSEPHINE BARSTOW (s)

Violetta (Traviata) 1968
Countess (Marriage of Figaro) 1969
Frasquita (Carmen) 1969
Fiordiligi (Così fan tutte) 1970
Mimi (Bohème) 1970
Amelia (Simon Boccanegra) 1970
Elizabeth (Don Carlos) 1973
Jenůfa (Jenůfa) 1975
Lisa (Queen of Spades) 1977
Ellen (Peter Grimes) 1978
Tatyana (Eugene Onegin) 1980
Tosca (Tosca) 1985

BRIDGET BARTLAM (m)

Flora (Traviata) 1971
3rd Boy (Magic Flute) 1971
Maddalena (Rigoletto) 1972

PATRICIA BARTLETT (s)

Marguerite (Faust) 1954
Mimi (Bohème) 1955
Nedda (Pagliacci) 1955
Rosalinda (Fledermaus) 1958

Abigail (Nabucco) 1959
Ortrud (Lohengrin) 1962

LANDO BARTOLINI (t)

Ernani (Ernani) 1984

NANCY BATEMAN (s)

Marenka (Bartered Bride) 1949
Marguerite (Faust) 1955

TOM BATEMAN (bar)

Micha (Bartered Bride) 1949
Coppelius (Tales of Hoffmann) 1950

CHRISTINE BEASLEY (s)

Katerina (Greek Passion) 1984

WYNFORD BEER (bar)

Zuniga (Carmen) 1949
Micha (Bartered Birde) 1950
Coppelius (Tales of Hoffmann) 1950
Gaston (Traviata) 1951

EMILE BELCOURT (t)

Pluto (Orpheus in the Underworld) 1976

CATRIONA BELL (m)

Olga (Eugene Onegin) 1982
Flowermaiden (Parsifal) 1983
Suzuki (Madam Butterfly) 1983

SHARON BENNETT (s)

Queen (Magic Flute) 1979

BEVERLEY BERGEN (s)

Dorabella (Così fan tutte) 1970
Rosalinda (Fledermaus) 1970
1st Lady (Magic Flute) 1971

LEON BERGER (bar)

Small Prisoner (House of the Dead) 1984

NOREEN BERRY (m)

Marcellina (Marriage of Figaro) 1963
Lady-in-Waiting (Macbeth) 1963
Miriam (Moses) 1965
Mamma (Parlour) 1966
Countess (Lulu) 1971
Mistress Page (Falstaff) 1972
Suzuki (Madam Butterfly) 1973
Marcellina (Barber of Seville) 1974
Emilia (Otello) 1975
Hostess (Boris Godunov) 1976

JONATHAN BEST (bs)

Sarastro (Magic Flute) 1983
Jago (Ernani) 1984
Masetto (Don Giovanni) 1984
Verdi's Messiah 1985

MATTHEW BEST (bs)

Ribbing (Ballo in Maschera) 1982
Colline (Bohème) 1984
Sparafucile (Rigoletto) 1985

ANTONIO BEVACQUA (t)

Duke (Rigoletto) 1977

ETHEL BEVAN (m)

Kate (Madam Butterfly) 1953

ANNE BEYNON (m)

Ceres (Orpheus in the Underworld) 1976
Venus (Orpheus in the Underworld) 1977

ROBERT BICKERSTAFF (bar)

Amonasro (Aida) 1971
Marcello (Bohème) 1974
Dutchman (Flying Dutchman) 1974
Grog (Grand Duchess of Gerolstein) 1975
Nourabad (Pearl Fishers) 1975
Belcore (Elisir d'Amore) 1976
Varlaam (Boris Godunov) 1976

HAROLD BLACKBURN (bs)

Colline (Bohème) 1955
Sparafucile (Rigoletto) 1959
Mayor (May Night) 1959
Basilio (Barber of Seville) 1971
King (Aida) 1971

JOYCE BLACKHAM (m)

Cherubino (Marriage of Figaro) 1963
Carmen (Carmen) 1968
Rosina (Barber of Seville) 1969
Amneris (Aida) 1970

DEREK BLACKWELL (t)

Erik (Flying Dutchman) 1974
Laca (Jenůfa) 1976

ANDREA BOLTON (s)

Despina (Così fan tutte) 1985

CHRISTOPHER BOOTH-JONES (bar)

Schaunard (Bohème) 1978
Figaro (Marriage of Figaro) 1978

IRIS BOURNE (s)

Viclinda (Lombardi) 1962
Abigail (Nabucco) 1963

ELIZABETH BOWEN (s)

Olympia/Antonia (Tales of Hoffmann) 1950
Frasquita (Carmen) 1952
Gilda (Rigoletto) 1952

KENNETH BOWEN (t)

Ottavio (Don Giovanni) 1967
Simpleton (Boris Godunov) 1969
Idomeneo (Idomeneo) 1974
Belmonte (Seraglio) 1976

MIRIAM BOWEN (s)

Pamina (Magic Flute) 1979
Gilda (Rigoletto) 1981

JAMES BOWMAN (c-t)

Oberon (Midsummer Night's Dream) 1978

ROBERT BOWMAN (t)

Missail (Boris Godunov) 1968

DENNIS BRANDT (t)

Alfredo (Traviata) 1963

JOHN BRECKNOCK (t)

Almaviva (Barber of Seville) 1977

CECIL BRIDGE (bs)

d'Obigny (Traviata) 1948
Strongman (Bartered Bride) 1949
Ceprano (Rigoletto) 1952
Old Gypsy (Trovatore) 1953
1st Consul (Battle) 1960
Murderer (Macbeth) 1963

ANN BRITTON (s)

Thibault (Don Carlos) 1973
Ida (Fledermaus) 1973

ESTHER BRODERICK (m)

Page (Rigoletto) 1953

DEBRIA BROWN (s)

Klytemnestra (Elektra) 1978

ETHEL BROWN (née Davies) (m)

Giovanna (Rigoletto) 1953
Marthe (Faust) 1959

FRANK BROWN (bs)

Roberto (Sicilian Vespers) 1954

HELENA HUGHES BROWN (s)

Lola (Cavalleria Rusticana) 1946

SANDRA BROWNE (m)

Fenena (Nabucco) 1972
Uma (Beach of Falesá) 1974
Dorabella (Così fan tutte) 1975

EVELYN BRUNNER (s)

Elizabeth (Don Carlos) 1973
Desdemona (Otello) 1975
Lisa (Queen of Spades) 1977

CHRISTINE BRYAN (m)

Wellgunde (Götterdämmerung) 1985

DELME BRYN-JONES (bar)

Macbeth (Macbeth) 1963
Germont (Traviata) 1965
Rigoletto (Rigoletto) 1968
Marcello (Bohème) 1970
Simon (Simon Boccangegra) 1970
Ford (Falstaff) 1971
Nabucco (Nabucco) 1972
Zurga (Pearl Fishers) 1973
Wiltshire (Beach of Falesá) 1974
Iago (Otello) 1975


ROGER BRYSON (bs)

Peachum (Threepenny Opera) 1984


CYNTHIA BUCHAN (m)

Olga (Eugene Onegin) 1980
Varvara (Katya Kabanova) 1982
Carmen (Carmen) 1985
Suzuki (Madam Butterfly) 1985


JANET BUDDEN (m)

Cherubino (Marriage of Figaro) 1970


ANNE BUNFORD (s)

Barbarina (Marriage of Figaro) 1965
Ida (Fledermaus) 1965
Hata (Bartered Bride) 1965


CLIFFORD BUNFORD (t)

Groomsman (Menna) 1953
Basilio (Marriage of Figaro) 1962


MICHAEL BURCH (t)

Verdi's Messiah 1985


MYRON BURNETT (t)

Ruiz (Trovatore) 1964
Basilio (Marriage of Figaro) 1964
Malcolm (Macbeth) 1964
1st Prisoner (Fidelio) 1964
Spoletta (Tosca) 1966
Pedrillo (Seraglio) 1966


NORMA BURROWES (s)

Eurydice (Orpheus in the Underworld) 1976
Gilda (Rigoletto) 1980


STUART BURROWS (t)

Ishmael (Nabucco) 1963
Malcolm (Macbeth) 1963
Rodolfo (Bohème) 1964
Macduff (Macbeth) 1964
Eleazor (Moses) 1965
Jenik (Bartered Bride) 1966
Ottavio (Don Giovanni) 1966
Ernesto (Don Pasquale) 1966
Duke (Rigoletto) 1968


EDWARD BYLES (t)

Pinkerton (Madam Butterfly) 1960
Rodolfo (Bohème) 1961
Arnold (William Tell) 1962
Oronte (Lombardi) 1963
Amenophis (Moses) 1965
Papa (Parlour) 1966
Tinca (Tabarro) 1966
Ernesto (Don Pasquale) 1967
Almaviva (Barber of Seville) 1968
Basilio (Marriage of Figaro) 1969
Remendado (Carmen) 1969
Caius (Falstaff) 1969
Monostatos (Magic Flute) 1971
Missail (Boris Godunov) 1971
Pang (Turandot) 1972
Father Galuchet (Beach of Falesá) 1974
Vitek (Makropoulos Case) 1978
Benda (Jacobin) 1980


CONNELL BYRNE (t)

Laca (Jenůfa) 1977


ELIZABETH BYRNE (s)

Aida (Drama of Aida) 1984
Gerhilde (Valkyrie) 1984
3rd Norn (Götterdämmerung) 1985


IAN CADDY (bar)

Pizarro (Fidelio) 1982


ALFRED CADY (bar)

Dancairo (Carmen) 1949


TERESA CAHILL (s)

Micaela (Carmen) 1970

DONALD CAMPBELL (bs)

Colline (Bohème) 1959
Sacristan (Tosca) 1959
Bonze (Madam Butterfly) 1959
2nd Consul (Battle) 1961

PHYLLIS CANNAN (m/s)

Suzuki (Madam Butterfly) 1979
Tchaikovsky at the Opera 1979
Kostelnicka (Jenůfa) 1984
Katerina (Greek Passion) 1984

APRIL CANTELO (s)

Countess (Marriage of Figaro) 1963
Ludmila (Bartered Bride) 1982

GABRIELLE CAPUS (s)

1st Girl (Marriage of Figaro) 1969
Lady-in-Waiting (Macbeth) 1969

CRISTINA CARLIN (s)

Musetta (Bohème) 1976

JOHN CAROLAN (t)

Faust (Mefistofele) 1957

ROBERT CARPENTER TURNER (bar)

Richard (Puritani) 1982
Goryanchikov (House of the Dead) 1982

JOHN CARR (t)

Boyar (Boris Godunov) 1969
Fiorello (Barber of Seville) 1969
1st Prisoner (Fidelio) 1969

CELESTINA CASAPIETRA (s)

Mimi (Bohème) 1976

JESSICA CASH (s)

Musetta (Bohème) 1971
Queen (Magic Flute) 1971

ALLEN CATHCART (t)

Laca (Jenůfa) 1975
Hermann (Queen of Spades) 1977

JANICE CHAPMAN (s)

Abigail (Nabucco) 1970
Aida (Aida) 1971

GEOFFREY CHARD (bar)

Luna (Trovatore) 1961
Germont (Traviata) 1963
Figaro (Barber of Seville) 1964
Falke (Fledermaus) 1966
Schaunard (Bohème) 1967
Sharpless (Madam Butterfly) 1967

ALAN CHARLES (bar)

Giovanni (Don Giovanni) 1967

GRAHAM CLARK (t)

Skuratov (House of the Dead) 1982

ESTHER CLEMENTS (m)

Siebel (Faust) 1948

GILLIAN CLENCH (s)

1st Girl (Marriage of Figaro) 1977
Saturnin (Song of Fortunio) 1979
Overseer (Elektra) 1979
Owl (Cunning Little Vixen) 1980
Sylviane (Merry Widow) 1984
Jenny (Threepenny Opera) 1984

EDITH COATES (m)

Grandmamma (Parlour) 1966
Hostess (Boris Godunov) 1968

TESSA COATES (m)

Page (Rigoletto) 1968
2nd Girl (Marriage of Figaro) 1969
Priestess (Aida) 1970

VINSON COLE (t)

Belmonte (Seraglio) 1976

ELIZABETH COLLIER (s)

Flowermaiden (Parsifal) 1983

MARIE COLLIER (s)

Tosca (Tosca) 1958
Cio-Cio-San (Madam Butterfly) 1959
Giorgetta (Tabarro) 1966

ANNE COLLINS (m)

Sosostris (Midsummer Marriage) 1977
Madam Arvidson (Ballo in Maschera) 1982
Dear Ivor 1983
Erda (Rhinegold) 1983
1st Norn (Siegfried) 1985
Erda (Götterdämmerung) 1985

KENNETH COLLINS (t)

Pedrillo (Seraglio) 1963
Radames (Aida) 1972
Ishmael (Nabucco) 1972
Calaf (Turandot) 1972
Pinkerton (Madam Butterfly) 1973
Carlos (Don Carlos) 1973
Nadir (Pearl Fishers) 1973
Rodolfo (Bohème) 1974
Gabriele Adorno (Simon Boccanegra) 1974
Erik (Flying Dutchman) 1974
des Grieux (Manon Lescaut) 1975
Manrico (Trovatore) 1976
Carlo (Masnadieri) 1977
An Evening with Puccini 1978
Ernani (Ernani) 1979
Cavaradossi (Tosca) 1980
Chénier (Andrea Chénier) 1982
Gustavus (Ballo in Maschera) 1983

NICOLAS COMMON (bar)

Morales (Carmen) 1968
Servant (Macbeth) 1969

ELIZABETH CONNELL (s)

Kostelnicka (Jenůfa) 1976

RACHEL COOK (m)

Dresser/Schoolboy (Lulu) 1972

RUSSELL COOPER (bar)

Frederick (Lohengrin) 1962

JANET COSTER (m)

Maddalena (Rigoletto) 1968
Carmen (Carmen) 1968
Amneris (Aida) 1970
Eboli (Don Carlos) 1973
Azucena (Trovatore) 1976

TOM COURT (bs)

Ivan (Fledermaus) 1950

CHARLES CRAIG (t)

Otello (Otello) 1975
Manrico (Trovatore) 1976

GLORIA CRANE (s)

Barbarina (Marriage of Figaro) 1977
Landry (Song of Fortunio) 1979
Damigella (Coronation of Poppea) 1980

NANCY CREIGHTON (s)

Gilda (Rigoletto) 1959

ZOE CRESSWELL (s)

Carmen (Carmen) 1947
Santuzza (Cavalleria Rusticana) 1948
Rosalinda (Fledermaus) 1950
Leonora (Trovatore) 1951
Cio-Cio-San (Madam Butterfly) 1953
Musetta (Bohème) 1955
Fenena (Nabucco) 1956
Giselda (Lombardi) 1957
Viclinda (Lombardi) 1957

RITA CULLIS (s)

2nd Boy (Magic Flute) 1974
Voice (Don Carlos) 1974
Musician (Manon Lescaut) 1975
Barena (Jenůfa) 1975
Miss Wordsworth (Albert Herring) 1976
Inez (Trovatore) 1976
Xenia (Boris Godunov) 1976
Diana (Orpheus in the Underworld) 1976
Leila (Pearl Fishers) 1977
Titania (Midsummer Night's Dream) 1978
Maidservant (Elektra) 1978
Niece (Peter Grimes) 1978
Musetta (Bohème) 1978
Miss Jessel (Turn of the Screw) 1979
Liu (Turandot) 1979

Kate (Madam Butterfly) 1979
Tchaikovsky at the Opera 1979
Virtue (Coronation of Poppea) 1980
Tatyana (Eugene Onegin) 1980
All for Love 1981
Falcon's Voice (Frau ohne Schatten) 1981
Countess (Marriage of Figaro) 1981
Lenio (Greek Passion) 1981
Gilda (Rigoletto) 1981
Marzellina (Fidelio) 1981
Pamina (Magic Flute) 1981
Anna (Don Giovanni) 1982
Flowermaiden (Parsifal) 1983
Ellen (Peter Grimes) 1983


LAURENCE DALE (t)

Ottavio (Don Giovanni) 1984
Ferrando (Così fan tutte) 1985


MILENA DAL PIVA (s)

Gilda (Rigoletto) 1977


MARIO D'ANNA (bar)

Scarpia (Tosca) 1980


BRUCE DARGAVEL (bar)

Sharpless (Madam Butterfly) 1958
Luna (Trovatore) 1958


JOY DAVIDSON (s)

Carmen (Carmen) 1968


ALLYN DAVIES (t)

Ruiz (Trovatore) 1961


ARNOLD DAVIES (bar)

Falke (Fledermaus) 1950
Dapertutto (Tales of Hoffmann) 1950
Luna (Trovatore) 1951
Germont (Traviata) 1951
Tonio (Pagliacci) 1951
Morales/Dancairo (Carmen) 1952
Escamillo (Carmen) 1952
Yamadori (Madam Butterfly) 1953
Monterone (Rigoletto) 1953
Krusina (Bartered Bride) 1954
Rigoletto (Rigoletto) 1954
Wagner (Faust) 1954
Roberto (Sicilian Vespers) 1955

ARTHUR DAVIES (bar)

Alfio (Cavalleria Rusticana) 1946
Tonio (Pagliacci) 1946
Escamillo (Carmen) 1947
Germont (Traviata) 1948
Bonze (Madam Butterfly) 1948


ARTHUR DAVIES (t)

Squeak (Billy Budd) 1972
1st Priest (Magic Flute) 1972
Goro (Madam Butterfly) 1973
Novice (Billy Budd) 1973
Arbace (Idomeneo) 1974
Nemorino (Elisir d'Amore) 1974
Steersman (Flying Dutchman) 1974
Almaviva (Barber of Seville) 1974
Edmondo (Manon Lescaut) 1975
Ferrando (Così fan tutte) 1975
Nadir (Pearl Fishers) 1975
Albert (Albert Herring) 1976
Orpheus (Orpheus in the Underworld) 1976
Jack (Midsummer Marriage) 1976
Tchekalinsky (Queen of Spades) 1977
Steva (Jenůfa) 1977
Lysander (Midsummer Night's Dream) 1978
Janek (Makropoulos Case) 1978
Quint (Turn of the Screw) 1979
Pong (Turandot) 1979
Shepherd (Tristan und Isolde) 1979
Tchaikovsky at the Opera 1979
Nero (Coronation of Poppea) 1980
Lensky (Eugene Onegin) 1980
Jiri (Jacobin) 1980
Prologue (Turn of the Screw) 1980
Fox (Cunning Little Vixen) 1980
Hunchbacked Brother (Frau ohne Schatten)
   1981
Yannakos (Greek Passion) 1981
Arthur (Puritani) 1982
Kudryash (Katya Kabanova) 1982
Boles (Peter Grimes) 1983
Jenik (Bartered Bride) 1983
Rodolfo (Bohème) 1984
José (Carmen) 1985
Pollione (Norma) 1985
Pinkerton (Madam Butterfly) 1985


BRYN DAVIES (t)

Pitichinaccio (Tales of Hoffmann) 1950

CHRISTOPHER DAVIES (bar)

Fiorello/Ambrogio (Barber of Seville) 1964
Schaunard (Bohème) 1964
Yamadori (Madam Butterfly) 1964


DERICK DAVIES (bar)

Bartolo (Barber of Seville) 1961
Bartolo (Marriage of Figaro) 1962
Douphol (Traviata) 1962
Yamadori (Madam Butterfly) 1962
High Commissioner (Madam Butterfly) 1962
Henry (Lohengrin) 1963
Figaro (Marriage of Figaro) 1963
Angelotti (Tosca) 1963
Schaunard (Bohème) 1964
Rocco (Fidelio) 1965
Grenvil (Traviata) 1965
Masetto (Don Giovanni) 1966


EDITH DAVIES (m)

Giovanna (Rigoletto) 1952


EIRIAN DAVIES (s)

Olga (Merry Widow) 1984
Barena (Jenůfa) 1984
Flora (Traviata) 1984
Woglinde (Götterdämmerung) 1985


GEOFFREY DAVIES (bar)

Dancairo (Carmen) 1947
Yamadori (Madam Butterfly) 1948
Bonze (Madam Butterfly) 1949
Miracle (Tales of Hoffmann) 1950
Mephistopheles (Faust) 1950
Sparafucile (Rigoletto) 1952


GEORGE DAVIES (bs)

High Commissioner (Madam Butterfly) 1948
Luther (Tales of Hoffmann) 1950


GERALD DAVIES (t)

Jenik (Bartered Bride) 1950
Duke (Rigoletto) 1953
Alfredo (Traviata) 1953
Faust (Faust) 1955
Pinkerton (Madam Butterfly) 1956


GLANVILLE DAVIES (bs)

Strongman (Bartered Bride) 1950
Mayor (Battle) 1960
Duncan (Macbeth) 1963


GRAHAM DAVIES (t)

Borsa (Rigoletto) 1952


IEUAN DAVIES (t)

Joseph (Traviata) 1968
Basilio (Marriage of Figaro) 1969
Malcolm (Macbeth) 1969
Ambrogio (Barber of Seville) 1970
Innkeeper (Falstaff) 1971
Simpleton (Boris Godunov) 1971
Emperor (Turandot) 1972
Blind (Fledermaus) 1973
Appia (Beach of Falesá) 1974
Dancing Master (Manon Lescaut) 1975
Nepomuc (Grand Duchess of Gerolstein) 1975
Messenger (Trovatore) 1976
Bacchus (Orpheus in the Underworld) 1976
Styx (Orpheus in the Underworld) 1977
Majordomo (Queen of Spades) 1977
1st Priest (Magic Flute) 1979
Servant (Ballo in Maschera) 1982


JOAN DAVIES (m)

Mistress Page (Falstaff) 1969
Hostess (Boris Godunov) 1976


LYNNE DAVIES (m)

Carmen (Carmen) 1949
Siebel (Faust) 1950


MARION DAVIES (s)

Nedda (Pagliacci) 1946


MARION DAVIES (m)

Orlofsky (Fledermaus) 1960


MARY DAVIES (s)

Emmie (Albert Herring) 1976
Bella (Midsummer Marriage) 1976
Mascha (Queen of Spades) 1977
Karolka (Jenůfa) 1977
Cherubino (Marriage of Figaro) 1978

Niece (Peter Grimes) 1978
Papagena (Magic Flute) 1979
Kristina (Makropoulos Case) 1979
Drusilla (Coronation of Poppea) 1980
Hen (Cunning Little Vixen) 1980
Susanna (Marriage of Figaro) 1981
Squire (Parsifal) 1983
Frasquita (Carmen) 1983
Lolo (Merry Widow) 1984
Valencienne (Merry Widow) 1984

MENAI DAVIES (m)

Amelia (Grand Duchess of Gerolstein)
1975
Marcellina (Barber of Seville) 1975
Grandmother (Jenufa) 1975
Mrs Herring (Albert Herring) 1975
Juno (Orpheus in the Underworld) 1977
Giovanna (Rigoletto) 1977
Governess (Queen of Spades) 1977
Marcellina (Marriage of Figaro) 1977
Confidante/Servant (Elektra) 1978
Auntie (Peter Grimes) 1978
Charwoman (Makropoulos Case) 1978
Mrs Grose (Turn of the Screw) 1979
Arnalta (Coronation of Poppea) 1980
Filipyevna (Eugene Onegin) 1980
Innkeeper's Wife/Hen (Cunning Little Vixen)
  1980
Gwen (Journey) 1981
Curra (Forza del Destino) 1981
Hata (Bartered Bride) 1982
Countess (Andrea Chénier) 1982
Mrs Peachum (Threepenny Opera) 1984

PARRY DAVIES (bar)

Strongman (Bartered Bride) 1954
Notary (Barber of Seville) 1956

RALPH DAVIES (bar)

Ivan (Fledermaus) 1960
Duncan (Macbeth) 1964
Elderberry (Parlour) 1966

RHIANNON DAVIES (m)

Flora (Traviata) 1966
Hata (Bartered Bride) 1966
Fenena (Nabucco) 1967
Suzuki (Madam Butterfly) 1967
Nurse (Boris Godunov) 1968

RHYDDERCH DAVIES (bs)

Sganarelle (Serch Yw'r Doctor) 1960
Bartolo (Marriage of Figaro) 1963

RITA DAVIES (s)

Frasquita (Carmen) 1947
Nedda (Pagliacci) 1948

RYLAND DAVIES (t)

Almaviva (Barber of Seville) 1964
Tamino (Magic Flute) 1974

SHIRLEY DAVIES (m)

Peasant (Traviata) 1957
Countess (Rigoletto) 1957

TUDOR DAVIES (t)

Canio (Pagliacci) 1946
Faust (Faust) 1946
Alfredo (Traviata) 1948

VIVIAN DAVIES (bar)

Marullo (Rigoletto) 1952
Ringmaster (Bartered Bride) 1954
Alcindoro (Bohème) 1955
Gaoler (Tosca) 1955
Grenvil (Traviata) 1955
Fiorello (Barber of Seville) 1956
d'Obigny (Traviata) 1957
Frosch (Fledermaus) 1959
Benoit (Bohème) 1961

JOHN DAVIS (t)

Notary (Barber of Seville) 1968

ANNE DAWSON (s)

Gilda (Rigoletto) 1985

ALLISON DEAKIN (s)

Jay (Cunning Little Vixen) 1980
Olga (Merry Widow) 1984

ROBERT DEAN (bar)

All for Love 1981
Macheath (Threepenny Opera) 1984

STAFFORD DEAN (bs)

Sparafucile (Rigoletto) 1972
Sarastro (Magic Flute) 1972
Philip II (Don Carlos) 1978
Seneca (Coronation of Poppea) 1980
Rocco (Fidelio) 1981

GRACE DE LA CRUZ (s)

Aida (Aida) 1970
Cio-Cio-San (Madam Butterfly) 1973

SOLANGE DE LA MOTTE (s)

Marguerite (Mefistofele) 1957

SETA DEL GRANDE (s)

Leonora (Trovatore) 1976

GREGORY DEMPSEY (t)

José (Carmen) 1969
Cassio (Otello) 1975
Steva (Jenůfa) 1975
Grigory (Boris Godunov) 1976

SUSAN DENNIS (s)

Adina (Elisir d'Amore) 1974

ADRIAN DE PEYER (t)

Eisenstein (Fledermaus) 1959

RHYS DEVLIN (bs)

Duncan (Macbeth) 1969
Officer (Barber of Seville) 1970
Alcindoro (Bohème) 1970
Servant (Traviata) 1971
Goll (Lulu) 1971
Bacchus (Orpheus in the Underworld) 1977

WILLIAM DICKIE (bar)

Figaro (Barber of Seville) 1956
Douphol (Traviata) 1958
Falke (Fledermaus) 1958
Tonio (Pagliacci) 1958
Nabucco (Nabucco) 1958
Sharpless (Madam Butterfly) 1962

MERIEL DICKINSON (m)

Madam Larina (Eugene Onegin) 1980

IVAN DIXON (t)

Turiddu (Cavalleria Rusticana) 1951

JOHN DOBSON (t)

Alfredo (Traviata) 1963
Luigi (Tabarro) 1966
Shuisky (Boris Godunov) 1968
Eisenstein (Fledermaus) 1970

ROBIN DONALD (t)

Rodolfo (Bohème) 1974

FREDERICK DONALDSON (t)

Pollione (Norma) 1985

EDMUND DONLEVY (bar)

Kecal (Bartered Bride) 1949
Frank (Fledermaus) 1950
Schaunard (Bohème) 1955
Angelotti (Tosca) 1955
Douphol (Traviata) 1955

HELENA DÖSE (s)

Tosca (Tosca) 1980

NIGEL DOUGLAS (t)

Alwa (Lulu) 1971
Vere (Billy Budd) 1972
Pluto (Orpheus in the Underworld) 1977
Hauk Sendorf (Makropoulos Case) 1978
Basil (Servants) 1980
Schoolmaster (Cunning Little Vixen) 1980
All for Love 1981
Shapkin (House of the Dead) 1982
Loge (Rhinegold) 1983

LYNE DOURIAN (m)

Amneris (Aida) 1970

RONALD DOWD (t)

Cavaradossi (Tosca) 1959
Arrigo (Battle) 1960

**LORNA ELIAS** (s)

Anna (Moses) 1965

**MARGRETA ELKINS** (m)

Pantalis (Mefistofele) 1957
Azucena (Trovatore) 1958
Lola (Cavalleria Rusticana) 1958
Rosina (Barber of Seville) 1959
Amneris (Aida) 1971

**BRIAN ELLIOT** (bs)

Usher (Rigoletto) 1968

**VICTORIA ELLIOTT** (s)

Cio-Cio-San (Madam Butterfly) 1958
Violetta (Traviata) 1949
Rosalinda (Fledermaus) 1950
Santuzza (Cavalleria Rusticana) 1951
Marguerite (Faust) 1951
Tosca (Tosca) 1956

**BRENT ELLIS** (bar)

Zurga (Pearl Fishers) 1977

**EVAN ELLIS** (t)

Giuseppe (Traviata) 1948
Vasek (Bartered Bride) 1949
Alfred (Fledermaus) 1950
Benoit (Bohème) 1955

**WARREN ELLSWORTH** (t)

Pinkerton (Madam Butterfly) 1981
Jenik (Bartered Bride) 1982
Parsifal (Parsifal) 1983
Siegmund (Valkyrie) 1984

**PABLO ELVIRA** (bar)

Scarpia (Tosca) 1980

**ROMANO EMILI** (t)

des Grieux (Manon Lescaut) 1975
Rodolfo (Bohème) 1976

**KENNETH ENGLAND** (bs)

Douphol (Traviata) 1951

All for Love 1981
Guardian (Frau ohne Schatten) 1981
Gilda (Rigoletto) 1981
Katerina (Greek Passion) 1981
Marzellina (Fidelio) 1981
Marenka (Bartered Bride) 1982
Tatyana (Eugene Onegin) 1982
Micaela (Carmen) 1983
Jenůfa (Jenůfa) 1984
Mimi (Bohème) 1984

**ANNE FINLEY** (s)

Leonore (Fidelio) 1965

**LINDA FINNIE** (m)

Madam Larina (Eugene Onegin) 1980

**KATE FLOWERS** (s)

Marenka (Bartered Bride) 1982
Micaela (Carmen) 1983
José's Carmen 1983
Valencienne (Merry Widow) 1984
Jenůfa (Jenůfa) 1984
Woodbird (Siegfried) 1985

**MICHAEL FOLLIS** (bs)

Sarastro (Magic Flute) 1971

**NICHOLAS FOLWELL** (bar)

Bosun (Billy Budd) 1978
Melot (Tristan und Isolde) 1979
d'Obigny (Traviata) 1979
Dog (Cunning Little Vixen) 1980
Ottone (Coronation of Poppea) 1980
Figaro (Marriage of Figaro) 1981
Fiorello (Barber of Seville) 1981
Melitone (Forza del Destino) 1981
Leone (Tamburlaine) 1982
Leporello (Don Giovanni) 1982
Small Prisoner (House of the Dead) 1982
Klingsor (Parsifal) 1983
Pizarro (Fidelio) 1983
Dancairo (Carmen) 1983
Alberich (Rhinegold) 1983
Schaunard (Bohème) 1984
Alberich (Siegfried) 1985
Alberich (Götterdämmerung) 1985

**JOHN FOWLER** (t)

Rodolfo (Bohème) 1984
Alfredo (Traviata) 1984
Duke (Rigoletto) 1985

**TOM FOX** (bar)

Escamillo (Carmen) 1985

**RENATO FRANCESCONI** (t)

Radames (Aida) 1971

**DONALD FRANCKE** (bs)

Micha (Bartered Bride) 1982

**ELIZABETH FRETWELL** (s)

Violetta (Traviata) 1958
Leonore (Fidelio) 1966

**MAURIZIO FRUSONI** (t)

Duke (Rigoletto) 1981
Alfredo (Traviata) 1981

**HEATHER FRYER** (m)

2nd Girl (Marriage of Figaro) 1978
Nutrice (Coronation of Poppea) 1980
Lotinka (Jacobin) 1980
Prostitute (House of the Dead) 1982
2nd Lady (Magic Flute) 1983

**DIANE FUGE** (s)

Chief Hen (Cunning Little Vixen) 1980

**YVONNE FULLER** (s)

Cherubino (Marriage of Figaro) 1972
Liu (Turandot) 1972
Elvira (Don Giovanni) 1972

**JANET GAIL** (s)

Micaela (Carmen) 1968
Rosalinda (Fledermaus) 1973

**ELIZABETH GALE** (s)

Blonde (Seraglio) 1976

ROBERT GARD (t)

Wagner/Nereus (Mefistofele) 1957


ALEXANDER GARDEN (bar)

Figaro (Barber of Seville) 1981


DON GARRARD (bs)

Ramfis (Aida) 1971
Marke (Tristan und Isolde) 1980
Father Guardian (Forza del Destino) 1981


ERIC GARRETT (bs)

Zuniga (Carmen) 1968
Animal Tamer/Schigolch (Lulu) 1971
Dulcamara (Elisir d'Amore) 1974
Geronte (Manon Lescaut) 1975


LESLEY GARRETT (s)

Nicola (Journey) 1981
Esmeralda (Bartered Bride) 1982


JOYCE GARTSIDE (s)

Marguerite (Faust) 1951
Mimi (Bohème) 1959


ELIZABETH GASKELL (m)

Kate (Madam Butterfly) 1985


ALEXANDER GAULD (bar)

Zurga (Pearl Fishers) 1976


PAMELA GEDDES (s)

Countess (Rigoletto) 1977
Rowan (Let's Make an Opera) 1978
Voice (Don Carlos) 1978
Sylvain (Song of Fortunio) 1979
Hen (Cunning Little Vixen) 1980


TIMOTHY GERMAN (t)

Parpignol (Bohème) 1978
Novice (Billy Budd) 1978
Mme Balandard (M. Choufleuri's At Home)
 1979
Friquet (Song of Fortunio) 1979
Giuseppe (Traviata) 1979
Maxim (Servants) 1980


Woodpecker (Cunning Little Vixen) 1980
Apparition (Frau ohne Schatten) 1981
Scott (Journey) 1981
Young Prisoner (House of the Dead) 1982
1st Knight (Parsifal) 1983
Fox (Cunning Little Vixen) 1983
Boles (Peter Grimes) 1983
Raoul de St Brioche (Merry Widow) 1984
Flavio (Norma) 1985
Borsa (Rigoletto) 1985


RACHEL GETTLER (m)

Adalgisa (Norma) 1985


EMIL GHERMAN (t)

Rodolfo (Bohème) 1974


CAROLE GIBB (s)

2nd Boy (Magic Flute) 1971
Zerlina (Don Giovanni) 1972
1st Lady (Magic Flute) 1974


JOHN GIBBS (bar)

Leporello (Don Giovanni) 1966
Charlton (Parlour) 1966
Escamillo (Carmen) 1967
Figaro (Marriage of Figaro) 1969
Bartolo (Barber of Seville) 1969
Donald (Billy Budd) 1972
Belcore (Elisir d'Amore) 1974


JOY HOODLESS GIOVANETTI (s)

Gilda (Rigoletto) 1953


STANLEY GITSHAM (bs)

Wagner (Faust) 1946
Zuniga (Carmen) 1947
Douphol (Traviata) 1948
Crespel (Tales of Hoffmann) 1950
Ferrando (Trovatore) 1951


PETER GLOSSOP (bar)

Luna (Trovatore) 1958
Scarpia (Tosca) 1960


MARGARET GLYN (s)

Esmeralda (Bartered Bride) 1949
Adele (Fledermaus) 1950

HOWELL GLYNNE (bs)

Kecal (Bartered Bride) 1950
Frosch (Fledermaus) 1955
Bartolo (Barber of Seville) 1956
Bartolo (Marriage of Figaro) 1962
Osmin (Seraglio) 1963

TITO GOBBI (bar)

Falstaff (Falstaff) 1972

VICTOR GODFREY (bar)

Zaccaria (Nabucco) 1972

JILL GOMEZ (s)

Jenifer (Midsummer Marriage) 1976

JOYCE GOODWIN (s)

Nedda (Pagliacci) 1959
Gilda (Rigoletto) 1959

BRIAN GORDON (c-t)

Andronicus (Tamburlaine) 1982

RITA GORR (m)

Kabanicha (Katya Kabanova) 1982

BEATRICE GOUGH (s)

Nedda (Pagliacci) 1946
Flora (Traviata) 1948
Frasquita (Carmen) 1949
Mrs Lillywhite (Parlour) 1966

EDNA GRAHAM (s)

Lida (Battle) 1961

LUCILLE GRAHAM (s)

Lucinde (Serch Yw'r Doctor) 1960

CLIFFORD GRANT (bs)

Zaccaria (Nabucco) 1967
Sarastro (Magic Flute) 1971
King (Aida) 1971

PETER GRANT (t)

Eisenstein (Fledermaus) 1960

LINDA ESTHER GRAY (s)

Isolde (Tristan und Isolde) 1979
Kundry (Parsifal) 1983

ANNA GREEN (s)

Isolde (Tristan und Isolde) 1979
Brünnhilde (Siegfried) 1985

EMYR GREEN (bs]

Frosch (Fledermaus) 1965
Micha (Bartered Bride) 1965
Antonio (Marriage of Figaro) 1965

BARBARA GREENWOOD (s)

Fenena (Nabucco) 1954
Siebel (Faust) 1954

BERNADETTE GREEVY (m)

Rosina (Barber of Seville) 1971
Maddalena (Rigoletto) 1972

KAY GRIFFEL (s)

Fiordiligi (Così fan tutte) 1975

GORONWY GRIFFITHS (t)

Giuseppe (Traviata) 1951

GWYN GRIFFITHS (bar)

Scarpia (Tosca) 1963
Pizarro (Fidelio) 1965
Michele (Tabarro) 1967
Ford (Falstaff) 1969

MARJORIE GRIFFITHS (m)

Kate (Madam Butterfly) 1948

MOIRA GRIFFITHS (m)

Nurse (Boris Godunov) 1971
Kate (Madam Butterfly) 1973
2nd Lady (Magic Flute) 1973

VALERIE GRIFFITHS (m)

Peasant (Traviata) 1958
Countess (Rigoletto) 1958
Shepherd Boy (Tosca) 1958
Kate (Madam Butterfly) 1958


MAUREEN GUY (m)

She-Ancient (Midsummer Marriage) 1976
Countess (Queen of Spades) 1977
Mrs Sedley (Peter Grimes) 1978


PHILLIP GUY-BROMLEY (bar)

Innkeeper (Cunning Little Vixen) 1980
Old Man/Off-stage Voice (Journey) 1981
Masetto (Don Giovanni) 1982
Cristian (Ballo in Maschera) 1982
Mathieu (Andrea Chénier) 1982
Morales (Carmen) 1983
Sergeant (Bohème) 1984


DAVID GWYNNE (bs)

Banquo (Macbeth) 1963
Basilio (Barber of Seville) 1964
Ferrando (Trovatore) 1964
Bonze (Madam Butterfly) 1964
Fernando (Fidelio) 1964
Colline (Bohème) 1964
Osiridis (Moses) 1965
Bartolo (Marriage of Figaro) 1965
Douphol (Traviata) 1965
Kecal (Bartered Bride) 1965
Commendatore (Don Giovanni) 1966
Micha (Bartered Bride) 1966
Talpa (Tabarro) 1966
Moses (Moses) 1966
Sacristan (Tosca) 1966
Zuniga (Carmen) 1967
Zaccaria (Nabucco) 1967
Sparafucile (Rigoletto) 1968
Pimen (Boris (Godunov) 1968
Pistol (Falstaff) 1969
King (Aida) 1970
Pietro (Simon Boccanegra) 1970
Fiesco (Simon Boccanegra) 1971
Sarastro (Magic Flute) 1971
Timur (Turandot) 1972
Ratcliffe (Billy Budd) 1972
Grand Inquisitor (Don Carlos) 1973
Neptune (Idomeneo) 1973
Daland (Flying Dutchman) 1974
Boum (Grand Duchess of Gerolstein) 1975

Geronte (Manon Lescaut) 1975
Lodovico (Otello) 1975
Budd (Albert Herring) 1976
Surin (Queen of Spades) 1977
Massimiliano (Masnadieri) 1977
Flint (Billy Budd) 1977
Quince (Midsummer Night's Dream) 1978
Swallow (Peter Grimes) 1978
Grenvil (Traviata) 1979
Tchaikovsky at the Opera 1979
Silva (Ernani) 1980
Gremin (Eugene Onegin) 1980
Vilem (Jacobin) 1980
Father Ambrose (Servants) 1980
Parson (Cunning Little Vixen) 1980
All for Love 1981
Old Man (Greek Passion) 1981
Father (Journey) 1981
Calatrava (Forza del Destino) 1981
Walton (Puritani) 1982
Dikoy (Katya Kabanova) 1982
Rocco (Fidelio) 1982
Prison Governor (House of the Dead) 1982
Titurel (Parsifal) 1983
Ramphis (Drama of Aida) 1983
Foreman (Jenůfa) 1984


PAUL GYTON (t)

Basilio (Marriage of Figaro) 1978
Petermann (M. Choufleuri's At Home) 1979
Mosquito (Cunning Little Vixen) 1980
Abbé (Andrea Chénier) 1982


MARGARET HAGGART (s)

Queen (Magic Flute) 1972
Gilda (Rigoletto) 1973
Musetta (Bohème) 1974


UNA HALE (s)

Nedda (Pagliacci) 1955


TERENCE HALL (bar)

Dancairo (Carmen) 1968


ALFRED HALLETT (t)

Oronte (Lombardi) 1956
Faust (Mefistofele) 1957

RALPH HAMER (bs)

Ceprano (Rigoletto) 1972
1st Mate (Billy Budd) 1972
Bonze (Madam Butterfly) 1973
Mandarin (Turandot) 1973
Naval Captain (Manon Lescaut) 1975
Ferrando (Trovatore) 1976
Vulcan (Orpheus in the Underworld) 1976
Snug (Midsummer Night's Dream) 1978
Dumas (Andrea Chénier) 1982
Blacksmith Prisoner (House of the Dead)
    1982
Customs Official (Bohème) 1984


MARK HAMILTON (t)

1st Priest (Magic Flute) 1974
Parpignol (Bohème) 1974
Maea (Beach of Falesá) 1974
Edmondo (Manon Lescaut) 1975
Ruiz (Trovatore) 1976
Apollo (Orpheus in the Underworld) 1976
Rolla (Masnadieri) 1977
Mercury (Orpheus in the Underworld) 1977
Duke (Rigoletto) 1977
Clem (Let's Make an Opera) 1978
Servant (Elektra) 1978
Rodolfo (Bohème) 1978
Gregor (Makropoulos Case) 1978
Red Whiskers (Billy Budd) 1978
Pinkerton (Madam Butterfly) 1978
Chrysodule Babylas (M. Choufleuri's At
    Home) 1979
Valentine (Song of Fortunio) 1979
Sailor (Tristan und Isolde) 1979
Riccardo (Ernani) 1979
Guard (House of the Dead) 1982


MARY HAMILTON (m)

Waltraute (Valkyrie) 1984


JOAN HAMMOND (s)

Cio-Cio-San (Madam Butterfly) 1958
Tosca (Tosca) 1959


DEREK HAMMOND-STROUD (bar)

Bartolo (Barber of Seville) 1971
Kecal (Bartered Bride) 1982


EILENE HANNAN (s)

Pamina (Magic Flute) 1979


BARBARA HARDING (s)

Mother Hen (May Night) 1959


DAVID HARDING (t)

Officer (Battle) 1960
Giuseppe (Traviata) 1962


ALISON HARGAN (s)

Pamina (Magic Flute) 1971


JOHN HARGREAVES (bar)

Rigoletto (Rigoletto) 1957₁


STUART HARLING (bar)

Almaviva (Marriage of Figaro) 1977
Onegin (Eugene Onegin) 1980


HEATHER HARPER (s)

Violetta (Traviata) 1957
Pannochka (May Night) 1959
Lida (Battle) 1960


NORMAN HARPER (t)

Lohengrin (Lohengrin) 1963
Arnold (William Tell) 1963


EIDDWEN HARRHY (s)

Poppea (Coronation of Poppea) 1980
Oriane (Servants) 1980
Gilda (Rigoletto) 1980
Eduige (Rodelinda) 1981
Cio-Cio-San (Madam Butterfly) 1981
Asteria (Tamburlaine) 1982


KATHRYN HARRIES (s)

Flowermaiden (Parsifal) 1983
Leonore (Fidelio) 1983
Sieglinde (Valkyrie) 1984
Adalgisa (Norma) 1985
Gutrune (Götterdämmerung) 1985


JOHN HARRIS (t)

Lamplighter (Manon Lescaut) 1975
Mayor (Albert Herring) 1976
Roderigo (Otello) 1976
Pedrillo (Seraglio) 1976

3rd Peasant (Boris Godunov) 1976
Ruiz (Trovatore) 1977
Arminio (Masnadieri) 1977
Borsa (Rigoletto) 1977
Parpignol (Bohème) 1977
Snout (Midsummer Night's Dream) 1978
Goro (Madam Butterfly) 1979
1st Soldier (Coronation of Poppea) 1980
Riccardo (Ernani) 1980
Sailor (Tristan und Isolde) 1980
Lensky (Eugene Onegin) 1980
Spoletta (Tosca) 1980
All for Love 1981
Michelis (Greek Passion) 1981
Monostatos (Magic Flute) 1981
Bruno (Puritani) 1982
L'Incroyable (Andrea Chénier) 1982
Squire (Parsifal) 1983
Woodpecker (Cunning Little Vixen) 1983
Mime (Rhinegold) 1983
Mime (Siegfried) 1985

IESTYN HARRY (t)

Turiddu (Cavalleria Rusticana) 1949
José (Carmen) 1949
Faust (Faust) 1950

ENID HARTLE (m)

Nurse (Boris Godunov) 1971

DAVID HARTLEY (bar)

Mark (Battle) 1961

JOHN HAUXVELL (bar)

High Commissioner (Madam Butterfly) 1958
Alfio (Cavalleria Rusticana) 1958
Silvio (Pagliacci) 1958
High Priest (Nabucco) 1959
Marcello (Bohème) 1960
Mark (Battle) 1961
Marullo (Rigoletto) 1968
Morales/Guide (Carmen) 1968
d'Obigny (Traviata) 1968
Germont (Traviata) 1968
Shchelkalov/Lavitsky (Boris Godunov) 1968
Escamillo (Carmen) 1968

JAMES HAWTHORNE (t)

Eisenstein (Fledermaus) 1965

GORONWY HAYES (bs)

Notary (Don Pasquale) 1966

QUENTIN HAYES (bar)

Morales (Carmen) 1985
Yamadori (Madam Butterfly) 1985

LORNA HAYWOOD (s)

Jenůfa (Jenůfa) 1975

THOMAS HEMSLEY (bar)

Bartolo (Barber of Seville) 1977
Kolenaty (Makropoulos Case) 1978
Zeta (Merry Widow) 1984
Alfonso (Così fan tutte) 1985

RAIMUND HERINCX (bar)

Mefistofele (Mefistofele) 1957
Douphol (Traviata) 1957
Germont (Traviata) 1957
Scarpia (Tosca) 1961
Pizarro (Fidelio) 1964
Nabucco (Nabucco) 1967
Kingfisher (Midsummer Marriage) 1976

ELAINE HEWITT (s)

1st Boy (Magic Flute) 1974
Wanda (Grand Duchess of Gerolstein) 1975
Karolka (Jenůfa) 1975
Blonde (Seraglio) 1976

DAVID HILLMAN (t)

Arvino (Lombardi) 1962
Belmonte (Seraglio) 1963
Fisherman (William Tell) 1963
Basilio (Marriage of Figaro) 1963
Alfredo (Traviata) 1968

ALAN HOLDICH (bar)

Khrushchov (Boris Godunov) 1968

MARK HOLLAND (bar)

Douphol (Traviata) 1984
Schaunard (Bohème) 1984
Carlo (Ernani) 1984
Marullo (Rigoletto) 1985
Sacristan (Tosca) 1985
Guglielmo (Così fan tutte) 1985

EUGENE HOLMES (bar)

Simon (Simon Boccanegra) 1974
Luna (Trovatore) 1978


JOHN HOLMES (bs)

Henry (Lohengrin) 1962
Kecal (Bartered Bride) 1965


DOROTHY HOOD (m)

Iris (Orpheus in the Underworld) 1976


EMELIE HOOK (s)

Leonora (Trovatore) 1952


ELAINE HOOKER (s)

Barbarina (Marriage of Figaro) 1969
Marcellina (Barber of Seville) 1970


TOM HOPKINS (t)

Turiddu (Cavalleria Rusticana) 1946
Faust (Faust) 1946
Canio (Pagliacci) 1947
Alfredo (Traviata) 1948


ANN HOWARD (m)

Azucena (Trovatore) 1964
Grand Duchess (Grand Duchess of
    Gerolstein) 1975


GWYNNE HOWELL (bs)

King (Aida) 1970
Colline (Bohème) 1974
Marke (Tristan und Isolde) 1979


ANNE HOWELLS (m)

Flora (Traviata) 1965
Orlofsky (Fledermaus) 1967


CEINWEN HOWELLS (m)

Siebel (Faust) 1955


VAUGHAN HOWELLS (c-t)

Tamburlaine (Tamburlaine) 1982


NEIL HOWLETT (bar)

Francesco (Masnadieri) 1977
Prus (Makropoulos Case) 1978


PAUL HUDSON (bs)

Rodrigo (Lulu) 1971
Sparafucile (Rigoletto) 1972
Monterone (Rigoletto) 1972
Monk (Don Carlos) 1973
Nourabad (Pearl Fishers) 1973
Speaker/2nd Priest (Magic Flute) 1974
Colline (Bohème) 1974
Basilio (Barber of Seville) 1974
He Ancient (Midsummer Marriage) 1976
Bottom (Midsummer Night's Dream) 1978
Hobson (Peter Grimes) 1978


DAVID HUGHES (t)

Alfredo (Traviata) 1965
Ottavio (Don Giovanni) 1966
Rodolfo (Bohème) 1967
José (Carmen) 1967


JANET HUGHES (m)

Augusta (Parlour) 1966
Barbarina (Marriage of Figaro) 1967
Feodor (Boris Godunov) 1968
Dresser/Schoolboy (Lulu) 1971


PATRICIA ANN HUGHES (m)
(some roles sung under the name PATRICIA
    LLEWELLYN)

3rd Lady (Magic Flute) 1971
Priestess (Aida) 1971
Giovanna (Rigoletto) 1972
Kate (Madam Butterfly) 1973
Nurse (Boris Godunov) 1976
Public Opinion (Orpheus in the Underworld)
    1977
Aunt (Jenůfa) 1984
Whore (Threepenny Opera) 1984
Giovanna (Rigoletto) 1985


GILLIAN HUMPHREYS (m)

Cherubino (Marriage of Figaro) 1967


BEVERLEY HUMPHREYS (s)

Rosina (Barber of Seville) 1977

RITA HUNTER (s)

Marcellina (Barber of Seville) 1959
Elsa (Lohengrin) 1963
Turandot (Turandot) 1979
Leonora (Trovatore) 1980

VALMAI HUNTER (s)

Molly (Fledermaus) 1958
Stepmother (May Night) 1959

ROSAMUND ILLING (s)

Oscar (Ballo in Maschera) 1982
Cio-Cio-San (Madam Butterfly) 1983

JACK IRONS (t)

Gaston (Traviata) 1962
Almaviva (Barber of Seville) 1964
Belmonte (Seraglio) 1964

RONALD JACKSON (bar)

Nabucco (Nabucco) 1952

ALICE JAMES (m)

Marthe (Faust) 1946
Annina (Traviata) 1948

EIRIAN JAMES (s)

3rd Boy (Magic Flute) 1971

FRANK JAMES (t)

Beppe (Pagliacci) 1946
José (Carmen) 1947
Pinkerton (Madam Butterfly) 1948
Eisenstein (Fledermaus) 1950

PETER JEFFES (t)

Tamino (Magic Flute) 1980
Nero (Coronation of Poppea) 1980

CELIA JEFFREYS (s)

Adele (Fledermaus) 1970
Musetta (Bohème) 1970
1st Boy (Magic Flute) 1971
Xenia (Boris Godunov) 1971
Papagena (Magic Flute) 1971
Zerlina (Don Giovanni) 1972

ANGELA JENKINS (s)

Adele (Fledermaus) 1966
Frasquita (Carmen) 1967

NEIL JENKINS (t)

Almaviva (Barber of Seville) 1974

HANS JOHANNSON (t)

Calaf (Turandot) 1972

KRISTIAN JOHANNSSON (t)

Cavaradossi (Tosca) 1985

IVOR JOHN (t)

Faust (Faust) 1946

LEONARD JOHN (bs)

Pirro (Lombardi) 1956
Grenvil (Traviata) 1957
2nd Consul (Battle) 1960

WILLIAM JOHNS (t)

Radames (Aida) 1970
Calaf (Turandot) 1972

PATRICIA JOHNSON (m)

Azucena (Trovatore) 1960
Orlofsky (Fledermaus) 1960

CYNTHIA JOHNSTON (s)

Gilda (Rigoletto) 1968

DAVID JOHNSTON (t)

Ophidis (Moses) 1966

JAMES JOHNSTON (t)

Manrico (Trovatore) 1952

PHILLIP JOLL (bar)

Orestes (Elektra) 1979
Electrician (Makropoulos Case) 1979
Kurwenal (Tristan und Isolde) 1979
Adolf (Jacobin) 1980
Monterone (Rigoletto) 1980

Patrice/Klein (Servants) 1980
Forester (Cunning Little Vixen) 1980
Kostandis (Greek Passion) 1981
Fernando (Fidelio) 1981
Onegin (Eugene Onegin) 1982
Amfortas (Parsifal) 1983
Wotan (Rhinegold) 1983
Wotan (Valkyrie) 1984
Wanderer (Siegfried) 1985


DAVID JONES (t)

Turiddu (Cavalleria Rusticana) 1948


DELLA JONES (m)

Rosina (Barber of Seville) 1977


EMRYS JONES (t)

Beppe (Pagliacci) 1951
Gaston (Traviata) 1951


FRED JONES (bar)

Hermann (Tales of Hoffmann) 1950


GEORGE JONES (bs)

Grenvil (Traviata) 1948


GWYNETH JONES (s)

Lady Macbeth (Macbeth) 1963
Leonore (Fidelio) 1964


HELEN JONES (s)

1st Girl (Marriage of Figaro) 1963


IONA JONES (s)

Anna (May Night) 1959


JENNIFER JONES (s)

Carmen (Carmen) 1983


KEITH JONES (t)

Orpheus (Orpheus in the Underworld) 1977


MARJORIE JONES (m)

Anna (Nabucco) 1958


MORGAN JONES (bs)

Gaoler (Tosca) 1961
Murderer (Macbeth) 1963
Osiridis (Moses) 1966


NORMA JONES (s)

Lola (Cavalleria Rusticana) 1959
Shepherd Boy (Tosca) 1959


NORMAN JONES (bar)

Mephistopheles (Faust) 1946
Frosch (Fledermaus) 1950
Douphol (Traviata) 1953


RODERICK JONES (bar)

Tonio (Pagliacci) 1951
Luna (Trovatore) 1953
Ivan (Menna) 1953
Nabucco (Nabucco) 1954
Scarpia (Tosca) 1955
Monforte (Sicilian Vespers) 1955


ROWLAND JONES (t)

José (Carmen) 1952
Faust (Faust) 1959
Clitandre (Serch Yw'r Doctor) 1960
Alfred (Fledermaus) 1960
Ishmael (Nabucco) 1960
Cavaradossi (Tosca) 1963
Manrico (Trovatore) 1964
Randall (Beach of Falesá) 1974
Puck (Grand Duchess of Gerolstein) 1975


SIDNEY JONES (t)

Gaston (Traviata) 1948


YOLANDE JONES (s)

Eduige (Rodelinda) 1981
1st Girl (Marriage of Figaro) 1981
Guardian (Frau ohne Schatten) 1981
Daughter (Journey) 1981
Alyeya (House of the Dead) 1982
Polly (Threepenny Opera) 1984


RHYDFEN JONES-EYNON (s)

Shepherd Boy (Tosca) 1963

WILLIAM JOSEPH (t)

Boyar (Boris Godunov) 1968
Guide (Carmen) 1968
Curzio (Marriage of Figaro) 1969
Gaston (Traviata) 1969

AVA JUNE (s)

Violetta (Traviata) 1968
Lady Billows (Albert Herring) 1977

STUART KALE (t)

Prince (Lulu) 1971
Ottavio (Don Giovanni) 1972
Red Whiskers (Billy Budd) 1972
Goro (Madam Butterfly) 1973
Paul (Grand Duchess of Gerolstein) 1975
Albert (Albert Herring) 1976
Styx (Orpheus in the Underworld) 1976
Vere (Billy Budd) 1977

HIROKO KASHIWAGI (s)

Rosina (Barber of Seville) 1974

MATTI KASTU (t)

Emperor (Frau ohne Schatten) 1981

MAUREEN KEETCH (s)

Leonora (Trovatore) 1964

DAVID KELLY (bs)

Commendatore (Don Giovanni) 1966
Monterone (Rigoletto) 1968
Varlaam (Boris Godunov) 1968
King (Aida) 1971

RODERICK KENNEDY (bs)

Theseus (Midsummer Night's Dream) 1978

JOHN KENTISH (t)

Distiller (May Night) 1960

PATRICIA KERN (m)

Martha (Mefistofele) 1957
Flora (Traviata) 1958
Maddalena (Rigoletto) 1958
Siebel (Faust) 1959

Cherubino (Marriage of Figaro) 1963
Rosina (Barber of Seville) 1964
Orlofsky (Fledermaus) 1965

JOHN KING (bs)

Captain (Eugene Onegin) 1980
Badger (Cunning Little Vixen) 1980
Servant (Traviata) 1981
Majordomo (Andrea Chénier) 1982
Pritschitsch (Merry Widow) 1984

MARGARET KINGSLEY (s)

Anna (Moses) 1966

JOHN KITCHINER (bar)

Almaviva (Marriage of Figaro) 1967
Zuniga (Carmen) 1968
d'Obigny (Traviata) 1968
Macbeth (Macbeth) 1969
Alfonso (Così fan tutte) 1970
Bartolo (Barber of Seville) 1970
Escamillo (Carmen) 1970

PETER KNAPP (bar)

Douphol (Traviata) 1971

ROBERTA KNIE (s)

Senta (Flying Dutchman) 1974

ANDREW KNIGHT (bar)

Falke (Fledermaus) 1973

GILLIAN KNIGHT (m)

Carmen (Carmen) 1970

OTAKAR KRAUS (bar)

Scarpia (Tosca) 1961
Germont (Traviata) 1966

REGINALD LACEY (t)

Joseph (Traviata) 1958

MARIE LANDIS (s)

Anna (Don Giovanni) 1968

ELIZABETH LANE (s)

Gilda (Rigoletto) 1972
Ilia (Idomeneo) 1973
Amelia (Simon Boccanegra) 1974
Constanze (Seraglio) 1976

MICHAEL LANGDON (bs)

Ferrando (Trovatore) 1951
Bonze (Madam Butterfly) 1953
Colline (Bohème) 1956
Basilio (Barber of Seville) 1956
Sparafucile (Rigoletto) 1957
Mephistopheles (Faust) 1959
Osmin (Seraglio) 1963
Moses (Moses) 1965
Commendatore (Don Giovanni) 1968
Rocco (Fidelio) 1969
Sarastro (Magic Flute) 1971
Ramfis (Aida) 1971
Daland (Flying Dutchman) 1975

PHILIP LANGRIDGE (t)

Prologue (Turn of the Screw) 1979

JOHN LANIGAN (t)

Alfredo (Traviata) 1964

LAURA LARNE (s)

Violetta (Traviata) 1948

ESTHER LATTER (s)

Marcellina (Barber of Seville) 1964
Lady-in-Waiting (Macbeth) 1964

MARTIN LAWRENCE (bs)

Mephistopheles (Faust) 1950

JEFFREY LAWTON (t)

Florestan (Fidelio) 1981
Ringmaster (Bartered Bride) 1982
Tikhon (Katya Kabanova) 1982
Judge (Ballo in Maschera) 1982
Large Prisoner (House of the Dead) 1982
Laca (Jenůfa) 1984
Manolios (Greek Passion) 1984
Siegfried (Siegfried) 1985
Siegfried (Götterdämmerung) 1985

YVONNE LEA (m)

Suzuki (Madam Butterfly) 1981

EVELYN LEAR (s)

Emilia (Makropoulos Case) 1979

CAROL LEATHERBY (m)

Kate (Madam Butterfly) 1973
3rd Boy (Magic Flute) 1974

ROBIN LEGGATE (t)

Camille (Merry Widow) 1984
Ottavio (Don Giovanni) 1984

THOMAS LEHERBERGER (t)

Belmonte (Seraglio) 1976

DAVID LENNOX (t)

Steve (Parlour) 1966

CHARLES LEWIS (t)

Squeak (Billy Budd) 1973
Guillot (Eugene Onegin) 1980

GLADYS LEWIS (s)

Gilda (Rigoletto) 1955

MICHAEL LEWIS (bar)

Donald (Billy Budd) 1978
Ping (Turandot) 1979
Zurga (Pearl Fishers) 1979

PATTI LEWIS (m)

Nicklaus (Tales of Hoffmann) 1950
Inez (Trovatore) 1951
Lola (Cavalleria Rusticana) 1951
Kate (Madam Butterfly) 1951
Carmen (Carmen) 1952
Maddalena (Rigoletto) 1953
Flora (Traviata) 1953
Gaynor (Menna) 1953
Hata (Bartered Bride) 1954
Sofia (Lombardi) 1956
Marcellina (Barber of Seville) 1956
Pantalis (Mefistofele) 1958

RICHARD LEWIS (t)

Gwyn (Menna) 1953

RONALD LEWIS (bar)

Marcello (Bohème) 1955
Alfio (Cavalleria Rusticana) 1956
Tonio (Pagliacci) 1956
Scarpia (Tosca) 1958
Rolando (Battle) 1960
Tell (William Tell) 1961
Figaro (Marriage of Figaro) 1962
Macbeth (Macbeth) 1963
Frederick (Lohengrin) 1964
Pharaoh (Moses) 1965
Michele (Tabarro) 1966

MARGARET LIDDELL (s)

Giannetta (Elisir d'Amore) 1976
Flora (Orpheus in the Underworld) 1976
Mayor's Wife (Jenůfa) 1977

ANNE LINSTRUM (s)

Musetta (Bohème) 1970

CLAIRE LIVINGSTONE (m)

Emilia (Otello) 1976

HAYDN LLEWELLYN (bs)

d'Obigny (Traviata) 1951

PATRICIA LLEWELLYN (m)

(See entry under PATRICIA ANN HUGHES)

ROBERT LLOYD (bs)

Sarastro (Magic Flute) 1972

MORFYDD LLOYD-DAVIES (s)

Micaela (Carmen) 1947

MARLENE LLOYD-JONES (s)

2nd Girl (Marriage of Figaro) 1964

JEAN LOOSEMORE (m)

Orange Seller (Carmen) 1969
Aunt (Jenůfa) 1975

FELICITY LOTT (s)

Countess (Marriage of Figaro) 1977
Jenifer (Midsummer Marriage) 1977
Governess (Turn of the Screw) 1979
Pamina (Magic Flute) 1979

GLENYS LOULI (s)

Carmen (Carmen) 1968

MARION LOWE (m)

Lisette (Serch Yw'r Doctor) 1960

GIANCARLO LUCCARDI (bs)

Ramfis (Aida) 1971
Timur (Turandot) 1972

WILLIAM McALPINE (t)

Faust (Faust) 1950

RODNEY MACANN (bar)

Speaker (Magic Flute) 1979
Grenvil (Traviata) 1979

MARION McCULLOUGH (m)

Flosshilde (Rhinegold) 1983
Margot (Merry Widow) 1984

KENNETH MACDONALD (t)

Alfredo (Traviata) 1959
Almaviva (Barber of Seville) 1960
Oronte (Lombardi) 1963
Ottavio (Don Giovanni) 1968

LOIS McDONALL (s)

Constanze (Seraglio) 1976

TOM McDONNELL (bar)

Onegin (Eugene Onegin) 1980

IAN McFADYEN (t)

Fisherman (William Tell) 1962

PATRICK McGUIGAN (bs)

Monterone (Rigoletto) 1968
Nikitich/Chernikovsky (Boris Godunov) 1968
Douphol (Traviata) 1969
Dancairo (Carmen) 1970

DONALD McINTYRE (bs)

Zaccaria (Nabucco) 1959
Gurnemanz (Parsifal) 1983ı

JAMES McKENNA (t)

Turiddu (Cavalleria Rusticana) 1951

WILLIAM MACKIE (bs)

Commendatore (Don Giovanni) 1982
Horn (Ballo in Maschera) 1982
Don Juan (House of the Dead) 1982
2nd Knight (Parsifal) 1983
Bonze (Madam Butterfly) 1983
Ramphis (Drama of Aida) 1984
Priester Fotis (Greek Passion) 1984
Colline (Bohème) 1984
Angelotti (Tosca) 1985

NEIL McKINNON (t)

Steersman (Flying Dutchman) 1974

MARIE McLAUGHLIN (s)

Susanna (Marriage of Figaro) 1981

HUGH MACLEOD (bar)

Yamadori (Madam Butterfly) 1983
Amonasro (Drama of Aida) 1983

GEORGE MACPHERSON (bs)

Angelotti (Tosca) 1968

ERIC MADDISON (t)

Abdullah (Nabucco) 1969
Parpignol (Bohème) 1970

CAROLYN MAIA (m)

Orlofsky (Fledermaus) 1970

STEPHEN MANTON (t)

Distiller (May Night) 1959
Basilio (Marriage of Figaro) 1962

ANTHONY MARLOWE (t)

Manrico (Trovatore) 1951
Faust (Faust) 1951
Turiddu (Cavalleria Rusticana) 1951

ADRIAN MARTIN (t)

Lensky (Eugene Onegin) 1982

ROBIN MARTIN-OLIVER (c-t)

Bertarido (Rodelinda) 1981
Tamburlaine (Tamburlaine) 1982

ANITA MARVIN (s)

Abigail (Nabucco) 1962

ANNE MASON (s)

2nd Girl (Marriage of Figaro) 1977
Trainbearer/Maid (Elektra) 1978
2nd Lady (Magic Flute) 1979

RALPH MASON (t)

Curzio (Marriage of Figaro) 1977
Balandard (M. Choufleuri's At Home) 1979
Babette (Song of Fortunio) 1979
1st Prisoner (Fidelio) 1981
Cherevin (House of the Dead) 1982
Remendado (Carmen) 1983

PETER MASSOCCHI (bs)

Peasant (Traviata) 1968
Antonio (Marriage of Figaro) 1970
Alcindoro (Bohème) 1970
Mitiukha (Boris Godunov) 1971
Theatre Director (Lulu) 1971
2nd Armoured Man (Magic Flute) 1971
Monterone (Rigoletto) 1972
2nd Mate (Billy Budd) 1972
High Commissioner (Madam Butterfly) 1973
Monk (Don Carlos) 1973
Neptune (Idomeneo) 1974
Pietro (Simon Boccanegra) 1974
Old Gypsy (Trovatore) 1976
Pan (Orpheus in the Underworld) 1976
Narumov (Queen of Spades) 1977

Black Bob (Let's Make an Opera) 1978
Orestes' Tutor (Elektra) 1978
He Ancient (Midsummer Marriage) 1978
Douphol (Traviata) 1979
Zaretsky (Eugene Onegin) 1980
Basilio (Barber of Seville) 1981
2nd Prisoner (Fidelio) 1981
Mayor (Forza del Destino) 1981
Micha (Bartered Bride) 1982
Fouquier-Tinville (Andrea Chénier) 1982
Swallow (Peter Grimes) 1983
Pimp (Threepenny Opera) 1984

ARNOLD MATTERS (bar)

Frank (Fledermaus) 1953
Procida (Sicilian Vespers) 1955
Monterone (Rigoletto) 1955
Bartolo (Barber of Seville) 1957

MICHAEL MAUREL (bar)

Figaro (Barber of Seville) 1964
Schaunard (Bohème) 1964
Falke (Fledermaus) 1965
Malatesta (Don Pasquale) 1966
Marcello (Bohème) 1967

ERMANNO MAURO (t)

Pinkerton (Madam Butterfly) 1973
Rodolfo (Bohème) 1974

DONALD MAXWELL (bar)

Anckarström (Ballo in Maschera) 1982
Shishkov (House of the Dead) 1982
Poacher (Cunning Little Vixen) 1983
Keene (Peter Grimes) 1983
Speaker (Magic Flute) 1983
Donner (Rhinegold) 1983
Amonasro (Drama of Aida) 1984
Marcello (Bohème) 1984
Carlos (Ernani) 1984
Rigoletto (Rigoletto) 1985

BERYL MAY (s)

Frasquita (Carmen) 1949

ANTHONY MEE (t)

Panait (Greek Passion) 1984
Ernani (Ernani) 1984

JOHANNA MEIER (s)

Isolde (Tristan und Isolde) 1980

MANI MEKLER (s)

Leonora (Trovatore) 1977

KERSTIN MEYER (s)

Klytemnestra (Elektra) 1979

MERVYN MEYRICK (t)

Manfredo (Sicilian Vespers) 1954
Tebaldo (Sicilian Vespers) 1955
Spoletta (Tosca) 1955

WALTER MIDGLEY (t)

Manrico (Trovatore) 1953
Rodolfo (Bohème) 1955
Cavaradossi (Tosca) 1955
Duke (Rigoletto) 1955
Oronte (Lombardi) 1962

KEVIN MILLER (t)

Eisenstein (Fledermaus) 1958
Orlofsky (Fledermaus) 1966

JAMES MILLER-COBURN (bar)

Fiorello (Barber of Seville) 1971
Masetto (Don Giovanni) 1972
Dulcamara (Elisir d'Amore) 1974
Mars (Orpheus in the Underworld) 1976
Bartolo (Barber of Seville) 1977
Bartolo (Marriage of Figaro) 1978
Uncle Yakuside (Madam Butterfly) 1978
Sacristan (Tosca) 1980
Cook Prisoner (House of the Dead) 1982
Dog (Cunning Little Vixen) 1983
Bogdanowitsch (Merry Widow) 1984
Benoit (Bohème) 1984
Brown (Threepenny Opera) 1984

APRILE MILLO (s)

Elvira (Ernani) 1984

BEVERLEY MILLS (m)

Bersi (Andrea Chénier) 1982
Dear Ivor 1983
Amneris (Drama of Aida) 1983

Mercedes (Carmen) 1983
José's Carmen 1983
Valencienne (Merry Widow) 1984
Zerlina (Don Giovanni) 1984

BRONWEN MILLS (s)

José's Carmen 1983

PHILIP MILLS (t)

Boris (Katya Kabanova) 1982

HERBERT MINETT (t)

Ruiz (Trovatore) 1951
Nathaniel (Tales of Hoffmann) 1950
Blind (Fledermaus) 1950

JOHN MITCHINSON (t)

Aegistus (Elektra) 1978
Grimes (Peter Grimes) 1978
Tristan (Tristan und Isolde) 1979
Manolios (Greek Passion) 1981
Filka Morozov (House of the Dead) 1982

JOHN MODENOS (bar)

Schön (Lulu) 1971

MARIA MOLL (s)

Leonora (Forza del Destino) 1982

MAUREEN MORELLE (m)

Rosina (Barber of Seville) 1964
Cherubino (Marriage of Figaro) 1965
Fenena (Nabucco) 1967
Suzuki (Madam Butterfly) 1967

ANNE MORGAN (m)

Inez (Trovatore) 1980
Old Woman (Greek Passion) 1981
Annina (Traviata) 1981
Feklusha (Katya Kabanova) 1982
Madelon (Andrea Chénier) 1982
Hen (Cunning Little Vixen) 1983
Schwertleite (Valkyrie) 1984
Mayor's Wife (Jenůfa) 1984
Whore (Threepenny Opera) 1984

ARWEL HUW MORGAN (bs)

Lictor (Coronation of Poppea) 1980
Helmsman (Tristan und Isolde) 1980
Ladas (Greek Passion) 1981
Ribbing (Ballo in Maschera) 1982
Fernando (Fidelio) 1983
Hobson (Peter Grimes) 1983
Sergeant (Bohème) 1984
Angelotti (Tosca) 1985

DUDLEY MORGAN (t)

Beppe (Pagliacci) 1951
Gaston (Traviata) 1951
Parpignol (Bohème) 1961

ERIC MORGAN (t)

Tebaldo (Sicilian Vespers) 1954

GERWYN MORGAN (bs)

High Priest (Nabucco) 1959
Colline (Bohème) 1960
Walter Furst (William Tell) 1961
Sacristan (Tosca) 1962
Melchtal (William Tell) 1962
Basilio (Barber of Seville) 1962
Grenvil (Traviata) 1962
Pasha (Seraglio) 1963
Banquo (Macbeth) 1964
Zuniga (Carmen) 1970

JOHN MORGAN (bar)

Silvio (Pagliacci) 1946
Valentine (Faust) 1946

MARGARET MORGAN (s)

Maid (Jenůfa) 1975
Nancy (Albert Herring) 1976
Minerva (Orpheus in the Underworld) 1976
Countess (Rigoletto) 1977
Hermia (Midsummer Night's Dream) 1978
Thibault (Don Carlos) 1978
Oscar (Ballo in Maschera) 1982
Squire (Parsifal) 1983
Chief Hen (Cunning Little Vixen) 1983
Praskowia (Merry Widow) 1984

MARIAN MORGAN (m)

Giovanna (Rigoletto) 1954

## NORMA MORGAN (s)

Nedda (Pagliacci) 1955
Countess (Marriage of Figaro) 1962
Flora (Traviata) 1963

## THOMAS A. MORGAN (bs)

Indian (Bartered Bride) 1949
Bethune (Sicilian Vespers) 1954
Sciarrone (Tosca) 1955
Wagner (Faust) 1955
Officer (Barber of Seville) 1956
Servant (Traviata) 1958
Customs Officer (Bohème) 1964

## VALERIE MORGAN (m)

Peasant (Traviata) 1959
Kate (Madam Butterfly) 1960

## ELSIE MORISON (s)

Menna (Menna) 1953

## GWYNETH MORRIS (m)

Marthe (Faust) 1950

## NORMA MORRIS (m)

Shepherd Boy (Tosca) 1961
Fenena (Nabucco) 1961
1st Girl (Marriage of Figaro) 1962

## SUSAN MORRIS (s)

Micaela (Carmen) 1968
Xenia (Boris Godunov) 1969
Countess (Marriage of Figaro) 1969
Anna (Nabucco) 1970

## RICHARD MORTON (t)

Cock (Cunning Little Vixen) 1980
Grimoaldo (Rodelinda) 1981
Basilio (Marriage of Figaro) 1981
Panait (Greek Passion) 1981
Almaviva (Barber of Seville) 1981
Jacquino (Fidelio) 1981
Tamino (Magic Flute) 1981
Bajazet (Tamburlaine) 1982
Ottavio (Don Giovanni) 1982
Froh (Rhinegold) 1983
Steva (Jenůfa) 1984

Yannakos (Greek Passion) 1984
Riccardo (Ernani) 1984

## GEOFFREY MOSES (bs)

Basilio (Barber of Seville) 1977
Pastor Moser (Masnadieri) 1977
Ratcliffe (Billy Budd) 1977
Quince (Midsummer Night's Dream) 1978
Colline (Bohème) 1978
Bonze (Madam Butterfly) 1978
Mandarin (Turandot) 1979 March
Helmsman (Tristan und Isolde) 1979
Nourabad (Pearl Fishers) 1979
Jago (Ernani) 1979
Sarastro (Magic Flute) 1980
Seneca (Coronation of Poppea) 1980
Angelotti (Tosca) 1980
Sparafucile (Rigoletto) 1980
Marke (Tristan und Isolde) 1980
Poacher (Cunning Little Vixen) 1980
Spirit Messenger (Frau ohne Schatten) 1981
Priester Fotis (Greek Passion) 1981
George (Puritani) 1982

## JULIAN MOYLE (bar)

Frank (Fledermaus) 1970
Almaviva (Marriage of Figaro) 1970
Paolo (Simon Boccanegra) 1971
Figaro (Barber of Seville) 1971
Shchelkalov/Lavitsky (Boris Godunov) 1971
Ford (Falstaff) 1971
Papageno (Magic Flute) 1971
Figaro (Marriage of Figaro) 1972
Ping (Turandot) 1972
Redburn (Billy Budd) 1972
Sharpless (Madam Butterfly) 1973
Trader Case (Beach of Falesá) 1974
Alfonso (Così fan tutte) 1975
Foreman (Jenůfa) 1975
Lescaut (Manon Lescaut) 1975
Gedge (Albert Herring) 1976
Nikitich/Chernikovsky (Boris Godunov)
   1976
Jupiter (Orpheus in the Underworld) 1976
Pasha (Seraglio) 1976
Dulcamara (Elisir d'Amore) 1977
King Fisher (Midsummer Marriage) 1977
Bartolo (Barber of Seville) 1977
Starveling (Midsummer Night's Dream) 1978
Yamadori (Madam Butterfly) 1978
Choufleur (M. Choufleuri's At Home) 1979
Fortunio (Song of Fortunio) 1979
Douphol (Traviata) 1979

Prus (Makropoulos Case) 1979
Tchaikovsky at the Opera 1979
Zaretsky (Eugene Onegin) 1980
Filip (Jacobin) 1980
Sacristan (Tosca) 1980
Hans Joseph (Servants) 1980
Badger (Cunning Little Vixen) 1980
One-armed Brother (Frau ohne Schatten) 1981
Patriarcheas (Greek Passion) 1981
Story Teller (Journey) 1981
Krusina (Bartered Bride) 1982
Kuligin (Katya Kabanova) 1982
Chekunov/Priest (House of the Dead) 1982
Njegus (Merry Widow) 1984

SUZANNE MURPHY (s)

Constanze (Seraglio) 1976
Adina (Elisir d'Amore) 1977
Amalia (Masnadieri) 1977
Gilda (Rigoletto) 1977
Lisa (Queen of Spades) 1977
Helena (Midsummer Night's Dream) 1978
Overseer (Elektra) 1978
Leonora (Trovatore) 1978
Elizabeth (Don Carlos) 1978
An Evening with Puccini 1978
Queen (Magic Flute) 1979
Jenifer (Midsummer Marriage) 1979
Violetta (Traviata) 1979
Elvira (Ernani) 1979
Julie (Jacobin) 1980
Rodelinda (Rodelinda) 1981
Elvira (Puritani) 1982
Amelia (Ballo in Maschera) 1982
Hanna (Merry Widow) 1984
Musetta (Bohème) 1984
Norma (Norma) 1985

DOREEN MURRAY (m)

Rosina (Barber of Seville) 1957
Ludmila (Bartered Bride) 1966

ALMA MYATT (m)

Mercedes (Carmen) 1967
Page (Rigoletto) 1968

JOHN MYRDDIN (t)

Hoffmann (Tales of Hoffmann) 1950
Manrico (Trovatore) 1952
José (Carmen) 1952

Abdullah (Nabucco) 1967
Parpignol (Bohème) 1967
Peasant (Boris Godunov) 1968

MERYN NANCE (s)

Giannetta (Elisir d'Amore) 1974
Fortuna (Orpheus in the Underworld) 1976

SYLVIA NEATE (s)

Page (Rigoletto) 1957

MARK NELSON (bs)

Innkeeper (Manon Lescaut) 1975
Grog (Grand Duchess of Gerolstein) 1975
Monk (Don Carlos) 1978
Sciarrone (Tosca) 1980
Schmidt (Andrea Chénier) 1982
Filch/Matthew (Threepenny Opera) 1984

MARGARET NEVILLE (s)

Mimi (Bohème) 1970
Pamina (Magic Flute) 1971
Gilda (Rigoletto) 1973
Leila (Pearl Fishers) 1975

HENRY NEWMAN (bar)

Yamadori (Madam Butterfly) 1973
Monterone (Rigoletto) 1973
Sharpless (Madam Butterfly) 1973
Bosun (Billy Budd) 1973
Zurga (Pearl Fishers) 1973
Schaunard (Bohème) 1974
Herald (Otello) 1975
Sid (Albert Herring) 1976
Shchelkalov/Lavitsky (Boris Godunov) 1976
Tomsky (Queen of Spades) 1977
Donald (Billy Budd) 1977
Demetrius (Midsummer Night's Dream) 1978
Marcello (Bohème) 1978
Speaker (Magic Flute) 1979
Germont (Traviata) 1979
Liberto (Coronation of Poppea) 1980
Bohus (Jacobin) 1980
Peter Jack (Servants) 1980
Scarpia (Tosca) 1980
Almaviva (Marriage of Figaro) 1981
Craig (Journey) 1981
Papageno (Magic Flute) 1981
Richard (Puritani) 1982

Fernando (Fidelio) 1982
Giovanni (Don Giovanni) 1982
Roucher (Andrea Chénier) 1982
Escamillo (Carmen) 1982
José's Carmen 1983

NORMA NEWTON (s)

Cio-Cio-San (Madam Butterfly) 1973

EVELYN NICHOLSON (s)

Ortlinde (Valkyrie) 1984
Elvira (Ernani) 1984

HARRY NICOLL (t)

Page (Coronation of Poppea) 1980
Vasek (Bartered Bride) Feb 1982

MARGARET NISBETT (s)

Adele (Fledermaus) 1958

NOEL NOBLE (bs)

Zaccaria (Nabucco) 1957

SHIRLEY NORRIS (s)

Ida (Fledermaus) 1954

BENT NORUP (bar)

Kurwenal (Tristan und Isolde) 1979

ETTORE NOVA (bar)

Scarpia (Tosca) 1982
Gérard (Andrea Chénier) 1982

MARIAN NOWAKOWSKI (bs)

Mephistopheles (Faust) 1959
Sparafucile (Rigoletto) 1959

ANTHONY NOWELL (bs)

High Priest (Nabucco) 1961
Huntsman (William Tell) 1961
Pirro (Lombardi) 1962
Doctor (Macbeth) 1963
High Priest (Nabucco) 1963
2nd Prisoner (Fidelio) 1964

CATHERINE OATES (s)

Abigail (Nabucco) 1963

FRANK OLEGARIO (bs)

Dansker (Billy Budd) 1972
Osmin (Seraglio) 1976

ALEXANDER OLIVER (t)

Alfred (Fledermaus) 1970
Monostatos (Magic Flute) 1971
Pong (Turandot) 1972
Arbace (Idomeneo) 1973
Pedrillo (Seraglio) 1976

DENNIS O'NEILL (t)

Alfredo (Traviata) 1979
Duke (Rigoletto) 1980
Arthur (Puritani) 1982
Gustavus (Ballo in Maschera) 1982
Pinkerton (Madam Butterfly) 1983

DOREEN O'NEILL (m)

Frantik (Cunning Little Vixen) 1980
Cherubino (Marriage of Figaro) 1981
Zerlina (Don Giovanni) 1982
Forester's Son (Cunning Little Vixen) 1983

ALAN OPIE (bar)

Falke (Fledermaus) 1970

CORNELIUS OPTHOF (bar)

Carlos (Ernani) 1979

MARIE-CLAIRE O'REIRDAN (s)

Woglinde (Rhinegold) 1983
Froufrou (Merry Widow) 1984

EDITH OSLER (s)

Gilda (Rigoletto) 1954
Menna (Menna) 1954

LUIGI OTTOLINI (t)

Radames (Aida) 1971
Calaf (Turandot) 1972

EIFON OWEN (bar)

Fiorello/Ambrogio (Barber of Seville) 1968

HANDEL OWEN (t)

1st Prisoner (Fidelio) 1965

RUTH PACKER (s)

Abigail (Nabucco) 1952
Violetta (Traviata) 1953
Elena (Sicilian Vespers) 1954

STEVEN PAGE (bar)

Cascada (Merry Widow) 1984

ELIZABETH PAINTER (s)

Raven (May Night) 1959

VASSILIA PAPANTONIOU (s)

Mimi (Bohème) 1974

DAVID PARKER (t)

Gaston (Traviata) 1957
Wagner/Nereus (Mefistofele) 1957
Abdullah (Nabucco) 1961
Parpignol (Bohème) 1961
Ishmael (Nabucco) 1962

MARY PARKER (s)

Marguerite (Faust) 1948

MOISES PARKER (t)

Alvaro (Forza del Destino) 1981

PATRICIA PARKER (m)

Cherubino (Marriage of Figaro) 1977

ANNE PASHLEY (s)

Jemmy (William Tell) 1963
Fenena (Nabucco) 1963
Marzellina (Fidelio) 1964
Esmeralda (Bartered Bride) 1965
Susanna (Marriage of Figaro) 1965
Zerlina (Don Giovanni) 1966
Louisa (Parlour) 1966

Micaela (Carmen) 1968
Feodor (Boris Godunov) 1968

JOAN PASSMORE (s)

Barbarina (Marriage of Figaro) 1964
Musetta (Bohème) 1964

JULIAN PATRICK (bar)

Pizarro (Fidelio) 1982

LAURIE PAYNE (bar)

Kalenik (May Night) 1959
Figaro (Barber of Seville) 1959
Falke (Fledermaus) 1960
Luna (Trovatore) 1960

PATRICIA PAYNE (m)

Florence (Albert Herring) 1976
Azucena (Trovatore) 1978
Nurse (Frau ohne Schatten) 1981
Madam Arvidson (Ballo in Maschera) 1983
Fricka (Rhinegold) 1983
Fricka (Valkyrie) 1984
Waltraute (Götterdämmerung) 1985

MARIA PELLEGRINI (s)

Aida (Aida) 1972
Manon (Manon Lescaut) 1975

NATALIE PEPPITT (m)

Peasant (Boris Godunov) 1969

JOHANNA PETERS (m)

Mistress Quickly (Falstaff) 1971
Florence (Albert Herring) 1976
Public Opinion (Orpheus in the Underworld) 1976

TREFOR PHELPS (bar)

Alfio (Cavalleria Rusticana) 1947
Silvio (Pagliacci) 1948

IVOR PHILLIPS (bs)

Priest (Madam Butterfly) 1958
Customs Official (Bohème) 1961

NORMAN PHILLIPS (bar)

Carlo (Forza del Destino) 1981

MONICA PICK-HIERONIMI (s)

Queen (Magic Flute) 1979

DONALD PILLEY (t)

Duke (Rigoletto) 1968

ROSALIND PLOWRIGHT (s)

Helena (Midsummer Night's Dream) 1978

EDDIE PLUNKETT (bar)

Morales (Carmen) 1949

MURIEL POINTON (m)

Lucia (Cavalleria Rusticana) 1948
Suzuki (Madam Butterfly) 1951
Marthe (Faust) 1951
Anna (Nabucco) 1952

BRUNO POLA (bar)

Luna (Trovatore) 1976

MOLLY POPE (m)

Inez (Trovatore) 1964
Kate (Madam Butterfly) 1964
Shepherd Boy (Tosca) 1964
Annina (Traviata) 1966
Orange Seller (Carmen) 1968
Marcellina (Marriage of Figaro) 1969
Mercedes (Carmen) 1969
Maid (Simon Boccanegra) 1970
2nd Lady (Magic Flute) 1971
Marcellina (Barber of Seville) 1971

BRYCHAN POWELL (t)

Arrigo (Sicilian Vespers) 1954
Manrico (Trovatore) 1956
Ishmael (Nabucco) 1962

CLAIRE POWELL (m)

Maddalena (Rigoletto) 1980
Marina (Servants) 1980
Rosina (Barber of Seville) 1981
Preziosilla (Forza del Destino) 1981

JOHN POWELL (t)

Parpignol (Bohème) 1960

RUTH PREECE (s)

Adele (Fledermaus) 1951
Micaela (Carmen) 1952

ELIZABETH-ANNE PRICE (m)

Glasha (Katya Kabanova) 1982
Clotilde (Norma) 1985

JANET PRICE (s)

Micaela (Carmen) 1968
Ilia (Idomeneo) 1973
Constanze (Seraglio) 1976

MARGARET PRICE (s)

Cherubino (Marriage of Figaro) 1962
Nannetta (Falstaff) 1969
Amelia (Simon Boccanegra) 1970
Mimi (Bohème) 1971
Pamina (Magic Flute) 1971

OLWEN PRICE (m)

Azucena (Trovatore) 1961
Marcellina (Marriage of Figaro) 1962
Hedda (William Tell) 1962
Marcellina (Barber of Seville) 1962
Sofia (Lombardi) 1962

PATRICIA PRICE (m)

Pauline (Queen of Spades) 1977
Hippolyta (Midsummer Night's Dream)
1978

BENIAMINO PRIOR (t)

Pinkerton (Madam Butterfly) 1973

LILIAN PROSSER-EVANS (s)

Mercedes (Carmen) 1949
Giulietta (Tales of Hoffmann) 1950
Santuzza (Cavalleria Rusticana) 1951
Anna (Nabucco) 1953
Viclinda (Lombardi) 1956

JEROME PRUETT (t)

Belmonte (Seraglio) 1976

HILARY PRYCE-JONES (s)

Marcellina (Barber of Seville) 1970
Barbarina (Marriage of Figaro) 1970
Ida (Fledermaus) 1970
1st Lady (Magic Flute) 1971

KENNETH PUGH (bs)

Murderer (Macbeth) 1969
Krushchov (Boris Godunov) 1969
2nd Prisoner (Fidelio) 1969
High Priest (Nabucco) 1970
Sergeant (Bohème) 1970
Pietro (Simon Boccanegra) 1970
Grenvil (Traviata) 1971
Sergeant (Manon Lescaut) 1975
Montano (Otello) 1975
Mayor (Jenůfa) 1975
Neptune (Orpheus in the Underworld) 1976
Surin (Queen of Spades) 1977
Theseus (Midsummer Night's Dream) 1978
Surgeon (Forza del Destino) 1981

ROSINA RAISBECK (s)

Giselda (Lombardi) 1956

GILLIAN RAMSDEN (s)

Feodor (Boris Godunov) 1976

JOHN RAWNSLEY (bar)

Figaro (Marriage of Figaro) 1977

SEAN REA (bs)

Budd (Albert Herring) 1977
Sparafucile (Rigoletto) 1985
Oroveso (Norma) 1985

PATRICIA REAKES (s)

Anna (Don Giovanni) 1966
Constanze (Seraglio) 1966

MARCELLA REALE (s)

Cio-Cio-San (Madam Butterfly) 1973

ARLEY REECE (t)

Hermann (Queen of Spades) 1977

DUNCAN REECE (bs)

Officer (Barber of Seville) 1964
High Commissioner (Madam Butterfly) 1964

KENNETH REES (bs)

Sergeant (Bohème) 1959

MORWEN REES (s)

Molly (Fledermaus) 1950

RICHARD REES (bs)

Leutold (William Tell) 1961
Herald (Lohengrin) 1962

ALBERTO REMEDIOS (t)

Otello (Otello) 1975

RAMON REMEDIOS (t)

Ishmael (Nabucco) 1968
Grigory (Boris Godunov) 1968
Alfredo (Traviata) 1969
Macduff (Macbeth) 1969
Gaston (Traviata) 1969
Almaviva (Barber of Seville) 1970
Tamino (Magic Flute) 1971
Painter (Lulu) 1971
Novice (Billy Budd) 1972
Ottavio (Don Giovanni) 1972
Duke (Rigoletto) 1972
Radames (Drama of Aida) 1984
Rodolfo (Bohème) 1984
Skuratov (House of the Dead) 1984

DAVID RENDALL (t)

Pinkerton (Madam Butterfly) 1985

SHEILA REX (m)

Martha (Mefistofele) 1961

GARETH RHYS-DAVIES (bs)

Innkeeper (Manon Lescaut) 1975
Khrushchov (Boris Godunov) 1976
Fiorello (Barber of Seville) 1977

Marullo (Rigoletto) 1977
Novice's Friend (Billy Budd) 1977
Indian (Bartered Bride) 1982
Fléville (Andrea Chénier) 1982
Dancairo (Carmen) 1983
d'Obigny (Traviata) 1984
Smith (Threepenny Opera) 1984

JENNIFER RHYS-DAVIES (s)

1st Lady (Magic Flute) 1979
Flora (Traviata) 1979
Fortune (Coronation of Poppea) 1980
Miss Jessel (Turn of the Screw) 1980
Forester's Wife (Cunning Little Vixen) 1980
Elvira (Don Giovanni) 1982

DAVID RHYS-EDWARDS (bs)

Micha (Bartered Bride) 1966
2nd Prisoner (Fidelio) 1966
Notary (Don Pasquale) 1966
Masetto (Don Giovanni) 1967
Alcindoro (Bohème) 1967
High Priest (Nabucco) 1967
High Commissioner (Madam Butterfly) 1967
Guide (Carmen) 1967
Talpa (Tabarro) 1967
Antonio (Marriage of Figaro) 1967
Ceprano (Rigoletto) 1968
Officer (Barber of Seville) 1968
Grenvil (Traviata) 1968
Mitiukha (Boris Godunov) 1968
Doctor (Macbeth) 1969
Nikitich (Boris Godunov) 1969
Basilio (Barber of Seville) 1970

JOHN RHYS-EVANS (bar)

Almaviva (Marriage of Figaro) 1963
Pasha (Seraglio) 1964

MYFANWY RICHARDS (m)

Siebel (Faust) 1946

STEPHEN RICHARDSON (bs)

Colline (Bohème) 1984
Oroveso (Norma) 1985

MARIO RINAUDO (bs)

Silva (Ernani) 1984

MICHAEL RIPPON (bs)

Bartolo (Marriage of Figaro) 1967
Bonze (Madam Butterfly) 1967
Leporello (Don Giovanni) 1968
Sacristan (Tosca) 1968
Donald (Billy Budd) 1973
Bartolo (Barber of Seville) 1974

ELIZABETH RITCHIE (s)

Flowermaiden (Parsifal) 1983

ERIC ROBERTS (bar)

Shchelkalov (Boris Godunov) 1971
Marullo (Rigoletto) 1972
Novice's Friend (Billy Budd) 1972
Papageno (Magic Flute) 1973
Falke (Fledermaus) 1973
Paul (Grand Duchess of Gerolstein) 1975
Guglielmo (Così fan tutte) 1975

GERAINT ROBERTS (t)

Michelis (Greek Passion) 1984

LANCEFORD ROBERTS (t)

Rodolfo (Bohème) 1977

DUNCAN ROBERTSON (t)

Levko (May Night) 1959

ALICE ROBICZEK (m)

Musetta (Bohème) 1967

ELIZABETH ROBINSON (s)

Cio-Cio-San (Madam Butterfly) 1967

FORBES ROBINSON (bs)

Giovanni (Don Giovanni) 1966
Figaro (Marriage of Figaro) 1967
Basilio (Barber of Seville) 1968
Boris (Boris Godunov) 1968
Fiesco (Simon Boccanegra) 1970
Claggart (Billy Budd) 1972
Philip II (Don Carlos) 1973
Dulcamara (Elisir d'Amore) 1974
Black Jack (Beach of Falesá) 1974
Colline (Bohème) 1974

Boum (Grand Duchess of Gerolstein) 1975
Osmin (Seraglio) 1976

**ELIZABETH ROBSON** (s)

Nannetta (Falstaff) 1971
Adina (Elisir d'Amore) 1976

**ANTHONY RODEN** (t)

Idamante (Idomeneo) 1973
Belmonte (Seraglio) 1976

**ANTHONY ROLFE JOHNSON** (t)

Tamino (Magic Flute) 1979
Lensky (Eugene Onegin) 1980
Bajazet (Tamburlaine) 1982

**EWART ROSSITER** (bar)

Morales (Carmen) 1947

**JOSEPH ROULEAU** (bs)

Ramfis (Aida) 1971

**SYLVIA ROWLANDS** (s)

Flora (Traviata) 1959

**WILLIAM RUSSELL** (t)

Remendado (Carmen) 1947
Franz (Tales of Hoffmann) 1950
Abdullah (Nabucco) 1952

**ELIZABETH RUST** (s)

Musetta (Bohème) 1959
Violetta (Traviata) 1962

**ANITA SARGENT** (m)

Mother's Voice (Tales of Hoffmann) 1950

**LAURA SARTI** (m)

Cherubino (Marriage of Figaro) 1963
Marcellina (Marriage of Figaro) 1969

**PETER SAVIDGE** (bar)

Leone (Tamburlaine) 1982
Dear Ivor 1983

Papageno (Magic Flute) 1983
Cascada (Merry Widow) 1984
Danilo (Merry Widow) 1984

**ROBERT SAVOIE** (bar)

Scarpia (Tosca) 1963
Figaro (Barber of Seville) 1964
Marcello (Bohème) 1964

**CATHERINE SAVORY** (m)

Giovanna (Ernani) 1979
2nd Lady (Magic Flute) 1979
Ottavia (Coronation of Poppea) 1980
Confidante (Elektra) 1980
Unulfo (Rodelinda) 1981
Voice from Above (Frau ohne Schatten) 1981
Nikolios (Greek Passion) 1981
Annina (Traviata) 1981
Henrietta (Puritani) 1982

**CAROLINE SAXON** (m)

(see entry under CAROLINE BAKER)

**RICO SERBO** (t)

Duke (Rigoletto) 1985

**ARTHUR SERVENT** (t)

Jenik (Bartered Bride) 1949
Canio (Pagliacci) 1951
Pinkerton (Madam Butterfly) 1951
Alfredo (Traviata) 1951

**NICOLA SHARKEY** (s)

Queen (Magic Flute) 1983

**TERENCE SHARPE** (bar)

Rigoletto (Rigoletto) 1968
Escamillo (Carmen) 1968
Macbeth (Macbeth) 1969
Germont (Traviata) 1969
Figaro (Barber of Seville) 1970
Nabucco (Nabucco) 1970
Amonasro (Aida) 1970
Marcello (Bohème) 1970
Simon (Simon Boccanegra) 1971
Ford (Falstaff) 1972
Posa (Don Carlos) 1973
Billy (Billy Budd) 1973

Belcore (Elisir d'Amore) 1974
Lescaut (Manon Lescaut) 1975
Guglielmo (Così fan tutte) 1975
Luna (Trovatore) 1976
Francesco (Masnadieri) 1977
Balstrode (Peter Grimes) 1978
An Evening with Puccini 1978
Carlos (Ernani) 1980
Gérard (Andrea Chénier) 1982

### JOHN SHAW (bar)

Rigoletto (Rigoletto) 1959
Tonio (Pagliacci) 1959
Nabucco (Nabucco) 1959
Scarpia (Tosca) 1959
Redburn (Billy Budd) 1972
Luna (Trovatore) 1976

### JULIA SHELLEY (s)

Adele (Fledermaus) 1960
Musetta (Bohème) 1960

### SHARMAN SHEPHERD (s)

Musetta (Bohème) 1974
Iza (Grand Duchess of Gerolstein) 1975
Hebe (Orpheus in the Underworld) 1976

### JOHN SHEPPARD (t)

Notary (Barber of Seville) 1970

### NEIL SHICOFF (t)

Duke (Rigoletto) 1977

### ERIC SHILLING (bar)

Bartolo (Barber of Seville) 1968

### WILLIAM SHIMELL (bar)

Giovanni (Don Giovanni) 1984
Sharpless (Madam Butterfly) 1985

### MARJORIE SHIRES (s)

Gilda (Rigoletto) 1955

### JOHN SHIRLEY-QUIRK (bar)

Almaviva (Marriage of Figaro) 1962

### TEGWYN SHORT (t)

Blind (Fledermaus) 1953
Ruiz (Trovatore) 1953
Abdullah (Nabucco) 1953
Goro (Madam Butterfly) 1953
Borsa (Rigoletto) 1953
Danieli (Sicilian Vespers) 1954
Beppe (Pagliacci) 1955
Benoit (Bohème) 1956
Priore (Lombardi) 1956
Spoletta (Tosca) 1959
Curzio (Marriage of Figaro) 1962
Ringmaster (Bartered Bride) 1965
Lillas Pastia (Carmen) 1967

### BARBARA SHUTTLEWORTH (s)

Leila (Pearl Fishers) 1973
Musetta (Bohème) 1974

### JOHN SIDFORD (t)

Goro (Madam Butterfly) 1948
Cochenille (Tales of Hoffmann) 1950
Giuseppe (Traviata) 1951

### ANNON LEE SILVER (s)

Gilda (Rigoletto) 1968

### ROBINA SILVOLLI (s)

1st Boy (Magic Flute) 1971
Page (Rigoletto) 1972
Voice (Don Carlos) 1973
Pomone (Orpheus in the Underworld) 1976

### JEANETTE SINCLAIR (s)

Mimi (Bohème) 1964

### MONICA SINCLAIR (m)

Sister-in-Law (May Night) 1959

### ILEANA SINNONE (s)

Mimi (Bohème) 1974

### EMLYN SMITH (t)

Remendado (Carmen) 1949
Cochenille (Tales of Hoffmann) 1950
Parpignol (Bohème) 1955

JENNIFER SMITH (s)

Countess (Marriage of Figaro) 1978

RUSSELL SMYTHE (bar)

Figaro (Barber of Seville) 1977
Yeletsky (Queen of Spades) 1977
Billy (Billy Budd) 1977
Almaviva (Marriage of Figaro) 1978
Keene (Peter Grimes) 1978
Electrician (Makropoulos Case) 1978
Herald (Don Carlos) 1978
Papageno (Magic Flute) 1979
d'Obigny (Traviata) 1979
Ottone (Coronation of Poppea) 1980
Onegin (Eugene Onegin) 1980
Garibaldo (Rodelinda) 1981
One-eyed Brother (Frau ohne Schatten) 1981

ELISABETH SÖDERSTRÖM (s)

Emilia (Makropoulos Case) 1978
Katya (Katya Kabanova) 1982

CLARE STANLEY (m)

Charlotte (Grand Duchess of Gerolstein)
  1975
Mayor's Wife (Jenůfa) 1975

JOHN STANLEY (t)

Curzio (Marriage of Figaro) 1969

RONALD STEAR (bs)

Mephistopheles (Faust) 1948
Frosch (Fledermaus) 1958
Sacristan (Tosca) 1958
Bonze (Madam Butterfly) 1958

NINA STEFANOVA (s)

Liu (Turandot) 1972
Cio-Cio-San (Madam Butterfly) 1973

JOAN STEPHENS (s)

Lola (Cavalleria Rusticana) 1948
Nedda (Pagliacci) 1949
Giulietta (Tales of Hoffmann) 1950
Siebel (Faust) 1950
Micaela (Carmen) 1952
Fenena (Nabucco) 1952

MADGE STEPHENS (s)

Musetta (Bohème) 1961
Rosalinda (Fledermaus) 1967

DENNIS STEPHENSON (t)

Alfredo (Traviata) 1952
Duke (Rigoletto) 1952

DONALD STEPHENSON (t)

Parsifal (Parsifal) 1983
Radames (Drama of Aida) 1983
José (Carmen) 1983

JEAN STEVENS (s)

Countess (Rigoletto) 1952
Adele (Fledermaus) 1953
Esmeralda (Bartered Bride) 1954

KENNETH STEVENSON (bs)

Basilio (Barber of Seville) 1961
Angelotti (Tosca) 1961
Bonze (Madam Butterfly) 1962

PAUL STRATHEARN (t)

Grimes (Peter Grimes) 1983
José's Carmen 1983
Laca (Jenůfa) 1984
Large Prisoner (House of the Dead) 1984

JACEK STRAUCH (bar)

Gunther (Götterdämmerung) 1985
Rigoletto (Rigoletto) 1985

SUZANNE STRETEN (s)

Thibault (Don Carlos) 1974
Olga (Grand Duchess of Gerolstein) 1975

DEBORAH STUART-ROBERTS (m)

Wellgunde (Götterdämmerung) 1985

JUDITH STUBBS (s)

Susanna (Marriage of Figaro) 1963
Jemmy (William Tell) 1963

FREDERICK STUDDEN (bs)

Schlemil/Luther (Tales of Hoffmann) 1950

MARION STUDHOLME (s)

Gilda (Rigoletto) 1957
Adele (Fledermaus) 1958

JEAN SUGRUE (s)

2nd Peasant (Boris Godunov) 1968

CRAIG SULLIVAN (t)

Radames (Aida) 1970

TOM SWIFT (t)

Manrico (Trovatore) 1977

MARTA SZIRMAY (m)

Azucena (Trovatore) 1980

DAVID TAGG (bar)

Peasant (Traviata) 1971
Priest (Madam Butterfly) 1973
Marullo (Rigoletto) 1973
Notary (Barber of Seville) 1975
Crabbe (Peter Grimes) 1978
Lerme (Don Carlos) 1978

ROBERT TEAR (t)

Jacquino (Fidelio) 1969
Simpleton (Boris Godunov) 1969

CHRISTINE TEARE (s)

Anna (Don Giovanni) 1982
Flowermaiden (Parsifal) 1983
Helmwige (Valkyrie) 1984
Musetta (Bohème) 1984
Verdi's Messiah 1985

ELIZABETH THIELMANN (s)

Cio-Cio-San (Madam Butterfly) 1953

ALBERT THOMAS (t)

Beppe (Pagliacci) 1948

EYNON THOMAS (bar)

Notary (Barber of Seville) 1961
Priest (Madam Butterfly) 1965

EVAN THOMAS (bs)

Bartolo (Barber of Seville) 1969
Douphol (Traviata) 1959
Ragotin (Serch Yw'r Doctor) 1960
Frank (Fledermaus) 1960
Yamadori/High Commissioner (Madam
    Butterfly) 1960
Mark (Battle) 1960
Angelotti (Tosca) 1960
Krusina (Bartered Bride) 1965
d'Obigny (Traviata) 1965

GLYNNE THOMAS (bar)

Speaker (Magic Flute) 1971
Amonasro (Aida) 1971
Monterone (Rigoletto) 1972
Mandarin (Turandot) 1972
Rigoletto (Rigoletto) 1972
Bosun (Billy Budd) 1972
Ping (Turandot) 1973

HILARY THOMAS (s)

Gilda (Rigoletto) 1977

KELVIN THOMAS (bar)

Bosun (Billy Budd) 1977

MARJORIE THOMAS (s)

2nd Girl (Marriage of Figaro) 1962

MURIEL THOMAS (m)

Mother's Voice (Tales of Hoffmann) 1950

ROBERT THOMAS (t)

José (Carmen) 1952
Faust (Faust) 1954
Duke (Rigoletto) 1958
Cavaradossi (Tosca) 1958
Pinkerton (Madam Butterfly) 1958
Turiddu (Cavalleria Rusticana) 1958
Rodolfo (Bohème) 1960
Ishmael (Nabucco) 1962
Lohengrin (Lohengrin) 1962
Macduff (Macbeth) 1963

Florestan (Fidelio) 1964
Jenik (Bartered Bride) 1965
Bardolph (Falstaff) 1969
Pong (Turandot) 1972
Missail (Boris Godunov) 1976


WILLIAM THOMAS (bs)

Vaudemont (Sicilian Vespers) 1954
Sacristan (Tosca) 1955


HEATHER THOMSON (s)

Tosca (Tosca) 1980


BESSIE THOROGOOD (m)

Marthe (Faust) 1948


PAULINE TINSLEY (s)

Susanna (Marriage of Figaro) 1962
Elsa (Lohengrin) 1962
Lady Macbeth (Macbeth) 1963
Sinaida (Moses) 1965
Elvira (Don Giovanni) 1966
Abigail (Nabucco) 1967
Aida (Aida) 1970
Turandot (Turandot) 1972
Kostelnicka (Jenůfa) 1975
Elektra (Elektra) 1978
Dyer's Wife (Frau ohne Schatten) 1981
Tosca (Tosca) 1981


ELIZABETH TIPPETT (s)

Pamina (Magic Flute) 1971


GABRIEL TODD (t)

Hoffmann (Tales of Hoffmann) 1950


ELIZABETH TOVEY (m)

Flora (Traviata) 1952
Anna (Nabucco) 1956
Kate (Madam Butterfly) 1956
Shepherd Boy (Tosca) 1957


VIVIEN TOWNLEY (s)

Jenůfa (Jenůfa) 1977
Mimi (Bohème) 1977
Servant (Elektra) 1978

JOHN TRANTER (bs)

Fasolt (Rhinegold) 1983
Grigoris (Greek Passion) 1984
Commendatore (Don Giovanni) 1984
Fafner (Siegfried) 1985
Hagen (Götterdämmerung) 1985


DAVID TREE (t)

Alfred (Fledermaus) 1951
Spoletta (Tosca) 1958
Goro (Madam Butterfly) 1958
Rudolf (William Tell) 1961
Curzio (Marriage of Figaro) 1962


JOHN TRELEAVEN (t)

Mercury (Orpheus in the Underworld) 1976
Mark (Midsummer Marriage) 1976
Nemorino (Elisir d'Amore) 1977
Arminio (Masnadieri) 1977
Nadir (Pearl Fishers) 1977
Red Whiskers (Billy Budd) 1977
Basilio (Marriage of Figaro) 1977
Flute (Midsummer Night's Dream) 1978
Boles (Peter Grimes) 1978
Pinkerton (Madam Butterfly) 1978
Tamino (Magic Flute) 1979
Alfredo (Traviata) 1978


STEWART TREVARTHEN (bs)

Schlemil (Tales of Hoffmann) 1950
Old Gypsy (Trovatore) 1951
High Commissioner (Madam Butterfly) 1951
Grenvil (Traviata) 1951


PEGGY TROMAN (m)

Fa'avao (Beach of Falesá) 1974
Maid (Simon Boccanegra) 1974
Mary (Flying Dutchman) 1974
Juno (Orpheus in the Underworld) 1976
Maid (Jenůfa) 1977
Maddalena (Rigoletto) 1977


JACQUE TRUSSEL (t)

José (Carmen) 1983


EDUARD TUMAGIAN (bar)

Rigoletto (Rigoletto) 1985

BERNARD TURGEON (bar)

Bartolo (Barber of Seville) 1961

BLANCHE TURNER (s)

Micaela (Carmen) 1949
Nedda (Pagliacci) 1956

ANDRE TURP (t)

Carlos (Don Carlos) 1973

MARGARET TYNES (s)

Aida (Aida) 1970

OSVALDO VALENTE (t)

Old Prisoner (House of the Dead) 1982

RICHARD VAN ALLAN (bs)

Sparafucile (Rigoletto) 1968
Basilio (Barber of Seville) 1968
Banquo (Macbeth) 1969
Zaccaria (Nabucco) 1969
Ramfis (Aida) 1970
Inquisitor (Don Carlos) 1974
Massimiliano (Masnadieri) 1977
Silva (Ernani) 1979
Grigoris (Greek Passion) 1981
Pizarro (Fidelio) 1981
Kecal (Bartered Bride) 1983

KYRA VANE (s)

Leonora (Trovatore) 1951
Tosca (Tosca) 1955

ADRIAN VAN LIMPT (t)

Ernani (Ernani) 1980
Gustavus (Ballo in Maschera) 1983

JOSEPH VARNEY (bs)

Fiorello (Barber of Seville) 1970
2nd Armoured Man (Magic Flute) 1971

ELIZABETH VAUGHAN (s)

Abigail (Nabucco) 1960
Musetta (Bohème) 1961
Jemmy (William Tell) 1961
Constanze (Seraglio) 1963

Mimi (Bohème) 1964
Violetta (Traviata) 1965
Alice (Falstaff) 1969
Cio-Cio-San (Madam Butterfly) 1973
Manon (Manon Lescaut) 1975
Leonora (Trovatore) 1976
Leonora (Forza del Destino) 1981
Tosca (Tosca) 1982
Maddalena (Andrea Chénier) 1982

WENDY VERCO (m)

Amneris (Drama of Aida) 1984
Rossweisse (Valkyrie) 1984
Maddalena (Rigoletto) 1985
Verdi's Messiah 1985

JOHN WAKEFIELD (t)

Levko (May Night) 1969
Alfredo (Traviata) 1962
Ishmael (Nabucco) 1970
Eisenstein (Fledermaus) 1970

NINIAN WALDEN (t)

José (Carmen) 1968

IAN WALLACE (bs)

Pasquale (Don Pasquale) 1967

DELIA WALLIS (m)

Cherubino (Marriage of Figaro) 1969
Flora (Traviata) 1969
Fenena (Nabucco) 1969
Mercedes (Carmen) 1969
Dorabella (Così fan tutte) 1985

TERENCE WALTERS (t)

Duncan (Macbeth) 1965
Malcolm (Macbeth) 1969
Andres (Carmen) 1969
Benoit (Bohème) 1970
Blind (Fledermaus) 1970
Captain (Simon Boccanegra) 1970
Gaston (Traviata) 1971
Shuisky (Boris Godunov) 1971
Messenger (Aida) 1971
Borsa (Rigoletto) 1972
Monostatos (Magic Flute) 1972
Yamadori (Madam Butterfly) 1973
Lerme (Don Carlos) 1973

Eisenstein (Fledermaus) 1973
Captain (Beach of Falesá) 1974
Fritz (Grand Duchess of Gerolstein) 1975
Mercury (Orpheus in the Underworld) 1976
Pluto (Orpheus in the Underworld) 1976

DAVID WARD (bs)

Zaccaria (Nabucco) 1957
Dutchman (Flying Dutchman) 1974

JOSEPH WARD (t)

Eisenstein (Fledermaus) 1967

LORNA WASHINGTON (s)

Guillaume (Song of Fortunio) 1979
Virtue (Coronation of Poppea) 1980
Barbarina (Marriage of Figaro) 1981
Despinio (Greek Passion) 1981
Niece (Peter Grimes) 1983
Hen (Cunning Little Vixen) 1983
Cloclo (Merry Widow) 1984

LILLIAN WATSON (s)

Papagena (Magic Flute) 1971
Zerlina (Don Giovanni) 1972
Thibault (Don Carlos) 1973
Adele (Fledermaus) 1973
Giannetta (Elisir d'Amore) 1974
Adina (Elisir d'Amore) 1974
Wanda (Grand Duchess of Gerolstein) 1975
Despina (Così fan tutte) 1975
Blonde (Seraglio) 1976

HELEN WATTS (m)

Mistress Quickly (Falstaff) 1969
Sosostris (Midsummer Marriage) 1976
Madam Larina (Eugene Onegin) 1980
Mrs Sedley (Peter Grimes) 1983

MARY WELLS (s)

Marguerite (Faust) 1959

SIV WENNBERG (s)

Senta (Flying Dutchman) 1975

VICTOR WHITE (t)

Arrigo (Sicilian Vespers) 1954
Canio (Pagliacci) 1955
Alfredo (Traviata) 1955

WILLARD WHITE (bs)

Osmin (Seraglio) 1976
Massimiliano (Masnadieri) 1977
Orestes (Elektra) 1978

GORDON WHYTE (bs)

Sergeant (Bohème) 1960
Indian (Bartered Bride) 1965
Customs Official (Bohème) 1970
d'Obigny (Traviata) 1971
Clown (Lulu) 1971
Jones (Billy Budd) 1972
Frosch (Fledermaus) 1973
Officer (Barber of Seville) 1977
Antonio (Marriage of Figaro) 1977
Old Retainer (Elektra) 1978
Priest (Madam Butterfly) 1979
Gaoler (Tosca) 1980
Peasant (Traviata) 1981
Kromow (Merry Widow) 1984
Pimp (Threepenny Opera) 1984

DENNIS WICKS (bs)

Rocco (Fidelio) 1964
Kecal (Bartered Bride) 1966

LESLIE WICKS (bs)

High Priest (Nabucco) 1952
Ivan (Fledermaus) 1953
High Commissioner (Madam Butterfly) 1953

ANNE WILKENS (m)

Brangäne (Tristan und Isolde) 1979

BEN WILLIAMS (bar)

Sergeant (Bohème) 1955

BETTY WILLIAMS (s)

Antonia (Tales of Hoffmann) 1950

BRANWEN WILLIAMS (s)

Barbarina (Marriage of Figaro) 1962

DONALD WILLIAMS (bs)

Servant (Macbeth) 1963
Ivan (Fledermaus) 1965

HAYDN WILLIAMS (bar)

Hermann (Tales of Hoffmann) 1950
Krusina (Bartered Bride) 1950
Gaoler (Tosca) 1966

LEONARD WILLIAMS (t)

Parpignol (Bohème) 1970
1st Priest (Magic Flute) 1971
Peasant (Boris Godunov) 1971
Manservant (Lulu) 1972
Borsa (Rigoletto) 1972

MALCOLM WILLIAMS (t)

Curzio (Marriage of Figaro) 1964
Parpignol (Bohème) 1964
Gaston (Macbeth) 1964
Malcolm (Macbeth) 1964
Jacquino (Fidelio) 1964
Ophidis (Moses) 1965
Vasek (Bartered Bride) 1965
Ballad Singer/Lover (Tabarro) 1966
Eleazor (Moses) 1966
Belmonte (Seraglio) 1966
Ishmael (Nabucco) 1967
Ottavio (Don Giovanni) 1967
Borsa (Rigoletto) 1968
Andres (Carmen) 1968
Simpleton (Boris Godunov) 1968

MARGARET WILLIAMS (s)

Santuzza (Cavalleria Rusticana) 1946
Marguerite (Faust) 1947

NEVILLE WYN WILLIAMS (t)

Spoletta (Tosca) 1968
Gaston (Traviata) 1968

RICHARD WILLIAMS (bar)

Crespel (Tales of Hoffmann) 1950

TOM WILLIAMS (bar)

Alfio (Cavalleria Rusticana) 1946
Escamillo (Carmen) 1947
Rigoletto (Rigoletto) 1952
Sharpless (Madam Butterfly) 1953

ANNE WILLIAMS-KING (s)

Aida (Drama of Aida) 1983
Amelia (Ballo in Maschera) 1983
Freia (Rhinegold) 1983
Lenio (Greek Passion) 1984
Mimi (Bohème) 1984
Gilda (Rigoletto) 1985

HELEN WILLIS (s)

Siegrune (Valkyrie) 1984

BARBARA WILSON (m)

Rosina (Barber of Seville) 1956

BRUCE WILSON (bar)

Sharpless (Madam Butterfly) 1948
Valentine (Faust) 1948
Krusina (Bartered Bride) 1949
Spalanzani/Dapertutto (Tales of Hoffmann)
    1950
Silvio (Pagliacci) 1951
Falke (Fledermaus) 1951

CATHERINE WILSON (s)

Rosina (Barber of Seville) 1960
Mimi (Bohème) 1967
Rosalinda (Fledermaus) 1967
Musetta (Bohème) 1977
Ellen (Peter Grimes) 1978

DAVID WILSON-JOHNSON (bs)

Speaker (Magic Flute) 1981

JOHN WINFIELD (t)

Goro (Madam Butterfly) 1967
Remendado (Carmen) 1967
Basilio (Marriage of Figaro) 1967

RONALD WOODHOUSE (t)

Gaston (Traviata) 1959

RAE WOODLAND (s)

Leonora (Trovatore) 1960
Marguerite (Mefistofele) 1961
Giselda (Lombardi) 1962
Alice (Falstaff) 1971
Elvira (Don Giovanni) 1972

Electra (Idomeneo) 1973
Lady Billows (Albert Herring) 1976

ELAINE WOODS (s)

Elvira (Don Giovanni) 1984
Fiordiligi (Così fan tutte) 1985

GWILYM YEOMAN (bs)

Micha (Bartered Bride) 1954
Ivan (Fledermaus) 1955

ALEXANDER YOUNG (t)

Idomeneo (Idomeneo) 1973
Belmonte (Seraglio) 1976

IAN YOUNG (t)

Parpignol (Bohème) 1970

MARILYN ZSCHAU (s)

Tosca (Tosca) 1982
Maddalena (Andrea Chénier) 1982

# GENERAL INDEX

# Mastering Project Management

## Applying Advanced Concepts of
- ## Systems Thinking
- ## Control and Evaluation
- ## Resource Allocation

James P. Lewis

McGraw-Hill

New York  San Francisco  Washington, D.C.  Auckland  Bogotá
Caracas  Lisbon  London  Madrid  Mexico City  Milan
Montreal  New Delhi  San Juan  Singapore
Sydney  Tokyo  Toronto

**Library of Congress Cataloging-in-Publication Data**

Author:         Lewis, James P.
Title:          Mastering project management : applying advanced concepts of systems
                thinking, control and evaluation, resource allocation / James P. Lewis.
Published:      New York : McGraw-Hill, 1998
Description:  p.     cm.
LC Call No.:  HD69.P75M37 1998
Dewey No.:   658.4'04—dc21
ISBN:          ISBN 0-7863-1188-6
Subjects:     Industrial project management.
Control No.  97-38133

*McGraw-Hill*

*A Division of The McGraw-Hill Companies*

5  6  7  8  9  0  DOC/DOC  0  2  1  0

ISBN 0-7863-1188-6   **Coventry University**

The sponsoring editor for this book was *Patrick Muller,* the editing supervisor was *John M.
Morriss,* and the production supervisor was *Suzanne W. B. Rapcavage.* It was set in Palatino
by *Judy Brown.*

Printed and bound by R. R. Donnelley & Sons Company.

This book is printed on recycled, acid-free paper containing a minimum of 50% recycled de-inked fiber.

*This book is dedicated to my friend*

*John Bailey*

*who knows how to manage
the project called "life."*

# CONTENTS

# FIGURE LIST

# PREFACE

The last I heard, Microsoft had sold around a million copies of Microsoft Project. That's a lot of people trying to schedule projects! And Microsoft does not account for all of them, although they probably have the lion's share of the market. So why all this interest in scheduling? You would think that with that many scheduling programs around, the world would run like a clock. But you still hear about projects being finished late, overspent, under scope, and at less-than-required performance. The simple fact is, project management is more than just scheduling.

There are, of course, true project managers and those who pretend to be. At the moment, it is the "in" thing to be a project manager.

This too shall pass.

When you work at the job for awhile, you find out it isn't what you expected. There are more or less two reactions to that realization: You either love the job or you hate it. There isn't much in between.

Project management can be challenging, exciting, and downright fun! It can also be a pain in every part of your anatomy. Part of it depends on whether you work for an organization that plays fair games or whether you are in one where all the games are rigged against you. The other factor is whether you take the time to learn your craft or whether you try to just "wing it." I'm sorry, but you can't just wing it as a project manager. The one thing I'm sure of is, even at its best, it's really hard work!

I spent 15 years doing it. I know.

Now I consult to a number of companies, working with their project managers to improve their performance. It's still hard work. But would it really be any fun if it were easy? I doubt it.

This book is written for those of you who are challenged by the game, who want to spend at least the next few years trying to master it. You have no doubt learned the ropes with PERT/CPM, work breakdown structures, and earned value analysis by now.

You may even feel comfortable with many of the behavioral skills needed to be effective as a project manager. So what's left to learn?

Well, the Project Management Institute, the professional association for people who think project management is fun, has identified nine areas of knowledge that are relevant. These are covered in the first chapter, so I won't go into them here. What I have tried to do is cover some topics that are not yet mainstream areas of project management—and go deeper into a few that are. These include decision analysis, risk management, quality in projects, dealing with uncertainty, and systems thinking—to name just a few.

I think these tools, techniques, and ideas will make your job as project manager even more interesting and, hopefully, a little easier. I could tell you, like Dilbert's boss (in Scott Adams's cartoon strip), once you have a grasp of these new tools, "go out there and maintain the status quo!" But I hope you can do better than that. I hope you can show your colleagues (and most important, your boss) that project management is a whole lot more than scheduling, and that it can really make a difference—if the discipline is mastered!

Hang in there!

Jim Lewis
Vinton, Virginia
November 1997

# ACKNOWLEDGMENTS

As all authors say in their acknowledgments, this book would not exist without the assistance and support of a number of people. Cynthia Zigmund was my acquisitions editor at McGraw-Hill when this book was conceived. Because of the success of my two previous books, she wondered if I might have another topic in mind. I wanted to do an advanced book, but didn't want to call it Advanced Project Management, so we finally decided on the present title, *Mastering Project Management*. Cynthia was very excited about the project.

The project was turned over to Patrick Muller when Cynthia took a job with another publisher, and Patrick has shown the same enthusiasm for the project that Cynthia did. He also has been very supportive throughout. It was a struggle to get this book finished. My father was in and out of the hospital with congestive heart failure and passed away on October 26, 1997. Because of the need to be with him, I missed several deadlines, proving the need for contingencies in managing projects. I appreciate the understanding of the McGraw-Hill staff during this trying time.

I want to thank Ben Thorp, who contributed two chapters to the book, for his contributions and also for a continuing dialogue on project management. Ben is a strong advocate of project management and is dedicated to making the discipline a central part of the culture at Chesapeake Corporation, where he is a vice president.

As has been true for all of my books, my wife, Lea Ann, has worked tirelessly on the illustrations for this book. This has become our trademark. Readers consistently tell me that the illustrations turn an otherwise dull looking book into something interesting. I greatly appreciate her dedication to these projects, which would not turn out nearly so well without her help. She is a natural project manager, being much more organized than I am.

I have dedicated the book to my friend, John Bailey. He attended a seminar that I taught at Brunel University, in Uxbridge,

England, in 1991, and invited me to dinner in London. It was my first trip to England, and John graciously showed me around London. Since then, we have become good friends, visiting each other about once a year. John is a very clever mechanical designer of hearing aid components and loves managing projects. Most importantly, he knows how to manage the project that we call "life," participating with his daughters in bands, outdoor outings, and attending cultural events. He is a consummate home remodeler and has transformed a small home that they recently purchased into a beautiful retreat from the busy world outside.

Finally, I have learned a lot from the thousands of students who have attended my seminars on project management over the years and from the clients with whom I consult on projects. They help me stay current, which would be very hard to do if all I did were teach seminars. They challenge me with questions and problems to be solved and make the job fun for me.

Again, as we say, many of the strengths of the book can be credited to these people. The weaknesses are entirely my own.

# PART ONE

## WHAT'S IT ALL ABOUT

# The Project Management Profession as a Discipline

Project management is more and more being recognized as a discipline that is distinct from general management. Furthermore, interest in the discipline as a profession is growing by leaps and bounds. In 1991, the Project Management Institute had about 5000 members. Now, in 1997, they have passed the 25,000 mark, and are adding members at an exponentially increasing rate!

Master's programs in project management are being started by universities throughout the United States and Canada, and noncredit certificate programs are very abundant. A number of corporations are endorsing the certification of project managers done by the Project Management Institute, and some are even requiring that contractors who work for them employ PMPs (project management professionals—see the next section) to run their projects. In addition, conferences on project managers are increasing in number and attendance is high. Will it be a fad, like so many other trends? I don't think so. It is hard to imagine organizations getting by without something like project management, no matter what they call it.

## PROJECT MANAGEMENT AS A CAREER PATH

Since this book is meant for readers who have been project managers for a while, I will not go into detail about the differences between general management and project management. I'm sure you know what they are. I would like to point out that I see a trend emerging in which project management will be seen as a highly desirable career path.

For several years I have been suggesting to my corporate clients involved in technology that they should consider setting up three career paths: general management, technical, and project management. In too many organizations, engineers, programmers, and scientists are being forced to become managers in order to make more money. Many of them have no desire or aptitude for managing. They would rather work with technology. It is their true love. They also need to feed their families, and when management is the only option open to them to increase their pay, they often take that choice. The net result is that the organization eventually loses a good technologist and gains a mediocre—or even poor—manager.

> Forcing technologists to become managers just so they can make more money is often a waste of good technical talent and turns out a bad manager in the process.

It is bad enough that these individuals become general managers. It is even worse, I believe, when they become project managers. The one thing that technologists often lack is human relations skills. They tend to be "things-oriented." Please understand that this is not universally true, but I believe it is true for a very large portion of the technical population, based on having worked with thousands of them.

Human relations skills just happen to be a major requirement for project managers. Since the project manager generally has a lot of responsibility and very little authority, she has to get work done through influence. She has to know how to deal with motivation, how to lead, how to handle decision-making in the team, how to communicate, negotiate, build teams, handle politics, and manage meetings. When potential project managers tell me that they hate that part of the job, I tell them to forget being project managers (and general managers too). I am certain that they won't be happy with the work, nor will they be very good at it.

On the other hand, I sometimes have individuals tell me they aren't very good at the human skills but would be glad to learn. I tell them to set goals for themselves to develop those skills, because they can all be learned.

> If you really hate dealing with "people" issues, don't be a manager.

I also believe that project management is going to be the new route to CEO positions. This is because project managers usually have to interface with almost every department in the company, and gain invaluable experience in doing so. In addition, the skills required to be effective as a project manager are so broad that the discipline gives you a good foundation for managing the entire enterprise. We will have to wait awhile to see if this is indeed true.

## THE PROJECT MANAGEMENT BODY OF KNOWLEDGE

Earlier, I mentioned the Project Management Institute. For those of you who are unfamiliar with PMI, it is the professional association in the U.S. Like most professional associations, they have tried to delineate what makes project management a distinct discipline, and in doing so, they have identified nine areas of knowledge that practitioners must have. These are listed and explained in the following table.

PMI offers a certificate designating the recipient as a Project Management Professional (PMP). To qualify, the applicant must pass a test on all areas of the Project Management Body of Knowledge (PMBOK). In addition, you must have two years' experience as a project manager. You also get so many points for contributions to the profession, such as writing books and articles. For information on certification, you can contact PMI at the number given in Resources for Project Managers.

Some organizations are beginning to require certification of their project managers. Others are specifying that if you are a contractor to them, you must employ a PMP to run the project. They

do not want to put their money at risk unless they have confidence
that the contractor will practice good project management methods.

| PMBOK Area | Deals with: |
|---|---|
| Scope management | The magnitude of the work involved in a project |
| Quality management | Ensuring that the work performed meets acceptable standards |
| Cost management | Making sure that the project stays within budget |
| Contract/procurement management | Subcontractor performance, purchasing of materials, equipment, and other resources |
| Time management | Scheduling all work to ensure that the project is completed on time |
| Risk management | Identifying risks, developing contingency plans, loss prevention |
| Human resources management | Recruiting, disciplining, performance appraisals, and protected-class individuals |
| Communications management | Every aspect of project communication, whether verbal, written, e-mail, or other forms |
| Project integration management | Plan development, execution, and change control |

## PROJECT MANAGEMENT MALPRACTICE

If you were accused of project management malpractice, how
would the prosecution make their case? What do we mean by
malpractice? Quite simply, malpractice
is failing to follow what is considered
proper methodology by the profession
itself. Every year doctors are sued for
malpractice, and the test always is
whether they followed standard medical practice.

**mal • prac • tice:**

Failing to follow
accepted
procedures in a
certain discipline.

Shortly after the Trans-Alaska
Pipeline was completed, there was a
lawsuit brought against the company
by its stockholders, alleging that they had mismanaged the project
and overspent the job by $1.6 billion (Cleland, 1985). Dr. David

Cleland, who is recognized as an expert in project management, was called in as an expert witness in the case. His job was to testify as to whether the management had indeed failed to manage properly. His answer was affirmative. The company tried to manage an $8-billion project with a rudimentary critical path diagram and no work breakdown structure. Furthermore, they failed to give Bechtel Corporation (a major contractor on the job) a clear delineation of their responsibility, accountability, and authority. For 15 months, every time a decision had to be made concerning Bechtel's part of the project, it had to pass through four layers of management on its way to the top. As we all know, getting anything through four layers of management is slow. By the time a decision could be made, the tundra would freeze and Bechtel would have to wait until the next season to implement whatever was decided.

I recently had a lawyer attend my project management seminar, and he asked if I expect more of this in the future. Sadly, I do. Since our society is so litigious, I'm sure more such cases will be tried sooner or later. What this means is that, as a project manager, you could find yourself in court defending your management of the project. If you are managing projects that might be subject to such lawsuits, your best defense is to be sure you are practicing accepted methodology.

## WHAT THIS BOOK OFFERS

I have previously written three books that cover much of the PMBOK subject matter. These books are *Project Planning, Scheduling and Control, Revised Edition; The Project Manager's Desk Reference;* and *Team-Based Project Management.* They provide the *essential* tools that you need to manage projects, but there are other tools that are useful. This book presents some of those tools and techniques that go beyond the basic methods. I believe that using these additional methods will help you become a master of project management.

> Our linear-causal view of the world just does not fit the reality in which we live.

Among the new tools, techniques, and methods is systems thinking. Peter Senge raised our awareness of the value of systems thinking in his book *The Fifth Discipline* (1990). He also strongly stressed the need for organizations to become learning organizations. While it is too large a topic to cover in much depth, I have tried to provide a brief introduction to systems thinking and how it can be applied to project management. I really believe the potential contribution is enormous, because our linear-causal view of the world just does not fit the reality in which we live.

It also occurred to me while I was writing this book that we talk about the role of the project manager in most books like this, but seldom do we talk about what managing is all about. I have been very impressed with the work of Henry Mintzberg and Peter Drucker, and decided to apply some of Mintzberg's ideas on managing to project management. I think what he has learned by shadowing managers applies equally well to project managers.

In line with that idea, I also have a chapter on power and politics for project managers. I know "politics" is a dirty word, but I also

> **Politics may be a dirty word, but it is a reality that we can't avoid as managers.**

know that politics is like death and taxes—things we can be certain of. So the only realistic thing that a project manager can do is learn how to recognize political dirty moves and deal with political issues in the most positive way possible. At the Boston University conference on project management the fellow who is managing the Boston Harbor waste treatment plant project told us that he spends about 40 percent of his time dealing with political issues. The dump trucks going to the site are tearing up the streets in a certain neighborhood. The noise is getting on people's nerves. Why can't they do this? Why can't they do that? If he weren't politically adept, he probably wouldn't have survived as long as he has.

Since all of us set out to succeed as project managers, it seems important to know how people define success and failure. If it were a nice, rational world, we would have an easy answer for this one. But the world is not so rational. There are projects that fail to meet their deadlines, come in over budget, under scope, and are still considered successful. Others meet all of the standard targets, but are called failures. What gives?

I also present a review of the standard tools of project management, for the benefit of those who may not have had in-depth training in them, and also to establish what I consider to be a baseline understanding needed to deal with other topics in this book. If you are already familiar with these, you can skim or skip this chapter.

Other topics include risk management, decision analysis, process improvement, managing vendors, project cost accounting (two chapters contributed by Ben Thorp), tracking progress, identifying customer requirements, and developing a shared understanding of the project in your team.

# 2
## CHAPTER

# The Job of Managing

In the 30-plus years of my career I have observed that there are a lot of people who want to be *managers,* but a lot of them don't want to actually *manage!* Part of the reason is that managers have status, some authority, and generally make more money than nonmanagers do. Even in technical organizations that claim to have dual career paths, the managerial path usually goes higher than the technical path, both in terms of hierarchical level and salary. In fact, I met a fellow a few years ago who had done a study for his M.B.A. degree on organizations with dual career paths, and he had found that the number of companies actually having such paths was very small, and in many cases the technical path was a dumping ground for individuals who could not make it in management.

> A lot of people want to be managers, but many of them don't want to manage.

## MAKING CHOICES

When I was about 14 years old, I got interested in electronics. I became a ham radio operator and built almost all of my equipment. I soon knew that I wanted to design radios as a career, but coming from a small town with only 90 students in the senior class, most of whom did not go to college, I had no idea how to go about becoming a radio designer. One of my friends told me that he was pretty sure you studied electrical engineering. Further, he said, he and two other of my friends were going to visit N.C. State University in Raleigh in a couple of weeks, and he suggested that maybe I should go along. Until then, going to college had never crossed my mind, because my family couldn't afford it.

But the idea had been planted, and I went with them to visit the school. I never applied anywhere else and was lucky enough to be accepted at NCSU. I got my degree in electrical engineering and then spent 15 years in two companies designing radio equipment.

What I discovered was that designing radios in industry is nothing like designing them for fun. I absolutely loved the design activity itself, but that was only part of the job. You had to make drawings of everything, compile bills of material, do endless testing to certify that the product met Federal Communications Commission requirements, and if you sold it in Canada or some other country, you had to test for their requirements as well. The design part I loved. The rest I hated.

At this point in my life, I wouldn't take anything for that 15 years in industry, because it has served as the foundation for my present career, which is training and consulting. I don't think you should teach or consult in something that you've never done, because I don't think you can understand the problems your clients have. So the experience was invaluable.

However, had I known what an electrical engineer actually does, I might not have taken that route. And this is the problem that many people have. They think they would like a certain job, career, or position, but they don't really know what the person does, and therefore often find that they made a bad choice. So if you are considering being a project manager, it would be helpful to know what they actually do, so you can make an informed choice.

## WHAT MANAGERS DO: MYTH AND REALITY

If you read any text on management, you will learn that managers plan, organize, direct, and control. They don't do any actual work themselves. That is done by other people. In fact, one of the most pervasive definitions of management is that they *get work done by other people.* It doesn't take much thought to realize how simplistic and unhelpful this definition is. Guards over chain gangs get work done through other people. Would you call that managing? I don't think so. Dictators, tyrants, bullies, and politicians get work done by other people, but again, they are not managing when they do it. It is pretty obvious that we need a better definition.

A proper definition should be congruent with reality, and not some platitude about what *should* be. Henry Mintzberg, a professor of management at McGill University in Canada, has written that ". . . it is surprising how little study there has been of what managers actually do." He goes on to say, "There has certainly been no shortage of material on what managers *should* do. . . . Unfortunately, in the absence of any real understanding of managerial work, much of this advice has proved false and wasteful. How can anyone possibly prescribe change in a phenomenon so complex as managerial work without first having a deep comprehension of it?" (Mintzberg, 1989, p. 7).

To answer the question, Mintzberg shadowed a number of managers, meticulously recording what they do, how long they do it, and with whom they do it. His findings are enlightening and certainly raise questions about the wisdom of the prescriptive material written by professors of management who have never managed. What I find in Mintzberg's book is confirmation of my own experience in managing. I have been both a department manager, with 63 people in my department (three of whom were supervisors of others), and a project manager. Much of what Mintzberg found to be true of department managers is also true of project managers, in my experience. I have summarized his principle findings in Table 2–1.

**T A B L E  2–1**

What Managers Do

| The Myth | The Reality |
|---|---|
| The manager is a reflective, systematic thinker. | Managers actually work at an unrelenting pace, on activities characterized by brevity, variety, and discontinuity. They are strongly oriented to action and dislike reflective activities. |
| The effective manager has no regular duties to perform. | In addition to handling exceptions, managers perform regular duties, including ritual and ceremony, negotiations, and processing the soft information that links the organization with its environment. |
| The senior manager needs aggregated information, which a formal management information system best provides. | Managers strongly favor oral media—namely telephone calls and meetings. |
| Management is, or is quickly becoming, a science and a profession. | How managers' do their work—to schedule time, process information, make decisions, and so on—remains locked deep inside their brains. |

## A DESCRIPTION OF MANAGERIAL WORK

The manager's job can best be described as a set of roles. These are organized sets of behaviors in which they engage. Mintzberg has identified 10 roles that fall into 3 categories.

> The manager's job can best be described as a set of roles.

### Interpersonal Roles

The first interpersonal role is the *figurehead* role. By virtue of his or her position as head of an organizational unit, every manager must perform some ceremonial duties. These can include having lunch with important customers, attending weddings of employees, and meeting with touring dignitaries. Some of these may seem trivial, but they are important to the smooth functioning of an organization and cannot be ignored by the manager. I would say that project managers have a certain number of these functions to carry out, so that this finding applies to project managers as well as to general managers.

The manager must also perform the *leader* role. Being in charge of an organizational unit, the manager is responsible for the work of the people in that unit. There may be both direct and indirect leadership roles to perform. Encouraging and motivating members of a project team would be a direct role in a pure project organization and an indirect role in a matrix. As we have all heard so often, project managers usually have a lot of responsibility but little formal authority, so they must use influence to get things done. Leadership itself involves a great deal of influence activity, so it is one of the most important roles for the project manager.

The third interpersonal role mentioned by Mintzberg is the *liaison* role. This is a role in which a manager makes contacts outside her vertical chain of command. There is no doubt that project managers engage in this role to a great extent. Some people call this the *boundary-crossing* role, because managers work outside the boundaries of their immediate unit. In fact, it is often the interfacing with people outside the unit that is critical to the success of project teams. One of the major functions of such interfacing is to gather information. In effect, the liaison role is devoted to building up the manager's own external information system—informal, private, oral—but nevertheless effective.

## Informational Roles

Through his interpersonal contacts, both with team members and with the network of contacts, the manager becomes the nerve center of his unit. He may not know everything, but he usually knows more than any one of his team members. Mintzberg found that managers spend nearly 40 percent of their contact time on activities devoted to the transmission of information. To a great extent, communication is the work of a manager.

As a *monitor*, the manager is always scanning the environment for information. Much of the information that the manager receives is in oral form and consists of gossip, hearsay, and speculation. This soft information can be very important in alerting the manager to problems before they occur.

Managers must *disseminate* information or it is of no use to the team. This is one area in which some managers fail, because they realize that information is power, and they try to keep it to themselves. The net result of this is that decisions cannot be made effectively by other members of the team but must be made by the manager. My favorite expression for this is "mushroom manager": he keeps people in the dark, feeds them a lot of nonsense, and when they grow up, he cuts them off at the knees and cans them.

The *spokesperson* role is one in which managers pass some of their information to people outside their units. This includes making presentations to higher-ranking managers, military officers in defense contracting projects, and sometimes to stockholders who are concerned about a major project.

## Decisional Roles

Information is the basic input to decision-making. Since the manager usually has more information than any single team member, she often plays a major role in making project decisions. Mintzberg has identified four decisional roles that the manager must perform.

The *entrepreneur* role is that of trying to improve the unit. In the monitor role, the manager is constantly on the lookout for good ideas. When she finds one, she may initiate a development project. This is the entrepreneur role. Even project managers may occasionally play this role, suggesting projects to senior managers. This would be especially true of technical project managers, who think of applications for technology and suggest new product development projects. We also find some corporations doing new business development projects, so that the project manager must play the entrepreneurial role to the hilt.

Another decisional role is that of *disturbance handler*. Managers are initiators in the entrepreneurial role. In the disturbance handler role, they are reacting to pressures in which change is outside their control. For the project manager, this can be changes in scope, accidents, loss of key personnel, and conflicts with functional managers over priorities.

The *resource allocator* role might be more the preserve of the functional manager than the project manager, but even project managers have responsibility for deciding who will get what in the project team. One of the most important resources that the manager allocates is his or her own time. Access to a manager exposes the person to the team's nerve center and decision-maker.

Finally, we have the role of *negotiator*. There can be no question of the importance of this role to project managers. Together with their leader role, this is the means of getting things done when you have no authority. Managers at all levels actually spend considerable time in negotiations, but negotiation is a way of life for the project manager.

### The Integrated Job

It is important to stress that the ten roles described by Mintzberg are not separable. They form a *gestalt,* an integrated whole. This does not mean that all managers give equal attention to all 10 roles. The function that the manager performs will dictate that more time be given to one role than the others. However, you cannot neglect one completely in any management job.

The fact that they do form an integrated whole is one reason for the difficulties of managing teams. "Two or three people cannot share a single managerial position unless they can act as one entity. That means they cannot divide up the ten roles unless they can very carefully reintegrate them" (Mintzberg, 1989, p. 22). The biggest problem is with the informational role. Unless there is full sharing of managerial information, team management breaks down. Since this is nearly impossible to achieve, we naturally can expect some problems with teams.

### PRESCRIPTIONS BASED ON REALITY

It has often been said that to be effective we must understand ourselves. Insight into management work is a step in that direction. Success depends on how well managers understand and respond to the pressures and dilemmas of the job. Mintzberg has suggested three specific areas of concern for managers. I believe all of these apply to project managers.

**1.** *The project manager must find systematic ways to share his or her privileged information.* This can be done through regular debriefing sessions with key team members, by maintaining a diary of important information for limited circulation, or by a memory dump to a dictating machine. To the degree that key team members have better information, they can make many of the decisions that would otherwise have to be made by the project manager. In her book *Leadership and the New Science* (1994) Margaret Wheatley has written that information is self-organizing and that teams can benefit greatly by having the same information at their disposal that the manager has.

**2.** *The project manager must avoid the pressures that would lead to superficiality by giving attention to issues that require it, by looking at the big picture, and by making use of analytical data.* This boils down to knowing what is a priority and what is not, so you don't spend as much time on the trivial many as you do on the vital few. Members of the team have time to deal with analysis of project status. The project manager must take full advantage of what these people have to offer and act on it appropriately.

**3.** *Project managers must gain control of their own time by turning obligations into an advantage and by turning those things they want to do into obligations.* There are a lot of things that managers are obligated to do that can be a waste of time. The effective manager makes the obligation into something positive. For example, a presentation can become an opportunity to lobby for resources for the team. A visit to a customer might be a chance to actually gain more business. If a manager initiates a project or subproject, he might obligate others to report back to him.

## A WORD OF CAUTION

It would be easy to conclude that because few managers really spend a lot of time planning, this is appropriate as well for project managers. Every major study I have seen on the correlates between what the project manager does and project success have shown planning to be vital. What may be important is that good project managers *facilitate* good project planning. They don't do it themselves. As I have written in all of my books, the first rule of planning is that the people who must do the work should do the planning. There are two principal reasons why this is true:

> Just because few managers do much planning does not mean that project managers should abandon planning. If you have no plan, you have no control!

1. They have no commitment to someone else's plan, not because of ego, but because it is generally not correct—either in estimates, sequencing, or in being inclusive of everything.

2. Collectively, the team will think of things that no one individual (namely, the project manager) would think of.

It is a fact that project managers are supposed to be in control, in the sense of getting results from the project team. And, since control is defined as comparing where you are to where you are supposed to be, so you can take corrective action when there is a deviation, it follows that if you have no plan, you cannot have control, since you have nothing to compare progress against. For that reason, planning is not an option—it is a requirement! Perhaps if more general managers spent time planning, we would have fewer organizations operating in crisis mode.

# 3

CHAPTER

# Power and Politics
# for Project Managers

To a lot of people in organizations, politics is a dirty word. When I was an engineer, my peers used to lament about politics. "I wish we could get rid of the politics," they would say. I agreed with them. However, I soon realized that politics is so much a part of every organization that the only thing to do is learn to deal with it.

No doubt you have been burned by some individual in an organization who was a ruthless, up-and-comer, who ran roughshod over you without blinking an eye. That is how we learn to hate politics. But politics doesn't have to be dirty, and I don't advocate that you play dirty.

**Principle:** The purpose of all political behavior is to develop and keep power.

## UNDERSTANDING POWER AND POLITICS

Before you can use politics in a way that supports your projects, you have to first acknowledge its existence and its impact on project success. Since the purpose of all political behavior is to develop and keep power, we should begin by understanding what is meant by power.

Power is the influence or control that a person has over others. Again, I know people who say, "I don't want to control anyone else, and I don't want anyone control ling me." It's a fine sentiment, but it does not change the fact that we are always influencing others and, therefore, exercising power over them, whether we want to or not.

**Power:** The influence or control over others that a person has.

One premise of human interaction is that you can't avoid influencing others. When you sit beside a person on a train, bus, or airplane, and the person stares out the window and never makes eye contact with you, that individual is communicating very clearly that she does not want to enter into a relationship with you. "Just leave me alone" is the message. And that usually works as an influence on the behavior of all but the most interpersonally unaware individuals, who insist on trying to talk to her anyway.

**Premise:** You can't *not* influence others!

No doubt you have been in a meeting or group in which a member sat and made faces while others talked. There are scowls and frowns, or just a single persistent look of disapproval. Even though he says nothing, that person has an influence on others. By the same token, you may have someone who sits smiling the entire time, nodding affirmatively once in a while. Everyone is influenced positively by that person. They think, "She's really one of us. She agrees with us." But either way, your interpretation of the person's nonverbal behavior can be wrong. The scowling person may simply feel unwell that day and may agree with the rest of you, and the smiling face may be thinking, "What a bunch of idiots!" The smile is one of condescension, not approval.

French and Raven (1959) identified five "faces" of power. These are shown in Table 3–1. Project managers who complain that they have a lot of responsibility but no authority are saying that they lack position power. They cannot tell people what to do and expect them to do it, because their position as project manager carries with it no "clout." Couillard (1995) has found that this truly is a problem in high-risk projects and suggests that organizations

**T A B L E  3–1**

The Five Faces of Power

| | |
|---|---|
| Expert | The ability to influence others because the person is recognized as an expert in some area. |
| Reward | The influence a person exercises because he or she has the ability to reward others. |
| Legitimate | One's position in an organization or group is a source of influence over others. |
| Referent | The power you have over another because that person identifies with you or feels attracted to you. |
| Coercion | Coercive power is the ability to force people to do something through fear of sanctions or punishment that might be inflicted on them for noncompliance. |

Cartwright & Zander (1968).

must give more authority to project managers who run such projects (see Chapter 11).

One way that project managers can have greater position power is to put them on an equal footing with functional managers. If project managers are drawn from functional groups and still report to functional managers, they have no clout. I discuss this in more detail in Chapter 6. The other aspect of this is that project managers should have input to the performance appraisals of team members. While the project manager may not evaluate the person's technical performance, she should be able to evaluate such dimensions as cooperation, timeliness of work, and contributions to the team. This automatically gives the project manager some power to reward (or punish) members of the team, and is one way of developing greater commitment to projects than is often found in organizations when the project manager has no input to performance appraisals.

> One way to give project managers some position power is to put them on the same level as functional managers.

Coercion power is one form that project managers can't use in most cases. In fact, coercive power is harder to use in organizations today than it might have been in the period from 1900 to 1960. Since the 1960s, people have been more mobile in their jobs, have had a greater sense of freedom, and have learned that they don't have to submit to coercion. This is not universally true, and you do find coercion being used by some managers. For it to work, the person being coerced must feel that he or she has no other job options and is therefore dependent on this manager for a living.

**Coercive power is not available to project managers in most cases.**

Project managers can sometimes use expert power, but even this base is fragile in some projects. When a project is multidisciplinary—that is, cuts across a number of technical specialties—it becomes very difficult for a project manager to understand all of them. This, then, limits her expert power over members of the team. What she might be seen as is an expert in managing projects, dealing with the politics of the organization, and being a provider of the resources that members of the team need in order to get the job done.

**Expert power is useful to project managers, but it must be real— not assumed.**

Reward power is often limited for project managers, if you consider rewards to be tangible things like pay increases. But rewards can be intangible—such as a pat on the back or recognition for good work—and there is no limit to the "amount" of such rewards that a manager can dispense. One word of caution, though. A pat on the back must be sincere. Attempts to "stroke" people as a behavioral reinforcement technique come across as phoney and usually create resentment and a decline in performance. So, if you don't mean it, don't say it!

## WHAT'S IN IT FOR ME?

There is a principle in psychology that people don't do anything unless there is something in it for themselves. Yes, that is true even when a person does a benevolent act—he gets a warm feeling for having done something good. Or he may avoid feeling guilty for not doing good. Either way, there is a payoff. If there is no payoff, he won't do it. You can take this to the bank, whether you like it or not. It doesn't make us cold, calculating human beings; it just explains how we behave.

The effective project manager must consider what's in it for me (WI-IFM) when dealing with other departments and stakeholders. These departments are not likely to help and support a project unless they perceive that it is in their interests to do so. As Pinto says, "The worst mistake project managers can make is to assume that the stakeholders will automatically appreciate and value the project as much as they themselves [meaning the project manager] do" (1996, p. 37).

> Project managers may not be able to dispense tangible rewards, but they can use intangible ones.

This proposition is supported by Baker and Menon (1995), who show how two projects failed because of politics and one succeeded for the same reason. One of the failures was the supercollider. The project leaders went around proclaiming the merits of the project to scientists (which was equivalent to preaching to the choir) but never tried to convince Congress. When the Clinton administration came into office, the supercollider was killed. So they say, "The story of the project needs to be told in a way that's clear not only to the technowizards but to the masses as well" (p. 20).

> You should *always* remember WIIFM when trying to influence people to do somthing you want done.

## USING INFLUENCE TO GET THE JOB DONE

When you have little or no authority, you have to get things done through influence or negotiation. And it turns out that this is true even when you do have authority. I have asked a number of company presidents and CEOs, "You have a lot of authority. Does your authority guarantee that people do what you want them to do." They always say no.

"Then what does get people to do what you want done?" I ask.

"They have to want to do it," is the answer given every time. "My job is to get them to want to do it."

What they are saying is that they still have to influence their people, in spite of the position power that they hold. If a company president has to do this, project managers can expect no better. So we had better hone our influence skills.

**in • flu • ence:**

**Power to sway or affect based on prestige, wealth, ability, or position.**

—*American Heritage*

The dictionary says that influence is to "sway or affect" the behavior of others. Robert Cialdini (1993) calls influence the psychology of persuasion. As a project manager, you have to use influence frequently, as I have already said, since you have no direct authority over a lot of the people with whom you deal.

Besides the members of your own organization, you have to deal with outsiders—vendors, customers, and partners in certain ventures. It is often necessary to influence these people. One way of doing this is to address the WIIFM issue, as discussed in the previous section. This is such a fundamental principle that it cannot be overlooked.

Besides WIIFM, there are other methods of exerting influence. One is through reciprocity. This is a very powerful way to gain influence in an organization. It is based on our belief that an exchange should, over time, be fair and balanced. I do something for you, and you, in turn, reciprocate. This rule is seldom discussed, but if it is violated, people become very upset. They feel cheated, and this is sometimes the cause of relationship damage. By building relationships in the organization, and by doing favors for others when it is appropriate, you build a "bank account" that you can draw on when you need something from others. I don't like to propose that this be done in a cold, calculating way, but you definitely need to be aware of the process and also be realistic about the need for the bank account. That is, if

**The rule of reciprocity is a powerful influence "tool."**

you never do favors for others, there is nothing for you to draw on if you need help.

Building relationships is itself a powerful way of building influence. We are far more willing to do things for people we like than for those we dislike or hardly know. A study at Bell Labs found that networking was a major factor in the success of engineers (Kelley and Caplan, 1993). Those who were most successful used the informal network to their advantage. However, it was not just that they were willing to call someone and ask for help that made the difference. These engineers took time to build alliances with other members of

> We are much more willing to do favors for people we know than those we don't know. Take time to build relationships!

Bell Labs *before* they needed help. Then when they called another engineer, they got a timely response. Those engineers who had not spent time building such alliances would call, but their calls would often not be answered for days. The finding of this study was considered so important that Bell Labs developed a program to train their engineers to use the informal network and to build relationships.

Good influencers are socially sensitive, articulate, and flexible (Pinto, 1996, p. 38). They can often read body language and can tell how another person is reacting to their proposals, so that they can "shift gears" if they detect that a particular approach isn't working. They also know when to use face-to-face methods and when a simple phone call will do. It is usually

> Good influencers are socially sensitive, articulate, and flexible.

harder for people to refuse a face-to-face request than one made by phone, so if you anticipate difficulty in getting something done, go talk to the person.

## DEALING WITH RESISTANCE

It is also important to know how to deal with resistance to your proposals. There are four approaches to dealing with resistance:

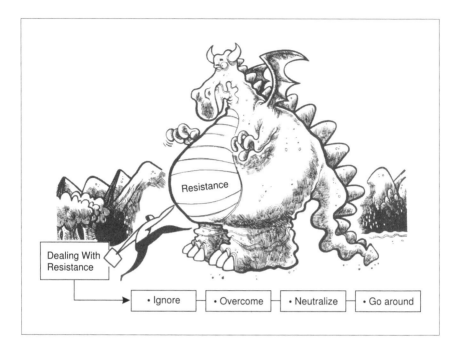

1. **Ignore**
2. **Overcome**
3. **Neutralize**
4. **Go around**

Ignoring resistance might be acceptable in some cases—when it is very weak or is being presented by people who can't do you much damage. However, be very careful not to underestimate that resistance. It just might be stronger than you think. We sometimes think that low-status members of our organizations can't do us much damage. But such people can sometimes incite others to resist. This is itself a political action and can build to a very strong force. Strikes sometimes develop in this way.

The next strategy, to overcome resistance, is the one most frequently tried. You try to convince a person or group through the force of argument that your proposal is good for them, but they aren't convinced. If you observe this being done by someone else, you will sometimes notice that the more pressure they exert to get the resisting party to acquiesce, the more resistant the party becomes. This is explained in systems thinking by saying that the interaction becomes a system that tries to balance itself. The stronger the force on one side becomes, the more the resisting force becomes. Thus, the resisting party just becomes more entrenched in resistance. When you see this happening, it is a good idea to back off, because continuing to push will get the person or group so entrenched in resistance that they can't change their position without losing face.

**If you push too hard, the person just pushes back and becomes entrenched in his resistance.**

In this instance, it is a good idea to try to neutralize the resistance. This does not mean to blast the person into oblivion, as much as you might want to. It means to find a way to make the resistance go away. The best approach that I know of is to proceed as follows:

"I understand that you have some concerns about my proposal," you say. "What would I have to do to convince you that it is a good proposal?"

The person can make two responses. One is that you will never convince him. When a person tells me that, I say, "Really. There's *nothing* I can do to convince you?" I place great emphasis on the word nothing. If the

**neu • tral • ize:** To find a way to make resistance go away.

person is willing to meet me part way, he will usually soften a bit and give me the second possible response. If he is unwilling to even meet me part way, then I might have to resort to one of the other approaches. And I might sometimes have to forget my proposal. You can't win all of the battles.

The second response you can get is for the person to say, "If you did xyz, that would convince me." If it is a reasonable suggestion and you can do it, you now know what to do. If it is something you can't do, you can now negotiate, which is discussed in the next section of this chapter.

The fourth approach to dealing with resistance is to go around it. This means go around the person to her boss and have her boss get her to cooperate. You sometimes have to do this in projects when you have a problem with a team member and have to go to her functional manager. It is always the least-preferred approach, in my opinion, because of the downside that it carries. You may win the battle and lose the war in using this approach. However, it may be necessary when the stakes are extremely high—for example, if a safety issue is involved.

There is another go-around method that can sometimes work. If you go to the person's peers and convince all of them of your position and let them put pressure on the person, this can sometimes work. It all depends on how easily the person is influenced by his peer group.

## NEGOTIATING SKILLS

No matter how much position power you have, a fact of life in organizations is that you have to influence and negotiate to achieve your objectives. Some people think of negotiation as being synonymous with compromise, but that is not correct. When possible, a negotiation should always take a win-win approach. In win-win, you try to see that both parties to the negotiation achieve their objectives to the degree possible. Yes, there may be some give-and-take. The problem with serious compromise, where each side gives up strongly desired objectives, is that they both feel cheated at the end. With win-win, less of such a feeling should exist.

> All project managers have to influence and negotiate to get the job done.

Win-lose, of course, is an attempt to run roughshod over the other person to get what you want. This approach always creates enemies and over the long run tends to become lose-lose. This is what happened in the fight between the machinists' union and management at Eastern Airlines. The union was determined not to let Lorenzo break their union, as he had done at Continental. They succeeded in doing this, but in the process, Eastern went under. When it was all over, they said, "We won." It was a hollow victory, in my opinion. They won the battle and lost the war.

Since a negotiation is always a conflict between the aims of two parties, conflict resolution and negotiation are nearly the same. If you are good at negotiating, you will usually be good at dealing with conflicts. Following are guidelines on how to approach either a conflict or a negotiation.

- Choose a neutral setting in which to discuss the problem. Your office is not the best place, since it automatically puts the other person at a disadvantage.
- State your sincere desire to resolve the conflict or difference to the satisfaction of the other person and yourself. (If you want to trash the other person, perhaps you should wait until you have cooled off before you begin. You can't fake it. If you want to stomp him or her, it will come out sooner or later.)
- Do not assume that you know the other person's motives, intentions, thoughts, or feelings. To do so is *mind-reading* and only makes the conflict worse.
- Deal with the issues, not the character of the person.
- Where values differences have caused the conflict, deal with the *tangible effects* of the difference, not the values themselves. You generally cannot change the other person's values. You can, however, ask that they take certain actions, etc.
- Practice *active listening.* Don't glibly say, "I understand." Demonstrate your understanding by rephrasing what the other person has said. Note also that, when the person feels you understand her, the problem is half solved in many cases. One of the frequent causes of conflict is the feeling that the other party does not understand or appreciate your concerns.
- State what you want as a request, not as a demand. Ask what the other person wants of you. If you cannot or will not comply with the other party's request, make a counterproposal. Try for win-win. Compromise only as a last resort.
- Keep in mind that the other person is not bad, mad, or crazy just because you have a difference. If you judge people, it is hard to remain objective and deal only with issues.

- Try to work on one issue at a time, when several exist. Begin with those for which it is likely to be easiest to reach agreement.
- Don't rush the process. Conflicts resolved in haste may come back to haunt you later.
- Once an agreement has been reached, ask the other party if there is anything which might prevent their complying with the agreement. Ask the same question of yourself. If there are any potential obstacles, try to find contingencies. This is called doing an "ecology check" at the end of the negotiation. Failure to do so can result in a failed resolution of the conflict.
- Don't make promises you can't keep. It is disastrous for a manager to promise something to an employee and then have his boss overrule him. If you need to check with your boss before making an agreement, say so and reconvene the meeting after you have seen your boss.

> **All behavior makes sense to the person doing the behaving.**

- *Always* give the other person a chance to save face. Never belittle his position. Remember, all behavior makes sense from the perspective of the actor, but not necessarily from the perspective of the observer. If you fail to observe this rule, you may "win" the negotiation and make an enemy for life. And in the corporate world, that person may be your boss one day, or at least wait for an opportunity to stab you in the back to retaliate for your humiliating him.

# 4

CHAPTER

# Dealing with Cultural Differences

**W**ith the advent of the global economy comes an increased interaction between people of different countries, and an increase in the need to deal with cultural differences. In addition, there is greater migration of people within the United States, and this, too, brings a greater mix of the cultures that exist within this country. One definition of culture is shown in the box. Another is that culture is the sum total of the attitudes, beliefs, values, behaviors, and traditions that a person has internalized.

Every organization has a culture unique to itself, and this is true of divisions within large corporations. The important thing to understand about culture is that in most cases there is nothing *absolutely* right or wrong about cultures—they just *are!* It is only in a relative sense that you can say something is wrong in another culture. (I am excluding such

**cul • ture:** The totality of socially transmitted behavior patterns, arts, beliefs, institutions, and all other products of human work and thought.

*—American Heritage*

33

glaring cultural differences as human rights abuses.) Naturally, not everyone agrees with my position. There are examples all around of people insisting that individuals from different cultures change to conform to the culture in which they are immersed at the moment. Some even go to another country and insist that the native people change their culture. One reason that some people in Europe dislike Americans is that we go there and insist that they do things *our* way!

This happened when missionaries went to the south sea islands and found that the women went around with their breasts uncovered. In the culture from which the missionaries came, this was shameful. To the islanders, it was a normal thing and there was no shame in it. The missionaries prevailed, however, and soon the women had their tops covered exactly as the women from Europe and America.

## SOME EXAMPLES

During my first trip to Thailand, I met a fellow from Norway who had been sent there by his company to manage a plant. He was single at the time, so he started dating a Thai woman. One evening he went to her home to take her out and asked where she would like to go? To his bewilderment, she exploded.

> When you violate a person's cultural expectations, you offend him or her.

"Why do you always ask what I want to do?" she shouted. "Why don't you make a decision like a man!"

The poor fellow stammered, "I was just trying to be polite."

"Well, don't be!" she said.

"But what if I want to go somewhere that you don't like?" he protested.

"It doesn't matter," she insisted. "We'll go there!"

Because he was violating her cultural expectations of a man, she got angry at him. If his Thai colleagues at work had known of his behavior, no doubt they also would have lost respect for him. As the old saying goes, "When in Rome, do as the Romans do."

This injunction has its own problems. I have a friend who lived in Hong Kong for about 10 years. He had only been there for a short time when there was a torrential rain storm, and he was trying to catch a taxi to his office. Naturally, so was everyone else. To his chagrin, every time a taxi would pull up to the curb, someone would jump in front of him and take the taxi. After this happened several times, he realized that this was the system—whoever grabbed the taxi first was entitled to it. So the next taxi that pulled up, he dived for and got inside. In the process, he just about trampled an elderly lady. He said that he was so embarrassed at violating his own cultural norm that for a long time afterwards, he couldn't jump in front of anyone to catch a cab.

In the early days of oil exploration in Arabic countries, Americans found that the people they were dealing with would move up very close to them when talking. The American would instinctively back up, and the Arab would move closer. In the Arabic culture body space is much closer than for Americans. I have been told that they like to stand close enough to literally smell each other's breath. We Americans prefer a larger distance so that we *can't* smell the other person's breath (we have a fear of this, which is why breath mints sell so well). In this interaction, *both* parties are feeling offended, because the other person is violating their cultural expectation.

On one of my trips to eastern Asia, I picked up a book on how Asian managers differ from Americans, and the book highlighted a number of cultural differences that sometimes cause conflict between Americans and Asians. One of these is the difference in perception of someone who is fat.

I had taught for Petronas, the oil company in Malaysia, and after the class had to catch a flight back to Singapore. The company had a driver take me to the airport, and he was driving a Volkswagen van. The customary thing to do is to get into the back seat, so I started to do so. The driver looked back at me and said, "You're kind of fat. Maybe you'd be more comfortable up here in the front."

Having just read about this, I was about to burst out laughing. I could just imagine this fellow coming to the U.S. and getting a job driving for a limousine service. One day he tells someone, "You're kind of fat. Would you like to sit up here?" The person is very offended, and the poor fellow is fired. His response: "What happened? I was just trying to be helpful."

And he was.

In east Asia, being fat is not a terrible thing as it is in our "Twiggy" society. We think that if you are a few pounds overweight, you should lose it immediately. You're a bad person! To the Asian, however, being fat is a sign of affluence. The reason is that for a long period in their history, only the wealthy could afford enough food to get fat (not to mention the fact that they generally eat a better diet than Americans, with less fat content).

> In east Asia, being fat is a sign of affluence.

I told this story in a seminar and during a break, a lady related a similar experience to me. She had gone to India to visit some friends, and she was a large woman. She had only been there a short time and was amazed to have people come up to her and ask, "How much do you weigh?" It was several days before someone explained the connection for her. They were trying to find out if she was a very affluent woman. In effect, they were asking, "Are you wealthy?" Even that question would be unacceptable in American society, but it is not in India.

## PROJECT EXAMPLES

A company hired an engineer from India to work in a project. One day the project manager came by his desk and asked how things were going. "Everything is fine," said the engineer, "except for my lab work. It's at a standstill."

"What's the problem?" asked the project manager.

"I don't have a technician to do the work," said the engineer.

"Oh, yes, we don't have enough technicians for every engineer to have one," explained the project manager. "I'm afraid you'll have to do your own lab work."

The engineer became indignant. "I don't do lab work," he said.

"Well, in this lab, all engineers have to do a certain amount of bench work," the project manager persisted. "I think you better get in there and do the work, so you can stay on schedule."

The engineer did as he was instructed, but he was really angry. What the project manager didn't understand was that this was demeaning to the engineer. In India, an engineer would never do bench work—it is considered beneath his status. Had the project manager understood this, he could have said, "If you're going to live in the U.S., you either have to find a company that has the luxury of a technician for every engineer or you have to adapt to our way of doing things. As it was, he thought the engineer was just being egotistical.

Another example: A project manager was doing work on a job that was a joint venture with a Japanese firm. He was discussing an issue with a Japanese engineer and asked if the fellow agreed with him on the issue. The engineer assured him that he did. Later on, he learned that the Japanese engineer had not really agreed about the issue but was merely being polite.

By way of understanding this, let me give some examples. When we hosted our first exchange student, who was from Japan, I asked her how to say *yes* and *no* in Japanese. "Well, yes is *hai*," she said, "and no is *eea*, but we don't like to say it." I didn't fully appreciate what she meant until a few years later. In Japanese society, saying no can be considered very rude, so when dealing with Japanese business people, be careful to determine if yes really means agreement or just politeness.

Although it isn't a project example, I frequently have dinner in a Japanese restaurant in Madison, Wisconsin. I was there one evening and the waitress, who is a native-born Japanese woman, was taking an order. The fellow asked for a specific beer. Her response was true Japanese.

"Maybe we don't have that kind," she said. "Maybe you'd prefer a different one."

I was really amused. She knew very well that she didn't have that specific kind of beer, but her cultural conditioning made it hard for her to say so. Instead, she had to soften it a bit.

In his book, *Dave Barry Does Japan,* Dave tells of a similar experience in Japan. He called a travel agent to book a flight. He told her where he wanted to go, and after a minute or so, she said, "You want to fly from *x* to *y*?"

"Yes."

"Perhaps you would prefer to take a train," she said.

"No, I want to fly," Dave insisted.

There was another pause. Then she said, "From *x* to *y*?"

"Yes."

"Perhaps you would prefer to take a train."

Dave said it took several iterations before he finally realized what she was telling him: "There are no flights from $x$ to $y$. If you want to go, you will have to take a train."

Another project example: A fellow was in Thailand on a job. He went to lunch one day with some of the facility managers, and when they came back, the factory workers were nowhere to be seen. When they found them, they were at the small temple that every factory has, and they were praying. It turned out that there was a problem in the plant and they were praying for its successful resolution. They had, however, told no one in management about the problem. Managers are expected to know these things.

An American project manager was working on a job in Mexico, to install some equipment in a plant. He finished the job and went away for the evening. When he came in the next morning, the local people had called in a priest, who was sprinkling holy water on the machine and blessing it.

These things seem strange to us because they are not part of our culture. But they are real to the countries involved, and we must respect them.

## BECOMING CULTURALLY AWARE

If you are going to run an international project, I strongly suggest that you try to learn as much as you can about the culture of the country with which you will be working. To find a source of information, you can call their embassy, check with some of the exchange student agencies that bring students from that country to stay in the U.S., or read a book on the subject. There are some protocol schools in areas like Washington, D. C. that teach Americans how to handle such issues.

For that matter, even if you don't run an international project, you may be faced with some of these issues. A fellow in Chicago told me that they had 21 different countries represented in his company. He needs a lot of cultural awareness to avoid problems.

# 5
CHAPTER

# Defining Success and Failure

It probably goes without saying that no one sets out to fail in managing a project. We all want our projects to be successful. However, it is not at all clear what is meant by success or failure. What is needed is an operational definition of these terms. An operational definition is one that has criteria that all parties involved can agree to use to define the outcome. How to develop operational definitions is covered in greater detail in Chapter 23, but for now, we need to agree on how to define success and failure in managing projects.

> When you fail to meet a target that was just pulled out of the air, should that be called a failure?

The most frequently used definition is that a project is a failure when it does not meet its cost, performance, time, or scope (C, P, T, S) targets. However, there are a couple of things wrong with this definition. First, where did the targets come from? When they are just "pulled out of the air," should failing to meet unrealistic targets be considered a failure? Second, even if you meet all of these targets, does the project solve

No one sets out
to fail in
managing a project.

the problem it was intended to solve? Does the customer use it? If not, was it really a success? As you can see, these are nontrivial questions.

Schutz, Sleven, and Pinto (1987) have identified four errors that can be made in solving projects, and as we have said, project management is problem solving on a large scale, so their concept applies equally well in this area. These are:

1. Type I error: Not taking an action when one should be taken.
2. Type II error: Taking an action when none should be taken.
3. Type III error: Taking the wrong action (solving the wrong problem).
4. Type IV error: Addressing the right problem, but the solution is not used.

Based on their terms, we can say that a project that meets its C, P, T, and S targets but is not used is either a Type III or Type IV error. In some cases, it is the fact that a Type III error has been made that ultimately causes the project to be a Type IV error. That is, we have solved the wrong problem, so no one uses the project. This happens on internal software projects sometimes when we talk to department managers about their requirements, implement the system based on their comments, but their people won't use the system because it does not really meet their needs.

## OTHER PERSPECTIVES

In their book *Learning from Failure: The Systems Approach,* Fortune and Peters (1995) say, "A simple definition of failure is something that has gone wrong, or not lived up to expectations. Moving a little way beyond this simple statement, various types or categories of failure can be identified" (p. 21).

> A simple definition of failure is that something has gone wrong or has not lived up to expectations.

They go on to establish four types of failures, much like Schutz, et al. These are shown in Table 5–1. Type 1 failures are those that we encounter every day. Examples are software that never worked properly or a new product that won't sell.

For Type 2 failures, the original objectives are met, but there are undesirable consequences or side effects that result. In step 4 of my general model of project management, choosing strategy is done by subjecting the candidate strategy to a number of tests, one of which is whether consequences are acceptable. This question is an attempt to help project

### T A B L E 5–1

Types of Failures

| | |
|---|---|
| Type 1 . . . . . . . . . . . . . . . . . . . . . . . . . | Objectives not met |
| Type 2 . . . . . . . . . . . . . . . . . . . . . . . . . | Undesirable side effects |
| Type 3 . . . . . . . . . . . . . . . . . . . . . . . . . | Designed failures |
| Type 4 . . . . . . . . . . . . . . . . . . . . . . . . . | Inappropriate objectives |

managers avoid Type 2 errors. Most of today's environmental problems are the consequences of solutions to problems we had yesterday. Fortune and Peters cite the drug thalidomide as an example of a product that seemed beneficial but caused numerous birth defects. More recently, we have breast implants, and the outcome has nearly destroyed Dow-Corning. So we are surrounded by many Type 2 errors.

The next category of failure is one that is intentional and, therefore, is not considered bad. A fuse that is designed to blow (fail) when a certain current level is exceeded by an appliance is an example. Sprinkler systems fail to hold water in pipes when a fire breaks out. These are called Type 3 failures.

The fourth category of failure is similar to Schutz, et al., Type III, solving the wrong problem. Examples include installing a conveyor to reduce breakage of manufactured goods that does not solve the breakage problem, but moves goods around the factory just fine; products that work fine but don't meet the needs of the market; and the Apple III computer, which was probably technically superior to the IBM-PC at the time but was not accepted in the marketplace because of IBM's superior name and because no software was available to run business applications. We might say the same about Beta format in video players. The format was technically superior to VHS, but because Sony tried to keep it proprietary, VHS was adopted by most manufacturers and Beta eventually died in the home entertainment market. (Most studio-quality recorders still use Beta format.)

> **It is extremely important that criteria be developed that are mutually agreed upon as definitions of success by major stakeholders before projects are started.**

As Fortune and Peters go on to say, almost all judgments about failure are subjective; they are colored by personal perception, circumstances, and expectations. I have a client company in which people lament that the actual person with whom they work in a customer organization will regard their work as successful, while that person's boss will call it a failure. No doubt this is often true where multiple stakeholders are involved, and it illustrates how important it is that criteria be developed that are mutually agreed upon as definitions of success before such projects are started.

## RESEARCH FINDINGS

In 1974, Murphy, Baker, and Fisher reported the results of a study of over 650 projects to determine the factors that affect project success. This study is summarized in Cleland and King's *Project Management Handbook.* They asked the question, "Why are some projects perceived as failures when they met the P, C, T, and S targets?" And "Why are others considered successes even when they are late and over budget?" Based on their study, they decided that success must be defined as follows:

> If the project meets the technical performance specifications and/or mission to be performed, and if there is a high level of satisfaction concerning the project outcome among key people in the parent organization, key people in the client organization, key people on the project team, and key users or clientele of the project effort, the project is considered an overall success (Baker, et al., 1974, p. 903).

The important word here is *perceptions.* If the right people perceive that the project was a success, then it was, for all practical purposes. Note that the definition does not include schedule and cost performance as criteria for success. The authors go on to say that one reason for this is that the research was conducted on completed projects. No doubt those not yet finished are under pressure to meet cost and schedule targets, but once a job is complete, if it satisfies a lot of key people in terms of satisfying their need, the missed cost and schedule targets become less important.

> If the right people consider a project a success, it is, for all practical purposes.

The study identified a number of variables that are important for perceived project success and a number that contribute to perceived project failure. An important finding was that for a project to be perceived as successful, many, if not most, of the variables associated with success must be present. Similarly, most, if not all, of the variables associated with failure must be absent.

They also confirmed something that contradicts what many managers seem to believe about project management: It is not just scheduling! PERT/CPM do contribute to project success, but the importance of scheduling is far outweighed by other factors, including the use of tools known as system management concepts. These include work breakdown structures, life-cycle planning, systems engineering, configuration management, and status reports. In fact, the overuse of PERT-CPM was found to hamper success! The reason is that the project manager spends so much time updating the schedule that day-to-day managing suffers.

Baker, et al. report that seven broad factors contribute to project success. This is based on a regression analysis of the data. Taken together, these seven factors explain 91 percent of the variance in perceived project success, which is strongly compelling. These are listed in Table 5-2. They are all statistically significant to a probability of less than 0.001. The table shows the standardized regression coefficient, together with the cumulative $R^2$ for each variable.

## T A B L E  5–2

Factors Which Contribute to Project Success

| DETERMINING FACTOR | REGRESSION COEFFICIENT | CUMULATIVE $R^2$ |
|---|---|---|
| Coordination and relations | +.347 | .773 |
| Adequacy of project structure and control | +.187 | .830 |
| Project uniqueness, importance, public exposure | +.145 | .877 |
| Success criteria salience and consensus | +.254 | .886 |
| Competitive and budgetary pressure | −.153 | .897 |
| Initial overoptimism, conceptual difficulty | −.215 | .905 |
| Internal capabilities buildup | +.084 | .911 |

## B O X  5–1

### COORDINATION AND RELATIONS FACTOR

Unity between project manager and functional managers
Project team spirit, sense of mission, goal commitment, and
    capability
Unity between project manager and public officials, client contact,
    and his superior
Project manager's human and administrative skills
Realistic progress reports
Supportive informal relations of team members
Authority of project manager
Adequacy of change procedures
Job security of project team
Project team participation in decision-making and major problem
    solving
Parent enthusiasm
Availability of back-up strategies

Note that a negative regression coefficient means that the direction of the effect is reversed. In other words, while increased coordination causes an increase in project success, an increase in competitive pressure will cause a *decrease* in project success.

Because coordination and relations alone account for 77 percent of the variance in perceived project success, it is instructive to take a closer look at just what this means. Box 5–1 contains a summary listing of the factors that make up the overall variable.

Since there are a number of factors that cause people to perceive a project as a failure, and since these must be avoided, I have listed these in Box 5–2.

**Project managers can achieve high levels of perceived success, even under adverse circumstances.**

Note again that you must *perform* those things that cause perceived project success and *avoid* doing those that cause perceived failure.

One final note about the study: Project managers are sometimes inclined to complain about their situation and say that they

**B O X  5–2**

---

### CHARACTERISTICS THAT AFFECT PERCEIVED PROJECT FAILURE

Insufficient use of progress/status reports
Use of superficial status reports
Inadequate project manager administrative, human, and technical
    skills
Insufficient project manager influence and authority
Poor coordination with client
Lack of rapport with client and parent organization
Client disinterest in budget criteria
Lack of project team participation in decision-making and problem
    solving
Excessive structuring within the project team
Job insecurity within the project team
Lack of team spirit and sense of mission within the project team
Parent organization stable, nondynamic, lacking strategic change
Poor coordination with parent organization
New "type" of project
Project more complex than parent has handled previously
Initial underfunding
Inability to freeze design early
Inability to close out the effort
Unrealistic project schedules
Inadequate change procedures

---

cannot succeed because of its adverse nature. The authors concluded that project managers actually can achieve high levels of
perceived project success, even under adverse circumstances, if
they properly attend to the factors listed in the tables.

## TARGETS AND VARIATION

I mentioned at the beginning of this chapter that failure is often
defined as not meeting the C, P, T, or S targets, but I question
whether it is failure to meet targets that have been set based upon
wishful thinking. Unless targets are realistic to begin with, everyone associated with a project is getting set up. If I, as a project

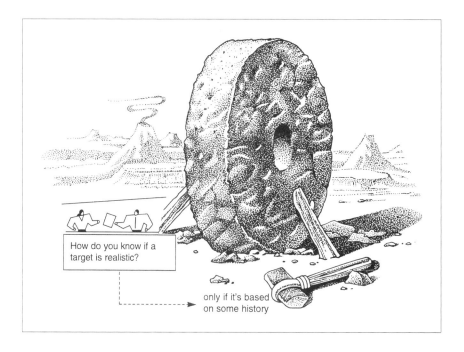

manager, agree to meet targets that I am pretty sure are unrealistic, because my manager puts pressure on me to do so, then we are both being set up. Eventually, when I can't meet the unrealistic target, my manager is going to be in trouble as well. So I have an obligation to insist on committing only to targets that are believed to be realistic.

> **We should understand that working times for *all* activities are probabilistic, not deterministic.**

How do you know if a target is realistic? You only know if it is based on some history. Until you make estimates at a level in a work breakdown structure where tasks are somewhat repeatable and you have some history on similar tasks, you are guessing. And even then, there are tolerances on all estimates. We should understand that working times for *all* activities are probabilistic, not deterministic. Yet we assign durations to activities based on best guesses, then link them together, and do deterministic calculations to find critical paths, float, and so on.

**B O X  5–3**

## SOME SOURCES OF VARIATION IN PROJECT WORK

Estimate of task duration is based on a small sample (it has only been done a few times before).

People are robbed from the project to put out fires on other projects.

The person for whom the original estimate was made is not available to do the work when the time comes.

Long stretches of overtime cause fatigue, which causes errors, which leads to more overtime, which leads to . . .

Sharing resources on multiple projects causes increased setup time, with corresponding decrease in work efficiency.

Work has to be done over because mistakes are made. May be due to poor planning, communication errors, etc.

Unexpected technical problems cause tasks to take longer than expected.

Illness, serious outside personal problems, child care, jury duty, etc.

A colleague of mine, Tom Conlon, has informally studied a number of networks to see how sensitive the deadline is to variations in various task durations and has been very surprised at some of the results. The critical path itself is often trivial in determining the end date for a project. It may well be some path that has a great deal of float that "sinks the ship," because it has a great deal of uncertainty (translate that into variability) associated with the work.

If you think about it, there is reason to wonder how any project is ever successful, as defined by coming in on schedule. I believe the only way this ever happens is that we vary the effort applied to meet the times. However, if you track both schedule performance and actual hours worked against original estimated hours, I think you will find that the price paid is in large variances of actual compared to estimated working hours. Consider the many causes of variation shown in Box 5–3.

Here, too, there are unrealistic expectations about what magnitude of variance is likely in project work. Many managers who have experience with department budgeting think that project budgets should be held to the same tight tolerances that are possi-

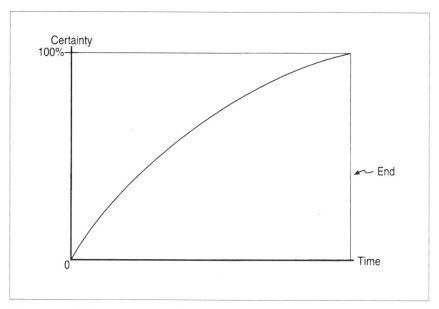

**Figure 5–1**  Ultimate certainty of project costs

ble with departments. But projects aren't budgeted the same way as departments. In a department, you budget for next year by looking at forecasted headcount. You tally up the salary increases you plan to give, add in the cost of rubber bands, paper clips, computers, and other supplies, and away you go. Such budgets can often be held to a few percent.

A project, on the other hand, is based on how much work has to be done, and that exact quantity is not well known at the outset, so labor costs cannot be accurately determined. There is a saying that the ultimate certainty of project cost increases the closer you get to the end. This is shown in Figure 5-1.

The one thing that we must all do is accept variability. It is a part of any process. You can reduce it over time, but you can never eliminate it. There is an injunction that is sometimes heard in organizations: You cannot go over budget—but neither can you come in under budget. Such an injunction is asking that people violate a law of nature. If they do it—that is, come in right on target—it is always through fancy footwork or pure accident. It is not because they were able to actually control work to achieve the result.

# 6

## CHAPTER

# Organizing for Project Management

Strictly speaking, the form of organization used to manage projects is usually not controlled by project managers, but by senior managers. However, it is important for project managers to understand the implications of various forms of organization and even to recommend to senior managers the structure that is best for their particular environment. In this chapter, we will examine some of the more common organizational forms and consider under what conditions they are appropriate.

## PROJECT ORGANIZATION

There are currently three general forms of organization structure used in projects. One is called *pure-project* form by most people. Another is the infamous *matrix*. The third is the so-called *virtual* organization. There are also a number of variations on these. Whatever form is used, the choice of structure is intended to make it possible for the project manager to control resources, communication, and coordination within the project team.

## Pure-Project Structure

In pure-project form, all members of the project team are assigned on a full-time basis. Their entire loyalty, then, is to the project. They report directly (or perhaps indirectly) to the project manager. In some cases they are scattered throughout the building. In others, they are all housed physically under one roof.

When projects are multidisciplinary, that is, involve team members from a number of different professions, trades, or specialties, pure-project organization is often used to ensure that everyone has complete dedication to the project. The most extreme form of pure-project organization is to have all members of the team co-located. This way, no one can reassign a team member to other work without going through the project manager. In addition, by having them close together, they can communicate with each other more effectively than if they are scattered all over the building. Studies have shown that people separated by more than 30 feet rarely communicate with each other. While this may no longer be true with the widespread use of e-mail, I still believe that there are significant differences between face-to-face communication and that done through e-mail.

There are a number of problems with pure-project format. For one thing, if the team is multidisciplinary, the project manager is going to have difficulty understanding the problems that some team members may have. It is impossible to be conversant in all disciplines. Further, when it comes time to do performance appraisals, since the project manager does not understand the work, she will have a hard time doing a valid appraisal. This is a disadvantage for the employee as well as the manager.

Another problem is that it can be nearly impossible to keep everyone level-loaded in a multidiscipline, pure-project team. You may only have enough work for one specialist to keep him occupied 25 percent of the time. What does he do the rest of the time? Chances are, he will spin his wheels doing nothing. This inefficiency has a direct, adverse impact on project costs.

When projects last for several years, members of pure-project teams tend to lose skills. The reason is that they are normally "housed" within their functional discipline, where they can exchange knowledge with their peers. If an individual is placed in a pure-project team, she may have no peers to talk with, so she finds it hard to keep up with what is going on in her field. She also has no one to ask for help if she gets stuck on a technical problem.

Pure-project is often used on fast-track projects. Couillard (1995) found that for projects that have high technical risk, this structure has a significant *negative influence* on project success. He found that matrix is better for such projects, presumably because technical expertise can be more easily drawn from a matrix structure than from the pure-project structure. (See also Chapter 11 on managing risk for more details of Couillard's study.)

## Virtual Organizations

In today's global economy, a number of organizations are running projects in which team members are scattered all over the U.S. and even the world. One example of this is in software development. It turns out that India has some excellent programmers, and their pay in India is considerably less than that of programmers in the U.S. A large number of these people are located in Bangalore, which has become the software capital of India. The beauty of such work is that the people can work independently. In addition, what they produce can be transported electronically, so a lot of the code that they write is sent by satellite broadcast.

When people are scattered all over the world, we call the resulting format a *virtual organization*. Some of the stories I have heard about this working arrangement lead me to believe that it should be called a virtual *dis*-organization, but regardless of my opinion, it is used frequently. One form is that people work at home. There really is no difference between working at home and having members of your team scattered throughout a huge building or in several buildings that are located on a large plot or possibly throughout town. Either way, people are in no position to conveniently talk face-to-face, so they must resort to e-mail or telephone.

There are enough companies that have experience with virtual organization that some consultants are emerging who specialize in helping organizations solve the special problems that result from this format. There are a few guidelines that seem universal. One is that frequent communications are absolutely essential, especially for members on the critical path in the project schedule. One company found that people on that path should be *virtually co-located*. This is another euphemism, but what it means to them is that these individuals must talk with each other daily in order to maintain coordination and communication at the required level.

Another guideline is that the entire group should be brought together near the beginning of the project for one face-to-face meeting. Otherwise, it is very hard for all the players to ever get to know each other. Ideally, this meeting would be the kick-off meeting for the project.

## Matrix Organization

I earlier called matrix "infamous." The reason is that this has traditionally been the most difficult to manage. It is the form in which project managers truly have a lot of responsibility but no authority. The reason for the term *matrix* is shown in Figure 6–1. In this arrangement, the company is organized by functions. That is, we

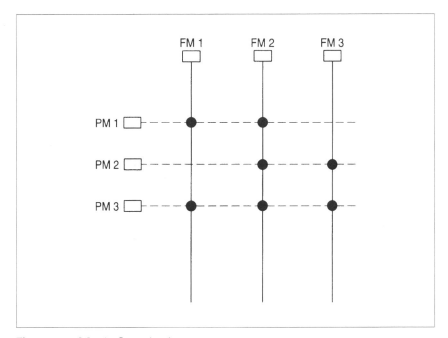

**Figure 6–1** Matrix Organization

have people grouped together to perform the various functions needed by the organization. As examples, we have marketing, engineering, production, accounting, and human resources grouped together. Within each of these groups (or departments, as we usually call them), there may be specialties. In human resources, for example, there may be a person who deals with benefits, another who handles recruitment, and someone else who handles grievances.

When project teams are formed, members are recruited from the functional departments. In pure matrix form, they do not leave their departments. Rather, they stay physically where they are and still report directly to their functional manager and indirectly to the project manager. This creates the one-person, two-boss system that almost everyone will advise you to avoid.

Why, then, do we use it?

Because it solves a lot of problems for project managers. In any multidisciplinary team, there will be team members performing work that the project manager knows nothing about. When you know nothing about the work of someone on your team, you have two problems. First, you cannot be certain that the person is performing either the right quantity or quality of work. This means that you cannot tell if the time estimates given to you by the team member are valid, nor whether the person is staying on schedule once the work starts. Furthermore, you cannot give the person a valid performance appraisal, since you know nothing about the technical aspects of his job. By having team members stay in their functional departments, the functional manager can review their performance and give them guidance on their work, besides being the project manager's go-between to judge whether the quantity of work being done by the person is sufficient.

Another advantage of matrix is that many projects do not need full-time effort from all team members. By leaving them in their functional groups, the functional manager can keep the individual properly loaded. Otherwise, if the person were assigned to the team full-time, the project manager would have to pay for dead time when the person had nothing to do.

Finally, one benefit of leaving people in their functional departments is that they can draw on each other for help when they need it. If you physically remove them from their departments, they may have no one to turn to for help when they are stumped on a technical issue. True, they can still call someone on the phone, but oftentimes, if the person has been away from the functional group for very long, he loses the connections that make it easy for him to ask his peers for help.

## PROBLEMS WITH MATRIX

As I said earlier, a number of authors have strongly advised against the use of matrix because of all the problems it presents. However, a recent study suggests that matrix should not be condemned out-of-hand. El-Najdawi and Liberatore (1997) presented the results of their survey of 29 project managers in corporations that are primary or secondary contractors to the U.S. Government and who use the matrix format. They found that goal conflict is the primary disadvantage of the matrix organization. This means conflicting goals between project managers and functional managers. The project manager naturally has only his or her own project goals to worry about, while the functional manager is trying to meet the goals of the functional department along with the goals of all projects that he or she is supporting. The conflict of goals leads to slow reaction time in making resource allocation decisions.

The authors also found that communicating long-range project objectives to functional managers is a significant concern. They therefore conclude that this indicates a need for project managers in matrix organizations to be very skilled at interfacing and communicating with functional managers in order to ease conflicts and clarify goals (p. 30). Their finding confirms what many of us have known for a long time: The relationship with functional managers is a key to success in this organizational structure.

El-Najdawi and Liberatore conclude that "the failure of matrix management is often a result of goal conflict between program and functional managers rather than a fundamental problem with the matrix structure itself" (p. 31).

## MAKING PROJECTS KING

Perhaps one of the reasons for problems with matrix is that, in most companies, the functional department is king and projects just present a nuisance to functional managers who must try to staff them. This might be acceptable when a company has only a very few projects going at any time. However, for those companies that live and die by projects, it seems to me that a simple change in perspective would be useful. That perspective is that the functional departments exist *primarily* to ensure that projects are successful. By making projects priority, functional managers would have to think seriously before they shuffle resources from one team to another or pull them off project teams to get functional department work done. In addition, you would elevate the project manager's role to one having status comparable to that of functional managers. I believe this thinking is needed in a lot of companies. El-Najdawi and Liberatore make the same case a little less strongly, saying ". . . the balance of power in matrix organizations in the military and aerospace industries must shift in favor of the program managers" (p. 31).

PART TWO

# TOOLS AND TECHNIQUES

# 7

## CHAPTER

# A Review of the Standard Tools

**B**ecause this book is intended to go beyond the standard tools of project management, a firm foundation in those tools is essential. Of course, to cover them in depth would be to write a book within a book on the subject, so this chapter will be a very brief review of how to plan, schedule, and control projects using work breakdown structures (WBS), critical path or PERT scheduling, and earned value analysis. If you need more in-depth treatment of any of these than is provided in this text, you should consult my introductory book, entitled *Project Planning, Scheduling, and Control*, Revised Edition, also published by McGraw-Hill.

Before getting into the *how* of managing projects, it might be helpful to first consider what we mean by project management. I define project management as the planning, scheduling, and controlling of activities to meet project objectives. These objectives will include cost, performance, time, and scope. The cost objective is normally called the project budget. Performance has to do with the quality of the work that is done. Time is the schedule, and most projects in today's world are deadline-driven. Scope is the magnitude of the work to be done. These are related as follows:

$$C = f(P, T, S)$$

This expression reads: Cost is a *function* of Performance, Time, and Scope. Ideally, we could write a true algebraic equation for these, but practically we cannot. We are always estimating the values of the variables. However, we do know that if this were an equation, we could assign values to any three of the variables, and the fourth one would be whatever the equation says it would be. To understand this better, consider Figure 7–1.

Note that if we assign values to the sides of the triangle, the area (scope) of the project is defined. In other words, you could say, "Here's what you will get for this cost, over this time, at this performance level. If you want more scope than is going to be achieved with this combination, you have to change one of the sides, usually cost."

I consider this relationship to be the most important thing that a project manager should know, because you are always making tradeoffs among them. A project manager should be prepared to show senior managers that they can pick three of the variables, but he or she (the project manager) gets to pick the remaining one.

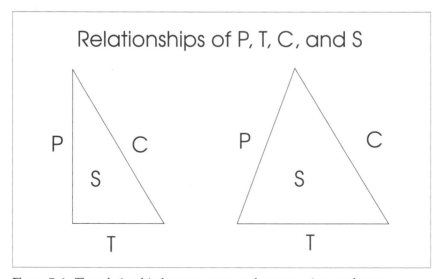

**Figure 7–1**  The relationship between cost, performance, time, and scope.

## A MODEL FOR MANAGING PROJECTS

If you are going to manage projects successfully, you need to follow some standard approach. This is sometimes called a project management *methodology* or simply a project management system. There are consulting firms that charge upwards of $100,000 for a methodology. I'm going to give you one in this book for a whole lot less. (If you want to send me a check for $100,000, I'll be glad to accept it.)

> A project is a job that is done one time. Cooking a meal is a project. Brain surgery is a project. Sending someone to the moon is also.

Before presenting my methodology, let me say that there *can* be a standard approach to running *any* kind of project, whether it be product development, construction, research, information systems, or whatever. Project management is a *disciplined thought process,* not to be confused with the content of what is being done. Two plus two equals four, no matter whether you apply it to finance, engineering, or foods. Furthermore, the same thought process can be applied to small, medium, or large projects. What differs between them is the amount of documentation required for various size projects. Small projects only require a few pages, whereas large ones require considerably more.

> **pro • blem:** A problem is a gap between where you are and where you want to be that is confronted by some obstacle(s). If there are no obstacles, there is no problem—only a desired goal.

In Figure 7–2 is my methodology for managing projects, shown as a flowchart. If you follow this process, it will enhance your chances of being successful with your projects. If you aren't used to reading flowcharts, just follow the arrows and be aware that diamonds are decision points, where questions get answered. The questions are framed to be answered "yes" or "no."

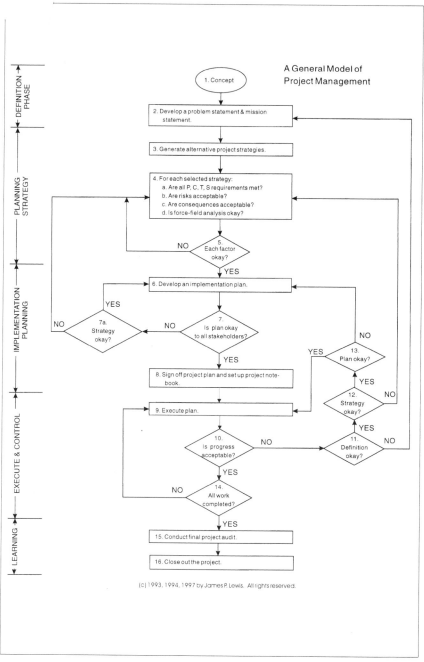

Figure 7–2 A general model of project management.

The first step is called the concept step. All projects begin as a concept. Someone has an idea for a project. The thing is that too often that concept is accepted as the final definition of what is to be done without ever questioning the validity of the idea. For that reason, step 2 involves defining the problem that will be solved by the project, determining the mission, and formulating a vision for the end result.

Step 2 calls for a problem statement. That is because all projects are done to solve some problem for the organization. Note, however, that we do not mean problem in a negative sense necessarily. Developing a new product is a project, by this definition, but a very positive one. So is reengineering an organization to improve a process. The point, however, is to define the problem correctly so that you don't make the mistake of developing the right solution for the *wrong problem*.

**Projects don't fail at the end, they fail at the beginning— usually at step 2 in my model.**

In fact, it is in step 2 that many projects go wrong. I often say that projects don't fail at the end, they fail at the beginning—right here in step 2. The reason is that we take for granted that we all understand the problem perfectly, when this is not the case at all.

Once the problem is correctly understood, you should try to visualize the problem as being solved. In other words, what would the world look like if the problem were solved? This image is called the vision for the project. If you

**vi • sion:** What the final result will look like.

were developing a new product, the vision would be what the new product is going to look like, how it will function, and so on. If you were re-engineering a process, you would visualize the new process as being more efficient, perhaps less wasteful, and so on.

**mis • sion:** What we are going to do and for whom.

Now that these two steps have been taken, writing the mission statement is simple—it is to solve the problem by achieving the vision. The formal statement should answer two questions: (1) What are we going to do? and (2) For whom are we doing it?

In step 3, you develop strategies for the project. There are two strategies that must be considered for most projects. One the project strategy itself. The second is the technical strategy that will be employed. Let's use "feeding your family" as an example of the two strategies. First, you can feed them by cooking from scratch, ordering home delivery, cooking frozen or canned foods, or going out to a restaurant (to name a few). These are all project strategies. If you choose to cook from scratch, technical strategy might be whether you cook on a conventional stove or microwave the food. You can also bake, broil, grill, or use convection cooking.

**stra • te • gy:** The approach to be employed in doing the project. Two strategies may be involved: *project* and *technical.*

Ideally, you would brainstorm a list of possible project and technical strategies in step 3 and then select the best combination in step 4. This selection is made through some analysis. First, can you meet your cost, performance, time, and scope targets? At this point in the planning process, this question cannot be answered very accurately. What can sometimes be done, however, is to reject certain approaches. This is done by realizing that you are fairly certain that you can't meet the targets with a particular strategy.

Next, you do a SWOT and risk analysis. What are our strengths, weaknesses, opportunities, and threats for this project, what risks are there, and can we deal with them. Risk management is covered in this book in Chapter 11.

The next issue is consequences. Are there unintended consequences of adopting this particular strategy for the project? For example, I know of a company that wanted to optimize the use of capital investment, so they decided to get rid of the machines that were used to make certain parts. They sold the machinery to a local shop with the understanding that they would buy their parts from the shop in the future. This worked fine until the machine shop ran out of raw materials and had to reorder. Then the shock hit!

When the company owned the machines, they bought raw materials through corporate purchasing. These were purchased in boxcar loads, then distributed to the divisions at substantial discounts. The small machine shop, however, was ordering a few hundred feet of stock at a time, and the price was considerably higher than that of a boxcar load. So naturally, the price increase was passed along to the company. This was an unintended consequence of a strategy to limit capital investment.

Finally, we are asked to do a force-field analysis, to determine if the strategy being considered will be acceptable to all stakeholders. An example of this comes from Avondale shipyards. During World War II, they were under pressure to produce ships as fast as possible. In looking at their process, they identified two problems in the way they had always built ships. When you build ships out of wood, you build them right-side up. When you make them out of steel, however, welding in the keel area requires that you literally stand on your head. Not only is this difficult, but it is hard to do good quality work. Furthermore, when you try to weld the sides, which are formed from heavy steel plate, the shape of the ship causes that plate to deform outwards, so that you again have quality problems with the welds.

Someone suggested that it would be easier to build steel boats upside down.

Can you imagine the response from some old-timer who has been building ships for a long time? "I've been building ships for nearly 40 years," he protests, "and we never built them upside down. Dumbest thing I ever heard of."

If this person is in a position of power in the company, he is a force to reckon with. Failing to consider that force and how to deal with it could easily cause the strategy to be jeopardized.

In step 5 we ask if the strategy is okay. If the answer is yes, we can proceed to implementation planning. If not, we cycle back into step 4 and select another combination of strategies to analyze until we finally find one that will work.

In step 6 we have to decide exactly how the project will be done. We answer the following basic questions:

1. What must be done?
2. Who will do each task?

3. How long will each activity take?

4. What will it cost?

5. In what order must things be done?

And so on. Answering these questions is the essence of implementation planning. That doesn't make answering them easy of course. In some cases, you can only answer some of these questions by reference to a crystal ball. Nevertheless, they must be answered.

In step 7 we ask if the plan is okay to all stakeholders. If it is, we can get the plan signed off (step 8) and set up in a project notebook. If not, we may have to change the strategy (step 7a) or just revise the implementation plan. The best way to get an approval of a plan is for the major stakeholders to have participated in putting the plan together.

**stake • holder:**

Anyone who has a vested interest in the project. This includes customers, financial managers, contributors, contractors, and so on.

In step 9 we can begin working on the project. As we do the work, we review progress periodically and ask if we are on target (step 10). Note that this question is asked for all four targets—cost, performance, time, and scope. If the answer is yes, we continue. The next question is whether the work is complete (step 15). So long as the answer is no, we just cycle back to step 9 and keep going until the answer finally is yes. Then we should do a final project review (step 16) before we consider the project to be absolutely complete.

Consider now the case in step 10 where the answer to the question is no. That is, progress is not acceptable. Now we are in the control mode. The first question we ask is whether the definition of the problem is okay. That is, are we on the right track, or have we defined the problem being solved incorrectly. If we have, we must return to step 2 and redefine the problem. This is a disaster. We have to start all over on the job. This won't happen too often, but it has to be in the model as a possibility.

If the definition is okay, we go to step 12 and ask if the strategy is okay. Remember, we have to ask this about both project and technical strategies, because either one can be a problem. For example, you might have farmed out some of the work to a contractor and you find that the contractor is doing poor quality work. You have to take steps to correct the problem, either by getting the contractor to improve his performance or by shifting the work to another contractor.

It might also be your technical strategy that is a problem, particularly if you were trying to employ some cutting-edge technology. You get into the execution stage and can't make it work. This is a pretty serious problem in some projects, because you have to start over on that part of the work and this can snowball throughout the project. I suggest that if you have questions about whether you can make a technology work, you should do a feasibility study before you launch a development project using that unproven technology. Whether the outcome of a feasibility study is yes or no, it is a success. On the other hand, when you launch a development project with unproven technology and get this far and can't make it work, that project will probably be deemed a failure.

If the strategy is okay, the next question (step 13) is whether the implementation plan is okay. If the answer is no, you are directed to change the plan, which then takes you back through the signoff process. This is for everyone's protection. The reasons that the plan is not okay can be numerous. Some of the more common ones are: (1) The scope changes; (2) The work has fallen behind and the schedule cannot be recovered; or (3) People have been pulled off the team to cover a changing priority somewhere else.

If the implementation plan *is* okay, notice that you are directed back to step 9. The implication here is that if the plan is okay but you are not on target, then you must not be following the plan, so you are told to get back in there and do it! The problem is, most of the time this situation happens because resources have been stolen from your project. In that case, the plan really is not okay unless the people can be made available. The way to bring this issue to a head is to do a "what-if" analysis with your scheduling software, present the results to senior management, and ask that they decide what to do.

## USING THE WORK BREAKDOWN STRUCTURE FOR PLANNING

When you get to step 6 of my methodology, you develop an implementation plan. This is where you dot all your i's and cross all your t's. The first question that might be asked is, "What must be done?" This is where the work breakdown structure comes in. As shown in Figure 7–3, the WBS breaks the project down into smaller and smaller units until you arrive at a level where decent estimates of time, resources, and costs can be made.

Again, if you are not familiar with how to construct the WBS, refer to my earlier book. Do note that the WBS should be constructed before scheduling and resource assignment is done.

## SCHEDULING THE WORK

The tool of choice for scheduling projects is critical path method (CPM). The critical path diagram makes use of arrows to show the order in which work is performed. The method also allows the determination of which path through the project is the longest one, and thereby we can tell the earliest finish for the entire job. This is shown in Figure 7–4.

The critical path diagram is absolutely necessary in order to find the longest path in a very large schedule. Trying to do this with a bar chart can be very misleading, because you might show things being done in parallel that simply can't be done that way. However, a CPM diagram is a terrible working tool. It should always be converted to a bar chart (also called a Gantt chart, after Henry Gantt, who formalized the notation for them). This is a nonissue, since all scheduling software automatically does this.

I would like to make one point about scheduling software. People seem to think that project management is primarily scheduling, and in line with that belief, that if you have a good scheduling package, you will be successful in managing projects. Nothing could be farther from the truth, as we have proven in the past 10 years. As I said in the Preface, Microsoft alone has sold about a million copies of Microsoft Project,™ and I expect that 999,000 projects that have been managed using the software have still come in late and over budget.

The software is just a tool, and without a proper understanding of project management methodology, all it will do is help

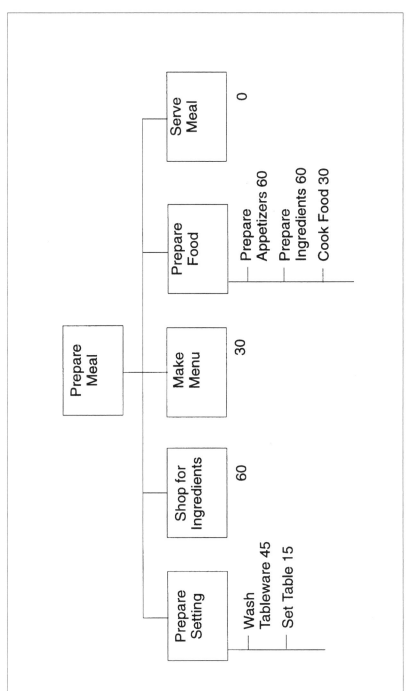

**Figure 7–3** A work breakdown structure for cooking a meal.

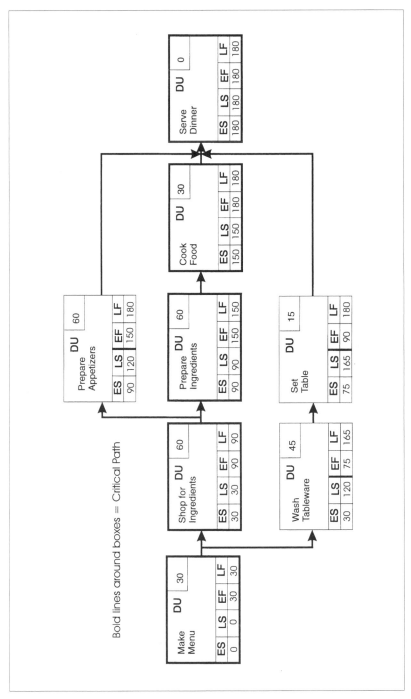

Bold lines around boxes = Critical Path

**Figure 7–4**  Critical path diagram for a project.

you document your failures! Furthermore, I don't believe that one size fits all (in clothing *or* in software), and too many organizations get trapped into standardizing on a single package that won't meet everyone's needs. It has been the experience of every company that I have worked with that when they do this, people simply refuse to use the software, and they have just wasted a lot of money.

> Without a proper understanding of project management methodology, all software will do is help you document your failures—with great precision, of course.

In addition, since the software is a tool, you cannot make a valid selection until you know what you are going to do with it in the first place! In other words, we have the cart before the horse. We first need to train people in how to manage projects, then let them select software that will be best for them.

Well, that's the end of that sermon.

## TRACKING PROGRESS

As far as I am concerned, the tool of choice for tracking progress in projects is earned value analysis. The method has its detractors, and it is not nearly as simple as just tracking the schedule, but it is much more robust.

Consider the progress report shown in Figure 7–5. Note that the dotted line drawn at January 20 is where we are supposed to be as of today. The shaded areas represent weekends, when we are not working. The critical path is shown as a solid black bar, while those tasks that have float are shown with hollow bars. Progress is shown by the small bar that runs inside the task bars. According to this schedule, task A is one day behind schedule. This is serious, since this task is on the critical path. Unless this time can be recovered, we know that the project will slip one day.

Task C is complete. Task D is one day ahead of schedule, and task E is right on target. That is, *if* all the work has really been done correctly. What is missing from this kind of report is whether cost, performance, and scope are really where they should be. We are

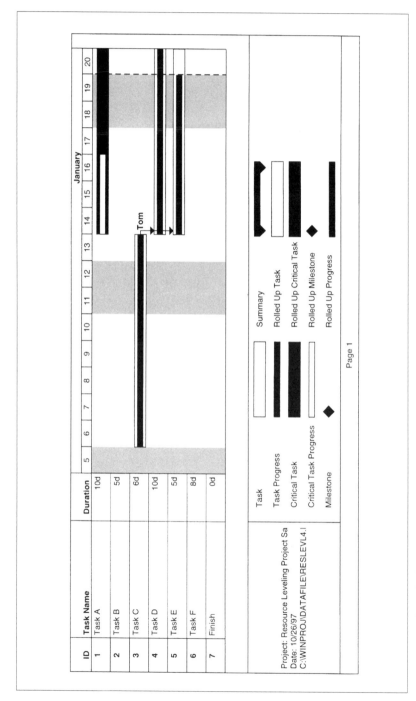

**Figure 7–5** Schedule showing progress.

forced to take on faith that they are correct, but this is not always the case.

There are some organizations that don't track project costs. They either assume that costs are correct or that they don't matter. These are both dangerous assumptions. If people were exactly 100 percent efficient all the time, then you could say that one hour invested yields one hour of productive work, but we know that this is seldom true. So we don't really know what we are getting for our investment unless we track actual work performed.

Does it matter?

Well, assume that you send your teen-age daughter to the grocery store with $100 and a grocery list, and she returns with four big bags of snacks (worth about $8) and she has spent the $100. Would you be happy? I doubt it.

> When you get only $8 worth of snacks for $100, your spending efficiency is extremely low. At this rate, you will go broke very efficiently!

You would say that what you *got* for your $100 was not enough. Your *spending efficiency* would be very low (only 8 percent). In fact, unless we know what we are getting for our money, we are going to get into serious trouble, whether the organization is a for-profit or not-for-profit one.

The other issue, of course, is quality of work (performance). This is incredibly hard to measure in many cases—especially for knowledge work, but some attempt must be made to assess quality or else the end result will be unacceptable. One indirect measure of quality is rework. It is likely that from 5 to 40 percent of design work (including software design) is rework. At 33 percent, which is often the case, this is equivalent to having one of every

> Rework is a direct measure of poor quality. At 33 percent, that is like having one of every three people on the job to just redo what the other two did wrong!

three designers on the job to just redo what the other two did wrong. Any improvement in quality (reducing rework) is a direct improvement in performance (call it productivity). In a later chapter, we will discuss how concepts from quality can be applied in project management.

What we would like, rather than the simple reporting of schedule progress, is an accounting for *what we got, how much effort was required,* and *how much effort was originally scheduled* to be done. This is best accomplished by translating everything into a dollar equivalent. For those familiar with earned value analysis, the terms used to measure progress are BCWS (budgeted cost of work scheduled), BCWP (budgeted cost of work performed), and ACWP (actual cost of work performed). These numbers give us the capability to tell where we are with regard to both work efficiency and spending efficiency and enable us to make some predictions about where the project is headed.

> **If you can't forecast the near term with any accuracy, you certainly can't forecast the far term with any better accuracy.**

For example, studies have found that, by the time a project is 15 percent of the way along the horizontal time line, if it is seriously in trouble, it is very likely to stay in trouble. You say, "Why can't I get it back on track?" The answer is simple. The original targets were *forecasts.* If you cannot forecast accurately only 15 percent ahead, then you are not likely to be any better further out. It is like the weather forecast. Tomorrow's forecast might be fairly accurate, but the one for a week from now is likely to be completely off. To confirm that this is true, 800 defense contracts that were in trouble 15 percent of the way along were analyzed, and not one ever got back on target!

Earned value analysis is covered in detail in my book cited previously. In a later chapter of this book, we will go into more depth on how EVA can be used to measure project status and forecast the future.

# 8
CHAPTER

# The Need for Systems Thinking in Project Management

**U**nless you are very young or in some way exceptional, you almost undoubtedly learned to think in linear-causal terms. I say this because a few schools are beginning to teach systems thinking, some at the urging of Dr. Jay Forrester, one of the pioneers of the discipline.

For most of us, however, the proposition that cause-effect relationships can be described as "A causes B" seems reasonable, and perhaps irrefutable. This has been so often our experience of the world that we seldom stop to think that things do not always operate in this manner. When an accident happens, we ask, "What caused it?" If two children get into a fight, we ask, "Who

> In human interaction, *A* causes *B* causes *A*.

started it?" Interestingly, if the children are asked, they may both point at each other, adamantly claiming, "He did!"

Adults tend to get frustrated at that response. When I was a child and my sister and I would have an altercation, my father would ask, "Who started it?" We would both accuse the other. He would get annoyed at this response and threaten to punish both of us if the *guilty party* didn't confess. In his mind, A causes B. It could not be possible that A causes B causes A, but that is exactly how it works in systems terms.

You might say that at the microsecond level, one party made the first move. However, there is communication at both the verbal and nonverbal levels, and the nonverbal channel is operating continuously in both directions. Since some, if not most, of the influence between humans is a function of the nonverbal channel, that influence is operating simultaneously, so again, it does not operate linearly, but circularly.

In systems thinking, you must abandon linear causality and talk in terms of circular causal effects. This is because systems involve *feedback,* which introduces circularity. This is shown in Figure 8–1. When you are heating your home in the winter, the thermostat senses the room temperature and tells the furnace to turn on when the temperature drops below the level at which the thermostat is set. As the heat causes the room to warm up, the thermostat sends another signal to the furnace, telling it to shut down.

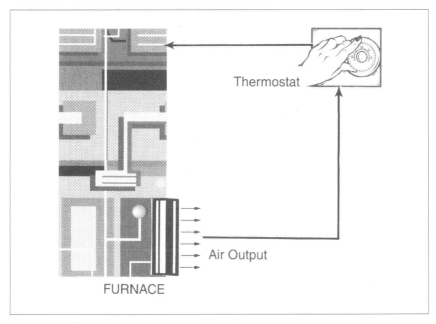

**Figure 8–1** Heating system.

We can say, then, that as the temperature drops, the furnace comes on and causes the temperature to rise, which causes the furnace to stop, and that causes the temperature to drop and so on, in a limitless number of cycles. Notice how convoluted our language becomes when we try to describe circularity. Our language itself is inherently linear. Notice:

Johnny hit the ball.

Johnny is the subject. The action is that he *hit*, and the object is the ball. Johnny is "A" in the equation A causes B, and the ball is "B." The causal link is *hit*. Notice that the verb hit can be replaced with all kinds of action descriptors: stole, dropped, held, threw, saw, accepted, liked, and so on.

It would be just as accurate to say that the ball hit Johnny's bat, as the bat swung through an arc, and rebounded at almost the same velocity at which it hit the bat. It would be just as accurate. But it would take forever to say anything.

Consider this sentence: Johnny cried until his mother gave him some cake, and then he smiled. It is a linear flow, but it does involve a reciprocal action. The action goes from A to B and back to A. Johnny's crying causes his mother to give him some cake, which causes him to smile. A causes B causes A.

## THE LANGUAGE OF MANAGING

This same linear-causal thinking carries over into managing. Managers are supposed to "make things happen." One common definition of managing is that "a manager gets work done through other people." This suggests that she is a causal agent and that she does no work herself. A causes B.

Now suppose the employee does not do what the manager has directed should be done? Then the manager will respond. She may give the directive again, probably in more forceful terms. If there is still no response, she may take disciplinary action. How do we understand this exchange in systems terms? The manager is A and the employee is B. A causes B causes A causes B causes A. The employee's response to the first directive causes the manager to give another directive, which elicits another response from the employee, which causes another directive (or discipline) from the manager, and so on.

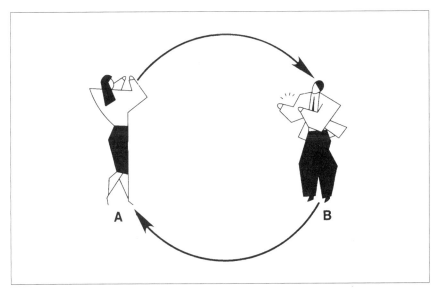

**Figure 8–2**  Circularity in human relations.

Causality in human relations, then, is circular and must be drawn as shown in Figure 8–2.

There are times when the action of one person causes the other person to do more of what he was doing and other times when the action causes him to do less. For example, behavioral reinforcement theory suggests that rewarding a person for performing well on the job will usually make him try to perform even better in the future. Thus, positive reinforcement (sometimes called positive "strokes") increases desired performance. This is shown as a graph in Figure 8–3.

Conversely, negative reinforcement should cause a behavior to diminish. If the behavior being displayed is undesired, then negative reinforcement should extinguish it. Unfortunately, there are times when desired behavior is also extinguished because it is negatively reinforced. See Figure 8–4.

It is interesting to consider the interaction between a manager and employee in terms of behavioral reinforcement. If a manager strokes an employee for good performance and the employee performs even better in the future, what effect does this have on the manager? She is rewarded for stroking the employee. What does

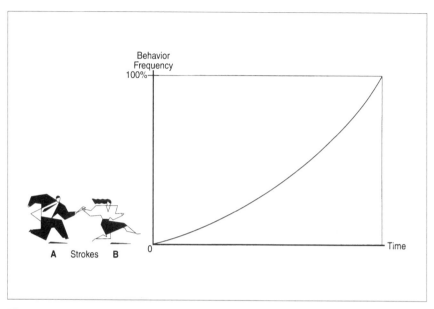

**Figure 8-3** Positive reinforcement increases desired behavior.

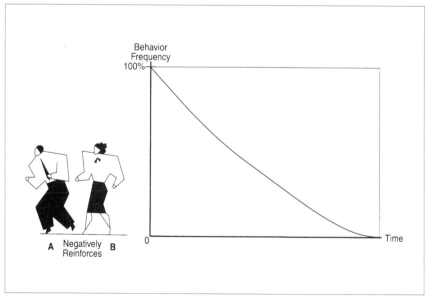

**Figure 8-4** Negative reinforcement extinguishes behavior.

she do? She strokes him even more. His performance improves. She is rewarded. She strokes the employee again, and so on. (Who is controlling whom?) This is called a *positive feedback loop*, in which each action is followed by a reaction of increasing strength. Can this go on forever? No.

Eventually the employee becomes satiated with strokes or the manager becomes fatigued from so much stroking. There are always limits to growth in any system. Note that as a person becomes satiated with strokes, each additional stroke loses some value. Thus, there is nonlinearity in the system. This is shown in Figure 8–5.

The opposite effect is also possible. An employee suffering from "stroke deficit disorder," a term I have borrowed from organization development specialist Lee Kleese (1996), values strokes much more highly than someone who is in "stroke overload." People tend to suffer from stroke deficit disorder at the left side of the curve in Figure 8–5 and to suffer stroke overload on the right side of the curve.

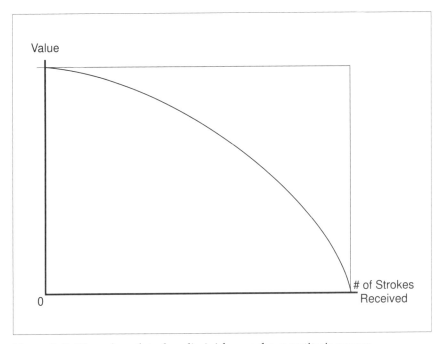

**Figure 8–5** The value of strokes diminishes as the quantity increases.

## CONTROL IN RELATIONSHIPS

In all human relations there is a constant struggle to define the relationship. There are basically two kinds of relationships, as defined by status. These are either symmetrical, meaning equal-status, or they are complementary, which is unequal-status. Every communication between two individuals carries a proposed definition of the relationship, as defined by status. Note that the communication can be verbal or nonverbal. If you have forgotten, nonverbal aspects of a communication include body gestures and/or posture, tone of voice, inflections, phrasing, and so on. Verbal communication is strictly the words themselves.

Consider the following question:

Can you *solve* the problem?

By stressing the word *solve,* the meaning is something like, "Is it possible for the problem to be solved at all, or is it likely that it will come back again.

Now suppose the stress is changed:

Can *you* solve the problem?

The meaning is very different. There seems to be doubt that this particular individual can solve the problem. Perhaps someone else can, but not this person. The meaning of the words has changed just by changing the stress on one word in the sentence.

Now suppose a supervisor says to an employee:

Have your report to me by 3 o'clock tomorrow.

This communication suggests that the supervisor sees the relation with this employee as very complementary (unequal status). Compare this to:

Would you please get your report to me by 3 o'clock tomorrow.

In both cases, the message is the same: The supervisor wants the report by 3 o'clock tomorrow. However, in the second case the relationship definition offered by the supervisor is more equal-status or symmetrical.

Does it matter?

Sometimes it does. In American culture, we recognize that there are status differentials between supervisors and employees, but we do not like them to be emphasized too strongly. If the employee feels that the supervisor is "coming on too strong," then he may get angry. This can result in a conflict in which the two try to define the relationship in mutually acceptable terms.

It is bad enough for us to have to interpret relationship definitions from the nonverbal component of a communication. It is even worse when a person offers a definition opposite the one he really wants.

## LET'S GO OUT FOR DINNER

Lee Kleese, whom I cited previously, has a wonderful example of this. You come home from work dead tired. Your significant other says, "Dear, I've had a really hard day and obviously you have too, so why don't we go out for dinner."

"That's a great idea," you say. "Where would you like to go?"

"I don't care. Where would you like to go?"

Now you say, "I don't care," but inside you're thinking, "If you loved me as much as I love you, you'd say steak."

"Well, if it really doesn't matter, I'd like to try that new Chinese restaurant. Everyone says it's really good."

There may be a momentary flash of disappointment on your face, but this quickly changes to a forced smile and you say, "Okay. Let's go."

Inside you're thinking, "Chinese! That doesn't have *anything* to do with steak. I'll go, but you owe me one."

Some time goes by. You come home from work again, dead tired, and your significant other says, "Dear, I'm really tired and you seem to be also. Why don't we go out to dinner."

"Great idea," you say. "Where would you like to go?"

"I don't care."

"Me either." But the little voice inside is saying, "If you loved me as much as I love you, you'd say *steak*."

"Well, if you really don't care, I'd like to try that Italian place on Vine Avenue. Margie says it's really good."

"Italian!" the little voice screams. "That doesn't have anything to do with steak."

This time, the little voice wins. "I don't want to eat Italian," you say. "I want to eat steak."

"Well, why didn't you say so?" says your significant other politely. "Let's go."

So you go eat steak.

Do you think you're going to enjoy it?

Not a chance!

Now the problem here is that you have offered a definition of your relationship with your significant other that is symmetrical. What you really would like to do, of course, is call the shots and choose steak. When your significant other chooses something else, you get upset. It would be much clearer if you had said, "Well, I'd like to have a steak. Maybe we can have steak this time and Chinese the next (or vice versa)." When you agree that one person chooses this time and the other chooses the next, that says the relationship is symmetrical over the long run but complementary for the specific choice. When both parties agree to this, there is no problem.

You notice that, in systems terms, the system is trying to adjust itself for stability. It turns out, though, that the most unstable system is one that is symmetrical. A tiny shift causes it to become complementary. A system that is inherently complementary, however, can experience shifts in either direction and will remain stable. This is why people who are highly concerned that they be treated as equal-status with everyone else are always being frustrated. They are constantly seeing signs that the relationship is unequal, and they attempt to restore balance. That attempt may be met with a counterresponse aimed at keeping the system unbalanced, and thus a conflict develops.

This is not to suggest that all relationships would be better if they were unequal-status. It is important that we recognize that no relationship can ever be totally equal all the time for every situation. The only thing we can achieve is equal status on the average.

## CONFLICT IN MANAGEMENT

Inevitably, there are conflicts in human relations. Conflict occurs when one person frustrates the concerns of another person. Those concerns include goals, values, self-interests, status, and control. This is one area in which systems thinking is essential if we are to understand and deal with such situations.

Remember the example of two children having an altercation? When asked who started it, each blamed the other. This is
because *each sees his own behavior as a response to the behavior of the
other child!* The way this works is shown in Figure 8–6.

Person A behaves. This is the arrow 1-2. Person B responds,
as sequence 2-3. Person A responds to that behavior as 3-4. This
goes on as a long series of interactions that we can call *move-countermove, move-countermove.* Now, as I have said previously, if you
ask each person why she behaved as she did, she will tell you that
she was only responding to the other person's behavior. Person A
sees the exchange as sequence 2-3-4, while person B sees it as 1-2-3.
This is called *punctuation* in communication (Watzlawick, Beavin,
and Jackson, 1967).

In some cases, once such an interaction begins, it becomes
almost impossible to stop. Each side sees his behavior as a response to that of the other. Such a sequence is called a *game without
end,* and naturally, we don't mean game in the fun sense. Exam-

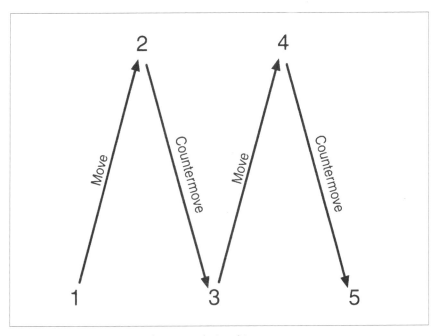

**Figure 8–6**  Punctuation in human relationships.

ples of such games without end are the Middle East conflict and the religious conflict that has gone on in Northern Ireland for so long. There have been many attempts to resolve those conflicts, and they have been only temporarily successful. The conflict breaks out all over again when one side makes a move that is seen by the other as similar to previous moves.

There is only one way to end a game without end, and that is to break the pattern. This was done by President Gorbachev in the arms race. In this game, the United States increases its weapons and the Soviet Union counters by doing the same. Over time, each country stockpiles massive quantities of weapons—by most estimates, enough to destroy all life on earth several times over. The cost to each country was enormous, and the money spent on weapons could not be used for improving the lives of the citizens of either country.

Finally Gorbachev realized that the Soviet Union could not continue this race indefinitely. They had limited resources (as does the U.S.). So he told President Reagan, "I am going to deprive you of an enemy." He did this by beginning to disarm the Soviet Union, without waiting for the U.S. to follow suit. This broke the move-countermove pattern. His countermove was exactly the opposite of what it had always been: Instead of increasing armaments, he decreased them, thus breaking the pattern.

In systems terminology, the exchange had been a reinforcing loop. Each move on one side caused a corresponding increasing move on the other. Gorbachev's action changed the system to a balancing loop initially. Later on, it became a reinforcing loop again, but this time in the opposite direction. As he decreased Soviet arms, we did the same. Of course, neither side is willing to decrease their arms to zero, since each has the potential to be attacked by someone other than their original foe.

This is an important lesson for project managers. When conflicts break out in our teams, it is often unproductive to try to get at causes. Each party will just blame the other. When this happens, it is more productive to find some way to break the pattern. This means you have to get at least one party to the conflict to abandon the normal behavioral response and do the opposite of what he has been doing. Here I am suggesting what you would do if you were mediating a conflict between two members of your team. If it is conflict between yourself as project manager and someone else and you want to resolve it, then you will have to break the pattern by behaving differently than you have been doing.

## THINKING IN SYSTEMS TERMS

The previous examples show that we must abandon linear thinking if we are to understand the dynamics of much of what happens in human affairs. This is especially true in project teams. In the next chapter, we will expand our understanding of systems thinking and introduce some tools that will help us understand how certain actions on our part can make our projects better and how some can actually make them worse.

# 9
CHAPTER

# Understanding Systems Thinking

**F**or several hundred years scientists have tried to understand the world through reductionist thinking. They initially believed that you could understand a thing by taking it apart and studying the components individually. After all, they reasoned, a machine is the sum of its parts, and Newtonian physics had led them to believe that the universe is a big clockwork mechanism.

At first glance, this sounds okay, until you begin to realize that a house is not the same as a pile of building materials. Furthermore, you cannot understand the qualities of a house by analyzing a single brick or an individual board that goes into the house. This is even more true of more complex aggregates of parts, such as biological organisms and complex machines.

> A house is not the same as a pile of building materials.

## WHAT IS A SYSTEM?

Even after you put all of the parts together, you still don't have a system. There is no active quality to a house. It just sits there. It may be cozy, comfortable, and great to live in, but it doesn't do anything! A system, on the other hand, is active. It does do something. In fact, a system is defined as follows:

A system is a collection of parts that interact
with each other to function as a whole.

The parts of a system, taken separately, are often useless. To be of value, they must be present and arranged correctly. If the arrangement and interaction of parts does not matter, then we are not dealing with a system, but with a "heap." Moreover, the definition of a system leads to an interesting conclusion: A system is actually *greater* than the sum of its parts. This has been called synergy and is one of the things that differentiates systems from nonsystems.

The human body is a large system, and it in turn contains a number of subsystems. The nervous system is a subsystem of the body. So is the circulatory system. When a system is part of a larger system, it is called a subsystem. Likewise, the earth is a part of the solar system, which is a part of a galaxy, and our galaxy is part of the collection of galaxies known as the universe.

Returning to human beings for a moment, note that a person is a complex system in her own right. Put her with a number of other individuals and have them work together to achieve a certain result, and you have a larger system called a team. It is true that you can study each member of the team individually, and you can describe their personalities, motivations, neuroses, and other characteristics. However, this understanding will not tell you a great deal about how the individual will function in the team, nor will it tell you a lot about the team as a system. Notice that I am not saying you will know nothing about the team, I am just saying that understanding will be limited.

The reason is in part because we are different persons in different settings. The attributes of a gear might not change when you assemble it into a clock. The attributes of human beings, however, are not so stable. I am a different person when teaching a seminar than when I am interacting with my family. Naturally, some characteristics are constant, but the differences make it hard to predict group behavior by observing individual behavior. I am also not the same in all teams. It is a very context-sensitive thing.

The importance of this for a project manager is that you have to be careful making predictions about what kind of project team you will have by looking only at individual team member qualities. As a simple example, you like Jane. You have worked with her before and found her to be reliable, hard-working, intelligent, cheerful, and resilient. You also like working with Bob. He is also very intelligent, extremely knowledgeable about a certain technology that you intend to employ, and he has very desirable work habits. You are certain that if you put these two on your team, you will have a dynamite combination!

The only thing is, Jane and Bob develop an immediate disliking for each other. There is an intense jealousy that manifests as sniping, competitiveness, and other acts of sabotage. Individually, they may be great. They may even be great for *you* to work with. It is just that the two of them can't work together.

Your dynamite combination is a disaster. - - - - - - - - - -▶ Jane and Bob take an immediate dislike for each other.

Again, the key to understanding systems is in that word *inter-act*. Jane and Bob interact with each other in a dysfunctional way. Naturally, for a team to be a good team, the members must interact in a harmonious, cooperative manner. So Jane and Bob together turn out to be a bad combination for your team.

## The key to understanding systems is in the word *interact*.

Now consider a simple interaction that most of us experience every day. You are driving a car. This forms a simple human-machine system. As you drive along, you approach a hill that you must climb. The car begins to slow down, so you press down on the accelerator and the car speeds up. When you have regained your original speed, you relax the pressure a bit and the car resumes a constant speed. When it reaches the top of the hill, you have to back off on the accelerator even more, or else the car will begin to speed up. This interaction between yourself and the car is a process called negative feedback. It is called negative because the feedback negates the change in system behavior. As the car slows down, your pressing the accelerator negates the change in speed. As the car speeds up, your letting up on the pedal negates the change in speed again. This can be diagramed as shown in Figure 9–1.

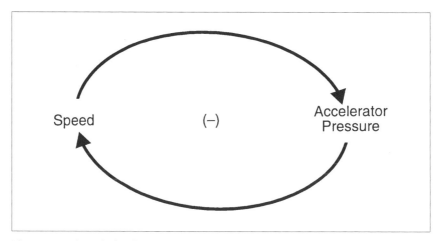

**Figure 9–1** Simple feedback system for driving a car.

Note that negative feedback does not have the colloquial meaning in this case. It is customary for people in organizations to talk about giving each other positive and negative feedback. By this they mean that they are either giving each other compliments (called positive feedback) or criticism (called negative feedback).

Returning to our example of driving a car, some people are able to maintain very good speed control going up and down hills. Others seem not to notice the feedback that tells them their speed is varying, so they speed up and slow down (even on level ground). When there is a lot of variation in a system, we say it is a *loose* system. Note that a self-stabilizing system does not prevent change, it just responds to change to try to minimize its effect on the system. The thermostat that turns your furnace on and off does this. It too has a certain amount of looseness. The room temperature may vary several degrees. The typical home thermostat only costs a few dollars. A system that would maintain temperature to a degree would cost many times more and probably wouldn't be worth the cost to most people. It is important to know the limits of a system.

Another characteristic of systems is reaction time. This is the amount of time it takes a signal to go around the loop. If it is too slow, the system can be damaged. An example is that if you touch a hot surface and don't feel it instantly, you can be seriously burned. This is, in fact, the problem with sunburn. It takes so long for you to realize that you are being burned that by that time, it is too late. The damage is done. This is analogous to placing a frog in a pot of water and slowly heating it up. The frog doesn't react. He just feels warmer, until the temperature is too hot. He lets himself be boiled. If you were to drop the frog into very hot water, however, he would jump out.

## ANTICIPATION

What if you can't afford the delay of even a fast-response system? For example, it is best not to get burned in the first place, rather than to react to being burned. Systems cope with this problem by reacting to *warnings*. Avoiding a growling dog is better than taking a chance that he might bite. Countries that wait until they are attacked to arm themselves may never get the chance. It is more

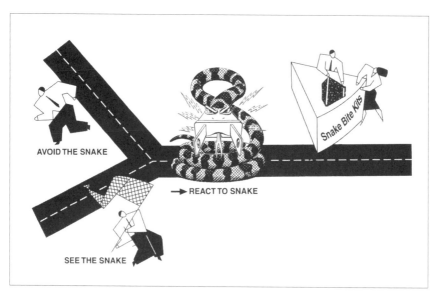

AVOID THE SNAKE

→ REACT TO SNAKE

SEE THE SNAKE

**Figure 9–2** Avoiding danger versus simply responding to it.

prudent to pay attention to intelligence reports that indicate imminent danger and arm in advance. Figure 9–2 shows the difference between avoiding danger and simply responding to it.

When systems only respond to problems, rather than anticipating them, it may be too late to deal with the problem, and the system is destroyed. The lesson for managers is that we should try to anticipate problems and deal with them ahead of time, rather than simply reacting to them. This is the difference between reactive and proactive management. This is also called risk management and is covered in Chapter 11.

## POSITIVE FEEDBACK

So far we have discussed systems that contain negative feedback loops. Negative feedback loops keep systems stable. They *resist* change. We often encounter such feedback systems when we try to change organizations. The French have a saying about such systems, which, roughly translated, is, "The more things change, the more they stay the same" (Watzlawick, Weakland, and Fisch, 1974). In fact, it seems that most systems employ negative feedback to protect themselves from being affected by outside influences. How then, do systems change, develop, or grow?

They contain some kind of positive feedback loop. Again, we are not referring to the colloquial use of the term, meaning to give someone positive strokes or compliments. Here, we mean that a small perturbation introduced into the system leads to a large system effect. Some examples include the growth of compound interest, rabbit populations, knowledge, personal power, and audio systems that howl at you. The audio system is diagrammed in Figure 9–3.

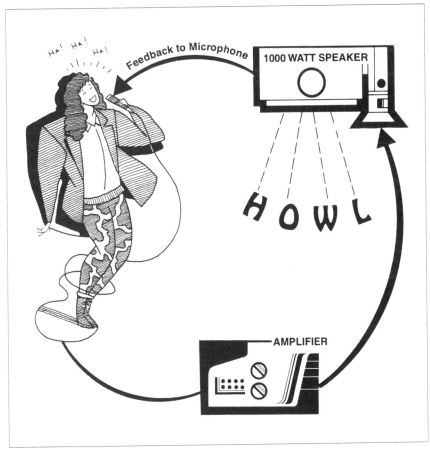

**Figure 9–3**  An audio system that howls.

When you speak into the microphone, the sound of your voice is amplified and fed to the speakers. The microphone picks up the sound from the speakers, amplifies it, and a positive loop is created. You might ask why the system does not get louder and louder. There are always limits to growth. In the case of an electronic system, the amplifier can only produce so much power, so when the sound reaches that level, it can go no higher. Rabbit populations can grow only so far. They reach a point at which there is not enough food to feed all of them. They either have to move to new areas or begin to starve. Even compound interest might reach a limit. The bank can only pay interest on deposits if they can lend the money to someone, so if they reach a point at which no one wants to borrow the money you have deposited, they would no longer be able to pay you interest on it. Of course, you would have to be a very large depositor indeed for this to happen.

## BUILDING COMPLEX SYSTEMS

Every complex system that you will ever encounter is built from the two basic elements—positive and negative feedback loops. Since this is true, when you see two systems that have the same loop structure, you can expect them to behave in very similar ways. The beauty of this is that we can learn how a system behaves in one area and transfer that knowledge to systems of the same structure in other areas.

As I explained in the previous section, positive loops would grow indefinitely if something didn't limit them. In the case of rabbits, it is the food supply. Consider a similar system composed of bacteria. These single-cell organisms multiply by dividing. In the right environment, a cell will divide in about one-half hour. The two cells will themselves divide in another half hour, so by then, you have four cells. This progression continues, so that you get 8, 16, 32, 64, 128, and so on. As incredible as it might seem, after only 10 hours, you will have more than a million cells!

This assumes that none of them die, of course. However, all living organisms do die, so to know how many bacteria you would have after a certain period, you must factor in the death rate. The overall system is shown in Figure 9–4.

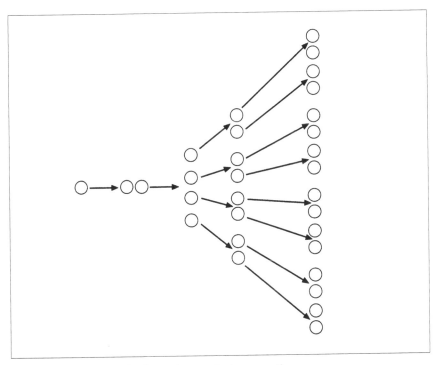

**Figure 9–4** A system for bacteria population growth.

As you can see, the two loops work against each other. If 10 bacteria are "born" and 6 die, the net increase in population is 4. However, if 12 die for every 10 that are born, the population will gradually decline. The overall system behavior is determined by which loop is stronger or dominant.

This basic model can be applied to other populations. A city grows or declines in the same way that bacteria do. However, in addition to being born and dying, people also move into and away from cities, so the situation is more complicated. In this case, you might have four loops, as shown in Figure 9–5.

We might also ask what controls the rate at which loops operate. For example, in the case of population growth, we would ask what affects the birth and death rates. If the population is one of animals, death would be affected by the food supply, predators, and disease. For simplicity, we can begin by adding the effect of food alone, to get the diagram in Figure 9–6.

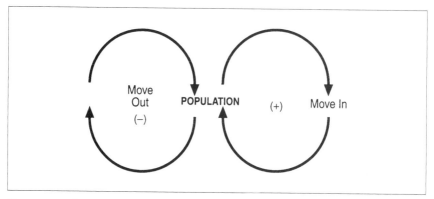

**Figure 9–5** Growth of a city.

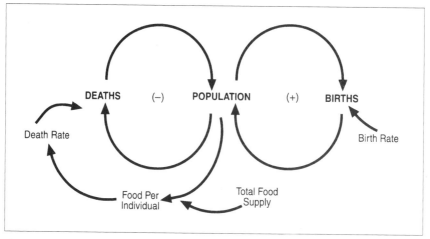

**Figure 9–6** Effect of food supply on death rates.

In the same way, we can add the effects of predators and disease to arrive at the system shown in Figure 9–7.

Is this everything? Not really. For animal populations, over-crowding introduces a significant factor (Maybe the same is true of human populations too). For example, when rabbits get too crowded, they may go into shock and die at the slightest stimu-lus—a loud noise, the sight of an enemy, or even another friendly rabbit. They literally die of fright or excitement. This means that if the other negative loops fail to control the population, the over-crowding loop takes over.

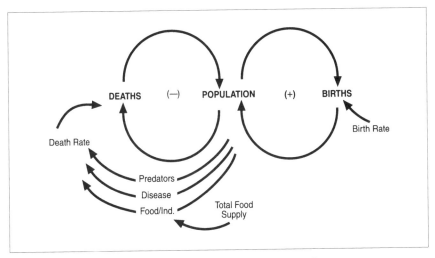

**Figure 9–7**  Effects of food, predators, and disease on death rates.

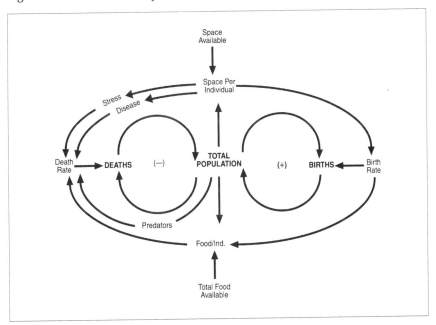

**Figure 9–8**  Major factors affecting animal populations.

In addition, some animals use the amount of food or space to control population by moderating the actual birth rate. Considering all of these factors together, we can construct a diagram like the one in Figure 9–8.

In this system, the loop that will eventually stop population growth depends on the particular situation. In some cases the loops all work together to control the positive loop. Sometimes a few do the major job and others are kept in reserve in case these fail.

One problem we have is that people sometimes intervene in a system to eliminate a negative feedback loop that they don't like. The next thing they know, a worse one takes its place. For example, if disease is reduced by medicine, and nothing is done to limit the birth rate, population might grow to the point where not enough food is available and famine occurs, which kills even more people. Even if the food supply is not a problem, we can already see the effects of people living longer because of improved health care. They now wind up in nursing homes or suffer Alzheimer's, which would not have struck them had they died younger.

> Any change that affects the relationship between the positive and negative loops is going to alter the long-term behavior of the system.

Most systems will balance themselves if left alone and will return to the balance point if disturbed. It is important to look for the balance point in complex systems. By understanding the nature of the positive and negative feedback loops, you can also differentiate between things that are going to affect the system only temporarily and things that will have a lasting effect. Any change, no matter how big, that does not change the important positive or negative loops of a system will be only temporary. Conversely, any change—no matter how small—that does affect the relationship between the positive and negative loops is going to alter the long-term behavior of the system.

From a practical point of view, this says that if we want to change a complex system, we must find a way to change the relationship between the loops that keep the system balanced. Otherwise, every change we try to make will end up being "resisted" by the system, which will just return to the status quo state.

That is a brief introduction to systems thinking. In the next chapter, we will look at ways to apply these ideas to projects.

# 10

## CHAPTER

# How to Apply Systems Thinking in Managing Projects

In the previous chapters, I showed how systems thinking can help us understand the dynamics of human interactions. Since project work is generally performed by people, it should be possible to apply systems concepts to the understanding and management of projects.

### FIXES THAT FAIL

Let's begin by considering a fairly common problem in projects. The work is falling behind schedule. It seems that the only thing to do is ask the person doing the work to increase his working hours each day, that is, to work a few hours of overtime to get back on track. He agrees. The first week, he works 12 hours a day and is making progress. The amount of work being done is definitely greater than what was previously accomplished. However, after a couple of weeks, you discover that he is making a lot of mistakes, and these must be corrected. Furthermore, his output is down from what it was the first week. In fact, you find that the amount of work he is turning out is just about equal to what he was doing in a normal 40-hour week before! You are actually losing, because he now has to spend time correcting the errors he has made, and this drops his output even more.

Something must be done.

You decide that if overtime is not the answer, then extra resources must be obtained. You convince your boss to assign a new person to help. To your amazement, the work accomplished by both of them is barely the same as for one person working alone, and there are considerably more errors being made. What is going on?

You talk to your original team member, and he says, "It's very simple. The guy you gave me knows nothing about what I'm doing, so I spent most of Monday getting him on board. Then I found that he's making a lot of mistakes, so I had to help correct those, and I'm still having to work overtime to take care of training him and to correct all the errors. I would be better off with no help at all!"

This is an example of a "fixes that fail." Having the person work overtime initially worked until the long-term effect of fatigue kicked in. Then the person started making more errors, which had to be corrected, which caused him to fall further behind, which required him to work harder, which caused more fatigue, and more errors, and on and on it goes. Then a helper was assigned to the project. The original worker had to train the helper, which dropped his productivity, which caused him to work harder, which made him more fatigued, and the helper made errors, which had to be corrected, which made him even more tired, and so on.

Another example. I know of a company, we'll call it Acme Electronics, that makes components that go into products manufactured by other companies. Occasionally, their customer has a problem with one of the components, and the design engineers are sent to the field to see if they can correct the problem. Since they are currently working on designing new components, that work comes to a standstill. They manage to correct the problem for the customer and return to work.

Unfortunately, the deadline for completing the current component design has not changed, but they have fallen behind. The only solution is to work hard to try to catch up. The result is the same as described previously in this chapter—they do poor quality work, which is not caught. The new component is released. The customer again has problems with the new part. The engineers are sent to the field to correct the problem. Current work comes to a standstill. They work hard to catch up, turn out another bad design, and the cycle begins all over again.

The common expression that describes this situation is fire-fighting. The engineers are doing a reasonable job of fire-fighting, but nothing is being done to prevent future fires.

## LEVELS OF UNDERSTANDING

There are numerous levels from which we can understand the world around us. Systems thinkers are concerned with four of these, as shown in Figure 10–1. At the level of *events* are things that occur on a day-to-day basis. Accidents happen, we go to work, eat lunch, perform a work task, or write a memo. In the case of the engineers, they correct a problem with a component—they put out a fire. This level is called *reactive,* because we are always reacting to the event rather than trying to control its occurrence.

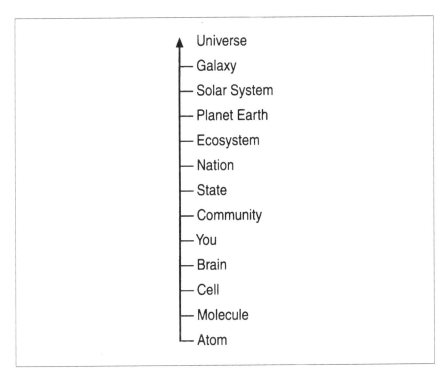

**Figure 10–1** Levels of understanding.

At the next level are *patterns of events.* In the case of our engineers, we begin to notice that the same pattern keeps happening. Note that patterns can only be seen over a period of time. When we see patterns developing, we might be able to be *adaptive* in our response. We give the engineers training in fire-fighting, so that when they have a fire, they can extinguish it quickly. This still does nothing to prevent fires.

At the *systemic structure* level we begin to ask what causes the patterns of events to occur. This level is called *creative,* because we might be able to prevent fires if we can understand the patterns. This level is future-oriented. By preventing fires, we create a different future than the one that would have occurred normally. At this level, we might decide to set up a fire-fighting group, separate from the design engineers. This would free the engineers from any fire-fighting so that they could concentrate on doing new designs really well, which over the long run should reduce the number of fires that break out.

The next tier is called the *shared vision* level. This level generates the structures that form patterns. This level is called *generative* and is truly future-oriented. At this level, we ask questions like, "What is the real role of design engineers? How should fire-fighting be handled? What trade-offs are we willing to make between resources devoted to design and those dedicated to fire-fighting?"

## THE TRAGEDY OF THE COMMONS

Complex systems have a lot of strengths, but they also are like everything else—you don't get anything for free. So complex systems also create their own set of problems. One of these is called the tragedy of the commons. In medieval England there were commons, or common pasture areas. This idea was brought to the United States by the colonists. Commons meant that all members of a community were entitled to graze their livestock there. The individual livestock owner soon begins to think, "The more cows I have, the better off I'll be, and since the grazing is free, I will increase my herd as fast as I can." This creates a positive feedback loop.

It also creates a situation that each individual is powerless to avoid. Each person tends to think the same way, so herds start growing. Soon they reach a point where the cows eat the grass faster than it can grow. Faced with nothing to eat, the animals crop the grass down to the roots, killing it, so that there is nothing at all to eat. Soon the cows are all starving and the entire village is faced with disaster.

Notice that it does no good for a single villager to voluntarily keep down the size of his herd. That just leaves more pasture for the others, who then have more incentive to add more cattle. Thus, the unselfish action will not prevent the disaster, and the person will just be poorer in the meantime, while his neighbors are prospering. The significant thing about this situation is that if every person makes the best decision from his own point of view, everyone winds up worse off!

Peter Block has pointed out that *enlightened* self interest would mean that every villager would do what is best for the village—not himself individually (Block, 1987). In doing so, he knows that he will benefit himself over the long run. Of course, it is very hard to get people to do this. People tend to look out for number 1, never realizing that their actions will eventually destroy themselves. We see this with many of the environmental problems that are being created today.

But what does this have to do with project management? One of the significant aspects of project management is that we are always competing for scarce resources to get our jobs done. If we realized that our real self-interest lies in cooperation rather than competition, our project teams would function better. Instead, we sometimes get locked into win-lose conflicts over resources. Each project manager wants to optimize his "herd" with no regard for the impact to other teams. From a systems point of view, anything that I do to help my organization in one area tends to help the entire system, and conversely, anything I do to hurt it hurts everyone.

I showed in Chapter 8 how we sometimes get locked into games without end because we set up a move-countermove interaction. Now that you understand negative feedback loops, you can see that such a system tends to balance itself and resists being changed. As I said at the end of Chapter 9, systems tend to return to the balance point if disturbed, so if you try to reduce the conflict, it just comes back after awhile. Unless you can interrupt the pattern, that is, disturb the negative feedback loop, the interaction will continue, unabated, forever! (Or until both parties get tired of it.)

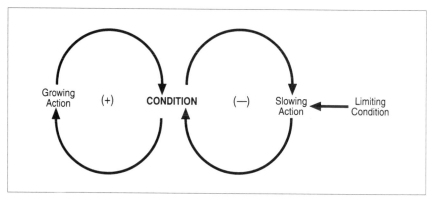

**Figure 10–2**  Limits to growth system structure.

## LIMITS TO GROWTH

In his book *The Fifth Discipline* (1990), Peter Senge presents a number of systems archetypes that appear over and over again in organizations, groups, and even in individual performance. One of these is the limits-to-growth model. This archetype is almost always found in situations where "growth bumps up against limits" (Senge, 1990, p. 96). Organizations grow for awhile, then stop growing. Teams get better for awhile, and then stop getting better. The same happens to individuals. Attempts to improve organizations through reengineering might succeed for awhile and then reach a limit.

This would certainly apply to project teams. In Chapter 23, I deal with improving processes in project teams. However, you might find that there are limits to the improvements you can achieve. We try to solve deadline problems by working longer hours, but as I showed at the beginning of this chapter, the stress and fatigue begin to slow our work speed and reduce quality, thus reducing the benefit of the longer hours.

A limits-to-growth system has a structure like the one shown in Figure 10–2.

## SHIFTING THE BURDEN

This archetype is prevalent throughout government and corporate organizations. There is a problem that causes symptoms that demand attention, but the underlying problem is difficult for people to address, either because it is obscure or costly to confront. So people shift the burden of the problem to other solutions. These are well-intentioned, easy fixes that seem efficient. However, the fixes just deal with the symptoms and leave the underlying problem unchanged.

One example of this at the personal level is when a person is overworked, possibly because the department is understaffed. She tries to juggle work, family, and her ongoing education, always running from one thing to another. When the workload increases beyond her capacity, the only real solution is to limit the workload. It might mean declining a promotion or prioritizing and making choices. Instead, she decides to juggle faster, tries to relieve her stress with alcohol or meditation, but neither provides a real solution. The problem persists, and so does the need for drinking.

We also see this in our attempts to deal with problem members of teams. Rather than dealing directly with the person, the manager tries to develop his human relations skills. Perhaps the HR department tries to intervene. They talk to the person, coach, counsel, and maybe "write him up." However, he persists in his problematic behavior. The real solution would be to remove him from the group (and probably the company), but no one wants to take that *hard medicine,* so the problem persists.

A system model for shifting the burden is shown in Figure 10–3.

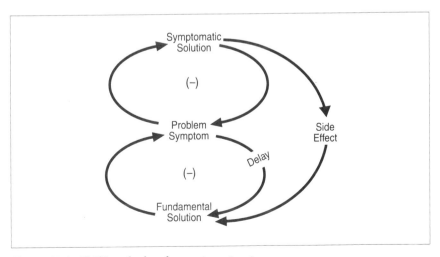

**Figure 10–3** Shifting the burden system structure.

I hope these examples show how systems thinking could be useful to project managers. For in-depth treatment of systems in organizations, I know of no better source than Senge's *The Fifth Discipline* and a companion book entitled *The Fifth Discipline Field-book* (Senge et al., 1994). You might also want to subscribe to *The Systems Thinker Newsletter*. See the listing for Pegasus Communications in the Resource Appendix for information.

# 11
## CHAPTER

# Managing Project Risks

**P**erhaps the most famous "law" of all is Murphy's Law, which is usually stated as, "Whatever can go wrong *will!*" Given that this seems to be true in the experience of most people, it seems reasonable to ask how one should deal with Murphy's Law. It seems clear that when something goes wrong, we have *the possibility of suffering harm or loss,* which is defined as *risk.* I therefore define risk as anything that can go wrong in a project, and since things that go wrong can cause me to suffer harm or loss, I then need to ask how we can manage risks in projects.

> **Principle:** We are all inclined to overestimate our ability and underestimate difficulties. As someone has said, "Even Murphy was an optimist!"

In my experience, this is a neglected area in managing projects. Of course, it is fair to ask if it really matters. My response is that it does matter, because when things go wrong unexpectedly, they throw you off balance and often cause major crises for your projects.

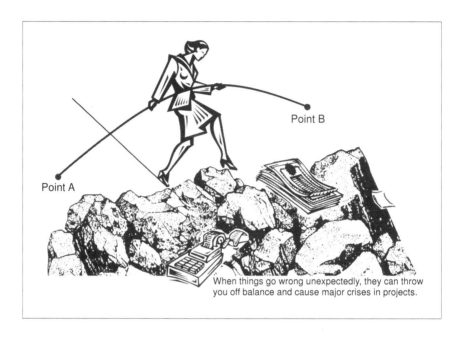

When things go wrong unexpectedly, they can throw you off balance and cause major crises in projects.

As an example, I have seen design engineers put all of their effort into a design that they couldn't make work. They never even *considered* the possibility! It may be that to consider that they might not be able to make the design work would be to admit their fallibility, and that might be too much for some perfectionist types to do. Whatever the reason, those engineers who encounter design problems are often thrown into the panic mode and may have to start over, since they have put "all of their eggs into one basket." Naturally, such a setback can have a serious impact on the project.

> "It is an unhappy fact of life that there are usually more things that can go wrong with a project than can unexpectedly go right."
>
> —John R. Schuyler (1995)

If you refer to my project methodology (the flowchart), you will see that there are two places in which risk management needs to be done. The first is in planning project strategy. The second is in implementation planning.

In planning strategy, you are trying to develop an approach for managing the project that may involve the choice of technology as well as an execution method. I have called these *project strategy* and *technical strategy* in Chapter 7. Both strategies have risks in most cases. When proven technology is being employed, the risks of failure are usually low. However, if cutting-edge technology is being applied, then the risks are much higher. Further, some project strategies have higher risks than others. For example, a "farm-out" project strategy might be more risky that one in which all work is done internally.

Either way, the first step in doing risk analysis is to identify what might go wrong. (This is true at both step 4 and step 6 of the flowchart.) When I do this with a team, I have them brainstorm a list of these and record them on a flip chart with no discussion or evaluation being done. To help them identify risks, I simply ask, "What could go wrong that could impact schedule, cost, performance, or scope in the project?"

## THREATS VERSUS RISKS

You will notice in step 4 of the flowchart that you are supposed to test a strategy against risks and SWOT analysis. SWOT stands for *s*trengths, *w*eaknesses, *o*pportunities, and *t*hreats. Unless you can manage risks, offset weaknesses, and contend with threats, your project strategy is likely to fail. The question is: What is the difference between threats and risks?

If you adopt a purist definition, risks are things that can happen without having any deliberate intention to cause harm behind them. Examples of risks might be accidents; acts of nature such as earthquakes, weather, and so on; losing key members of the team; fires; escalating labor rates or inflation; changes in the exchange rate for international projects; political instability, and so on. A threat is something that is done by a competitor or adversary to offset whatever you have done. For example, when an airline tries to capture a route by offering a very low fare, they are usually unsuccessful because the competition just matches their fare and nobody gains any more market share. While threats and risks are technically different, for the purposes of managing projects, they can be lumped together in the same analysis.

## IT IS BEST TO AVOID RISK

It seems reasonable to say that it is always better to avoid risk than it is to manage it (Levine, 1995, p. 30). This should be done through better planning, not by avoiding a good opportunity. As I said above, you begin by identifying what can go wrong that might affect time, cost, performance, or scope in your project. Then you ask what might be done to avoid these effects. If it is not possible to avoid the effect, can you reduce the impact?

> "It seems reasonable to say that it is always better to avoid risk than it is to manage it."
>
> —Harvey Levine

As an example, weather can hold up projects and cannot be avoided. The solution is to examine the weather history for the area and time of year and to build into the schedule a reasonable amount of delay. If the weather is better than usual, you will get ahead of schedule, and conversely.

It is helpful to have some measure of the impact a risk or threat might have on the project.

On the other hand, I would rather avoid the risk of putting an inexperienced project manager on a highly important project than to try to manage the risk once I have done so. Prevention is always less expensive than failure, as is discussed in Chapter 22 on quality.

## QUANTIFYING RISKS AND THREATS

It is helpful to have some measure of the impact a risk or threat might have on a project. Naturally, most of these cannot be quantified in any really objective way, but we can use a subjective method that seems to work fairly well. The approach was first devised by engineers to identify where product designs might fail and is therefore called failure mode effects analysis, or FMEA. For any of you who are math-challenged, this is a foreboding sounding term, but don't be intimidated by it. The approach is really very simple and requires nothing more difficult than multiplication.

I am going to call the approach project risk analysis and management, because I want to emphasize that it is not enough to simply *identify* risks—you have to manage them as well. Furthermore, I am lumping risks and threats together, so I don't have to keep saying "risks and threats" every time. From now on, you will understand that "risks" refers to both.

## ASSESSING PROBABILITY

Once we have brainstormed a list of risks, we have to estimate the probability that they might occur. To do so, we use the information shown as Table 11–1. In the FMEA terminology, something that goes wrong is referred to as a failure. I have changed that word to "occurrence," since the word "failure" does not always apply. For example, political unrest that might affect an international project is not a failure but an occurrence or event. You will note that the probability scale is a logarithmic scale, whereas the remaining scales are linear.

The next thing that we need to consider is how severe the effect of the event or occurrence is on the project. An event that has a high probability of happening but a low impact on the project is of little concern, whereas an event that is low probability but se-

**T A B L E  11–1**

Probability of Occurrence

| Probability of Occurrence | Possible Occurrence Rates | Rank |
|---|---|---|
| Very High: Occurrence is almost certain | ≥ 1 in 2 | 10 |
| | 1 in 3 | 9 |
| High: Repeated occurrences possible | 1 in 8 | 8 |
| | 1 in 20 | 7 |
| Moderate: Occasional occurrences | 1 in 80 | 6 |
| | 1 in 400 | 5 |
| | 1 in 2,000 | 4 |
| Low: Relatively few occurrences | 1 in 15,000 | 3 |
| | 1 in 150,000 | 2 |
| Remote: Occurrence is unlikely | ≤ 1 in 1,500,000 | 1 |

vere impact is of great concern. In this table, you will note the word "customer" is used several times. For this analysis, *customer* can mean an actual customer for the project or your company management, whichever is appropriate. See Table 11–2.

The next thing we want to look at is how easy it is to detect that the event is going to happen before it actually takes place. For example, if the oil runs out of your car while you are driving it, the effect will be severe. If you have an oil gauge, you should be able to see that the oil pressure is getting low and take action before the situation becomes serious. If you have a broken oil gauge or an indicator light that comes on at some threshold level, it is not as easy to detect the problem beforehand.

In projects, things like bad weather can be predicted with some accuracy, and steps can be taken to compensate. Accidents, however, tend to happen without warning, so they are harder to deal with. Table 11–3 is used to measure the detection capability of a risk in a project. Note that this scale is reversed; that is, the more certain it is that you can detect a hazard, the lower the number.

**T A B L E  11–2**

## Severity of the Effect

| Effect | Criteria: Severity of Effect | Rank |
|---|---|---|
| Hazardous-without warning | Project severely impacted, possible cancellation, with no warning. | 10 |
| Hazardous-with warning | Project severely impacted, possible cancellation, with warning. | 9 |
| Very High | Major impact on project schedule, budget, or performance; may cause severe delays, overruns, or degradation of performance. | 8 |
| High | Project schedule, budget, or performance impacted significantly; job can be completed, but customer will be very dissatisfied. | 7 |
| Moderate | Project schedule, budget, or performance impacted some; customer will be dissatisfied. | 6 |
| Low | Project schedule, budget, or performance impacted slightly; customer will be mildly dissatisfied. | 5 |
| Very Low | Some impact to project; customer will be aware of impact. | 4 |
| Minor | Small impact to project; average customer will be aware of impact. | 3 |
| Very Minor | Impact so small that it would be noticed only by a very discriminating customer. | 2 |
| None | No effect. | 1 |

**T A B L E  11–3**

## Detection Capability

| Detection | Rank |
|---|---|
| Absolute Uncertainty | 10 |
| Very Remote | 9 |
| Remote | 8 |
| Very Low | 7 |
| Low | 6 |
| Moderate | 5 |
| Moderately High | 4 |
| High | 3 |
| Very High | 2 |
| Almost Certain | 1 |

## THE RISK PROBABILITY NUMBER

For each risk that you have identified, you now have three measures—a probability level, severity measure, and detection capability index. These three numbers are multiplied to obtain a risk probability number (RPN). The higher that number, the more serious the risk. To show how this works, consider the three risks shown in Figure 11–1.

The general approach to dealing with high RPNs is to ask whether any of the three individual components can be reduced. That is, can risk or severity be lowered and/or can detection be increased (which will lower its number). As an example, we can reduce the probability of a weather delay in a project by doing it during a calendar period that historically has good weather. We can reduce severity of weather delays by padding the schedule, and we can increase our ability to detect forthcoming bad weather by paying close attention to weather forecasts.

For the examples in our table, the RPN for bad weather is so small that it can be ignored. However, the other two risks have significant RPNs, and we should consider what to do. First, let's examine loss of a key team member. While it has a probability of only 2, it has a high severity and high detection. As a general rule, whenever severity is high, regardless of the RPN, special attention should be given to this particular risk.

A possible example of this is the *Challenger* disaster. It was believed by some members of the team that the probability of O-ring failure at the low launch temperature was quite low. However, the severity of failure was a 10, because the astronauts on board would be killed. Because of this fact alone, greater caution should have been exercised. It has been my experience that when

| Identified Risk | P | S | D | RPN |
|---|---|---|---|---|
| Bad weather | 3 | 2 | 4 | 24 |
| Loss of key team member | 2 | 8 | 8 | 128 |
| Technology won't work | 6 | 10 | 8 | 480 |

**Figure 11–1**  Risk analysis for a project.

people think the probability of something is low, they throw caution to the wind. An example is that some people think the probability that they will have an automobile accident is very low, so they take chances with their driving—and get killed or seriously injured.

The severity of losing a key team member can be reduced if we have someone available to cover for her. This is what live theatrical productions do. They have an understudy who can play the part of a regular performer in the event of illness or accident. We might not be able to reduce detection in this case, but reducing severity alone might be enough.

The third risk in the table is that technology won't work. There are a couple of possibilities in this case. First, the probability of failure is shown as six points, which is moderate. This might not give us too much cause for concern. However, if probability of technology failure were higher, say around eight or nine points, then I would suggest that a feasibility study be conducted before any kind of application of that technology be attempted. A basic premise is that discovery and development should be separated, if you are to have control over project schedules.

Even if we have low probability, the severity of a technology failure can be very high. One way to deal with this is to be ready with an alternate. In some very high-risk projects, where it was not possible to do feasibility studies, I have known some companies that have launched parallel development paths. The first technology that could be made to work was the one they continued with. This obviously costs a lot of money and would only be done where time is more important than cost, which is true in some situations.

Finally, can we detect failure of technology with any ease? Perhaps not. However, it might be prudent to establish some decision criteria about how many failures will be tolerated before an approach is abandoned in favor of one that is more certain. This can be a blow to the ego of a professional, but in business, we must do what is prudent rather than what is necessarily self-serving. An exception might be an attempt to develop a vaccine for a disease such as AIDS. However, even here, we must ask if repeated failures at a particular approach might not dictate adopting an alternative strategy.

## DEVELOPING CONTINGENCY PLANS

As I stated earlier, it is not enough to identify and quantify risks. The idea is to manage them. This might be done in three ways:

1. Risk avoidance
2. Mitigation (reduction, such as using air bags)
3. Transfer (such as in loss prevention through insurance)

### Risk Avoidance

In the case of risk aversion or avoidance, we want to avoid the risk altogether. In the case of the *Challenger,* the decision to delay the launch until the temperature warmed up would be an example of risk avoidance.

Japanese manufacturing has for many years employed "fool-proofing" as a risk-avoidance strategy. The idea is to set up the assembly process so that it cannot be done incorrectly. One example was that they occasionally would start to install a gas tank in a car only to find that one of the four mounting brackets had not been welded onto the tank. The solution was to set up a fixture to hold the tank while the brackets were being welded onto it. Feelers were attached to detect the presence of the brackets. If all four brackets were not in place, the welding machine would not weld any of them.

In construction projects, we pad the schedule with rain delay days, based on weather history for the area and time of year. This way, we avoid the risk that we will be delayed by bad weather. In engineering design, I mentioned using parallel design strategies to avoid the possibility that the deadline might be missed because one strategy proves difficult to implement. In any project, risk aversion or avoidance might be the most preferable strategy to follow.

### Mitigation or Risk Reduction

If we can think of contingencies in the event that a risk takes place, we can mitigate the effect. Placing air bags in cars is an attempt to reduce the severity of an accident, should one occur. Stafford Beer

(1981) has argued that seat belts and air bags in cars actually give drivers a false sense of security. We have defined the problem as protecting the driver from being harmed if he is in an accident. Beer argues that it would perhaps be better to redefine the problem as how to keep a driver from having an accident in the first place (risk avoidance). He suggests that if we lined the dash board of the car with spikes, making it very clear that an accident has serious consequences, we might give drivers incentive to be more careful. His suggestion is not without merit.

In projects that involve procurement, sole-sourcing is a risk to consider. The alternative is to second-source all procured parts or equipment. That way, if a supplier can't deliver on time or at the specified price, the second supplier might be able to. This can be thought of as either risk avoidance or mitigation.

Temporary workers are used as backups for critical personnel who become ill or are injured. Overtime is used as a contingency when tasks take longer than estimated. This is one reason why overtime should not be planned into a project to meet original targets, if possible. Rather, it should be kept in reserve as a contingency.

Another possible contingency is to reduce scope to permit the team to meet the original target date, then come back later and incorporate deferred work to finish the job.

Having a fire evacuation plan in a building can be thought of as a contingency and also a loss-prevention plan.

## Loss Prevention

Insurance is one way of protecting against loss in the event that a risk manifests. Having alternative sites available into which a group can move in the event of a disaster is a loss-prevention strategy. Backup personnel can also be thought of as loss avoidance. If someone else can do the work, then when a key person is ill, there will be no loss to the project. Of course, this is difficult to do with highly skilled personnel.

## Cost Contingency

Cost contingency is also called management reserve. Unfortunately, it is misunderstood. Too often it is believed that management reserve is there to cover poor performance. This is incorrect. Management reserve is a fund that is part of a project budget to cover the cost of unidentified work. All projects should have a work budget to cover the cost of identified work and a management reserve to cover work not yet identified. In addition, on projects that are paid for by a customer, there will be a component of the total job cost called *margin*. This is the intended profit for the job. Poor performance eats into margin, not management reserve.

The management reserve account is not touched unless we identify new work to be done. This is a change in scope, of course. At that point, money is transferred from the management reserve account into the work budget, and performance is subsequently tracked against the revised budget. A log should be maintained of all scope changes and their effect on the work budget, management reserve, and margin (if the change has such an effect). In customer-funded projects, the customer may be required to pay for scope changes so that there is no impact to the management reserve account.

Schuyler (1995) has developed a list of possible ways to mitigate or avoid risks. These are shown in Box 11–1.

## PROJECT MANAGEMENT APPROACH AS A FUNCTION OF RISK

As Jean Couillard (1995) has written, much of the literature on managing projects proposes a uniform set of tools and methods to manage all kinds of projects. A study by Couillard confirms a suggestion by McFarlan (1981) that the nature of the project should dictate the proper tools and methods. Risk, in particular, is a characteristic that should determine the best management approach.

Couillard found that if project risk is not considered, standard PERT/CPM techniques, project monitoring, and control do not have a significant influence on project success. However, in high-risk projects, these techniques *do* have a significant influence on success. In high-risk projects, using PERT/CPM, which increases the frequency of project monitoring and control, does improve the likelihood of project success. He concludes that high-risk projects should be more closely planned, monitored, and controlled than low-risk projects.

## B O X 11–1

### WAYS OF MITIGATING OR AVOIDING RISKS

**Portfolio Risks**

Share risks by having partners

Spread risks over time

Participate in many ventures

Group complementary risks into portfolios

Seek lower-risk ventures

Specialize and concentrate in a single, well-known area

Increase the company's capitalization

**Commodity Prices**

Hedge or fix in the futures markets

Use long- or short-term sales (price and volume) contracts

Tailor contracts for risk sharing

**Interest Rate and Exchange Rate**

Use swaps, floors, ceilings, collars, and other hedging instruments

Restructure the balance sheet

Denominate or index certain transactions in a foreign currency

**Environmental Hazards**

Buy insurance

Increase safety margins

Develop and test an incident response program

**Operational Risks**

Hire contractors under turnkey contracts

Tailor risk-sharing contract clauses

Use safety margins; overbuild and overspecify designs

Have backup and redundant equipment

Increase training

Operate with redirect and bail-out options

Conduct tests, pilot programs, and trials

**Analysis Risks (Reducing Evaluation Error)**

Use better techniques (i.e., decision analysis)

Seek additional information

Monitor key and indicator variables

Validate models

Include evaluation practices along with project post-reviews

Develop redundant models with alternative approaches and people

Involve multiple disciplines, and communicate cross-discipline

Provide better training and tools

The study also showed that when technical risk is high, pure-project organization structure (see Chapter 6) has a significant *negative influence* on project success. It turns out that matrix structure is better for such projects, presumably because technical expertise can be more easily drawn from a matrix structure than the pure-project (or stand-alone) structure.

To measure success, Couillard employed the factors shown in Table 11–4. Based on the findings of Baker et al. (1974) (reported in Chapter 5), his measures seem to be appropriate, as the point is that project success should be called *perceived* success, since the quantitative measures alone (cost, performance, time, scope) do not always correlate with whether a project is judged successful or not. As you can see, Couillard is explicit in calling the measures *subjective*.

**When technical risk is high, matrix is better than pure-project organization.**

Altogether, Couillard used 17 factors to indicate aspects of project management. These are shown in Table 11–5.

Using regression analysis, Couillard concluded that communication patterns and project goal understanding significantly influence all six measures of project success (Table 11–4). This supports the frequent suggestion in the literature that you must have a clear, shared understanding of the project mission in order

**T A B L E  11–4**

Project Success Measures

| | |
|---|---|
| Tech 1 | The subjective measurement of technical success relative to the initial requirement |
| Tech 2 | The subjective measure of technical success compared to other projects in DND |
| Cost | The subjective measure of budget over/underrun |
| Time | The subjective measure of schedule over/underrun |
| Process | The level of satisfaction with the process by which the project was managed; a successful project is one that requires minimal conflict and crisis management (Might and Fisher, 1985) |
| Overall | The subjective measure of overall project success |

Source: Adapted from Jean Couillard, "The Role of Project Risk in Determining Project Management Approach," *Project Management Journal*, December 1995, pp. 3–15. (Used with permission.)

**T A B L E    11–5**

Management Factors

| Project Manager Experience | Project Management Method | Project Management Tools and Techniques |
|---|---|---|
| Number of projects managed | Project goals understanding | WBS utilization |
| Responsibility index | Level of PM authority and responsibility | PERT/CPM utilization |
| | Level of PD authority and responsibility | C/SCSC utilization |
| | Organizational structure | Periodic technical reports |
| | Senior management involvement | Periodic cost reports |
| | Communication patterns | Periodic schedule reports |
| | Problem handling | Frequency of project monitoring |
| | Project team support | |

Source: Adapted from Jean Couillard, "The Role of Project Risk in Determining Project Management Approach," *Project Management Journal,* December 1995, pp. 3–15. (Used with permission.)

to be successful. Good communication within the team is also essential.

The authority given to the project manager to make decisions at the project level was also a factor, as were support received from the project team and problem handling by the team. This offers some support to the complaint by project managers that they have a lot of responsibility and no authority. Based on this finding, senior managers should be sure to give the project manager the needed authority to deal with project issues directly.

Project managers in the study were also asked to assess project risk with regard to three objectives: technical performance, schedule, and cost. He used a three-point scale in which risk was rated as low, medium, and high. It was found that more-experienced project managers are generally assigned to the high-risk projects. Also, PERT/CPM, C/SCSC, and periodic technical reports are more frequently used in high-risk projects.

## Technical Risk

When technical risk is high, project success is influenced by project manager authority, communication, team support, and problem handling. As previously mentioned, pure-project structure is also negatively correlated with success when technical risk is high.

## Cost Risk

When cost risk is high, project success is influenced by understanding of project goals by the team, project manager authority, team support, and communication.

## Schedule Risk

If schedule risk is high, two factors are important: the project manager's experience and the frequency of monitoring progress.

## CONCLUSION

Many success factors in projects center around human relationships, which says that project managers must master these skills no matter the project risk. High-risk projects need more careful planning, monitoring, and controlling than do low-risk projects. In general, if you have any one or a combination of technical, cost, or schedule risks, it seems prudent to follow these guidelines:

1. Emphasize team support.
2. Give the project manager appropriate authority.
3. Improve problem handling and communication.
4. Avoid the pure-project structure.
5. Increase the frequency of project monitoring.
6. Use WBS, PERT/CPM, and C/SCSC.
7. Establish clear project goals for the team.
8. Select an experienced project manager.

# 12
## CHAPTER

# Improving Decisions
# in Projects

Like all managers, project managers must make many decisions every day. For example, in planning the project, step 4 of the model requires that a project strategy be selected from a list made in step 3. There are four criteria that should be considered when making this choice. These include whether the choice will meet cost, performance, time, and scope targets; whether risks are acceptable; whether consequences are acceptable; and whether the force-field analysis can pass muster.

> "Decision-makers should be judged on the quality of the decision-making approach that they follow."
>
> —Marvin Patterson

## THE STEPS TO EFFECTIVE DECISIONS

Marvin Patterson (1993) has written that decision-makers should be judged on the quality of the decision-making *approach* that they follow, not on the quality of the decision outcomes themselves. The reason is that all decision-making is done

DECISION . . .
A choice
from among
several
alternatives

under uncertainty, and the decision-maker is always trying to esti-mate the probability of an outcome. If decision-making were deter-ministic, rather than probabilistic, then it would be a trivial exercise.

As an example of the problem facing any decision-maker, we need to understand expected value. The expected value of a choice made under uncertainty is given by multiplying the probability of the outcome by its payoff or cost. Thus, we have:

$$EV = P \times \$$$

where:

$EV$ = the expected value of the outcome
$P$ = the probability of the outcome
$ = the payoff or cost if the outcome occurs

Now let's assume that a manager is trying to decide which of two projects to invest in. One project has a 50-50 likelihood of success but will net the company $400,000 if it is successful. The other has a 90 percent chance of success, with a payoff of $150,000. Both projects will require an investment of about $50,000. If either one fails, of course, the company will lose the investment, not to mention the opportunity represented by the loss, which could have been applied somewhere else. Which project should she take? If we label the projects 1 and 2, the expected value for each is shown as follows:

$$EV_1 = 0.5 \times \$400,000 = \$200,000$$

$$EV_2 = 0.9 \times \$150,000 = \$135,000$$

Based on expected value of the outcome, the first project would be the better risk, with an $EV$ of $200,000. But which choice do you think most decision-makers would make? Probably the second one, because it has a higher probability of success.

The difficulty is that corporate America is largely risk-averse. If the manager chooses project 1 and it bombs, she is likely to be fired or at least severely reprimanded. However, over her career, if she made "project 1" choices, she would be more successful than the manager who always makes "project 2" choices, which are safer. Expected value computations give the decision-maker a tool with which to judge choices quantitatively.

We will return to this method later in the chapter. First, however, we should examine the general approach that should be followed in making decisions. In their book, *Decision-Making,* Janis and Mann (1977) outlined a series of steps that a person should follow to improve the quality of his or her decisions. These are presented as follows:

The decision-maker, to the best of his or her ability, and within his/her information-processing capabilities:

1. Thoroughly canvasses a wide range of alternative courses of action
2. Surveys the full range of objectives to be fulfilled and the values implicated by the choice
3. Carefully weighs whatever he/she knows about the costs and risks of negative consequences, as well as the positive consequences, that would flow from each alternative
4. Intensively searches for new information relevant to further evaluation of the alternatives
5. Correctly assimilates and takes account of any new information or expert judgment to which she or he is exposed, even when the information or judgment does not support the course of action which she or he initially prefers
6. Reexamines the positive and negative consequences of all known alternatives, including those originally regarded as unacceptable, before making a decision
7. Makes detailed provisions for implementing or executing the chosen course of action, with special attention to contingency plans that might be required if various known risks were to materialize

## TOOLS FOR DECISION MAKING

All too often decisions are made based on intuition alone. If they could be evaluated—both quantitatively *and* qualitatively—a project manager would be more certain that the right choice has been made and would feel more confident about the ultimate outcome for the project. In fact, such an approach does exist, and a software package has been developed that makes the process very easy to apply. Furthermore, it can be applied individually or with a project team. It is called the "analytical hierarchy," and Dr. Thomas L. Saaty (1995) of the University of Pittsburgh is its author.

## PAIRED COMPARISONS

The basis for the approach is called "paired-comparisons." When we are trying to make a choice from among a number of alternatives, what we are doing in essence is trying to rank the choices from best to worst so that we can pick the best one. To rank a list of choices requires that some criterion be used as the basis of ranking. Some examples of criteria might be: cost, quality, speed, performance, durability, appearance, flexibility, acceptability, and ease-of-use. If only one criterion is applied to do the ranking, then making a choice is fairly simple. However, few choices ever involve a single criterion, so what we might find is that an alternative is best for cost but has the worst performance, or it has the best appearance but poorest quality, and so on. For that reason, working with multiple criteria is very difficult, and having software that will handle such complex problems if very helpful.

We will get to the multiple criteria case later on, but for now, let's focus on single criteria. Let's say that we want to rank a group of employees by using their cooperativeness as a criterion. If we could accurately measure cooperativeness, then the ranking would be easy. However, like many criteria, it is difficult to measure such a variable. What *is* fairly easy is to compare each employee to every other employee in the group, and simply ask, "Which one is more cooperative?" This is best done using a matrix, as shown in Figure 12–1. I have done this for six employees.

The matrix is set up so that the columns correspond to the rows. That is, column 1 represents Jane, column 2 Bill, and so on. Comparisons are made across rows. Naturally comparing a person to himself does not make sense, so the letter x is placed down the diagonal. Once this is done, begin on row 1 by asking whether

| Person | 1 | 2 | 3 | 4 | 5 | 6 | Total | Rank |
|--------|---|---|---|---|---|---|-------|------|
| 1. Jane | x | 1 | 1 | 0 | 0 | 0 | 2 | 4 |
| 2. Bill | 0 | x | 0 | 1 | 1 | 1 | 3 | 2 |
| 3. Shawna | 0 | 1 | x | 1 | 1 | 1 | 4 | 1 |
| 4. Andrew | 1 | 0 | 0 | x | 0 | 0 | 1 | 6 |
| 5. Melissa | 1 | 0 | 0 | 1 | x | 0 | 2 | 5 |
| 6. Trent | 1 | 0 | 0 | 1 | 1 | x | 3 | 3 |

**Figure 12–1** Ranking of team members using cooperativeness as a criterion.

Jane is more cooperative than Bill. If she is, we put a 1 in column 2, which has been done. Is she more cooperative than Shawna? Yes, so we place a 1 in column 3. For the next three columns, we have zeros, meaning that Jane is *not* more cooperative than these three team members.

Now when we get to row 2 we immediately see that we are asking if Bill is more cooperative than Jane, which was asked on row 1 in reverse. In fact, all of column 1 is going to be the inverse of row 1, so we can immediately fill in that column, then proceed with the rest of row 2. Similarly, you can fill in each row above the diagonal, then fill in the column with the same number with the inverse of its row. Then you total the rows, and the row with the highest total is ranked 1, next highest total is ranked 2, and so on.

We can clearly see that Shawna is the highest ranked person, with 4 points. Then we have a tie between Bill and Trent. That tie has been broken inside the matrix. If you look on row 2, where we ask if Bill is more cooperative than Trent, you find that the answer is yes, so Bill ranks one step above Trent. Similarly, there is a tie between Jane and Melissa, which has been broken in the matrix in Melissa's favor.

## THE ANALYTICAL HIERARCHY

Dr. Saaty has extended the application of paired comparisons to include cases in which some aspects of the problem are quantitative and others are qualitative. Because the analysis involves matrix algebra, it is a challenge to do manually. So Dr. Saaty developed a software program called Expert Choice™ to do the analysis. It is available from Expert Choice, Inc. by calling 412-682-3844. You can also download a demo version by visiting their website: http://www.expertchoice.com.

Using the Expert Choice software, I ranked employees as was done in the preceding section. As before, Shawna ranks number 1 and Melissa ranks at the bottom.

In Figure 12–2 is a printout from Expert Choice showing the paired comparison matrix, together with a bar graph of their rankings.

This is a very simple example, and Expert Choice is not needed to do the employee ranking, but its use shows that it ar-

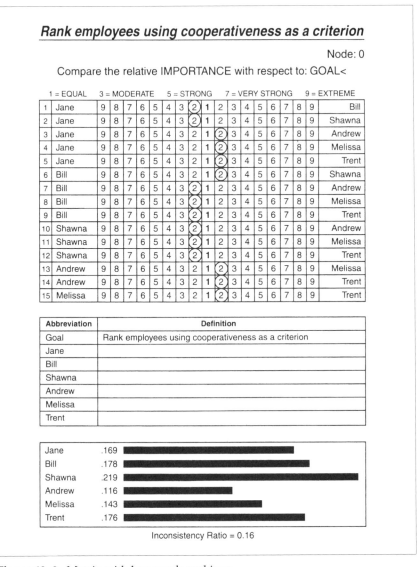

**Figure 12–2** Matrix with bar graph rankings.

rives at the same outcome as a manually done paired-comparison. For more complex problems, the software is invaluable. Applications include choosing software, choosing computers, selecting project strategy, and so on.

## DECISION ANALYSIS IN PROJECTS

Most decisions in projects involve committing resources, such as time and money. In the early stages of a project, you may be doing a feasibility study, in which decisions involve technical and economic viability. As project planning begins, risk analysis becomes important. Finally, there are the day-to-day decisions that must be made during the implementation of the project, through the closeout phase.

Although many situations will always involve a subjective evaluation of possibilities, Expert Choice and decision analysis methods are designed to help sort through a complex array of choices. Psychologists have found that humans can only deal with seven ± two bits of information at one time—that is, from five to nine. Some individuals can deal with nine, others with no more than five. When situations involve consideration of more than nine elements of information, we become overwhelmed. In this case, decision analysis is helpful.

A typical decision analysis involves the following steps (Schuyler, 1995):

- ◆ Determine the decision alternatives.
- ◆ For each alternative, identify the possible outcomes and the outcome values.
- ◆ Assess the probabilities (or distributions) for the various chance events.
- ◆ Solve for the expected monetary value (EMV) of each alternative.
- ◆ Implement the best alternative.

As an example, suppose you have developed a project plan and are examining risk (see Chapter 11). You identify something that could go wrong. It can have a low, medium, or high impact on the project if it happens. To represent the possibilities, you draw a decision tree like the one shown in Figure 12–3.

You believe that the probability of the event happening is only 30 percent (or 0.30). This means that there is a 0.70 probability that it won't happen. There are three options you can use to correct for the problem if it does happen, each with it's own probability and associated cost. Using a decision tree, we can calculate the

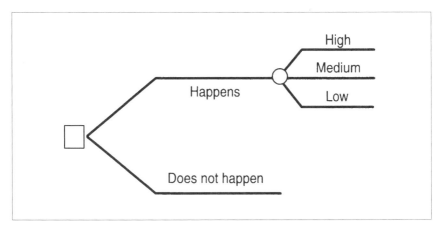

**Figure 12–3**  Simple contingency decision tree.

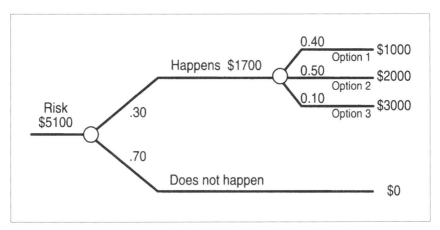

**Figure 12–4**  Expected value of the risk if nothing is done about it.

expected value (EV) of the risk if nothing is done to avoid it ahead of time. This is shown in the decision tree in Figure 12–4. Note that this is a cost impact to the project if it happens.

Whatever alternatives we consider must reduce the EV cost by more than the cost of implementing action. You could decide now to go ahead and apply option 1, rather than waiting to see if the risk materializes. However, it will cost you an additional $500 to implement option 1, whereas going with your current plan will cost nothing. Is this a good course of action?

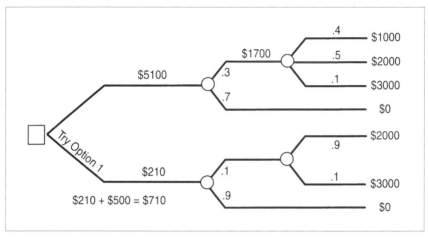

**Figure 12–5**  Decision tree showing option 1 being implemented initially.

Figure 12–5 shows the decision model in which we try option 1 initially. If we do apply option 1, we estimate that we reduce the risk of still having a problem from 0.3 to 0.1. We also increase the probability of option 2 from 0.5 to 0.9. The expected value of implementing option 1 initially is $210, but since actually implementing the option costs $500, the total cost to the project is expected to be $710. Since this is significantly less than the $5100 expected value (cost) to the project if nothing is done, it is clear that implementing option 1 from the very beginning is a good move.

If you want to go beyond decision analysis, you might want to consider preference theory. Since not all managers have the same attitude toward risk, preference theory allows the individual to tailor expected value computations to his or her own inclination to take risk. See Hammond (1975), for example.

PART THREE

# PLANNING

# 13

## CHAPTER

# Developing a Shared Understanding of a Project

The first title I wrote for this chapter was How to Develop a Shared Vision with Your Team. I changed it to shared understanding because the word "vision" has been used by so many people in so many ways that when people hear it, they are put off. What we want with any project team is that all members be going in the same direction, heading for the same destination. I don't care whether you call it "vision" or "peanut butter," there must exist a shared understanding of the project or you will not achieve the result you want.

> A primary purpose of planning is to produce a shared understanding of the project in the team.

The difficulty of doing this should not be taken lightly. It no longer surprises me when project managers tell me that they have been working on a project for three months and just learned that key members of their team are not on the same page with them. I have seen it time and time again. I am also not surprised, when I suggest that we write out the mission statement and vision statement in a team, that they protest that this is not necessary. "We all know what the mission is," they say.

My response is that if this is true, it is a mere formality to put it on paper, and it will only take a few minutes. I insist that we do it, because I know they are usually wrong in believing that a shared understanding exists, and even if they are right, there is no harm in doing the exercise. Never once have we been able to write a clear statement in a few minutes. If there are six people or twenty people in the room, you have almost as many perceptions of where the project is headed.

The other thing that I have found, as I suggested at the beginning of this chapter, is that different meanings of the words have been used, so confusion is rampant. I want to clearly define what I mean in this chapter. I don't propose that my definitions are gospel and that everyone else is wrong. I simply know that unless we all agree on the meaning of the words we use, we can't possibly communicate with each other.

## MISSION, VISION, PROBLEM STATEMENT

If you refer to the first two steps of my model for managing projects, which I have extracted and show in Figure 13–1, you will see that a project almost always begins as a concept, which must be turned into a concrete definition of what the project is going to be. I have also found that most projects tend to fail at this step. The reason is that people want to "get on with it" and do not want to spend time on this step. As I have said, they usually think they all understand and agree on what they are going to do, so there is no need to waste time going over ground that they have already covered.

You will see in Figure 13–1 that three things must be done. A problem statement, vision, and mission statement must be developed. Why a problem statement? Because, as J. M. Juran has said, a project is a problem scheduled for solution. That is, every project is done to solve a problem that the organization has. However, we do not mean problem in the negative sense necessarily. Developing a new product is a problem, albeit a very positive one.

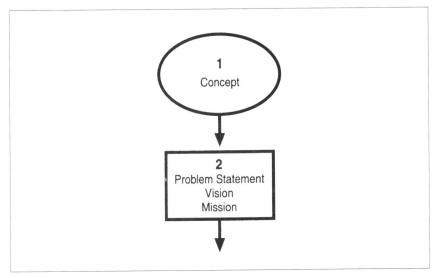

**Figure 13–1**  Steps 1 and 2 from the general model.

## PROBLEM OR PROJECT DEFINITION

The team cannot develop a vision for the project until they understand the needs of clients. Chapter 14 covers defining clients' needs in more detail, so I will not say much about the process here. Suffice it to say that you must begin by identifying key project stakeholders, then identify their needs. A stakeholder is anyone who has a vested interest in the project. These include customers, contributors, senior managers in your organization, key suppliers, and so on. Key stakeholders are those with the greatest influence on the project. Once these have been identified, you can examine their needs.

## DEVELOPING A VISION

Once you formulate a problem statement, you next should develop a vision for the situation that would exist if the problem were solved. There are two reasons for this. One is that you won't know the problem is solved unless you understand the conditions that would exist if it were solved. Second, having a vision for the desired end state creates a driving force that pulls or drives the team toward the final result. A shared vision can be a powerful motivating force and should not be underestimated in this regard. It lends a sense of purpose to a team, and purpose itself is very powerful. The mission for the team, in fact, is to achieve the vision.

**vi • sion:** a positive mental image of the future.

This is shown in Figure 13–2, compliments of my colleague John Carretti of Chesapeake Company.

To add more substance to the idea of vision, Peg Thoms (1997) has written, ". . . a shared vision refers to an image that a group of people—for example, a project team—hold in common, an image of how the project will look, work, and be received by the customers when it is completed. Technically, it is unlikely that all of the people in a group will have exactly the same mental image, but it will be similar if the vision is developed as a group" (p. 33). The key here is that the vision be developed by the group—the *entire* group, if possible, not the elite members alone, but all of them. The reason is simple: Unless every member—from lowest status to highest status member of the team—shares the vision, fragmentation of effort is likely to occur at some step in the project.

The common complaint in large teams is that this is impractical. "You can't get 50 people together in one place to work on vision," howl the protestors. "It's impractical!" I'm sorry, that is not true. Practitioners all over the world have done so with groups much larger than 50, and the results are outstanding. In fact, there is no other way to achieve the same result that is accomplished by having the entire group work on developing a shared vision. When a few people work on a vision and then try to communicate it to others, it just never has the same impact. People to whom the vision is communicated either (1) don't get it, (2) don't agree with it, or (3) don't buy into it, because "it is *their* vision, not ours." When they participate in developing it, however, it is "ours," not theirs, and commitment is the result of that ownership.

No doubt, it is difficult to determine who all members of the team will be from the very beginning of a project, so some of the later additions will not have participated in formulating the vision. However, if most of the group was involved, they will collectively be able to communicate the vision much better than could be done

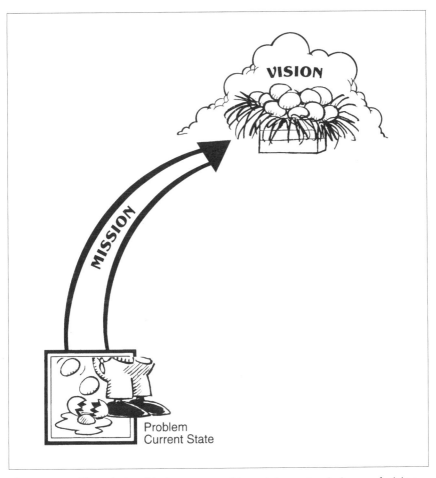

**Figure 13–2**  The relationship between problem statement, mission, and vision.

by the project manager alone. In fact, a shared vision that is important to a group is contagious. In no time at all, new members of a
team will be "infected" by it.

## HOW TO DEVELOP A SHARED UNDERSTANDING

When a core project team is formed, you should explain the assignment and the overall objectives of the organization for the
project. Let them know that there will be another meeting in a few
days to develop a shared understanding of the project. I personally

prefer to avoid the words vision and mission because of the negative baggage they carry. The term "shared understanding," on the other hand, is more palatable. Or I might say that we are going to meet to be sure we are all on the "same page together" in our understanding of the project.

The meeting to develop a shared vision should be well planned and managed. If possible, a facilitator skilled in group process should lead the team through the steps. The process that I am going to outline is a derivative of what is called the "future search conference." The format was originally developed by Emery and Trist in the 1950s and has been used worldwide with all kinds of groups to plan future outcomes. Perhaps one of the strongest advocates for future search today is organization development practitioner Marvin Weisbord (Weisbord and Janoff, 1995).

The idea behind the future search meeting is very simple: The best way in which an organization can arrive at an ideal future is to get the entire membership together in one place and let them plan that future themselves. In addition, the group should begin by designing the *ideal* scenario, and then, if necessary, they can settle for less. It is always easy to give up things if need be. It is harder to go the other way.

> **The best way an organization can arrive at an ideal future is to have the entire membership plan it themselves.**

For groups larger than nine, subgroups are formed. The guiding rule is that working groups should be sized between five and nine, so for large groups, small subgroups are set up and given assignments. The facilitator gives them assignments, which are always time limited. They need ample working space so that they are not on top of each other when they do their assignments, so a large room is necessary. Alternatively, break-out rooms can be used. They need a flip chart for each subgroup and lots of colored felt markers, drafting tape, and any other media that can be used for creative thinking.

The first step in the process is to identify all of the attributes of the project deliverable. If it is a product, what will it be like? How will it work? How will the customer use it? How will it compare to other similar products? If the project is to move a facility, the questions might be: How would we conduct the ideal move? Who would do various parts? How would timing have to work? How do we move people so they can be functional immediately after the move?

The best "tool" for identifying all of the attributes of a project outcome/deliverable is probably the mind map. You begin by writing the name of the project in an oval, then start listing major attributes around it. These will, in turn, make you think of related ideas, which are clustered around the major attributes, and so on, until everything has been covered. There is an example in Figure 13–3. If you would like to read a book on the many uses of mind maps, I highly recommend Tony Buzan's *The Mind Map Book* (1993).

Once the mind map is finished, you can now have the group describe the ideal scenario, which would optimize all attributes that have been listed in the map. There are creative ways to do this. They can draw a picture of a product, write a commercial and present it, or design a brochure. If it is moving a facility, they can put on a skit that demonstrates how the move is to be accom-

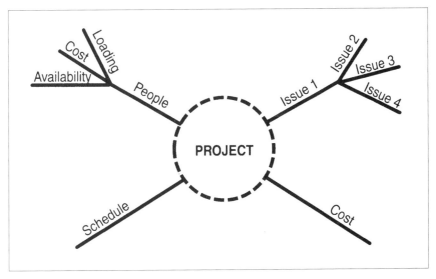

**Figure 13–3**  A mind map for a project.

plished. For other scenarios, they can write songs, poems, skits, commercials, rap pieces, and so on. These are all presented by small groups for the others.

I worked with a group of school principals once to design the ideal school. They went away in their subgroups and wrote songs, skits, and a Charles Kuralt on-the-road interview. These were then presented. The amazing thing about this process is that there are usually very similar core ideas presented. You would almost swear that the groups colluded to develop their presentations. Furthermore, by the time all groups have finished, you have a wealth of ideas that can now be drawn on by the entire group. These can now be incorporated into the overall end result.

The process creates an enormous amount of energy. Just yesterday I co-facilitated a version of one of these on a Saturday, and at 3:00 p.m., people were at a higher energy level than you would ever expect after working all day. And they understood their project much better than they ever would have if we had communicated it to them. In addition, there were several good strategies developed by subgroups, so that the project manager will now be able to work with them to select the best strategy to be implemented later on.

## COMPLETING THE PROCESS

The team now has an ideal vision for the project. Naturally, we generally cannot "go for broke" in most projects, so we will probably forego some attributes. One way to do this is to place those attributes in three categories. These are labeled must-have, want, and nice-to-have. I have shown this in Figure 13–4, to illustrate the relationship between problem statement, vision, and mission in a slightly different way than was done in Figure 13–2.

Having done all of this, you can now proceed to step 3 in my general model of managing projects, which is to develop a project strategy.

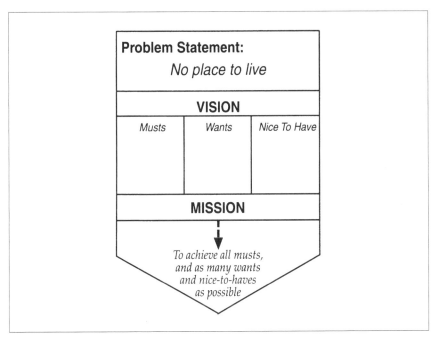

**Figure 13–4** Problem statement, vision, mission.

# 14
## CHAPTER

# Identifying Customer Requirements

Every project team has the same ultimate mission that an organization has—to meet the needs of customers. In case you still have not resolved for yourself the apparent conflict between making a profit and meeting customer needs, perhaps this will help: The primary *motive* of a business is to make a profit. It's *mission* is to meet customer needs. Naturally, they must both be accomplished. The difficulty is that if we get focused on profits as our mission, we may do short-sighted things that will make us more money in the short term but cost us our customers in the long term.

As an example, a restaurant needs to turn its tables as fast as possible during lunch time to maximize its sales. So the manager tells the chef, "Don't take too long to prepare each meal. Keep it short. Turn up the temperature on the stove so the food cooks fast." He also tells the serving staff, "Get them in and out as fast as possible."

> The *motive* of a business is to make a profit. The *mission* is to meet the needs of customers.

Of course, the end result is that the food is poor quality and the serving staff border on being rude. Sooner or later, word gets around and the business dies.

## WHO IS THE CUSTOMER?

The next point that is important is to define "customer." Essentially, a customer is defined as anyone who uses what the project team produces. That means that there can be more than one customer. A product development group produces prototypes and drawings for manufacturing to use to make the final product. The manufacturing department is a customer of the design team. So is the ultimate customer, who buys the product. Each has different needs. The design team has to meet all of those needs.

The following definitions might help in understanding the different categories of customers and their needs. There are three categories:

1. *Internal customers* are those people inside your company who use something you produce. Often they are next-in-line. For a product-development group, this would be the manufacturing department, who take the drawings produced for a new product and actually make it from those drawings.

2. *Intermediate customers* are usually external to the company but not the final end-user of the product or service. They will typically be distributors of products.

3. *External customers* are considered to be the users of the product or service being delivered by the company.

**stake • hold • er:**

**Anyone who has a vested interest in the project.**

In some cases, it might be better to say that we must satisfy all of the "stakeholders" for a project, since we will eventually be judged by them. A stakeholder is anyone who has a vested interest in the project. This includes contributors, actual customers, financial people who are funding the project, and perhaps the community outside the organization.

If we are to meet the needs of our customers, however, we must have some way of knowing what those needs really are. This is easier said than done. If you ask the customer, you can't always get a good answer, because the customer really isn't sure what she needs. All she knows is that she has a problem, and she is hoping you can solve it. This means, of course, that you have to translate the customer's need into a solution.

Note that we are also using the word "needs" to mean both actual needs as well as what the customer *wants*. Following the restaurant example, I might need nutritious food and want it to taste good. I might also want to be treated a certain way by the serving staff. Taken together, these define for me the *quality* of the experience I have with the restaurant. Deming and others have said that *only* the customer can tell you what quality means. So when we are doing a project in which we try to satisfy the customer, we are sure to have to meet her needs, wants, and expectations.

> **Principle:** *Only* the customer can tell you what quality is for the product or service you provide.

In some cases, we are solving a problem for the customer. Here again, the customer might not know exactly what the problem is. You must sometimes begin with the *symptoms* that tell the customer she has a problem to begin with. I say this because it is through symptoms that we know we have problems. For example, someone says, "Sales are down this month." That is a symptom of a problem, not the problem itself. Until we know what is causing sales to be down, we cannot correct it. It could be the sales staff has had a number of illnesses, or the market is depressed just now, or perhaps a competitor is undercutting your price.

> **Principle:** The way you define a problem determines the approach you will use to solve it.

The thing is, the way a problem is defined determines the approach that we will take to solve it, so it is vitally important that we define the problem being solved by the project, or identify customer needs, wants, and expectations, before we go beyond step 2 in the flowchart.

In fact, it is failure to properly handle step 2 that is the cause of many project failures. I often say that projects don't fail at the end, they fail at the beginning. Quality time spent on this step will pay dividends later on.

## THE NEED FOR FIRST-HAND UNDERSTANDING OF THE CUSTOMER

I believe that every member of a project team should have a first-hand understanding of customer requirements. In saying this, I have absolutely no intention of usurping the role of the marketing department or other group that is responsible for telling you what the customer expects of you. Those individuals have an important role to play.

However, in the typical scenario, the marketing department has someone interview customers, conduct a focus group or survey, and then develop a written description of what the customer wants. Invariably, the marketing person has to *translate,* because the customer often does not know what he or she wants. She only knows that she has a problem that must be addressed and is looking to the provider to develop a product or service that will solve that problem or meet her need. This means that the marketing group can *mistranslate* what they think the customer wants.

In any case, the marketing department develops their specification and it is passed on to the product development group. Now another translation takes place. The product developers interpret the written spec into what *they* think it represents as a product, and there is room for another error. Is it any wonder that by the time the customer gets the final result, it is nothing like what she wanted?

The importance of understanding the customer first-hand was brought home to me about three years after I started my career as an engineer. I worked for a small company that made land-mobile radio equipment, and we sold some units to the police department of a major city. They had some technical difficulties with one of the radios, and I was sent to correct the problem. While I was working on the radio, I was approached by a very large police officer.

If you can't call for backup, you've really got a problem.

"You work for Aerotron?" he asked.

I told him that I did.

"Good. I'd like to give you some feedback on this hand-held unit," he said.

"Okay," I said.

"You see these little tiny knobs," he said, pointing to the top of the radio.

I nodded my affirmation.

"You can't get ahold of these little knobs when you have a hand as big as mine," he said, holding up a big paw. "Especially when you have gloves on," he continued.

I told him he had a good point.

"You know what the real problem is with this radio?" he asked.

I didn't.

He looked me directly in the eye and said, "When you hit somebody with this thing, the case cracks, and you can't call for backup."

> "The *real* problem with this radio is that when you hit somebody with it, the case cracks, and you can't call for backup."
>
> —Police Officer

I said something to the effect that we hadn't designed it to be used as a billy stick."

"Maybe not," he said, "but when somebody jumps you in an alley, you hit him with whatever you have handy. When it's the radio, and the case cracks, then you can't call for backup and you've really got a problem."

Now like it or not, this is a real-world situation. The radio design was changed to make it withstand a higher impact, and the problem was apparently solved. Consider, however, an engineer who is shown the impact spec without understanding the reason for it.

"What idiot wrote this?" he says. "We aren't supposed to be designing a club!"

Little does he know.

Over the years I have experienced numerous incidents in which first-hand understanding of the customer has made a significant difference in how the designers have developed their products. One scientist that I know visited a lab in which his products were used and came away totally transformed. He got so many new ideas that it will take him years to develop all of them.

## SOME CAUTIONS

Since I believe strongly in first-hand understanding of customers, I encouraged one of my clients to start a customer involvement program (CIP). The program was designed to get technical people into the field to visit customers. They usually went along with a sales or marketing person. The first mistake we made, however, was that we didn't teach the techies to *listen*. So as soon as a customer made a critical comment about a previous product, the technical person got defensive, started explaining why the customer was wrong, and lost the opportunity to learn from what the customer had to say.

> **Before you send employees to the field to talk to customers, teach them to *listen*.**

Another problem is failing to distinguish between customer requirements and product features. A study conducted by Product Development Consulting and the Business Roundtable was reported in the *PM Network* April 1995 issue. They surveyed 4000 companies in a wide range of industries, including electromechanical systems, medical, aerospace/defense, components, automotive, computer, and services. One-third of the responses were from "best-in-class" companies, this being based on sales volume and market share. This group was contrasted with average performers to determine differences in practice.

> **We must distinguish between customer requirements and product features.**

The best-in-class pass on requirements. The others specify features. For example, there is a significant difference between telling a designer that the customer wants to be able to change channels in the dark and "put a light on the remote." The customer requirement allows the designer to exercise some creativity in solving the problem, whereas the other is a rote solution. As Sheila Mello, a principal at Product Development Consulting, remarked, "Given a directive, engineers are destined to produce 'me too' products. But when provided with an in-depth view of customers' needs, they are likely to create 'delighters'" (*PM Network*, April 1995, p. 49).

Another interesting finding from the study is that understanding customer needs does not necessarily mean interviewing more people. On average, best-in-class companies were found to gather data from around 10 customers, compared with 24 for average performers. Furthermore, the best companies were more likely to interview customers in-depth rather than to use focus groups.

The problem with focus groups is that members of the group influence each other, so you don't know for sure if a customer really had a specific need or it just sounded good when someone else said it. Also, by conducting interviews at the customer's worksite, the interviewer can gain first-hand knowledge of the environment and how the customer might apply the product. This was one of the things that struck the scientist mentioned earlier. He saw how the customer actually worked, and this gave him a lot of ideas on how to improve the design of his products.

Finally, the study found that best-in-class companies focus on the total product, taking into account various factors that influence product success, such as product-specific sales and service strategies. The less effective companies tend to focus only on product development skills and technology core competencies. The bottom line is that businesses that want to become market leaders must develop a companywide vision of their customers' complete needs.

## THE NEED FOR CONCURRENT PROJECT MANAGEMENT

Not only are there problems in understanding outside customers but there are still problems in meeting the needs of inside customers. When the marketing department develops a product specification and hands it off to product developers, who have no direct contact with customers, we say the specification has been "thrown over the wall." In fact, in a typical product development scenario, you have a sequence like the one shown in Figure 14–1.

Now, before you say, "I'm not in product development, so I can skip this," let me suggest that you read on. I believe what I am going to discuss applies to all projects.

The walls between the various groups should be thought of as the walls of silos, not cubicles. The reason is that you can see over a cubicle wall and even converse. With a silo, the walls are too tall to permit conversation, so when people live in silos, they are isolated from the rest of the world.

As I said above, in this situation, marketing throws the product spec over the wall to product developers, who look at it and break out in hives. They throw it back over the wall to marketing, protesting that they can't possibly develop a product with *these*

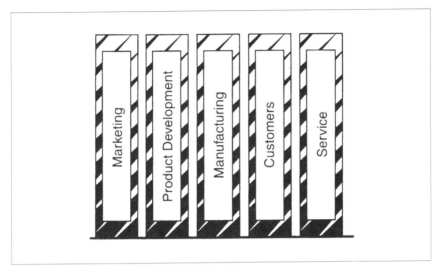

**Figure 14–1**  Groups involved in product development.

specs to sell for the desired price. This process might go through several back-and-forth cycles before a spec is finally agreed upon.

Then the product developers design the product and throw their drawings over the wall to manufacturing. The people in manufacturing look at the drawings and throw them back over the wall to product development. "We can't make this thing in our plant," they protest.

"Not our problem," say the product developers. "We designed it. You guys have to build it."

This also goes through several cycles, and occasionally some redesign is necessary before manufacturing agrees that they can build the product.

Then the product is shipped. The customer takes one look at it and says, "What is this? Who came up with this idea? This isn't what we need."

Again, the product might have to go back for more redesign to solve this problem.

Finally, the customer accepts the product, but this is not the end of the line. Eventually, the product breaks. The customer takes it to a service shop. The repair people take one look at it and they also break out in hives.

"You can't work on this thing!" they protest.

As an example, a number of cars and vans have been designed that had spark plugs positioned so that they could not be reached without pulling the engine out of the vehicle or cutting a hole through the firewall. Wouldn't that be a shock if you were the customer? You take your car in to have the plugs changed, which should be a routine servicing job, and they tell you it will cost about $500 dollars in labor to take the engine out—just to change a $5 plug!

One auto company solved this problem in a very inimitable style: They put a platinum-point plug in the one position that couldn't be reached. That way, you don't have to change the plug but once in 100,000 miles. Hopefully, by then you will have traded the vehicle and it will be someone else's problem!

This entire throw-it-over-the-wall scenario is ridiculous, and fortunately a lot of organizations abandoned it long ago. However, I find it is still alive and well in entirely too many companies. If yours is one of them, I urge you to practice concurrency, as shown in Figure 14–2.

The only way to solve the problem is for everyone involved—from concept through final disposal of the product—to be involved in the process throughout. This is why the process is called concurrent—everyone is involved at every step.

This way, manufacturing can provide guidance to product development on how the product should be designed to make it manufacturable. And service can do the same so that it can be repaired when it finally breaks down. And the customer can give guidance on how the product should be designed in order to best meet her needs.

**Rather than abandon concurrency because of its difficulty, learn to manage consensus.**

The problem is, if you have ever tried this, it is extremely difficult to make it work. As Dilbert has said in one of Scott Adams's cartoon strips, "The difficulty of getting agree ment goes up as the exponent of the number of people involved." So the inclination is to throw out the process and go back to throw-it-over-the-wall.

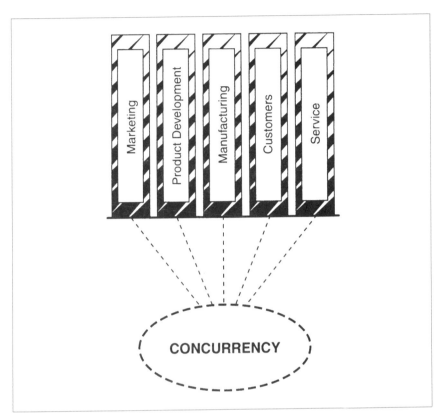

**Figure 14–2**  Concurrent project management.

That is the wrong response. Rather than throw out the process because it is difficult, we need to learn to manage consensus. Unfortunately, we find that many people don't seem to know how to do this. They generally resort to majority rule, by voting, and this always leads to problems if the issue is a serious one. A couple of things are likely to happen. One, as soon as a problem crops up, the outvoted members will say, "I told you so." Second, even if there are no problems, the dissenters will often refuse to support the majority approach or may even try to sabotage it to prove that they were right.

But how do you get everyone to agree on anything?

You don't. That is too high an order. What consensus must mean is that every member of the group must be able to say,

"While I don't entirely agree with the majority, I have heard you, and you have listened to me, and I am willing to support the approach you want to take."

This is as good as you can do with a group. The key word is *support*. Every member must be willing to say she or he will support the approach. If anyone can't do that, then you need to try to find an alternative that everyone can support or try to convince the person to go along with the majority, or—in some rare cases—just overrule them. It's not a good thing, but you occasionally have to do it. Naturally, if you need the person's support later on, you aren't likely to get it.

## USING THE QUALITY FUNCTION DEPLOYMENT MATRIX

One tool that is helpful in understanding stakeholder requirements is the quality function deployment matrix (QFD). It is sometimes called the "house of quality." The name itself is enough to scare anyone to death. Quite simply, it should be called a correlation matrix, in which we look at customer concerns (whether they be needs or wants) and product or service features and ask which of these have correlations.

In *The QFD Book* (1993), Guinta and Praizler suggest that QFD should be used to answer three questions:

1. What are the qualities or characteristics that the customer wants?
2. What functions must this product serve, and what functions must we use to provide this product or service?
3. Given the resources that we have available, how can we best provide (deploy) what our customer wants?

QFD is used to translate broad product requirements or specifications into specific action assignments. This is done through the use of a number of matrices. It helps teams determine the right methods, tools, and order in which they should be used. Note also that you do not have to be developing products to use QFD to advantage. You can be developing a new service or trying to solve almost any kind of problem. In fact, throughout the remainder of this chapter, the term *product* will be used to mean product or service in general.

When QFD is used properly, it results in shorter product development cycles (or shorter times to solve problems), provides lower costs and greater productivity in making products, and helps us break out of the paradigm that says higher quality products mean higher costs. In fact, improving quality of a product usually leads to lower production costs. The reason—elimination of scrap, rework, and warranty costs.

A major benefit of QFD is that it virtually eliminates the throw-it-over-the-wall approach discussed earlier, because it brings together people and data from many places—customers, marketing, product development, manufacturing, field service, and so on. By using this collective knowledge, companies can identify what will work and what won't. Since as much as 80 percent of project cost is determined in this early phase, the QFD assessment can greatly reduce program costs and development time—simultaneously!

According to Guinta and Praizler, companies that use QFD for product development have achieved a 50 percent reduction in costs, 33 percent reduction in development time, and 200 percent increase in productivity (1993, p. 14).

Although the full-blown QFD process can get fairly complicated, the essence of the approach is simple. Customer needs are correlated with product or service features. I am using the word *need* to stand for musts, wants, and nice-to-haves that were discussed in Chapter 13. Furthermore, the customer ranks his needs so that the project team can be sure to satisfy them in order of importance. If tradeoffs must be made, we can do it with the lower-priority items rather than the high-priority ones.

As an example of a QFD matrix, consider the one shown in Figure 14–3. This one is for a hotel. Down the left side we list customer needs. In this case, we have a mixture of musts, wants, and nice-to-haves. Across the top, we have a list of some of the features of a hotel that might satisfy customer needs. In each cell, we put a +, *, 0, – or – – to indicate the relationship between the feature and the customer need. A + means that there is a positive correlation between the feature and satisfaction of the need. A * is a strong positive correlation. A 0 means no relationship. A – sign is a negative. That is, there is actually a negative relationship between the feature and the customer's need. Finally, a – – is a strong negative correlation.

| + = CORRELATION<br>✳ = STRONG CORRELATION<br>0 = NO CORRELATION | Individual Temp. Control | Lighting | Furnishings | Cable TV | Room Service Menu | Courteous Staff | Airport Courtesy Van | Rank |
|---|---|---|---|---|---|---|---|---|
| Comfort | ✳ | + | ✳ | 0 | ✳ | 0 | + | 2 |
| Service | 0 | 0 | 0 | 0 | ✳ | ✳ | ✳ | 3 |
| Price for Value | ✳ | ✳ | ✳ | ✳ | ✳ | ✳ | ✳ | 5 |
| Security | 0 | 0 | 0 | 0 | 0 | 0 | 0 | 1 |
| Able to Read or Work Comfortably | 0 | ✳ | ✳ | 0 | 0 | 0 | 0 | 4 |
| Access to Telephone / Computer | 0 | 0 | + | 0 | 0 | 0 | 0 | 6 |
| Convenience | 0 | 0 | 0 | 0 | ✳ | 0 | ✳ | 7 |
| In-Hotel Entertainment | 0 | 0 | 0 | ✳ | + | 0 | 0 | 8 |

**Figure 14–3** QFD matrix for a hotel.

Now we can see in Figure 14–3 that the customer's most important concern is with security, but none of the hotel features correlate with security. Clearly, the team that did this analysis has missed something and now must go back to the drawing board. Also, notice that convenience is negatively correlated with quietness. If the hotel is near a freeway, it is convenient, but the freeway noise might be a problem.

One of the key ideas of QFD is that we should give the customer those features that have correlations *with things he cares about* and not give him things that he either cares nothing about or that at least have very low correlations! I have known product developers who wanted to incorporate features in the design because the developer thought it was nifty, but the customer didn't want it and would have to pay for it if it were included. We need to be customer-driven, not designer-driven.

One problem with QFD is that you can generate an enormous amount of data, and it can quickly become overwhelming. You don't want to go into analysis paralysis and get nothing done, so you have to use judgment as to when the analysis should be stopped.

As I said earlier, QFD can get very involved in its full-blown form. For an in-depth treatment, I strongly recommend *The QFD Book,* by Guinta and Praizler (1993).

# 15

CHAPTER

# Managing Resources
# in Project Scheduling

It has been estimated that of the million people who have bought Microsoft Project, only a few percent are using the resource leveling feature. I would concur with that estimate. Of the thousand people who attend my classes every year, only a small number are doing much with resource allocation. They have tried assigning people to tasks, even leveling them, but the situation is so complex that many of them give up.

The problem is, this is the key to meeting a schedule. If you don't have adequate resources, your schedules are not realistic, and in my opinion, a wrong schedule is worse than no

**If you can't manage resources, your schedule is unrealistic.**

schedule because it sets up an unrealistic expectation that causes frustration when the deadline is missed. As you may know, developing critical path diagrams involves a hidden assumption that you have unlimited resources. This is because each task is estimated independently of the others. Then when you do your diagram, you are supposed to show what is logically possible to do.

At some point, you have two tasks that can logically be done in parallel. However, the same person is assigned to both of them. If that assignment is full-time on each, then you have the individual double-scheduled, which won't work. The hidden assumption was that you had two of this person available, when you really only had one. So unless you manage the allocation of resources, you wind up with a schedule that can't be met.

## ASSIGNING RESOURCES TO TASKS

The first problem in scheduling is estimating task durations. This is discussed in detail in Chapter 24. What we must begin with is the number of working hours (or days or weeks) that will be required to complete a task with a certain person assigned to it. If you can't assign a specific person to a task at the planning stage because you don't know who will actually do the task when the time comes, then you will have to assign a *skill-category* to the task. This means that you would assume the person assigned is going to be someone from the required discipline having a certain level of skills. Members of that discipline would then have to estimate how long the task would take a person having those skills. It isn't perfect, but it's the best you can do sometimes.

Next you have to ask if the person will be assigned to the task on a full-time or part-time basis. Let's begin by assuming a full-time assignment. The person will work on the assigned task and nothing else until it is complete. I know this is very unrealistic in most organizations. Most people are working on many assignments at once. Still, this is the best it can be, so we start here, just to see that even with the best of situations, there are still problems to resolve.

## What does full-time really mean?

The first one is, what do you mean by full-time? If we assume we are scheduling people to work a standard 8-hour day, 40-hour week (which you really should do—keeping overtime in reserve as a way of handling unexpected problems), then you could say that a task requiring 16 hours of working time would span two days. However, this assumption would get you into trouble. If the working time required is really 16 hours, it will take more than two days to accomplish it, because nobody works 8 productive hours each day.

The industrial engineers reduce the 8-hour day by 20 percent to account for what they call *personal, fatigue,* and *delays* (PF&D). People need to take occasional breaks (personal), they get tired (fatigue), and their work is held up by other people, unavailability of materials, information, or other resources (delays). Thus, a standard 8-hour day yields only 6.4 hours of productive work. This means that our 16-hour task will span 2.5 days. If the person starts first thing Monday morning, he will finish around noon on Wednesday.

At this point, we better evaluate the assumption that people are available even 80 percent of their time to do productive work. I was told by a fellow that his company became frustrated because they missed so many project deadlines and couldn't understand why. They seemed to have enough resources, based on the 80 percent assumption.

**Typical availability of knowledge workers for project work is 40 to 60 percent.**

As a test of their assumption, they gave each project member a log sheet and told them to record, once an hour, what they had been doing during the previous hour. They did this for two weeks. To their surprise, they found that many of their team members were working on project assignments only 25 percent of the time! No wonder nothing was getting done on time! With people working on projects only 25 percent of the time, rather than 80 percent, the calendar time required to finish a task is at least 3.2 times longer than planned.

Since he told me this, I have surveyed several hundred people informally, and they tell me that they experience similar situations. At best, they tell me that the availability of people to do project work is about 50 to 60 percent.

What robs the time? A lot of factors are involved. Just to list a few, we have meetings that have nothing to do with the project, nonproject assignments, training classes, interruptions from people, giving help to people working on other assignments, working on proposals for future projects, working on next year's budget, and solving problems in old projects that you thought were complete, but you're the only person left who knows anything about it. One factor that stands out as a major issue is sharing the person with other projects. We will discuss this one in more detail later on.

The lesson, of course, is that you must be realistic about how much time a person really has available to work on your project, or your calendar times will be grossly inaccurate. The only way anyone is available to work 80 percent on a project is if you can figuratively tie them to a desk and keep them there. In factory environments, the 80 percent figure is often accurate, since that is essentially the situation for a worker; he or she is not free to wander around or be assigned other things to do. For knowledge workers, however, 80 percent is unrealistic.

## THE EFFECTS OF MULTIPLE PROJECTS ON PRODUCTIVITY

Another reason why resources are not available more than 80 percent of the time is that they are shared with other projects. Informal surveys of my seminar participants indicates that most of them have team members working on from two to six projects at the same time, with the norm being about four projects. This means that team members are available to work on a given project only 20 percent of the time.

If this were a linear effect, it would be bad enough, but it is not linear. To illustrate, suppose I assigned you a task that you could complete in six working hours if you could work straight through until you finished it. Of course, this is a pretty long stretch, so you would probably work three or four hours in the morning and finish it in the afternoon. Would it still take six hours? No. The reason is that you would have to spend a few minutes getting reoriented to the task after taking a break. It may be only a few minutes, but it does reduce your productivity.

Now suppose, because of working conditions, that you have to work on the task two hours today, another two tomorrow, and two more the third day. Now the task will take even longer than it would by splitting it into two chunks. The reorientation time is called *setup time* in manufacturing, and we learned years ago that setup time is a total waste. Every minute of setup time eliminated is a minute gained for productive work.

This shows why we have problems with multiple projects. People are constantly shifting back and forth from one project to another. Time management studies have found that if you get interrupted by a person (face-to-face or by phone) while you are working on a task, you may need 15 to 20 minutes to get reoriented to it. If you get interrupted three times in one hour, you may lose most of that hour, even though the total time taken by the interruptions was only five minutes each.

> Setup time adds no value to a process. Eliminate setup time and improve productivity.

Not only do you lose productivity because of setup time, but consider the time spent in meetings for each project a person is on. It is usually a minimum of one hour per week for each project. And, as we know, many meetings are virtually nonproductive, so having people work on several projects at once also increases time wasted in meetings.

Experience has shown that there are big gains to be made by reducing the number of projects that people are working on. One company found that by having people work on one project as a primary project, with a secondary project that they could work on if they had some dead time, their productivity nearly doubled.

It can be very hard to get senior management to buy into this notion. They get trapped into thinking that everything must be done at once, not realizing that if they would prioritize projects and do them in priority order, they would get everything done in the same calendar time and at higher efficiency and higher quality.

## QUEUING THEORY AND RESOURCE MANAGEMENT

Another thing that adversely affects projects is the lean-mean paradigm that is so prevalent in organizations today. As a brief historical perspective, you might think back to the 1980s and remember that many companies had layer upon layer of management. This was probably the ultimate consequence of the belief that a manager could only directly supervise about six people. Over time, organizations became little pyramids of one manager who had six people reporting to her, and each of them in turn had six people reporting to them, and so on.

This might have been necessary in the early days of the industrial revolution, when many workers had little education and required a lot of supervision, but it had ceased to be true by the 1980s. Nevertheless, we clung to it, because the paradigm was that span of control should be limited to six direct reports, and that was that.

> A lot of organizations have binged on "trimming fat" to the point that they may die of anorexia.

Then people began realizing that this was no longer true, and a wave of reductions in middle management followed. The metaphor was that we were getting rid of *excess* "fat," and we were. The result was highly positive for business: The bottom-line showed *immediate* improvement, and rightfully so. If you eliminate costs without affecting sales revenues, you have automatically increased profits.

> Insanity is defined as continuing to do what you've always done and expecting to get a different result. I think mindlessness is continuing to do something that has worked in the past and expecting it to get the same results as it always has.

Because that first dose of cost-cutting felt so good, managers were quick to apply more of it. When you find something that works, it is natural to try it again, so they did. Now we are in the midst of the lean-mean paradigm. Companies have cut every expendable person they can identify.

Trouble is, some of them long ago got rid of *all* the fat, so now they're cutting muscle.

In addition, since this is a biological metaphor, we know that you don't want to remove all of the fat from any organism. The fat provides reserve energy for hard times. But we have failed to realize this.

So what does queuing theory have to do with the situation. Queuing theory deals with things like highway capacity, production line capacity, and so on. If you have ever tried to get onto a major high-

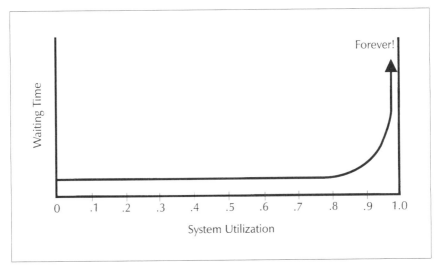

**Figure 15-1** Waiting time as a function of system utilization.

way during rush hour, when everyone else in the whole world was also trying to get onto it, you understand what happens when any system is at its limits. The amount of time you must wait to get onto the highway gets very high at rush hour. At other times of the day, it is insignificant. Figure 15-1 shows how this works. As the capacity of a system approaches 100 percent, the waiting time to use that system approaches infinity!

This same idea can be applied to a resource pool. As we load people up to their limit, the time new projects must wait to be started approaches infinity. Yet many managers think that the only way to be productive is to keep people working at 100 percent (or even greater) capacity. And when people try to say they're overloaded, some of the very macho managers tell them to quit complaining, they're lucky to have jobs.

## THE WONDERFUL BENEFITS OF OVERTIME

When faced with the fact that there are only so many hours in the day to get things done, we sometimes wish we could increase the number of hours. We do this by having people work overtime. In many organizations, professional people are expected to work 50-

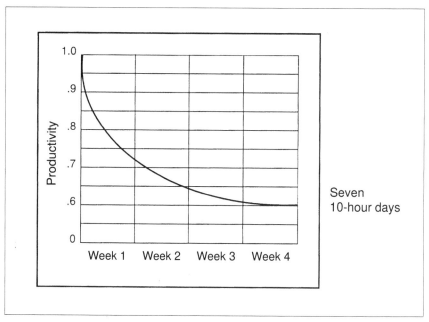

**Figure 15–2** Decline in productivity with overtime.

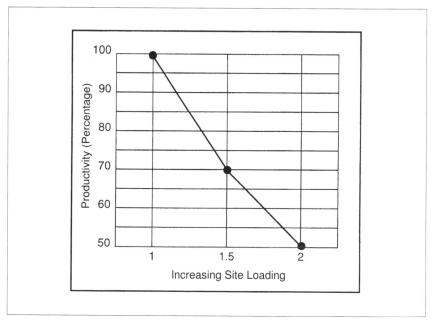

**Figure 15–3** Decline in productivity with site loading.

and 60-hour weeks routinely. After all, they're paid the big bucks, so we want to get our money's worth from them.

Here, too, we are being penny-wise and pound-foolish. Studies show that after people have worked 10 to 15 hours of overtime each week for several weeks in a row, their productivity drops back to what they would normally do in 40 hours, and their error rates go up. This is true for both factory workers and knowledge workers. It is possible to work overtime for one week and gain productive output. But people get tired after so many weeks of this, and fatigue takes its toll on performance.

> After working several weeks of 50 to 60 hours, productivity falls to the normal 40-hour level and errors go up.

For this reason, it is very bad practice to plan a project so that long stretches of overtime are required to meet the original end date. Not only will productivity drop rapidly, but if unforseen problems occur, you can't use overtime to solve them, as people are already working all they can stand.

Just to see the effect of overtime, consider the curves in Figure 15–2. While these are for construction work, you can be sure that similar effects would exist for other kinds of work.

Figure 15–3 shows the impact of having too many workers on a construction site. While this might seem to be strictly true for construction, how about the problems that people encounter with having too many people in a department, not enough desks, office equipment, and so on? I believe it is a similar effect. These are all factors that we should consider in trying to accelerate projects.

## THE NEED TO SHARPEN THE SAW

Stephen Covey, in his book *The 7 Habits of Highly Effective People* says that effective people spend some time sharpening the saw. They do not work all the time. His metaphor comes from the fact that if you saw wood for an extended period without stopping to sharpen the saw blade, it gets dull and won't cut very effectively any more. Over a period of time, the woodcutter who keeps his saw sharpened will generally cut more wood than the one who cuts wood continuously.

It has always struck me as odd that we treat our capital resources better than our human resources in a lot of companies.
When I was in college, I worked summers in a shipping department that was housed in an old cotton mill. Those old mills were
not air conditioned, and in July the temperature in North Carolina
can easily be 95 outside, which results in an inside temperature of
100 to 105 degrees. Needless to say,
you can't move at extreme speed in
that temperature, or you'll have a heat
stroke.

> We treat our capital resources better than we do our human resources.

In many of the old factories, air
conditioning was out of the question.
Costs too much was the belief. Yet people were moving at a snail's pace. I al-
ways thought the increased productivity that would have been
achieved in an air-conditioned building would far offset the cost.
But what do I know?

Then along came computers and numerically controlled machinery. These blow up if they get too hot, so guess what—they
had to be housed in air-conditioned offices. On top of that, in the
1960s, when the computers were being installed, smoking around
the computer was banned. Yet you could puff away around your
coworkers.

The message here is simple: If you want to get maximum
value from your most valuable resource of all—a human being—
you must make it possible for him or her to sharpen the saw once
in awhile. This is not just a soft-hearted humanitarian plea; it just
makes good business sense!

## APPROACHES TO RESOURCE LEVELING

Consider the bar chart schedule shown in Figure 15–4. Activity A
is a critical path task. Activity B has a duration of three weeks and
has one week of float. Activity C has a duration of two weeks and
has three weeks of float. These durations are based on having two
people available to work on A, one on B, and one on C, full-time
for each task. However, we only have three workers available. This
clearly means that the job cannot be completed as scheduled.

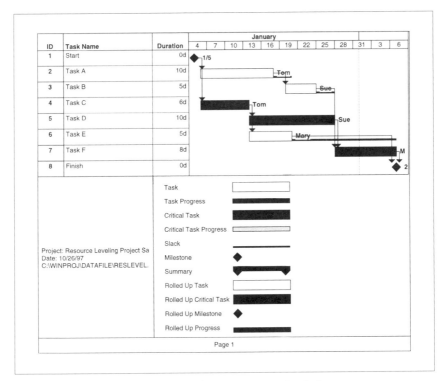

**Figure 15–4**  Bar chart schedule with resources overloaded.

Note that I am assuming what would be called *generic* or *pooled* resources in this example. Generic resources are people who can all do the same work. This is possible in some crafts, such as plumbing, carpentry, or electrical wiring, but would often not be true for specialists, such as engineers, certain machinists, and other professionals. In the case of specialists, you must assign specific individuals to tasks. We will consider that case further on.

Now suppose you were going to manually allocate resources so that no one is overloaded. How would you go about it? Well, you might begin by assigning two people to Activity A, since it is on the critical path. We know that if this task is not completed on time, the project will slip, so we must begin here.

This leaves one person to do B and C. It occurs to you that you might assign that person to work on each task half-time. If you do that, you will have to double the durations of each task, which would work for C, since it has enough float, but would not work for B. Doubling durations, of course, assumes that time is a linear function of resources assigned, which is itself a faulty assumption in many cases.

Since changing durations appears unfeasible, you might next ask, "Since I need another person, maybe I can just get one and be done with it." So you ask the powers that be in your company, and they tell you that three people is all you can have. You still are in a bind.

The next thing you might try is assigning that one person to either B or C, but which one? You might think that you should assign the person to B, because it is longer than C. It turns out that B is the correct choice, but you have made it for the wrong reason. The best thing to consider is the float available to each task. You did this when you assigned two people to task A, which has no float. The most common rule for assigning resources is called a *minimum-float* rule. Assign resources to those tasks that have the least float, then the next-smallest amount, and so on, until resources are exhausted. Then those tasks that have float and no resources can slip without (hopefully) impacting the deadline.

Now it is easy to see in Figure 15–4 that this works very nicely. Activity C has enough float that you can slide it over to the point at which task B is complete, and then resources will be available to do task C. Fortunately, this happens just at the point where C runs out of float. This is shown in Figure 15–5. Note also that because activity C has run out of float, it is now on the critical path. This is shown by making the bar solid color.

You also realize that this is a very clean example. It will never happen this way in a real-world project! What will happen is that task C will run out of float before B is complete, and now you have a dilemma. If you slip C any more, it will cause the project deadline to slip. What do you do in that case?

## TIME-CRITICAL VERSUS RESOURCE-CRITICAL ALLOCATION

In the above example, we assumed that you were allocating resources manually, that is, without benefit of a computer. Ulti-

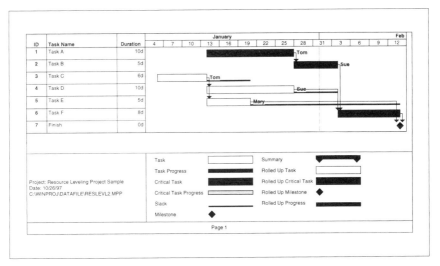

**Figure 15–5**   Bar chart with resource overload resolved.

mately, however, this is impractical. As the number of tasks and resources increases, the solution to overloads becomes very difficult, and only a computer can solve the problem. So computers have to be programmed to level-load resources, and the most common allocation rule (or heuristic, as it is sometimes called) is the minimum-float rule that we applied in the previous example.

In addition, the computer must be programmed to do either time-critical or resource-critical leveling. Under time-critical conditions, once a task runs out of float, the computer will stop moving it, since to do so would slip the end date for the project. When this condition exists, you will have to find a way to deal with the remaining overloads. It may be that you can work people overtime for a brief spurt to resolve the problem, since working someone overtime is equivalent to adding resources to the project.

# 16

## CHAPTER

# Scheduling Uncertainty in Projects

In projects where most activities are fairly well defined, scheduling is straightforward. You estimate durations, work out the sequencing of tasks, and let the computer find your critical path and calculate your slack. But this is not true for projects that have activities that can branch in several directions, based on the outcome of that task. This is typical of research projects. You run an experiment. Depending on the outcome, you may run another experiment, start a new task, or abandon the work altogether. Such junctions in projects are called *conditional branches,* and they defy our best efforts to schedule them *deterministically.*

### DESIGN OF EXPERIMENTS

Somewhat related to conditional branches is the situation in which you are not quite sure how to make something work. You try an approach and it doesn't work, so you try something else. It doesn't work either. Several questions arise. How many iterations do you try before you give up? How do you know what order to try things in? How do you know that you didn't miss the exact combination of things that would have solved the problem? And, perhaps most important for project managers, how do you schedule such a situation?

This kind of problem is encountered frequently in engineering design and science projects of various kinds, such as pharmaceuticals. I can always tell that a person is dealing with this kind of problem when he asks me, "How do you deal with a loop in a schedule network?"

"Why do you have a loop?" I ask.

"Well, I'm trying to find just the right combination of insulator and contacts to make a circuit breaker that will have a certain capacity. So you try one combination and it doesn't work, so you have to try another and another until you finally find the right one."

When one engineer asked me about this, I said, "Why don't you use design-of-experiments?"

"Somebody told me it was more expensive than just trying different combinations," he said.

"Somebody misled you," I said. "Unless you are just plain lucky and hit the right combination the first try, design-of-experiments (DOE) is always more cost effective. Besides, without using DOE, you have no way of knowing if your approach is really the best one or just one that happens to work. With proper DOE, you can answer a host of questions in a fairly short time and have a very robust outcome."

> **Design-of-experiments is always more cost effective than cut-and-try.**

He was convinced, and sure enough, the outcome of his work was very positive.

I was asked this same question by a scientist. He wanted to know how to schedule loops when you are doing critical experiments. I asked him also why he didn't use DOE. His response floored me.

"What's that?" he asked.

This was when I learned that life sciences majors do not routinely receive training in statistical procedures. And this is also true in some engineering programs. So project managers need to be aware of the approach so that they can suggest its use when it is appropriate.

The approach that these individuals were suggesting is equivalent to a loop called "design-test-redesign," which can go on for an undetermined number of cycles. Standard PERT/CPM scheduling software will not handle loops. In fact, if you accidentally insert a loop into a critical path diagram, most software programs will immediately tell you that you have a logic violation, and you must correct it before the program can tell where the critical path is.

There have been some sophisticated scheduling programs written to handle conditional branches and loops, but they were mostly used by defense contractors, they ran on mainframes, and so far as I know, are not available in microcomputer versions. So you can't handle these situations with the scheduling software.

However, you don't need to. The answer to the design-test-redesign problem is to employ design-of-experiments to answer your questions. Now this is a seminar in itself, and I don't intend to tell how to do design-of-experiments (DOE) in this book, but I do want to outline the basic procedure.

Suppose you were managing a project to determine what combination of fertilizer and seed variety would give the best crop yield. You plant a field with combination $F_1S_1$ (fertilizer 1, seed 1) irrigate it, and when it is harvested, you record the results. Next season, you plant a field with combination $F_1S_2$ (fertilizer 1, seed 2), harvest it, and record the results. You continue this process until you have tried all the combinations available to you.

First of all, you will be a very old researcher if there are very many combinations, but besides that, you have not controlled for a couple of major factors that affect crop growth—sunlight, rainfall, and temperature. (Even if you irrigate, the rainfall variation will still be a factor.) Fortunately, there is a better way. In Figure 16–1 you will see a field that has been divided up into a number of equal-area plots. In each plot, you plant a different combination of fertilizer and seed. At the end of the season, you harvest all of the plots and see which one has the best yield. In this way, the sunlight, rainfall, and temperature will have been uniformly distributed across all of the plots, so their effects are controlled and cease to be a factor in different crop yields. Now you can definitely tell which combination of seed and fertilizer is best.

Another example: Suppose your project is to determine if sales of a product can be increased best by a sale, combined with a

| $F_1S_1$ | $F_1S_2$ | $F_1S_3$ | $F_1S_4$ | $F_1S_5$ |
|---|---|---|---|---|
| $F_2S_1$ | ... | ... | ... | ... |
| $F_3S_1$ | ... | ... | ... | ... |
| $F_4S_1$ | ... | ... | ... | ... |
| $F_5S_1$ | ... | ... | ... | $F_5S_5$ |

**Figure 16–1**  Field planted with different combinations of fertilizer and seed.

particular advertising campaign, or by a giveaway and a different advertising approach. You would have four possible combinations of these. They could be represented by $S,A_1$, $S,A_2$, $G,A_1$, and $G,A_2$. Now the problem is that people differ greatly in their responses to various things, so unless you have a way to account for the variability in people, you can't answer the question.

To test this situation, you need four groups of people so that each group can be administered a different *treatment*. This is shown in Figure 16–2. Groups 1 and 3 will be exposed to the sale and both ad approaches, while groups 2 and 4 will be exposed to the giveaway and the two ad approaches. To determine which combination is most effective in increasing sales of the product, we measure how much product is sold to each group after they have been exposed to the various treatments, then we do an analysis

|  | Sale | Giveaway |
|---|---|---|
| Ad 2 | Group 1 | Group 2 |
| Ad 1 | Group 3 | Group 4 |

**Figure 16–2**  Test of various combinations of sales campaigns.

called analysis of variance, or ANOVA. If the variation in sales *between* groups is greater than the variation *within,* and if that difference is statistically significant, then we can say that one treatment is better than the others.

By statistically significant, we mean that the difference would not have a high probability of occurring by chance alone, so that most likely we can account for it because the treatment actually caused the variation.

Good DOE is an extremely powerful way to answer questions that cannot be answered any other way. However, the design should be set up by someone very well schooled in principles of statistics, because it is easy to contaminate your results through an inappropriate procedure. We assume in the above experiment, for example, that the population is randomly distributed through the four groups for age, race, and sex. But suppose we actually did the group 1 treatment in an area that is inhabited largely by retired persons. Then we have contaminated the experiment, because the assumption is that all four groups are homogeneous, that is, they are all the same. If group 1 is mostly retired persons and the rest of the groups are mixed in terms of age, then we would expect the behavior of people in group 1 to be different from the other groups. This would be like having a small area of a large plot of land be very alkaline, whereas the rest of the plot is not.

DOE does not guarantee that you will answer your questions in one pass, but it improves the likelihood. Furthermore, once you have done a number of such experiments, you begin to build history on how long an experiment typically takes, and you can estimate durations with better accuracy. It will never be as good as well-defined tasks, however.

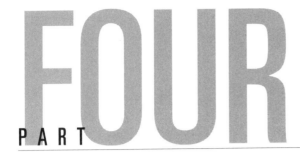
PART FOUR

CONTROL

# 17 CHAPTER

# Tracking Progress to Achieve Project Control

If you are going to keep a project on schedule, budget, within scope, and meet quality requirements, you must have a way to measure where you are for each variable of interest. This is much easier said than done. When you are doing work that has some tangible nature, you can measure progress fairly well, but when you are trying to measure knowledge-work progress, it gets more difficult.

## DEVELOPING PROJECT METRICS

There are some guidelines on developing metrics that should be followed. Otherwise, you can fool yourself. Metrics tend to encourage people to behave in ways that make the measures most favorable. For that reason metrics must be chosen to encourage the behavior actually desired by the organization. Otherwise, you will encourage people to do what you *don't want!*

**me • trics:** Measures.

Marvin Patterson (1993) relates several examples of problems being created because of metrics. In one instance a company wanted to measure the productivity of keyboard operators, so they attached keystroke counters on the keyboards. One day the super-visor of the group walked in during lunch hour and noticed one of the op-erators having her lunch, while holding down the spacebar on her keyboard with her thumb. Because holding down a key causes it to generate a continuous stream of characters, she was generat-ing a lot of keystrokes, but none of them were useful!

**What kind of behavior are you trying to encourage?**

Another company wanted to set up incentives for their divisions to develop more new products in less time, so they told the executives that they would receive bonuses based on how many new products their units produced each year. One division caught on to the fact that the way corporate knew they had developed a new product was by seeing a new part number in their catalog. They quickly responded by repackaging old products, assigning a new number, and for a couple of years, they collected bonuses without actually producing anything new!

For a set of metrics to be effective, they must meet four criteria:

## Relevance

The metric must provide information on factors that are *important* to the project. Collecting data that are not important is a waste of time. For example, it may not matter very much how many changes an engineer makes to a design *before* it is released, but it certainly makes a difference *after* it is released.

## Completeness

The set of metrics should include *all* factors important to the project. If you leave one out, the others will be optimized, but at the expense of the one omitted. "Every important aspect of the operation under scrutiny should be measured" (Patterson, 1993, p. 29). While we want the minimum number of metrics that will do the job, nothing should be omitted that is critical to success.

## Timeliness

Timeliness is a function of how quickly the project can change. Nyquist sampling criteria says that if something is changing and you cannot monitor it continuously, then you must sample at least twice as often as the change occurs in order to know what is happening. Thus, if a project can change once weekly, you would have to measure it twice weekly. (This will be discussed in more detail later in the chapter. ) Measures need not be absolutely precise to be useful, but they should be timely enough so that decisions based on them are effective. Failing to get information in a timely fashion is like having someone navigate for you while you are driving, and a second after you pass a turn, your errant navigator says, "Oops, you should have turned back there!"

## Elegance

Metrics can be a serious burden to a project because of the serious overhead cost incurred. For that reason, they should be designed to provide a maximum level of insight into the project with a minimum amount of data. This is commonly called the KISS principle—keep it simple, Sam. In my view, I want to do the absolute minimum that will allow me to successfully control project progress.

## KINDS OF METRICS

There are at least three kinds of metrics that are important in projects: *process metrics, personnel performance metrics,* and *management performance metrics.*

## Process Metrics

Processes have attributes called *state variables*. These are analogous to the state variables of a physical system, such as a spring-mass system. The states of such a system are the positions and velocities of the masses in the system. You can predict the behavior of the system if you know the parameters and state variables at any given time. Project management processes have similar state vari-

| REWORK | SPEED | QUALITY | # OF SCOPE CHANGES | CUSTOMER SATISFACTION |

**Figure 17–1** Metrics appropriate for projects.

ables. If these can be established, they will serve as process metrics, which can be tracked so that the process can be understood and controlled.

Some examples of project metrics that are important are shown in Figure 17–1. However, you have to apply these with caution. For example, when you ask people to do a job faster, they will sometimes do poor quality work in order to finish faster. I have seen this happen in product development especially. The admonition must be, "Do it faster without sacrificing quality."

Number of scope changes is also not a good measure unless you factor in the impact on the project of the change. You could have several small scope changes that make almost no difference to the job. Or you could have just one change that almost sinks it.

Customer satisfaction is an excellent measure, if you can get that information. As was mentioned in Chapter 5, success of projects is generally a function of whether customers are happy with the outcome, so it is really *perceived success* that we are looking at.

It is outside the scope of this book to lower personnel and management performance metrics. Our focus will be on process metrics only. Later in this chapter, we will use other measures of progress to keep the job on track. This will include earned value measures.

## THE TYPICAL PROGRESS REPORTING SYSTEM

I recently sat through a project status reporting meeting held by a client. It essentially went like this:

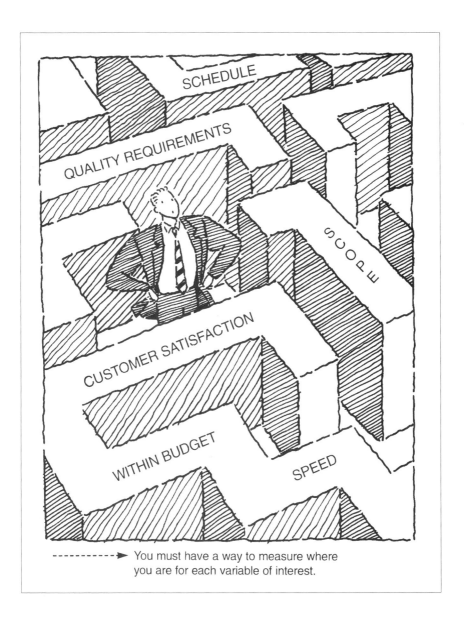

------------▶ You must have a way to measure where you are for each variable of interest.

"How is project x?"
"It's okay."
"Good, let's move on to project y. How's it doing?"
"Okay."

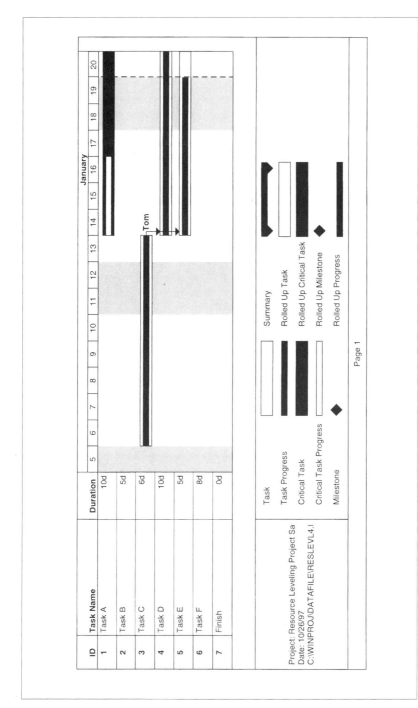

**Figure 17–2** Schedule with progress shown.

You get the message. There are four variables that we care about, as has been discussed in previous chapters: cost, performance, schedule or (time), and scope. Saying that a project is okay does not tell us anything about the status of these variables.

A step above the system of reporting progress as okay or not-okay is to report schedule performance only. This is done as shown in Figure 17–2. This report is from Microsoft Project™, but most scheduling software reports progress in a similar way. The small bars that run inside the schedule bars show how far along you are.

In this example, the date on which progress is being measured is January 20. The shaded areas at January 5, 11, 12, 18, and 19 are weekends, in which no work is being done. From this report, we can see that the tasks have the status shown in Table 17–1.

The problem with this report is that the information is very limited. First of all, we know nothing about performance or scope. We must take for granted that the quality of work being done is correct, as well as the scope of work. Furthermore, we know nothing about what was done to achieve the result. By this, I mean that we don't know the cost—whether it is expressed in monetary terms or simply working hours expended.

There are companies that don't track project costs in any form. They consider that the people doing the work are on the payroll, so it doesn't matter. I'm sorry, it does matter. Every hour spent on one activity is an hour lost to some other work that might be done. Only someone with an endless pot of gold can be in a position to not care about costs.

**T A B L E  17–1**

Task Status for Sample Schedule

| Task | Status |
|------|--------|
| A | Behind one day |
| B | Not started |
| C | Complete |
| D | One day ahead |
| E | Right on target |

In any case, knowing that a person is on schedule, but that he worked twice as many hours to get there as he had planned, tells me that his work is not going well and that the project may be in jeopardy. The sooner I know this, the sooner I can address the problem and make a decision about what should be done. Conversely, if I find that a person is only taking half the time to get the job done, then I can begin to think about what this will ultimately mean to the project. So whether you know about labor costs or not does not matter. You can always track hours expended and make adjustments based upon that data.

> Knowing that a person has worked twice as many hours as planned, even though he is on schedule, tells me he might be in jeopardy.

## EARNED VALUE ANALYSIS

Measuring progress using earned value was first done in manufacturing as part of standard cost systems. It goes like this. Suppose you are making widgets, and each widget has a value of $50. You are supposed to have made 1000 of them by noon today. When I check with you, I find that you have only made 800 widgets, all of them good. How much are they worth to me? Clearly they are worth 800 × $50 or $40,000. I tell you then that I will give you credit for having produced $40,000 worth of widgets for me, and I call this *earned value*.

How are you doing? Well, since you have made only $40,000 worth of widgets and you should have made $50,000, you are behind schedule by $10,000 worth of widgets. What that represents in time is a function of how many widgets you can make per day. If you can normally make about $5000 worth of widgets per day, then you are behind by two days.

With this comparison, I know the schedule status of the work you are doing, but I don't know how much effort you have spent to make the 800 widgets. Do I care? You bet! If you are working too many hours, my costs are high and it will affect my profits. So I ask how many hours you have worked to produce the 800 widgets.

"You don't want to know," you say.

## THE PURPOSE OF VARIANCE ANALYSIS

When progress is monitored, three questions should always be asked:

1. What is the actual status of the project?
2. What caused the deviation? (When there is one)
3. What should be done about it?

It is not enough to simply monitor progress in a project. When a significant deviation from plan occurs, *something* must be done in response. There are three responses that can be made:

1. Ignore the deviation.
2. Take corrective action to get back on target
3. Revise the plan.

Note the word *significant*—what is meant by significant should be determined in the planning stage of a project. In general, a deviation should exceed at least 5 percent to be considered significant, as most control systems cannot maintain a tighter tolerance.

"Maybe not," I reply, "but I have to know, so tell me the bad news."

"Well, we've worked 1200 hours to produce the 800 widgets, and our loaded labor rate is $50 per hour, so the labor cost is $60,000." Now I know how bad off I am. You have produced $40,000 worth of widgets for me and spent $60,000 to do it, so you are over-spent by $20,000 on labor. In fact, not only are you overspent, but behind schedule as well. This is the worst position you can be in. It is bad enough to be overspent but to be behind on the work as well is really a problem.

Note that these measures do not involve material costs. The true cost of a manufactured product, building, or road is the material and labor costs combined. Do we care? Of course. However, what we are

**loaded labor rate:** Direct labor cost plus overhead. To salaries, you add the costs of heat, water, lights, benefits, and so on, to get loaded labor rates.

tracking is *work* progress, and we track material costs in another account. We would also do the same with capital and other expenses in projects.

There seems to be some confusion about the word "value." Isn't the value of a widget what I can sell it for? Yes, but there are two uses of the word involved here. If you are working for me and I pay you $50 per hour, loaded labor, I value every hour that you work for me at $50. If I can only sell what you produce in an hour for $50, I don't have a profitable enterprise. This is why I am concerned if you take longer to do your work than we have estimated. If we estimated that it would take an hour and it actually takes an hour and fifteen minutes, then at a $50 per hour labor rate, the actual cost of labor would be $62.50. That will decrease my profit by $12.50. So I definitely care about the value of the work that you do for me.

> Nobody sets out to create salvage value. What we want is end-result value!

I know a project management consultant, a specialist in software, who objects to earned value analysis being applied to software. He says that there is no salvage value in unfinished code. That may be true, but it misses the point of progress measures. Every step in a process should add value. If it does not, it should be eliminated. Nobody sets out to create salvage value in the first place. Salvage value is a measure of what you can get if you abandon a project. What we want to create is end-result value!

Using the consultant's argument, I could say the same for almost anything. There is no salvage value in unfinished buildings or roads. Using earned value to measure progress is like saying that you are half-way to a destination. There may be no salvage value in being part-way to a destination, but it tells you how much further you have to go and whether you are making reasonable progress. If you had estimated that you were going to average 50 miles per hour and find that you are actually only averaging 25 miles per hour, then you aren't doing very well. You can expect that your trip is going to take twice as long as you planned unless you can get your average speed up to a higher level.

## THE MEASURES USED

When we estimate that you can make 1000 widgets for me by noon today, and each has a value of $50, we call the $50,000 value of these widgets budgeted cost of work scheduled, or BCWS. This is your target. Since control is exercised by comparing planned effort to actual, when I look at how many widgets you have actually made, I can tell if you are on track and whether anything needs to be done if you are off. So when we find that you have only made $40,000 worth of widgets, we know that you are behind. The amount of widgets that you have produced is called budgeted cost of work performed, or BCWP. If we take the difference between the scheduled work and performed work, we have your *schedule variance*. This is written as:

$$\text{Schedule Variance} = BCWP - BCWS$$

For our example, we have:

$$\text{Schedule Variance} = \$40{,}000 - \$50{,}000 = -\$10{,}000.$$

That is, you are behind schedule by $10,000 worth of work, which is indicated by the minus sign on the $10,000 figure. This is standard accounting practice, to show an unfavorable variance as a negative.

In the same way, we said that we could compare what you actually spent to the target and have an idea about cost variance. We call the actual spending figure actual cost of work performed, or ACWP. *Cost variance* is calculated as follows:

$$\text{Cost Variance} = BCWP - ACWP$$

For our example, we have:

$$\text{Cost Variance} = \$40{,}000 - \$60{,}000 = -\$20{,}000.$$

Thus, you are overspent by $20,000. Notice that the cost variance is a composite variance. You are behind schedule by $10,000 worth of work. You have also put in $10,000 more effort than we estimated, so the total cost variance is the sum of the two. This is shown in Figure 17–3.

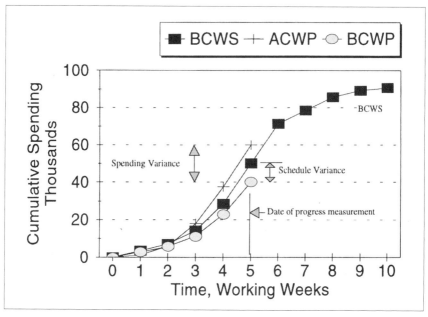

**Figure 17-3**  Project is behind schedule and overspent.

## TRACKING KNOWLEDGE WORK

This system works nicely for tracking tangible work. You can count widgets and inspect them to see if they are good quality. With knowledge work, it is a great deal harder. How do you quantify what you have done? For example, if you were writing this book, and you estimate that it will have 300 manuscript pages when finished and you have 100 written, are you one-third of the way there? No way. Or you are writing code. You think that there will be 10,000 lines when it is all finished. The programmers have written 8000 lines. Are they 80 percent complete? I doubt it.

> Knowledge work tasks should have durations no greater than 1 to 3 weeks.

The problem with both of these examples is that they are at too high a level in the project. In order to track progress, you need to "chunk down" the work into increments that can be measured with some precision. In terms of the work breakdown structure (WBS), you need to get down to a low enough level where work has durations that do not exceed 1 to 3 weeks for engineering or programming, or possibly days for some tasks.

Let's see how this works by taking writing a book as an example. I generally write chapter drafts, then come back and do final editing once all chapters are written. For a lot of chapters, I can write one a day. The final edit might take a half day per chapter. There are also figures to develop, and these are generally done last. I can't tell from the beginning how many figures I will have, but maybe I think it will be at least two per chapter, and I estimate that they will require two hours each to do. So I need 20 to 25 figures, at two hours each, or 40 to 50 hours for that part. Since I am working on this by myself, everything will be done in series, no need for a critical path schedule.

If we make a task list, it will look like Table 17–2.

## T A B L E 17–2

Task List

| Task | Time, Days | Total Days | BCWS |
|------|-----------|-----------|------|
| Write Chapter 1 | 1 | 1 | 400 |
| Chapter 2 | 1 | 2 | 800 |
| Chapter 3 | 1 | 3 | 1200 |
| Chapter 4 | 1 ½ | 4 ½ | 1800 |
| Chapter 5 | 1 ½ | 6 | 2400 |
| Chapter 6 | 1 | 7 | 2800 |
| Chapter 7 | 1 | 8 | 3200 |
| Chapter 8 | 1 | 9 | 3600 |
| Chapter 9 | 1 | 10 | 4000 |
| Edit 1 & 2 | 1 | 11 | 4400 |
| Edit 3 & 4 | 1 | 12 | 4800 |
| Edit 5 & 6 | 1 | 13 | 5200 |
| Edit 7 & 8 | 1 | 14 | 5600 |
| Edit 9 & 10 | 1 | 15 | 6000 |
| Index | ½ | 15 ½ | 6200 |
| Figures 1–4 | 1 | 16 ½ | 6600 |
| Figures 5–8 | 1 | 17 ½ | 7000 |
| Figures 9–12 | 1 | 18 ½ | 7400 |
| Figures 13–16 | 1 | 19 ½ | 7800 |
| Figures 17–20 | 1 | 20 ½ | 8200 |
| Final Work | 1 ½ | 22 | 8800 |

The nice thing about this system is that as each part is completed, I can see it, touch it, check it out. The question is, how do I value the progress I have made? The simplest system is to take a ratio between the total of 22 days and whatever has been completed to-date. It isn't perfect, but it is better than nothing. So when I have completed Chapter 1, I get 1/22, or approximately 5 percent credit. If I want to use earned value, I have to establish a BCWS baseline, which is shown in the final column of the table. I have valued my time at $50 per hour and consider a day to be eight hours, so each day I am supposed to accomplish $400 in work. This gives a linear rate of work, which is never quite correct, but it is good enough for most purposes.

Now suppose at the end of the first day I don't have Chapter 1 complete. Should I get partial credit? You could estimate and assign a partial credit, but it is better to wait until the chapter is complete and then you get credit for the entire thing. So let's say at the end of the second day you have finished both Chapters 1 and 2. Then if you plot progress, it would look like the graph shown in Figure 17–4.

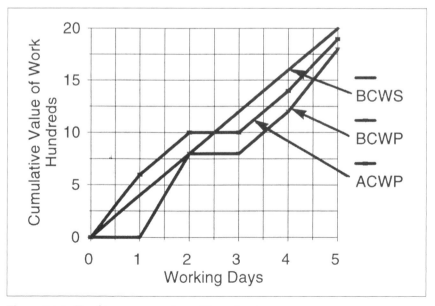

**Figure 17–4** Tracking progress in writing a book.

It turns out that at the end of the first day, I have actually spent 12 hours writing, so my ACWP for that day is $600. This means that I am behind schedule and overspent. At the end of day 2, I am back on schedule but still overspent. Then I encounter a problem. I don't get to work on the book the next day, so BCWP and ACWP move horizontally. The next two days I do reasonably well. Then another two days when no work is done, so ACWP and BCWP again turn horizontal. At this point, even if I were to start making linear progress, the progress curves would fall below the BCWS curve, and wherever BCWP reaches $8800 would be the forecasted end date for the project. It would be a two-day slip as presently shown.

This same approach can be used in engineering design, software development, research projects, and so on. The proper approach is to break work down to very small increments, so that some marker can be used to show that work is complete. In engineering design, for example, my first step might be a conceptual design, which I estimate will take one week. When it is done, I should be able to see it on paper. The next step is to build a model of the paper design. Time—two weeks. When it is finished, I can touch it. Next step, test it. Again, about one week. Result—a report on paper that tells the test outcome.

Another example: I am doing scientific research. My first step is a literature review. Estimated time is about two weeks to identify papers to read. End of that period, I have a list of papers and maybe even copies of all of them. Next step, read them. Estimated time, two weeks. The reading pile should be empty at that time. Then I want to do some experiments. How long will they take? The ones I have planned will take a week, but after I see the results I may want to do additional experiments, so I can't plan this one as well as for the design project. In fact, this brings up a very important point—you should always separate development from discovery, because discovery is very difficult to time-limit. That doesn't mean that you can't plan discovery projects, it just means that it must be done in phases and no exact times can be placed on the overall project.

> **Don't waste time doing detailed planning of work that will take place a year from now.**

This also brings up a good point for most projects. If you are going to break work down to daily or weekly increments, you only want to do so for short periods. If a project is going to last for a year, you only want small increments for a few months at most, because you can't see very far ahead with any accuracy. To plan work that will occur a year from now to increments of weeks is a waste of time. So you do what is called phased planning, as in the research project. As you get to the end of the first phase, you plan the next phase in detail, and so on. This is also called a rolling plan.

## TRACKING EARNED VALUE GRAPHICALLY

You may want to present tracking data graphically so that you can see trends. Consider the curves in the graph shown in Figure 17–5. BCWS is the baseline plan for the project. It is derived directly from the scheduled work. ACWP can be seen to be going high, while BCWP is going low. That is, the project is getting behind schedule and is simultaneously overspending. It does appear that BCWP is turning back toward the BCWS curve, so perhaps the work will be caught up in a few weeks, but it may be at the ex-

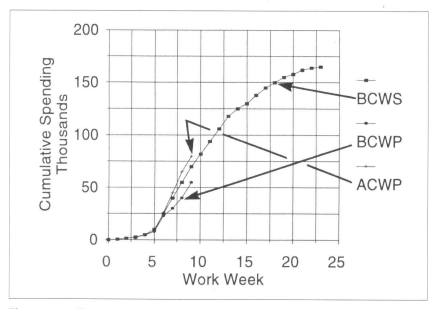

**Figure 17–5** Earned value curves for project Echo.

**T A B L E  17–3**

Earned Value Combinations

| Combination | Status | Likely Cause |
|---|---|---|
| BCWP > BCWS and ACWP < BCWS | Ahead of schedule and underspent | Conservative estimate or lucky break |
| BCWP < BCWS and ACWP = BCWS | Behind schedule and spending correctly | Not enough resources applied to do the work |
| BCWP > BCWS and ACWP = BCWS | Ahead of schedule and spending correctly | More resources applied than originally planned |
| BCWP >BCWS and BCWS < ACWP < BCWP | Ahead of schedule and slightly underspent | More resources applied at greater-than-expected efficiency |

> means "greater than;" < means "less-than"

pense of going over budget. Be careful about making linear projections of these curves to find the final state of the project, since most projects do not progress linearly, as is shown by the curvature in the BCWS curve.

All possible combinations of progress can be shown by these curves. In Table 17–3 are interpretations for most of the combinations. You should be able to figure out the few not covered in the table.

## INDICES OF PERFORMANCE

The three earned value variables can be used to calculate indices of performance. One is called the schedule performance index (SPI), and the other is the cost performance index (CPI). These are calculated using the following formulas:

$$SPI = \frac{BCWP}{BCWS}$$

$$CPI = \frac{BCWP}{ACWP}$$

The SPI is essentially a measure of work efficiency. If you are accomplishing as much work as you had planned to do, then your efficiency is 100 percent. If it is less than planned, you will have less than 100 percent and conversely. The CPI can be thought of as spending efficiency. It is what you got for what it cost you. If you buy $90 worth of goods and pay $100 for them, then your spending efficiency is 0.90.

If the SPI and CPI are multiplied together, you get an overall measure of project performance called the critical ratio. The critical ratio then, is:

$$CR = CPI \times SPI$$

You can see that this number should be 1.0 if everything is going according to plan. If it is larger than 1.0, you are performing better than plan, and conversely. You can also see that the CPI could be a bit low and the SPI a bit large and still get a CR equal to 1.0. That is, you are spending a little more than planned but getting more work done than planned, so that the net result balances out. The reverse situation could be true as well.

Meredith and Mantell (1985) suggested that the critical ratio can be plotted on a periodic basis and that control limits could be established so that determinations can be made based about project status. This is shown in Figure 17–6. If you are not familiar

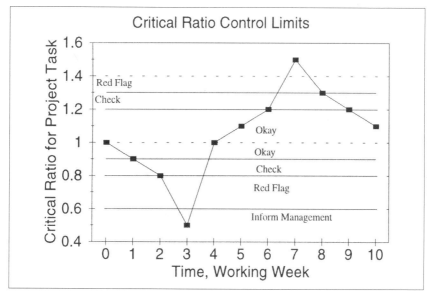

**Figure 17–6**  A control chart for the critical ratio.

with control charts, you might want to consult one of the many texts on statistical process control, such as Juran and Gryna (1980).

Most scheduling software packages offer earned value reports. Microsoft Project, SuperProject, Timeline, Project Workbench, and others all do basic earned value reports. However, most do not employ the critical ratio. If you know how to program in Microsoft's macro language, you can calculate the CR. Or you can dump the earned value data to an Excel spreadsheet (like the one in Figure 17–7) and calculate it there. By having the spreadsheet test the CR against the control limits shown in Figure 17–5, you can place the words "NA," "okay," "check," or "red flag" in the far right column, so that by scanning that column, you can detect your trouble spots immediately.

### Earned Value Report

Project No.: 1201  Date: 20-Feb-95  FILE: BALIREPT.WB1
Description: Bali Book  Page_____ of _____
Prepared by: John Miller  Signed:

| WBS # | Cumulative-to-date | | | Variance | | At Completion | | | Critical Ratio | Action Required |
| | BCWS | BCWP | ACWP | Sched. | Cost | Budgeted | Latest Est. | Variance | | |
|---|---|---|---|---|---|---|---|---|---|---|
| Recruit | 900 | 900 | 930 | 0 | (30) | 900 | 930 | (30) | 0.97 | O.K. |
| Travel | | | | 0 | 0 | | | 0 | NA | NA |
| Pack | 480 | 480 | 420 | 0 | 60 | 480 | 420 | 60 | 1.14 | O.K. |
| VISAs | | | | 0 | 0 | | | 0 | NA | NA |
| Staff | | | | 0 | 0 | | | 0 | NA | NA |
| Survey | 2,700 | 2,400 | 2,550 | (300) | (150) | 3,000 | 3,150 | (150) | 0.84 | CHECK |
| Interview | 1,500 | 1,500 | 1,350 | 0 | 150 | 1,500 | 1,350 | 150 | 1.11 | O.K. |
| Reports | | | | 0 | 0 | 1,500 | 1,500 | 0 | NA | NA |
| Local | 1,800 | 1,200 | 1,200 | (600) | 0 | 3,000 | 3,150 | (150) | 0.67 | RED FLAG |
| Photos | 1,500 | 1,250 | 1,250 | (250) | 0 | 5,000 | 5,000 | 0 | 0.83 | CHECK |
| Develop | | | | 0 | 0 | 1,250 | 1,250 | 0 | NA | NA |
| Select | | | | 0 | 0 | 600 | 600 | 0 | NA | NA |
| Print | | | | 0 | 0 | 1,000 | 1,000 | 0 | NA | NA |
| Draft | | | | 0 | 0 | 18,000 | 18,000 | 0 | NA | NA |
| Review | | | | 0 | 0 | 3,000 | 3,000 | 0 | NA | NA |
| Revise | | | | 0 | 0 | 9,000 | 9,000 | 0 | NA | NA |
| F.Edit | | | | 0 | 0 | 1,500 | 1,500 | 0 | NA | NA |
| Captions | | | | 0 | 0 | 300 | 300 | 0 | NA | NA |
| Typeset | | | | 0 | 0 | 2,000 | 2,000 | 0 | NA | NA |
| Pasteup | | | | 0 | 0 | 3,000 | 3,000 | 0 | NA | NA |
| Proof | | | | ·0 | 0 | 3,000 | 3,000 | 0 | NA | NA |
| | | | | 0 | 0 | | | 0 | NA | NA |
| TOTAL | 8,880 | 7,730 | 7,700 | (1,150) | 30 | 58,030 | 58,150 | (120) | 0.87 | CHECK |

NOTE: Negative variance is unfavorable || If Critical Ratio < 0.6, INFORM MANAGEMENT!
( ) = NEGATIVE VALUES

**Figure 17–7**  Spreadsheet that calculates critical ratio.

## FORECASTING FINAL COST AND SCHEDULE RESULTS

There are a couple of ways to forecast final results for a project. One is to replan based on what has been learned to-date. Another is to calculate forecast results using earned value data. Perhaps the best would be to do both.

The most common and most accepted of the statistical forecasting methods is to use the cumulative CPI estimate at completion. The formula for making this projection follows:

$$\$EAC = \frac{BAC - BCWP}{Cumulative\ CPI} + ACWP$$

Using this formula, we can calculate the $EAC for my book project. On day 7, the BCWS for my project is $2800, the BCWP is $1800, and the ACWP is $1900. Inserting these into the formula gives:

$$\$EAC = \frac{8800 - 1800}{0.95} + 1900$$

This calculates to an EAC of $9268, so the project will go over budget by $468, or slightly more than one day's work.

Fleming and Koppelman (1997) report that researchers have found the cumulative CPI to be very stable from as early as 15 to 20 percent into the project's time line. In fact, they cite Christensen (1994) as saying that the cumulative CPI does not change more than 10 percent once a project is 20 percent complete. In most cases, it gets worse, not better. One outcome of this finding is that you can forecast that a project is going to stay in trouble if it is already in trouble just 15 to 20 percent along the way. The explanation is simple. Your plan was a forecast (estimate). If you cannot estimate accurately over the near term, then you aren't going to do any better over the far term. Thus, the earned value method gives early warning that a project is headed for disaster.

> If a project is in trouble 15 percent of the way along the horizontal time line, it is going to stay in trouble.

Forecasting where you will be with the schedule is best done using critical path method. If you report progress against all tasks, the software will show the impact on the overall schedule. However, if a task has slipped and you now expect that its duration has changed, you should revise the task duration, then let the software update your projection. It may be that changing the duration of a task that originally had float will now place it on the critical path. Of course, it goes without saying that anything on the critical path that slips will cause a one-for-one slip of the end date, unless it can be recovered somehow.

## OTHER TRACKING METHODS

Another way to show how a project is proceeding is to use a run chart. You can plot any four of the project variables (P, C, T, S) using this approach. The chart in Figure 17–8 shows a plot of fraction of work completed each week for a hypothetical project called Echo. To plot fraction of work completed, you divide the amount of work completed to date by the amount of work scheduled to be completed. This could be called percentage of scheduled work actually completed and is equivalent to the ratio BCWP/BCWS.

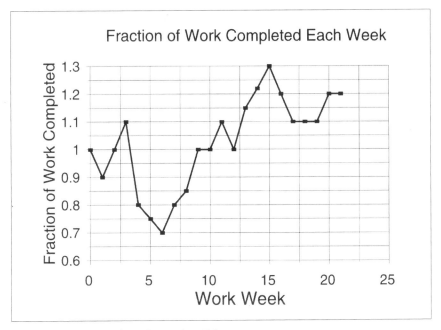

**Figure 17–8**  A run chart for project Echo.

From this chart you can see that starting in week 3, there is a downward trend. People are clearly having trouble. Then they somehow begin to recover and there is an upward trend that peaks in week 15, then falls back a bit. Since work following week 12 is being performed at a greater rate than scheduled, it is likely that the project will finish early, possibly by week 21, rather than as scheduled on week 23. This chart is highly unlikely to occur in reality, because the team is in a lot of trouble early-on, but it illustrates the approach.

There are two guidelines for interpreting run charts to detect meaningful systemic changes:

1. Since it is expected that there would be approximately the same number of points above the *average* line as there are below it, a good rule of thumb is that if there is a run of seven consecutive points on one side of the average, something significant may be happening and it would probably be a good idea to call "time out."

2. A second test is to see whether a run of seven or more intervals is steadily increasing or decreasing without reversals in direction. As in (1), such a pattern is not likely to occur by chance, thereby indicating [that] something needs to be investigated (Kiemele & Schmidt, 1993, p. 2–25).

To track quality, you might want to record rework hours. It is likely that most projects will incur from 5 to 40 percent rework. If you are improving your project management process, you should see a decline in rework. A run chart that tracks hours spent on rework is shown in Figure 17–9.

If you compare Figure 17–8 with Figure 17–9, you will notice that the curve showing rework hours is almost a mirror image of the progress curve. This suggests that one reason the team was not making good progress prior to week 10 is because they were making a number of errors that had to be corrected. After week 10, they had reduced the rework significantly, and progress reflects this. These figures would be for a very small team.

Other indicators of project quality might be documentation changes, engineering changes, design revisions, customer complaints, test failures, number of software bugs, and so on.

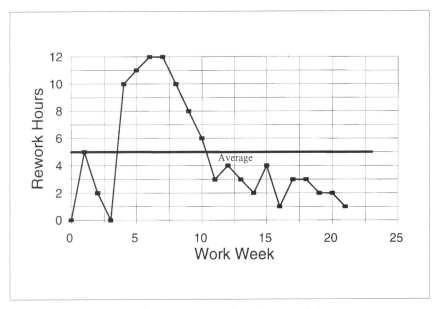

**Figure 17–9**  A run chart for project Echo showing rework hours.

It is also useful to track the number of scope changes in a project, but you need to capture the impact of a scope change for this to be meaningful. You might be able to absorb a dozen small scope changes with almost no project impact, while a single change in scope might nearly sink the project. Since scope changes result in additional work, you can track impact by looking at the dollar value of the extra work required (or the number of working hours, if you don't have dollar figures). You can also show impact by any slip in schedule that results.

The other issue that should be addressed is what caused the scope change. If it was environmental changes that no one could foresee, then the changes are probably legitimate. On longer duration projects, the world is going to move around before you can finish the project. Competitors bring out products that necessitate changes in your design if you are going to be able to compete. This is understandable, although you sometimes should go ahead and freeze a design without the competitive feature, release it, and then start a new project to add that feature. It all depends on how critical that feature is for product sales.

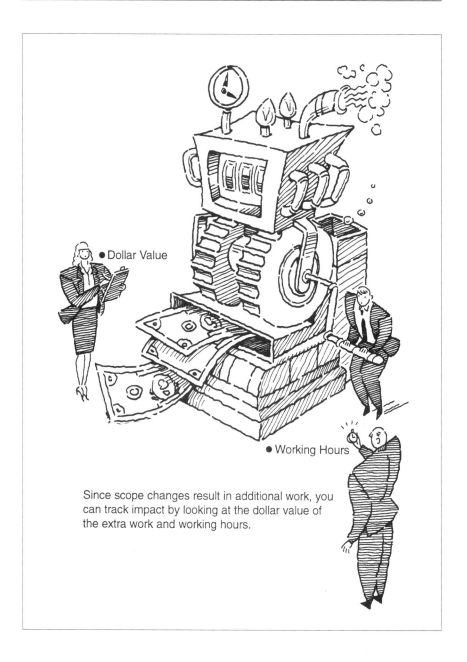

● Dollar Value

● Working Hours

Since scope changes result in additional work, you can track impact by looking at the dollar value of the extra work and working hours.

On the other hand, if changes were required because not enough time was spent up front in defining the project, these are wasteful and should be avoided in the future.

## HOW OFTEN SHOULD PROGRESS BE MEASURED?

This question is one that could probably be answered, "It all depends." If it is a long duration project, it may be sufficient to measure progress monthly. On a job that has a duration of a few months, weekly might be in order. For a project that is going to last no more than a few weeks, such as a maintenance project, we would probably want to check progress daily.

If it were possible, we would like to monitor progress continuously. The reason can be seen by examining Figure 17–10. The essence of control is feedback. We compare where we are to where we are supposed to be, then take corrective action if deviations exist. In mathematical terms, if a deviation is represented by the sinusoid shown as a solid line in Figure 17–10, the feedback signal will be the dashed line. Because the dashed line is equal in amplitude and opposite in phase to the initial variation, the two curves cancel each other out. This causes the net variation to drop to zero.

Suppose the deviation represents project spending on labor. A positive deviation means that spending has gone too high, while

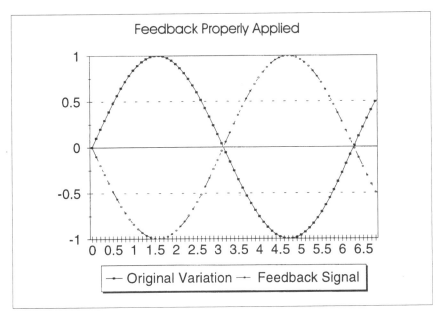

**Figure 17–10**  Variation in project variables.

a negative swing means it is too low. When it is too high, we are getting more work done than called for by the plan. This might not be a problem, but this is not always true. Getting ahead on project work can sometimes create problems downstream. Conversely, if spending is too low, we are undoubtedly falling behind, unless the work is being done at greater-than-expected efficiency. This would also signal a problem.

What we are dealing with is information. We learn about project spending through reports that often come from the accounting department, and these are sometimes received only monthly. This can create a situation like that which exists when you are driving with a friend navigating for you, and about two seconds after you pass a turnoff point, your friend says, "Oops, you should have turned back there." The feedback has come too late, and now you have to take a circuitous route to get back on track.

Suppose you receive spending reports monthly, and you have just received the latest one. It is shown in Figure 17–11. It says that spending was high for the month. You decide to cut back. The problem is, you are cutting back from this point forward. If

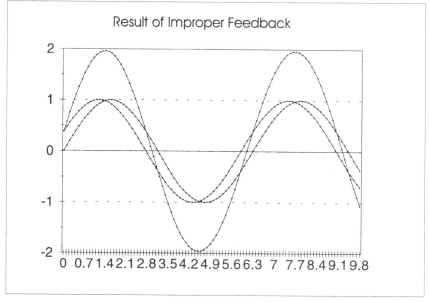

**Figure 17–11**  Delayed feedback.

the project is already entering a phase in which spending is going low, then your correction is only going to make matters worse. You would have been better off to do nothing.

Of course, I am simplifying the example. I am pretending that you could get continuous data on progress, but that it is delayed by one month, so that your correction makes things worse. Since you are getting one data dump for an entire month, the real situation won't work as I have said. I am simply trying to illustrate the essence of the problem caused by delayed feedback.

I said earlier that we would like to monitor progress continuously. What we are doing is sampling. In the case just mentioned, we get data for the project for an entire month. Suppose we monitored progress by going around to everyone and asking how they are doing. However, we don't do it every day. Perhaps the site is remote and we can only go there monthly. There are deviations taking place, but on the days that we visit the site, everything is right on target. This is shown in Figure 17–12.

What we are doing is sampling at the zero crossings. This will cause us to report zero deviations, when, in fact, there are devia-

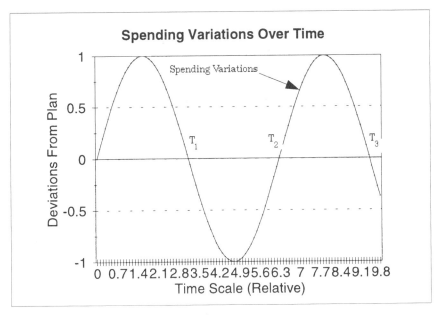

**Figure 17–12** Sampling at zero crossings.

tions taking place. The question is, how often should we sample to know what is going on? There is a branch of communication theory that does offer some guidance. Nyquist established that you must sample at least twice the rate of change of the signal if you are going to have any idea what it is actually doing. If we add sample points T, T, and T, as shown in Figure 17–13, we will be able to tell in which directions the deviations are moving. We don't know if the deviation has the form of an instantaneous change (represented in Figure 17–14 by a square wave), or whether it varies sinusoidally or as a triangle wave (Figures 17–13 and 17–15). We do know that it isn't standing still!

The only difficulty is, we don't know how often the deviations occur unless we first monitor continuously, and furthermore, it is not likely that the rate of change stays constant, so how do you apply Nyquist's sampling criterion?

If every member of your project team has a clear understanding of his or her work assignment and has a personal plan for doing that work, together with guidelines on acceptable variances,

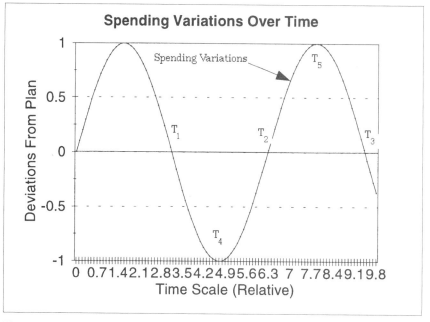

**Figure 17–13** More sampling points.

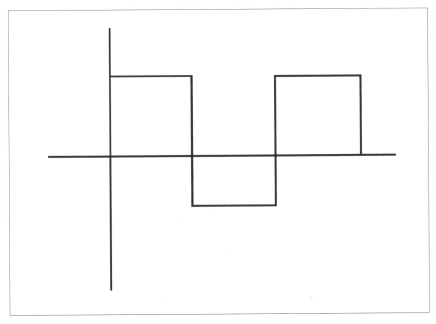

**Figure 17–14**  Square wave.

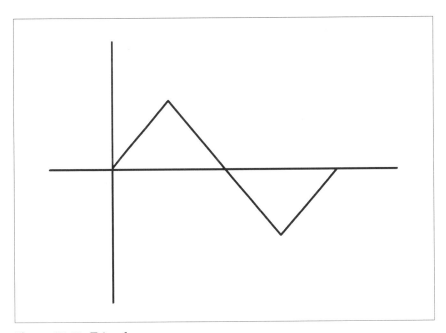

**Figure 17–15**  Triangle wave.

then the person can monitor his own progress and take corrective action whenever necessary. If a deviation goes outside acceptable limits, he knows to check with you, the project manager, or with his functional manager to decide what must be done. If this system is followed, then the person is monitoring himself continuously, and you can rely on sampling to discover any unnoticed glitches, and sampling becomes a check-and-balance to the system.

# 18

## CHAPTER

# Accounting and Cost Control

**(This chapter was written by Ben Thorp, Vice President, Chesapeake Corporation.)**

**C**ost control can be no better than the plan and the budget. Thomas Blackburn, Vice President of Kraft Operation, said to me once, "Without a plan, everything is a deviation." If the project manager is thinking about accounting and cost control and has uneasy feelings about the plan and the budget, then it is best to revisit those subjects using the principles discussed in other chapters. The four most common reasons for cost control issues are (1) poor budgeting, (2) uncertainty about cost status, (3) scope creep, and (4) unforeseen problems. Each one of these will be discussed using more familiar terms. Unforeseen problems will be largely covered under the subject of contingency.

> "Without a plan, everything is a deviation."
> —Thomas Blackburn

### CONTROL AGAINST BUDGET

The budget needs to be broken down into whatever level of detail is necessary to track the project. Reviewing the plan and the work breakdown structure should indicate the level of detail desired.

The most common error is to not have enough detail or to not have it in the right place. For example, budgeting by area is not enough detail. One needs to break out major pieces of equipment, their installation, their connection to the process, their digital control (if any), service, and training. These areas may need more detail. Connection to the processes can have mechanical, piping, electrical, and instrument budgets. Breaking the whole project down by major equipment, etc., is not good enough unless it's a small project. There should be detailed budgets for each "unit operation." Sometimes, subunit operations are important. For example, in a solid fuel boiler, one subarea could be fuel storage and boiler feed. Another could be the boiler itself, and a third could be ash handling and distribution.

The budget log must be in at least as much detail as the original estimate and frequently in more detail. One must then track deviations from each line item to develop a sense of the total impact of being over on some and under on others. It is typical to be under budget on large single-item purchases (which come at the front of a project) and over budget on softer items like "installation" or "connection" (which come late in the project). This is because quotes are obtained for the larger items and the low bid is not usually used for the estimate. Items like installation or connection are factored or estimated from databases which may not be representative of the project at hand. These pluses and minuses must be tracked.

> Contingency funds should not be used to pay for sloppy estimating. They should be used to pay for undiscovered work.

One way to track these is a budget adjustment entry (BAE), which is the fourth column on the spreadsheet after budget (see Figure 18–3). This budget adjustment must be carefully controlled, and a budget adjustment process (BAP) is recommended. A budget adjustment process is shown in Figure 18–1. A budget adjustment entry is shown in Figure 18–2. If the pluses and minuses for any one category (e.g., installation) or any one area (e.g., boiler) exceed the original budget, then the project manager needs to identify equal savings from budget or needs to seek supplemental

## BUDGET ADJUSTMENT PROCESS (BAP)

### DEFINITION

Budget adjustment estimate (BAE) is a description and estimated cost of a change, which is to become an entry.

### PROCEDURES

A BAE shall be prepared by the Project Engineer or his designee for any change or potential change that may result in the following:

More than a $10,000* change in cost in the budget

Equipment additions or deletions.

Account additions or deletions.

As requested by members of the project team.

The attached form will be used. Detailed estimates should be attached, as appropriate. Each estimate will be prepared in an unbiased and professional manner.

The BAE should be submitted to the Project Leader or Facility Department Representative for review and further submission to the Project Manager.

The Project Manager will determine if a Scope Change Request needs to be prepared, or dependent on approval levels, accept or reject the BAE.

A BAE log will be the responsibility of the Project Engineer or designee, along with a copy of all the backup, etc.

If the BAE is approved or disapproved and a Scope Change Request is not necessary, the Project Manager's secretary shall distribute approved copies to the entire project team and send the original to the project file kept by the Project Engineer or designee.

If the BAE requires a Scope Change Request, it should be returned to the Project Leader or Facility Department Representative for preparation of the Scope Change Request. The BAE should then be attached as backup to the Change of Scope. The Scope Change Request approvals shall then be followed.

### USE

The BAE is used to recognize and document a change. It will communicate to all the team members the changes.

It will force discussions around the impact of a change.

BAE's should not be used to keep forecasted variances to a minimum.

---

*The level should be determined for each project.

**Figure 18–1** Budget adjustment process.

**BUDGET ADJUSTMENT ENTRY**          NO. _____

                                     FILE NO. _____

Location  _____  Project Title _____

        BAE Title _____

To: _____ Date: _____

From: _____ Estimated By: _____

Reviewed By: _____

        Your approval is requested for the following change:

REASON FOR CHANGE (Including deficiencies with current situation)

DESCRIPTION OF CHANGE:

| Budget Category | Estimate $ (Plus) or Minus | | | |
|---|---|---|---|---|
|  | Equipment | Labor | Material | Total |
|  |  |  |  |  |
|  |  |  |  |  |
|  |  |  |  |  |
|  |  |  |  |  |
|  |  |  |  |  |

Account No. _____    Previous BAE Total _____

                                   This Change _____

                                   New BAE Total _____

_____ Not Approved _____(Date)

_____ Not a Change of Scope      Estimate Accuracy m(+/-) _____

_____ Change of Scope

Approval of Requested Change

_____   _____   _____

Project Manager                       Project Sponsor   (If over $100,000)

Type

_____ A = Facility Oversight       _____ D = Result of Detail Engineering

_____ B = Engineering Oversight    _____ E = Marketing Change

_____ C = Estimate Oversight

**Figure 18–2**  Budget adjustment request.

funding. *The use of contingency funds to make up for poor budgeting is not recommended.* Contingency, or management reserve, is for undiscovered work, as was discussed in Chapter 11. We will revisit it later in this chapter. This is an important principle that needs to be practiced with great vigor. Contingency is for unknowns, not for poor budgets.

## COMMITMENT TRACKING

All experienced capital project managers know they must track their budgets as commitments are made. Waiting for bills to be paid and posted delays entry. Bills paid represents accounting, but this process is of little value in cost control. It's a little like not totaling the points in Saturday's game until Monday morning. The game is long over before the score is known. Accounting by bills posted gives significant *uncertainty* about cost status. This uncertainty can cause inexperienced project managers to spend more than they should and can cause experienced project managers to spend less. Unfortunately, most plant, mill, and business systems do accounting on a bills-posted basis, so project managers must track commitments manually, using the fifth column (Figure 18–3) in their budget log. It can be done manually, special software can be designed, or current systems can be "adjusted" so that they enter the value of purchase orders in the commitment column.

> You need to track your budget as commitments are made. Waiting for bills to be paid creates too much delay.

Whatever system is used, this column must be kept accurate and up to date. It is the only way a project manager can know where her project is at any instant. It is a "real time" method of understanding status against budget. A literature search failed to reveal much written about the subject of commitment tracking or commitment accounting, but it is widely practiced and used.

This method of tracking gets difficult if "open purchase orders" are used. Open purchase orders are an expediency which should be avoided for this and other reasons. It is also important to note that some of the "business enterprise" systems do not have

| Acme Company | | | | |
|---|---|---|---|---|
| Project: Project Manager: | | | | |
| Account No. | Description | Original Budget | Current Budget | Committed to-date |
| | | | | |
| | | | | |
| | | | | |
| | | | | |
| | | | | |
| | | | | |
| | | | | |
| | | | | |
| | | | | |
| | | | | |
| | | | | |
| | | | | |
| | | | | |
| | | | | |
| | | | | |
| | | | | |
| | | | | BudgetIog |

**Figure 18–3**  Budget and cost control log.

a commitment tracking feature, and one is very difficult to install because of the "tight integration" of these systems. Figure 18–3 shows important columns of our budget and cost control log as it has developed through this point in the chapter.

## SCOPE CREEP

Scope creep is the single most important cause of a deviation from budget. The two driving forces are lack of detailed scope definition and a host of stakeholders wanting to make the project better or more efficient or more operating-cost-effective. Scope creep can also be driven by the legislative process when new laws are passed or regulations added between the time the estimate was made and startup. Whatever the reason, it is important to have an effective cost control mechanism in place to deal with the *pervasive driving force of scope creep.* In Figure 18–4 is a scope change log for a project. Figure 18–5 shows a scope change process, and Figure 18–6 shows a scope change request.

| Scope Change Log Project: | | | | | | |
|---|---|---|---|---|---|---|
| Date | Nature of Change | Requested by | Impact to project | Approval Document No. | Cost of Change | Paid for by |
| | | | | | | |
| | | | | | | |
| | | | | | | |
| | | | | | | |
| | | | | | | |
| | | | | | | |
| | | | | | | |
| | | | | | | |
| | | | | | | |
| | | | | | | |
| | | | | | | |
| | | | | | | |
| | | | | | | |
| | | | | | | |
| | | | | | | |

Scopechange

**Figure 18–4**  A scope change log form.

Project managers must be firm about this process. They must not permit any commitment or any expenditure until scope change approval is obtained. There are some gray areas between a budget adjustment and a scope change. Lets take a couple of examples to understand this important difference. First, assume that a pump and motor used in the project was esti-mated for a feed rate of say 5000 gpm. If the process dictates it should be 6000 gpm and this was a missed estimate, then the difference in cost is usually considered to be a budget estimate. If someone wants the feed rate to be 8000 gpm because we need more steam for the old part of the plant (when none was originally scoped), then this is a scope change.

> All projects must have a control mechanism to deal with scope creep.

It may be very legitimate and it may be the right thing to do for the company, but the project manager must have the discipline and the character to insist on a signed scope change document. If it's "so right," then those with approval authority will recognize it

---

### SCOPE CHANGE PROCESS

#### DEFINITION

The Scope Change Process starts with a A Scope Change Request (SCR).

A SCR is any discretionary change from the original Scope and estimate of the appropriation requisition.

#### PROCEDURES

A SCR will be prepared by the Project Leader or Facility department Representative on the attached form, as requested by the Project Manager. The Project Leader shall obtain all stakeholder's agreement prior to submission of the SCR. The first step in preparing a SCR is preparation of the BAR.

After approval or disapproval, the SCR will be transmitted to all the team members by the Project Manager. Once notified of the approval, all parties will proceed with the changed work.

#### USE

A SCR shall not be prepared for items that are necessary to carry out the original intended Scope which are a result of new information such as detailed design, field information, regulations, estimating errors, etc.

The SCR shall be used to inform and gain the appropriate approvals prior to making any discretionary change in a project. A SCR should be prepared for items which do not impact the budget.

---

**Figure 18–5**  Scope change process.

and formally approve it. You can see that this gets to be an involved process. The more detailed and specific the scope, the easier it is to judge if it is a budget adjustment or a scope change.

Another example will indicate how outside forces can impact decisions. Suppose a project manager gets a request to install a backup pump which is completely redundant. If the request is for operational convenience, it's a scope change. If the request is because the state or insurance codes require it, then it is probably a budget adjustment. This is because the engineer should have known code and should have allowed for the pump. Some will call for the use of contingency funds, but as will be seen in the next section, that is not the intended use of contingency.

**SCOPE CHANGE REQUEST**　　　　NO. _____

　　　　　　　　　　　　　　　　　FILE NO. _____

　　　　　　　　　　　　　　　　　PROJECT NO. _____

Location _____　Project Title _____

Scope Change Title _____

Purpose _____

_____

_____

As Proposed in AR Scope _____

_____

_____

As Proposed in Scope Change _____

_____

_____

　　　Capital Cost (Increase) or Decrease　　$ _____

　　　New Cumulative Scope change Balance　$ _____

　　　Source of Funding _____

Approved

_____　　_____
　　　　To $50,000　　　　　　　Date

_____　　_____
　　　　To $100,000　　　　　　Date

_____　　_____
　　　　To $200,000　　　　　　Date

_____　　_____
　　　　To $300,000　　　　　　Date

_____　　_____
　　　　To $400,000　　　　　　Date

_____　　_____
　　　　To $800,000　　　　　　Date

**Figure 18–6** Scope change request.

## CONTINGENCY OR MANAGEMENT RESERVE

The most useful definition of contingency is that it is money set aside to pay for work or equipment that were unknown and unknowable during estimating. This is a hard rule but one that results in better estimates and control. If in the redundant pump example the code changed between estimating and construction, then the cost of the second pump was unknown and unknowable. It requires a scope change, but the funding comes from the contingency budget. There are a host of project requirements that may be unknown at the time of budgeting. Experienced project managers know many of these areas and take great pains to evaluate them but cannot possibly evaluate all of them. Examples include:

1. Buried structures
2. Soil conditions different from test borings
3. Undetected soil contamination
4. Conditions inside tanks
5. Conditions inside structures
6. Inordinate weather conditions
7. Changes in workman's compensation or insurance rates

The level of unknowns is higher in rebuild situations than new construction, and different contingency levels are frequently used. A good database can help document a reasonable contingency level.

> You should never use more contingency than the amount of work already completed in the project.

There are a couple of "golden rules" around contingency. The first is worth restating. Contingency is for unknowns, not for errors of omission (it should have been known) or errors of budgeting. Second, one should never use more contingency than the amount of work already completed in the project. That is, if the project is 35 percent complete, one should have used no more than 35 percent of the contingency budget. Because most "unknowns" show up late in the project, some project managers have an even tougher rule of thumb. They say that the contingency used should be no more than half of the percentage complete, until the very end of the project. This means that if a project is 35 percent complete, one should have used no more than 17.5 percent of the contingency budget.

Saving contingency for the end of the project is an excellent idea for two reasons. First, one never knows what startup problems will be encountered. Startup problems must be resolved quickly, and you don't want to wait for funding changes during startup. Second, when the project is being closed, any unused contingency will be used to cover budget adjustment entries if the sum of the changes is greater than the original budget.

## ACCURACY OF ESTIMATES

There is yet another reason for using different levels of contingency, which is not strictly part of cost control but which will be covered here because it can be a cost control mechanism. Experienced project managers know that the level of accuracy of estimates can be improved with increasing detail (and cost). Some firms have formalized this process. A system used by Dr. Jaako Pöyry and Paul Talvio, of Jaako Pöyry, Inc., as related to me privately, typically uses three levels. The first level, say E1, is a quick "back of the envelope" estimate based on similar projects. It generally takes a few hours or days to prepare. The E1 level is regarded as having a ± 40 percent accuracy because even the exact site of the job may be unknown. This level of accuracy may be okay for evaluating alternatives or looking at the conceptual merits of an idea.

The second level, say E2, is a factored or parametric estimate. This level is regarded as having a ± 20 percent accuracy and is used to judge feasibility, or to choose between closer alternatives. This estimate generally takes weeks to prepare.

The third level, say E3, is a "board quality estimate." It requires a site to be identified, flow sheets to be completed, and Piping and Instrument Drawings to be done in as much detail as possible. Estimates are prepared from budget quotes. This means the three types of specifications (mechanical, life, and performance) must be developed. This estimate can take months and up to

3 percent of the total installed cost to develop. The E3 estimate is regarded to have an accuracy of ± 10 percent.

The accuracy of any level is highly dependent on the accuracy of a database, and this illustrates the importance of establishing and maintaining an accurate database. Some clients require a +0, minus 10 percent level of accuracy, sometimes called E4. This requires more complete engineering, bid packages, and firm quotes, usually with guaranteed time limits. Even more funds may be required for this level of estimating.

The usual problem is that some marketing opportunity, competitive move, or cash surplus requires that a project be scoped and estimated for "board approval" in less time than "board quality estimates" take. Engineers and estimators frequently complain when this happens but usually provide a number—an estimate. They frequently fail to communicate its accuracy, and when the project is approved, some unsuspecting project manager inherits a nightmare.

One solution is to communicate the accuracy of the estimate and get board approval for wide limits or make the adjustment in contingency. If the quick estimate is at an E2 level (± 20 percent), then there will be 10 percent more unknowns than for an E3 level *because the E2 lacks detail.* Therefore, if E3 estimates have a contingency of 7 percent, an E2 can have the same total budget accuracy by having a contingency of 17 percent.

If the process is explained to the board and if the project is truly urgent, then workable budgets will be established. This "level of accuracy" budgeting shows one reason why the definition of contingency as "unknowns" is so useful, but the concept does require a level of estimating expertise that is sophisticated.

## PROJECT ACCOUNTING

Figure 18–7 shows a portion of a budget log. Columns have been added for "expended to date" (bills paid), required to complete, projected final cost, and variance. Projected final cost is the sum of expended to date and required to complete, which *is always an independent estimate.* Please note that the budget log in Figure 18–7 is one detailed sheet on process construction. It is one of many sheets of the budget log. As you can see, the accounting process is

| Acme Company | | | | | | | | |
|---|---|---|---|---|---|---|---|---|
| Project:                    Project Manager: | | | | | | | | |
| Account No. | Description | Original Budget | Current Budget | Committed to-date | Expended to-date | Required to complete | Projected final cost | Variance over- or underrun |
|  |  |  |  |  |  |  |  |  |
|  |  |  |  |  |  |  |  |  |
|  |  |  |  |  |  |  |  |  |
|  |  |  |  |  |  |  |  |  |
|  |  |  |  |  |  |  |  |  |
|  |  |  |  |  |  |  |  |  |
|  |  |  |  |  |  |  |  |  |
|  |  |  |  |  |  |  |  |  |
|  |  |  |  |  |  |  |  |  |
|  |  |  |  |  |  |  |  |  |
|  |  |  |  |  |  |  |  |  |
|  |  |  |  |  |  |  |  |  |
|  |  |  |  |  |  |  |  |  |
|  |  |  |  |  |  |  |  |  |
|  |  |  |  |  |  |  |  |  |

Budgetlogfinal

**Figure 18–7**   Portion of a budget log.

quite detailed and takes professional financial skills to complete. Large projects require at least one full-time, trained financial person plus necessary support staff. This phase of project accounting is not covered in detail here.

## PROJECT AUDITS

It is an excellent idea for the project manager to request an "in-process audit" early in the project, say at the 10 to 20 percent of completion stage. This audit should focus on the project procedures established and practiced. The audit should answer two questions: (1) Are all of the established procedures adequate? (2) Are they being followed? This early audit will help the team understand the importance of the discipline of project management. It will help the project manager establish or strengthen any systems or procedures necessary to facilitate the discipline of project management. Since the purpose of the audit is partly training and strengthening, a verbal feedback from the audit team to the project team can be very helpful if a positive environment can be created. With 80 to 90 percent of the project remaining, the team can make changes which will benefit the entire project. Holding this kind of a review at the 80 to 90 percent of completion stage is not helpful to the project or the team.

A final review at the end of the project is useful for accumulating learning and to record this for the benefit of the team members and future teams. This audit information can be added to the financial audit, which will be done typically 6 to 12 months after startup or commissioning. See Chapter 21 on conducting process reviews.

# 19

## CHAPTER

# Change Control in Projects

**A**ny change made to a project during the implementation stage is likely to pose a threat to progress in some way. The impact can be to any one or more of the cost, sched-ule, performance, or scope targets. The project manager has a dual responsibil-ity in dealing with changes: (1) to keep the client informed about the impact of the change, and (2) to protect himself and the team from being "beaten up" at the end of the project when they miss original targets because changes were made.

> Changes made to projects during the implementation stage always pose a threat to progress.

One of the most common requests for change during a project is additional scope. This can happen for three basic reasons:

1. The initial plan did not include the scope, because it was forgotten.

2. Something was learned about a technical issue during the project that suggested a change. Or work is discov-

ered, such as asbestos removal, that was not known during the planning stage. (See Chapter 18.)

3. The world moves around during the project life cycle and changes to the project are required to stay competitive.

The first of these can be avoided by doing a better job of planning up front. The second two are pretty much unavoidable, but should not be casually made. Everyone should understand the impact to the project before a scope change is agreed to. If the customer agrees that the change is worth the impact, then a change to the plan is made that will incorporate the scope revision, and all stakeholders affected by the change will sign the change approval form. A form for such use is shown in Figure 19–1.

This form has a feature not seen on many change approval forms. By checking the box in front of a position description, you can indicate who must sign the form. That way, not every person indicated need approve a change. I suggest that a policy be adopted that requires a person to sign a project approval only if he or she is taking responsibility for some aspect of the job. Signatures should not be an ego thing. It takes a lot of time to route a change request through an organization, and this can severely impact project responsiveness. It is useful to have a project change board meeting on a regular basis if a lot of project changes are being made in an organization. That way, a change can wait for the regular meeting unless it is urgent, in which case it can be walked around for signatures.

Another feature is the impact box at the top of the form, which shows whether the impact of a change will be to schedule, cost, quality, or scope. In some organizations, another field needs to be added. That is the impact on inventory. Is a change going to obsolete parts in inventory, which will then have to be scrapped? If so, what is the cost impact, and can it be avoided?

## CHANGES THAT NEED CONTROL PROCEDURES

The way to decide whether a change needs formal approval is to ask whether the proposed change would alter any information on

## Project Change Approval

| Project Name: | Project Number: | Date: July 31, 1997 |
|---|---|---|
| Project Manager:<br>Requested by: | Department: | Change in:<br>□ Scope   □ Schedule<br>□ Budget  □ Performance |

### Deviation Information

Description of change being requested:

Reason for change:

Effect on schedule:

Effect on cost (budget):

Effect on performance (quality):

Effect on scope:

| Class | Distribution of Estimated Cost Deviation | The Requested Change is: | |
|---|---|---|---|
| Capital | | □ Absolutely necessary to achieve desired results | □ Scope reduction that will not impact original targets |
| Non-capital | | □ Discretionary - provides benefits beyond the original target | □ Scope reduction that will impact original targets |

### Required Approvals □

| | | |
|---|---|---|
| □ Project Leader/Manager (type name) | Sign: | Date: |
| □ General Manager (type name) | Sign: | Date: |
| □ Concerned Dept. Manager (type name) | Sign: | Date: |
| □ Controller (type name) | Sign: | Date: |
| □ Concerned Vice President (type name) | Sign: | Date: |
| □ President (type name) | Sign: | Date: |
| □ Other (type name) | Sign: | Date: |

**Figure 19–1** Project change approval form.

a document that has already been issued to authorize work. By this definition, a formal procedure should be applied whenever a change would affect:

## To decide if a change needs formal approval, ask whether the change would alter any information on a document that has already been issued to authorize work.

- ◆ The contract document or any of its attachments. Such a change would be called a contract variation.
- ◆ A purchase order that has already been issued. The change would probably be called a purchase order amendment.
- ◆ Any drawing or specification that has been issued for manufacturing, purchasing, or construction.

## CONTROL PROCEDURES FOR ENGINEERING CHANGES

Before a proposed engineering change is approved, it is customary to assess the risks such a change might cause, including technical, manufacturing or construction, commercial, safety, reliability, time scale, costs, and inventory. This assessment must usually be done by a change board, since no one individual is likely to be able to assess the impact in all areas.

The project manager should designate someone to keep a register of all such changes and to record when they have been implemented. A standard change form like the one shown above would be used to request the change. When engineering documents are changed, revision numbers must be updated and logged. Before the advent of computer-aided engineering, it was easy to control drawing revisions because the master was housed in a central file. Now anyone can print out a drawing, and there is no assurance that it is the latest version unless the revision number is checked against the log.

## Before approving an engineering change, ask what risk such a change might cause.

Most organizations recognize a point in the design process beyond which a change will cause a serious impact on costs and/or progress. At that point the design is frozen. The change board will then refuse to approve any change to the product unless they are convinced that there are compelling reasons for doing so, such as safety or a customer-funded request. Ideally, even the customer should be bound by a design freeze, or should be made to pay heavily for violating it.

## LOGGING CHANGES IN PROJECT SCOPE

In Chapter 11, it was pointed out that management reserve is to be used to pay for undiscovered work, but this is only for internally funded projects. If customers ask for changes to project scope, they are usually required to pay for them. A log should be kept of all scope changes made in a project. The log should document the nature of the change, who requested it, the impact to the project, dates on which the change was incorporated, the number of the approval document that authorized the change, the cost of the change, and who pays for it. A suitable form was shown in Figure 18–4.

The form on page 231 should be used to authorize changes in project scope. Together with the log, these constitute a history of changes and causes of those changes for future reference.

CHAPTER

# Managing Vendors in Projects

**(This chapter was written by Ben Thorp, Vice President, Chesapeake Corporation.)**

In projects that involve partnering with vendors, the vendor actually becomes a member of the project team in a sense. Such vendors must be managed exactly as you would manage any resource in your team. Naturally, you don't have direct control over vendors, but then you often don't have such control over internal resources either.

**Owner:** The organization doing the project.

You also need to manage vendors when you have large capital equipment projects in which the vendor is delivering long-lead capital equipment. Because of the large investments in these projects, it is very important that all efforts between vendor and customer (namely your company) be well managed.

This is by no means meant to suggest that a "command and control" method is advocated, especially in a partnering arrangement. A good partnering arrangement is only achieved by clearly defining goals, roles, and processes, and that is the focus of this chapter.

There are two points that need to be made. First, the accountability for all projects resides *totally* with the owner. Second, the most typical form of relationship between owner and supplier is contractual. This contractual arrangement must be well understood by the project manager and owner alike.

> **To manage vendors does not mean to adopt a "command and control" approach.**

The message to new project managers or sponsors is that the owner must take control of the process, which is shown in Figure 20–1. He must define the decision-making process and stakeholder roles. Major stakeholders include production, finance, engineering, technical, and vendors. Each of these stakeholder groups has its own culture and each needs to be addressed uniquely. Owners must take control by clearly and completely defining their needs and desires (musts and wants) and ensuring that they are in specifications, bid packages, orders, contracts, and the like. This will require owners to take control of agenda-setting in meetings so that the required output is obtained. Partnering or teaming is a preferred method of working, but it cannot take precedence over managing the project.

> **Sponsor:** The person in the organization who "drives" the project.

## RESOURCE DOCUMENTS

There are three primary resource documents that need to be prepared as early as possible. The first is an *internal document* which defines the level of approval, the time required for approval, and the level of documentation needed for an approval to be granted. This simple document can save hundreds, even thousands of hours of hunting down the right person for approval and in expediting delivery because the purchase order could not be issued in a timely manner. It can also save rework caused by the approving individual wanting to see more (or less) in order to sign. Does the approver want to see three bids, just know that three bids have

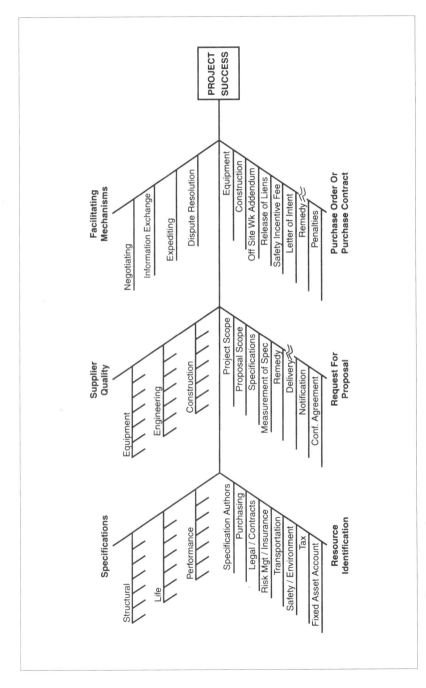

**Figure 20–1** Owner controls process.

been obtained, or is it satisfactory to know that the supplier has been the low bidder for the required quality on the last two jobs and the unit prices are the same for this job?

The second document identifies resources for the vendor management function by name either inside or outside of the owner's firm. Typical resources include individuals dealing with the issues shown in Figure 20–2.

Performance specification author
Safety
Purchasing
Transportation
Legal
Tax
Risk management/insurance
Fixed asset accounting

**Figure 20–2**  Issues that must be addressed in a project.

Every purchase order can have issues requiring input from one or all of these resources. Therefore, the resource needs to be *defined* and *available.*

The final document needed is a material coordination plan. This plan can be started early—around permitting—but can only be completed after all of the components are known. It can be a detailed description or it can be a simple spreadsheet where each function (e.g., air permit) or service (soil reports) or component (storm sewer) is listed. Columns would then be created for who will request, purchase, ship, expedite, inspect, construct, and approve. Where multiple ship-to sites are involved, another column will need to be added. See the example in Figure 20–3.

## SPECIFICATIONS

The project team will need to discuss three very different types of specifications, namely:

Structural specifications
Life specifications
Performance specifications, including training

**Material Coordination Plan**
(Sample, abbreviated form)

| Project: | | | | | | | Date issued: | |
|---|---|---|---|---|---|---|---|---|
| | Requested | Purchased | Expedited | Received | Installed | Inspected | Checkout | Acceptance |
| Gen. Requirem'ts | | | | | | | | |
| Site Work | | | | | | | | |
| Foundations | | | | | | | | |
| Masonry | | | | | | | | |
| Carpentry | | | | | | | | |
| Doors & Fixtures | | | | | | | | |
| Finishes | | | | | | | | |
| Equipment | | | | | | | | |
| Mechanical | | | | | | | | |
| Elec. & Inst. | | | | | | | | |
| Piping | | | | | | | | |
| Safety | | | | | | | | |
| Environmental | | | | | | | | |
| | | | | | | | | |

File: PMFORMS\Material Coordination

Instructions for use: List names of responsible parties in each cell and add any sub-components of each item in column 1 from the Work Breakdown Structure.

**Figure 20–3** Sample spreadsheet.

Historically, we have put emphasis on the structural specifications—typically type of material and strength or rigidity of the structure. Many firms have a comprehensive specification "library" for these. Those are still very appropriate. We are now adding to that certain life criteria for the product being delivered by the vendor. In automotive, we are talking about seven-year warranties on the "drive train" and 100,000 miles between tune-ups. There are industrial equivalents which must be converted into specifications. Figure 20–4 shows some life issues which need to be considered.

Life of machinery
Life of components
Repair frequency
Interchangability of spares
Minimum spare inventory

**Figure 20–4** Life issues for deliverables.

However, the most critical specification for production machinery is *performance itself*. Specifications are normally written by engineers, but performance requirements are usually best understood by operations personnel, so this is an area that requires a team effort. Throughput models and run-rate models are sometimes helpful. That is, given certain input raw materials and conditions, what is the output and what is the tolerance around that output? What are the sustained and peak output rates? What is the average uptime? What training is required? What are the outcomes of the training (e.g., what do operators and mechanics need to do to run the facility). These conditions will become part of the bid package and eventually part of the purchase order or contract. When preparing all of the specifications, it helps to think about how a good contract will reflect them. The contract should answer these questions:

> ## Contracts without remedies are often without value.

What are the performance specifications?

How will they be measured? What are the criteria and conditions?

What is the remedy when something is out of specification?

*Contracts without remedies are often without value,* except to the lawyers who will use the legal system to write what you forgot.

Specifications may also apply to intermediate steps, including, but not limited to, issues such as those shown in Figure 20–5.

---

♦ Drawing submittal
♦ Certified drawings
♦ Shipment date
♦ Percent complete shipment
♦ Inspection
♦ Installation
♦ Startup
♦ Dates for full compliance to specification

---

**Figure 20–5**  Issues that must be covered.

Remember, each needs a definition of how performance will be measured and what the remedy will be if vendor performance is unsatisfactory. The consequences of a missed milestone date can often have large project consequences, even if the final ship date is met. For example, equipment that requires cavities or special mountings in a building might require certified drawings before the building drawings can/should be certified. A delay in equipment drawings could delay the whole building or the entire project. What is then the appropriate remedy? This can be determined through competitive bidding and negotiation, if it is in the bid package.

## SUPPLIER QUALITY

There is more written about this subject than perhaps any other subject in this chapter. This will be kept short and deal with a few principles. The first principle is that good projects have good suppliers. The second principle is that you need a system to define what is important to you and to do it in the most objective way possible. If this has been previously done by your corporation and you have preferred suppliers, selected suppliers, or partnerships, then you can proceed to the *supplier selection* section of this chapter. If not, you need to develop supplier evaluation mechanisms for at least equipment, engineering, and construction. Some of the evaluations will be for products (hard or soft), and some will be for services. These evaluations can be quite different.

**Good projects have good suppliers.**

In setting up evaluation mechanisms, you need to determine whether they will be made on the content of presentations (often future expected results) or on the evaluation of past performance. For example, will contractor safety be judged by the promised safety programs or will it be judged by his experience modifier rate (EMR) to his Workers Compensation Insurance Premium?

For equipment, typical areas that can be evaluated are shown in Figure 20–6.

- Quality
- Cost of use (price is a default)
- Delivery
- Service
- Business practices
- Ethics
- Technology/development
- Training

**Figure 20–6**  Equipment evaluation areas.

For the engineering activity, typical areas that can be evaluated include those shown in Figure 20–7.

- Process expertise
- Design expertise
- Drawing quality (errors per drawing)
- Custom design expertise
- Modules design capability
- Long-term operation and maintenance
- Alignment with owner
- Ethics
- Design safety
- Standards & procedures
- Timeliness

**Figure 20–7**  Engineering areas to evaluate.

To evaluate contracting work, consider the list shown in Figure 20–8.

- Safety (EMR, etc.)
- Quality control
- Ethics
- Planning/scheduling
- Billing accuracy, backup, and timeliness
- Financial stability
- Craftsman training
- Supervisors' skills
- Dispute resolution
- Relationship with subcontractors

**Figure 20–8**  Contracting evaluation areas.

Having a uniform system of evaluation will result in at least three positive outcomes. First, the team will have a more consistent evaluation process. Second, unqualified suppliers will be eliminated. Finally, there will be a way to *objectively* evaluate "favorite suppliers" who are suggested by someone, including management.

## REQUEST FOR PROPOSALS

When RFPs are issued, they should be complete and should only go to qualified suppliers. A qualified supplier is one that you would buy from if they provide the best response to the RFP. There is a lot of debate over this issue. There has been a practice in which suppliers are asked to bid on a job, even though the company knows that they will never be awarded the contract, simply because they aren't qualified. However, they are almost certain to bid lower than anyone else. That low bid is then held up to desired contractors as an incentive to go lower. The bidder

> The effort of including stalking horses in your bid system is probably not worthwhile.

who initially gave the lowest bid is called a "stalking horse." Most of the leading companies have concluded that the wasted effort of including stalking horses is not worth the value of the time spent.

A request for proposal should include the items shown in Figure 20–9.

- ◆ Outline of total project
- ◆ Scope of work for the RFP
- ◆ Structural specifications
- ◆ Life specifications
- ◆ Performance specifications
- ◆ Measurement of specification
- ◆ Remedies
- ◆ Delivery of information
- ◆ Delivery of materials/services
- ◆ Shipment methods
- ◆ Installation services
- ◆ Startup services
- ◆ Payment schedule
- ◆ Recommended spares
- ◆ Insurance coverage
- ◆ Evaluation criteria
- ◆ Notification procedures
- ◆ Names of key personnel
- ◆ Confidentiality agreements

**Figure 20–9**  Items to include in RFPs.

There will always be questions from bidders about RFPs, and a list of these should be maintained and the same answer given to all bidders. One method that has been used to shorten this process is to invite all bidders to a single meeting. Another advantage is that the number and quality of questions improves. One potential disadvantage is that all bidders are known to each other.

## SUPPLIER SELECTION

A well prepared RFP can make this process relatively straightforward. If the evaluation criteria have been stated objectively and weighted, each bid can be scored and totaled. If one uses a Kepner-Tregoe (1965) process (in which you list musts, wants, and nice-to-haves), the musts should be scored and totaled first. It is always a good idea to decide up front what range of totals will be considered equal. For example, if there are 10 factors of 10 points each, then one knows that an 87 is the same as an 88. Another method is to say all musts need to be fully met, and anyone falling below 100 is a candidate for elimination. It is typical for the evaluation process to sort leaders from average responses and to identify clear candidates for elimination. Assuming there are several bidders that warrant further consideration, a ranking of the wants is in order. Experience shows that it is wise to keep more than one bidder before entering into the next process, which is negotiation. There are technical and commercial insights that can be obtained from the negotiation process. These can change the evaluation. Furthermore, changes can sometimes unseat the leading bidder. For example, their delivery can change due to a new order, or critical personnel can be assigned to other projects.

Negative things can happen during this process. Competitive bids can show that one or more of the specifications was incorrect or missing. The delivery dates or estimated cost can be grossly in error. If the deviation is small, amended bids can be requested. If the deviation changes the scope, new RFPs may be needed. If the deviation changes project economics, the project may need to be changed or even canceled. Project managers or teams might be disappointed by a canceled project, but experienced project managers know this is a better outcome than having to manage a bad project.

## NEGOTIATION

This is the point at which an owner's *wants* and *musts* have to be reconciled with the bidders' capabilities and desires. Everyone agrees that at this point in the project, the owner has the advantage. Wise use of power will create a win-win situation. Unwise use of power is likely to create a win-lose situation or even a lose-lose situation. *The key questions should be resolved in favor of what's best for the project.* What's best is usually that all of the project wants are met by a strong supplier who is capable of dedicating the resources needed to make the project a

> Key questions should be resolved in favor of what's best for the project.

success. Too many times, bidders accept conditions that cannot be met in order to secure an order. When this condition becomes apparent, the project is headed for trouble. The project mission and vision must include vendor success and eliminate "getting something for nothing" thinking.

There are many approaches to negotiation. One successful approach is to break the negotiations into "technical" and "commercial" parts. The specifications should be negotiated first, because their resolution could change the price. If special materials of construction are needed, the price may increase. If an owner is willing to accept a standard offering, the price may go down. Once all of the specification issues have been resolved, the commercial negotiations can begin. Here, all items that will appear in the purchase order must be discussed and agreed to, especially performance specifications, test conditions, and remedies. *After negotiations are complete, there should be no surprises for the owner or the successful bidder.*

The remedy deserves some special discussion because of the realities that occur when performance is not met. At this point, the project can be practically over. Usually, the budget has been spent. The same is true for the suppliers' budget. These forces can "seduce" both the owner's project team and the bidder to try a series of "low cost" fixes that can take weeks or usually months. When performance specs are missed, it is usually wise to invite higher levels of management on both sides to the solution meeting. Ide-

After negotiations are complete, there should be no surprises for the owner or the successful bidder.

ally, the time allowed to implement the remedy is addressed in the purchase order or contract. If the bidder is unwilling or unable to resolve the performance issue, then the owner can implement and charge back all or a percentage of the costs to the bidder. Some contracts have a liquidated-damages clause in which the cost of the equipment or service is discounted until the owner achieves their original financial returns. Most bidders will insist on a limitation-of-liability clause. These conditions are all resolved through negotiation with the goal of creating a win-win situation. One form of a win-win is to negotiate penalty clauses for late delivery, poor performance, and so on. In return, there are incentive clauses for perfect delivery (early delivery can sometimes cause staging problems), good startup, above-average performance, or outstanding safety performance. The owner typically benefits from all of these, and sharing an unplanned benefit is easier than many would expect.

There are a number of negotiating processes that can be used, and most are satisfactory if the process is fair, ethical, and well understood by all stakeholders. Getting everyone at the same office on the same day is not in itself brutal. It may be very time efficient. Getting everyone there to "shop the low price" is at least unfair. Most experienced teams like to devote a half day to a day per major bidder and to separate close competitors by at least an evening. This is because there are usually many items to resolve, and it takes intense focus to get through the major issues.

## THE PURCHASE ORDER/PURCHASE CONTRACT

There are a large number of contract forms, and it takes an experienced project team to know what form to use and why. There are two general recommendations. First, the owner should have his contract forms reviewed and modified by expert outside legal counsel who have experience in litigating contracts. This is a special skill that may require a slightly higher fee—once. However, it could save millions over time. Second, the owner should use his stationery and his contract as a starting point.

It is beyond the scope of this book to delve into contract law. It is not beyond the scope of this book to note that the owner has the responsibility and accountability that dictates he be good at contract negotiation and contract implementation. An experienced project manager will know the contracts better than the process or the equipment being purchased.

The major types of purchase contracts include those components listed in Figure 20–10 below. The elements to be addressed include those listed in Part 5. Your most critical projects should have your best contracts personnel, who can typically be shared across a number of projects.

Acceptance Certificate
Affidavit and Release of Liens
Construction Agreement, Cost Plus Fixed Fee
Construction Agreement, Cost Plus Percentage Fee
Construction Agreement, Lump Sum
Contractor's Performance Incentive Fee
Contractor's Safety Incentive Fee
Corporation Consultation
General Conditions, Cost Plus Fixed Fee
General Conditions, Cost Plus Percentage Fee
General Conditions, Lump Sum
Individual Consultant
Letter of Intent
On-Site Work Addendum
Purchase Order (Cost Reimbursable Construction)
Purchase Order (Equipment Supplier)
Purchase Order (Firm Price Construction)
Renewable Construction Agreement
Renewable Engineering Agreement
Request for Contractor's Affidavit

**Figure 20–10**  Components of purchase contracts.

## INFORMATION EXCHANGE

There are two forms of information exchange, one external and one internal. External exchange of information requires that the owner examine the project, the location of the project, and the types of information that will be exchanged. The key questions are: What information is confidential? and How confidential? On the one hand, there can be a completely public project like building a park. On the other hand, a project can require high levels of security and in-depth security clearance for all workers. In most projects there is considerable information which the owner wants to keep confidential. This means that confidentiality agreements need to be signed with each company receiving this information. For very sensitive information, it is worth considering agreements for each person receiving the information. These agreements should state how confidential information will be identified and marked. Restrictions on copying the information need to be included in the contract and on the markings. Verbal confidential information is usually confirmed in memo, or it is noted in meeting minutes. All official meeting administrators need to be aware of the policies established. The owner needs to keep a log of all confidential information distributed and at the end of the project may want to reclaim all of it. The owner's IT (information technology) or IS (information systems) person should be consulted for the best way to handle confidential information that may be transmitted electronically.

Internal document distribution is usually the larger job. This is actually a communications function and should be approached in that fashion. The most common document control device is a spreadsheet with the "documents" listed in the first column and potential recipients listed in subsequent columns. Facility files and central files are critical recipients. Correspondence and meeting notes are critical "documents." Figure 20–11 shows a typical document distribution matrix. This matrix should be reviewed with all

| Distribution of Documents (Sample, abbreviated form) | | | | | | | | | |
|---|---|---|---|---|---|---|---|---|---|
| Project: | | | | | | Date issued: | | | |
| Document Name | Project Secretary | Project Team* | Facility Engineer | Project Receiving | Accounts Payable | Project Files | Vendors* | Project Sponsor | Others (Specify) |
| Proj. Procedure | 1 | 1 | 1 | 1 | 1 | 1 | 1 | 1 | |
| Meeting Minutes | 1 | 1 | 1 | 0 | 0 | 1 | 1 | 1 | |
| Specifications & Bill of Materials | 1 | 1 | 1 | 1 | 0 | 1 | 1 | 0 | |
| Request for Proposals | 1 | 1 | 1 | 0 | 0 | 1 | NA | 0 | |
| Proposals | 1 | 1 | 1 | 0 | 0 | 1 | NA | 0 | |
| Progress Reports | 1 | 1 | 1 | 0 | 0 | 1 | 1 | 1 | |
| Audits | 1 | 1 | 0 | 0 | 0 | 1 | 1 | 1 | |
| Closeout | 1 | 1 | 1 | 1 | 1 | 1 | 1 | 1 | |
| Others (specify) | | | | | | | | | |

File: PMFORMS\Document Distribution

**Figure 20–11** Document distribution matrix.

stakeholders up front and decisions agreed to by the project manager. Once this is done, each document can be coded as to its type (e.g., bill of material) and a process can be put in place for support personnel to make immediate distribution.

There should never be a bottleneck in communications, especially document distribution. E-mail can facilitate distribution. Here it is necessary to make sure that all recipients and the receiving system have the capability to receive documents sent by the version of the software the sender is using. This is particularly true for attachments to E-mail. It is frustrating to receive files that cannot be "opened."

Project review meetings are a critical communication mechanism. They are best when the meeting forum is open and critical stakeholders are present. See Chapter 21 on conducting project reviews.

Typically, the project plan is the yardstick, and various groups report project status or tracking against "the plan." These meetings should be scheduled in advance and the agenda well planned. If the project manager does all the talking, she learns very little. The agenda should be structured so that the meeting is a status report and coordination meeting with problems identified and well defined but not necessarily solved in the meeting. Separate meetings can be established for problem solving. Status of safety, schedule, cost, and coordination are typical agenda items. Using earned value analysis to measure project status is a very useful approach. Minutes should be taken and issued promptly. The minutes should reflect action items with responsibility and timetables. Projects have a relatively short life, and actions take on a new meaning.

## EXPEDITING

It is best to start with the premise that there is always something on the critical path and that events of the project could change the critical path. Therefore, expediting skills will be needed. Once critical path items are known, it can be determined if expediting will be done by the owner, the supplier, or a third party. Early decisions and arrangements will allow this function the lead time it needs to be successful. It is sometimes necessary to book special trucks, trains, boats, or planes. It is sometimes expeditious to use a port of entry familiar to the expediter. It may also be necessary to obtain state permits to haul "oversized" loads. All of this takes time to plan and execute. The worst time to engage expediting service is after a critical date is missed.

## DISPUTE RESOLUTION

Disputes can occur at many levels. They need to be thought about up front and procedures put in place so that disputes are identified and resolved in a professional manner. *In no event should a dispute become disruptive to the project.* Dispute resolution procedures should be included in every purchase order and in every contract.

There are a number of procedures that can be used, but two important principles should be observed. First, the problem must be accurately stated and documented. Experience has shown that many disputes arise from

> A dispute should never become disruptive to the project.

an inaccurate or unclear description of the problem. Second, all parties should agree ahead of time on the dispute resolution process and agree to follow it.

One process will be outlined here, but as previously stated, there are others. The first step is to establish a detailed definition of the problem, which all parties can support. The easy first step is frequently overlooked. The second step is to apply the principles of the purchase order or contract to the problem. This shows the importance of including quantifiable definitions of the three types of specifications in each purchase order or contract.

The third step is to negotiate a resolution of the problem. Use of established negotiating techniques can be of value at this step. The fourth step is to delegate the resolution to higher levels of management on each side. As you can see, it is helpful if the contract specifies the exact level of higher management by title or name. Typically, this will be someone who can approve a scope or funding change. The final step is to take the dispute to an "independent third party." Some choose arbitration. Others have noted that arbitration has a leveling or averaging impact and have specifically deleted this from all contracts. Their reasoning is that significant effort should be put into developing good contracts and selecting good suppliers, which results in few disputes. In the instance of an unresolved dispute, the legal system can be used to achieve an equitable resolution.

# 21

## CHAPTER

# Conducting Project Reviews

Throughout the life of a project, there are various reviews that should be conducted. The timing, manner, and follow-up of these reviews is important to the success of the project and subsequent ones.

There are three kinds of reviews that might be done on a project. These are listed in the following table:

**Project Reviews and Their Nature**

| | |
|---|---|
| Status | Looks at the status of cost, performance, schedule, and scope |
| Design | Examines a product, service, or software design to see if it meets requirements |
| Process | Examines project processes and asks if they can be improved |

## STATUS REVIEWS

The most frequent review is the status review. There are two levels of this review—cursory and comprehensive. A cursory review might be held weekly, whereas a comprehensive one might be monthly. How often status reviews should be held is a judgment call, but my suggestion would be that for projects of less than a year's duration, a weekly cursory review is about right, with a monthly comprehensive review. For projects of greater than a one-year duration, monthly reviews are probably okay unless problems exist. When problems occur in a project, more frequent reviews are generally held until the problem is corrected. Care should be taken not to fall into the trap of micromanaging—unless the team is in so much trouble that it is required.

I also do not consider a review to be sufficient that goes like this:

"How is project googleplex going?"

"Okay."

"Great. How about project sillyputty?"

"It's okay."

The only way such a review can be valid is if "okay" is backed up with some numerical data that is meaningful. This means that the project manager knows something about the actual level of cost, performance, time, and scope. In too many cases people tell you they are on target when they are nowhere close, so measures are necessary. This topic is covered in Chapter 17.

I do consider that reporting on projects should be on an exception basis. That is, I need to report on deviations that are greater than my variance thresholds and tell what the potential impact might be and what is being done about them. A reporting form like the one in Figure 21–1 captures this. The form should be filled out *only* to report deviations. If no deviations exist, then a periodic report that says everything is okay, backed up by numerical data, is sufficient. You do need that report, since no information is uninformative.

## CORRECTING PROBLEMS RATHER THAN PLACING BLAME

There are times when someone in a project team does something totally stupid or unprofessional. In such a case, that person deserves to be sanctioned. However, I am very opposed to the organization that operates in the blame-and-punishment mode all the time. If you are always looking for witches, you generally find them. If people know they are going to be trashed for every slip, then they will try to protect themselves by hiding those problems,

## Project Progress Report

| Project: | Prepared by: |
|---|---|
| For the period from        to | Date: |

Accomplishments for this report period are:




We are ☐ ahead, ☐ behind, ☐ on schedule

| List any changes to project objectives: | List any changes in our business climate that might affect your project: |
|---|---|

What problems do we face that were originally unanticipated?


| What needs to be changed? | List anyone whose approval is needed for those changes: |
|---|---|

| List any additional *anticipated* problems: | Action steps which I plan to take: |
|---|---|

Comments:


PROGRESS.61

**Figure 21–1** Progress report form.

and this may mean that the problems will only reveal themselves when the situation is too serious to correct easily.

Status reviews should always be conducted in a problem-solving mode. We want to know (1) what problems exist, (2) what is causing them, and (3) what must be done to solve them. Notice that the word "what" is used in each case. It is a good idea to delete the word "why" from your vocabulary. When you ask someone why a problem exists, you almost always arouse a bit of defensiveness. I personally think we become conditioned to be defensive when we hear the word "why," since our parents often asked why we did some unacceptable thing, then trashed us after we explained. So the sequence that we expect is:

1. Why did you do this very forbidden thing?
2. I don't know. The devil made me do it.
3. That's not acceptable as an answer. Go to your room! You're grounded for 100 years!

So, since we don't want to be grounded for 100 years when we do something unacceptable in projects, we try to hide it, blame it on the guy in the next cubicle, or pretend we didn't notice it if someone finds out.

> **Status reviews should always be conducted in a problem-solving mode.**

Once problems are identified, you should follow standard problem-solving procedure to deal with them. It is amazing to me how we often totally ignore this process. We need to get to the root cause of the problem rather than dealing with a symptom. Then we should generate alternative solutions. Next a solution should be selected, tried, and revised if it doesn't work. Often, what is done is a lot of flailing around that only makes the situation worse. The most serious error is self-deception, in which we convince ourselves that the situation is not so bad. The ship is sinking, but since it is going down very slowly, there is no need for concern.

## THE DESIGN REVIEW

Whether you are designing a new product, writing software, developing a new service, or planning to move a facility, the purpose of a design review is to ensure that the final "deliverable," or outcome of the project, is on track. Will it do what it is supposed to do? Are there performance issues that must be addressed? If it is an actual product being developed (I am considering software a product), and it appears unlikely that it will meet the original specifications, do these need to be changed? If they are, will the customer still accept them? Design reviews are usually conducted at major milestones in a project.

To some degree, the design review is focused on the P component of the cost, performance, time, and scope equation. If we do not perform the design work correctly, then the product will not do what it is supposed to do. That being the case, the project may be headed for serious trouble.

In the chapter on defining success and failure, we saw that one definition of failure is that the deliverable is not accepted by the customer. We can get through on time, within budget, on scope, but if the thing does not work correctly and the customer rejects it, then the project might be deemed a failure. The question is: How critical is the performance issue? If it is serious and we cannot achieve the required performance, should the project be canceled? Marvin Patterson, formerly vice president of product development at Hewlett-Packard, says that the most productive thing you can do is cancel a losing product development project *as early as possible* (Patterson, 1993). Cut your losses and get on with something else!

This is one area in which technical people can fool themselves. They are convinced that they can make it work, if just given enough time. Their egos won't let them admit that the thing doesn't work, that they have no clue how to make it work, and that even if they are given forever, they still might not be able to make it work. So they plod on, ever hopeful of success. There is a difference between a positive mental attitude, wishful thinking, and correct assessment of reality. It is certainly hard to tell sometimes. Success *might* be just around the corner.

This is where peer review is useful, if you can get peers to be honest with each other. Unfortunately, we find that people in technical professions tend to be reluctant to trash someone else's work. It may be a fear of reciprocation, or it may be an honest concern that solving problems is unpredictable, so they don't want to advise pulling the plug too soon. Whatever the case, peer review is the best you have, but it's not always as objective as it should be, so sometimes nontechnical managers must make judgments to shut down a project over the protest of the technical people. You will be public enemy number one, but you may save the company a lot of money.

To ensure a proper evaluation of a design, ANSI N45.2.11 and ANSI/ASME NQA-1 have established design review criteria. These criteria are widely used and should be adopted for any program involving a design review. They are shown in Figure 21–2.

---

**DESIGN REVIEW ELEMENTS**

1. Were the inputs correctly selected and incorporated into design?
2. Are assumptions necessary to perform the design activity adequately described and reason able? Where necessary, are the assumptions identified for subsequent reverifications when the detailed design activities are completed?
3. Are the appropriate quality and quality assurance requirements specified?
4. Are the applicable codes, standards, and regulatory requirements—including issue and addenda—properly identified, and are their requirements for design met?
5. Have applicable construction and operating experience been considered?
6. Have the design interface requirements been satisfied?
7. Was an appropriate design method used?
8. Is the output reasonable compared to the inputs?
9. Are the specified parts, equipment, and processes suitable for the required application?
10. Are the specified materials compatible with each other and the design environmental conditions to which the material will be exposed?
11. Have adequate maintenance features and requirements been specified?
12. Are accessibility and other design provisions adequate for performance of needed maintenance and repair?
13. Has adequate accessibility been provided to perform the in-service inspection expected to be required during the plant life?
14. Has the design properly considered radiation exposure to the public and plant personnel?
15. Are the acceptance criteria incorporated in the design documents sufficient to allow verification that design requirements have been satisfactorily accomplished?
16. Have adequate preoperational and subsequent periodic test requirements been appropriately specified?
17. Are adequate handling, storage, cleaning, and shipping requirements specified?
18. Are adequate identification requirements specified?
19. Are requirements for record preparation review, acceptance, retention, etc., adequately specified?

---

**Figure 21–2**  Design review elements.

(Excerpt from ANSI N45.2.11 and ANSI/ASME NQA-1) Reprinted by permission of American Society of Mechanical Engineers.

When products are being designed for manufacture, the review must include conditions of manufacturability and serviceability. The specifics of the manufacturing process should consider tooling, economics of special machinery and processes, and integration of the design with manufacturing to ensure overall optimization. As in the ANSI guidelines for serviceability and warranty, in Figure 21–2, there are considerations such as ease-of-access, safety to operators and maintenance personnel, and protection from damage due to inadvertent use. To confirm proper scope and technical content, a scope description must be available against which comparisons can be made.

It should be noted that these conditions are for formal design reviews. Project managers are encouraged to practice MBWA (management by walking around) throughout the life of the project in order to have a feeling for whether the work is proceeding well in terms of design quality. It may be too late to easily correct minor problems inexpensively if you wait until a formal design review to identify them.

## PROCESS REVIEWS

Process reviews are focused on *how* we are doing what we are doing. Can the work process be improved in any way? What things are we doing that we want to keep on doing? Chapter 23 is devoted to process improvement, so in this chapter, I want to just deal with how the process review should be conducted.

A process is a way of doing something. Communication is a process. Leadership is a process. So are decision-making, problem-solving, meeting management, and planning. (For a more complete listing, see Chapter 23.) Process reviews should be held at major milestones in a project or every three months, whichever comes first. The reason for the three month rule is that this seems to be about the limit of people's memories. For very short projects, you might have a process review once a month.

The important thing to remember in process reviews is that you are trying to maintain what is being done well and improve those processes that need improvement. You are not out to get someone! So the process review should be conducted by asking two questions:

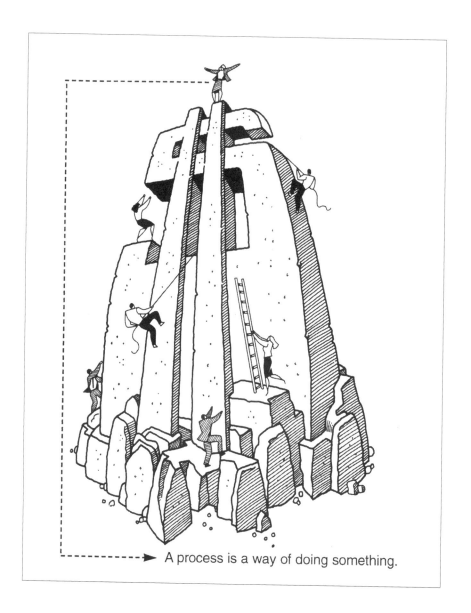

A process is a way of doing something.

1. What are we doing well so far?
2. What would we like to improve?

Notice that I do not ask, "What are we doing wrong?" We may not be doing anything wrong, but we can almost always improve. I also do not like the method of writing a plus sign (+) on one flip chart page and a minus sign (–) on another to indicate okay and needs improvement. A minus has a connotation of things being done wrong, and when you suggest that things are being done wrong, people tend to get defensive. When that happens, you will never hear about things that should be improved.

As a matter of fact, one of the biggest barriers to doing process reviews is the aversion that people have to "airing their dirty laundry." This is especially true when you suggest that what we learn in one group should be shared with other teams so that they can take advantage of it. People don't want to do this. Yet learning is expensive, and an organization needs to take advantage of all learning.

I suggest that companies should have periodic reviews, perhaps quarterly, in which project managers share with each other in a public forum what they have learned. If organizations could adopt the approach used by the army to review themselves, they could improve tremendously. This can be done by adopting a rule that *after anything significant happens, we will take the time to ask what we can learn from it.*

Years ago I knew a fellow who was consulting with a glass company to help them improve their quality. One day he went into the plant and everyone was celebrating.

"What's going on?" he asked.

"We just had a great day," someone said.

"Tell me about it."

"Well, we just had an 85 percent yield," said the person.

"How did you do it?" asked the consultant.

"We don't know," was the response.

Clearly, if they don't know, they can't repeat it. And this happens all too often in organizations everywhere.

## WHO SHOULD CONDUCT THE REVIEW?

Process reviews can be conducted by the project manager or by an outside facilitator. There are advantages either way. If you, as project manager, have good group process skills, then you can conduct the review. One downside is that leadership is a process and should be open for improvement, and that means the group will have to give you feedback on your leadership style. Unless the group is used to doing this, they may be very hesitant to do so. They don't know what the repercussions will be. If that is the case, an outside facilitator might get better information.

# 22 CHAPTER

# Managing Quality in Projects

As I have pointed out a number of times throughout this book, there are four variables that we always deal with in projects: cost, performance, time, and scope. Cost and time get most of the attention, scope is next, and performance (quality of work done) is dead last. In fact, when you put enough pressure on people to meet deadlines, stay on budget, and do all of the work assigned, they invariably sacrifice quality. One problem with this is that we don't know about it until it is much too late to do anything about it.

A project manager at a steel mill told me once, "If you finish a project a little late, go over budget, and maybe don't quite have all the scope you origi-

> If you finish late, over budget, and below scope, and the thing still works, you will probably be forgiven.

nally promised, but the thing still works, you'll generally be forgiven. On the other hand, if all these things happen and it doesn't work on top of that, then you're in serious trouble." He makes a very good point.

It is now 17 years since the quality "movement" started in the United States, and I find people seem to be losing interest in quality. They have been part of so many program-of-the-month efforts to improve quality that they are a bit glazed over. Yet, if we lose sight of quality, we ultimately wind up in trouble.

## WHAT IS IT ANYWAY?

After all these years of quality improvement, I still find people mistaking quality for sophistication. So it seems that we should revisit the definition of quality before going on. After all, if we don't have the same understanding of the word, much of the discussion won't make any sense.

**Quality is meeting the needs of the customer.**

There are two common definitions of quality. One is that quality is conformance to specifications or requirements. The other is that quality is meeting the needs of the customer. Some people call this "fit for use." Both definitions arrive at the same point, if you understand that the specifications or requirements must be developed in such a way that the customer's needs will be met if specs and/or requirements are met.

Another axiom of quality is that *only the customer can tell you what quality means to him or her.* Sometimes technical people want to shove their idea of quality down the customer's throat, but that is not the quality way. As we discussed in Chapter 14, QFD is one approach for determining those factors that must be met in order for the customer to be satisfied with a product or service.

**Only the customer can tell you what quality means.**

Quality management is the managing of all functions and activities necessary to determine and achieve quality (fitness for use). Like functional managers, project managers must also manage for quality. Failing to do so can be costly.

In several places I have written that many experts estimate that as much as 30 percent of the cost to develop new products is rework. This is not surprising to those of us who have been associated with the quality movement since its early days in the 1980s. We knew back then that from 5 to 40 percent of factory effort to produce products goes into scrap and rework. Rework is total waste. It is lost to the factory, since it cannot be reclaimed. Scrap is not quite totally wasted, because there is some salvage value to the waste product. The impact of this is that if you have 100 plants, all making the same products, and your scrap and rework total 30 percent, then this is equivalent of having 30 plants working full time to turn out nothing!

> Rework is an inverse measure of quality!

Hopefully, you won't find too many plants today with such high scrap and rework figures. If they have applied quality improvement methods to their manufacturing processes, they should have largely eliminated these problems. Trouble is, we haven't applied the things we learned in factories to knowledge work processes—at least not until recently.

Although Deming argued that we need to improve all processes, the awareness that this meant processes outside manufacturing seems to have been missed until it was provoked by Hammer's and Champy's book *Reengineering the Organization* (1993). They made managers aware that the same improvements that have been made in manufacturing can be made in other areas of the organization. The focus is on *processes*—the way in which we get work done. In Chapter 23, I discuss improving those processes that specifically affect project management. However, within projects themselves, there are work processes that should be examined for improvement opportunities.

## QUALITY COSTS

The term quality costs is actually misleading. What we are really concerned with is the cost of *poor quality,* or the cost of nonconformance to our requirements. For the purpose of brevity, however, I will use the term quality costs to mean the cost of poor quality.

Quality costs can be divided into three categories. These are easy to remember by using the acronym PAF. This means *prevention, appraisal,* and *failure.* Prevention costs are normally considered to be quality assurance costs. These are the costs of any action taken to prevent or reduce defects and failures. Included would be the cost of planning and managing quality systems and the preventive elements of such systems.

Appraisal means inspection. These are the costs of determining what level of quality has been achieved. They include such factors as:

1. Inspection and testing
2. Vendor control
3. Checking documents
4. Process validation
5. Checking specifications
6. Product sampling

Failure costs are the costs of nonconformance. These are the result of doing things wrong, and include:

1. Repairs and rework
2. Loss of customers
3. Warranty costs
4. Increased insurance costs
5. Investigating the causes of defects

A typical distribution for these costs is shown in Figure 22–1. Note that appraisal and failure can exceed profits. Thus, any reduction in failure and appraisal costs can go directly to profits. This is discussed in the next section.

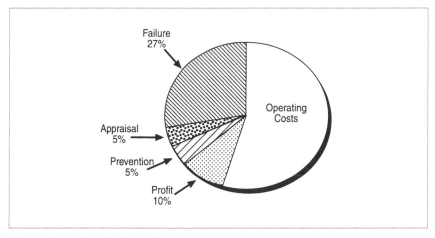

**Figure 22–1** Distribution of business costs.

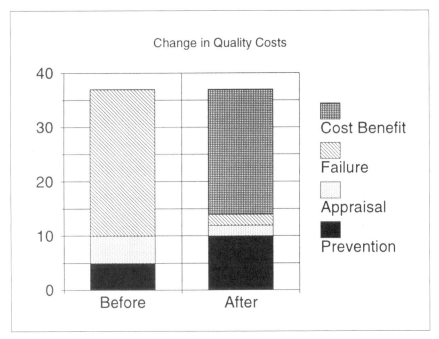

**Figure 22–2** Cost benefit of improved quality.

## THE BENEFIT OF QUALITY IMPROVEMENT

Before the application of quality improvement methods, it is commonplace to find that the cost of appraisal and failure is 80 percent of total quality cost, while prevention is only 20 percent. By increasing prevention costs, that is, doing things that will prevent problems, you can reduce the cost of appraisal and failure and gain a net cost benefit for the organization, which translates directly into a bottom line profit. This is shown in Figure 22–2. Notice that we have not totally eliminated inspection (appraisal). The long-term objective would be to eliminate inspection, but you may never completely get there.

## QUALITY MANAGEMENT PRINCIPLES AND PRACTICES

There are three principles of quality management that must be applied in order to have an effective system:

1. *Quality is everyone's business.* Every function in an organization must be performed in accordance with quality principles.
2. *Do it right the first time every time.* Phil Crosby, a former vice president of quality at ITT, was fond of saying that it always costs less to do it right the first time than to do it over. Rework is wasted effort and can be expensive, as has been mentioned before. It should be noted, however, that management must ensure that systems, equipment, and services used by employees to do their work are capable of sustaining the level of quality desired. If not, it is management's responsibility to replace these with the proper ones.
3. *Communicate and cooperate.* Everybody should know what to do, where they fit within the organization, and with whom they interface. In projects, this is achieved by proper planning, role definition, and coordination.

## DEVELOPING A QUALITY SYSTEM FOR A PROJECT

Assuming that the organization has an overall quality system, there needs to be one specific to projects. If no overall system exists in the organization, then it will be next to impossible to achieve project quality of the desired level. Furthermore, a project quality system cannot stand alone and do the job.

A quality system is also known as a quality plan. Developing a quality plan for a project will depend on the total project work scope. Like the overall project plan, you should begin with defining your quality objectives. What is the system intended to achieve?

The quality plan should be part of the overall project documentation and should detail the specific quality practices, resources, and activities relevant to a particular product, service, contract, or project. The company's overall quality system will need some modification to suit each project. These can be additions to or reduction of the company system. For example, if only design activities are engaged in, then the company's system dealing with design would be adapted for the project.

## DETAILED PROCEDURES

Procedures should exist that, if followed, will ensure that work is done right the first time. Ideally, such procedures should be developed only by personnel familiar with the particular activities and functions. Each procedure should define the purpose and scope of the relevant activity and specify how it is to be properly performed. Sometimes the quality assurance department has to develop these, though this is not the best approach. Note that the project manager is ultimately responsible for the quality of the project on completion.

PART FIVE

# OPTIMIZING PROJECT PERFORMANCE

# 23 CHAPTER

# Improving Project Management Processes

There is a saying in psychology that says a lot about the need for performance improvement. It goes: If you always do what you've always done, you'll always get what you always got. The corollary to this is: If you have tried something repeatedly and have not gotten the desired result, try something different!

Dr. W. Edwards Deming used to say that there are two kinds of organizations—those that are getting better and those that are dying. If you're standing still, you're dying; you just don't know it yet. Your competition isn't standing still, so if you are, they will eventually pass you by. He used this point to argue for continuous improvement in organizations. The same can be applied to overall companies or groups within them. This includes project teams.

> If you always do what you've always done, you'll always get what you always got.

No sports team with any credibility would go an entire season without trying to improve. They practice to simply maintain status quo—they try to get better. To do this, they practice, watch game films to give players feedback on past performance, coach the players, try new plays, and change players and coaches if need be. In fact, the most dangerous place a team can be is successful, because they become complacent. They think they are on top and nobody can drag them down. The same is true of organizations. Judith Bardwick wrote a book entitled *Danger in the Comfort Zone* that echoes this idea.

Yet project teams seldom stop to ask if they can improve. In fact, this is one of the major causes of project failure. Team building is the forgotten side of project management. We get so focused on the task at hand that we totally forget about process issues. This is a concern for *what* must be done to the exclusion of concern for the *how* it is being done. The flaw is that process issues will always affect task performance, to quote Marvin Weisbord.

> "Process issues will *always* affect task performance."
> —Marvin Weisbord

One pressure that is being felt by many project managers today is to get their jobs done faster and cheaper at the same time, while holding performance and scope constant. At first glance, this sounds contradictory, since there is usually an inverse relationship between reducing time in a project and the cost to do the work. That is, as we try to do the work faster, the costs tend to go up. This is shown in Figure 23–1.

However, this curve is drawn assuming that the processes of doing work remain unchanged and all we are doing is adding resources to the team. That being the case, you cannot simultaneously reduce time and costs both.

On the other hand, by changing the process by which work is done, you can reduce both at the same time. Note also that doing work correctly the first time will help achieve this result. Elsewhere, I have written that the typical rework cost in a project ranges from 5 to 40 percent. Rework is totally wasted. As one chief engineer said, when the rework in a project is 30 percent, that is equivalent to having one person out of every three on the staff to just redo what the other two did wrong. If you reduce the rework, you get the job done faster and cheaper at the same time.

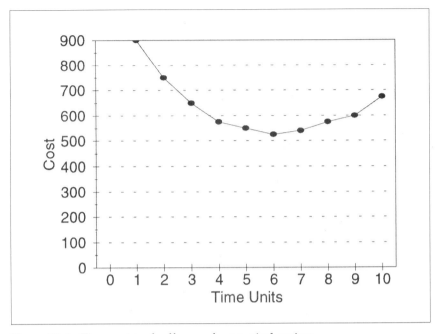

**Figure 23–1**  Time-cost tradeoff curve for a typical project.

One of the contributors to rework is definitely a process issue. It is how well the project is defined and planned at the very beginning. The tendency here is to avoid the initial pain of planning. Unfortunately, you pay now or pay later, and it is almost always cheaper to pay now than later. As my colleague Bob Wysocki jokes, "You pain now or pain later." This is shown in Figure 23–2. Good project planning causes a lot of pain at the beginning, but the pain diminishes as the project progresses. With no planning or cursory planning, there is not much pain at the beginning, but it grows significantly as the project goes ahead.

You might remember, from our discussion of systems issues, that one reason for this is that as rework goes up, more overtime is required, which causes greater fatigue, which leads to more errors that have to be corrected (reworked), which means more overtime, and on and on. It is a vicious spiral, getting progressively worse. This is indicated graphically by the exponential increase in pain.

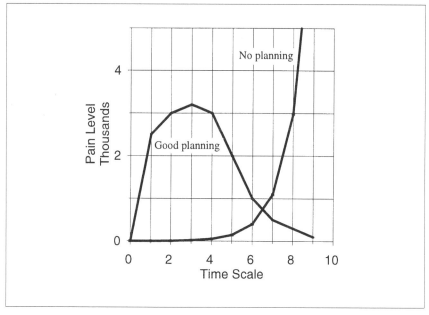

**Figure 23–2**  Pain curve in project management.

## IDENTIFYING PROCESSES

A process is a way of doing something. In Egyptian times, a form of writing called hieroglyphics was invented. Each symbol initially stood for a word, or maybe an idea. This same kind of system was invented by the Chinese. The problem is that you need to remember about 1800 of these to have a good working vocabulary. Eventually, alphabets were invented, which permitted words to be built up from letters, so that with a knowledge of 26 to 30 characters, you could represent any word in the language. This also meant that the way you write those symbols changed. Hieroglyphics are often painted with a brush. Alphabetical characters can be easily written with stylus, pen, or brush. They can also be typed. Thus, the invention of the typewriter speeded up the process of putting words on paper. More recently, the invention of computers has taken us a step further. All of these steps were refinements of the process of conveying ideas to others through written means.

All process improvements tend to follow an S-curve, as shown in Figure 23–3. Initially, gains in process improvement are

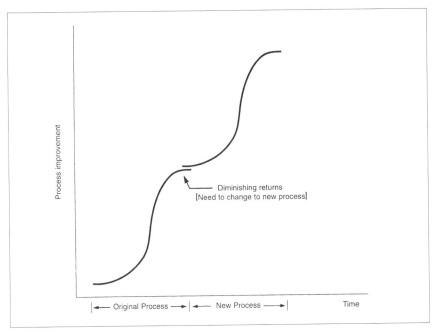

**Figure 23–3**  Process improvement curves.

hard to come by. Then considerable progress is made. Finally, the gains become harder and harder to achieve. We sometimes say that we are *pushing the envelope* at either the beginning or end of the process improvement curve.

Notice that when the end of a process improvement cycle is reached and the gains become difficult to achieve, it is time to throw out the old process and invent an entirely new one. Unfortunately, some managers get hung up trying to improve a process that should be eliminated because it is at the end of its improvement cycle, but they don't realize this.

> There is no point in trying to improve a process that should be replaced altogether.

Interestingly, organizations that are just getting started with formal project management are down on the low side of the process improvement curve, and they experience significant startup difficulty. This sometimes causes them to throw out the process entirely, because they are experiencing too much initial pain. They don't realize that they will soon cross the peak if they stick with it, and will then be in for an easy ride down the right-hand slope of the pain curve (Figure 23–2).

Following is a list of some of the processes involved in getting projects done. None of these are meant to have to do with technical aspects of the work. They are all a part of the project management process only.

### Some of the Processes of Project Management

| | | |
|---|---|---|
| Communicating | Decision Making | Leadership |
| Negotiating | Problem Solving | Creative Thinking |
| Scheduling | Planning | The Work Itself |
| Monitoring Status | Change Control | Meetings |
| Team Building | Conflict Resolution | Administrative |

## SOME PRINCIPLES OF PROCESS IMPROVEMENT

The first idea that I believe is useful to consider in process improvement is that if we have learned how to improve processes in one domain, we should be able to apply some of what was learned there to other processes. Part of the reason for this is that processes must conform to some of the rules of system behavior, which we discussed in Chapter 9. In that chapter we found that systems that have similar structures can be expected to behave similarly, regardless of the content involved in the system process.

For that reason, since we have had so much experience with process improvement in manufacturing, we should be able to adopt some of the procedures used in that area and apply them to improving project management processes. In a previous section of this chapter, I mentioned the pressure to get projects completed quicker. There have been a number of books written in recent years on speeding up the product development process. These include *Accelerating Innovation* (Patterson, 1993), *Developing Products in Half the Time* (Smith & Reinertsen, 1995), and *Revolutionizing Product Development* (Wheelwright & Clark, 1992), to name just a few. As I have noted elsewhere, however, product development should not be confused with project management. Similar pressures to speed up projects are being felt in all kinds of projects, not just in product development.

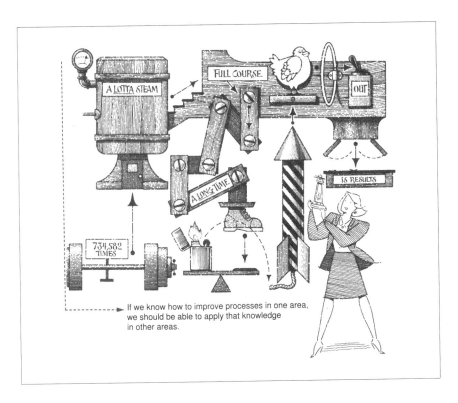

If we know how to improve processes in one area, we should be able to apply that knowledge in other areas.

One of the first points that must be made about improving a process is that it should be running smoothly already, or it is nearly impossible to tell if it has been improved. If you are familiar with statistical process control (SPC) methodology, we would say that the process should be in control before you begin changing it. The second point is that it requires good planning to improve a process, and this, in turn, requires that the process be well-understood. We will discuss understanding processes in the next section.

Patterson lists a number of things that can be done to reduce manufacturing time, and it is instructive to examine these with respect to projects. I have adapted his list, as shown in Table 23–1 (Patterson, 1993, p. 101).

Improve process quality. Anything that you can do to reduce errors that lead to rework will improve overall process performance, especially speed. Improvements in planning generally reduce errors due to false starts. Time spent planning must be balanced, of course. It is not productive if the team goes into analysis paralysis because they are afraid to make any planning errors.

**T A B L E  23–1**

Actions That Reduce Manufacturing Cycle Time

- ◆ Improve process quality (in particular, minimize rework)
- ◆ Implement concurrent processes
- ◆ Add value as rapidly as possible at each step
- ◆ Improve quality and timeliness of incoming materials
- ◆ Eliminate work that adds no value
- ◆ Minimize changeover time (reduce setup time)
- ◆ Eliminate bottlenecks

*Implement concurrent processes.* If we can do as many things as possible in parallel rather than in series, we can speed up project work. Care must be taken to balance risk with gains in speed. When interdependent tasks are performed concurrently, you definitely increase risk that costs will be incurred because the work done in one step negates that done in the (normally subsequent) next step.

*Add value as rapidly as possible at each process step.* In manufacturing, raw materials themselves have almost no value to customers. It is only after they have been formed, shaped, machined, stamped, or molded that they have value. In projects, the same idea would apply. Every step in the project should increase the value of the final product that will be delivered to the customer. Related to this idea, perhaps as a corollary, is the point about *eliminating any step that adds no value.* Setup time, for example, is an operation that provides no value, but may have to be done if a single machine is used for multiple tasks. The longer the run of parts on that machine before a changeover is made, the smaller the setup time as a percentage of the total. The same is true of people. If we can reduce the interruptions and transitions that they experience, the more productive they become.

> Every step in a project should add value to the end "product," or it should be eliminated.

One example of eliminating steps that add no value is in iterating over and over to make something work. Elsewhere, I have discussed using design of experiments to eliminate the design-test-redesign iteration that creates an endless loop in projects. Wherever feasible, this approach is preferable to multiple iterations.

Another subject that is near and dear to the hearts of many of us is the wastefulness of meetings. For goodness sake, get a copy of *Mining Group Gold* by Tom Kaiser (1995) and practice his model in running your meetings. It will improve your efficiency tremendously. The model is also available on film from CRM Films. See the Resources section in Appendix A for ordering information.

*Improve quality and timeliness of incoming materials.* A manufacturer who receives shoddy raw materials can hardly produce quality products. Considerable time and money were once spent on incoming inspection of materials. Selection of good vendors and partnership arrangements can greatly improve the quality of incoming goods and reduce later incurred cost of poor quality manufactured product. In the same way, projects of any kind need good raw materials with which to work. When projects are done primarily by knowledge workers, this means *the right information at the right time.* If the information arrives too late, it will be of no benefit to the current job. If it arrives too early, it may not be recognized as relevant, though if an error is to be made, it should be made in the direction of too early as opposed to too late. A good reference librarian can be an immense help for this issue. What is needed is akin to a just-in-time (JIT) information system.

*Streamline the flow of materials.* In manufacturing, modern assembly lines are characterized by the well-planned flow of materials from beginning to end. Good project planning should result in the same smooth flow of information or work from one stage to another. For local project teams, this means that all members of the team have access to information on a timely basis through a local area network (LAN). For dispersed teams, a wide area network (WAN) is needed.

*Eliminate bottlenecks.* A bottleneck is a point in a process that restricts the flow of materials. In construction projects, bottlenecks are often caused by agencies that must approve building plans or perform environmental impact studies or archaeological surveys. You often can't eliminate these or speed them up, since you have no control over them. About all you can do is work around them.

Sometimes a single support group becomes a bottleneck because they are servicing so many teams that they lack capacity to do it well. Bottlenecks are resolved by identifying the root cause of the limited capacity and then investing in the resources needed to bring capacity up to the required level. Needless to say, the economy of keeping a support group "lean and mean" can be greatly offset by the loss of time in dependent teams. However, since project managers are not always able to influence the powers that be to deal with bottlenecks properly, the best defense is to have work that can be productively done while waiting for other work to clear the bottleneck.

## OPERATIONAL DEFINITIONS OF PROBLEMS

I cannot stress strongly enough how important it is that problems be defined correctly so that we solve the right problem. It should be clear that such a definition must be one that everyone understands and agrees with. Unless everyone has the same understanding of a problem, there is no way to solve it. What is needed is an operational definition. An operational definition establishes a language that communicates the same meaning to everyone involved in solving the problem. Since our focus here is on improving processes, this language will specifically apply to the processes we are trying to improve. Words such as "defective," "unsafe," or "inadequate" have no meaning unless they are operationally defined.

> Unless everyone has the same understanding of a problem, it is almost impossible to solve it.

To illustrate how confusion can be caused by the absence of operational definitions, consider a label on a shirt that reads "75% cotton." What does this mean? Is it three-quarters cotton, on the average, throughout the shirt? Or is it three-quarters cotton applied to shirts over a month's production? Is it three-quarters by linear measure or by weight? If by weight, at what humidity? Does humidity affect the noncotton component the same as the cotton?

Another example: The team says communication is poor. What does this mean? Communication consists of transmitting and receiving. Is transmission the problem, or is it receiving? Is the person talking using precise language? Or are listeners not paying attention? Is the transmission being affected by noise, so that it is not received properly? What are the tangible effects of the communication? Misunderstandings, missed dates, work done incorrectly, or conflicts? Until we arrive at a shared understanding of what is meant by "poor communication," we can't possibly solve the problem.

A given operational definition is not necessarily right or wrong. It's importance lies in its acceptance by all parties involved in trying to deal with the process. As conditions change, the operational definition may change to meet new needs.

An operational definition consists of:

1. A criterion to be applied to an object or to a group
2. A test of the object or of the group
3. A decision as to whether the object or group did or did not meet the criterion

The project team is told that they are expected to do their work on time and within budget, while maintaining performance as expected and doing the predefined amount (scope) of work. This statement is loaded with problems. What does on time and within budget mean? Can there be a tolerance? If so, how much? If not, we are expecting the impossible, because all processes vary. To expect people to get work done *exactly* on time is unrealistic. In the first place, where did the time frame come from? It was an estimate, so by definition, it is not exact.

Now, if we know that we can typically achieve schedule and budget tolerances of ± 10 percent, then we can operationally define on time and within budget as being within this tolerance. By the same token, we must operationally define performance requirements. If the person is writing software, how do you define the performance requirement? Less than so many bugs in the entire program? It executes at a certain speed? It has no more than $x$ lines of code? All of the above?

Here is an example of actually applying the conditions to arrive at an operational definition. A salesperson is told that her performance will be judged with respect to the percentage of change in this year's sales over last year's sales. What does this mean? Average percentage sales each month? Each week? For each product? Percentage between December 31, 1997 and December 31, 1998? How are we measuring sales? Is it gross, net, gross profit, net profit. You get the picture.

Step 1: Develop a criterion for percentage change in sales.

A percentage change in sales is the difference between 1998 sales (January 1, 1998 to December 31, 1998) and 1997 sales (January 1, 1997 to December 31, 1997):

$$\text{Percentage change } (97 - 98) = (S98 - S97)/S97$$

where:
    S98 = dollar sales volume for January 1–December 31, 1998
    S97 = dollar sales volume for January 1–December 31, 1997.

S97 is measured in constant dollars.

Steps 2 and 3. Test the decision on percentage change in sales. This will be done by looking at 1997 and 1998 sales figures and performing the computations.

## AN EXAMPLE OF IDENTIFYING A PROCESS PROBLEM

The team has missed the last two project milestones. The project manager is feeling the heat to make sure this does not happen again, as the project deadline is highly critical to the business and if milestones are slipping, it is likely that the end date will be missed. To help identify the possible cause or causes of this problem, you might want to use an Ishikawa diagram, which is shown in generic form in Figure 23–4. The model is also called a fishbone or cause-effect diagram. The problem you are trying to solve is noted in the box to the right and possible causes are listed on the "bones" of the diagram, grouped according to general categories. This list is usually generated through brainstorming.

Once the list has been created, you classify each variable with a C, N, or X, as follows:

C (Constant):        These are variables that we intend to
                     hold constant so that we can achieve
                     the desired response, or possibly to
                     reduce extraneous variation in the
                     response. For each of these variables,
                     we need a standard operating procedure
                     to tell us how the variable is being
                     controlled.

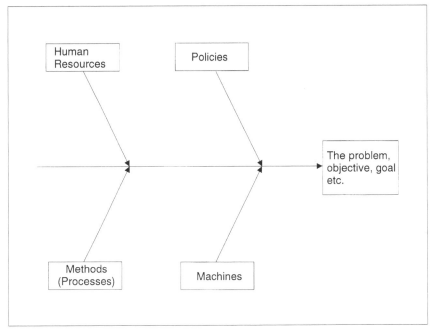

**Figure 23–4**  The generic Ishikawa diagram.

N (Noise):                These are uncontrolled variables.
                          They cause "noise" in the system.
                          Although they do affect system
                          response, they are too difficult or too
                          expensive to hold constant.

X (Experimental):  If an experiment is to be run, these are
                          the factors to be investigated. Not all
                          cause-and-effect diagrams will contain
                          X factors. However, a variable that is a
                          C today could become an X tomorrow
                          if we decide to investigate the effect
                          experimentally (and vice versa).

In using the Ishikawa diagram or any other approach, you have to be careful not to fall into the trap of having people give you causes at too high a level. For example, you ask your group to tell you what they think are problems affecting project team performance, and you get a list like the following:

1. Lack of leadership
2. Poor communication
3. Unclear mission and objectives
4. Inadequate workspace
5. Lack of training

The difficulty with this list is that people have concluded that lack of leadership is a cause, based on some lower-level cause. At this point, you don't know what the real problems are to which your team is attributing the causes. To understand the real problem, you now need to ask, "What *effect* is lack of leadership (or any of the others) having on our team?" The person says, "I think members of the team are demoralized just now."

She is attributing low morale to lack of leadership. But is that true? We would have to look more closely to determine if some aspect of the leader's behavior is causing morale problems. In all likelihood, there may be other factors in the situation that are causing the morale effect.

Once you have identified the root cause of a problem, the solution is often fairly obvious, although it is not always easy to implement. As examples, if your car is running rough and you find that a sparkplug is broken, then all you need to do is replace the plug and the problem is solved. If sales are down because you are in a recession, however, you can't necessarily solve the problem, even though you know its cause. I also might know that an employee is performing poorly because she has a really rotten attitude, but that knowledge won't necessarily help me solve the problem.

For our example of missed deadlines, here is the procedure you would follow:

1. The project manager calls a meeting to solve the problem of missed deadlines, and the Ishikawa diagram shown in Figure 23–5 is generated. As the diagram shows, there are not many causes under Policies and Machines, but several under each of the other two categories. The question is: What do you do with these guesses at possible causes?

2. The next step in the process is to allow people time to ponder the causes before evaluating them. Some questions to consider at this time are:

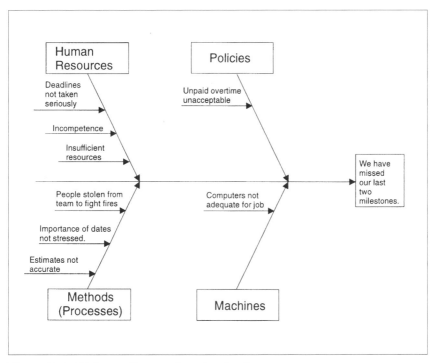

**Figure 23–5**  Ishikawa diagram for missed milestones.

- ◆ Is this cause a variable or an attribute? A variable is one that has continuous measures, such as pounds, feet, and so on. An attribute is present or not present, such as a scratch, dent, or hole.
- ◆ Has the cause been operationally defined?
- ◆ Does this cause interact with other causes?
3. Once people have had time to think about the issue, the next step is to circle likely causes on the diagram. This will always be based on judgment initially. Once this is done, you can rank them in order of most likely to least likely. Paired comparisons is a good technique to use to rank the causes.
4. Finally, you need to verify the cause. You can do this in a variety of ways. Begin by gathering data to see if the most likely cause actually has a significant impact on the problem. If not, then look at the next most likely cause,

and so on. You can also design experiments to manipulate variables to see if they have an effect, when they are amenable to such treatment. A full treatment of such methods is outside the scope of this book. For more in-depth information, you might want to consult Gitlow et al., 1989, or Schmidt et al., 1996.

# 24

## CHAPTER

# Improving Estimating Capability

In my seminars on project management, I have the class do an estimate. It goes like this. Suppose I give you a standard 52 card deck of playing cards that has been well shuffled. I ask you to sort those cards back into numerical order by suit, so that all of the diamonds, hearts, spades, and clubs are in numerical order. How long do you think it will take the typical person to sort a deck of cards?

Each person in the class writes down a number, and then I poll them to get the range. It generally varies from about 1 minute to as much as 10 minutes. Usually, the larger the group, the greater the variation. Ranges of 5 to 1 to as much as 20 to 1 have been obtained.

"Now suppose this group represents the Jim Lewis Card Sorting Company," I say. "I am the manager, and you are my troops. The reason we exist is that occasionally a truck load of playing cards overturns somewhere, and the cards get all shuffled up. They are mostly undamaged, so the company wants to recover them, but that means sorting them back into decks. I have just been asked to quote them on what we charge per deck to sort cards, and you have given me a 10 to 1 range on times. What should I quote?" (Naturally the overturned truck situation would be much worse than my example, because the cards would be totally scrambled. So my situation is a best-case scenario.)

It is clear that if I quote 1 minute per deck, this is probably too low. I will get the job but lose a lot of money. Conversely, 10 minutes is probably too high, so if I quote that amount of time, I probably won't get the job. What am I to do?

The problem is, we don't have any data on which to base our estimates. When I ask the class how they did their estimates, they say that they imagined how they would go about the process and estimated how long each step would take. Certainly, in the absence of data, all you can do is apply a mental model to the problem.

I also ask if they were to poll people back home for an estimate of work that they typically do, would they get similar ranges. Most agree that this would be so. Then how are we to run a business with so much variation in estimates?

The answer is, we are going to have problems. Actually, the answer is that we already *do* have problems. One of the 10 major causes of project failure is that estimates are best guesses, made without consulting historical data. The reason for this is simple—most companies don't have good history on activity durations. So there is nothing to consult but memory, and you are in real trouble if you rely on people's memories!

As an example, I just finished writing a draft of the chapter entitled Tracking Progress to Achieve Project Control. I started yesterday morning around 7 A.M. and finished this morning at 10 A.M. But that is *calendar time.* I know I stopped a number of times to answer the phone. I took several breaks. I got on the Internet and checked on the weather, searched for some information, and so on. In short, I don't know how many total *working hours* it took to do that chapter, and this is just for one day! Think how hard it would be to reconstruct if I went back in memory to one day last week.

## HOW ACCURATE MUST AN ESTIMATE BE?

There certainly is no single answer to this question. Project justifications are often made using return on investment (ROI), net present value (NPV), or breakeven (BE) analysis. Each organization has its own rules on what these figures must be to justify doing a project. I once facilitated an end-of-project review for a large capital equipment project and saw that the initial ROI projection steadily declined throughout the life of the project, so that by the end of the job, there was very little ROI left. Had this been known at the outset, the project probably would not have seen the light of day.

## A LESSON FROM ROYAL DUTCH SHELL

At one time Royal Dutch Shell was having problems with the forecasting accuracy of young geologists. Oil wells are drilled based upon analysis of geological and seismic survey data. Drilling a dry well is very expensive, and you naturally want to minimize the number of these that you drill. The "hit rate" for experienced geologists is not extremely good, but it was far better than for the entry-level geologists.

Finally, the company had an idea. They brought new geologists in for a training session. They began by giving them data for wells that had already been drilled (without telling them this) and asked them to make a forecast. The trainees studied the data and made a recommendation. Then the trainer told them what had actually happened. With this kind of feedback, they were soon making as good predictions as the senior geologists, and the company hadn't had to drill another dry well! This illustrates a very important point—no learning takes place without feedback.

It also suggests that we could all improve the estimating ability of our personnel if we would conduct a similar program. I find that in many companies people make estimates for how long it will take them to do a job, but never track the actual time, so they have no way of knowing if they were right, and consequently, they never improve their estimates. What you get from most people in companies, when you ask how long some task will take, is calendar time. They are pretty sure they can get the job done in a few hours, but know that it will take all week to work it in, so they tell you they will have the work done by the end of the week. This is fine if calendar time is all that matters, but if you also want to know what the effort cost, you are out in the cold.

In order to improve estimating capability, you have to estimate a task duration, track the actual working time taken to do the

To improve estimating capability, track the "actual" working time it took to do the task.

task, and feed back that information to the person who is doing the work. In addition, the time should be recorded for future reference. Otherwise, six months from now, you may have forgotten how long it took.

The problem is, one sample is not enough. From statistics, we know that the average time it takes to perform a task cannot be determined by doing it only one time. Generally, at least 25 samples are required to know the task average duration and the standard deviation. So collecting enough data to have a reasonable database will take some time. Most organizations find that it takes several years to collect enough data to improve their estimates.

## MOVING TARGETS

One concern is that in many projects, technology is changing so fast that by the time you collect enough history to know how long tasks take to complete, the history is obsolete, because new technology has emerged. In other words, you are always shooting at moving targets.

In terms of the work breakdown structure, this argument is only true at high levels of the WBS. As you go further down in the WBS, you do reach a point where tasks become repetitive. A drafting supervisor can usually tell how long it will take to make a D-size drawing of a mechanical or electronic assembly, for example, because her department has done so many of them. A technician can tell how long it takes to run certain tests. Even a designer can tell how long it takes to design small circuits, even though the technology being employed is new.

So if we track at low enough levels in the WBS, we can build a database that has meaning. There is an important factor to consider here. The data on actual time spent working on the task must be accurate. This means that it should be recorded daily. The best approach is to record as you go, like an attorney does, but most people find this hard to do. Failing this, they should at least write down what they have done during the day to the nearest hour. At loaded labor rates of $50 to $100 an hour, costs add up very quickly.

## FACTORS AFFECTING WORKING TIMES

A number of things affect how long it actually takes a person to do work. These include learning curves, setup time, fatigue, and skill level. In the card-sorting example that I mentioned earlier, you could expect that a person would get faster at sorting cards the more times he does the task. This improvement in performance is called a learning curve. If you have such tasks in projects, you might want to consider performance improvement over time. A learning curve is shown in Figure 24–1.

Setup time in knowledge work is a function of how many times a task gets interrupted. The time management experts say that if a person doing knowledge work gets interrupted, it typically takes 15 to 20 minutes to get reoriented to his work. For that reason, several phone or personal interruptions in one hour can just about kill that time!

Other task interruptions come from having people work on too many projects at one time, so that they are constantly shifting gears. Moreover, the overhead of meetings takes its toll. When you work on several projects, you may easily spend an hour or more

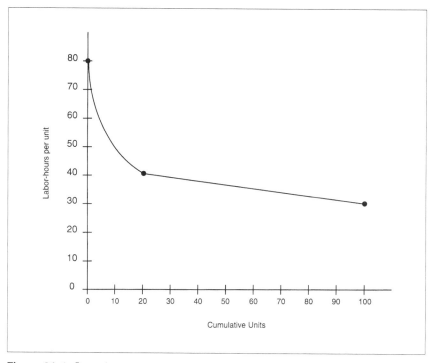

**Figure 24–1**  Learning curve.

each week attending meetings for each project. This takes away time from getting project work done, and because meetings are often so badly managed, you lose in that additional way.

Fatigue is often not figured in knowledge projects. In construction projects, fatigue factors are understood much better (see Chapter 15). Estimates are sometimes made based on full-productivity performance of people, even though they are expected to work overtime routinely. In these cases, estimated times are seldom met.

Skill level of the person doing the work is also a factor. A more-skilled person should be faster than one of lesser skill. This is often covered by a multiplier: a number greater than one for higher skill or a number less than one for a lower-skilled person.

# 25
## CHAPTER

# Managing Innovation in Projects*

**W**hether you are in an organization that produces new products or does construction work, there is a need for innovation. Those organizations that offer the best array of innovative products and services have a competitive advantage over those who continue to offer the "same-old-same-old." In order for a team to be innovative, the climate in which they operate must support innovation, and some climates do just the opposite.

**in • no • va • tion: The act of introducing something new.**

Corporate America is largely risk-averse. We push managers to deliver short-term profits—monthly or quarterly—and many truly innovative efforts require long-term investments before a payoff is achieved, and this may adversely affect short-term profitability. No doubt there are many innovative people in most organizations, but they will be restrained by a risk-averse climate.

---

\* Some of the material in this chapter is also contained in my book *Team-Based Project Management.*

## THE INTELLECTUAL PROCESS

As I have shown in Chapter 23 on process improvement, there is no doubt that we need to improve project performance. The four objectives of a project are cost, performance, time, and scope, as was outlined in Chapter 7. Further, as was explained in that chapter, these are related as follows:

$$C = f\,(P,\ T,\ S)$$

which reads, "Cost is a function of performance, time, and scope."

As I pointed out in Chapter 23, there is a tremendous pressure to reduce time. This is especially true in product development. Target reductions in time are as much as 50 percent. That is, get it done in half the time.

Further, the pressure is on to *simultaneously* reduce cost. At first glance, this seems contradictory, since reductions in time are often achieved by applying more resources, which raises costs. As I showed in Chapter 23, however, if we change the process by which the work is done, we can reduce both time and cost simultaneously. In product development, that process is largely intellectual, so this suggests something that seems strange at first glance—you have to improve the intellectual process, or you have to *think faster!*

> If you want to improve the intellectual process, you have to think faster.

Naturally, you might argue that thinking speed can't be improved, but in a sense, it can. Furthermore, some of the thinking process can be aided by computers. This was done in designing the 777 airplane at Boeing. Using three-dimensional computer modeling, engineers could tell before a model was built that there was an interference between two components inside a wing. This greatly speeded up the design process (Sabbagh, 1996).

Now, before you dismiss the idea that the actual thought process can be improved, let me suggest that you study the literature on innovation or creative thinking. A number of works are listed in the reading list by de Bono, Michalco, von Oech, and others. I have applied these techniques individually and in groups, with excellent results. In one case, a group of about seven scientists worked for two hours to generate ideas to solve some problems that concerned them, and they developed so many ideas that the team leader (chief scientist) said it would probably take another year to work through all of them. He was elated at the outcome.

It is important to note that I am not referring just to the old group brainstorming approach that has been around for a long time. Brainstorming is just one of a family of approaches for groups. There are also a number of techniques that can be applied by individuals. Creativity is not necessarily better with groups than with individuals. In fact, very few really new inventions have ever been developed by groups. Invariably, they are the product of one person thinking individually.

The conclusion to draw from all of this is that teams can benefit from training in the methods of innovation, since most people have not been exposed to these.

## THE ENVIRONMENT ITSELF

Although it is outside the scope of this book to get into much detail, the working environment itself plays a part in making people more innovative. Some organizations have built special rooms in which groups can work to generate innovative ideas. These are usually brightly colored, may have walls with Lego\#170 panels, usually have large white boards and a multitude of media, such as modeling clay, colored markers, and construction paper. Some innovation experts also say that a good way to start a group is to show cartoons for a few minutes, to get them laughing, because laughter is so strongly part of the creative mindset (Hall, 1995).

## ADAPTERS AND INNOVATORS: DIFFERENCES IN COGNITIVE STYLE AND PERSONALITY

Michael J. Kirton has studied the creative-thinking process and determined that there are two aspects, one called the *level* of the intellectual process and the other called the *style* of problem-solving. Level has to do with one's intelligence, experience, and so on. Style, however, is a single dimension, anchored on one end by innovators and on the other by adapters.

Adapters, when confronted with a problem, tend to turn to conventional rules, practices, and perceptions of the group to which they belong. This can be a working group, cultural group, or professional or occupational group. They then derive their ideas from the established procedures of this group. If there is no ready-made answer provided by a collection of conventional responses, the adapter will try to adapt or stretch a conventional response until it can be used to solve the problem. Thus, much of the behavior of adapters is in the category of improving existing methods, or "doing better" what is already done. This is a strategy that tends to dominate management (Drucker, 1969). This has been exemplified since 1980 by the continuous improvement process advocated by Dr. Deming. The flaw in continuous improvement is that you eventually reach a point at which a process should no longer be improved. It should be eliminated.

Innovation is the characteristic behavior of individuals who, when they have a problem, try to reorganize or restructure the problem and to approach it in a new light. In doing so, they try to divorce themselves from preconceived notions about the nature of

The flaw in continuous improvement is that you eventually reach a point at which a process should no longer be improved, but should be eliminated.

the problem and its solution. Their approach can be called "doing things differently," instead of "doing things better."

## Relationships between Innovators and Adapters

Because of their different styles in solving problems, it can be expected that innovators and adapters might have conflicts in teams, and this is sometimes the case. Adapters tend to see innovators as abrasive, insensitive, and disruptive. They are always wanting to change things, always creating havoc. Innovators see adapters as stuffy and unenterprising. They are hung up on systems, rules, and norms of behavior that seem restrictive and ineffective to the innovators. So, when the extreme innovator meets the extreme adapter, sparks are likely to fly.

## Organizational Climate and Innovation

As I have said earlier, organization climate affects how much innovation is expressed. In general, organizations are inclined to encourage bureaucracy and adaptation in order to minimize risk. This is especially true of large organizations. Weber (1970) has written that the aims of bureaucratic organizations are precision, reliability, and efficiency. Such organizations exert fairly constant pressure on managers to be methodical, prudent (this often means risk-averse), and disciplined. They are also expected to maintain a high degree of conformity. Note that these are qualities that are generally ascribed to the adapter personality. For a strong adapter, the longer an institutional practice has existed, the more he takes it for granted. So when a problem arises, he does not consider changing the structure of the organization. Rather, he tries to find a solution within that structure.

The innovator, on the other hand, might challenge the existing structure and propose solutions that appear more risky and less sound to adapters. This makes the innovator seem less concerned with company needs and less concerned with the effect on others of his solutions.

What this means, of course, is that bureaucratic organizations tend to support adapters more than innovators, thus making incremental change the norm and making it hard to implement step-function or large-scale change. Innovators in such organizations often feel unappreciated and may very well leave, thus moving the majority of the population in the direction of adaptation and reducing its capacity for innovation. In a stable world, the stodgy bureaucracy can survive, but in a topsy-turvy, turbulent world, incremental change is often insufficient for survival. Yet the very person who might be able to save the stiff-necked bureaucracy is likely to be resisted and resented.

## SOFTWARE FOR INNOVATION

There have been a lot of techniques developed to help individuals and groups generate large numbers of ideas quickly. One of the best known is Synectics, developed and taught by the Synectics Corporation. Now a software product has been developed that is based on principles from Synectics. It is called MindLink Problem Solver and can be used by individuals or groups to solve problems.

In the problem-solving literature, we find that there are two kinds of problems—open-ended and close-ended. A close-ended problem has a single solution, whereas an open-ended one can be solved many different ways. As an example, a math problem is close-ended. So is a troubleshooting problem: Once you find what is broken, you can make a repair.

As you can imagine, most of the problems in this world are open-ended, yet most of our training is aimed at solving close-ended problems. The problem caused by this focus is that we want to frame all of our problems as close-ended and apply the tools of close-ended problem-solving. Unfortunately, those tools are not very effective for solving open-ended problems.

MindLink Problem Solver is used to solve primarily open-ended problems. These are called creative problems. These cover a wide range of applications in organizations, including the following:

- Strategic Planning
- Product Development
- Market Positioning
- Process Reengineering

- Total Quality Management
- Human Resource Planning
- Training Course Development
- Personal Career Planning

The program works by serving as a personal or small group facilitator and helps spur people on to new and creative ideas. It is available for both Windows™ and Mac platforms. As of this writing (January 1997), the Windows version is $299. Information can be obtained by calling 800-253-1844.

# G L O S S A R Y

**Activity**   The work or effort needed to achieve a result. It consumes time and usually consumes resources.

**Activity Description**   A statement specifying what must be done to achieve a desired result.

**Activity-on-Arrow**   A network diagram showing sequence of activities, in which each activity is represented by an arrow, with a circle representing a node or event at each end.

**Activity-on-Node**   A network diagram showing sequence of activities, in which each activity is represented by a box or circle (that is, a *node*), and these are interconnected with arrows to show precedence of work.

**Authority**   The legitimate power given to a person in an organization to use resources to reach an objective and to exercise discipline.

**Backward Pass**   Calculations made working backward through a network from the latest event to the beginning event to calculate event late times. A forward pass calculation determines early times.

**Change Order**   A document which authorizes a change in some aspect of a project.

**Control**   The practice of monitoring progress against a plan so that corrective steps can be taken when a deviation from plan occurs.

**CPM**   An acronym for critical path method. A network diagramming method which shows the longest series of activities in a project, thereby determining the earliest completion for the project.

**Crashing**   An attempt to reduce activity or total project duration, usually by adding resources.

**Critical Path**   The longest sequential path of activities which are absolutely essential for completion of the project. It will also have no slack, or float.

**Dependency**   The next task or group of tasks cannot begin until preceding work has been completed, thus the word "dependent," or dependency.

**Deviation**   Any variation from planned performance. The deviation can be in terms of schedule, cost, performance, or scope of work. Deviation analysis is the heart of exercising project control.

**Dummy Activity**   A zero-duration element in a network showing a logic linkage. A dummy does not consume time or resources, but simply indicates precedence.

**Duration**   The time it takes to complete an activity.

**Earliest Finish**   The earliest time that an activity can be completed.

**Earliest Start**   The earliest time that an activity can be started.

**Estimate**  A forecast or guess about how long an activity will take, how many resources might be required, or how much it will cost.

**Event**  A point in time. An event is binary. It is either achieved or not, whereas an activity can be partially complete. An event can be the start or finish of an activity.

**Feedback**  Information derived from observation of project activities, which is used to analyze the status of the job and take corrective action if necessary.

**Float**  A measure of how much an activity can be delayed before it begins to impact the project finish date.

**Forward Pass Method**  The method used to calculate the earliest start time for each activity in a network diagram.

**Free Float**  The amount of time that an activity can be delayed without affecting succeeding activities.

**Gantt Chart**  A bar chart which indicates the time required to complete each activity in a project. It is named for Henry L. Gantt, who first developed a complete notational system for displaying progress with bar charts.

**Hammock Activity**  A single activity which actually represents a group of activities. It "hangs" between two events and is used to report progress on the composite which it represents.

**Histogram**  A vertical bar chart showing (usually) resource allocation levels over time in a project.

**Inexcusable Delays**  Project delays that are attributable to negligence on the part of the contractor, which lead in many cases to penalty payments.

**Latest Finish**  The latest time that an activity can be finished without extending the end date for a project.

**Latest Start**  The latest time that an activity can start without extending the end date for a project.

**Learning Curve**  The time it takes humans to learn an activity well enough to achieve optimum performance can be displayed by curves, which must be factored into estimates of activity durations in order to achieve planned completion dates.

**Leveling**  An attempt to smooth the use of resources, whether people, materials, or equipment, to avoid large peaks and valleys in their usage.

**Life Cycle**  The phases which a project goes through from concept through completion. The nature of the project changes during each phase.

**Matrix Organization**  A method of drawing people from functional departments within an organization for assignment to a project team, but without removing them from their physical location. The project manager in such a structure is said to have *dotted-line* authority over team members.

**Milestone**  An event of special importance, usually representing the completion of a major phase of project work. Reviews are often scheduled at milestones.

**Most Likely Time**  The most realistic time estimate for completing an activity under normal conditions.

**Negative Float or Slack**   A condition in a network in which the *earliest time* for an event is actually later than its *latest time*. This happens when the project has a constrained end date which is earlier than can be achieved, or when an activity uses up its float and is still delayed.

**Node**   A point in a network connected to other points by one or more arrows. In activity-on-arrow notation, the node contains at least one event. In activity-on-node notation, the node represents an activity, and the arrows show the sequence in which they must be performed.

**PERT**   An acronym which stands for program evaluation and review technique. PERT makes use of network diagrams as does CPM, but in addition applies statistics to activities to try and estimate the probabilities of completion of project work.

**Pessimistic Time**   Roughly speaking, this is the *worst-case* time to complete an activity. The term has a more precise meaning, which is defined in the PERT literature.

**Phase**   A major component or segment of a project.

**Precedence Diagram**   An activity-on-node diagram.

**Queue**   Waiting time.

**Resource Allocation**   The assignment of people, equipment, facilities, or materials to a project. Unless adequate resources are provided, project work cannot be completed on schedule, thus resource allocation is a significant component of project scheduling.

**Resource Pool**   A group of people who can generally do the same work; therefore, they can be chosen randomly for assignment to a project.

**Risk**   The possibility that something can go wrong and interfere with the completion of project work.

**Scope**   The magnitude of work which must be done to complete a project.

**Slack**   Same as float. The amount of time a task can be delayed before it impacts the finish time for a project.

**Subproject**   A small project within a larger one.

**Statement of Work**   A description of work to be performed.

**Time Now**   The current calendar date from which a network analysis, report, or update is being made.

**Time Standard**   The time allowed for the completion of a task.

**Variance**   Any deviation of project work from what was planned. Variance can be around costs, time, performance, or project scope.

**Work Breakdown Structure**   A method of subdividing work into smaller and smaller increments to permit accurate estimates of durations, resource requirements, and costs.

# RESOURCES

Following is a list of sources of information, books, and professional associations which may be helpful in managing projects. Not all are specifically aimed at project management, but you may find them helpful anyway.

**The Business Reader:** This is a mailorder bookstore specializing in business books. If it's on business, the chances are they have it! P.O. Box 3627 • Williamsburg, VA 23187 • Tel. (757) 258-4746

**CRM Films:** A good source of films for training, including *Mining Group Gold, The Abilene Paradox,* and many others. 2215 Faraday Avenue • Carlsbad, CA 92008 • Tel. (800) 421-0833

**The Lewis Institute, Inc.:** Founded by the author, the institute provides training in project management, team building, and related courses. The core program is Project Management: Tools, Principles, Practices and has been attended by around 13,000 managers worldwide. 302 Chestnut Mountain Dr. • Vinton, VA 24179 • Tel. (540) 890-1560 • FAX: (540) 890-7470 • CompuServe 74124,2267 • http://www.lewisinstitute.com

**MindWare:** The store for the other 90 percent of your brain. A source of tools, books, and other materials for helping enhance learning and creativity in organizations. They have a nice catalog listing their materials. 6142 Olson Mem. Hwy. • Golden Valley, MN 55422 • Tel. (800) 999-0398 • FAX: (612) 595-8852

**Morasco, Vincent:** A newspaper clipping service that operates on a pay-per-use basis. You pay only for the clippings you actually use. A good source of up-to-the-minute information. Vincent Morasco • 3 Cedar Street • Batavia, NY 14020 • (716) 343-2544

**Pegasus Communications:** Publishers of *The Systems Thinker,* a monthly newsletter. They also have videos by Russell Ackoff and Peter Senge, among others. P.O. Box 943 • Oxford, OH 45056-0943 • Tel. (800) 636-3796 • FAX: (905) 764-7983

**Pfeiffer & Company:** A source of training programs, training materials, instruments, and books on management. 350 Sansome Street, 5th Floor • San Francisco, CA 94104 • Tel. (800) 274-4434 • FAX: (800) 569-0443

**Pimsleur International:** The most effective way to learn a language on your own is with the cassettes using a method developed by Dr. Paul Pimsleur. Learning is virtually painless. 30 Monument Square, Suite 135 • Concord, MA 01742 • Tel. (800) 222-5860 • FAX: (508) 371-2935

**Project Management Institute:** The professional association for project managers. Over 25,000 members nationwide as of July 1997. They have local chapters in most major U.S. cities and a number of countries. 130 S. State Road • Upper Darby, PA 19082 • Tel. (610) 734-3330 • FAX: (610) 734-3266

# REFERENCES

Baker, Bruce; Murphy, David; and Fisher, Dalmar. Factors Affecting Project Success. In David I. Cleland and William R. King (Eds.) *Project Management Handbook* (2d Ed.). New York: Van Nostrand Reinhold, 1988.

Baker, Bud, and Menon, Raj. Politics and Project Performance: The Fourth Dimension of Project Management. *PM Network,* November 1995, pp. 16–21.

Beer, Stafford. *Brain of the Firm* (2d Ed.). New York: Wiley, 1981.

Block, Peter. *The Empowered Manager.* San Francisco: Jossey-Bass, 1987.

Buzan, Tony. *The Mind Map Book.* New York: Dutton, 1993.

Cartwright, Dorwin, and Zander, Alvin. *Group Dynamics.* New York: Harper and Row, 1968.

Cialdini, Robert B. *Influence: The Power of Persuasion* (Rev. Ed.). New York: Quill, 1993.

Couillard, Jean. The Role of Project Risk in Determining Project Management Approach. *Project Management Journal,* December 1995, pp. 3–15.

Dail, Hardy. Job Acceleration: What Does It Really Cost? *The Journal of the American Institute of Constructors, 10,* No. 1. 1986.

El-Najdawi, Mohammad, and Liberatore, Matthew. Matrix Management Effectiveness: An Update for Research and Engineering Organizations. *Project Management Journal, 28,* No. 1, March 1997, pp. 25–31.

Farson, Richard. *Management of the Absurd: Paradoxes in Leadership.* New York: Simon & Schuster, 1996.

Fleming, Quentin, and Koppelman, Joel. *Earned Value Project Management.* Upper Darby, PA: The Project Management Institute, 1996.

Fortune, Joyce, and Peters, Geoff. *Learning from Failure: The Systems Approach.* Chichester, England: John Wiley & Sons, 1995.

French, J., and Raven, B. The Bases of Social Power. In D. Cartwright (Ed.), *Studies in Social Power,* pp. 118–149. Ann Arbor, MI: University of Michigan, 1959.

Gitlow, Howard, et al. *Tools and Methods for the Improvement of Quality.* Burr Ridge, IL: Irwin, 1989.

Hammer, Michael, and Champy, James. *Reengineering the Corporation.* New York: Harper, 1993.

Hammond, III, John S. Better Decisions with Preference Theory. In *Harvard Business Review on Management.* New York: Harper & Row, 1975.

*Harvard Business Review on Management.* (No editor listed) New York: Harper & Row, 1975.

Janis, Irving, and Mann, Leon. *Decision Making.* New York: The Free Press, 1977.

Juran, J. M., and Gryna, Frank. *Quality Planning and Analysis.* New York: McGraw-Hill, 1980.

Kayser, Tom. *Mining Group Gold.* New York: McGraw-Hill, 1995.

Kelley, Robert, and Caplan, Janet. How Bell Labs Creates Star Performers. *Harvard Business Review*, July–August 1993, pp. 128–139.

Kepner, Charles, and Tregoe, Benjamin. *The Rational Manager.* Princeton, NJ: Kepner-Tregoe, 1965.

Levine, Harvey. Risk Management for Dummies: Managing Schedule, Cost and Technical Risk and Contingency. *PM Network,* October 1995, pp. 30–32.

Lewis, James. *Fundamentals of Project Management.* New York: AMACOM, 1993.

Lewis, James. *How to Build and Manage a Winning Project Team.* New York: AMACOM, 1993.

Lewis, James. *Project Planning, Scheduling, and Control* (Rev. Ed.). New York: McGraw-Hill, 1995.

Lewis, James. *The Project Manager's Desk Reference.* New York: McGraw-Hill, 1993.

Lewis, James. *Team-Based Project Management.* New York: AMACOM, 1997.

Lock, Dennis (Ed.). *Gower Handbook of Project Management* (2d Ed.). Hampshire, England: Gower, 1994.

Meredith, Jack, and Mantel, Jr., Samuel. *Project Management: A Managerial Approach.* New York: Wiley, 1985.

Might, R. J., and Fisher, W. A. The Role of Structural Factors in Determining Project Management Success. *IEEE Transactions on Engineering Management, EM-32,* No. 2, May 1993, pp. 71–77.

Mintzberg, Henry. *Mintzberg on Management.* New York: The Free Press, 1989.

Murphy, David; Baker, Bruce; and Fisher, Dalmar. *Determinants of Project Success.* Springfield, VA: National Technical Information Services, Accession No.: N-74-30392, September 15, 1974.

Patterson, Marvin. *Accelerating Innovation: Improving the Processes of Product Development.* New York: Van Nostrand Reinhold, 1993.

Pinto, Jeffrey K. Power and Politics: Managerial Implications. *PM Network,* August 1996, pp. 36–39.

Pinto, Jeffrey K. *Power and Politics in Project Management.* Upper Darby, PA: Project Management Institute, 1996.

Saaty, Thomas L. *Decision Making for Leaders.* Pittsburgh: RWS Publications, 1995.

Schmidt, Stephen; Kiemele, Mark; and Berdine, Ronald. *Knowledge-Based Management.* Colorado Springs, CO: Air Academy Press, 1996.

Schultz, R. L.; Slevin, Dennis; and Pinto, Jeffrey. Strategy and Tactics in a Process Model of Project Implementation. *Interfaces,* May–June 1987, pp. 34–46.

Schuyler, John R. Decision Analysis in Projects: Summary and Recommendations. *PM Network,* October 1995, pp. 23–28.

Senge, Peter. *The Fifth Discipline.* New York: Doubleday Currency, 1990.

Senge, Peter, et al. *The Fifth Discipline Fieldbook.* New York: Doubleday Currency, 1994.

Smith, Preston, and Reinertsen, Donald. *Developing Products in Half the Time.* New York: Van Nostrand Reinhold, 1995.

Thoms, Peg. Creating a Shared Vision with a Project Team. *PM Network,* January 1997, pp. 33–35.

Watzlawick, Paul; Beavin, Janet; and Jackson, Don. *Pragmatics of Human Communication.* New York: Norton, 1967.

Watzlawick, Paul; Weakland, John; and Fisch, Richard. *Change: Principles of Problem Formulation and Problem Resolution.* New York: Norton, 1974.

Weisbord, Marvin, and Janoff, Sandra. *Future Search.* San Francisco: Berrett-Koehler, 1995.

Wheelwright, Steven, and Clark, Kim. *Revolutionizing Product Development.* New York: Free Press, 1992.

Wheatley, Margaret. *Leadership and the New Science.* San Francisco: Berrett-Koehler, 1994.

# INDEX

# ABOUT THE AUTHOR

**James P. Lewis, Ph.D.,** is the founder of The Lewis Institute, Inc., an association of professionals providing project management and behavioral consulting and training throughout the United States, Canada, Mexico, England, and Asia. This includes team building, project management, engineering management, and problem solving to several *Fortune* 100 and 500 companies in the United States.

An outstanding workshop leader, he has trained more than 16,000 managers and supervisors since 1981, drawing on his many years of firsthand experience as a manager with ITT Telecommunications and Aerotron, Inc., where he held positions including product engineering manager, chief engineer, and project manager. He also served as quality manager for ITT Telecom during the last two years of his industrial career. During his 15 years as an electrical engineer, Jim designed and developed a variety of communications equipment for application in land, sea, and mobile environments. He holds a joint patent on a programmable memory for a transceiver.

He has published numerous articles on managing as well as four books on project management: *How to Build & Manage An Effective Project Team* and *Fundamentals of Project Management*, both published by the American Management Association; and *Project Planning, Scheduling and Control, Revised Edition* and *The Project Manager's Desk Reference*, published by McGraw-Hill. He holds a B.S. in Electrical Engineering and M.S. and Ph.D. degrees in Psychology, all from North Carolina State University.

Jim is married to the former Lea Ann McDowell, and they live in Vinton, Virginia, in the Blue Ridge Mountains. Although they have no children of their own, they have three exchange-student "daughters," Yukiko Bono of Japan, Katarina Sigerud of Sweden, and Susi Mraz of Austria.

You can contact Jim at the Lewis Institute, Inc. See the Resources for Project Managers section for phone numbers and e-mail address.